16th International Conference on Cognition and Exploratory Learning in Digital Age (CELDA 2019)

Cagliari, Italy
7 - 9 November 2019

Editors:

Demetrios G. Sampson
Dirk Ifenthaler
Pedro Isaias
Maria Lidia Mascia
Luis Rodrigues

ISBN: 978-1-7138-0306-5

Printed from e-media with permission by:

Curran Associates, Inc.
57 Morehouse Lane
Red Hook, NY 12571

Some format issues inherent in the e-media version may also appear in this print version.

International Association for Development of the Information Society (IADIS)
Rua Sao Sebastiao Da Pedreira
No. 100, 30, 1050-209
Lisbon, Portugal

Phone: 351 21 3151373
Fax: 351 21 3151244

secretariat@iadis.org

Additional copies of this publication are available from:

Curran Associates, Inc.
57 Morehouse Lane
Red Hook, NY 12571 USA
Phone: 845-758-0400
Fax: 845-758-2633
Email: curran@proceedings.com
Web: www.proceedings.com

PROCEEDINGS OF THE 16th INTERNATIONAL CONFERENCE on

COGNITION AND EXPLORATORY LEARNING IN THE DIGITAL AGE (CELDA 2019)

CAGLIARI, ITALY

NOVEMBER 7-9, 2019

Organised by

iadis

international association for development of the information society

Co-Organised by

As a member of Crossref (a non-profit membership organization for scholarly publishing working with the purpose to make content easy to find, link, cite and assess) each published paper in this book of proceedings will be allocated a DOI (Digital Object Identifier) number for its fast and easy citation and indexation.

Edited by Demetrios G. Sampson, Dirk Ifenthaler, Pedro Isaías and Maria Lidia Mascia

Associate Editor: Luís Rodrigues

TABLE OF CONTENTS

SHORT PAPERS

REFLECTION PAPER

FOREWORD

These proceedings contain the papers of the 16th International Conference on Cognition and Exploratory Learning in the Digital Age (CELDA 2019), held during 7 to 9 November 2019, which has been organized by the International Association for Development of the Information Society (IADIS) and co-organised by University Degli Studi di Cagliari, Italy.

The CELDA conference aims to address the main issues concerned with evolving learning processes and supporting pedagogies and applications in the digital age. There have been advances in both cognitive psychology and computing that have affected the educational arena. The convergence of these two disciplines is increasing at a fast pace and affecting academia and professional practice in many ways.

Paradigms such as just-in-time learning, constructivism, student-centered learning and collaborative approaches have emerged and are being supported by technological advancements such as simulations, virtual reality and multi-agent systems. These developments have created both opportunities and areas of serious concerns. This conference aims to cover both technological as well as pedagogical issues related to these developments. Main tracks have been identified. However innovative contributions that do not easily fit into these areas will also be considered as long as they are directly related to the overall theme of the conference – cognition and exploratory learning in the digital age.

The following areas are represented in the submissions for CELDA 2019:

- Acquisition of Expertise
- Assessing Progress of Learning in Complex Domains
- Assessment of Exploratory Learning Approaches
- Assessment of Exploratory Technologies
- Cognition in Education
- Collaborative Learning
- Educational Psychology
- Exploratory Technologies (Simulations, VR, i-TV, etc.)
- Just-in-time and Learning-on-Demand
- Learner Communities and Peer-Support
- Learning Communities & Web Service Technologies Pedagogical issues related with Learning Objects
- Learning Paradigms in Academia
- Learning Paradigms in the Corporate Sector
- Life-long Learning
- Student-centered Learning
- Technology and Mental Models
- Technology
- Learning and Expertise
- Virtual University

The CELDA 2019 Conference received 87 submissions from more than 25 countries. Each submission was reviewed in a double-blind review process by at least two independent reviewers to ensure quality and maintain high standards. Out of the papers submitted, 48 were accepted as full papers for an acceptance rate of 55%; 15 were accepted as short papers and 1 was accepted as reflection paper. Authors of the best published papers in the CELDA 2019 proceedings will be invited to publish extended versions of their papers in a book from Springer.

In addition to the presentation of full, short and reflection papers, the conference also includes one keynote presentation from an internationally distinguished researcher. We would therefore like to express our gratitude to this year keynote speaker: Dr. Baltasar Fernández Manjón, Director of the e-Learning Research Group e-UCM, Complutense University of Madrid (UCM), Spain.

A successful conference requires the effort of many individuals. We would like to thank the members of the Program Committee for their hard work in reviewing and selecting the papers that appear in this book. We are especially grateful to the authors who submitted their papers to this conference and to the presenters who provided the substance of this meeting. We wish to thank all members of our organizing committee.

Last but not least, we hope that participants enjoy Cagliari and their time with colleagues from all over the world.

Pedro Isaías, The University of New South Wales (UNSW Sydney), Australia
Maria Lidia Mascia, University Degli Studi di Cagliari, Italy
Conference Co-Chairs

Demetrios G. Sampson, University of Piraeus, Greece & Curtin University, Australia
Dirk Ifenthaler, University of Mannheim, Germany & Curtin University, Australia
Program Co-Chairs

Cagliari, Italy
November 2019

PROGRAM COMMITTEE

CONFERENCE CO-CHAIRS

Pedro Isaías, The University of New South Wales (UNSW Sydney), Australia
Maria Lidia Mascia, University Degli Studi di Cagliari, Italy

PROGRAM CO-CHAIRS

Demetrios G Sampson, University of Piraeus, Greece & Curtin University, Australia
Dirk Ifenthaler, University of Mannheim, Germany & Curtin University, Australia

COMMITTEE MEMBERS

Ah-Choo Koo, Multimedia Univerisity, Malaysia
Alke Martens, University of Rostock, Germany
Anthony Y. H. Liao, Asia University, Taiwan
Aparna Lalingkar, International Institute of Information Technology, India
Arif Altun, Hacettepe University, Turkey
Baltasar Fernandez, Universidad Complutense de Madrid, Spain
Carol H. C Chu, Soochow University, Taiwan
ChanMin Kim, Penn State University, USA
Charalampos Karagiannidis, University of Thessaly, Greece
Chien Sing Lee, Sunway University, Malaysia
Chih-Hung Lai, National Dong Hwa University, Taiwan
Chun-Wang Wei, Kaohsiung Medical University, Taiwan
Davinia Hernandez-Leo, Universitat Pompeu Fabra, Spain
Farshad Badie, Aalborg University, Denmark
Flavio Manganello, National Research Council, Italy
Giuliana Dettori, National Research Council, Italy
Giuliana Guazzaroni, University Politecnica Delle Marche, Italy
I-Fang Liu, National Central University, Taiwan
Imran Zualkernan, American University of Sharjah, United Arab Emirates
Jirarat Sitthiworachart, King Mongkut Institute of Technology Ladkrabang, Thailand
Juan Felipe Calderon, Universidad Andres Bello, Chile
Katherine Sinitsa, Int. Res. Training Center for Info. Technologies and Systems, Ukraine
Kuo-Liang Ou, National Hsin-chu University of Education, Taiwan
Kyparisia Papanikolaou, School of Pedagogical and Technological Education, Greece
Lence Miloseva, Goce Delcev University, Macedonia
Luis Anido, University of Vigo, Spain
Maiga Chang, Athabasca University, Canada
Michael Verhaart, TANZ eCampus, EIT (Hawkes Bay), Open Polytechinc, New Zealand
Ming-Chi Liu, Feng Chia University, Taiwan
Ming-Puu Chen, National Taiwan Normal University, Taiwan
Minjeong Kim, Dankook University, Republic of Korea
Monica Landoni, University of Lugano, Switzerland
Ni Chang, Indiana University South Bend, USA

KEYNOTE LECTURE

GAME LEARNING ANALYTICS FOR EVIDENCE-BASED SERIOUS GAMES

Dr. Baltasar Fernández Manjón,
Director of the e-Learning Research Group e-UCM,
Complutense University of Madrid (UCM), Spain

Abstract

The applications of data science techniques to game learning analytics data obtained from serious games can provide a more scientific approach to improve the serious games lifecycle. Honing on the game analytics data is possible to use an evidence-based approach to the design, evaluation and deployment of serious games. For instance, the use of game analytics techniques on the users gameplay interaction data can be applied to systematize the evaluation of games, and allow both teachers and institutions to make better evidence-based decisions. The talk will address some of the new possibilities offered by game learning analytics and what are the requirements (e.g. standards) for its generalization in real settings (including some of the ethical implications).

FULL PAPERS

USING COOPERATIVE TEACHING TECHNIQUES IN ENGINEERING COURSES. THE JIGSAW CASE

Maria-Cristina Marinescu[1] and Jose L. Marzo[2]
[1]*CASE, Barcelona Supercomputing Center, Jordi Girona, 29, 08034, Barcelona, Spain*
[2]*Institute of Informatics and Applications, University of Girona, Plaça Sant Domenec 3, 17004, Girona, Spain*

ABSTRACT

Students everywhere are increasingly expecting to learn content that is immediately relevant to the degree they are preparing for. The negative implication of this is that they generally lack the motivation to study the fundamentals and understand in-depth material that they may not yet see the use for. Based on our previous experience with inquiry-based learning methodologies, and given the course content and the number of students in class we felt that a collaborative inquiry-based approach would encourage students to actively participate in their learning, motivate them to learn differently than in traditional ways, and inspire them to share information with their classmates. Results using the Jigsaw methodology show that some of the more positive effects were teamwork and "being forced to understand and prepare well enough to be able to explain clearly to your colleagues". On the negative side, some students found the number of presentations to be excessive and some thought that they knew less about the material that they had not prepared themselves than they would have known had they followed a traditional teaching method.

KEYWORDS

Autonomous Learning, Collaborative Learning, Active Learning, Jigsaw

1. INTRODUCTION

The lack of general technical motivation of undergraduates in the third year of the Design and development of videogames degree at the University of Girona, Spain, triggered our search for non-traditional teaching-learning techniques to make them more interested and increase class participation. An important factor in our decision was the desire to complement the purely technical skills students acquire during the course with skills directed to the effective monitoring, selection, and analysis of information, decision-making in complex problems, and teamwork.

Based on our previous experience with inquiry-based learning methodologies, such as problem-based learning, course content, and the number of students in class, we considered that a collaborative inquiry-based approach may work well. After further reading we decided to adopt the Jigsaw method.

We set up the experiment with third year undergraduates in the Cloud computing and distributed systems for videogames course'. This is a rather technical course in the curriculum of the videogame design and implementation specialization, but it lends itself to the learning various topics independently. One of the concerns with the Jigsaw method – as with most collaborative methods – is that, after a certain age, students are already settled into their roles as leaders or followers which, in turn, could make it harder for them to work in collaborative environments that lack hierarchy. This is yet another reason why we chose to see how third year students would adapt to this methodology. To limit the possibility of negative outcomes for some of the students, we decided to apply the Jigsaw method to only part of the course contents – specifically to Optical Networking, which stands for an eighth of the course content and grade. The idea is to later validate these results with even older students in a course of the Master's program at another Spanish university, in which 10 to 25 students typically register.

This paper is organized as follows: Section II is an abbreviated introduction to the literature of collaborative and inquiry-based methods. Section III presents our case study and Section IV introduces the method, including the questionnaires that students were asked to fill out after each Jigsaw session. Results are presented in Section V. Section VI draws conclusions and sketches out future work.

2. BACKGROUND

2.1 Collaborative Learning

Collaborative learning techniques are based on student cooperation to achieve a common goal. This class of techniques presents the student with the challenge of explaining concepts to fellow groupmates who may not know or understand the material. While doing this, students develop their communication, argumentation, and debating skills. Cooperative learning is based on the premise that the students can learn better by doing and by working with each other than from the instructor presentations, Slavin, 1995) (McConnel, 1996) (Jones, 2007) and (Pow Sang, 2016).

In collaborative learning environments, students do not rely solely on their teachers. They are not motivated only by their teachers' approval or praise and they do not wait for correction, advice, or instruction on part of their instructors to advance. Instead, the focus is shifted to working in pairs and groups, and the teacher acts as a facilitator rather than a deliverer of knowledge (Zarei, 2016).

2.2 Active and Inquiry-Based Learning

Active learning is intended to address the problem of passive students usually losing concentration 10-15 minutes into a 50-minute lecture (Stuart, 1978). The methodology is based on the hypothesis that if a student is actively involved in reading, writing, discussing, problem solving, or interacting via questions, he/she will pay more attention throughout the class.

Inquiry-based learning focuses on the student investigating a question or a problem and using evidence-based reasoning and creativity to obtain the answers, which he/she then must present and defend (Guido, 2017). From the teacher's viewpoint, this methodology is supposed to not only create curiosity about a subject, but also to elicit critical thinking and understanding on part of the students. The tools at the teacher's disposal are usually guided research, document analysis, and question-and-answer sessions, and they may be used in the form of i) case studies, ii) group projects, iii) research projects, iv) field work - especially for science lessons, and/or v) unique exercises tailored to the students' needs (16). In this work, we mainly address point iv).

2.3 Jigsaw

Jigsaw is a collaborative inquiry-based learning technique proposed by (Aronson, 1978). It consists of dividing the learning material into different tasks and the class into different teams, each containing a number of students usually equal to (or greater than) the number of tasks. Each student in a Jigsaw team will have to perform one of the tasks, which will eventually be integrated by the team to complete the learning process. The methodology iterates between task-based and team-based work. Task-based work is performed in groups of increasing size, starting with individual work and ending with all the students that were assigned to a specific task contrasting and complementing their understanding to reach common ground. After each such phase, each student returns to their corresponding Jigsaw team and presents a report.

This technique takes advantage of learning by teaching. In learning by teaching, Student A teaches Student B about a particular subject. Not only does B learn from this process – and from A's knowledge, but A also learns as he must clearly articulate his understanding to B.

The results of a number of investigations support the positive impact Jigsaw has during the teaching/learning process. In (Sharan, 1980), a study on the effect the Jigsaw Classroom method has was carried out on learners' attitudes and achievements. Jigsaw helped create interdependence among learners as a result of the learning task being divided up amongst them. The results of the study showed a significant change in learners' attitudes towards their fellow classmates as well as a heightened perception of self.

Jigsaw also shows the potential to increase learners' active participation and communication skills (Sahin, 2010). (Durmus, 2008) reports that the effect of Jigsaw on students' performance leads them to conclude that it should be used in all phases of education thanks to its positive influence as compared to traditional learning. In (Felder, 1998), the sequential and global dichotomy learning style, among others, is defined. Most formal education involves presenting material in a logically ordered progression. Some students are comfortable with this system; they learn sequentially, mastering the material (more or less) as it is presented. Others, however, may be lost for weeks, until suddenly they "get it". Jigsaw helps to combine the two types of learning and the benefits of both.

In all such studies, the Jigsaw technique encourages students to better participate in their learning, motivates them to learn larger amounts of material faster than in traditional ways, and inspires them to share information with their classmates.

3. OUR APPROACH

3.1 Case Study

We developed the present study with the 12 third year undergraduates registered in the Cloud computing and distributed systems course of the "Design and development of videogames" specialization during the 2019 Spring quarter. In many engineering disciplines, the learning process is based on incrementally building new knowledge on top of concepts that are already fully understood. This makes the process of selecting a set of topics that could be independently studied a major challenge. We selected Optical Networking because it can be more easily split into independent subtopics as follows:

- Optical fiber (transmission, type of fibers, wavelength multiplexing)
- Optical components (multiplexors/demultiplexers and transponders, amplifiers and switching fabrics)
- Types of optical networks ("circuits", bursts, packets)

These topics can be studied initially in any order, then they could be used as the Jigsaw pieces. The learning process starts with online content search based on a set of keywords that the teacher provides for each subtopic.

3.2 Organization of the Experiment

(Felder, 2003) states that learning techniques should focus on structured cooperative learning that targets five criteria: positive interdependence, individual accountability, face-to-face interaction, the use of appropriate interpersonal skills, and self-assessment towards the continuing goals. These criteria form the basis for planning and managing cooperative learning methods that have been identified as leading to positive impact, not only by increasing students' achievement, but also by enhancing other complementary and fundamental skills such as motivation, positive interaction, cooperation, leadership, decision-making capabilities, tolerance and trust, and the ability to think critically.

We have adopted this hypothesis and considered that Jigsaw is a good candidate for testing it. We have organized the experiment as follows.

We first defined three expert groups for each of the three subtopics introduced in Section III. Students were organized into four teams with each team consisting of one expert for each subtopic. We formed the expert groups randomly as a way for students to learn how to collaborate, discuss, and debate with any partner (Nooritawati, 2010). Each student was also randomly assigned to a team. As a notation, student C2 from Team 2 was assigned to subtopic C.

3.3 Jigsaw Phases

To carry out the Jigsaw activity, students followed the ensuing phases over three consecutive weeks:

1. Every student works individually on his subtopic and delivers a short report to the instructor. Reports are evaluated.
2. During class, students present their findings (on their assigned subtopics) to their team members, who worked on different subtopics, in four simultaneous meetings. Each team meeting thus consists of three presentations covering all the subtopics. Each student is required to make a note of missing points, misunderstandings, etc., from the presentation so as to be able to address them in the future.
3. Students assigned to the same subtopic meet in pairs, i.e. A1+A2, B1+B2, etc. Each pair of students pools their revised material (from their team meetings) and refines it until they converge to the same

material. They then send their integrated material to the teacher. This results in six reports (two per subtopic) for evaluation.

4. During class, each pair of subtopic-specific students presents the improved material to the larger groups consisting of all the members of their teams (e.g. in mixed team 1&2, student pairs A1+A2, B1+B2, and C1+C2).
5. The four students assigned to each subtopic meet and put together their material for the final version and then send a report for evaluation.
6. In a "plenary" meeting during class, three presentations – one for each subtopic - are made. The instructor also evaluates students based on their oral skills, discussions, and possibly other factors that become apparent during this meeting. This is the only time when the instructor is present for all the activities, as all previous phases occur in parallel presentations during class.

3.4 Evaluation of the Activity

Despite the Jigsaw literature indicating all the positive impacts the methodology has on the students, we could not risk treating individuals as statistics to avoid any significant negative impact on the grades of those students who may not find Jigsaw productive for them, we weighted this activity so it only counted 10% towards the final course grade. . This grade is computed as an average of the following four grades:

1. Report from phase 1, graded as individual work.
2. Report from phase 3, graded as work in pairs.
3. Report from phase 5, graded as work of the four-author groups.
4. Final class presentation, individual assessment.

It is important to say that none of the students were familiar with the Jigsaw technique; it was a new concept for all of them.

3.5 Learning Objectives and Competences

Among the competences of the course (as defined in the course syllabus), the Jigsaw activity addresses the following:

- Knowledge and application of the characteristics, functionalities, and structure of distributed systems, computer networks, and the Internet. Ability to design and implement applications based on this knowledge.
- Analyze complex situations and design strategies to address them.
- Compile and select information efficiently.
- Teamwork.
- Decision-making.

4. RESULTS

While the reports and presentations are quantitative measures of how well the students adapted to this method to reach fundamental skills and course competences, the students' own perceptions are equally important. For this reason, we sent a survey to all the students after each presentation. Replies were voluntary. The idea was to try to capture not just a result at a point in time, but also to understand how the students felt about the methodology and their fellow students during this activity, and whether they found Jigsaw motivating.

4.1 First Jigsaw Survey

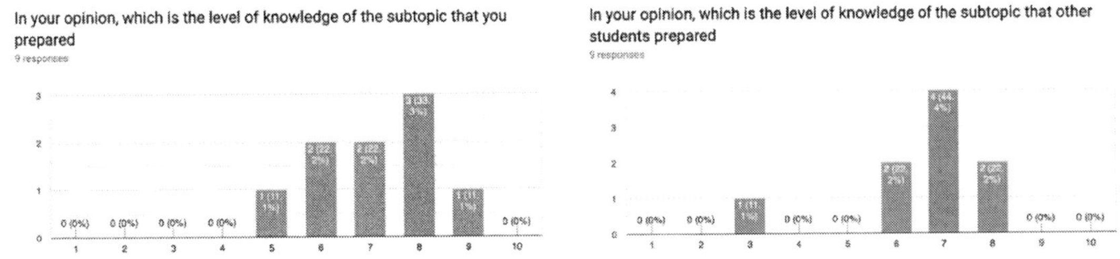

Figure 1. Results from the first survey

From Figure 1, it would seem that students think they are all above average and place their peers into two categories: those who are equally good, (but with a sharper distribution), or those who were very badly prepared. In the results for the question: 'The preparation of your topic is better/equal/worse in relation to the others' topics', 89% said "equal", and 11% said "better".

Summary of *positive comments* (in free text):

Question 1: What aspect of the Jigsaw activity do you like most?

This question elicited free written answers. We summarize the answers below. Noted in **bold** are the most relevant comments.

1. Having to follow different threads to find the necessary information
2. Teamwork, discussion, and the fact that team members change.
3. The explanations of other students are always more easily understood from the outset because they tend to use words that are less formal than those of the teacher.
4. Conducting the first phases in small groups gives more freedom to speak openly with the other person.
5. **Putting together the information synthesized by different people helps one realize that there were things that went unnoticed or that one didn´t give them the importance they have.**

Summary of *negative comments* (in free text):

Question 2: What aspect of the Jigsaw activity do you not like?

This question elicited free written answers which we have summarized below and noted in **bold** the most relevant comment among the answers.

1. Requires too many sessions spent on topics that are not rich/complex enough.
2. Requires a minimum of preparation on part of each student, otherwise one learns very little.
3. The feeling of not being sure whether the information you worked on is good (or that you´re not missing information) until you put all the pieces together.
4. **It can become quite repetitive explaining everything many times.**
5. That we use PBL (project-based learning), the student probably meant "collaborative learning".

4.2 Second Jigsaw Survey

Table 1. Results from the second survey

Questions and answers	After the second session, your knowledge on the subtopic that you prepared has increased:	After the second session, your knowledge on the subtopic that your colleagues prepared has increased
Some	33%	44%
A little	56%	56%
Did not increase	11%	

In Table 1 we see that students tend to think that they have learned less from the assembled information during their second meeting of their subtopic than from the second presentations of the other topics. This is a positive result that says that the material that one prepares and discusses is learned quicker (during the first session) than understanding material presented by others but not worked on by oneself.

4.3 Third Jigsaw Survey

Summary of *positive comments* (in free text):

1. Having to prepare the subject by ourselves improved understanding; comparing one's work with the others and putting it together makes one realize what things they hadn't paid much attention to.
2. Easier to understand the subject.
3. You learn the subject you have prepared 100% after explaining it three times.
4. Being forced to understand and prepare well enough to be able to explain clearly to your colleagues.

Summary of *negative comments* (in free text):

1. It´s a good methodology at the beginning, but it becomes too repetitive if all "experts" in the group summarize more or less the same information.
2. Too many presentations; with a couple it's enough.
3. Some more directed help if we don´t find what we need, or we want to find out more.
4. The content of the other students is equal to or worse than that in a traditional class.
5. The level of knowledge is a bit limited due to finding little information online compared to what we could have learned with a traditional method.
6. When taking the exam, it is assumed that there´s a level of knowledge about things that some groups may not have discussed. This happened in this exam and I don't think it's OK.

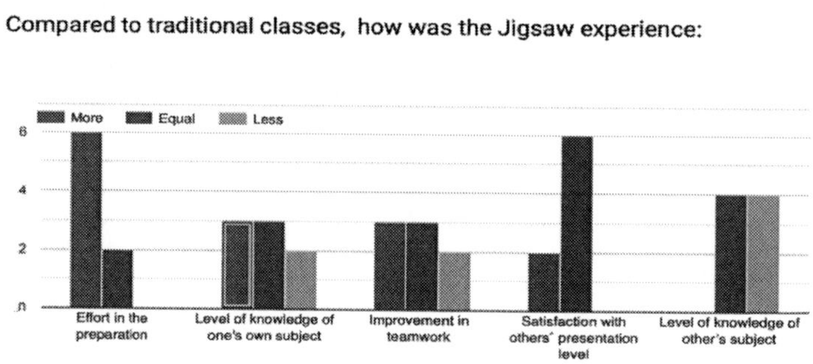

Figure 2. Results from the third survey

Figure 2 shows that a significant number of students considered that they acquired less knowledge about the subtopics they had not prepared than if they had been taught using a traditional method. We believe that this is linked to the fact that some students also lacked some background to understand whether they covered all the relevant material. One lesson learned is that the teacher may need to provide more directed support in some cases. One possible way to do that would be via quizzes that students could take online for themselves. The points covered in the quizzes would need to cover all the material that the teacher thinks necessary for the students to fully understand the class material – including that which was explained by other students. The results of the quizzes are not seen by the teacher.

As a last thought for interpreting the student answers, these are the *impressions* as related by the students. Thus, they may, or may not, reflect reality. These results must be taken as an indication rather than a recipe; more work is needed to fully understand this feedback.

5. CONCLUSION

This work presents a study with the 12 third year undergraduates registered in the Cloud computing and distributed systems course of the "Design and development of video games" specialization at the University of Girona, Spain. Although this is a technical course in the curriculum, it lends itself to the possibility of learning various topics independently. We chose to implement the Jigsaw methodology to increase students' understanding, motivation, cooperation and leadership skills, decision-making capabilities, tolerance and trust, and their ability to think critically.

Our results show that students valued most the fact that preparing and presenting the material by themselves made them understand the subject really well and – encouragingly – that contrasting and complementing information as part of a group made them discover aspects that they had originally not paid attention to. Small groups also gave them the freedom to speak more openly. Our conclusion was that most students adapted rather well to working in groups.

On the negative side, the main impression was that there were too many presentations for a small amount of material (subtopics). Additionally, some students felt that they were not sure whether the information they discovered by themselves was complete and of good enough quality, and they would have liked to have had some more directed help when they needed it. We think that the first observation they made can be resolved by better adjusting the quantity of material and the number of teams and teammates. The second observation could be addressed by providing some form of self-assessment (for instance, online quizzes) directed towards covering a set of teacher-selected points. This could be a way to support those students who feel they need more guidance in a more problem-directed manner.

Finally, there were some contradictions. Students frequently complain about traditional teaching methods, but when they have to follow an alternative method, some reach the conclusion that the traditional one was in fact better. This may be the result of statistics over a reduced number of data points (i.e. students), a real issue for certain learning styles, or a consequence of the way the questions were formulated in our surveys. In the future we will refine these surveys and apply this method to other courses to obtain more data points, which would allow for a more precise analysis, with better results in the classroom. We will also validate these results with Master students, in an effort to see whether age does seem to play a role in the sense that the literature suggests – that older students find it harder to adapt to more flexible, hierarchy-less environments.

ACKNOWLEDGEMENT

This work has been partially supported by the *Generalitat de Catalunya* research support program SGR-1469] and the *Ministerio de Economia, Industria, y Competitividad* (TIN2016- 78473-C3-2-R).

REFERENCES

Aronson, E. 1978. *The Jigsaw Classroom,* Sage, Beverly Hills, CA, USA.

Dumus, Kilic. 2008. The Effect of the Jigsaw Technique on Learning the Concepts of the Principles and Methods of Teaching. World Applied Sciences Journal, Vol. Supple 1. pp. 108-114.

Felder, R.M., and Silverman, L.K.1988. *Learning and teaching styles in engineering education.* Engineering Education, 78:4, 674–681. 1988.

Felder, R.M. and Brent, R. 2003. *Designing and teaching courses to satisfy ABET Engineering criteria.* Journal on Engineering Education. Vol. 92 (1) pp. 7-25.

Guido, M. 2017. *All About Inquiry-Based Learning: Definition, Benefits and Strategies.* https://www.prodigygame.com/blog/inquiry-based-learning-definition-benefits-strategies/

Jones, L. 2007. *The student-centered classroom.* Cambridge University Press. Cambridge, UK.

Kousa, Maan. 2015. *Jigsaw Cooperative Learning in Engineering Classrooms.* IEEE Global Engineering Education Conference (EDUCON).

McConnell, Jeffrey J. 1996. *Active learning and its use in computer science.* In Proceedings of the 1st conference on Integrating technology into computer science education (ITiCSE '96). ACM, New York, USA, 52-54.

Moreillon, J. 2007. Collaborative strategies for teaching reading comprehension: Maximizing your impact. American Library Association, Chicago, USA.

Nooritawati Md Tahir, Kama Azura Othman. 2010. *The Jigsaw Cooperative Method amongst Electrical Engineering Students.* 2nd International Congress on Engineering Education. Kuala Lumpur, Malaysia.

Pow-Sang, José Antonio. 2016. *The Jigsaw technique to teach object-oriented design: A replication study with graduate students.* IEEE Global Engineering Education Conference (EDUCON) pp. 1212-1217.

Sahin, A. 2010. Effects of jigsaw II technique on academic achievement and attitudes to written expression course. Educational Research and Reviews, Vol. 5, pp. 777-787.

Sharan, S. 1980. Cooperative learning in small groups: Recent methods and effects on achievement, attitudes, and ethnic relations. Review of educational research, Vol. 50 (2). pp. 241-271.

Slavin, R. E. 1995. Cooperative learning: Theory, research, and practice. Allyn and Bacon, Boston, USA.

Stuart, J. and Rutherford, R. 1978. *Medical Student Concentration During Lectures.* The Lancet, Vol. 2, September. pp. 514-516.

Zarei, Abbas Ali and Adbi, Venus. 2016, Blended Learning, Computer-based, and Conventional Reading Instruction Affecting EFL Learners' Self-regulation and Critical Thinking. International Journal of Humanities and Cultural Studies.

CYBERNETICS AND PRECURSORS OF PROMOTING CRITICAL THINKING - A WAY TO CHANGE THE SCHOOL

Teodora Surubaru and Dorin Isoc
GRAUR – Group for Reform and University Alternative, Cluj-Napoca, Romania

ABSTRACT

The requirement to assure the teaching of critical thinking put the school in front of its own weaknesses. A profound criticism highlights limitations, hindrances and obstacles that are difficult to pass without the personal efforts of the teachers. Following criticism, one can identify a set of requirements that would allow for improvement and upgrading. This set of requirements builds the specification of a cybernetic system developed to help the training process promoting the critical thinking. The new cybernetic system diminishes the role of the teacher as coordinator in approaching the field of interest, inclusively the building of the recommended bibliographic list and interventions in crises. The main stages of the training sessions coordinated by the cybernetic system aim at a) building a set of problems by the students; b) the classification of all proposed problems according to their opportunity established by the voting group; c) solving the proposed problems by the students; d) evaluating, by vote, all the solutions offered for the proposed problems. Using the formulated specification and the established operating algorithm the operating scheme of the cybernetic system is being built. The proposed scheme is intended to monitor and manage the training process. The results interpretation highlights the absolute novelty of such a system and analyzes how it satisfies the original specification. One observes the generality of the concept, the way it meets the requirement of promoting critical thinking, the fact that the promotion is made gradually and continuously.

KEYWORDS

Training, Critical Thinking, Cybernetics, Criticism, Evaluation, Problem Building, Problem Solving

1. INTRODUCTION

The technological evolution of society, as well as of human relations, entails an increase in the degree of adaptation of the school. It is worth mentioning that the school is losing more and more of the training resources taken over by the electronic environment and other ways of training the workforce. All these resources and means have a significant influence on the student's future, the future specialist. Moreover, this influence isn't a uniform one neither on individuals nor on groups of individuals.

Thus, the school finds itself among many variables: the technological evolution determines the lack of specific knowledge and skills, the level of formal and informal learning of the student is always different and differs from individual to individual, the amount of information increases and changes its coordinates in the space training, at less and less frequent time periods.

In the school modernization strategy a key role is the choice of a higher standard. In this case, learning "critical thinking" seems to be a provocative ideal.

In this sense, the definition introduced by (Scriven and Paul, 1987) appears as a true specification of the notion. We note in particular that the achievement of the objective does not seem possible from a simple reform or maneuver on a long-standing social system, but the definition is a set of tangible in time sub-objectives.

> *„...critical thinking is the intellectually disciplined process of actively and skillfully conceptualizing, applying, analyzing, synthesizing, and/or evaluating information gathered from, or generated by, observation, experience, reflection, reasoning, or communication, as a guide to belief and action. In its exemplary form, it is based on universal intellectual values that transcend subject matter divisions: clarity, accuracy, precision, consistency, relevance, sound evidence, good reasons, depth, breadth, and fairness....*"

In fact, many references (Mandernach, 2006) (Saeed, 2012), (Snyder and Snyder, 2008) highlight realistically those hindrances that prevent the current school from reaching such an objective.

Together with other researchers, (Snyder and Snyder, 2008) emphasizes the role of questions and problems in addressing learning "critical thinking." However, there is a tendency to introduce surrogate solutions without fundamental changes to the conventional school, and also the tendency to keep the teacher at the heart of the concerns when it comes to school.

Far from reducing school to the mere accumulation of knowledge, it is undeniable that any training process begins and is a stage of acquiring knowledge. At this stage of training, it is essential how the teacher and the student are positioned and cooperate, how the relationships between the teacher and the group of students are.

The evolution of the school never changed the relationship between the teacher and the student, never changed their role in the training process. It may be possible to insist on some changes in the form in which these roles happen, and by accentuating new requirements such as creativity, which could be added to traditional tasks (Iba et al, 2011).

In this context, the emergence of software occurs as a revolution through the volume of resources and the new communication possibilities (Klamma et al, 2007). Still, however, the student-teacher relationship does not change in essence.

A more realistic vision on the school (Dewey, 2004) occurs when looking at the analysis of its purpose, the ability to stimulate thinking. In these situations, it quickly concludes that school is not the one that stimulates, but rather that, which inhibits thinking. When we talk more about school and the one that inhibits thinking, it is inevitable not to insist that it's the teacher. He/she is who can develop the ability to think or, on the contrary. He is the one who looks for the problems and assumes responsibility for the applied guidance on future results.

> „...*A large part of the art of instruction lies in making the difficulty of new problems large enough to challenge thought, and small enough so that, in addition to the confusion naturally attending the novel elements, there shall be luminous familiar spots from which helpful suggestions may spring...*"

This latter conclusion is the one that puts the most important diagnosis on the school framework. In the traditional view, the teacher possesses and insists on arrogating the exclusivity of the right to know everything, to be the master of the problems and the victim of the solutions. The teacher is a victim because his/her problems almost never coincide with the real problems of the student.

The subject of this research is situated in the school area, of the necessity to systematically promote "critical thinking", the argumentation of some ways of intervention on the organization and functioning of the training process in order to make it more efficient for the benefit of the student and to materialize the requirements in a dedicated cybernetic system.

In the second chapter a criticism is made on some aspects of functional training systems. The finality of the critique is to identify the requirements of a specification of the interventions the author wishes to suggest and the cybernetic system to develop.

The third chapter introduces a set of principles that should underpin a cybernetic system. It is noteworthy that these principles take into account both the elements of specification introduced and the requirements that can build critical thinking. The criteria have a mixed pedagogical - technical - organizational structure.

The fourth chapter describes the functional scheme of the cybernetic system dedicated to the training process and its main working algorithm. Although succinctly, the presentation is sufficiently explicit to allow a series of consistent interpretations, further found in the fifth chapter. Interpretations emphasize how the proposed technical solution addresses the multiple requirements previously analyzed. Finally, in the conclusions chapter are synthesized those elements of contribution that are meant to solve the problem of critical thinking through the systematic generation of precursors.

The essential contribution of the article is its first coherent presentation of the elements of a complex cybernetic system that eliminates the teacher as a human factor responsible for the acquisition of critical thinking and replaces it with the group of all the students working under a procedure and under the control of the machine. The whole of the students is especially performing precisely because they are responsible for generating problems, but also for building solutions with reference to a segment of knowledge and reality judiciously chosen by the teacher.

2. A CRITICISM OF CONVENTIONAL TRAINING SYSTEMS

In the following, the analysis of the current training system is carried out especially in terms of a technical system. Other, even interesting, aspects are approached only to the extent that they have consequences in the training technique.

Building a technical system, be it a socio-cybernetic system, requires a set of objectives and a fair reporting at a current context and stage.

Obviously, the training process has several component parts, but its destination is to ensure the acquisition of knowledge and skills. If acquiring skills involves a controlled exercise, when it comes to acquiring knowledge in school, the main form of current action involves passing it through lectures, university courses or assimilated forms. We will encompass all these forms of transmission of knowledge under the generic name of "training". In addition, the call to the name of "instructor" will also be generic for any quality of teacher or assimilated, and the same for the name of "student" for any person who is in a position to acquire knowledge systematically in an organized form based on a group of individuals.

Conventionally, the relationship between the instructor and the student assumes the student's interest, the instructor's competence and a volume of knowledge to assimilate by specific forms. The collaboration between the instructor and the student has also no other premises than the student's supposed interest.

A criticism of conventional training systems can only consider criteria that address their functionality.

2.1 The Lack of Actuality and Efficiency of the Lecture Technique

In (Isoc and Isoc, 2010) an analysis of the general relationship between the instructor and the student is made through the sources of knowledge and the way these sources affect the student's initial level of knowledge. The conclusion of the study is that, over time, the instructor has gradually lost the exclusivity of knowledge sources through the emergence of media vectors, such as radio, television, computer, internet.

The main consequence is that the initial level of knowledge of any subject with which the student comes to school is no longer void and differs from person to person. In this way, the effectiveness of the trainer's work is becoming relative. Under the same conditions, it is increasingly difficult for the school to meet the individualized requirements of each student.

2.2 Lack of Personalized Training

In general, training happens through groups and thus, all individual results are marked by the intrinsic nature of the quality of the student and his / her colleagues. Through quality of the student is also understood the volume and quality of knowledge acquired a priori by the student from the resources available to inform.

The student's individual quality and then, the quality of the student group affect the quality of the training. A student with better initial information will have a better evolution. Better initial student information will ease training, but at the same time, it will focus on certain topics, often different from the teacher's priorities.

Most often, the instructor is the one who presumes the student's needs and imagines his or her own ways to make his / her best presentation (Bergin, 2000).

One can thus talk about a lack of adjustment between the student's actual topics of interest and the topics of interest proposed by the instructor. As the student represents a certain vision of the labor market, the lack of adjustment becomes a potential conflict within the school between new and old, between useful and less useful.

The greater the distance between the students 'topics of interest and the themes of the instructors' interest, the less is the school's efficiency.

This identifies the need for adaptation between the instructor and his students as a way to improve the school. Practically, each student series can direct the instructor's activity to specific chapters of a common knowledge pool or to the need to enrich the knowledge base asked for the training.

2.3 Lack of Use of the Latent Potential of the Group of Students

Conventional school puts the instructor in the core of its action. It is the classic vision and it has proven effective in historical times long gone. By repositioning the school's actors before the sources of knowledge, the process of "democratizing" the sources of knowledge, the role of the instructor decreases. Instead, the formative role of interaction within a group accentuates in front of a volume of knowledge.

Collaboration can thus gain more from the classical role of the instructor. Collaboration can be a natural solution to trigger the latent potential of the group of students. When it comes to engineering, for example, collaboration is not just a desideratum; it becomes a necessity imposed by the standards of the profession.

2.4 The Difficulty of Acquiring "Critical Thinking"

Defined within a desideratum, "critical thinking" is the one that has the lowest chances to be acquired in conventional school under the conditions of conventional education systems.

If we take only the conclusions of a single reference (Saeed et al, 2012), the conventional school represents, both in the form of organization in classes and through education instructors, a background incompatibility with "critical thinking" training.

We remember here (Snyder and Snyder, 2008) that there are sufficient evidences that "critical thinking" is not properly assessed in the context of the traditional school. Thus, the hindrances to inefficiency correctly identifies: a) lack of training of trainers, b) lack of information; c) preconceived ideas from both instructors and students; d) time constraints. It identifies further the need to increase the efforts of the instructor and the students' reaction as a point where they can intervene. Finally, the practical solution is given, namely, the questioning.

It is obvious that the lack of effects lies in the absence of a coherent project that justifies and further bases the intervention.

2.5 Lack of Adaptation to the Needs of Lifelong Learning

It is increasingly difficult to see a person's professional and social development without taking into account the need for lifelong learning. However, the achievement of continuous learning also implies some particular aspects. Their simple mention is found in any work in the field (Klamma el al, 2007). We remind them, as these issues relates to the subject.

There are discussions about the difference between adult learning and youth learning, about the difference between formal and in-formal learning, about collaborative learning platforms and their role in providing customized solutions.

2.6 An Interpretation of Criticism - Specification of Modernization Intervention

Because of the criticism, there are some conclusions that can offer new solutions for the modernization of the training process and the training structures.

Information technology becomes part of the training process not only by allowing access to information:

1. Training cannot ignore the diversity of students' initial levels of knowledge.
2. Training requires metering as objective as possible of indicators to properly relate the effects of training to the real needs of students.
3. Training needs to be the one that takes at the right moment new knowledge and sources of knowledge customized to the needs of society.
4. It is necessary for the instructor's activity to become more efficient in the process of coordinating the acquisition of knowledge.
5. It is unnatural that the instructor should support the entire quality of the school and the training.
6. The organizational and economic considerations of the training process cannot be ignored at any time. It is worth noting here indicators such as the size of the study groups, the achievement of an expected degree of satisfaction, the efficiency of the school in the areas of activity of the group of students in relation

to the instructor. These indicators cannot be ignored in designing a training system.

7. Training has ceased to be an art. Training should be conducted in the area of efficient procedures from which information technology naturally belongs.

3. PRINCIPLES OF MODERNIZATION INTERVENTION

Here are some of the principles that will underpin the modernization of the training process. It is insisted that the purpose of the research is to build a socio-cybernetic system through which the school can better ensure "critical thinking".

3.1 Critical Analysis Priority Principle

The whole approach is based on the principle of critical analysis as a form of training development.

The essence of the principle describes with the recapture of the role of an instructor, which after Dewey, quoted in (Giles and Eyler, 1994) should be

> „...*to provide the materials and the conditions by which organic curiosity will be directed into investigations that have an aim and that produce results in the way of increase of knowledge, and by which social inquisitiveness will be converted into ability to find out things known to others, an ability to ask questions of books as well as of persons*...".

During the implementation, the principle will be found in that the entire training process is based on the question or problem; and on the problem management task.

The question or problem is a lack of knowledge, explicitly expressed in relation to a volume of information suggested by the instructor. The complexity of the problem may be lower or higher. The way the problem is formulated is a free one and the only condition that is required is that the text of the problem is readable and understandable to any reader. The problems are read and evaluated firstly by the students.

3.2 Principle of Priority of Interested Competence of Group

Such a principle is introduced in the context of training and collaboration and occurs with reference to a group of people.

A possible statement of the principle of priority of interested competence could be:

> *Any action of a group of individuals interested in a joint activity is more competent than the action of any of its members considered separately.*

Specifically, the training group consists, conventionally, of the instructor and the members of the student group. It will assume that if the group's professional opinion is permissible as a whole, then it manifests itself as a competence that is superior to the competence of each individual, so it is superior, including to the competence of the instructor.

Competence manifests itself in two ways. A first way is that in front of a problem formulated by a student, each member of the training group has all the conditions to provide a response, a solution.

On the other hand, competence will materialize in the fact that it is admitted that each member of the training group can give an appreciation of the degree to which a problem or a solution meets the needs of each individual. This appreciation is called the opportunity of the problem and the extent to which a solution offered for a problem is usable, will be called usability of the solution.

Expression of the individual position will be done through a quantitative vote expressed in different stages of the training process.

3.3 Principle of Operational Constraints of Critical Action

Professional training through specialized entities involves the presence of two less algorithmic features. It is about personal interest and the occurrence of synergy manifestations.

Each feature in turn has a beneficial character and needs to be taken into account. Although these characteristics are also present in the conventional forms of the school, they are less exploited explicitly.

This time, the existence of a technical implementation allows the materialization of means by which the two characteristics become functional means.

|The personal interest will relate to the application of a mandatory action regime for certain stages of work and will be stimulated by the introduction of quantitative voting as a means of measurement.

Being a cybernetic system, the driven process is seen in its entire dynamic. It therefore seems natural to take into account that school, and the training takes place over time, and all the component parts that interact, including the training group and the instructor, act in time by means of own or imposed dynamics.

Constraints at the temporal variable have priority before other possible constraints.

3.4 Principle of Objective Measurements in the Training Process

Cybernetics produces controllable results only if the state of the controlled system is objective and reproducible. As state means a set of defined variables, the cybernetic system cannot exist outside of a state variables measurement subsystem.

4. IMPLEMENTATION OF THE CYBERNETIC SYSTEM

The effect of the connections and the proposed algorithm results from the description in Figure 1. The basic element of the socio-cybernetic system is the instructor-student relationship.

The instructor-student relationship is no\ necessarily straightforward. However, the relationship always involves the existence of a motivation, of a specific interest for each party. It is to note that always the relationship has a procedural character. Conventionally, the relationship between the instructor and the student is an instructor-stimulated one.

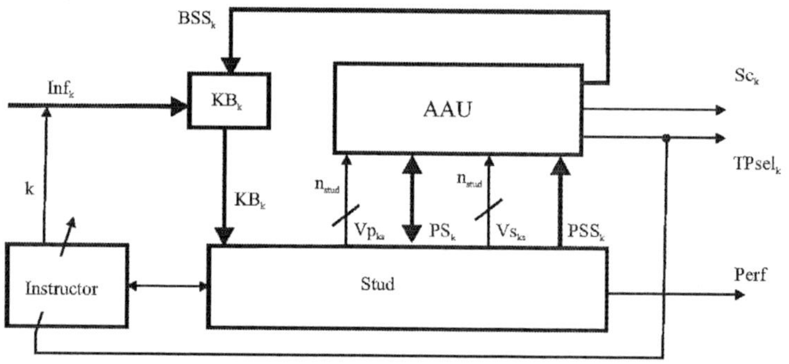

Figure 1. The block diagram of the self-adaptive socio-cyber training system

Without being explicit as such, the relationship between the instructor and the student responds to social desiderata, along with a series of individual desires of development and development of each student.

In the new vision, the instructor is the one who offers the training theme and then receives the request to adapt the training process from the group of students he is working with.

In the block diagram of Figure 1, one identifies Inf_k - the information planned for approach at time moment k; KB_k - the knowledge base built under the coordination of the instructor in order to support the training process; Sc_k - the set of opportunity degrees of the proposed problems and the usability degrees of the offered solutions; $TPsel_k$ - the set of unresolved problems at k cycle; BSS_k - the set of selected solutions to be introduced into the KB_k knowledge base at the end of step k; *AAU* - the self-adapting unit; *nstud* - number of students of the working group; *Stud* - group of students in training activity; PS_k - the set of problems generated by student activity in k-cycle of the self-adjusting system; Vp_{ks} - the qualifying votes of students for the proposed problems from step k; Vs_{ks} - student votes to evaluate solutions for the problems proposed in step k; PSS_k - the set of solutions offered for the problems proposed by the students; *Perf* - the performance indicator of the training system. One insists that the solutions formulated by the students are also built by the action of the students.

The instructor's activity takes place over a time period in training sessions that correspond to cycles $k = 1, 2, \ldots$ In each work cycle, k, the instructor discusses an Inf_k amount of information. Over time, in relation to the training process, a knowledge base, KB_k for the k cycle, also built on steps, can be identified.

$$KB_k = KB_{k-1} + Inf_k \tag{1}$$

The sequence of work stages, attached to each work cycle k, follows a step path described as in Algorithm 1.

Step 1: Students are provided, in co-operation with the instructor, with the information to be approached Inf_k.
Step 2: Each student is invited to formulate at least one problem with reference to work information.
Step 3: All students decide by vote on the degree of opportunity for each built problem.
Step 4: One builds the PB_k problem base associated to k step.
Step 5: Each student can offer solutions, PSS_k for one or more of the built problems.
Step 6: Students decide by vote on the usability of each solution offered.
Step 7: The opportunity scores of the problems and the usability scores of the solutions from k step are automatically integrated into the activity score of each student of the training group.
Step 8: Set of unresolved problems *TPsel* are given to instructor for priority treatment.

End of Algorithm 1

Algorithm 1. Work steps attached to each training k cycle

5. INTERPRETATIONS, DISCUSSIONS, RESULTS

Although not specifically insisted, the proposed system is based on cybernetic principles. Among these principles, for this work, it is essential the providing of assistance and constant monitoring of the work of all actors involved.

By the provided algorithm of this system essential changes are produced in the structure and nature of the training process:

i. The instructor ceases to be the centre of the training activity. Its role diminishes to coordinate the themes to be addressed, to achieve the purpose of the training activity, and to intervene in special situations.
ii. By the nature of the built self-adaptive system, the problems become essential. Problems are formulated based on the training theme, without being limited by it. Students propose the problems without the teacher's influence.
iii. The problems suggested by the students reflect their real interest in the topic in question. The set of problems can be classified based on the interested competence principle and corresponds indirectly to the difficulty of the proposed problems.
iv. The students of training group offer solutions to the proposed problems. It should not be forgotten, that they have knowledge of the activity support given by the instructor. In this way, their solutions are built on their own perception.
v. The evaluation of the solutions offered to the proposed problems has as a criterion the usability related to the expectations and the interest of the students. The relevance of usability is ensured by the vote of all students who still respect once again the principle of interested competence.
vi. Turned into a coach, the instructor can rethink the "game schedule" after each training cycle. The "game scheme" involves associations of bibliographic references whereby topics of interest are covered as accurately and specifically as possible by the training group.

The proposed solution is not, in itself, a form, a mechanism for acquiring "critical thinking", but it is a possible collection of precursors to do that.

Once the system is used, there is the student's experience in addressing and refining the techniques of "critical thinking" development, such as the five steps of the IDEAS process suggested by (Facione, 1998).

In the above, it should be added that both the texts of the problems and the texts of the solutions can be admitted only in written form and drafted according to norms that emphasize the stages of reasoning and context reporting.

One aspect worthy to be emphasized is that the "source of problems" is inexhaustible and is maintained in this state precisely by the freshness and lack of prejudice that any human being presents before a new theme in the absence of too many hindrances before the experience.

It emphasizes that achieving an electronic service from the developed cybernetic system eliminates the conventional school hours as the only condition is to ensure the transparency of the working stages and this is implicit.

One aspect of the experiments and simulations already carried out concerns the sizing of the training teams. It turns out that a number of 10-15 students per training group seem to be optimal. The limitation is not technical, but the optimization issue remains open and will probably be readjusted after a significant number of completed training sessions.

The principles outlined and how to conceive the cybernetic concept lie at the heart of the CyberTrainer training service.

6. CONCLUDING REMARKS

The extent of the requirements imposed on school, and in particular the imperative of promoting "critical thinking", highlighted the lack of adaptability of the traditional school. Following detailed functional analyzes, the obsolete role of the instructor confirms reported to the new conditions and the new requirements. Therefore, a specification of a training system is developed that could eliminate the persisting shortcomings.

The training system, based on cyber-grounds, shifts the role of the trainer to coach and focuses on successive modules of problem-building steps, followed by actions to classify their opportunity to the students of the training group, with steps to build solutions for these issues, followed by actions to evaluate built-in solutions. Students develop both, problems and solutions.

Suggested work is an operational precursor of "critical thinking" and has the consequence of involving the entire training group under the conditions of full transparency.

It is worth mentioning that with the monitoring and coordination of the training activity, the cybernetic system also has a module for integrating the students' activity scores on each cycle introduced.

The role of the instructor is limited to establishing the training plan and building the list of reference bibliographies.

The generalization of the cybernetic training system in a public service allows it to be extended from schools of all categories to continuous education activities, to specific training activities for elderly.

REFERENCES

Bergin, J., 2000, July. Fourteen Pedagogical Patterns. In *EuroPLoP*, pp.1-49.

Dewey, J., 2004. *Democracy and education.* Courier Corporation.

Facione, P.A., 1998. Critical thinking: What it is and why it counts. *Retrieved June, 9*, p.2004.

Giles Jr, D.E. and Eyler, J., 1994. The theoretical roots of service-learning in John Dewey: Toward a theory of service-learning. *Michigan Journal of Community Service Learning, 1*(1), p.7.

Iba, T., et al, 2011, October. Pedagogical patterns for creative learning. In: *Proceedings of the 18th conference on pattern languages of programs,* p. 28.

Isoc, D., and Isoc, T., 2010, A new adaptive teaching method for engineering school. *Journal Plus Education / Educația Plus. 6*(2), pp. 124–131.

Klamma, R., et al, 2007. Social software for life-long learning. *Educational technology & society, 10*(3), pp.72-83.

Mandernach, B.J., 2006. Thinking critically about critical thinking: Integrating online tools to promote critical thinking. *Insight: A collection of faculty scholarship, 1*, pp.41-50.

Saadé, R.G., et al, 2012. Critical thinking in E-learning environments. *Computers in Human Behavior, 28*(5), pp.1608-1617.

Snyder, L.G. and Snyder, M.J., 2008. Teaching critical thinking and problem solving skills. *The Journal of Research in Business Education, 50*(2), p.90.

EXAMINING LANGUAGE-AGNOSTIC METHODS OF AUTOMATIC CODING IN THE COMMUNITY OF INQUIRY FRAMEWORK

Yuta Taniguchi[1], Shin'ichi Konomi[2] and Yoshiko Goda[3]
[1]*Faculty of Information Science and Electrical Engineering, Kyushu University, Japan*
[2]*Faculty of Arts and Science, Kyushu University, Japan*
[3]*Research Center for Instructional Systems, Kumamoto University, Japan*

ABSTRACT

This study discusses the automatic coding methods of the Community of Inquiry (CoI) framework for multilingual contexts, in particular. In universities, foreign students cannot be overlooked, and learning systems are also required to work in multilingual situations. However, none of the existing work has addressed the lack of language-agnostic and automatic coding algorithms for the CoI framework, even though the framework is widely used to assess student-generated texts. In this study, we investigate the performance of a data-driven text tokenization algorithm for automatic coding. Using a real-world dataset, we compare the prediction performance of the language-independent tokenizer with a language-dependent tokenizer. Our experiments show the data-driven tokenizer to be comparable to its competitor, and a classification algorithm with this tokenizer could achieve high prediction performance for many CoI indicators. We believe that our experimental results are informative and could provide a baseline for future research.

KEYWORDS

CSCL, CoI Framework, Coding, NLP, Prediction

1. INTRODUCTION

Texts are fundamental elements of an educational context and provide rich information for improving learning and teaching. For instance, reflective learning journals are useful for understanding students' learning, and chat-like messages between students are found in online forums and computer-supported collaborative learning (CSCL) environments. Such chat messages are important as sensors, especially in a CSCL setting, for knowing about the kinds of activities in which students are participating, or how well group work is progressing, etc. To implement an effective CSCL environment, visualization is a useful solution for the enhancement of collaborative learning performance and contributions. A serious problem in CSCL is that of social loafing (Latané et al. 1979), in which some learners are not engaged in collaborative learning activities, because of the non-visualization of their contributions to collaborative work. Therefore, utilizing such textual data is indispensable for tailoring collaborative learning effectively.

One of the important problems associated with such student-generated texts is the automatic coding of texts. Some research exists which has tackled this problem (Zehner et al. 2016), but none of the studies considered the problem in a multilingual setting. Many natural language processing techniques depend on a language's properties; thus, it is not easy to apply an automatic coding algorithm developed for a Western language to an East Asian text dataset. Since education can no longer be separated from the global context, it is crucial that a system work uniformly in any language. Hence, the language-agnostic analysis of educational text data is important and still a challenging task.

The specific focus of this study is the coding of the Community of Inquiry (CoI) framework (Rourke et al. 1999; Garrison, Anderson, and Archer 1999; Anderson et al. 2001). This framework is composed of three elements: social presence, cognitive presence, and teaching presence. The framework has been used in many studies to investigate and evaluate the effect of learning communities and collaborative learning environments (e.g., Yamada 2010; Yamada and Kitamura 2011). Despite their usefulness, automatic coding algorithms of CoI have not been investigated as much. Several studies have indicated that visualization of collaborative learning situations could enhance the awareness of social presence (e.g., Yamada et al. 2016; Yamada et al. 2016). However, categorization accuracy and prediction rate are low, depending on social presence categories. In order to improve the accuracy, automatically-coding algorithm should be improved. For this reason, in this study, we examine methods of coding some CoI components automatically, especially in multilingual situations. Our major concern in this study is tokenization. Tokenization is a type of preprocessing of natural language texts that splits a given sentence into smaller tokens. The most frequently used type of token is the word, since it is relatively easy to identify and considered to be a rich source of meaning. Having said that, words are not always a good unit for characterizing texts, and different units have been proposed (Okanohara and Tsujii 2009; Zhai et al. 2011). Furthermore, tokenization is a fundamental problem in East Asian languages, in which words are not separated by spaces. For such languages, morphological analysis is applied to obtain reasonable sentence splits. However, it is not possible to achieve language-agnostic automatic coding with such analyzers.

Therefore, in this study, we examine the performance of a data-driven tokenization algorithm compared with a Japanese morphological analyzer. Among the many indicators introduced by the CoI framework, we focus on those for social presence and cognitive presence. We formulate the automatic coding problem as a multi-label binary classification problem and then evaluate the prediction performance of some combinations of tokenizers and classifiers with a real-world dataset obtained on our CSCL platform and manually annotated.

2. METHOD

2.1 Classifiers

The task we consider in this study is as follows. There are 13 cognitive presence indicators and 18 social presence indicators, and we want to automatically determine which indicators a given sentence contains, as human annotators do. Since such indicators can be considered as a type of label, our classification task is a general multi-label classification problem. In this study, we adopt the binary relevance approach (Read et al. 2011). With this approach, we regard our task as 31 independent uni-label classification tasks. We train 31 independent uni-label classifiers for each label and then use them to predict each label one by one.

We use two types of classifiers which have shown high performance in text classification tasks. One is random forests (Breiman 2001) classifier, a type of ensemble method based on bagging decision trees. XGBoost (Chen and Guestrin 2016) is the other classifier we use in this study; it is also based on decision trees but uses the gradient boosting technique.

Please note that our experiment aims to compare tokenization methods, not these classifiers, so we do not invest much effort in tuning classifiers, e.g., grid search of hyperparameters. Our experimentation uses existing programming libraries for machine learning, Scikit-learn (Pedregosa et al. 2011), and we mainly use the default parameters of classifiers.

2.2 Tokenization

We compare two tokenization methods: MeCab (Kudo, Yamamoto, and Matsumoto 2004) and SentencePiece (Kudo and Richardson 2018). MeCab is a popular morphological analyzer for tokenizing Japanese sentences. Its model's parameters are pre-trained from a large text corpus and provided as a dictionary. While it can achieve higher tokenization quality for formal texts, it is known to fail with more casual texts. In other words, the tokenization results vary significantly depending on the dictionary, which is why there are some dictionaries for MeCab. Therefore, we expect that it is also hard for MeCab to tokenize chat messages.

SentencePiece is a relatively new tokenization method developed mainly for neural machine translations. It is an unsupervised text tokenizer we can consider as a data-driven approach. It builds a probabilistic language model from an input corpus of texts to tokenize on the fly, and then it segments texts into sub-word pieces. Unlike supervised approaches, this algorithm does not need a pre-tokenized dataset, and thus it is essentially language agnostic. This fact suggests that SentencePiece is more suitable for a text corpus such as ours, in which texts written in different languages are mixed.

Another important point of the SentencePiece algorithm is that it requires the number of tokens to be specified in advance, while this is not required in the case of MeCab. Since this setting is considered to affect the classification results significantly, we try different numbers. We put a limit on the size of vocabularies obtained from both of the tokenizers as follows. In the case of the MeCab tokenizer, we first tokenize all sentences from a corpus and count every token's occurrences. Then, we reject infrequent tokens and choose the most frequent k tokens as the vocabulary. However, for the case of SentencePiece, we simply let it choose optimal k tokens. We set k to 1500, 3500, and 5500.

Prior to tokenization, we apply two normalization processes to all the texts so that we can ignore non-essential variations of texts. One is case conversion, during which we convert all capital letters to their corresponding lower-case letters. The other is Unicode normalization. We employ Normalization Form Compatibility Composition (NFKC) normalization. Through the latter, we can treat different forms of some letters often observed in Japanese texts consistently.

After tokenization, however, we omit the usual preprocessing steps of natural language processing, e.g., stop word removal, in this study, because our purpose is to investigate the possibility of language-independent processing of chat messages, and we want to avoid language-dependent preprocessing as much as possible. Another reason for preserving stop words is because we are *not* classifying chat messages by their topics but by chat method. For example, the phrases "how about" and "what if" are usually deleted as stop words, but they might provide good hints for coding the cognitive presence of "suggestions for consideration" (corresponding to label 24). Therefore, we preserve all of the obtained tokens for better classification results.

2.3 Evaluation

Tokenized chat messages are converted into feature vectors and then passed to a classifier. We use the vector space model as a representation of chat texts and TF-IDF (Salton and Buckley 1988) as a term weighting method. The TF-IDF feature consists of term frequency (TF) and inverse document frequency (IDF). The former works as an indicator of the importance of a word within a document (a chat message, in our case). The latter suppresses topic-irrelevant words, i.e., stop words, and it is important for our settings without stop word removal. Depending on the maximum number of tokens, the resulting feature vectors have different dimensionality.

```
for each label {
    for each split of CV {
        training_dataset, test_dataset = get_dataset_for_this_split()
        for each vocabulary size {
            for each tokenizer {
                tokenized_training_dataset, vocabulary = tokenize_with(tokenizer, training
                tokenized_test_dataset = tokenize_with(tokenizer, est_dataset, vocabulary)
                for each classifier {
                    train(classifier, tokenized_training_dataset)
                    evaluate_with(classifier, tokenized_test_dataset)
                }
            }
        }
    }
}
```

Figure 1. The pseudo code of our evaluation procedure. Please note that we use a vocabulary learned during tokenization of the training dataset for tokenizing the test dataset

Table 1. Labels to be assigned to every chat message. There are two types of labels corresponding to social and cognitive presence indicators. The former is shown in the upper table, while the latter is shown in the lower table. We ignore labels that have no more than 10 positive instances, i.e., five labels are ignored in our experiment

ID	Description	#Positives	Ignored?
1	emotion	293	no
2	humor	26	no
3	selfdisclosure	74	no
4	paralanguage	938	no
5	value	944	no
6	thread	3	yes
7	quoting	1	yes
8	reference	110	no
9	question	652	no
10	appreciation	60	no
11	agreement	384	no
12	disagreement	46	no
13	advice	1	yes
14	vocatives	121	no
15	inclusive	231	no
16	phatics	312	no
17	social sharing	142	no
18	reflection	4	yes

ID	Description	#Positives	Ignored?
19	recognize problem	375	no
20	sense of puzzlement	257	no
21	exploration within the online community	1244	no
22	exploration within a single message	24	no
23	information exchange	527	no
24	suggestions for consideration	308	no
25	leaps to conclusions	216	no
26	integration among group members	76	no
27	integration within a single message	4	yes
28	connecting ideas synthesis	189	no
29	creating solutions	39	no
30	vicarious application to real-world testing solutions	288	no
31	defending solutions	20	no

To evaluate the classification results, cross-validation (Kohavi 1995) is a widely used method that can average the effect of different dataset splits. In this study, we use stratified 10-fold cross-validation. Since each label has a very different number of positive samples, as shown in Table 1, we decided to conduct cross-validation separately for each label. Furthermore, some labels have only a small number of positive instances, and we cannot evaluate classification for them. Therefore, we abandoned evaluations of labels with less than 10 positive instances. As a result, we conduct an evaluation of 26 labels; 14 are social presence indicators, and 12 are cognitive presence indicators. As an evaluation metric, we employ ROC AUC (Fawcett 2006). Figure 1 shows the whole picture of our evaluation procedure. Please note that we use a vocabulary learned during tokenization of the training dataset for tokenizing the test dataset.

2.4 Labeled Dataset

We use manually labeled chat texts as a training and test dataset for our experiments. Following the coding scheme used in Shea et al. 2010, we give 31 binary labels to every chat message collected on our CSCL platform. The dataset is composed of 3,251 chat messages, written in Japanese and/or English. However, please note that there are messages consisting of words that are neither English nor Japanese. They are written using the alphabet, but the characters are used as phonetic symbols to express the pronunciation of Japanese words. In our group chat system, we use emoticons represented in special notation such as "(smile)" or "(cat)" in the dataset. To prevent them from being tokenized into multiple tokens, we added them to MeCab and SentencePiece tokenizers as pre-defined tokens.

3. RESULTS

Table 2 shows the major outcomes of our experiment. The table shows the area under the receiver operating characteristic curve (AUC ROC) values for every combination of a label (row) and prediction method (column). A prediction method is defined as a combination of three components: a classifier, tokenizer, and the number of tokens. In the table, the darker the background, the better the prediction performance. Again, please note that we do not tune any hyperparameters of the classifiers, and comparison between random forests and XGBoost does not make sense.

First, we compare the results of MeCab and those of SentencePiece. Basically SentencePiece-based predictive models are comparable to MeCab-based ones, and sometimes they have greater performance. Relatively speaking, MeCab-based models have no obvious disadvantages over the competitor, while SentencePiece has some cases of its performance being clearly poorer (see the cases of label 2, label 22, and label 26).

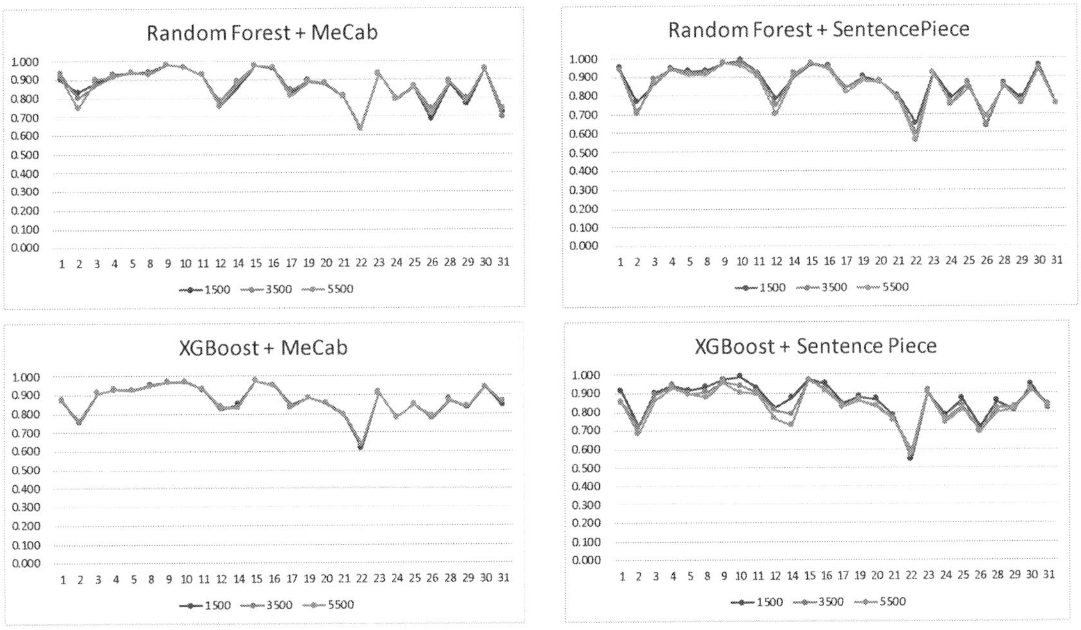

Figure 2. Visual comparison of the stability of different vocabulary sizes. The most robust combination is XGBoost + MeCab, while the other combinations using SentencePiece are relatively unstable

Second, regarding the effects of vocabulary sizes, we see no large differences in performance, except for certain cases. For example, in the case of the combination of label 12 and SentencePiece and that of label 2 and MeCab, the performance decreases as vocabulary size increases. However, it is difficult to say which vocabulary size we should use for the best performance. In terms of performance stability, Figure 2 provides a visual comparison of the stability of different vocabulary sizes. In the figure, we can easily see the different tendencies: the combinations using SentencePiece are relatively unstable, and, in addition, the combination of XGBoost + MeCab is the most robust.

Table 2. The core outcome from our experiment. In the table, the darker the background, the better the prediction performance. Please note that we do not tune any hyperparameters of these classifiers; comparing them does not make sense

	Random Forests						XGBoost					
	MeCab			SentencePiece			MeCab			SentencePiece		
Label ID	1500	3500	5500	1500	3500	5500	1500	3500	5500	1500	3500	5500
1	0.899	0.931	0.919	0.949	0.940	0.940	0.874	0.871	0.872	0.912	0.857	0.849
2	0.831	0.799	0.747	0.766	0.704	0.712	0.753	0.760	0.759	0.722	0.717	0.681
3	0.885	0.873	0.902	0.860	0.890	0.866	0.910	0.910	0.911	0.901	0.892	0.858
4	0.927	0.925	0.914	0.947	0.940	0.941	0.928	0.931	0.930	0.944	0.936	0.931
5	0.937	0.936	0.939	0.932	0.921	0.913	0.925	0.926	0.924	0.912	0.899	0.894
8	0.940	0.938	0.927	0.933	0.920	0.913	0.951	0.946	0.947	0.934	0.903	0.875
9	0.979	0.978	0.978	0.976	0.974	0.974	0.968	0.968	0.967	0.971	0.960	0.955
10	0.965	0.965	0.966	0.988	0.978	0.959	0.971	0.971	0.970	0.987	0.939	0.902
11	0.925	0.925	0.924	0.922	0.917	0.898	0.927	0.929	0.932	0.926	0.904	0.895
12	0.757	0.783	0.755	0.782	0.748	0.701	0.823	0.824	0.833	0.818	0.807	0.762
14	0.862	0.888	0.875	0.899	0.918	0.902	0.847	0.831	0.830	0.873	0.787	0.724
15	0.975	0.974	0.975	0.967	0.971	0.971	0.975	0.975	0.974	0.971	0.970	0.973
16	0.960	0.964	0.964	0.955	0.954	0.944	0.951	0.953	0.951	0.949	0.921	0.911
17	0.828	0.840	0.808	0.840	0.840	0.817	0.846	0.832	0.838	0.843	0.835	0.824
19	0.892	0.889	0.887	0.899	0.884	0.880	0.884	0.883	0.882	0.877	0.861	0.859
20	0.873	0.875	0.880	0.869	0.870	0.872	0.855	0.856	0.855	0.866	0.831	0.828
21	0.805	0.808	0.807	0.798	0.789	0.780	0.789	0.792	0.789	0.776	0.763	0.754
22	0.638	0.642	0.630	0.648	0.596	0.556	0.614	0.634	0.634	0.542	0.591	0.568
23	0.931	0.932	0.928	0.921	0.918	0.917	0.911	0.910	0.907	0.906	0.910	0.904
24	0.790	0.796	0.789	0.793	0.759	0.752	0.776	0.777	0.775	0.779	0.756	0.741
25	0.858	0.863	0.859	0.867	0.866	0.841	0.847	0.848	0.846	0.866	0.831	0.813
26	0.683	0.740	0.712	0.638	0.643	0.687	0.778	0.770	0.783	0.715	0.689	0.693
28	0.878	0.886	0.882	0.861	0.858	0.846	0.873	0.866	0.870	0.852	0.819	0.795
29	0.764	0.797	0.788	0.786	0.755	0.767	0.827	0.836	0.834	0.804	0.824	0.812
30	0.955	0.956	0.953	0.959	0.947	0.945	0.939	0.940	0.940	0.942	0.918	0.913
31	0.722	0.699	0.739	0.758	0.755	0.755	0.841	0.861	0.860	0.813	0.835	0.820

Finally, comparing labels, we can see relatively clearer differences in predictive performance. Table 2 shows that label 22 is the hardest to predict, followed by labels 2, 12, 26, and 31 is the second hardest. This label corresponds to the indicator “exploration within a single message.” Furthermore, when we compare social indicators and cognitive indicators, there are more labels of social indicators in which AUC values are over 0.9 than cognitive indicators. These results suggest that a more advanced analysis of text messages is required, rather than traditional unigram TF-IDF features.

We conclude as follows. 1) We can use SentencePiece as a language-agnostic alternative to MeCab for tokenizing multilingual chat texts; it has comparable performance for providing useful tokens to predictors, despite being an unsupervised algorithm. 2) We need not be as sensitive to vocabulary sizes when using XGBoost with MeCab; however, we must carefully choose one when using SentencePiece as the tokenizer. 3) We found many labels could be predicted fairly well although some labels, especially those of cognitive presence indicators, require a deeper understanding of the texts.

4. CONCLUSION

In this paper, we discussed the multi-label classification problem of group chat messages collected from a collaborative learning support system. Our task was different from usual text categorization problems on two points: 1) our target labels are social presence and cognitive presence indicators, not chat topics, and 2) chat messages consist of both Japanese and English texts requiring language-agnostic treatment. We examined SentencePiece, an unsupervised tokenizer in classification, and our experiments showed that many labels could be predicted with it, although it slightly lacked robustness. We also found that cognitive presence indicators were harder to predict than social presence ones.

Limitations of our research include the facts that the classification method only considers word-level (unigram) features and that no contextual information is considered. Recent developments in natural language processing proposed neural network-based methods which consider contextual information. Such a model could improve the prediction performance of labels that require more contextual consideration. Therefore, our investigation does not present the maximum performance of social and cognitive labeling tasks but merely a baseline. Furthermore, because of the small size of our dataset, five labels with few positive instances were not examined during our experiments. Thus, our conclusions cannot be applied these labels.

ACKNOWLEDGEMENT

This work was supported by JSPS KAKENHI Grant Number JP19H01716.

REFERENCES

Anderson, T., Liam, R., Garrison, D.R. and Archer, W., 2001. Assessing Teaching Presence in a Computer Conferencing Context. *In Journal of Asynchronous Learning Networks*, Vol. 5, No. 2.

Breiman, L., 2001. Random Forests. *In Machine Learning*, Vol. 45, No. 1, pp. 5–32.

Chen, T. and Carlos G., 2016. XGBoost: A Scalable Tree Boosting System. *Proceedings of the 22nd ACM SIGKDD International Conference on Knowledge Discovery and Data Mining*, pp. 785–794.

Fawcett, T., 2006. An Introduction to ROC Analysis. *In Pattern Recognition Letters*, Vol. 27, No. 8, pp. 861–874.

Garrison, D.R., Anderson, T. and Archer, W., 1999. Critical Inquiry in a Text-Based Environment: Computer Conferencing in Higher Education. *In The Internet and Higher Education*, Vol. 2, No.2, pp. 87–105.

Kohavi, R., 1995. A Study of Cross-validation and Bootstrap for Accuracy Estimation and Model Selection. *Proceedings of the 14th International Joint Conference on Artificial Intelligence*, Vol. 2, pp. 1137–1143.

Kudo, T. and John R., 2018. SentencePiece: A Simple and Language Independent Subword Tokenizer and Detokenizer for Neural Text Processing. *Proceedings of the 2018 Conference on Empirical Methods in Natural Language Processing*, pp. 66–71.

Kudo, T., Kaoru Y., and Yuji M., 2004. Applying Conditional Random Fields to Japanese Morphological Analysis. *Proceedings of the 2004 Conference on Empirical Methods in Natural Language Processing*, pp. 230–237.

Latané, B., Williams, K. and Harkins, S., 1979. Many Hands Make Light the Work: The Causes and Consequences of Social Loafing, *In Journal of Personality and Social Psychology*, Vol. 37, No. 6, pp. 822–832.

Okanohara, D. and Jun'ichi T., 2009. Text Categorization with all Substring Features. *Proceedings of the 2009 SIAM International Conference on Data Mining*, pp. 838–846.

Pedregosa, F., Varoquaux, G., Gramfort, A., Michel, V., Thirion, B., Grisel, O., Blondel, M., Prettenhofer, P., Weiss, R., Dubourg, V. and Vanderplas, J., 2011. Scikit-learn: Machine Learning in Python. *In Journal of Machine Learning Research*, Vol. 12, pp. 2825–2830.

Read, J., Pfahringer, B., Holmes, G. and Frank, E., 2011. Classifier Chains for Multi-label Classification. *In Machine Learning*, Vol. 85, No. 3, p. 333.

Rourke, L., Anderson, T., Garrison, D.R. and Archer, W., 1999. Assessing Social Presence in Asynchronous Text-based Computer Conferencing. *In The Journal of Distance Education*, Vol. 14, No. 2, pp. 50–71.

Salton, G. and Christopher B., 1988. Term-weighting Approaches in Automatic Text Retrieval. *In Information Processing & Management*, Vol. 24, No. 5, pp. 513–523.

Shea, P., Hayes, S., Vickers, J., Gozza-Cohen, M., Uzuner, S., Mehta, R., Valchova, A. and Rangan, P., 2010. A Re-examination of the Community of Inquiry Framework: Social Network and Content Analysis. *In The Internet and Higher Education*, Vol. 13, No. 1, pp. 10–21.

Yamada M. and Kitamura S., 2011. The Role of Social Presence in Interactive Learning with Social Software. *Proceedings of Social Media Tools and Platforms in Learning Environments*, pp. 325–335.

Yamada M., 2010. Development and Evaluation of CSCL Based on Social Presence. *Proceedings of E-Learn: World Conference on E-Learning in Corporate, Government, Healthcare, and Higher Education*, pp. 2304–2309.

Yamada M., Goda Y., Matsukawa H., Hata K., and Yasunami S., 2016. A Computer-Supported Collaborative Learning Design for Quality Interaction. *In IEEE Multimedia*, Vol. 23, pp. 48–59.

Yamada M., Kaneko K., Goda Y., 2016. Social Presence Visualizer: Development of the Collaboration Facilitation Module on CSCL. *Proceedings of International Conference on Collaboration Technologies*, Vol. 647, pp. 174–189.

Zehner, F., Sälzer, C., and Goldhammer, F., 2016. Automatic Coding of Short Text Responses via Clustering in Educational Assessment. *In Educational and Psychological Measurement*, Vol. 76, No. 2, pp. 280–303.

Zhai, Z., Xu, H., Kang, B. and Jia, P., 2011. Exploiting Effective Features for Chinese Sentiment Classification. *In Expert Systems with Applications*, Vol. 38, No. 8, pp. 9139–9146.

WHAT PREDICTS CHEATING AMONG STUDENTS? A CROSS CULTURAL COMPARISON BETWEEN ONLINE AND FACE-TO-FACE COURSES

Yovav Eshet[1], Yehuda Peled[2], Keren Grinautski[3] and Casimir Barczyk[4]
[1]*PhD, Interdisciplinary Department, Zefat Academic College, 11 Jerusalem St, POB: 160, Zefat, 1320611, Israel*
[2]*PhD, Information Studies, Western Galilee College, POB: 2125, Akko 2412100, Israel*
[3]*MBA, School of Management, University of Haifa, Haifa 3190501, Israel*
[4]*PhD, School of Management, Purdue University Calumet, Hammond IN 46323, United States*

ABSTRACT

Many researchers have dwelled on the phenomenon of academic dishonesty (AD) or unethical behaviors within the academic environment. While this phenomenon can be explained by various factors, the current study investigates and presents a new structural model for determinants of AD. The predictors of AD that were found in the context of traditional and distance-learning courses in higher education are types of motivation, students' attitudes, personality traits, and cultural backgrounds (presented by country according to Hofstede's cultural dimensions theory). This study was conducted using a survey method of 2,357 students studying in six different academic institutes. Using structural equation modeling (SEM) the results indicate that the surveyed students tend to engage less in AD in online courses than in face-to-face courses. This notion is contrary to the traditional views and the research literature, therefore, having important practical implications for educators, institution and researchers dealing with course design development and institutional policy concerning pedagogical uses of digital technology.

KEYWORDS

Academic Dishonesty, Distance Learning, Online Courses, Motivation

1. INTRODUCTION

One of the largest and fastest growing segments of education is online learning (Kincey, Farmer, Wiltsher, McKenzie & Mbiza, 2019). A study by Higher Education Reports Babson Survey Research Group in 2018 revealed a growth at public institutions grew by 7.3 percent, and private non-profit institutions grew by 7.1 percent in United States (Seaman, Allen, and Seaman, 2018). Convenience and flexibility are what students' value when deciding to enroll in online courses. (Toufaily, Zalan, & Lee, 2018). Copious research suggests that online and classroom-based instruction result in equivalent outcomes for student in most higher education settings. (Shea & Bidjerano, 2018).

Academic dishonesty (AD) is a long-standing, culturally dependent, universal phenomenon relate to what is right or wrong (Martin, Rao, and Sloan, 2011; Peled and Khaldi, 2013). It is an important issue in education (Yang, Huang, and Chen, 2013) that continues to be a pervasive problem in the academic arena (Arnold, 2016), as most students have engaged in academic misconduct at some point of their careers (Stuber-McEwen, Wiseley, and Hoggatt, 2009). According to Jones (2011), the 92% of surveyed students report that they had cheated at least once or knew someone who had.

The scholarly research ascertains that online cheating is prevalent over traditional forms (Chuang, 2015; Fontaine, 2012; Kennedy, Nowak, Raghuraman, Thomas, and Davis, 2000). For example, Kennedy et al. (2000) surveyed students in many different academic areas and showed that 64% of 69 faculty members, and 57% out of 172 students, felt that cheating was easier in online exams. The belief that cheating is easier in online exams is also indicated in the research of King, Guyette and Piotrowski (2009) where 73.6% of 121 undergraduate business students agreed that it was easier to cheat online.

Many reports show that students admit that they are more likely to cheat in online courses. Chapman and colleagues (Chapman, Davis, Toy, and Wright, 2004) found that 24% of 824 business students indicated that they had cheated on an electronic exam, and that 42% of them claimed that if given the opportunity, they would cheat in electronic exams. Students also indicated that electronic testing was one of the several important, situational determinants related to the probability of cheating. Lanier (2006) found that 41.1% of the students surveyed admitted to cheating in online courses. Watson and Sottile (2010) surveyed undergraduate and graduate students across many academic fields and found that students were significantly more likely to obtain answers from other students during an online test or quiz.

To test traditional beliefs that online cheating prevails over traditional forms of cheating, and focusing on students cheating propensity, we surveyed 2,357 undergraduate students, enrolled in online courses, and compared to face to face courses. We have controlled the following predictor variables - personality traits, motivation, attitude toward academic dishonesty and cultural differences (by country).

The scholarly research has addressed various factors explaining the concept of AD. One such factor relates to the quick development in the field of Instructional Technology, which has resulted in the proliferation of online courses. Since these courses lessen the personal contact between students and faculty members, students are provided with a greater opportunity to engage in academic misconduct (Peterson, 2019; Walker, 2010). Thus, online courses, in contrast to traditional classroom courses, may contribute to students engaging in higher levels of dishonesty. The reason for this is that they feel more "distant" or separated from others (Kelley and Bonner, 2005).

Other studies have determined the availability and the accessibility of digital information as factors affecting AD (Cole et al, 2018). Some claim that this has made plagiarism more common due to the ease of copying and pasting the work of others while claiming it is one's own (Lehman and DuFrene, 2011; Walker, 2010). The students' lack of perception and understanding of institutional policy regarding academic dishonesty (Ewing, Anast, and Roehling, 2016; Şendağ, Duran, and Fraser, 2012) may be another element encouraging misbehavior.

The scholarly research has also shown that: societal factors, achievement goal approaches to motivation, internal and external motivation, external pressures to meet high standards of performance or deadlines, the desire to excel, fear of failure, or the lack of personal integrity, may explain dishonest behavior in the academic setting (Griebeler, 2019; Imran and Ayobami, 2011; Maeda, 2019; McCabe, Trevino, and Butterfield, 2001; Ramlan et al, 2019; Van Yperen, Hamstra, and Van der Klauw, 2011).

Additional explanations are the individual's desire to attain social acceptance, to keep up with peers, to further advance in their careers, to please others, or to protect their livelihood (Imran and Ayobami, 2011; McCabe et al., 2001; Van Yperen et al., 2011).

Several studies showed that the type of course (face-to-face vs. online) (Eshet, Grinautski, Peled, and Barczyk, 2014; Spaulding, 2011) and the different personality traits (Giluk and Postlethwaite, 2015; Wilks, Cruz, and Sousa, 2016) determine the intensity of AD. Despite the extensive academic literature, one of the most fundamental questions in this field remains not fully answered: what are the factors that predict students' propensity to engage in AD? This research is expected to provide a substantial contribution to the understanding of unethical behavior in the academic environment. The findings show that academic misconduct can be predicted and explained by the type of course in which students are enrolled, their background characteristics, type of motivation, personality traits, their instructor's attitude towards AD, and their cultural background (presented by country).

1.1 Hypotheses

Hypothesis 1. There will be level differences in the various motivational types between students that learn in traditional settings and those that are e-learners, which in turn, result in differences in the cheating propensity. E-learners will show higher levels of intrinsic motivation and have less propensity to engage in academic misconduct than students in traditional face-to-face settings.

Hypothesis 2. There will be differences in students' levels of Academic dishonesty based on their predominant personality traits.

Hypothesis 3. There will be differences in the level of Academic dishonesty based on faculty members' attitudes towards dishonest behaviors.

Hypothesis 4. Uncertainty avoidance will have an impact on academic misconduct, thus, Israeli students will report less incidence of Academic dishonesty than their counterparts in the United States do.

The basic research question underlying the four hypotheses detailed above is: which factors affect a students' tendency to engage in academic misconduct?

2. METHOD

2.1 Research Settings and Participants

The sample consisted of 2,475 students: 841 participants from the two abovementioned USA academic institutions and 1,634 from the four abovementioned colleges in the North of Israel. About two thirds (69%) of the participants were women and a third (31%) were men. Their ages ranged between 17 and 64 (M = 26.54 years). A third of the participants (33%) were freshmen, 35% sophomores, 16% juniors, 13% seniors, and 3% were graduate students. About a third of the participants in USA (36%) enrolled to online courses, while 64% enrolled to face-to-face courses.

A similar distribution can be seen in Israel, 37% enrolled to online courses, while 63% enrolled to face-to-face courses. Five percent of the participants were excluded from the analysis because their survey instruments were incomplete (less than 80%) or carelessly completed. Missing values were replaced by the variable average. The final data set consisted of 2,357 participants.

2.2 Survey Instrument

A five-part survey instrument measured the following variables: AD, motivational orientation, personality traits, attitude measures, and socio-demographic status.

2.3 Independent Variables

Motivational orientation - this part of the survey instrument contained 16 items that were compiled from the Academic Self-Regulation Questionnaire (SRQ-A) (Ryan and Connell, 1989). Four types of motivation are examined in the questionnaire: identified regulation, introjected regulation, external regulation, and intrinsic motivation on a four-point Likert scale (α=0.75).

Personality traits - this part of the survey included the TIPI scale developed by Gosling, Rentfrow, and Swann (2003), which consisted of 10 items designed to assess the participants' personality traits. Every trait consisted of two statements (α=0.63).

Attitude measures - this part of the questionnaire was designed to measure the attitudes of lecturers towards AD based on Coalter and colleagues' (2007) survey that included 30 questions on a five-point Likert scale (α=0.76).

Perceived opportunity - this part of the questionnaire was based on the Perceived Opportunity Scale by Bolin (2004) on a five-point Likert scale (α=0.73).

Acting - this part of the questionnaire was based on Shipley's (2009) Academic Dishonesty Survey (Penalty and Self Report items) with Cronbach's alpha of 0.72.

Socio-demographic variables – the questionnaire also contained a series of demographic items that related to the participants' age, gender, grade point average, and type of course enrollment (elective versus required and on-line versus face-to-face).

2.4 Dependent Variable

Academic dishonesty - Using the Academic Integrity Inventory, this part of the survey instrument included questions about Likelihood of considering misconduct (Kisamore, Stone, and Jawahar, 2007), based on 5 items with a reliability of α=0.75. The engagement in each academically dishonest behavior, is measured using an Academic Dishonesty Scale (Bolin, 2004), based on 10 items, with a reliability of α=0.91.

2.5 Procedure

A printed version of the survey instrument was administered in traditional face-to-face courses and an on-line version of the same in the e-learning courses. We used the stratified sampling method. The survey instruments were coded and grouped according to the location of the participants' college or university.

2.6 Results

Descriptive statistics and a correlation matrix summarizing the study variables are presented in Table 1 (see Appendix A). All measures of AD (consisting of items related to forms of misconduct, plagiarism, and cheating) and covariates (four types of motivation and most of the socio-demographic variables) were correlated with one another (Table 1).

Table 1. Correlation matrix of the study variables

Variables		1	2	3	4	5	6	7	8	9	10	11	12	13	14	15	16	17	18
1. External Motivation		==																	
2. Introjected Regulation		.486***	==																
3. Identified Regulation		.187***	.629***	==															
4. Intrinsic Motivation		.314***	.273***	.230***	==														
5. Extraversion		-.045*	-.052*	-.058*	.070**	==													
6. Agreeableness		-.101***	-.060**	-.055*	.052*	-.053*	==												
7. Conscientiousness		-.015	.056*	.058*	.142***	.108***	.200***	==											
8. Emotional Stability		-.076**	-.078**	-.013	.072**	.149***	.278***	.339***	==										
9. Openness to Experiences		-.016	.047*	.063**	.076**	.329***	.147***	.302***	.220***	==									
10. Attitude Measures		-.018	.244***	.269***	.066**	.003	.138***	.097***	.049*	.172**	==								
11. Perceived Opportunity		-.015	.198***	.224***	.084***	-.020	.112***	.069**	.042	.127***	.550***	==							
12. Taking Action		-.115***	.064**	.161***	.035	-.029	.046*	.016	-.006	.053*	.252***	.161***	==						
13. Course Type		47.50**	89.61***	216.70***	229.76***	32.61**	23.78*	38.07***	30.48**	22.80*	191.33***	201.84***	50.08	==					
14. Age		-.130***	-.073**	-.030	.156***	.084***	.171***	.063**	.140***	.079**	.027	.053*	.027	141.98***	==				
15. Gender		24.17	35.41	12.87	49.99***	16.13	55.41***	41.27***	24.05*	18.53	127.47	87.49*	47.57	.025	102.96***	==			
16. Grade point average		-.028	-.187***	-.258***	.030	-.006	.056*	.086**	.050	-.098***	-.218***	-.202***	-.082**	725.53***	.079**	225.38***	==		
17. Required vs. Elective (1. Required; 0. Elective)		22.16	35.49	36.77***	30.06**	6.62	19.59	6.77	19.20	9.05	97.88	96.57**	85.60***	.266***	79.95**	.024	347.39***	==	
18. Academic dishonesty		.065**	-.047*	-.071**	-.124***	-.023	-.174***	-.135***	-.102***	-.096***	-.151***	-.216***	.002	343.47***	-.192***	198.21	.045	214.43**	==
USA	Mean	2.57	3.11	3.59	2.50	4.39	4.82	5.60	4.79	5.42	3.74	3.61	3.38	0.64	25.20	0.37	74.19	0.68	2.57
	S.D.	0.65	0.61	0.62	0.74	1.52	1.25	1.22	1.37	1.14	0.49	0.65	0.72	0.48	7.46	0.48	12.98	0.47	0.65
	N	799	800	800	798	797	798	796	797	796	798	783	795	801	750	783	698	764	799
Israel	N	2.64	2.64	2.81	2.85	4.69	5.08	5.88	5.13	5.19	3.24	3.11	2.87	0.63	27.24	0.28	83.75	0.77	1.95
	S.D.	0.64	0.64	0.94	0.73	1.35	1.11	1.12	1.24	1.11	0.43	0.63	0.67	0.48	7.82	0.45	7.22	0.42	0.63
	N	1.548	1.549	1.552	1.548	1.130	1.129	1.131	1.129	1.130	1.098	1.075	1.086	1.556	1.424	1.451	997	1.556	1.476
Independent T test		-2.75**	17.24***	21.14***	-10.69***	-4.65***	-4.96***	-5.31***	-5.86***	4.63***	24.04***	17.28***	16.14***	==	-5.88***	==	-19.65***	==	0.33
Cohen's d effect size		0.09	0.61	0.74	0.38	0.17	0.18	0.19	0.21	0.16	0.85	0.80	0.56	==	0.21	==	0.57	==	==

T-test analyses between countries (USA and Israel) were conducted with the study variables (Table 1). The results indicate that there is a significant difference between the USA and Israel in external motivation [$t_{(2355)}=-2.75$, p=.006], intrinsic motivation [$t_{(2355)}=-10.69$, p=.000], extraversion [$t_{(2355)}=-4.65$, p=.000], agreeableness [$t_{(2355)}=-4.96$, p=.000], conscientiousness [$t_{(2355)}=-5.31$, p=.000], emotional stability [$t_{(2355)}=-5.86$, p=.000], age [$t_{(2355)}=-5.88$, p=.000], and grade point average [$t_{(2355)}=-19.65$, p=.000], with higher levels found in Israel compared to the USA. Also, a significant difference between USA and Israel was found in introjected regulation [$t_{(2355)}=17.24$, p=.000], identified regulation [$t_{(2355)}=21.14$, p=.000], openness to experience [$t_{(2355)}=4.63$, p=.000], attitude measures [$t_{(2355)}=24.04$, p=.000], perceived opportunity [$t_{(2355)}=17.28$, p=.000], and taking action [$t_{(2355)}=16.14$, p=.000], with higher levels found in the USA compared to Israel.

2.7 Plan of Analysis

Full information maximum likelihood estimates were computed by means of the Analysis of Moment Structures (AMOS) program (Arbuckle and Wothke, 1999). Structural models linking types of motivation, culture (presented by country), course type (face-to-face vs. online), age, gender, grade point average, type of course enrollment (required vs. elective), and AD were tested, the results of which are summarized in Figure 1. The model was examined for goodness of fit using χ^2, comparative fit index (CFI), and root mean square error of approximation (RMSEA) fit indices. CFI values above 0.90 and 0.95 indicate adequate and good model fit, respectively, and RMSEA values below 0.08 and 0.05 indicate adequate and good model fit, respectively (Browne and Cudeck, 1992; Hu andBentler, 1999; Kline, 1998). CFI = .991, RMSEA = 0.045). The structural model is diagrammed in Figure 1.

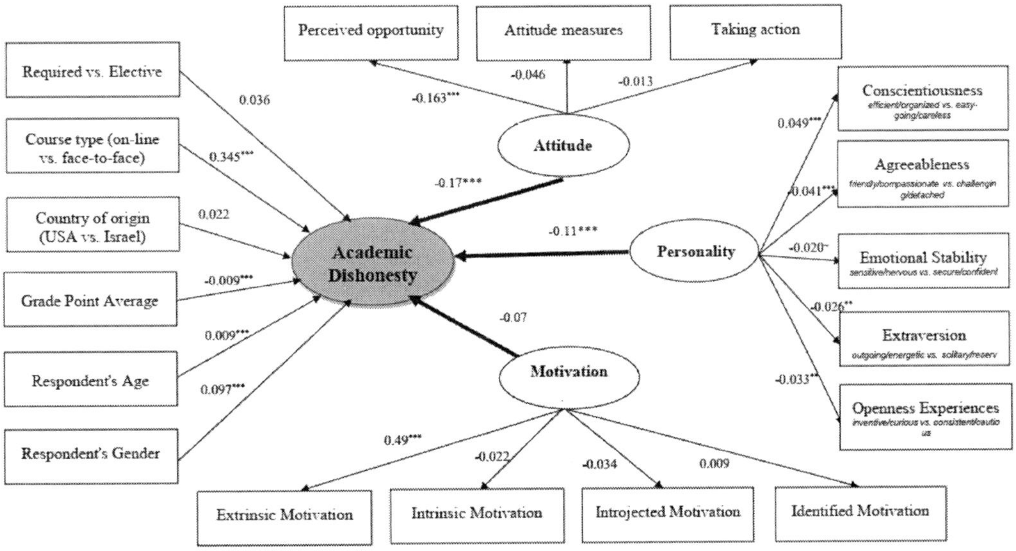

Figure 1. Structural model for determinants of academic dishonesty with standardized Coefficients

The results of the AD analysis indicate that the variance in students' propensity to engage in AD is explained by the research variables: students' motivational orientation, students' personality traits, attitudes of lecturers towards academic dishonesty, students' perception of the opportunities to cheat, students' attitude towards punishment for acts of academic dishonesty, type of course (on-line vs. face-to-face), gender, age, grade point average, and type of course enrollment (elective vs. required). As shown in Figure 1, course type is the variable that has the largest impact on AD. Surveyed students in on-line courses tend to engage less in academic misconduct than their counterparts in face-to-face courses.

Other variables that were found to have a significant influence on the dependent variable are divided. Some have a positive impact and others have a negative one. More specifically, the personality trait of extraversion and extrinsic motivation increase the students' tendency to cheat, while this tendency increases with age. By contrast, the other Big Five personality traits (conscientiousness, emotional stability, agreeableness, and openness to experience), as well as studying in academic institutions that consider acts of academic misconduct as very serious offences, and act upon them with severity, lessen the inclination to engage in dishonest behaviors.

3. CONCLUSION

This research suggests that our understanding of the factors that influence AD needs to be adjusted. The essence of this study is to investigate which variables (type of course to which students are enrolled, background characteristics, type of motivation, personality traits, instructor's attitude towards AD, and cultural background [presented by country]) help predict and determine academic misconduct.

We empirically tested four hypotheses, of which three of them were confirmed by the survey's data; the fourth is proved wrong by evidence. We have found that: (1) e-learners exhibited less propensity to engage in AD if compared to their counterparts in face-to-face courses; (2) personality traits explained the students' willingness to engage in dishonest behaviors; (3) faculty members' attitudes toward AD explained to which extent were students willing to engage in dishonest behaviors; (4) both Israeli and USA students had the same level when engaging in AD conduct. Although when asked if they would not report misbehavior, only

29% of the American students answered yes, 57% of their Israeli colleagues would not report on a peer's misconduct. This may be due to both, the different manners people interpret whistle blowing on a peer misbehavior, and their ethical sensitivity, on the one hand, and on the positive or negative outcome (McIntosh et al., 2017), on the other hand.

Although, some researchers have asserted that distance learning environments provide and promote opportunities for AD compared to traditional learning environments (e.g., Cole, Shelley, and Swartz, 2012, pp. 1-19; Shachar and Neumann, 2010). Others reject this claim altogether (Black, Greaser, and Dawson, 2008). The findings of this study show that students tend to cheat more in face-to-face classroom settings. Furthermore, course type was found to have the greatest impact on AD among all other examined factors.

These results may be interpreted according to Yang et al. (2013) and Geddes (2011), who found that students who participate in online courses have a higher motivation to learn or are able to learn independently, which could substantially reduce their desire to cheat compared to students participating in traditional face-to-face classroom settings. Another possible explanation for these results is that more intrinsically motivated students self-select online as opposed to traditional classroom courses.

On-line instruction is thought to facilitate increasing levels of intrinsic motivation. Thus, it is not surprising that e-learning students manifest significantly higher levels of intrinsic motivation and significantly lower levels of extrinsic motivation than traditional classroom students do.

Conscientious students have less need to cheat, since they tend to be better prepared academically and can resist cheating. They may be achievement-oriented, but at the same time, responsible, honest, and able to regulate their behavior. Similarly, emotional stability can also help students avoid unethical academic behaviors, since students that are high on this trait have a sense of security, which allows them to be less influenced by stressful conditions. In addition, a significant negative correlation between the personality trait of agreeableness and AD indicates that the more students are cooperative with others, the less likely they are to be academically dishonest. Agreeableness is associated with the ability to create good relationships and conform to group norms. By contrast, highly extroverted students tend to be talkative, aggressive, verbal, sociable, bold, assertive, unrestrained, confident, attention-seeking, and domineering (De Raad, 2000). Thus, the positive influence of the personality traits of extraversion and emotional stability as predictors

for AD can be interpreted by the notion that unlike extraversion, these traits enable students to withhold the tendency to cheat.

In line with the research literature we hold that understanding the factors influencing AD is a crucial issue. Moreover, it has important implications for both, institutional policies, and course design. Nonetheless, contrary to traditional views ascribing online cheating a prevalence over face to face courses our findings show that the antecedents of AD need to be revised.

Consequently, we conclude that online courses are not a predominant factor in the prediction of misbehavior. Next, we show that the principal variables predicting the tendency to cheat are related to personality traits, faculty's attitudes, and institutional policies. The study's practical implications are related to course design and institutional policy.

REFERENCES

Arbuckle, J., and Wothke, W., 1999. *AMOS 4.0 User's Reference Guide*. Small Waters Corporation, Chicago, USA.

Arnold, I.J., 2016. Cheating at online formative tests: Does it pay off? *The Internet and Higher Education*, Vol. 29, pp. 98-106.

Black, E.W., Greaser, J., and Dawson, K., 2008. Academic dishonesty in traditional and online Classrooms: Does the "media equation" hold true? *Journal of Asynchronous Learning Networks*, Vol, 12, No. 3-4, pp. 23-30.

Bolin, A., 2004. Self-control, perceived opportunity, and attitudes as predictors of academic dishonesty. *Journal of Psychology Interdisciplinary and Applied*, Vol. 138, No. 2, pp. 101-114.

Browne, M.W., and Cudeck, R., 1992. Alternative ways of assessing model fit. *Sociological Methods and Research*, Vol. 21, pp. 230-258.

Chapman, K. et al, 2004. Academic integrity in the business school environment: I'll get by with a little help from my friends. *Journal of Marketing Education*, Vol. 26, No. 3, pp. 236-249.

Chuang, C.Y., 2015. *Improving Proctoring by Using Non-Verbal Cues During Remotely Administrated Exams*. Arizona State University, USA.

Coalter, T. et al, 2007. Factors that influence faculty actions: A study on faculty responses to academic dishonesty. *International Journal for the Scholarship of Teaching and Learning*, Vol. 1, No. 1, pp. 1-19.

Cole, M.T. et al, 2012. *Academic Integrity and Student Satisfaction in an Online Environment. Cases on Online Learning Communities and Beyond: Investigations and Applications*. IGI Global, Hershey, USA.

Cole, M.T. et al, 2018. In Re Launching a New Vision in Education and e-Learning: Fostering a Culture of Academic Integrity in e-Learning. *Smart Education and e-Learning*, pp. 151-164.

De Raad, B., 2000. *The Big Five Personality Factors: The Psycholexical Approach to Personality*. Hogrefe and Huber Publisher.

Eshet, Y. et al, 2014. No more excuses - personality traits and academic dishonesty in online courses. *Journal of Statistical Science and Application*, Vol. 2, pp. 111-118.

Ewing, H. et al, 2016. Addressing plagiarism in online programmes at a health sciences university: A case study. *Assessment and Evaluation in Higher Education*, Vol. 41, No. 4, pp. 575-585.

Fontaine, J., 2012. Online classes see cheating go high-tech. *The Chronicle of Higher Education*, Vol. 58, No. 38, pp. A1-A2.

Geddes, K.A., 2011. Academic dishonesty among gifted and high-achieving students. *The Gifted Child Today*, Vol. 34, No. 2, pp. 50-56.

Giluk, T.L., and Postlethwaite, B.E., 2015. Big five personality and academic dishonesty: A meta-analytic review. *Personality and Individual Differences*, Vol. 72, pp. 59-67.

Gosling, S.D. et al, 2003. A very brief measure of the big five personality domains. *Journal of Research in Personality*, Vol. 37, pp. 504-528.

Griebeler, M.C., 2019. "But everybody's doing it!": A model of peer effects on student cheating. *Theory and Decision*, Vol. 86, No, 2, pp. 259-281.

Hu, L., and Bentler, P.M., 1999. Cutoff criteria for fit indexes in covariance structure analysis: Conventional criteria versus new alternatives. *Structural Equation Modeling*, Vol. 6, pp. 1-55.

Imran, A.M., and Ayobami, O.R., 2011. Academic dishonesty among tertiary institution students: An exploration of the societal influences using SEM analysis. *International Journal of Education*, Vol. 3, No. 2, pp. 1-15.

Jones, D.L., 2011. Academic dishonesty: Are more students cheating? *Business Communication Quarterly*, Vol. 74, No. 2, pp. 141.

Kelley, K., and Bonner, K., 2005. Distance education and academic dishonesty: Faculty and administrator perception and responses. *Journal of Asynchronous Learning Networks*, Vol. 9, pp. 43-52.

Kennedy, K. et al, 2000. Academic dishonesty and distance learning: Student and faculty views. *College Student Journal*, Vol. 34, No. 2, pp. 309-314.

Kincey, S.D., Farmer, E.D., Wiltsher, C.Y., McKenzie, D. & Mbiza, S.T. 2019, "From Chalkboard to Digital Media: The Evolution of Technology and Its Relationship to Minority Students' Learning Experiences", *The Journal of Faculty Development,* vol. 33, no. 1, pp. 65-75.

King, C. et al, 2009. Online exams and cheating: An empirical analysis of business students' views. *The Journal of Educators Online*, Vol. 6, No. 1.

Kisamore, J.L. et al. 2007. Academic integrity: The relationship between individual and situational factors on misconduct contemplations. *Journal of Business Ethics*, Vol. 75, pp. 381-394.

Kline, R.B., 1998. *Principles and Practice of Structural Equation Modeling*. Guilford, New York, USA.

Lanier, M.M., 2006. Academic integrity and distance learning. *Journal of Criminal Justice Education*, Vol. 17, No. 2, pp. 244-261.

Lehman, C.M., and DuFrene, D., 2011. *Business Communication* (16th ed.). South-Western/Cengage Learning, Mason, OH, USA.

Martin, D.E. et al, 2011. Ethnicity, acculturation, and plagiarism: A criterion study of unethical academic conduct. *Human Organization*, Vol. 70, No. 1, pp. 88-96.

Maeda, M., 2019. Exam cheating among Cambodian students: When, how, and why it happens. *A Journal of Comparative and International Education*.

McCabe, D.L. et al, 2001. Cheating in academic institutions: A decade of research. *Ethics and Behavior*, Vol. 11, pp. 219-232.

McIntosh, T. et al, 2017. To whistleblow or not to whistleblow: Affective and cognitive differences in reporting peers and Advisors. *Science and Engineering Ethics*, pp. 1-40.

Peled, Y., and Khaldi, S., 2013. Are discrimination, survival and tradition sufficient argument for academic dishonesty? Discrimination, Survival and Tradition as Argumentation for Academic Dishonesty. *Educational Practice and Theory*, Vol. 35, No. 1, pp. 41-61.

Peterson, J., 2019. An Analysis of Academic Dishonesty in Online Classes. *Mid-Western Educational Researcher*, Vol, 31, No. 1, pp. 24-36.

Ramla, M. et al, 2019. Spiritual intelligence and academic dishonesty: The Malaysian higher education student perspectives. *European Journal of Education Studies*, Vol. 6, No. 2, pp. 205-222.

Ryan, R.M., and Connell, J.P., 1989. Perceived locus of causality and internalization: Examining reasons for acting in two domains. *Journal of Personality and Social Psychology*, Vol. 57, pp. 749-761.

Seaman, J.E., Allen, I.E. and Seaman, J., 2018. Grade Increase: Tracking Distance Education in the United States. *Babson Survey Research Group.*

Şendağ, S. et al, 2012. Surveying the extent of involvement in online academic dishonesty (e-dishonesty) related practices among university students and the rationale students provide: One university's experience. *Computers in Human Behavior*, Vol. 28, No. 3, pp. 849-860.

Shachar, M., and Neumann, Y., 2010. Twenty years of research on the academic performance differences between traditional and distance learning: Summative meta-analysis and trend examination. *MERLOT Journal of Online Learning and Teaching*, Vol. 6, No. 2.

Shea, P. & Bidjerano, T. 2018, "Online Course Enrollment in Community College and Degree Completion: The Tipping Point", *International Review of Research in Open and Distance Learning*, vol. 19, no. 2.

Shipley, L.J., 2009. Academic and professional dishonesty: Student views of cheating in the classroom and on the job. *Journalism and Mass Communication Educator*, Vol. 64, No. 1, pp. 39-53.

Stuber-McEwen, D. et al, 2009. Point, click, and cheat: Frequency and type of academic dishonesty in the virtual classroom. *Online Journal of Distance Learning Administration*, Vol. 12, No. 3.

Toufaily, E., Zalan, T. & Lee, D. 2018, "What do learners value in online education? An emerging market perspective", *The e - Journal of Business Education & Scholarship of Teaching,* vol. 12, no. 2, pp. 24-39.

Van Yperen, N.W. et al, 2011. To win, or not to lose, at any cost: The impact of achievement goals on cheating. *British Journal of Management*. Vol. 22, No. s1, pp. S5–S15.

Walker, J., 2010. Measuring plagiarism: Researching what students do, not what they say they do. *Studies in Higher Education*, Vol. 35, pp. 41-59.

Watson, G., and Sottile, J., 2010. Cheating in the digital age: Do students cheat more in online courses? *Online Journal of Distance Learning Administration*, Vol. 12, No. 4.

Wilks, D.C. et al, 2016. Personality traits and plagiarism: An empirical study with Portuguese undergraduate students. *Journal of Academic Ethics*, Vol. 14, No. 3, pp. 231-241.

Yang, S.C. et al, 2013. An investigation of college students' perceptions of academic dishonesty, reasons for dishonesty, achievement goals, and willingness to report dishonest behavior. *Ethics and Behavior*, Vol. 23, No. 6, pp. 501-522.

COLLABORATIVE LEARNING: COLLEGIATE PEDAGOGY UTILIZING WEB CONFERENCING

Joan Ann Swanson[1], Susan L. Renes[2] and Anthony T. Strange[3]
[1]*Skidmore College, Saratoga Springs, NY, USA*
[2]*University of Alaska Fairbanks, Fairbanks, Alaska, USA*
[3]*Wayland Baptist University, Plainview, Texas, USA*

ABSTRACT

This study was completed in two phases, the first of which employed systematic literature analysis of collegiate instructional use of web conferencing followed by a case study of a multi-campus collaborative course utilizing web conferencing. Results provide implications for collegiate educators seeking to employ web conferencing for synchronous instruction and collaborative learning experiences. Additionally, while the study revealed a foundational base for empirical studies related to collegiate pedagogical use of web conferencing, this study also served to expose the need for more sophisticated, generalizable studies regarding web conferencing.

KEYWORDS

Collegiate Instruction, Web Conferencing, Collaboration, Pedagogy

1. INTRODUCTION

We exist in places. Places are where we live, work, learn, create, travel to and imagine. While we often think of place in terms of a physical context, Hutchison (2004) notes that places can be a socially constructed reality. He remarks that the "significance of place is often enhanced by the personalities and idiosyncrasies of the individuals who populate a place" (p.11). The place in which learning occurs for today's college students is evolving in large part due to technological advances. The traditional classroom has morphed into any setting in which a screen can capture synchronous or asynchronous instructional activity. This online place is both a locality and special representation of community building and learning. Bringing together individuals in an online setting allows for a reimagining of the learning place. Technology such as web conferencing allows for a mode of social construction which has the ability to move far beyond the constructs of one geographic setting. Advances in modern technology now enable synchronous e-learning through online conferencing, however, empirical studies involving web conferencing for collegiate instruction are still limited (Kang & Shin, 2015). This study seeks to provide an analysis of how the movement toward web conferencing for educational purposes has impacted the place of collegiate academia.

2. WEB CONFERENCING IN THE COLLEGIATE SETTING

Educators are having increased opportunities for synchronous, multimodal communication within academic settings as technological advancements provide web-based communication learning tools. In the 1990s new technologies surfaced on college campuses which allowed for a limited number of users to have real-time communication and collaboration via the internet (Business Matters, 2015). With the introduction of internet services like Skype and iChat, telecommunications became available for free in the 2000s, and by 2010 video conferencing was put to the Cloud and freely available via mobile devices (ezTalks, 2017). The use of video and web conferencing has gained in popularity in both the traditional and online classrooms as an e-learning tool. Web conferencing involves the use of real-time video conferencing software that enables individuals to interact virtually and can be accomplished using any technological device that provides a screen enabling the sight of others and sound to hear them. The scope of web conferencing ranges from being the vehicle for a guest speaker, a virtual field trip, group collaboration space, online synchronous instruction time or even virtual office hours. Video and web conferencing can be supplemental for face-to-face courses, or the vehicle to deliver a blended portion of a course or an entire online course.

2.1 Video Conferencing versus Web Conferencing

Confusing video and web conferencing is understandable as they deliver similar opportunities. While both involve real-time communication between two or more parties from laptops, desktops or mobile devices, there are subtle differences (See Table 1). Video conferencing has traditionally required special equipment for two-way, high quality video and audio sharing with limited file sharing for specific, controlled audiences. Web conferencing allows for live feed through a web browser that is not limited to a geographical location or number of participants. Web conferencing tends to be less expensive and offers collaborative communication, polls, surveys, whiteboard features and media streaming (Eli, 2017; Erwin, 2019). The course needs will dictate the type of conferencing chosen. For the purposes of this study, web conferencing will be the focus as it has the advantages of being used globally, is less expensive, and offers more academic pedagogical tools.

Table 1. Web and Video Conferencing Contrast

	Web Conferencing	Video Conferencing
Purpose	Content sharing; ideal for face-to-face, impromptu meetings and delivering large amounts of information	Communication; ideal at face-to-face communication for groups and collaboration, provides real-time
Technical Quality	Internet connection is needed and works across many geographic locations, sometimes has frozen images and pixilation due to low bandwidth hence limiting interaction	High quality images and sound, most similar to face-to-face, broadcast from one stationary location on a room-based system, specialized equipment needed
Ease of Use	Authorization not required, only a browser needed, cheaper than video conferencing, webcast (one-way, non-interactive) or webinar conference, allows collaborative communication, polls, surveys and whiteboard features	Created by an administrator who creates user accounts for every user and issues personal credentials for all users
Tools Needed	Any device connecting to the web	Requires a PC, camera and a microphone
Users	Unlimited users	Limited number of viewers by conferencing server's capacity
Application	Presentations, online trainings, distance learning	Regular meetings, discussions

(Ch, 2019; Eli, 2017; Erwin, 2019; ezTalks, 2017)

2.2 Web-based Pedagogy

Web-based pedagogy involves extending and enriching learning communities beyond the traditional setting. Stevenson and Hedberg (2011) acknowledge tremendous growth in internet-informed pedagogies due to the expansion of web tool availability and cloud computing. Wang and colleagues (2013) suggest that synchronous interaction in the collegiate academic arena aids in bridging both geographic and cultural gaps. Similarly, Muepi (2014) contends web-based technologies are now allowing for expanded world-wide multicultural exchanges and education.

3. STATEMENT OF THE PROBLEM - CHALLENGES IN HIGHER EDUCATION

In an era of globalization, higher education is facing many challenges to stay current technologically and keep students engaged and motivated. "Bridging the geographical divide between on campus, off campus, rural, and remote learners has been an ongoing challenge for many universities often resulting in a different learning experience based on the mode of study" (Martin & Broadley2018, p. 55). Knight, et al. (2004) caution the application of banking-model pedagogy and literacy in the online setting could be limiting and detrimental to culturally diverse groups. Martin and Broadley (2018), however propose that the use of distributed learning supported through video and web conferencing will assist in "real time student-centered learning experiences with diverse student perspectives" (p. 55). Additionally, Stevenson and Hedberg (2011) remark that "despite the inherent challenges for adoption within the institution, Web 2.0 technologies do more to unify people across divides – generational, economic, geopolitical and digital – than they do to separate them" (p. 324).

While web conferencing has so much potential, another challenge within higher education is to assist instructors and students to develop the competencies needed to successfully engage in such synchronous activities. Bower, (2011) notes synchronous collaboration competencies need to be developed for multimodal education which includes operational, interactional, managerial, and design abilities. Effectively managing groups and interactions as well as the technology necessitates some level of skill development by all parties. The instructor must then design the learning environment and activities which will support optimal learning. Bower (2011) illustrates that teaching effectively in web conferencing environments does have challenges that can potentially lead to misunderstandings or misuses if institutions do not prepare faculty and students in developing necessary competencies.

The purpose of this study is to understand more fully the place web conferencing currently has pedagogically in the collegiate setting through systematic literature review and a case study utilizing web conferencing. The study was guided by the following research questions:

1. What is the scope of empirical studies about web conferencing in the collegiate instructional setting between 2000 and May 2019?
2. What lessons can be gleaned from a collaborative class case study experience in which web conferencing was utilized?

4. METHODS

This study sought to investigate the use of web conferencing for collegiate instruction. The research was conducted into phases using two methodologies: systematic literature review and a collegiate case study. The systematic literature review approach was useful in identifying, selecting and critically analyzing previous empirical studies concerned with the use of web conferencing for instructional purposes (Grant & Booth, 2009). The second methodology utilized a study approach (Creswell, 2007) and included data collection using course documentation, archival records, interviews, direct observation, participant observation and physical artifacts (Stake, 1995).

4.1 Phase 1 – Systematic Literature Review

Data related to web conferencing for collegiate instruction was collected using a contemporary systematic literature review ranging from the year 2000, when video and web conferencing began to be utilized in higher education through the present, 2019. The Ebsco database was used and specific searches were completed using Academic Search Complete, Education Search Complete, ERIC, and PsycINFO. The selection process was guided with the following criteria: papers published between January 2000 and May 2019, papers published in peer-reviewed journals, papers published in English; and papers including the key words web conferencing and college. Relevant, empirical publications were chosen resulting for analysis (N=76).

4.2 Phase 2 – Case Study

Three collegiate instructors, representing three higher education institutions collaborated for a cross-institution experience in an effort to establish a learning community place that stretched beyond the borders of one institution in one locale, to multiple regions and individual representations. This collegiate learning community adopted the guiding framework provided by West and Williams (2017) which includes access, relationships, visions, and functions.

4.2.1 Phase 2 – Case Study Participants and Procedure

The case study participants included students enrolled in higher education course work at three separate institutions located in Alaska, New York, and South Carolina. The participants were registered for a course at their home institution and then met three times throughout the semester for a combined synchronous web conference course session between the three institutions. Students were assigned an introductory activity, pre-class session readings, and activities including post-class reflections where students were able to respond to each other. Each of the three synchronous sessions was led by one of the lead faculty members from the different institutions and conducted through the Zoom platform. Each participant was enrolled in a private WordPress (WordPress.com) website which hosted all course related materials including required media, assignment descriptions and readings, as well as a depository for assignments.

The web conferencing tool Zoom (https://zoom.us/) was used to facilitate the collaborative classes. Students across all three geographic locations joined online at the appointed times, having completed the pre-class session work which served as a basis for the discussions and activities commenced in the hour-long synchronous time. Ground rules were reviewed for discussion times and for ease of facilitating discussion. When a speaker was vocalizing, the Zoom web conferencing program automatically enlarged their image in the center of the screen and all others were minimized in a frame around the perimeter of the screen. At different points in the course, for the purpose of the discussion, screen sharing allowed for documents and images to be viewed as well. All synchronous web conferenced class sessions were also recorded for students and instructors to review.

5. RESULTS AND ANALYSIS

5.1 Phase 1 - Results

To explore the ways in which web conferencing was being utilized for collegiate instruction, a systematic literature review of educational databases was conducted searching for empirical studies about collegiate web conferencing, which yielded (N=76) articles with only four of the articles having lead authors publishing more than one publication. These results first indicated a limited number of research specialists focusing in on the use of web conferencing. The methodology utilized was mainly qualitative (55%), followed by mixed methods (24%) and quantitative (21%). While some studies were mixed methods, using more than one type of method to collect data, the largest amount of studies involved questionnaires or surveys (36%), followed by case studies (22%) and interviews (12%). Additionally, other methods noted included observations (10%), correlational studies (9%), experimental studies (5%) and narrative or systematic literature reviews (6%). The most frequently used methodology was qualitative, these studies reflected largely on detailed observations and descriptions of data relating to web conferencing in collegiate settings. The data complexities analyzed within the represented systematic literature review were found to be especially useful to describe the human experience in these online environments.

The content area in which the reported studies were associated varied a great deal. While most studies focused upon one course, there were 18% that were multi-discipline focused, looking globally across a campus. The content areas most represented in web conferencing studies over the past 19 years were Education (16%), Medical/Health (12%), Business (8%) and Library related (6%). Other content areas in which web conferencing was studied included: counseling, engineering, geography, history, chemistry, club events, communication, computer programming, criminology, environmental science, math, music, psychology, social work, tutoring, study abroad, and writing.

The most common web conferencing platform or tool reported was Adobe Connect (33%), followed by Blackboard Collaborative (16%), Skype (7%), and Eluminate Live! (5%). A total of 17 other tools were also reported however each was only used in one study. The variety of tools utilized indicates there is no singular consensus on the best platform for web conferencing. This is reflective of the proprietary nature of web conferencing tools and that only two seem to have broken into the collegiate technology market in a stronger manner. Since most educational institutions have an established Learning Management System, it would behoove them to further enrich their products with web conferencing tools, similar to the Blackboard Collaborate extension.

Many of the studies described within this literature review did not report a subject size (50% of studies reported an N=x), however, a majority of those who did report the number of participants dealt with smaller subject sizes, which is common among case studies, also strongly represented in this review. A total of 62% of studies reported under 100 subjects, and 44% had 36 and under for the number of subjects. Considering most college courses contain 40 students or less, the smaller number of subjects in studies involving college courses is commensurate with the typical population.

5.2 Phase 2 – Results

Data analysis in phase two involved the researchers reviewing the recordings of the collaborative classes and reviewing the written submissions of students and faculty. Additionally, analysis was conducted within the theoretical frameworks of access, relationships, vision, and function (West and Williams 2017).

The collaborative class was set up to deliberately concentrate on topics which are difficult to discuss. The first class theme focused upon the awareness of our own personal perspectives. Often we hear or believe only a single story about others, when in fact lives are composed of many overlapping stories. The second class theme was about resolving conflict. The last class theme was cultural sensitivity. Students were assigned pre-class work involving watching a media presentation, readings, and completing experiential activities related to the topics. Students were also to come to class having prepared responses to discussion questions, and following the class were required to post reflection pieces. These reflections were then available to be commented upon by other members of class, thus extending interactions. Examples of post-class reflections included the following comments which revealed both vulnerability and growth (See Table 2).

Table 2. Student Reflection Samples

Student 1: I don't think differences should separate and divide people. I think acceptance is a large trend in the world right now and there are a lot of movements trying to increase cohesion between different groups of people. I believe a lot of great opportunities are lost when people decide to divide themselves based on ethnic, cultural, socioeconomic, religious, mental or physical differences.
Student 2: I think that this impacts my work as a teacher because I cannot simply ignore my students' identities. I should not lump all Asian students under one moniker just like I should not lump all people who identify as queer under the idea of gay or being gay. The population of non-cis-straight people is much larger than gay and lesbian, similar to how other populations have branches and subcultures that should be respected. I recognize that I cannot know the entire history of every individual culture that my students may have, but I can put the effort into discussing their cultures and identities with them and researching a little about each of their cultures in order to make sure I am not just assuming they experience life in a certain way or that they identify in a certain way.
Student 3: This experience, the combination of the classroom experiment and my thought processing exercise, evoked feelings of helplessness, a sense of frustration, and feelings of being "outside" the group, or set apart by a difference. It also evoked feelings of empathy as I considered how being blind might impact my own daily life and change the way I live. This experience reminded me of the importance of mindfulness in listening to clients, considering the daily obstacles and roadblocks they may be facing that might be overlooked or missed by anyone not having experience with a disability. As a society, we tend to "other" anyone with a disability. The label of disabled has been used to justify exclusion and derision, in the same way that race, and gender were used previously. ...We view this other able-ness as negative, a weakness, instead of recognizing there is more than one way to navigate the world and experience life that is neither wrong nor less valuable.
Student 4: Like many of the people Chimamanda Ngozi Adichie has encountered in her lifetime, I too was told a single story about other places, whether they were about different continents or different states. I grew up in New York City and as a child I identified anywhere outside of the city as the "countryside." Even suburban areas I dismissed as rural. The term "redneck" was often used in my environment to describe and stereotype people who lived in the southern states. Many people in the city can be very elitist, and I was definitely guilty of this while I was living there. But after high school I was able to travel and go outside of my little city bubble and humanize the places I use to dismiss or overlook. I finally saw that people are more similar than different, but for some reason we like to focus on the differences, maybe to feel better about ourselves and to put ourselves on a pedestal.

5.2.1 Access

On the outset of the course, each member of the community was required to present an "Introduction Selfie" on the course website. This could include their image or anything they felt was representative of them. Additionally, they were to note their home institution, major and why they chose that particular image. This served to humanize and acquaint all course members. Each member of the community had access to each other via course communications. There was also a common meeting place for collaborative sessions, discussions, and access to materials. Regardless of the location of the student, access and opportunity for participation was equal.

The course served to break barriers through web conferencing. For example, in Alaska and other rural areas, web conferencing increases access to higher education. In Alaska, where the communities and the demographics and culture of those communities are so varied, classes such as this increase a student's ability to work following graduation, as they have a better idea of other situations.

5.2.2 Relationships

Each person regardless of their locale was an accepted member of the course community and had opportunity to share knowledge, dialogue, and learning experiences. It was established that this was a "safe" community in which members were respectful of each other's differences – especially as topics were broached which challenged personal perspectives and experiences.

5.2.3 Vision

The vision for the collaborative learning community was to learn and grow both individually and collectively while examining many topics from multiple understandings, perspectives, and backgrounds. These were hard topics to discuss but enriching to watch the engagement of students across a wide geographic and cultural span.

5.2.4 Function

The function of the collaborative class was to socially and digitally create a space in which students could share projects and assignments while also breaching distance and cultural barriers. A Faculty Expectations handout was distributed at the individual institutions that stated the instructor's expectations regarding the class in general, and the interactions between students in the room, as well as distance students. The following ground rules were set up for discussion times: listen with focus and attention; speak without interruption; refrain from giving unsolicited advice or commentary; use I statements; avoid generalizing about people or groups; assume good intentions; and respect difference.

The instructor had to be vigilant about including all of the students in the conversations and activities. If something happened in the classroom that distance students could not see or experience, the instructor explained what just happened so they were not left to feel outside the classroom. The instructors also allowed the distance students plenty of time to talk about their location and how the various concepts being studied might differ elsewhere.

6. DISCUSSION

Digital technologies, especially web conferencing, allow students to participate in classes in a highly interactive manner in real-time, using a variety of mobile devices as well as traditional lap top or personal computers. Incorporating these web-based technologies encourages collaboration and communication not only between students and teachers but student-to-student. Additionally, communication and collaboration as noted in this case study potentially spans across campuses as well. Web conferencing as described in both the systematic literature review and case study serves to increase accessibility and opportunity for diversity in learning experiences.

The web conferencing experience in the collaborative class enriched students' perspectives and exposed students to a diverse range of fellow students and situations. One instructor noted, "I think in Alaska students get a much richer experience than they would otherwise; learning from others who are in remote locations, they come to appreciate the differences in access to health care and limitations in travel, etc. as well as the particular benefits and problems of living remotely in Alaska." Another instructor noted a student from New

York City commented on how they realized their perspectives of other students prior to the collaborative class discussions were inaccurate.

The nature of a course being hosted through web conferencing, such as the collaborative class case study, ultimately adds pedagogical and methodological variety to instruction. Faculty need to focus more on student-centered and active learning activities in which collaborative learning can occur within groups and across groups locally and remotely. More authentic tasks and problem-solving via web technology connections potentially promotes developing 21st Century skills for a more global society.

In addition to the benefits of collaboration, the collaborative web conferencing class was financially feasible for each institution with no extra cost for individual students. Since all interactions were web-based, using Zoom and a WordPress website, there were no extra costs and all tuition remained at the home institution for each school.

6.1 Suggestions for Organizing Web Conferencing and Collaborative Experiences

The faculty involved in the collaborative course experience which utilized web conferencing were able to tackle this new experience together, strategizing procedures and protocols, sharing plans, concepts, and sharing the instructional presentation load. Recommendations for web conferencing and collaborative experiences should first be clear with their goal or objective – beyond just an opportunity to use new technology. In this case study, there were many logistical hurdles that were conquered, but it took time and organization centered upon the purpose for the experience. Since the technological tools will vary across institutions, the faculty involved in this study recommends that instructors practice prior to the first instructional session. Step-by-step instructions on how to access the tools and materials should be provided. Also, on the outset of the course, instructors should establish protocol for how the class will function, ground rules for interactions, and lastly provide a trouble shooting resource and technical support person for assistance.

7. CONCLUSION

The systematic literature review revealed many holes in the knowledge base about web conferencing as a collegiate pedagogical tool. Even though it has been actively used since the year 2000, the documentation about the foundation for pedagogical practices is fragmented. Empirical studies are quite limited over the 19-year span, with very few quantitative studies. Additionally, there has been little analysis of the pedagogical effectiveness of web conferencing in singular disciplines. While case studies and singular uses within disciplines can serve to provide individual in-depth knowledge about experiences using web conferencing, these results are more difficult to generalize across other collegiate situations. This study served to expose the need for more sophisticated, generalizable studies regarding web conferencing.

One limitation of this study could be the exclusion of literature review related specifically to video conferencing. The researchers focused upon web conferencing as a more amenable vehicle for synchronous pedagogy. However, future studies will encompass video conferencing as well.

An instructor, teaching in two formats (face-to-face and simultaneously web conferencing) must constantly being paying attention to the local and remote students. Instructors and higher education institutions have to ask themselves why they are instituting web conferencing. Why are they seeking to offer this option? It's optimal to be able to offer options that allow students to take classes the way they learn the best. Distance or web conferencing pedagogy adds a new dimension to education, one that increases access and therefore opportunities to many students who might not otherwise be able to take advantage of education past the secondary level. Web conferencing and collaborative classes also allow for the opportunity for students across geographic and cultural spans to interact, thus promoting and extending diversity acceptance. The goal of web conferencing and collaborative classes is construct a new place of social reality which increases learning and moves far beyond the physical constructs of one geographic setting and any singular pedagogy. Berens (2012) concludes, "It doesn't matter to me if my classroom is a little rectangle in a building or a little rectangle above my keyboard. Doors are rectangles; rectangles are portals. We walk through." Collegiate educators are challenged to venture into a new place for learning experiences, including web conferencing and collaborative teaching situations.

REFERENCES

Berens, K. I., 2012. *The new learning is ancient.* Retrieved from http://kathiiberens.com/2012/12/03/ancient/

Bower, M. 2011. Synchronous collaboration competencies in web-conferencing environments – their impact on the learning process. *Distance Education, Vol.*32, No. 1, pp 63-83.

Business Matters, 2015. *The history of video conferencing.* Retrieved from https://www.bmmagazine.co.uk/tech/history-video-conferencing/

Ch, R. 2019. *What is the difference between web conferencing and video conferencing?* Retrieved from https://www.quora.com/What-is-the-difference-between-web-conferencing-and-video-conferencing

Creswell, J. W. 2007. *Qualitative inquiry and research design: Choosing among five approaches.* Sage, Thousand Oaks, CA.

Eli, B. 2017. *Understanding the difference between web conferencing and video conferencing.* Retrieved from https://www.eztalks.com/video-conference/difference-between-web-conferencing-and-video-conferencing.html

Erwin, J. 2019. *What is the difference between video and web conferencing?* Premiere Global Services, Inc. Retrieved from https://www.pgi.com/resources/articles/what-is-the-difference-between-video-and-web-conferencing/

ezTalks, 2017. *A Brief History of Video Conferencing from 1964 to 2017.* Retrieved from https://www.eztalks.com/video-conference/history-of-video-conferencing.html

Grant, M. J. & Booth, A., 2009. A typology of reviews: An analysis of 14 review types and associated methodologies. *Health Information & Libraries Journal, Vol.* 26, No. 2, pp 91-108.

Hutchison, D., 2004. *A natural history of place in education.* Teachers College Press, New York, NY

Kang, M. & Shin, W.S. (2015). An empirical investigation of student acceptance of synchronous e-learning in an online university. *Journal of Educational computing Research,* Vol.52, No.4, pp 475-495.

Knight, M. G., Dixon, I. R., Norton, N. E. L., & Bentley, C. (2004). Extending learning communities: New technologies, multiple literacies, and cultural blind pedagogies. *The Urban Review*, Vol. 36, No. 2, pp101-118.

Martin, R., & Broadley, T. 2018. New generation distributed learning: Models of connecting students across distance and cultural boundaries. *Austrailian and International Journal of Rural Educaiton*, Vol.28, No. 1, pp 55-72.

Mupepi, M. G. 2014. A schematic description of the nature of video-conferencing and Internet exchange: Enhancing global understanding. *International Journal of Web-Based Learning and Teaching Technologies,* Vol.9, No.1, pp 33-40.

Stake, R. 1995. *The art of case study research.* Sage, Thousand Oaks, CA.

Stevenson, M. & Hedberg, J., 2011. 'Head in the clouds: a review of current and future potential for cloud-enabled pedagogies'. *Educational Media International*, Vol. 48, No. 4, pp. 321–333

Wang, C. X., Jaeger, D., Liu, J., Guo, X., & Xie, N. (2013). Using synchronous technology to enrich student learning. *TechTrends*, Vol.57, No.1, pp 20-25.

West, R. E. & Williams, G. S. 2017. "I don't think that word means what you think it means": A proposed framework for defining learning communities. *Educational Technology Research Development,* Vol.7, pp 1-14. https://doi.org/10.1007/s11423-017-9535-0

NETWORK ANALYTICS OF COLLABORATIVE PROBLEM-SOLVING

Simon Kerrigan[1], Shihui Feng[2], Rupa Vuthaluru[1], Dirk Ifenthaler[1,3,*] and David Gibson[1]

[1]*Curtin University, Australia*

[2]*University of Hong Kong, Hong Kong*

[3]*University of Mannheim, Germany*

ABSTRACT

Problem-solving and collaboration are regarded as an essential part of 21st Century Skills. This study describes a task-focused approach to network analysis of trace data from collaborative problem-solving in a digital learning environment. The analysis framework builds and expands upon previous analyses of social ties as well as discourse analysis and adds new metrics of collaborative learning, problem-solving and personal learning. Using three forms of evidence - actions and use of resources, communications and constructed products - the article outlines and illustrates a framework for characterising individual and team performance on a team project as a basis for documenting individual and team behaviours linked to personal learning, collaboration and team problem solving. This study provides a preliminary demonstration of the effectiveness of network analysis on quantifying and visualizing individual-level and group-level performance in computer-mediated collaborative learning.

KEYWORDS

Collaborative Problem-Solving, Data Analytics, Network Analysis, Challenge-Based Learning

1. INTRODUCTION

Problems vary in terms of their structure. Jonassen (1997) classifies problems on a continuum from well-structured to ill-structured. Well-structured problems have a well-defined initial state, a known goal state or solution, and a constrained set of known procedures for solving a class of problems. In contrast, the solutions to ill-structured problems are neither predictable nor convergent because they often possess aspects that are unknown. Additionally, they possess multiple solutions or solution strategies or often no solutions at all (Funke, 2012). Jonassen (2011) reiterates that structuredness of a problem often overlaps with complexity: Ill-structured problems tend to be more complex, especially those emerging from everyday practice, whereas most well-structured problems tend to be less complex. The complexity of a problem is determined by the number of functions, or variables it involves; the degree of connectivity among these variables; the type of functional relationships between these properties; and the stability of the properties of the problem over time (Funke, 1991). Simple problems are composed of few variables, while ill-structured problems may include many variables that may interact in unpredictable ways. When the conditions of a problem change, a person must continuously adapt his or her understanding of the problem while searching for new solutions, because the old solutions may no longer be viable. Static problems are those in which the factors are stable over time while ill-structured problems tend to be more dynamic (Seel, Ifenthaler, & Pirnay-Dummer, 2009). Hence, in order to successfully solve complex and ill-structured problems, the person involved in problem-solving must be able to view and simulate the dynamic problem system in its entirety imagining the events that would take place if a particular action were to be performed (Eseryel, Ifenthaler, & Ge, 2013). It has been argued convincingly that all games serve as situated problem-solving environments, in which players are immersed in a culture and way of thinking (Eseryel, Ge, Ifenthaler, & Law, 2011; Gee, 2003).

*Corresponding author: dirk@ifenthaler.info

Collaboration is an essential part in most working environments because it encompasses different views, multiple skills, diverse experiences, analytical judgments, and rich knowledge. Common characteristics of definitions of a collaborative team include at least two involved individuals, common objectives, shared responsibility and interdependence as well as optimal performance (Ifenthaler, 2014). Empirical research shows that through the use of combined resources, teams can successfully handle problems that otherwise would be too complex for a single individual (Badke-Schaub, Neumann, & Lauche, 2011; Cannon-Bowers & Salas, 2001). Digital learning environments, and especially games, designed for team performance, often are characterised by integrated, media-rich contexts with multiple layers of interaction with peers as well as computational resources, which provides a foundation for authentic performance of individual and team-based problem-solving processes with attendant opportunities for unobtrusive observation and documentation of strategies, tools, communications, intentional actions and artefacts (Clarke-Midura, Code, Dede, Mayrath, & Zap, 2012).

A *network* (or graph) is constructed from a set of *vertices* whose relationships are represented by *edges*. Basics of graph theory are necessary to describe the properties of such a network (Diestel, 2000). Various measures from network or graph theory have been applied to assess individual as well as team problem representations and, in addition, to track the development of problem-solving over time (Clariana, 2010). Appropriate structural measures include (a) *number of vertices*, (b) *number of edges*, (c) *connectedness*, (d) *ruggedness*, (e) *diameter*, (f) number of cycles, or (g) *average degree of vertices* (Ifenthaler, 2010).

Both, problem-solving and collaboration are regarded as an essential part of 21st Century Skills (Griffin, McGaw, & Care, 2012). In this article, we briefly define network measures of personal learning, collaboration and problem-solving and integrate them into a trajectory analysis based on a discrete series of network states of team behaviour evolving during collaborative problem-solving. The case-study illustrates a semester-long collaborative problem-solving task where six teams of three students were engaged, leading to high performing and low performing teams being identified.

2. DIMENSIONS OF PERSONAL LEARNING, COLLABORATION AND PROBLEM-SOLVING

The domain model of a learning analysis or assessment is a conceptual representation of the key indicators that experts "might see people say, do, or make as evidence, and situations and activities that evoke it—in short, the elements of assessment arguments" (Mislevy, 2011, p13). For the analysis discussed here, the dimensions of the domain model are personal learning, collaboration and problem solving, which have been defined along with evidence indicators (Gibson, Irving, & Seifert, 2018). We will refer to these as the 'theory-based evidence targets.'

Personal learning: acquisition of knowledge (e.g. new insights, capacities for thinking, acting and employing skills) that is evidenced for outside observers as well as an individual's own reflection and metacognition (Friedrichs & Gibson, 2003). Evidence targets:

PL1: Sharing experience
PL2: Expressing and examining diverse concepts
PL3: Articulating, applying and building understanding
PL4: Communicating new powers and creations

Collaboration: coordinated group activity resulting from continuous attempts to construct and maintain a shared conception of a problem (Roschelle & Teasley, 1995). *Evidence targets:*

C1: Establishing and maintaining shared understanding
C2: Taking appropriate action to solve the problem
C3: Establishing and maintaining team organization

Problem solving: cognitive processing directed at achieving a goal when no solution method is obvious (Mayer & Wittrock, 1996). *Evidence targets:*

PS1: Exploring and understanding
PS2: Representing and formulating
PS3: Planning and executing
PS4: Monitoring and reflecting

3. RESEARCH QUESTIONS

The focus of exploratory data analysis in this research is to determine the challenges and potential of fine-grained time-sensitive analyses of collaborative problem-solving tasks to inform an understanding of the structural, correlational and causal relationships of students achieving learning outcomes. In particular, to what extent can network analyses and related measures assist in the characterisation and prediction of learning processes and learning outcomes (Ifenthaler, 2010)? Guiding the research are five research questions concerning how network analysis can assist in characterising learning in a collaborative problem-solving context:

1. Task Participation – who does what to help the team accomplish it objectives, how team members relate to and divide up the task, and which task activities and outcomes involved which team members?
2. Attention to Feedback for Improvement – how do teams differ in resiliency and the percentage of feedback used to improve, how do teams differ in the type of feedback requested and received
3. Completion Paths – how do teams differ with respect to time to completion, what variability do they exhibit in starting and ending times, and sequence of tasks
4. Use of Time – how do teams differ in their use of time during a long-term project with 24-7 access, which subtasks take the teams more time than others, how to the teams differ in overall time
5. Learning Outcomes – the extent of coverage of outcomes per team member, quality and amount of evidence of achievement of outcomes

4. METHOD

4.1 Participants and Context

Participants in the study were $N = 18$ students in their last year of high school enrolled in a semester-long Vocational Education and Training programme (VET) leading to a certificate in Business Practice with a focus on Health and Workplace Safety and Social Media in Communication. VET programs provide students with learning experiences that are often tailored towards workplace experience, or niche subject content that is not covered in a traditional high school syllabus. Students self-formed into five teams of 3 or 4 members and chose an organisation that they wished to represent in a business scenario. The main task was to research the company and deliver a social media communications plan that effectively educated the company's employees on workplace health and safety legislation rights and responsibilities. The assignment was structured through a series of 17 primary tasks and 76 sub-tasks, referred to as artefacts, which included research, written and design-based work.

The teacher created the project framework, including the design of tasks and sub-tasks linked to learning outcomes, in the Challenge platform, a web-based, mobile-ready application platform for active digital learning experiences and event-level data collection (Gibson & Jakl, 2015). Challenge integrates with Cisco WebEx Teams (https://www.webex.com/downloads.html) to provide each team with telecommunications capability for working globally, including a whiteboard, file sharing and teleconference facilities automatically organised by the Challenge platform into the main deliverables in the curriculum design.

The students in this study used the platform to form teams, upload files, chat with team members and complete the assigned tasks for the project. The analyses presented here are based on data collected from student's interactions with the platform, in particular, the creation and submission of artefacts and other inputs required by the tasks, communications among the team members and with the teacher about how to organize the work, and the instructor-judged quality of the team's product as well as the team's self-evaluation of their project. Data for the research team's analyses were collected from log-files and evidence stored on the platform (e.g., uploaded files and the content of page interactions, chat discussions, and written responses to prompts). Analyses and findings of the research team were validated by inspection and protocol review by the instructor as well as by cross-validation of multiple measures presented below.

4.2 Data Handling and Analytics

The data used in this study for exploring group collaborative problem-solving was collected from Challenge platform and Webex Teams platforms, merged into one dataset, which was straightforward given the similarities in data structure. Raw transcripts (communications) and trace data (actions and artefacts) were capable of being downloaded at any time for any time frame. Each time that a team member (user) contributed towards an assignment artefact, an interaction transaction was captured by the Challenge platform. Data collected from the Challenge platform included (a) timestamp converted to local time, (b) the user responsible for the interaction, (c) the team of the user, (d) the task they were working on, (e) the artefact they were working on, (f) the content they provided to this artefact and (g) the status of the interaction noted as *visible* (current state), *archived* (saved previous edited version) or *published* (submitted as final state) content. In addition, the communication data among team members was also collected from the Webex Teams platform, including (a) timestamp converted to local time, (b) the user posting the message, (c) the team of the user, and (d) the message content posted to the group. A manually edited column for linking events to tasks and artefacts was manually added and applied to messages in the WebEx Teams data where a student or teacher directly and unambiguously referred to a specific assignment task or artefact. This link allowed analysts to measure the effectiveness and response time to teacher feedback.

The networks modelling the interactions between individual students and artefacts were constructed for analysing individual participation and shared contribution in group collaboration. Two sets of nodes in the network include individual students and task artefacts. The links in the networks represent the interactions between agents and artefacts. There is no link within the same set of nodes (e.g. students to students or artefacts to artefacts) in the network. Bipartite networks, a technique that has been widely used to present the affiliation relationship in social problems, such as personal recommendation (Zhou, Ren, Medo, & Zhang, 2007), were constructed with this approach and used for measuring individual-level and group-level network structures of group collaboration,. Since we are interested in studying the interactive relationships between students and sub-tasks in group collaboration, the number of samples of data per team is the product of the total number of sub-tasks and number of students (e.g. several hundred samples per team). Strength of connections between a student node and an artefact node is considered as a weighted line that summarizes effort (e.g. time and number of interactions) and indicates the relative contribution of a student to an artefact. In addition, three levels of distributions were created to represent artefacts where one, two, or three people had interacted. Implications of the naturally occurring task distributions (e.g. for setting empirical probabilities in future studies) for assessment and social network analysis of collaborative problem solving are under preparation.

5. RESULTS

The page limit of the CELDA conference does not allow to present all findings of the above mentioned research questions. The CELDA presentation, however, will include the full coverage of research questions and related findings.

5.1 Task Participation

In collaborative learning, group members ideally need to complete key assigned artefacts together in order to achieve the identified learning outcomes. For example, a team cannot acquire or demonstrate any state of collaboration (C1, C2, C3) if they work independently and do not share their work with each other. The visualization of the bipartite networks for a high performing (HP) and low performing (LP) team is presented below (see Figures 1 and 2). The node sets of team members (e.g., person agents – red nodes) are presented in relationship to artefacts classified as 1-person (green nodes), 2-person (yellow nodes) and 3-person (blue nodes) artefacts. In the high performance (HP) team, members worked on more 2-person artefacts compared to the low performance (LP) team. In addition, there was no 3-person artefact in the LP team, in spite of the fact that the relevant team evaluation artefact required all group members to participate.

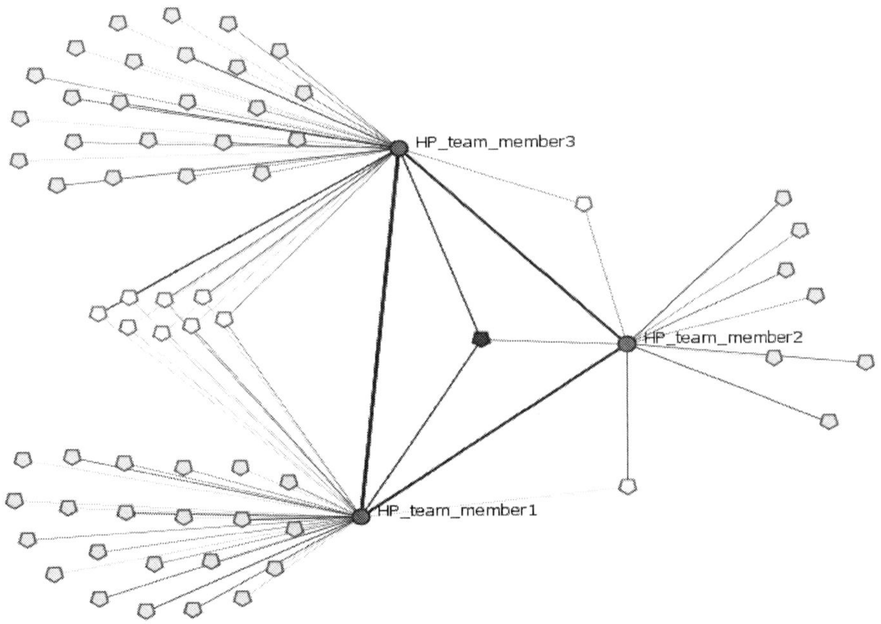

Figure 1. Individual and team task participation in the HP team; semester summary

Examining the extent to which team members worked together on tasks compared to work done on their own, the HP team showed a relatively balanced participation distribution of artefact creation by two members and fewer contributions by a third team member. Incidentally, this appears to be new objective evidence of interpersonal status hierarchies within social expectations states theory (Berger, Cohen, & Zelditch, 1966). Importantly, there were ten instances where HP team members worked on 2-person artefacts and all team members took part in paired production activity. In addition, the HP team self-evaluation included participation by all members. The automatically documented evidence from the Challenge platform is thus strongly linked to the theoretical framework of personal learning in a collaborative problem-solving context.

In comparison, the lowest performing team exhibited a spread of individual workloads among team members but created only 4 artefacts in pairs (Figure 2). There was no instance of all team members working together on an artefact. Team self-evaluation, for example, was 'filled out' by only one team member. This suggests that while individual members took some appropriate actions to solve the problem (C2), there is a lack of evidence of an effort to establish a shared understanding (C1) and maintain team organisation (C3), and this is reflected in the team's overall low performance.

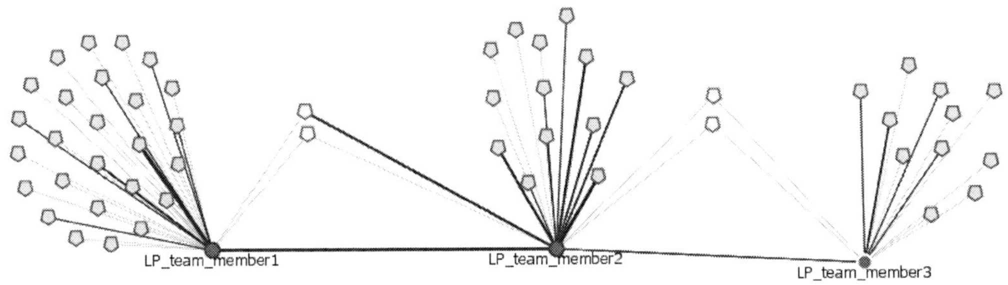

Figure 2. Individual and team task participation in the LP team; semester summary

These network graphs of task participation and distribution (Figure 1 and 2) are summary pictures of the semester-long project, so are missing important dynamic information, which we discuss below in the time series analyses.

5.2 Completion Paths

The tasks in Challenge were displayed in a listed order for teams to complete but students were free to start and finish tasks in whatever order they wanted. This provided an opportunity to analyse whether teams differed in their approach to taking appropriate action and planning and executing (C2 and PS3). The general trend in all groups was to start tasks in the order provided by the framework, but the teams exhibited much more variability in the order of completed tasks.

The data concerning completion was computed based on the last time an artefact was touched by any team member, thus capturing the order of any final check by the team. We did not consider the interval from first touch to last touch the actual time on task, because the team could have conducted a last-minute final look at everything. Instead, a time ordered list was created and sequenced with each team's task interactions (any time the task page was opened or the artefact was edited or uploaded) throughout the project duration. An average duration and sequence order was calculated for each task and subtask, to identify where along the project completion path most of the team's work occurred. Sorting the tasks by their average sequence value produced an order in which teams started and completed work on the various subtasks (see Figure 3).

The HP team evidenced one of the highest correlations to the benchmark ordering of task in both start and completion order. This suggests that the high performing team methodically approached their work (C3) which may have assisted them in being a high performing team. The LP team on the other hand, exhibited more deviation from the suggested structure in both task start and completion time, and appeared to be less methodical in how they went about completing the tasks; evidenced also by their depth and timing of responses to instructor feedback (C2) and the timing of team member participation (C1). The LP team's ordering caused some tasks to be completed 'out of logical order.' For example, the LP team completed some of the research tasks (Social Media Sites Research) after some of the design-based tasks that were supposed to be research-based (Social Media Summary) suggesting poor organisation and lack of cohesion among the group. This lack of structure (C1) and team cohesiveness (C3) might be a part of why the LP team struggled to create a high-quality final product.

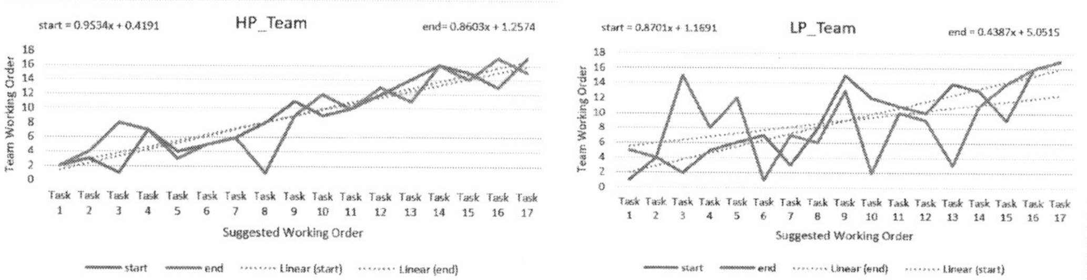

Figure 3. Completion paths of the high performing (HP versus low performing (LP) team

6. DISCUSSION AND CONCLUSION

Network analysis and graph theory have proven to be an appropriate analysis approach for educational applications. Pathfinder and combined techniques (Durso & Coggins, 1990; Schvaneveldt, 1990) provide a reliable representation of knowledge structures and analysis of learning by using pairwise similarity ratings among concepts to create networks. These networks are based on proximity data among entities and are determined by calculating the proximities that best fit within the network. Additionally, graph theory can be applied to almost every area of educational diagnostics. Picard (1980) introduced a promising approach for the design and analysis of questionnaires using graph theory. Furthermore, graph theory has been successfully applied for instructional planning (Hsia, Shie, & Chen, 2008) and evaluation purposes (Xenos & Papadopoulos, 2007).

The current study shows that network-based analyses provide an objective way to represent and evaluate individual participation and contribution during collaborative problem-solving. Network analysis was also found useful for examining the intensity of team-level collaboration by utilising the density property of a bipartite network consisting of agents (team members) and artefacts (team tasks and work products). Furthermore, the analysis of dynamic team networks revealed the periodic changes of individual engagement and group coordination during each stage of a long-term team project, which provided information that in the future could be by instructors to deliver timely intervention and guidance (Ifenthaler, Gibson, & Dobozy, 2018).

Limitations of the study are the low number of participants and teams (even with hundreds of samples over time per team), limited external validity of the findings because the case was limited to one classroom), and labour-intensive manual data processing and analysis. Future research will focus on larger sample sizes and automated analysis techniques.

ACKNOWLEDGEMENT

This research is supported by Curtin University's UNESCO Chair of Data Science in Higher Education Learning and Teaching (https://research.curtin.edu.au/unesco/).

REFERENCES

Badke-Schaub, P., Neumann, A., & Lauche, K. (2011). An observation-based method for measuring the sharedness of mental models in teams. In M. Boos, M. O. Kolbe, P. M. Kappeler, & T. Ellwart (Eds.), *Coordination in human and primate groups* (pp. 177–197). Berlin: Springer.

Cannon-Bowers, J. A., & Salas, E. (2001). Reflections on shared cognition. *Journal of Organizational Behavior, 22*(2), 195–202.

Clariana, R. B. (2010). Deriving individual and group knowledge structure from network diagrams and from essays. In D. Ifenthaler, P. Pirnay-Dummer, & N. M. Seel (Eds.), *Computer-based diagnostics and systematic analysis of knowledge* (pp. 117-130). New York: Springer.

Clarke-Midura, J., Code, J., Dede, C., Mayrath, M., & Zap, N. (2012). Thinking outside the bubble: Virtual performance assessments for measuring complex learning. In M. Mayrath, J. Clarke-Midura, D. Robinson, & G. Schraw (Eds.), *Technology-based assessments for 21st century skills* (pp. 125–148). Charlotte, NC: Information Age Publishers.

Diestel, R. (2000). *Graph theory*. New York, NY: Springer.

Durso, F. T., & Coggins, K. A. (1990). Graphs in social and psychological sciences: Empirical contributions to Pathfinder. In R. W. Schvaneveldt (Ed.), *Pathfinder associative networks: Studies in knowledge organization* (pp. 31-51). Norwood, NJ: Ablex Publishing Corportion.

Eseryel, D., Ge, X., Ifenthaler, D., & Law, V. (2011). Dynamic modeling as cognitive regulation scaffold for complex problem solving skill acquisition in an educational massively multiplayer online game environment. *Journal of Educational Computing Research, 45*(3), 265-287.

Eseryel, D., Ifenthaler, D., & Ge, X. (2013). Validation study of a method for assessing complex ill-structured problem solving by using causal representations. *Educational Technology Research and Development, 61*(3), 443–463. doi:10.1007/s11423-013-9297-2

Funke, J. (1991). Solving complex problems: Exploration and control of complex problems. In R. J. Sternberg & P. A. Frensch (Eds.), *Complex problem solving: Principles and mechanisms* (pp. 185–222). Hillsdale, NJ: Lawrence Erlbaum.

Funke, J. (2012). Complex problem solving. In N. M. Seel (Ed.), *The encyclopedia of the sciences of learning* (Vol. 3, pp. 682–685). New York, NY: Springer.

Gee, J. P. (2003). *What video games have to teach us about learning and literacy*. New York: Palgrave-Macmillan.

Gibson, D. C., & Jackl, P. (2015). Theoretical considerations for game-based e-learning analytics. In T. Reiners & L. Wood (Eds.), *Gamification in education and business* (pp. 403–416). New York, NY: Springer.

Griffin, P., McGaw, B., & Care, E. (Eds.). (2012). *Assessment and teaching of 21st century skills*. Amsterdam: Springer.

Hsia, T. C., Shie, A. J., & Chen, L. C. (2008). Course planning of extension education to meet market demand by using data mining techniques – an example of Chinkuo technology university in Taiwan. *Expert Systems with Applications, 34*(1), 596-602.

Ifenthaler, D. (2010). Scope of graphical indices in educational diagnostics. In D. Ifenthaler, P. Pirnay-Dummer, & N. M. Seel (Eds.), *Computer-based diagnostics and systematic analysis of knowledge* (pp. 213–234). New York, NY: Springer.

Ifenthaler, D. (2014). Toward automated computer-based visualization and assessment of team-based performance. *Journal of Educational Psychology, 106*(3), 651-665. doi:10.1037/a0035505

Ifenthaler, D., Gibson, D. C., & Dobozy, E. (2018). Informing learning design through analytics: Applying network graph analysis. *Australasian Journal of Educational Technology, 34*(2), 117–132. doi:10.14742/ajet.3767

Jonassen, D. H. (1997). Instructional design models for well-structured and ill-structured problem-solving learning outcomes. *Educational Technology Research and Development, 45*(1), 65-94.

Jonassen, D. H. (2011). *Learning to solve problems. A handbook for designing problem-solving learning environments.* New York: Routledge.

Picard, C. F. (1980). *Graphs and questionnaires.* Amsterdam: North-Holland Publishing Company.

Schvaneveldt, R. W. (1990). *Pathfinder associative networks: Studies in knowledge organization.* Norwood, NJ: Ablex Publishing Corporation.

Seel, N. M., Ifenthaler, D., & Pirnay-Dummer, P. (2009). Mental models and problem solving: Technological solutions for measurement and assessment of the development of expertise. In P. Blumschein, W. Hung, D. H. Jonassen, & J. Strobel (Eds.), *Model-based approaches to learning: Using systems models and simulations to improve understanding and problem solving in complex domains* (pp. 17-40). Rotterdam: Sense Publishers.

Xenos, M., & Papadopoulos, T. (2007). Computer aided evaluation of higher education tutors' performance. *Studies in Educational Evaluation, 33*(2), 175-196.

OPEN DISTANCE LEARNING AND IMMERSIVE TECHNOLOGIES: A LITERATURE ANALYSIS

Afika Ntaba and Mmaki Jantjies
University of the Western Cape, South Africa

ABSTRACT

Open and distance learning (ODL) education provides an opportunity for prospective students who require flexibility in education enabling learning without traditional face to face lecture sessions. Previous literature indicated that there has been a growing curiosity amongst educators, researchers, and pedagogues on employing modern visualization technologies to enrich current educational experiences for students who do not attend face to face lessons. This study aims to explore how new immersive technology can be used to enhance the experience of distance learning. Using a systematic literature review, findings were presented in the form of a thematic discussion looking at journal articles between the year 2000 to October 2018. Following a review of 40 articles which were included in the qualitative synthesis, this study investigated the challenges experienced in open distance learning experience, in an attempt to form the basis of interlinking the use of Virtual and Augmented Reality (AR) technologies to enhance the distance learning experience. Findings revealed ODL presently employs various Information and Communication Tools (ICT) which are comprised of technological resources that assist the facilitation of lecturer and student interaction. However, these ICTs do not fully assist in enhancing the DL experience. Results from the review found that the adoption of Augmented and Virtual Reality (VR) in higher education contributed to learner engagement and enhanced learning outcomes. Moreover, literature revealed that immersive learning is best utilized as a complement to traditional learning as opposed to a replacement.

KEYWORDS

Immersive Technology, Virtual Reality, Augmented Reality, Distance Learning

1. INTRODUCTION

Al-Arimi (2014) defines distance learning (DL) as a discipline in education that is centered on the pedagogy, technology and teaching design methodology that is effective in providing education to learners. UNISA (2018) which is South Africa's largest long-distance educational institutions, articulates that traditionally distance education could be related to correspondence courses, where the learning institution and the learner would make use of postal services as a means of exchanging learning material as well as communication-related to the process. Baukal (2010) states that DL can be asynchronous, where the learner engages with the academic material at a time suitable to them (e.g. viewing videotaped lectures). DL can also be synchronous, where the learner is engaging with a teacher in real-time through technology such as teleconferencing and webinars.

It is crucial to investigate why individuals enroll in higher education distance learning institutions. This objective will form the basis of understanding the student experience discussed in this paper. Simpson and Anderson (2012) report that the first distance learners were primarily composed of women and the working class motivated by a lack of adequate services from formal institutions and also having to work in order to pay for fees. The reasons for enrolling in distance learning has since evolved over the years. Rodrigues et al. (2014) states that individuals that enroll in distance learning seek to adopt an educational framework that is not restricted to a physical classroom, is not costly, and most importantly, has a high level of flexibility. Distance learners seek to make better use of their time, have geographic independence and also often require a flexible schedule (Rodrigues et al., 2014).

Leszczyński et al. (2017) details the benefits of DL as time saving and providing access to an extensive variety of learners, flexible learning hours, the prospect of modifying academic content to the individual learner, and decreased education cost in the long run. Markova et al. (2017) found that the primary reason that had influenced student's decision to choose DL to be the prospect of being able to combine their studies and employment, followed by the opportunity to study from home, and lastly the flexibility of "school hours". DL is, therefore, preferred by students who would be unable to attend lectures on a daily basis due to their other responsibilities and/or lack of resources. Yasmin (2013) cites how DL has been effective in reducing several barriers to traditional learning, namely inaccessibility due to geographical locations, previous subpar educational completion and financial restrictions. Since the advent of distance learning as an alternative means of formal education, there have been a number of significant transformations in not only the provision of education in distance education but also the learning experience by students. According to Van Antwerpen (2015), ODL presents learners with an opportunity to engage in an environment free of physical interaction. Distance learning presents a significant opportunity for the prospective student who seeks flexibility in education, however, it is not without its challenges. Pozdnyakova and Pozdnyak (2016) speculate that these challenges are predominantly related to the lack of corporeal co-presence between the student and lecturer or tutor. Croft et al. (2010) substantiates this perspective by reflecting on the absence of physical interaction, due to temporal separation, which may invoke feelings of isolation in the student. Croft et al. (2010) further elaborates that this lack of interaction lessens the value of the learning experience.

1.1 Research Question and Objectives

Over the years there has been an increase in the number of courses offered online as well as the number of students enrolled for these courses. However, distance learning students still face a number of challenges with the administrative and the learning processes throughout their studies. Distance learning institutions' lack of interaction has led to distance learners as having been characterized as having feelings of isolation (Zaborova & Markova, 2016 cited in Markova et al., 2017). Mbatha (2013) recommends consistent communication and interaction, especially in the presentation of course material, in distance learning. Although learner support services exist in such institutions (face-to-face tutorials, video and satellite broadcasting, and counselling services), these services are not always effective in addressing such challenges. In view of the above, it is essential to both ascertain and identify these challenges, in order to proceed to examine possible apparatuses that can be employed in enhancing the ODL learning experience. This study will thus only focus on the learning experiences of ODL learning students and how immersive technologies can be used to address these challenges.

Various technology tools have been employed in education, with the goal of enhancing and increasing the quality of the learning experience. In the modern world, learning institutions have looked to employ technology tools that will further stimulate active learner engagement with academic content. Immersive learning technology tools, (which involve the use of gaming, simulations and AR and VR) have largely been used in education in most recent years in order to provide immersive learning experiences.

This paper aims to answer the primary research question; ***How can open and distance learning be enhanced using virtual and augmented reality technologies?***

Three research objectives have been outlined in order to answer the primary research question. The first objective is to investigate the challenges that are currently being experienced in distance learning. Second, to determine what ICT tools are currently being used to support distance learning. Third objective, to investigate how augmented and virtual reality is currently being used to enhance higher education. A systematic literature review will be employed to address these objectives.

The study builds on work that support the use of modern technologies in the enhancement of DL courses. In a study conducted by Mawn et al. (2011), the author states that the study is evidence that field- experiments can be incorporated in the DL science coursework. "Distance learning opportunities such as these can enable students to increase their science content knowledge while also developing scientific process skills, all while doing so on their own schedules and from varied locations (Mawn et al., 2011, p145).

2. DESIGN AND METHODOLOGY

This study made use of a qualitative research methodology through a systematic literature review. Qualitative data predominantly refers to data collection methods (eg. Interviews) or data analysis approaches that produce non-numerical data (Saunders et al., 2009). The study aims to comprehend the challenges experienced in distance learning while establishing the role that immersive technologies such as virtual reality can play in bridging these challenges.

2.1 Data Collection

A total amount of 40 papers were chosen for this paper. The Research papers were analyzed in this study included the following words "distance education", "immersive learning" "distance learning challenges", "practical modules distance learning", "distance learning experience", "distance learning South Africa", "distance learning technology", "virtual reality higher learning", "augmented reality higher learning". Various search engines were utilized to find these articles; Taylor and Francis, Science Direct, Researchgate and EBSCO Host were primarily made use of. Other articles were found on Google Scholar and IEEE and through journal articles that were under review. The selection of keywords was then followed by an inclusion and exclusion criteria. Okoloi and Schabram (2010) articulate that this stage of the search is centered on two categories of practical criteria: according to whether the research paper's content is relevant to the primary research question. Okoloi and Schabram (2010) emphasize the importance of this section as it is imperative that the researcher justify how the research can be considered as being extensive given the exclusion criteria. The first criteria were the language of the articles. This was specifically included as the authors mainly had access to English language articles. The time frame for selecting the articles ranging from 2000 to 2018 in order to compare the differing views of researchers throughout the years and additionally to ensure that the most relevant and recently updated data was used. Okoloi and Schabram (2010) substantiate this reasoning as they state that it is essential that the selection be broad enough so as to incorporate a satisfactory amount of articles that can adequately answer the primary research question. Conversely, the review needs to be practically manageable, taking into consideration the researcher's limitations of time, money, and personnel. Table 1 presents the inclusion and exclusion criteria of the paper.

Table 1. Inclusion and exclusion criteria for journal selection

Criteria	Inclusion	Exclusion
1.Language of papers	Articles must be written in English	Articles written in other language except English
2.Time frame (date of publication)	Articles must be published between 2000 to 2018	Articles published before 2000
3. Type of publication	Peer reviewed journal articles, conference papers or reports	Books, magazines and opinion pieces
4.Phenomenon of interest: Distance Education	Higher education institutions that offer distance education	Traditional higher education
5. Phenomenon of interest: Immersive learning	Institutions where immersive learning has been used	Institutions that used AR and VR but not for the purpose of learning. (Businesses)
6. Setting/ population: distance learning	Distance learning students	Full-Time students
7. Relevance to distance education	Articles are relevant to distance learning experience	Articles are insignificant to the study

2.1.1 Data Extraction

The extraction and analysis of data was guided by the research objectives that have been set out. The study utilized a thematic analysis in order to extract and analyses data. The use of a thematic analysis is advantageous as JBI (2014) states that a thematic synthesis allows the researcher to make inferences focused on common elements that address the research objectives. Table three below is an example of a data extraction and categorization table. Articles are numbered and categorized according to the relevant concepts discussed in the article. The category section of the table is related to the outlined objectives that each article may potentially assist in addressing. These outlined objectives were classified as distance learning challenges; distance learning technology tools, and immersive learning. Within the first and second objective, three themes were identified; psychological challenges, teaching style and interaction. These themes assisted in the extracting of relevant data in the articles, addressing the objectives of the study and essentially highlighting and validating the statement of the research problem. Additionally, through the review of articles, the findings revealed another theme "Towards immersive technology use in ODL" which highlights practical ODL courses. The third objective aimed to articulate how immersive learning has been utilized in higher education while highlighting the both the positive and negative aspects of its adoption. Initially, the themes were categorized as Immersive learning challenges and immersive learning advantages. Subsequently, through further scrutiny these themes were further dissected into areas of use, learning outcomes, learner engagement, and adoption challenges.

3. SYSTEMATIC LITERATURE REVIEW THEMATIC DISCUSSION

3.1 Distance Learning

3.1.1 Psychological Challenges

Distance learning institutions have a vast array of students that make use of a variation of learning styles. This poses a challenge in the provision of learning as distance learning tends to make use of the "one size fits all" method (Croft et al., 2010). For example, aural learners may be disadvantaged as they would most likely fair better in traditional lecture rooms, while visual learners are more likely to prefer making use of the internet. It is imperative to seek alternative methods of relating course material, at the risk of creating intellectual isolation in students (Croft, et al., 2010). Simpson (2013) supports this argument by stating how evidence indicates that distance learning educators focus on the distribution of course material as opposed to than the learning experience. Simpson (2013) further elaborates that this challenge can also be attributed to the unsatisfactory graduation rate in higher distance learning institutions, in comparison to traditional institutions. Advocates of DL maintain that distance learning can be as effective or may even surpass traditional learning (Markova, et al., 2017). Zaborova & Markova (2016) critique DL, having noted that learners in virtual environments tend to exhibit feelings of confusion, isolation and frustration. Gravani (2015) details that DL students expressed their feelings regarding the learning experience as being: disappointing, filled with anxiety, constant tiredness, pressure, marginalization, and relegation. Koutsoupidou (2014) reports that the most significant drawback of DL is the psychological issues associated with the course for both the learner and the lecturer. Koutsoupidou (2014) further elaborates that isolation may become a restrictive factor in for learners' enthusiasm for the course and may even serve as justification for them dropping out.

3.1.2 Distance Learning Instruction Tools

Distance learning has become one of the most prevalent factors that have encouraged the frequent use of information and communication technologies (ICT) in institutions of higher education (Markova et al., 2017). Koutsoupidou (2015) states that digital tools are imperative with regards to the comprehension of a variation of open distance learning courses. Guri-Rosenblit (2009) supports this notion by detailing that Technological devices, from printed letters, radio, compact disc players, television and video to the modern internet-based learning, technology has always fashioned the construction of engagement between learners, educators and the academic content that is taught in ODL settings.

Online courses have improved promptly in higher institutions of learning with technology and the internet replacing the traditional face-to-face interaction. According to Rodrigues et al. (2014) distance learning is dependent on modern-day teaching practices which are comprised of technological resources that assist the facilitation of communication between lecturer and students. Numerous resources are currently available to assist the DL learner; university learning management systems, e-libraries, e-database, online- textbooks, video conferencing facilities, email and printed material (Markova et al., 2017). However, these resources are not available in all distance education institutions. Alternatively, in other institutions teaching and the provision of course material is carried out through the use of tutorial classes, e-learning, and audio course material. Markova et al. (2017) reports that DL lecturers often made use of online lectures, tests, exams, and course paper presentations but seldom made use of interactive training methods. Markova et al. (2017) further argue that in order to improve the quality of student knowledge in DL, it is imperative to enhance the level of instruction and to also seek new methods of educating as opposed to replicating traditional methods. Dede (2014) argues that the rapid growth of technology will have a considerable effect on Distance learning education. Martín-Gutiérrez et al. (2015) support this by reporting there has been a keen interest amongst educators, researchers, and pedagogues on utilizing new visualization methods to enhance current education frameworks. Modern technology that currently exhibits the most potential is virtual and augmented reality (AR).

3.2 Immersive Learning

3.2.1 Areas of Use

The evolution of the internet prompted a surge in the use of online teaching programs and the use of technology in education; these have reshaped the traditional education system. Technology tools such as AR, for example, make it possible to interlink real-world aspects by capturing them using a camera with multimedia factors for instance "text, images, video or three-dimensional models and animations." (Martín- Gutiérrez, et al., 2015). AR and VR present an opportunity to enhance the distance learning student experience. Additionally, it displays prospects of possibly assisting in the challenges experienced by the DL students. Herrington et al. (2007) reported that a sizeable amount of various institutions was incorporating simulations into their educational environment. Realistic simulations were commonly used in education settings that are deemed to have "high stakes", these sectors comprise of space training, medical education, and piloting. Rizov & Rizova (2015) substantiates this as the author asserts that is possible for augmented reality to be implemented and be beneficial to various disciplines, such as medicine, education, and architecture. "Alien Contact!" is a scenario-based simulation, was employed to enhance mathematical thinking capabilities (Dunleavy et al., 2009; Mitchell, 2011). Gamification and role-play-based AR has been implemented to increase motivation and a sense of realisticness in medical science (Rosenbaum et al., 2007). The aforementioned is an indication of the potential that immersive learning has in the enhancing of the ODL learning experience as Mawn et al. (2011) had emphasized the necessity to not only enhance theoretical knowledge but to also hone the learning of practical skills. The use of AR in education may be relatively new, however, there are several AR applications that may be utilized in various learning contexts.

VR similarly to AR has been employed in various educational contexts. A virtual exercise was implemented in a microbiology course, Flint and Stewart (2010) deduced that learners not only enjoyed the virtual exercise, but it also met the objectives, was relatively inexpensive for the university, and its speed was 10 times than that of a traditional laboratory exercise (Flint and Stewart 2010). There was, however, a large emphasis on student's prior knowledge of laboratory techniques, therefore Flint and Stewart (2010) do not recommend the use of virtual laboratories in isolation as a replacement for traditional laboratories. Additionally, several researchers have studied the use of virtual laboratories as a supplement. Dalgarno et al. (2009) intended on familiarizing chemistry learners, who were studying from a distance, by utilizing a virtual environment. Dalgarno et al. (2009) reported that students stated that the virtual laboratory would be an effective tool to assist with the advancement of their familiarity with the traditional chemistry laboratory. Koretsky et al. (2011) provided a different application of supplementary virtual environments. There was no physical laboratory counterpart for the virtual exercise in which Koretsky et al. (2011) presented engineering learners with laboratory settings and practices that depicted industry more realistically than the traditional laboratory could. Koretsky et al. (2011 p.567) concluded that 'virtual laboratories can facilitate a broader experience for students'. Koretsky et al. (2011) further elaborated that the various sorts of experiments (physical vs. virtual) direct learners' consciousness of their learning towards various factors, for example; "laboratory procedures in traditional laboratories versus critical thinking and higher-order cognition in virtual laboratories".

3.2.2 Learning Outcomes

One of the aforementioned challenges experienced by distance learners is the feeling of isolation. Rizov & Rizova (2015) conducted research on the use of augmented reality as a teaching tool; positive results were reported in the initial implementation of the application of augmented reality as an instruction tool. This indication may suggest a possible solution to the feeling of isolation experienced by students. Rizov & Rizova, (2015) states that making use of tools that depict the modern world is beneficial as it assists in maintaining learner's interests. Herrington et al. (2007, p13) reports that "the task is the crucial component of immersion and engagement in higher-order learning." When suitable technologies are utilized as cognitive instruments to find solutions to challenging problems, the learning obligation is shifted to the student as opposed to the engineer of the virtual world. Herrington et al. (2007) thus concludes that the onus is on the student to determine the method on how to complete the task. Taking into account that learning method is deemed to be reflective (Herrington et al., 2007), the use of virtual worlds may prove to be beneficial in addressing the DL challenge highlighted by Simpson (2013) of educators focusing on the distribution of content as opposed to the learning experience. However, Lee et al. (2017) reports that when making use of virtual reality primarily for the delivery of content, only a marginal benefit exists in terms of content absorption. Lee et al. (2017) further details that despite this, it should not be assumed that virtual reality is ineffective. Martín-Gutiérrez et al. (2015) conducted a study that focused on the following teaching contexts; the utilization of electrical apparatus in the laboratory, analyzing and interpretation of illustrations for reviewing installations, and autonomous learning of course work. Motivated students were reported to have had a positive academic performance. The positive outcomes and feedback from students from the use of new technology correlates with Leszczyński et al. (2017) study of an emergency medicine DL course. Leszczyński et al. (2017) found that students are enthusiastic about the use of modern methods of education, value the substantive quality and innovation presented by these new materials and are quick to adjust to new technologies. The use of immersive technology in education has been found to enrich the skills that students are expected to obtain. Patiar et al. (2017) study asserts that the VFT enabled learners to improve both their cognitive and attitudinal skills too. Moreover, the VFT tool aids learners' personal development and presents opportunities for independent knowledge seekers by modifying learners' experience of reality. Webster (2016) examined a US Army traditional lecture an immersive virtual reality-based multimedia teaching, in terms of attaining declarative knowledge. The VR instruction tool was found to offer high time-compressed training, it was able to be customized to the students' knowledge level, can permit numerous repetitions that are needed in order to increase mastery (Webster, 2016). Immersive technologies can be seen as an appropriate measure to address a DL experience challenge detailed by Croft et al. (2010). The challenge is the use of a "one size fits all" teaching approach made use by educators, that in turn, impacts influence the students' ability to assimilate information (Croft et al., 2010). Rizov & Rizova, (2015) corroborated this as the authors reported that educators expressed that AR succeeded in decreasing the amount of time spent attempting to assist students in assimilating information.

3.2.3 Learner Engagement

Learner engagement is essential in the provision of the academic content, therefore students who take in interest in the course material are more likely to find value in the learning process. Rizov & Rizova (2015) conducted a test on students based on their knowledge of engineering graphics. However, Rizov & Rizova, (2015) reports that after educators employed augmented reality in assisting with the displaying of space objects, positive growth in the results could be viewed. Furthermore, Rizov & Rizova (2015) noted a benefit that physical interaction between students and the application contributed further to the learning of various geometric shapes in the cosmos. Contrastingly a study conducted by Dyrberg et al. (2017 p.358) aimed to examine "a pilot study on student attitude, motivation and self-efficacy when using the virtual laboratory programme Labster." Dyrberg et al. (2017) details that students found less value in interacting in the virtual laboratory in comparison to participating in a traditional laboratory. Dyrberg et al. (2017) reports that the cases appeared to be less engaging, motivating and useful in comparison to doing traditional laboratory work. This also contradicts Flint and Stewart (2010) whose study found that learners in a microbiology course experienced increased enjoyment with a virtual laboratory as opposed to a traditional laboratory. The results by Dyrberg et al. (2017) do, however, support the findings by Dalgarno et al. (2009) who reported that virtual laboratories can be employed when familiarizing students with virtual laboratory before the official sessions. Dyrberg et al. (2017) reported that learners had notably greater confidence when conducting laboratory experiments.

3.2.4 Adoption Challenges

Researchers have varying opinions on the feasibility of successfully implementing immersive technologies in education. Although there are several studies that have reported the successful use of immersive technologies, there are researchers who still remain hesitant regarding immersive learning. Saleem et al. (2017) highlighted a significant issue that the prolonged use of these devices (immersive and wearable devices) may cause health issues. Saleem et al. (2017) indicates that the health issues are related to skin allergies, rashes, etc. additionally the weight of the device is also a significant concern as to whether the device can be easily carried and be mobile. Herrington et al. (2007) state that provision immersive learning technology simulations is exceedingly expensive, thus resulting in their use being limited. Conversely, Martín-Gutiérrez et al. (2015) stated augmented reality is a relatively inexpensive technology that assists in delivering course work in a more appealing manner to students. In a recent study, Saleem et al. (2017) reported that IDC (a firm providing global market intelligence) estimated in 2014 that the need for immersive and wearable devices would increase up to 112million units by 2018, with Google glasses being the most expensive device ranging around 1500$. Saleem et al. (2017) note that in certain countries this may be viewed as an affordable price, however, the rest of the world may not be on par with these prices, particularly in developing particularly developing countries. Despite the various benefits, the cost factor may significantly impede the adoption of AR and VR in ODL in a developing country such as South Africa.

Ellaway et al. (2003) referred to access as a possible limitation to the application of virtual environments in the classroom. Ellaway et al. (2003) expounds on this argument stating that even though the internet has become predominant in all aspects of modern-day society, there are noteworthy setbacks that may affect the potential users when accessing the system, for example, the lack of networked computing equipment. Ellaway et al. (2003) highlights staff development as another possible hindrance to the application of a virtual environment in education. In order to facilitate system development, the staff will require technical training on the system. Saleem et al. (2017) further elaborates on access in the context of connectivity as the study reports that the devices require a continuous data update which involves the use of an Internet connection. This poses a challenge as developing and even some developed countries are unable to provide all of its citizens with adequate Internet. Saleem et al. (2017, p692) reports that in 2013 "a mere 42% of the global population had internet access. When narrowed down to the continents 13% of the population in North America had no access, 28% in Australia, 30% in Europe, 48% in Latin America, 52% in the Middle East, 64% in Asia, and 74% in Africa still did not have access to the Internet."

Taking into account these limitations researchermarkovs have still found the use of immersive learning in higher education learning, particularly in courses that require practical engagement, as significantly beneficial in improving the learning experience (Baukal, 2010; Güven 2014; Mawn et al., 2011). Ellaway et al. (2003) however, reported that although virtual learning environments are able to provide exceptional support for the complex, dispersed and integrated practices of medical education, investment, community commitment and stakeholder buy-in will remain the most critical hindrance to implementation. Without these factors, VLEs will be inclined to linger on the periphery, to only be utilized by enthusiasts and early adopters only. Porter et al. (2016) cited the adoption innovation patterns that may possibly impede or facilitate the implementation of an immersive environment in higher education. Porter et al. (2016) reported that innovators and early adopters could be influenced through the provision of infrastructure and assistance, and in addition to clarifying the rationale for implementing blended learning. The early majority was reported to be influenced by evaluation data. The conclusion of the report on the late majority suggested that adequate training and support in a safe environment would result in their support.

4. DISCUSSION

Cornelius et al. (2008) stated that in the modern world, it would be rare to find a "fulltime student". Instructors were aware of the unavoidable need to meet the modern student's needs; students who work part-time, study from the convenience of their house, and or in their workplace, residence halls, and also those who fall in the gap of being unable to access computing resources. This description supported the statement by Rodrigues et al. (2014) detailing why individuals became distance learners. Despite the advantages presented by distance learners, the distance learners were confronted with numerous challenges that affected their learning experience (Markova et al., 2017; Gravani 2015; Koutsoupidou, 2014) these challenges included psychological challenges; feelings of isolation, anxiety marginalization, a lack of efficient in-depth content delivery, physical interaction when having a dialogue, rigid course materials and learning methods. Although there were several technology tools such as; e-libraries, e-database, online-textbooks, video conferencing and email (Markova et al., 2017), learners were still found to experience these challenges.

Cornelius et al. (2008) affirmed that a virtual environment presented an opportunity for educators to meet the needs of the modern student while, at the same time, affording students with several, not all, of the components of a real-life environmental experience. Although a virtual environment may not have been able to compare to a real visit to space, a national park, an aquarium, the amazon or a historical site, it did offer

students an opportunity to obtain a realistic perspective with reference to the module that they are learning. AR and VR have exhibited several benefits that may assist in enhancing the distance learning experience. The majority of the studies (Rizov & Rizova ,2015; Herrington et al., 2007; Martín-Gutiérrez et al., 2015; Patiar et al., 2017; Webster, 2016) indicated that the adoption of immersive learning in higher education fostered an increase in learner engagement, a better assimilation of course content and a better development of practical skills. Bower et al. (2014) argued that the use of virtual reality may be of more use to educational courses that rely on the development of practical skills as opposed to modules that were based on content absorption. Studies which focused on courses in ODL that required the development of practical skills (Baukal, 2010; Güven 2014; Mawn et al., 2011), substantiated the argument by Bower et al. (2014).

The most significant factors that may have potentially impeded the adoption and application of immersive technology in ODL are funding, health factors and accessibility or a lack thereof, in both developed and developing countries. However, recent advancements in mobile computing and operational performance had brought about an increased allocation of resources to the development of mobile AR systems (Bower et al., 2014; Johnson et al., 2010). Augmented reality had, therefore, become more commonly available to the general public, in comparison to previously, when it had been exclusively located in high-end laboratory research and industry. One of the challenges faced by distance learning students is the feeling of isolation, which stems from a lack of interaction and a "blanket" teaching style. Bower et al. (2014) maintained that the more intelligent and advanced augmented reality became, it would possess the ability to alert lecturers and tutors to a pupil's learning needs, possible behavioural concerns, and recommend an applicable course of action in real-time.

It is essential to note that the studies that made use of AR and VR in higher education did not implement immersive tools in isolation. Singh et al. (2002) maintained that the augmentation of traditional practices in higher education learning must be viewed as a tool to enrich teaching and learning and not as a complete replacement of traditional learning. Cornelius et al. (2008) substantiated this notion stating that virtual environments should only be considered as complements or supplements to the existing teaching methods and not as a replacement. This statement also satisfied the main objective of this study which is to answer the primary research question; "How can open and distance learning be enhanced using virtual and augmented reality technologies?" Additionally, Ellaway et al. (2003) reported that when aiming to take full advantage of the educational learning outcomes of immersive learning, it would be essential that the virtual learning environment (VLE) is aligned with the practices and outcomes of the course. The course must inform the VLEs and VLEs need to be modifiable to meet course outcomes and not to modify them to meet VLE limitations.

5. CONCLUSION

This study investigated how immersive technologies (AR and VR), may be used to enhance the distance learning experience. The study presented a mini systematic literature review in which a thematic discussion was implemented. The themes for the thematic discussion were informed by the three research objectives which were (1) to investigate the challenges that are currently being experienced in distance learning (2) to determine what ICT tools are currently being used to support distance learning (3), to investigate how AR and VR is currently being used to enhance higher education. The aims were achieved through a selection of journal articles that met the inclusion and exclusion criteria. Literature findings revealed that the most prevalent challenges amongst ODL students were psychological challenges; feelings of isolation, anxiety marginalization, a lack of efficient in depth content delivery, rigid course materials and learning methods. Learners still experienced challenges with the ODL learning experience regardless of having had technology tools that are currently being employed in ODL (e-libraries, e-database, online-textbooks, and video conferencing) to improve the learning experience. Additionally, the literature revealed that there has been several uses of AR and VR in higher education, however, it is more beneficial when employed in courses that require the development of practical skills. Various authors noted that although immersive learning presents various advantages in the learning environment, AR and VR should not be used as a replacement for traditional teaching but rather as a supplement. AR and VR was found to have contributed to learner engagement and enhanced learning outcomes but there are still several significant challenges that may still impede the adoption of immersive learning in ODL. The outlined aims of the study were achieved however, in order to fully answer the primary research question, future studies should be focused on how to address the adoption challenges of AR and VR, especially in developing countries. Furthermore, future studies should additionally focus on providing a framework for the adoption of AR and VR in ODL.

REFERENCES

Al-Arimi, A.M.A.K., 2014. Distance learning. Procedia-Social and Behavioral Sciences, 152, pp.82-88. Baukal, C.E., 2010.

Behavioral Sciences, 182, pp.685-691.

Bower, M., Howe, C., McCredie, N., Robinson, A. and Grover, D., 2014. Augmented Reality in education–cases, places and potentials. Educational Media International, 51(1), pp.1-15.

Continuing engineering education through distance learning. European Journal of Engineering Education, 35(2), pp.225-233.

Cornelius, S., Medyckyj-Scott, D., Forrest, D., Williams, A. and Mackaness, W., 2008. The virtual placement: an alternative to the traditional work placement in the geographical sciences?. Journal of Geography in Higher Education, 32(2), pp.287-302.

Craft, N., Dalton, A. and Grant, M. (2010). Overcoming Isolation in Distance Learning: Building a Learning Community through Time and Space. Journal for Education in the Built Environment, 5(1), pp.27-64.

Dalgarno, B., Bishop, A.G., Adlong, W. and Bedgood Jr, D.R., 2009. Effectiveness of a virtual laboratory as a preparatory resource for distance education chemistry students. Computers & Education, 53(3), pp.853-865.

Dede, CJ (2014). The Evolution of Distance Learning, Journal of Research on Computing in Education, 22:3, 247-264, DOI: 10.1080/08886504.1990.10781919

Dunleavy, M., Dede, C. and Mitchell, R., 2009. Affordances and limitations of immersive participatory Augmented reality simulations for teaching and learning. Journal of science Education and Technology, 18(1), pp.7-22.

Dyrberg, N.R., Treusch, A.H. and Wiegand, C., 2017. Virtual laboratories in science education: students' motivation and experiences in two tertiary biology courses. Journal of Biological Education, 51(4), pp.358-374.

Ellaway, R., Dewhurst, D. and Cumming, A., 2003. Managing and supporting medical education with a virtual learning environment: The Edinburgh Electronic Medical Curriculum. Medical Teacher, 25(4), pp.372- 380.

Flint, S. and Stewart, T., 2010. Food microbiology—design and testing of a virtual laboratory exercise. Journal of Food Science Education, 9(4), pp.84-89.

Gravani, M.N., 2015. Adult learning in a distance education context: Theoretical and methodological challenges. International Journal of Lifelong Education, 34(2), pp.172-193.

Guri-Rosenblit, S., 2009. Distance education in the digital age: Common misconceptions and challenging tasks. Journal of distance education, 23(2), pp.105-122.

Güven, M., 2014. Distance learning as an effective tool for medical interpreting training in Turkey. Open Learning: The Journal of Open, Distance and e-Learning, 29(2), pp.116-130. Ham, V. and Davey, R., 2005. Our first time: Two higher education tutors reflect on becoming a 'virtual teacher'. Innovations in Education and Teaching International, 42(3), pp.257-264.

Herrington, J., Reeves, T.C. and Oliver, R., 2007. Immersive learning technologies: Realism and online authentic learning. Journal of Computing in Higher Education, 19(1), pp.80-99.

Johnson, L., Smith, R., Levine, A., & Haywood, K. (2010). The 2010 Horizon Report: Australia – New Zealand Edition. Austin, Texas: T. N. M. Consortium.

Koretsky, M., Kelly, C. and Gummer, E., 2011. Student perceptions of learning in the laboratory: Comparison of industrially situated virtual laboratories to capstone physical laboratories. Journal of Engineering Education, 100(3), pp.540-573.

Koutsoupidou, T., 2014. Online distance learning and music training: benefits, drawbacks and challenges. Open Learning:

Lee, S.H., Sergueeva, K., Catangui, M. and Kandaurova, M., 2017. Assessing Google Cardboard virtual reality as a content delivery system in business classrooms. Journal of Education for Business, 92(4), pp.153-160.

Leszczyński, P., Charuta, A., Gotlib, J., Kołodziejczak, B., Roszak, M. and Zacharuk, T., 2017. Distance Learning Methods in Continuing Education of Paramedics. Studies in Logic, Grammar and Rhetoric, 51(1), pp.53-70.

Letseka, M. and Pitsoe, V., 2014. The challenges and prospects of access to higher education at UNISA. Studies in Higher Education, 39(10), pp.1942-1954.

Markova, T., Glazkova, I. and Zaborova, E., 2017. Quality issues of online distance learning. Procedia-Social and

Martín-Gutiérrez, J., Fabiani, P., Benesova, W., Meneses, M.D. and Mora, C.E., 2015. Augmented reality to promote collaborative and autonomous learning in higher education. Computers in Human Behavior, 51, pp.752-761.

Mawn, M.V., Carrico, P., Charuk, K., Stote, K.S. and Lawrence, B., 2011. Hands-on and online: scientific explorations through distance learning. Open Learning, 26(2), pp.135-146.

Mitchell, R., 2011.Alien Contact!: Exploring teacher implementation of an augmented reality curricular unit. Journal of Computers in Mathematics and Science Teaching, 30(3), pp.271-302.

Mounton, J., 2001. How to succeed in your masters and doctoral studies. Van Schaik. p. 166

Mouton, J. and Babbie, E., 2004. The practice of social research. Cape Town: Wadsworth. p. 76 & p. 84

Patiar, A., Ma, E., Kensbock, S. and Cox, R., 2017. Students' perceptions of quality and satisfaction with virtual field trips of hotels. Journal of Hospitality and Tourism Management, 31, pp.134-141.

Porter, W.W., Graham, C.R., Bodily, R.G. and Sandberg, D.S., 2016. A qualitative analysis of institutional drivers and barriers to blended learning adoption in higher education. The internet and Higher education, 28, pp.17-27.

Pozdnyakova, O. and Pozdnyakov, A., 2017. Adult Students' Problems in the Distance Learning. Procedia Engineering, 178, pp.243-248.

Rizov, D. and Rizova, D. (2015). Augmented reality as a teaching tool in higher education. International Journal of Cognitive Research in Science, Engineering and Education, 3(1), pp.7-16.

Rodrigues, S.J., Affonso, S.A., Quinelato, E. and Montiel, J.M., 2014. Distance learning in undergraduate education: the challenges of building a collaborative environment. Procedia-Social and Behavioral Sciences, 116, pp.3499-3501. Rosenbaum, E., Klopfer, E. and Perry, J., 2007. On location learning: Authentic applied science with networked augmented realities. Journal of Science Education and Technology, 16(1), pp.31-45.

Saunders, M., Lewis, P. and Thornhill, A., 2009. Understanding research philosophies and approaches. Research methods for business students, 4, pp.106-135.

Siddaway, A. (2014). What is a Systematic Literature Review and How do I do one? | p. 11/13. [online] cybermanual.com. Available at: http://www.cybermanual.com/what-is-a-systematic-literature-review-and-how-do-i-do-one.html?page=11 [Accessed 20 May 2018].

Simpson, M. and Anderson, B., 2012. History and heritage in open, flexible and distance education. Journal of Open, Flexible, and Distance Learning, 16(2), pp.1-10.

Simpson, O. (2013). Student retention in distance education: are we failing our students? Open Learning: The Journal of Open, Distance and e-Learning, 28(2), pp.105-119.

Singh, G., O'Donoghue, J. and Betts, C., 2002. A UK study into the potential effects of virtual education: does online learning spell an end for on-campus learning?. Behaviour & Information Technology, 21(3), pp.223-229.

The Journal of Open, Distance and e-Learning, 29(3), pp.243-255.

ADAPTIVE SMART TV AS A SOCIAL LANGUAGE LEARNING PLATFORM

María José Naranjo Sánchez, Mª Mercedes Rico Garcia, Héctor Sánchez Santamaría and Jesús Salguero Serrat
Universtiy of Extreadura, Centro Universitario de Mérida
Santa Teresa de Jornet, 38, 06800 Mérida, Spain

ABSTRACT

With the recent emergence of the interactive TV, the iTV starts to gain ground as a learning social media forgotten in the last decades due to previously existing applications (smart phones, tablets, laptops) that surpassed it. The TV has always been used as a means of transmission and family conciliatory, but, at the same time, the necessary feedback, as well as its adaptation to the users' preferences, language level, and age have always been lacking in every learning process that smart televisions can currently provide. In this sense, it seems necessary, on the one hand, to investigate the different characteristics and capabilities of smart televisions and, on the other, to design educational learning pills for English language learning through adaptive smart TVs. To achieve the aforementioned objectives an interactive methodology based on family/ peer gaming will be presented as a way to awake collective and social learning. The expected results will be an application developed with Hybrid Broadcast Broadband technology including a content recommendation system designed considering the user's preferences and a set of educational pills created by a team of linguists and experts in language and methodology. To conclude, this project seeks to promote language learning acquisition in a fun and entertaining way and enhance the experience with their television which has been a traditional model representing bond and time to gather around family and friends.

KEYWORDS

Social Learning, Smart TV, Design, Teaching and Learning, Education

1. INTRODUCTION

Today, four screens coexist in many Spanish homes: the television, the computer, the smartphone and the tablet. All these devices have network capabilities, they can access the Internet and communicate with each other, however, for many years TV technology has advanced little beyond its functionality while other devices such as tablets, smartphones, and laptops have risen dramatically. As Catherine Regina et al. (2016) suggest: 'Mobile language learning approaches are clearly in demand and will continue to grow in use as more people turn to smartphones or tablets as a primary computing device.' For this reason, the television has lost its exclusivity as an audiovisual and entertaining device and remained obsolete for the habitual dissemination of multimedia content, although its use continues to be active and frequent in homes, mainly due to its proximity, its place based on family experience, and ultimately, to its social component.

The analogical blackout and the later arrival of the DTT (Digital Terrestrial Television) seemed to draw the favorable scenario for the traditional television channels to develop a new concept of television: interactive TV. However, most audiovisual operators have ignored this functionality of DTT as demonstrated by the almost anecdotal percentage of DTT tuners with MHP (Multimedia Home Platform) that has been commercialized.

These screens, despite the current technological advancement in terms of image and sound quality, allow us to store large amounts of information, interact with the user and operate from a small remote control with a keyboard. Smart televisions nowadays offer us connectivity, making it possible to convert our old television into a complete multimedia entertainment center without missing any other device.

Thus, the way of enjoying television has changed in the recent years and the possibility of interacting through mobile devices has opened up many paths in the educational field. With regard to the role of foreign languages in education, it is worth mentioning 'The potential of television as an educational tool has been widely recognized in terms of early childhood education, since the launch, for example, of Sesame Street and Play School more than 30 years ago…' (Wood, 2003; Tuula Rajavaara 2005; Pavlov, R & Paneva, D., 2006; Vásquez, E., & Bejarano, A., 2011).

Although Television viewing was traditionally the dominant leisure activity for many people (Abadía, I., 2011), there has not been much exposition of language learning resources on TV; in contrast, tablets have become increasingly popular over the past decade due to it multifaceted aspect and variety of tasks that can be undertaken. So, if the television has the appropriate technology to work effectively as a mobile device, we must extend its use to reach the typical motivations for watching TV, such as passing time, companionship, relaxation along with the new added value which is changing the traditional learning style.

Television has been an important device in our daily life for a number of reasons. It is recognized that television is a source of entertainment where family/peers gather, converse, share feelings and thoughts. This social component, seen as its potential, will be the source to enhance the effectiveness of a language learning situation, specially, by presenting real facts that may draw the attention and interest of the users. Furthermore, it can be a powerful learning tool for all age people, particularly teenagers to develop closer attitude and relationships with peers and family members, and at the same time, foster their language learning styles and strengthen their cultural knowledge. Likewise, iTV can also help the elderly who sometimes feel isolated given the fact that the younger generation, the so called digital natives, millennials, or tech savvy are hooked to mobile technology all time and live in a desired social isolation. Thus, these two groups' limitations can be minimized by integrating themselves into the social value of TV intended to entertain the public. This issue is also raised in Renuka Bhattacharjee's work (2017): 'Some television programs are made to raise social awareness. The educational telenovela is one form of edutainment which is very much popular in Latin America. Miguel Sabido has combined communication theory with health and education messages to educate all people throughout Latin America in terms of family planning, literacy, and other current or socially relevant topics.'

According to a project of Northwestern University in the United States (Megan Wood, 2003), it is noted that students are much more likely to retain the knowledge gained from television programs and videos than from lectures. While teachers now make frequent use of other popular technologies such as the Internet and multimedia, it is important to note that television has had a longer and more wide reaching effect on the lives of students. In consonance with S.S Chandra & Rajendra K. Sharma (2004), one of the most important agencies of informal education is the television; the television has become an important means to informal education in most advanced countries. Most people spend their leisure time in front of the television, and thus absorb a lot of knowledge and information without having to make any great effort. Given these highlights, further development would be more than desirable.

In this light, the STVALL project, funded by the Regional Government of Extremadura (Spain), aims to develop an English teaching platform for interactive televisions which offer personalized training pills to all age users regardless their starting level of English and also taking into consideration their interests and preferences. The platform is based on HbbTV technology because it is available in a great number of televisions in Europe, and particularly, Spain.

This study explores how television as an instructional medium can be integrated with EFL learning and teaching within a social context (at home without setting fixed previous objectives), as well as, its integration in formal education by incorporating newer teaching methodologies based on social and cooperative learning such as Project based-learning, flipped classrooms and gamification under technological environments. In section 1 we have provided an introduction to interactive TV, education, and social learning. The following sections are distributed as follows: section 2 presents the research objectives. Section 3 describes STVALL project including the project's objectives, platform, and learning modes. Section 4 outlines the results, and finally, section 5 summarizes the key findings so far.

2. RESEARCH OBJECTIVES

This study seeks to investigate how the teaching and learning of English can effectively be integrated into Television leisure and education offer. The 2016 NMC Horizon Report on Higher Education in the US (Johnson et al.) lists the blending of formal and non-formal education learning as one of the major challenges in education today. Students are prone to gain easily the necessary skills, knowledge, and motivation to be autonomous learners, being able to use the learning approaches and resources that suit them best. In this light, this device has been always part of everyone's house and we all have sat around to experience a sense of socialization sharing attitudes, thoughts and feelings while watching, discussing and commenting any programme. In addition, the hyper-connected generation, the new potentialities of the mobile devices and the new global vision have given room to fully integrated iTVs. So, our project pretends to:

- 1. Provide new methodologies based on social and collaborative settings.
- 2. Stimulate individual and group learning in an entertaining way.
- 3. Provide flexibility of time and space in learning.
- 4. Reinforce and expand on content being taught.
- 5. Improve the English language
- 6. Increase users' motivation to learn.
- 7. Provide collaborative and social learning to massive audiences

3. STVALL PROJECT

As a support of this research, the STVALL project aims, on the one hand, to develop an educational platform for personalized interactive teaching of languages through iTV. The architecture of the platform (see figure 1) is divided into two distinct blocks: (1) the user (client part) that interacts with the intelligent system, and (2) the server where the educational content and individual user profiles are stored, and where the adaptation engine and the author web tool for the construction of training pills are resided. The adaptation engine comprises the recommendation motor and the evaluation system.

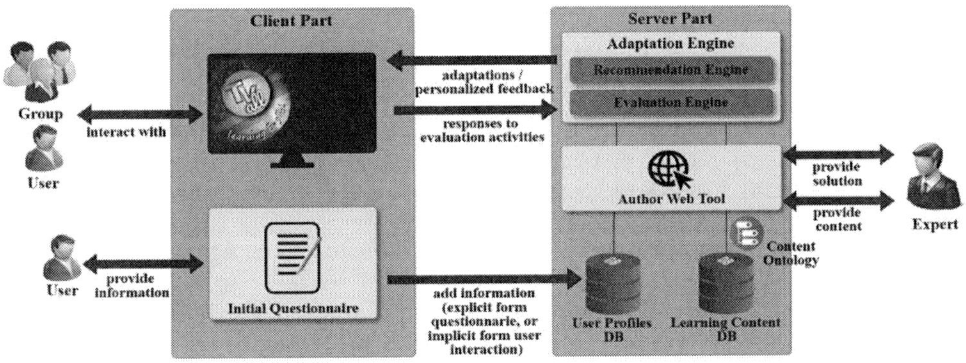

Figure 1. Structure of the STVALL project

3.1 Platform

According to the functioning of the platform, the first time users access the platform, they complete an initial questionnaire to create their own profile. The relevant information to create the profile will be formed taking into consideration personal data (full name, age, gender), the English language level they want to reach, along with a selection of topics to determine the user's preferences. Users can choose more than one, these being the options: (1) geography and history; (2) art, literature and culture; (3) science and nature; (4) entertainment, sports, film and television and (5); English language. The information about time devoted for the tasks and the ones already done, correct and incorrect answers, attempts of each assignment, score obtained and the percentage of exercises done applied for the skills listening, writing and reading will be recorded. These data allow the recommendation system to work effectively.

Figure 2. Platform

This system is used to recommend appropriate learning materials to learners based on the learner's profile and also the work carried out by each individual, providing personalization based on their current situation and experience. Additionally, linguists and experts in language and methodology can access the platform to create activities, modify and delete tasks that were previously created. Pending activities in need of feedback will be also corrected and commented by experts.

3.2 Learning Modes

The STVALL platform has three learning modes: individual, if it is a single user who accesses the platform (individual access); collaborative if it is a group who access the platform and all of them want to jointly solve the same training activities; and finally, competitive, if the group of students wants to contrast their English language and cultural knowledge (gaming).

As for the individual learning mode, it allows the user to improve their language and cultural level working with the different skills through training activities, particularly, training pills. Once the student accesses this mode, after being completed the questionnaire, the recommendation engine selects a set of assignments that meet the requirements chosen in the previous survey. Each correct task gets a score which is added to the record of the user. In case of mistakes or not completing the task appropriately, the user may improve the score by repeating the activities when the recommendation engine sends the task back again. However, this process occurs when the user ends up the bank of recommended activities for their user model. Undoubtedly, the maximum score assigned for the repeated activity is considerably reduced, getting fewer points than the first time done.

In the collaborative learning mode, again the users fill in the profiles so that the recommendation engine can build a joint user model based on each of the individual involved in the game. As in the previous mode, training pills of different themes and modalities are presented, but in this option they jointly solve them promoting social learning through collaboration and connectivism. When they leave the platform, the engine adds to each individual user model the progress made by the group, adding the points obtained and adding to their history the activities carried out.

Finally, we present the competitiveness mode which is based on group games and which connects with the new active methodologies and where competitiveness, rewards (points or badges) and motivation play an important role in learning. In this case, invited users register and already registered users select their profiles to start the activities regarding their user model. The learning of the lower level student will be favoured when different profiles are created; and the most common topics to all the members of the group will be more likely to be displayed, but without discarding the tasks with preferred themes for each of the individual members. Each participant plays in their turn adding points provided correct answers. The user who first reaches the maximum score will be the winner of the game. Once finished, the engine stores the progress of each registered user, adding the training pills made to their history and adding the points won to their total score.

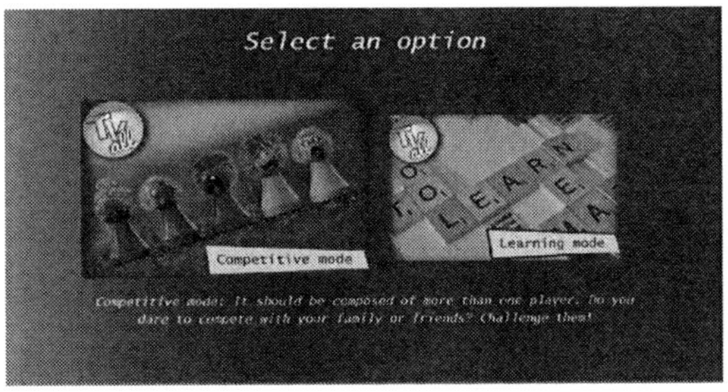

Figure 3. Learning modes

4. RESULTS: LANGUAGE LEARNING DESIGN THROUGH ADAPTIVE ITV

To complete the whole project, different research techniques were used to obtain the data for this study. These included a previous study of the literature of adaptive and interactive TV carried out by the department of Computer Systems and Telematics Engineering, followed by the development of the English teaching platform based on HbbTV technology. The language learning platform is the main result for the objectives 1, 2, 3, 6, 7 mentioned in section 2.

The remaining objectives 4 and 5 lead to creating content to be taught to improve the English language and likewise expand the knowledge providing collaborating and social learning to massive audiences. Thus, for the linguistic and culture content, the language experts selected the topics for the training pills, designed the activities and assessed them. The selected areas of study are:

1. Geography and history;
2. Art, literature and culture;
3. Science and nature;
4. Entertainment, sports, film and television and;
5. English language.

Our purpose as language specialist is to work with learning pills to foster the communicative and social approach that can be maximized from the iTV since learning a language is about more than just memorizing vocabulary lists and verb tense forms.

From the methodological approach, we adhere to the ecological theory (Van Lier, L., 2012) of language learning, dynamic games (in any of the modalities), collaborative learning and connectivism, adaptation of the contents to the user profiles according to their age, preferences and English level.

Hence, the team of language experts has been responsible for feeding the platform with around 500 training activities in each mode (interactive and non-interactive activities) with a total of around 1000 tasks. For each activity the system stores the subject (the 5 categories mentioned above), the linguistic level required by the user according to the Common European Framework of Reference for Languages (A1/A2, B1/B2), the modality (reading, listening, speaking, writing), the type of discourse (monological or dialogical), the type of text (narration, description, argumentation, instructions, biographies, advertising, informative or comic texts), and if it is oriented to child or adult audience.

As noted before, another function of the team of experts is to assess the evaluation activities with pre-recorded feedback. The expert will receive notifications of pending evaluation activities when accessing the platform. Immediate solutions will be provided to users, allowing, in addition, a more personalized and motivating learning. The training activities for each of the topics mentioned above are classified in:

- Non-interactive or presentation mode activities, where the student only visualize the training content offered in the activity (listening and reading). These activities are short (the videos last around one minute, and texts are brief, no more than 150 words) to avoid unnecessary scrolls in the screen which will hinder the purpose of the training pills and iTV functionality. No feedback is included.

Figure 4. Non-interactive activity

- Interactive or evaluation with immediate feedback tasks, where the student must provide some answer to the question arisen. The feedback can be offered by the evaluation engine without the intervention of the expert. When presenting speaking and writing activities, the feedback can be given by peers, promoting self-evaluation or by experts.

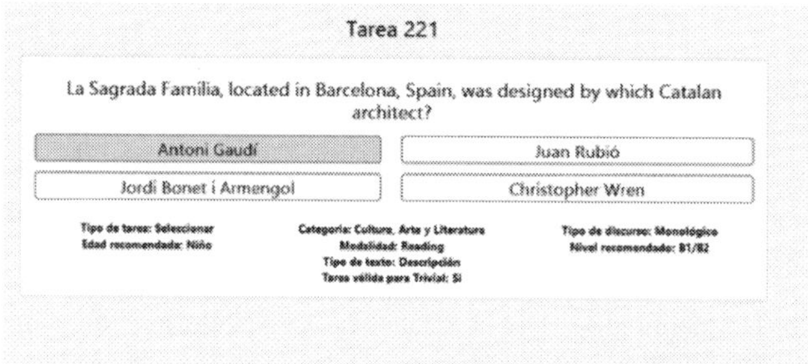

Figure 5. Interactive activity with immediate feedback

- Interactive or evaluation with pre-recorded feedback activities, where feedback cannot be automatically offered by the evaluation engine without the intervention of the human expert (long texts and speaking).

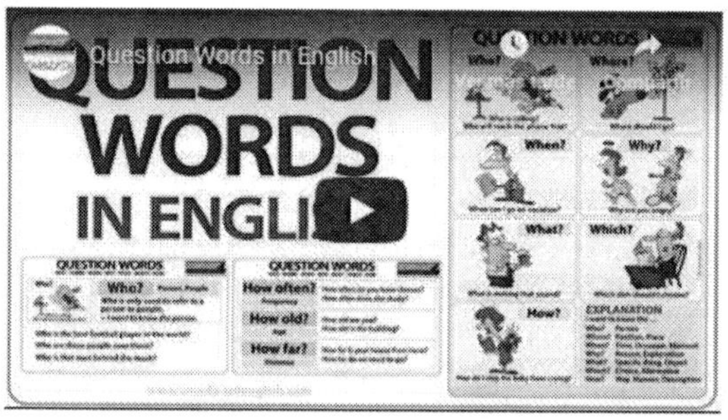

Figure 6. Interactive activity with pre-recorded feedback

The language experts have designed the following types of activities considering that pills are short inputs aiming at entertaining the users: activities with resources: image, video, audio (around 30 and 50 seconds); matching exercise; fill in the blank spaces; select the correct answer for the interactive tasks with immediate feedback. For non-interactive activities the ones presented are video (no more than 60 seconds) and text input.

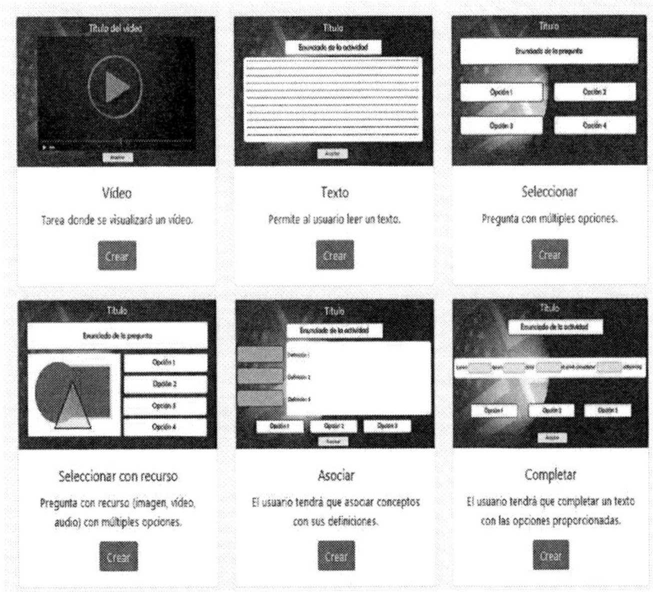

Figure 7. Different types of activities designed

After the review of literature about the strengths and weaknesses of mobile applications in comparison to the iTV, focusing on their trends, challenges and opportunities and our depiction of how the teaching and learning of English can effectively work into Television leisure and education, we hope to offer qualitative and quantitative results about the learning improvement of the sample that will be tested in short. Similar research justifies the learning improvement of t-learning applications developed (Dos Santos, D.T. et al, 2006; Souza, Maicon & Bizelli, José, 2012).

5. CONCLUSION

Although television has always been seen as a tool of indirect teaching and learning in the past- video presentations, films, series, and any kind of input have been used to promote intellectual and cultural growth in classrooms-, the originality of the proposal lies in the analysis of the effectiveness and use of educational content through television, in an environment that allows interactive, group and personalized learning within the scope of any user. In the last few years, teaching through television has become more popular and has reached a higher level of sophistication. For that purpose an English teaching platform based on HbbTV technology for interactive television offering personalized training pills to a user or a group of users have been created. The findings may reveal that users acknowledge the importance of using TV as a means of transmission and family/peer conciliatory. In addition, it meets the requirements of the traditional use of TVs, the socializing factor. Currently, we cannot provide quantitative results since this proposal is in its first phases; qualitative and quantitative results will be studied soon. Thus, further lines of research may lie in the implementation of the iTV with a social purpose in public or private channels and a later the analysis of user's data and so that all citizens have the opportunity to acquire skills and attitudes, promoting the sustainable development of knowledge and values through educational content in an interactive environment.

ACKNOWLEDGEMENT

This project has been co-financed by the Ministry of Economy and Infrastructure of Junta de Extremadura and by the European Regional Development Fund (ERDF) of Extremadura (Ref. IB16160).

REFERENCES

Abadía, I. 2011. Revisión de lineamientos para el desarrollo de contenido educativo para televisión digital interactiva. Revista S&T, 10(20), 71-104.

Dos Santos, D.T. et al, 2006. Digital TV and Distance Learning: Potentials and Limitations. Proceedings - Frontiers in Education Conference. Conference: Frontiers in Education Conference, 36th Annual. DOI: 10.1109/FIE.2006.322670

Johnson, L. et al. 2016. NMC Horizon Report: 2016 Higher Education Edition. Austin, Texas: The New Media Consortium. Retrieved from http://www.nmc.org/publication/nmc-horizon-report-2016-higher-education-edition/

Pavlov, R. & Paneva, D., 2006. Interactive TV-based learning, models and standards. HUBUSKA Open Workshop Semantic Web and Knowledge Technologies, 70–99. Varna.

Rajavaara, Tuula, 2005. Television … as a tool of learning. Examples from the Finnish broadcaster, YLE.

Regina C. et al, 2016. A review of mobile language learning applications: trends, challenges and opportunities. Eurocall Review. Retrieved from https://polipapers.upv.es/index.php/eurocall/article/view/6402/7213

Renuka, B., 2017. International Journal of Innovative Research and Advanced Studies (Ijiras). 178-183. Retrieved from http://www.ijiras.com/2017/Vol_4-Issue_1/paper_37.pdf

S.S Chandra & Rajendra K. Sharma, 2004. Sociology of Education. Delhi: Atlantic Publishers and Distributors.

Sabido, M., 1989. Soap operas in Mexico. Paper presented to the Entertainment for Social Change Conference, at Annenberg School of Communications, University of Southern California, Los Angeles.

Souza, Maicon & Bizelli, José, 2012. Televisão digital interativa na educação: desenvolvimento de um conteúdo complementar ao ensino. Revista Ibero-Americana de Estudos em Educação , ISSN-e 1982-5587, Vol. 7, Nº. 1, 2012, págs. 84-97.

Van Lier, L., 2012. Language learning: An ecological – semiotic approach. In E. Hinkel (Ed.), *Handbook of second language teaching and learning (Second Edition)*. Mahwah, NJ: Erlbaum.

Vásquez, E., García, A., & Bejarano, A., 2011. Contenidos Educativos Para Televisión Digital. Sesiones LACLO2011 - SESION 13: Desarrollos de Contenidos.

Wood, M., 2003. Using television to educate, stimulate and disseminate. Curriculum and Leadership Journal.

UNIVERSITY TUTORING ACTIONS USING AN INTEGRATED ONLINE PLATFORM

Cecilia Fissore, Francesco Floris, Marina Marchisio and Sergio Rabellino
University of Turin, Italy

ABSTRACT

University tutoring consists of a set of heterogeneous actions aimed to support students, upon entering the University and throughout their academic life. The tutoring implements the resources needed to cope with possible difficulties in each phase of the training process. It also provides information and advice to better address the study course, prepares paths for the recovery of learning gaps, and provides assistance for the preparation of the thesis. Its main purpose is to remove any possible obstacles to a profitable attendance at courses, also through initiatives related to the attitudes and needs of individuals. The research group of University of Turin has designed and developed a model of online tutoring, carried out via an online Moodle platform integrated with a web conference service for the Disciplinary Tutoring of the University of Turin. The main aim of the project, called TutoratoOnline, is to reduce the number of students starting the second academic year with a low number of passed exams, by helping students with the lessons they find more difficult. Through the platform, various and many synchronous and asynchronous tutoring activities were offered to students. The aim of this paper is to discuss and analyze the multiple tutoring activities carried out through the platform and the multiple teaching strategies used, and to discuss how their variety is associated with a greater students engagement.

KEYWORDS

E-learning, Integrated Online Platform, Online Tutoring, University Tutoring, Virtual Learning Environment

1. INTRODUCTION

University tutoring involves a heterogeneous set of actions aimed to support students throughout their academic life, implementing the resources to face possible difficulties in each phase of the training process. The university tutoring must also give information and advice to better address the study course, prepare paths for the recovery of learning gaps, and provide assistance for the preparation of the thesis. Its main purpose is to remove any obstacles to a profitable attendance at courses, also through initiatives related to the attitudes and needs of individuals (Giuliani et al., 2015). Each University organizes their own tutoring model according to their needs and possibilities. New trends and challenges in the world of education invite to experiment with new learning paradigms based on blended and collaborative models, which involve active learning (Felder and Brent, 2009) and which stimulate the development of higher cognitive abilities indicated by the Bloom taxonomy (Krathwohl, 2002). These teaching approaches, such as Problem-Based Learning, Task-Based Learning, Project-Based Learning and Cooperative Learning, are the result of the characteristics and developments of the Information and Communication Age (Bozzo, 2012). At the same time, the use of ICT and computer networks to support training processes is constantly growing and a variety of educational approaches have emerged that uses the online tools as a virtual space capable of hosting a collaborative learning community. In particular, the evolution of online tutoring shows that success does not only depend on the tool selected to create the virtual learning environment, but also on the acquisition of a new culture that considers these practices as a further possibility and not in antagonism or as an alternative to face-to-face training (Trentin, 2003; Turrentine and Macdonald, 2006). In the academic year 2016/2017 the University of Turin enhanced the existing tutoring activities (disciplinary tutoring in attendance, reception activities for first year students, study assistance for enrolled students, advice on the training offer and study plans, support in finding information on international mobility) by offering students an online tutoring service. The main objective of this project, called "TutoratoOnline", is to reduce the number of students starting the second academic year with a low number of exams passed, helping students in the lessons which they may find more difficult. The online tutoring model that the research group of University of Turin has designed and developed is based on a student-centered didactic and blended approach, which combines traditional face-to-face classroom tutoring with online platform activities. The tool we chose to offer all the tutoring activities is the Moodle Virtual Learning Environment. The University of Turin carried out multiple experiences in the field of tutoring and adaptive teaching (Barana et al., 2017b; Barana et al., in press 2019; Barana et al., 2019a; Barana et al., 2019b), e-learning (Brancaccio et al., 2016; Brancaccio et al., 2019; Marchisio et al., 2019a) and in the development of Virtual Learning Environments (Barana et al., 2017a; Bruschi et al., 2018; Marchisio et al., 2019b). The research group also designed and developed the online Moodle platform of the project (available at the link: https://tutoratoonline.orientamente.unito.it/) integrated with a web conference service for the Disciplinary Tutoring of the University of Turin. On the platform students are offered synchronous and asynchronous support for 55 courses of 25 different bachelor's degree courses, adopting a blended learning approach that combines traditional face-to-face classroom tutoring with online platform activities. The aim of this paper is to discuss an analyse the multiple tutoring activities carried out through the platform and the multiple teaching strategies used, and to discuss how their variety produces a greater engagement of students.

2. THEORETICAL FRAMEWORK

Student-centered learning is an educational approach focused on each student's interests, abilities and learning styles. According to this theory, learning is not so much the transmission of knowledge from the teacher to the student, as an active process of acquiring the most suitable principles and strategies to achieve one's goals. This knowledge process, in which the teacher acts as a facilitator of learning, can be carried out through a wide range of activities, including dialogue and experience (Bozzo, 2012). The characteristics of a constructivist learning environment are: the centrality of the student's role, the functionality of the teacher as a facilitator rather than a source of knowledge and the stimulation of motivation and autonomous investigation. Student-centered learning requires students to be active and responsible participants in their own learning. A pedagogical approach close to constructionism is an experiential learning. This approach is able to integrate the theoretical and practical elements of learning into a vision that emphasizes the importance of the student's active and responsible contribution and the value of direct experience. Constructivism, student-centered learning and experiential learning provide interesting guidelines for the creation of personalized and strongly located learning paths. Johnson et al. (2012) present the adaptation of pedagogical models to new forms of communication and research, as well as the production and publication of information, and the massive introduction of new media technologies in all disciplinary and professional fields as significant challenges for education. The analysis by Johnson et al. on third-level education perspectives identifies as key trends the growing expectation of a collaborative and delocalized use of information technologies, the proliferation of electronic resources, the increase in the establishment of contacts and mediated relations from computer, and consequently the revision of the roles of teacher and student. In the last years, the use of e-learning technologies has increased considerably, making possible new learning methodologies based mainly on Virtual Learning Environments, which are increasingly customizable (Impedovo et al., 2011). Virtual Learning Environments, such as the Moodle Learning Management System, allow to have a learning environment that fulfills the constructivist and experiential ideal: it allows students to create and publish their own works, immediately usable and shared within the community, to compare the work and to actively collaborate with the teacher or other students.

Historically, online tutoring began with emailing, but this model of tutoring, as well as the face-to-face lesson, suggested to the student that each question had to be answered with a direct answer. According to a constructivist perspective, the purpose of training should not be a mere communication of knowledge, but it should include a set of educational actions which ensure that each student can identify the knowledge they need. The same can be done for tutoring actions: we could include a review of theoretical contents but also reflection activities, group discussions, development of students' learning with the use of concept maps, correction of exercises, test simulations in preparation for the exam and discussions on concepts, principles and critical skills (Ferreira M., 2013). When students evaluate their own learning, learning becomes an incentive and they become active agents of their own learning. With the availability of new tools, new tutoring models can be used, in both asynchronous and synchronous formats, in which the student does not only passively receive explanations but tests himself to evaluate its knowledge and skills. With online tutoring models, space and time problems can be solved (Turrentine and Macdonald, 2006). For example, we consider those cases where the space-time unity becomes a big obstacle to participating in a training event, or when e-learning methods prove to be more effective because they allow dismounting and separately playing the two components -"space" (I do as much as possible on my own, perhaps assisted remotely or involved in a learning group) and "time" (when the conditions on their border allow it). The online tutoring also allows to engage students who cannot take part to the face-to-face activities, as well as working students, thus involving a higher number of students and offering all students the same possibilities.

3. TUTORING THROUGH THE ONLINE PLATFORM

Basing on this theoretical framework, the research group of University of Turin has designed and implemented a model of tutoring for the Disciplinary Tutoring of the University of Turin, in the "Tutorato Online" project. The first experimental edition of the project (2017-2018) involved a small number of courses and included exclusively online tutoring activities (Barana et al., 2018). The activities were in synchronous form – upon agreeing the day and time with the tutor, students had the possibility to fix an online appointment to have explanations on a specific topic and they could also connect to online tutorials requested by other students to listen to explanations; moreover, in asynchronous form, students had the possibility to ask questions and doubts in a forum and to submit writing, exercises or problems and have them corrected. In the second edition of the project (2018-2019), tutoring activities were activated for 55 courses of 25 different disciplines, for a total of 81 collaborations carried out by 77 tutors. The tutors were mainly graduates, and in some cases undergraduates, of the Master Degree. The small gap between the age of tutors and students helps in the action of tutoring and in achieving these objectives, since students are much closer in age to the tutors than to the teachers (Giraudo et al., 2014). The tutors followed a 3 hours course on the use of the Moodle Learning Virtual Environment and on the use of the Adobe Connect web conferencing service, so that they were able to work independently with the students creating their virtual learning communities. The tutors also received a 2 hours pedagogical training on the role of the tutor. In this second edition, we chose to use a blended learning approach also including face-to-face tutoring, in order to develop a model that could adapt to the different types of teaching involved (in which students are not used to using technologies during their studies) and in order to support and encourage students to use the platform. All the tutoring activities (face-to-face or online) were carried out using the platform, so as to take advantage of all its potential and have a complete tracking of the participation of the students. All the students of the University of Torino can access the platform with their UniTo credentials, then check if the course they are interested in is on the platform and, if so, register for the tutoring. A special dashboard was designed and developed by the research group in order to facilitate the search for the course (Barana et al., 2018). When students enrol in a course, they are asked to fill in a short questionnaire. The questions in the initial questionnaire are: Name and surname, Degree courses, Which year are you registered? (first/second/third/supplementary years), Have you already tried to take this exam? (Yes No), If yes, how many times? (One, Two, Three, More than three times).

Since all the courses on the platform belong to the first year of the three-year degree courses, but are in fact accessible to all students independently of the year, the initial questionnaire allows an overview of the students enrolled in the various tutoring courses. The format of tutoring courses is composed of an introduction to the course, where information is given about the teaching, the initial questionnaire, a forum for tutor communications and a forum for student requests. Each course has four sections, one for each type of activity: face-to-face tutoring, online tutoring, task delivery, teaching material.

Synchronous activities:

- **Face-to-face tutoring**: the tutor gives a lesson to a group of students according to a shared calendar, or offers a private consultation upon request. The platform is used to publish the tutoring calendar and to remind students of the appointment, to alert them of program changes or to request an appointment from the tutor through the forums. In addition, students are required to book their face-to-face tutoring, through the Moodle "Reservation" activity. In this way the tutor can know how many students will there be in the classroom, thus planning the teaching activity accordingly, and use the list of students to prepare the signature sheet.

- **Online tutoring**: similar to the face-to-face tutoring, but it takes place entirely online via the Adobe Connect web conference tool, through which the tutor has the possibility to share the screen of his PC and the audio with the participants during the online meetings.

Asynchronous activities:

- **Online tutoring through forums**: the tutor answers the questions asked by the students, requests for further information or assistance with the use of the platform.
- **Task submission**: in this section there is an assignment activity, always open, which enables a teacher to communicate tasks, collect work and provide grades and feedback. The tutor can decide to set up tutoring activities through exercises to perform and submit and therefore use more delivery tools with specific availability. Students can submit exercises or papers and have them corrected by the tutor.
- **Test/Teaching material**: in this section the tutor makes available to the students tests for the consolidation of knowledge in preparation for the exam, as well as teaching material of his own creation, validated by the teaching professor before publication.

Each tutor, together with the teaching professor, was able to choose which tutoring activity to carry out (choosing only one, more than one or all of them) based on the characteristics of the teaching, the needs of the students and the type of final exam. They could also choose to carry out tutoring activities in parallel with the lessons, at the end of the lessons, before the exams or after the exams, to help the students who did not pass the exam. At the beginning of the project they had to present the program of tutoring actions but, in case of need, they could modify it during the project. The platform also hosts a community of tutors who, within the training course, can talk to each other about the activities carried out and refer to the managers of the platform for any doubts on the use of the Moodle platform. This course is also used for monthly reporting of tutors and monitoring of student attendance at tutoring activities. To access the platform, any mobile devices (tablet, smartphone) or a PC can be used. Lastly, the platform has an integrated HelpDesk service managed and monitored by the research group, to offer support to all its users (for example access problems, questions on how to use the platform, etc.). The helpdesk service is always active.

4. METHODOLOGIES

The platform currently counts 4899 registered users. In this paper we have considered only the second edition of the project, in which 3329 students enrolled in a tutoring course. Several data were used to study the multiple tutoring activities carried out through the platform and the multiple teaching strategies used, and to discuss how their variety is linked to greater student engagement: subdivision of the number of students enrolled in the 55 tutoring courses on the platform, answers to the initial questionnaire in each course completed by the students, activities carried out by students at the courses registered through the Moodle logging system and tutoring activities carried out in the various courses. To classify the activities carried out by tutors in the various tutoring courses, the Excel summary file of all the activities reported by the 77 tutors in the 81 collaborations was analysed. The reported activities were compared with the activities present in the course. The classification of the courses was made after the project ended. To derive the number of students enrolled in each course and the number of each student's logs the block "Configurable Reports" was used, a Moodle custom reports builder suitable for admins or teachers. This block allows the creation of custom reports, such as courses reports - with information regarding courses - users reports - with information regarding users and their activity in a course - and custom SQL Reports to create your own type of reports. The R software was used to analyze the 3329 students responses to the initial questionnaire and to perform statistical tests.

5. RESULTS

Each Study Course of the University of Turin has identified the courses in which the students had the most difficulty in taking the final exam. 55 courses of 25 different Study Courses were identified, belonging to 5 different Departments. There were 55 tutoring courses, one for each teaching. The types of teaching involved (Figure 1) can be divided into 3 macro-categories: linguistic (7), scientific (21) and humanistic (27).

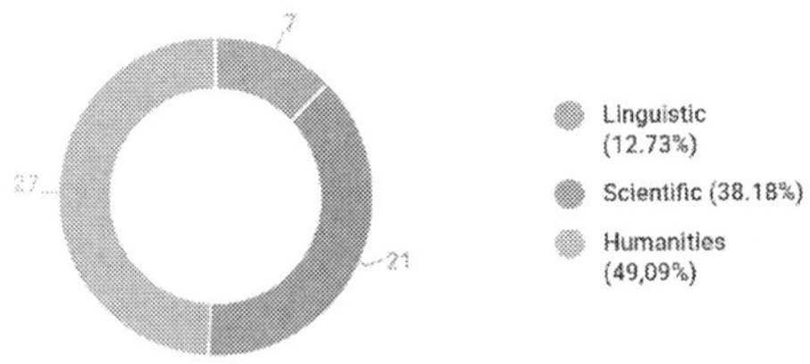

Figure 1. Types of courses involved for tutoring

To get an overview of which tutoring activities were used, we classified each course according to the four types of tutoring activities: face-to-face tutoring, online tutoring, task submission, test/teaching material. In the overview shown in table 1, there is an "X" when an activity has been carried out and for each case the number of tutoring courses is reported. This first classification shows that in most courses more than one tutoring activity was used. Most courses have chosen to have face-to-face tutoring but in blended mode, alternating it with online activities. A good number of courses also carried out online tutoring. Ten courses held exclusively face-to-face tutoring and three courses held exclusively online tutoring.

Table 1. Overview of the type of tutoring activity proposed in the tutoring courses

Type of tutoring activity				Number of tutoring courses
Presence tutoring	Online tutoring	Task submission	Test/Teaching material	
X			X	15
X		X	X	10
X				11
X	X	X	X	5
X		X		6
X	X	X		2
X	X		X	2
	X	X	X	2
X	X			1
	X		X	1

The analysis of the data of the initial questionnaire compiled by the 3329 students enrolled in a platform course (Figure 2) shows that, as expected, most of the students are enrolled in the first year, but there are also, students of the following years and students of supplementary years. All students completed the questionnaire only once, so no student enrolled in more than one tutoring course. Out of 3329 students, 796 students have already tried to take the exam of the chosen tutoring course: 447 once, 194 twice, 67 three times and 88 more than three times.

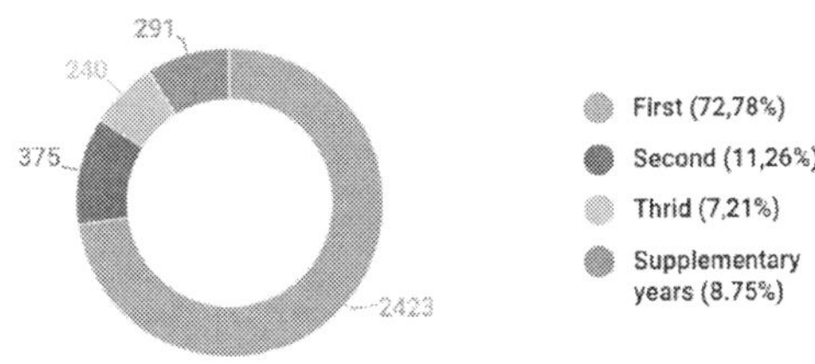

Figure 2. Students' answer to the question "Which year are you registered in?" of the initial questionnaire

Table 2 shows the connection between the two questions "Which year are you registered in?" and "Have you already tried to take this exam?", in each cell the absolute frequency, percentage, row percentage and column percentage are addressed. It emerges that a good number of first-year students enrolled in the tutoring course after failing the exam. Second and third year students are equitably split between those who had already taken the exam and those who had not yet taken the exam. It is interesting to note that there is a good percentage of supplementary years students who have never taken the exam.

Table 2. Connection between the questions "Which year are you registered?" and "Have you already tried to take this exam?"

	Already taken the exam		
Year of course enrollment	No	Yes	Total
Fist year	2130	293	2423
	87,9	12,1	
	84,1	36,8	
Second year	194	181	375
	51,7	48,3	
	7,7	22,7	
Third year	101	139	240
	42,1	57,9	
	4,0	17,5	
Supplementary years	108	183	291
	37,1	62,9	
	4,3	23,0	
Total	2533	796	3329

To analyze the engagement of students in the tutoring activities and the use of the platform, for each student registered on the platform we extracted the activities logs within the tutoring course. The tutors had a total of 40 hours (in the case of graduates) and 100 hours (in the case of students of the master's degree). They could use these hours for the whole duration of the one-year project. In some cases, the activities were concentrated only in some months of the academic year (close to the exams or in parallel with the lessons of the first or second semester) in other cases, tutors carried out activities for the entire duration of the project. The duration of the activities varies considerably, on average the tutoring face-to-face lessons lasted 2 hours but for the online activities the duration of the activities depended on the participation and the request of the students. As shown in Table 3, the range of Logs of 3329 students is very wide: there are students who have logged in very few times and have therefore hardly used the platform and students who have logged in many times and thus really took advantage of the platform. On average, a student logged in 95 times and the interquartile range - that is the width of the range of values containing the "central" half of the observed values - is 76. The first aspect we have studied is whether there is a correlation between the number of logs and the year of enrolment of the students previously analyzed. Since the Log distributions for the four groups "first year", "second year", "third year", "supplementary years" are not normal, we performed the non-parametric Kruskal-Wallis test to verify the equality of the medians. The value of the p-value is 0.005 and therefore there is sufficient statistical evidence to reject the hypothesis that the medians are equal for each group. Then we considered only two groups dividing students between "first year" and "subsequent years" and we studied if there is a correlation between the group and the number of Logs. With the Wilcox test we got a p-value of 0.6433. The test therefore leads us to state that the median of the first year student logs is not statistically different from the median of the student log of the other years. This result confirms that, even if the courses were exclusively designed for the first year students, the students of the first year and subsequent years equally benefited of the tutoring service.

Table 3. Summary of Logs of course activity of all students

Min.	1st Qu.	Median	Mean	3rd Qu.	Max.
7	31	55,5	94,79	107	1975

A second aspect that we have studied is whether the number of student Logs depends on the type of activities carried out during the tutoring course. We started from the subdivision of the courses into the four categories, shown in Table 1, grouping the last two cases into a single "online activity" case and creating the following new subdivision with the respective course numbers: "Only face-to-face and online without activity" (1), "face-to-face and online activities" (9), "only online with activities" (3), "face-to-face only with activities" (31) and "face-to-face only" (11). For each category we then divided the number of Logs of students enrolled in a course in that category into two classes "a few logs" and "many logs" depending on whether the value is less or more than the median of the Logs of that category (Table 4).

Table 4. Log classification in the various sub-categories of types of activities performed

	Presence and online no activity	Presence and online with activity	Online with activity	Presence with activity	Only presence
Few Logs	1	1	1	15	9
Many Log	0	8	2	16	1

To see if there is a correlation between the student logs and the use of online activities we have grouped these five categories into the two macro categories "online" (44) and "face-to-face" (11), where in the "face-to-face" category courses were included that only provided face-to-face tutoring. For the "online" category there are 26 courses in "many logs" and 18 courses in "a few logs", for the "face-to-face" category there are 10 courses in "a few logs" and a course in "many logs". The value of the p-value of the Fischer Test equal to 0.005 leads us to reject the independence between the type of course and the number of activities logs. This result confirms that in the courses in which we have a posteriori observed that only face-to-face tutoring was performed - without the use of online tutoring or platform activities -, the use of the platform was limited to make appointment with tutors and students were thus not encouraged to use the platform to ask questions in the forum or ask for corrections, meaning they did not take full advantage of its potential.

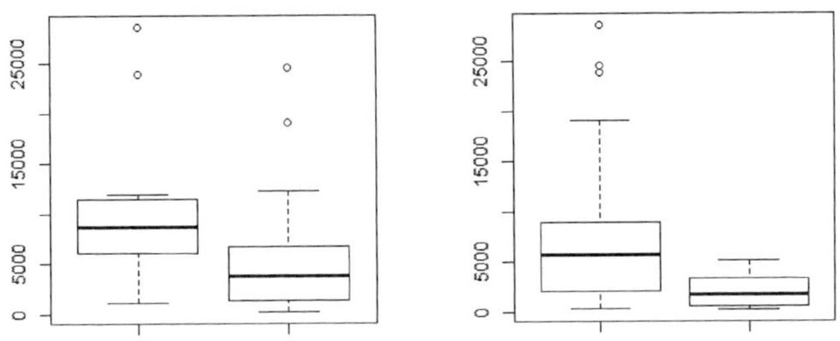

Figure 3. Boxplots of student Logs divided into the two categories: the 1st (left) and the 2nd (right)

We performed a new analysis with the two new macro categories "online2" (13) and "face-to-face2" (41), entering in the "online2" category all the courses that used the online tutoring (synchronous and asynchronous) and in the other all the courses that have not used it. We ran the Fisher test again to check the independence between the new course category and the number of activities logs. With this subdivision the value of the p-value greater than 0.05 indicates that the test does not provide any evidence against the assumption of independence. Comparison tests were then performed for the mean of the logs (Figure 3) between the two macro categories of courses for both classifications previously mentioned. In both cases there is statistical evidence that the average of the logs in courses classified as "online" is greater than the one of "face-to-face". This result shows, in the first case, that the use of online activities tailored to and at the request of the student stimulates the active engagement of the students. In the second case, since there is online activity in both categories, synchronous online tutoring seems to take on greater weight in the engagement of students.

6. CONCLUSION

The disciplinary tutoring carried out using the online platform made possible a blended tutoring, which alternated tutors, face-to-face or online, (synchronous and asynchronous) to asynchronous platform activities. The platform is used for all tutoring activities: synchronous activities (face-to-face tutoring and online tutoring) and asynchronous activities (online tutoring through forums, task submission, test/teaching material). In this way, a learning based on the needs and engagement of the student is promoted. The platform also made it possible to monitor the attendance of students in tutoring activities and that of the activities carried out by the tutors. 3329 students enrolled in a tutoring course. The analysis shows that all students, both in the first year and in the following years, actively participated in the tutoring activities and used the platform. It also emerged that student participation may depend on the type of activity performed, differentiating between online and non-online activities. At the end of the academic year an evaluation of the tutoring activities will also be conducted in relation to passing the final exams, using also psychological variables to explore the differences between users and non-users of the platform. The analysis of this paper shows the potential of tutoring activity through an online platform integrated with a web conference service.

REFERENCES

Barana, A., Bogino, A., Fioravera, M., Marchisio, M., Rabellino, S., 2017a. Open Platform of self-paced MOOCs for the continual improvement of Academic Guidance and Knowledge Strengthening in Tertiary Education. *Journal of e-Learning and Knowledge Society* 13, pp. 109–119.

Barana, A., Boffo, S., Gagliardi, F., Garuti, R., Marchisio, M., Empowering Engagement in a Technology Enhanced Learning Environment, in press 2019.

Barana, A., Fioravera, M., Marchisio, M., Rabellino, S., 2017b. Adaptive Teaching Supported by ICTs to Reduce the School Failure in the Project "Scuola Dei Compiti". *Proceedings of 2017 IEEE 41st Annual Computer Software and Applications Conference (COMPSAC)*. IEEE, pp. 432–437.

Barana, A., Fissore, C., Marchisio, M., Rabellino, S., 2018. Online Tutoring to Enhance University Success. *Exploring the Micro, the Meso and the Macro. Proceedings of the European Distanceand E-Learning Network 2018 Annual Conference*. Genova, Italia, pp. 755–763.

Barana, A., Marchisio, M., Rabellino, S., 2019a. Empowering Engagement through automatic formative assessment. *Proceedings of 2019 IEEE 43st Annual Computer Software and Applications Conference (COMPSAC)*, pp. 216-225

Barana A., Marchisio M., Sacchet M., 2019b. Advantages of Using Automatic Formative Assessment for Learning Mathematics. *Draaijer S., Joosten-ten Brinke D., Ras E. (eds) Technology Enhanced Assessment. TEA 2018. Communications in Computer and Information Science*, 1014. Springer, Cham, pp. 180-198.

Bozzo, L., 2012. Il blended learning all'Università: sperimentazione di un paradigma di apprendimento esperienziale costruttivista. *Atti di Didamatica 2012*.

Brancaccio, A., Esposito, M., Marchisio, M., Pardini, C., 2016. L'efficacia dell'apprendimento in rete degli immigrati digitali. L'esperienza SMART per le discipline scientifiche. *MONDO DIGITALE* 15, 10.

Brancaccio, A., Esposito, M., Marchisio, M., Sacchet, M., Pardini, C., 2019. Open professional development of math teachers through an online course. *Proceedings of 13th International Conference on e-Learning*. Porto, Portugal, pp. 131-138.

Bruschi, B., Cantino, V., Cavallo Perin, R., Culasso, F., Giors, B., Marchisio, M., Marello, C., Milani, M., Operti, L., Parola, A., Rabellino, S., Sacchet, M., Scomparin, L., 2018. Start@unito: a Supporting Model for High School Students Enrolling to University. *Presented at the IADIS International Conference Cognition and Exploratory Learning in Digital Age 2018*, pp. 307–312.

Felder, R.M., Brent, R., 2009. Active Learning: An Introduction. *ASQ Higher Education Brief.* Vol. 2, No. 4, pp. 1-5.

Giraudo, M.T., Marchisio, M., Pardini, C., 2014. Tutoring con le nuove tecnologie per ridurre l'insuccesso scolastico e favorire l'apprendimento della matematica nella scuola secondaria. *Mondo Digitale* 13, pp. 834–843.

Giuliani, A., Moretti, G., Morini, A., 2015. Servizi di tutorato didattico e Obblighi Formativi Aggiuntivi, un'indagine empirica esplorativa: il caso del Dipartimento di Scienze della Formazione dell'Università Roma Tre.

Impedovo, S., Campanella, P., Facchini, G., Pirlo, G., Modugno, R., Sarcinella, L., 2011. Learning Management Systems: un'analisi comparativa delle piattaforme open-source e proprietarie. *Atti di Didamatica 2011*.

Johnson, L., Adams, S., Cummins, M., 2012. *The NMC Horizon Report: 2012 Higher Education Edition*. The New Media Consortium, Austin, Texas.

Krathwohl, D.R., 2002. A Revision of Bloom's Taxonomy: An Overview. *Theory Into Practice*. Vol. 41, No. 4, 212–218.

Marchisio, M., Operti, L., Rabellino, S., Sacchet, M., 2019a. Start@unito: Open Online Courses for Improving Access and for Enhancing Success in Higher Education. *Proceedings of the 11th International Conference on Computer Supported Education (CSEDU 2019)*, pp. 639–646.

Marchisio, M., Sacchet, M., Salusso, D., 2019b. Instructional design to "train the trainers": the Start@unito project at the university of turin. *Proceedings of 13th International Conference on e-Learning*. Porto, Portugal, pp. 195-202.

Trentin, G., 2003. Gestire la complessità dei sistemi di e-learning. *Atti del Convegno Didamatica 2003*. Genova, pp. 1–8.

Turrentine, P., Macdonald, L., 2006. Tutoring Online: Increasing Effectiveness with Best Practices. *NADE Digest* Vol. 2, No. 2, pp. 9–18.

THE DEVELOPMENT OF STUDENTS' ALGORITHMIC COMPETENCE BY MEANS OF ELECTRONIC LEARNING RESOURCES

Evgenia V. Baranova[1], Irina V. Simonova[1], Mikhail I. Bocharov[2] and Victoria V. Zabolotnaia[3]
[1]Herzen State Pedagogical University of Russia
Moika River, 48, St. Petersburg, 191186, Russia
[2]Moscow City University
Vtoroy Selskohoziajstvenny proezd, 4, Moscow, 129226, Russia
[3]Transnistrian State University named after T.G. Shevchenko
Gagarina 12, Rybnita, 5500, Moldova

ABSTRACT

The problem of development of algorithmic competence of students – future Computer Science teachers as a component of information competence is investigated. The aim of the study is to identify the conditions for effective algorithmization and programming learning, involving a modular representation of the content, blended learning, allocated in accordance with the B. Bloom's taxonomy classes of problems in Computer Science and Methods of its Teaching and the use of electronic learning resources. This paper specifies the concept of algorithmic competence of university students – students' readiness to design algorithms and programs, their use in professional activities in the process of Computer Science teaching, electronic learning resources (ELR) design, self-education in the field of Computer Science. Classes of problems for algorithmic competence development in accordance with B. Bloom's taxonomy (knowledge, comprehension, application, analysis, synthesis and evaluation) are identified. Classes of problems correspond to ELR of a certain structure and content. The efficiency of ELR use in students' algorithmic competence development is statistically confirmed.

KEYWORDS

Algorithmic Competence, B. Bloom's Taxonomy, Computer Science Teacher Training, Blended Learning, Electronic Learning Resources

1. INTRODUCTION

The development of blended and electronic learning create the prerequisites for improving the efficiency of training, strengthening, which is of crucial importance for the younger generation, motivation, suggest the necessity to change the ways of working with information. The aim of the study is to identify approaches to the development of algorithmic component of information technology competence of students, future Computer Science teachers. We understand algorithmic competence as the readiness of students to design algorithms and programs, their use in professional activities in the process of Computer Science teaching, electronic learning resources (ELR) design, self-education in the Computer Science field. The development of algorithmic competence in the training of teachers is carried out on a staged basis in various modules of the educational program. The article considers two major modules "Foundations of Computer Science and Programming Techniques" and "Theories and Methods of Computer Science teaching at school". The content of the first module is aimed at the formation of students' theoretical knowledge in the field of Computer Science and algorithmic competence development. The content of the methodical module is aimed at the development of methodical competence of the future Computer Science teacher. We also reveal the system of concepts of General methods of teaching taking into account interdisciplinary connections of Pedagogy and Psychology with the subject "Computer science". Recent changes in educational are closely connected with the introduction of social media in the learning process (Thoma, Hutchison, Johnson, Johnson, Stromer, 2017).

In-service teachers and academic researchers investigate the questions of media literacy (Velasquez, Mier, Rivera, Marin-Gutierrez, 2017), and the connection between students' engagement into media environment, their motivation (Zylka, Christoph, Kroehne, Hartig, Goldhammer, 2015) and progress (Pounaki, Givi, Fahimnia, 2017).

The main means of algorithmic competence development, according to the authors, is a system of problems in Computer Science and Methods of its Teaching. The system of problems is developed by the authors and is based on the B. Bloom's taxonomy of pedagogical objectives. According to B. Bloom, the taxonomy covering the cognitive domain includes six categories of objectives: knowledge, comprehension, application, analysis, synthesis, and evaluation (Bloom, B. S.; Engelhart, M. D.; Furst, E. J.; Hill, W. H.; Krathwohl, D. R., 1956). Bloom's taxonomy can help assessment in class, as well as assignment development to exercise student's learning in all orders of thinking, including aspects of information searching (Jansen B., Booth D., Smith B., 2009).

The article describes sample problems of the selected modules and corresponding electronic learning resources. The results of the pedagogical experiment prove the effectiveness of ELR for students' algorithmic competence development.

2. RESULTS

The research and practical experience in the implementation of Computer Science teachers' training showed the advantage of modular and blended learning. This approach contributes to a flexible system of training, ensures the implementation of individual educational routes and takes into account information technology development. The analysis of various studies shows (.Harin Sellahewa. 2015; Phil Maguire, Rebecca Maguire & Robert Kelly, 2017; Baranova E.V. & Simonova I.V. , 2018.) the relevance of the design of educational learning materials for blended learning implementation, including ELR. This approach will allow to vary the forms of blended learning: online study mode, "flipped classes", etc.

The designed model of training is aimed at students' algorithmic competence development and is based on the B. Bloom's taxonomy of pedagogical objectives. This determines the logic of the formation of classes of problems, the readiness to their solving develops in students in the direction from reproductive activity to partly searching and researching. The structure, content and functional of ELR should correspond to the selected classes of problems. The use of ELR provides an opportunity to individualize the rhythm of learning, its place and time. The inclusion of resources in the LMS ensures ELR systematization, the ability to manage training activities, both in the classroom and in the online study mode, allows teachers to carry out tutoring, implement group discussion of tasks to perform. The ELR system allows each student to determine his initial level of algorithmic competence development and build a comprehended individual educational path.

Hereunder we are going to describe the developed by the authors content, sample problems, ELR aimed at students' algorithmic competence development.

2.1 Module "Foundations of Computer Science and Programming Techniques"

The module content is aimed at the formation of students' theoretical knowledge in the field of Computer science and the development of algorithmic competence. Students study the concepts of the Theory of Algorithms, Mathematical Logic, Formal Languages and Grammars, Relational Algebra, Information Theory, etc. The module implements interdisciplinary connections with the mathematical module, which studies the mathematical apparatus that forms the basis of Theoretical Computer Science.

The development of algorithmic competence is carried out in the disciplines devoted to the study of modern programming paradigms and involves students' mastery of algorithmic and programming methods. Students form knowledge of basic concepts, principles and methods of programming, on the basis of which they develop the ability to design information models, algorithms, data structures, databases, computer programs, information systems and web resources for solving by means of information technology problems from various fields, including the field of future professional teaching activities.

The study of basic concepts, principles, algorithms of compilation theory contributes to the formation of students' systematic understanding of the sources of syntax errors and skills to develop syntactically correct programs.

The peculiarity of the discipline is the need for individualization of learning, taking into account different competence levels of students in the programming field: more than 50% of students do not have or have a vague notion of this type of activity, only 10% of students usually have notion of programming and are ready to successfully solve complex problems.

Conditions for the formation of individual educational routes of students are provided with a set of sample problems of different complexity levels and electronic learning resources presented in LMS Moodle. Table 1 presents module sample problems and corresponding ELR associated with the B. Bloom's categories.

Table 1. Sample problems and electronic learning resources

Module "Foundations of Computer Science and Programming Techniques"		
B. Bloom's categories	**Computer Science sample problems in accordance with pedagogic objectives**	**Electronic learning recourses to achieve pedagogic objectives**
knowledge	performing basic operations with data presented by various structures;	"Data structure" containing a description of data structures, basic access operations, examples that illustrate ways of access and results of operations;
comprehension application	design of algorithms (computational) and programs based on the known mathematical apparatus; design of algorithms and programs modeling phenomena, processes, behavior of objects from different areas;	"Processing algorithms of data structures", containing a brief description of basic data processing algorithms presented in different structures, interactive demos, self-assessment questions;
analysis synthesis evaluation	design of algorithms and programs for the analysis of data presented in various structures and for the formation of data according to a given scheme; design of multi-module programs for solving educational and professional problems related to future professional activities	"Information systems and web resources" containing a brief description of design stages, examples of implementation stages in the form of ready-made applications; the integrated resource "Syntax analyzer" aimed at the development of students' concepts and algorithms of Theoretical Computer Science

2.1.1 Sample Problems for Students

The achievement of learning objectives is carried out by using a system of sample problems designed to develop students' algorithmic competence, including the readiness to describe and create data structures of different complexity levels, to develop and implement algorithms for solving problems from different fields. The first type of problems involves performing basic data operations represented by various structures: arrays, lists, records, object classes, database tables, etc. To solve these problems, students should know the appropriate syntactic structures, the results of the execution, including the control structures of the programming language under studies. For example, when learning object-oriented paradigm (OOP) programming languages, the central data structure is object class. To solve the problems students should know the basic principles of OOP (encapsulation, inheritance, polymorphism), class structure, ways of description and access to the fields and methods of the class.

The problems of the second type are focused on identifying the formation of algorithmic competence at the level of comprehension and involve the design of computational algorithms and programs based on the known mathematical apparatus. These are, for example, approximate calculations, calculation of series sums, matrix processing, calculation of geometric objects parameters, etc. At this stage students should be ready to interpret the mathematical module, implement a "translation" from the language of Mathematics to the language of Computer Science.

The problems of the third type involve the design of algorithms and programs that simulate phenomena, processes, behavior of objects from various fields. When solving such problems, the formation of algorithmic competence at the level of application, the readiness of students to solve problems in new situations based on known facts, models and rules are verified. This type includes software implementation of simple models describing phenomena from various spheres of knowledge, science and technology, the design of fragments of game situations, etc.

At the next, fourth stage, the readiness to analyze the data, to identify the relationship of the data elements, to determine the principles of data organization is formed. The problems of the fourth type include the design of algorithms and programs for analyzing data presented in various structures, and the formation of data according to a specified scheme: algorithms for searching and sorting, creation of object classes with a specified behavior, creation by means of SQL language of related data sets according to a specified scheme.

The synthesis category in Bloom's taxonomy of pedagogic objectives involves the ability to combine elements to produce a whole that is a novel, includes the design of the action plan, the production of a new product. When teaching algorithmization and programming with such a new product, the result of educational activities of students is a computer program. The problems of the fifth type involve the development of multi-modular computer programs, including those for solving educational and professional problems.

With regard to the training of future teachers in the field of Computer Science, it can be electronic learning resources on various topics of school subjects, information systems and web resources for the organization and management of the educational process, testing systems, etc. It is assumed that the sequence of actions of students in the process of information systems design is close to the stages of the life cycle and includes the analysis of the subject area, design, software implementation, testing.

2.1.2 Electronic Learning Recourses

For mastering the module a system of electronic learning resources has been designed to improve the efficiency of students' learning the content of the module and achieve learning objectives. The resource "Data structure" contains a systematic description of the studied data structures, basic operations of access to the elements of data structures, examples, illustrating the ways to access and the results of operations. Depending on the studied data structures programming language operators of the selected paradigm, SQL statements, etc. are described. The resource contains tasks of a reproductive nature: to describe the structure representing the data of a specified type, the object class performing a certain functional, the structure of related tables representing the abstraction of some subject area.

The resource "Processing algorithms of data structures" contains a brief description of the basic data processing algorithms presented in various structures, interactive demos – software applications that simulate the operation of algorithms. Such computer models provide a visual display of the algorithms operation for various data sets, allow students on the basis of experiments with different data sets to understand the essence of algorithms. For example, to evaluate the effectiveness of sorting methods, to understand the peculiarities of the execution of statements over the data of the database, to learn how to understand the results of executing complex queries of the SQL language, etc. The included in the resource tasks involve the modification of the considered algorithms for use in the new environment.

The electronic learning resource "Information systems and web resources" is used at the final stage of learning and is aimed at developing students' readiness for independent design of algorithms and programs that implement the specified functional. The resource contains a brief description of the design stages including design of specifications, information model, database structure, software implementation, testing. Professionally performed examples of software applications will help students learn how to analyze the subject area, create their own software products and evaluate their quality.

The integrated electronic learning resource "Syntax analyzer" developed by the following authors (Baranova E. V., Elizarova I. K., 2014), includes several software modules representing important concepts and algorithms of Theoretical Computer Science. First of all, these are models of compiler components: lexis and syntax analyzers, code generator. Working with models, students learn methods of analysis and syntax parsing of chains of formal grammars that describe the sentences of the programming language. Mastering compilation techniques allows students to learn how to design syntactically correct programs. The models use complex data structures to represent the components of formal grammars, trees, graphs. Students learn to analyze algorithms of Theoretical Computer Science, evaluate their effectiveness, "predict" the results of algorithms for different data sets. The resource is of interdisciplinary nature. It is also used in learning process of the mathematical module for mastering various concepts of Discrete Mathematics and methodical module as a tool for teaching Computer Science in the profession-oriented school.

The described system of problems and electronic learning resources is used during the whole period of training of students in the field of algorithmization and programming. By the end of training, the level of algorithmic competence formation in students allows them to independently analyze the subject area, design data structures and algorithms, create a new software product, evaluate its quality. The most capable and motivated students perform final qualification work on the creation and use of electronic learning resources in the educational process.

2.2 Module "Theories and Methods of Computer Science Teaching at School"

The module content is aimed at the development of methodological competence of the future Computer Science teacher, reveals the system of concepts of teaching methods taking into account interdisciplinary connections with the module "Foundations of Computer Science and Programming Techniques" as well as Pedagogy and Psychology. It describes the stages of content development of the school subject "Computer Science" in connection with the development of the science of information and information processes, the computer as a universal means of information processing, software. The content highlights the concept of "information", "algorithm", "model" and problem classes which solving requires comprehension and application of these concepts. Classifications, visual illustrations and demonstrations, schemes, computer models and presentations are used. The types of problems of the school subject "Computer Science" in which the major content line is "Algorithmization and programming" are considered. Methods and techniques, forms and means of education aimed at improving the efficiency of pupils' mastering the educational material are discussed.

Table 2. Sample problems and electronic learning resources

Module "Theories and methods of Computer Science teaching at school"		
B. Bloom's categories	**Problems of Methods of Computer Science teaching at school in accordance with pedagogic objectives**	**Electronic learning recourses to achieve pedagogic objectives**
knowledge comprehension analysis	Knowledge formation about basic peculiarities of Computer Science teaching at school, the structure and functions of the methodical system of education: objectives, content, forms, methods, teaching techniques.	"Methodical system of Computer Science teaching at school" contains texts of lectures, scientific articles, authors of textbooks of Computer Science for school etc.
comprehension application analysis	Formation of skills to describe plans and notes of Computer Science lessons and to explain problem solving using schemes, drawings, computer models; to analyze methodical materials, lessons of teachers.	"Educational learning materials for the Computer Science lesson at school" contains examples of lesson plans of Computer Science teachers, links to video lessons etc.
analysis synthesis evaluation	Formation of skills to adapt and create sets of educational problems for Computer Science lessons, tasks and tests using IT tools; to make a plan and to test the prepared materials with pupils; to participate in discussions.	"Network services for creating multimedia educational content" contains detailed instructions for creating graphic, animations, processing of audio and video objects.

2.2.1 Sample Problems for Students

Methodical competence development of the future Computer Science teacher involves learning of a set of definitions of major concepts revealing the structure and functions of the methodical system of education: objectives, content, forms, methods, means of teaching and knowledge of basic peculiarities of teaching Computer Science at school, knowledge of concepts and sample problems of the school subject at all levels of school education: primary, secondary, senior. In the course of training to achieve this objective the tasks that contribute to the memorization and comprehension of the logical relationship of the major concepts are used. The tasks involve the construction of logical schemes of concepts within one or more topics in accordance with the textbook material of secondary and senior school, self-construction of working definitions of the concepts "computer", "information", "algorithm", "model", etc. The result of the tasks fulfilling is required to be done with the use of computer tools: logical structure editors, text and table editor.

The leading activity of the Computer Science teacher is planning of the content of training for the entire period of secondary and senior school, making up of educational and thematic plans for the semester and lesson plans. Sample problems for teaching students this activity are making up a thematic plan on the subject of "Computer Science" for one semester (term); creation of a technological map in support of this plan for the organization of individual educational route of pupils; methods of teaching necessary for the lesson; analysis of video lessons of Computer Science teachers according to the given criteria; own judgment of the achieved lesson objectives, of the quality of teaching tools used, and of methods of pupils' motivating. Such skills are formed in the design process of sets of differentiated tasks for pupils. The future teacher should be able to design and describe the plan and scenario of the network discussion dedicated to actual problems of Computer Science teaching at school, motivation to study modern Computer Science directions, behavior ethics in network communities, etc.

2.2.2 Electronic Learning Resources

Electronic learning resources have been developed to support students' independent work and provide individual educational routes for mastering the module material. The resources include systematized theoretical material on topics and presentations focusing on the major aspects of the topic, conclusions, questions and tasks for self-reflection, and tests. Students' practical activity in mastering the subject is supported by laboratory work. The resources are implemented in LMS Moodle.

The resource "Methodical system of Computer Science teaching at school" contains lectures, scientific articles on the methods of Computer Science teaching, articles with the concepts of authors of Computer Science textbooks for school, videos with speeches of scientists and practitioners at thematic conferences, links to video Computer Science lessons, implemented in various conditions of equipping with IT tools and pupils' needs using various pedagogical technologies, bibliography to be studied by students and links to sources, solving problems examples. These materials can be used to perform sample tasks, the list of which is presented in the resource.

The resource "Educational learning materials for the Computer Science lesson at school" contains examples of Computer Science teachers' lesson plans, links to video lessons with an explanation of how to solve complex problems, links to Internet resources with relevant information about new methods and means of Computer Science teaching at school, a set of computer presentations for lessons dedicated to certain topics, a set of computer models in support of solving cross-subject problems, analysis examples of Computer Science lessons according to specified criteria as well as examples of doing the tasks by students of previous years of study.

The resource "Network services for creating multimedia educational content" contains detailed instructions for creating graphic illustrations, animations, processing of audio and video objects, using freely distributed network services, examples of objects created by students of previous years of study, examples of their use in Computer Science lessons, test tasks for each topic for self-reflection, tasks for independent work. The resource is implemented as a web-site with free access and it is used by students throughout the whole period of training to create educational learning materials for lessons: video fragments of lessons, animated videos explaining the training material, infographics and graphic illustrations for lessons (Simonova I., Ustiugova T., Yakovleva O., 2017).

3. EXPERIMENT

Two groups of students of the 2-4 courses, trained in the study field of Teacher education, specialization "Computer Science and Information Technologies in Education", took part in the experiment to assess students' readiness to solve the allocated classes of the problems aimed at algorithmic competence development. The control group consisted of 48, while the experimental group of 52 students.

Before the experiment both groups received initial training in Computer Science and Teaching Methods. At the beginning of the 2nd course, both groups had to solve problems of Computer Science and Methodology, focused on the achievement of various categories of achievement of B. Bloom's pedagogic objectives. Table 3 presents the results of the tasks performed by the students of the control and experimental groups. The analysis of the results (Table 3) shows that there were no significant differences between the readiness levels of students of both groups to solve sample problems. It should be noted that the problems related to the analysis, synthesis and evaluation of data cause great difficulties for students.

Further training in the experimental group was carried out in the form of blended learning and was based on the application of the described ELR classes. ELRs were not used in the control group. After the modules study completion the final test was carried out, including the same tasks for both groups. The tasks of the control group were aimed at checking the achievement of B. Bloom's pedagogic objectives.

Table 3. Experimental data on the development of students' readiness to solve classes of problems

Percentage of students managing to solve the problems / B. Bloom's categories	Before the experiment		After the experiment	
	Control group	**Experimental group**	**Control group**	**Experimental group**
Knowledge	0,7708	0,6731	0,6667	0,9615
Comprehension and application	0,8125	0,8269	0,5417	0,7692
Analysis	0,5625	0,6538	0,5625	0,8462
Synthesis and evaluation	0,3125	0,2692	0,3333	0,5192

The analysis of the results of the final test (Table 3) showed that the results to achieve all pedagogic objectives in the control and experimental group increased. The increment in the experimental group is significantly higher. On the basis of the data given in Table 3 we obtained the following Fisher's ration test (F-test) values which are presented in Table 4 that shows differences in students' readiness to solve problems in Computer Science and Methodology focused on achieving different B. Bloom's categories between the experimental and control groups before and after the experiment.

Table 4. Fisher' ratio test value for assessing differences in students' readiness to solve classes of problems between the experimental and control groups

B. Bloom's categories	Fisher ratio test value (φ – Fisher's angular transformation) Differences between the experimental and control groups	
	Before the experiment	**After the experiment**
Knowledge	1,0939	4,1775
Comprehension and application	0,1875	2,4240
Analysis	0,9364	3,1942
Synthesis and evaluation	0,4763	1,8900

The critical Fisher's ratio test (F-test) value for 1% of the significance level $\varphi_{cr} = 2{,}31$ and for 5% of the significance level $\varphi_{cr} = 1{,}64$. Before the experiment there were no statistically significant differences in all four categories of the studied features in the control and experimental groups at the specified significance level, since all empirical Fisher's ratio test values before the experiment were lower than the critical value.

The value of the Fisher's angular transformation after the experiment is higher than the critical value equal to about 2.31 to achieve the first three pedagogic objectives and higher than the critical value equal to 1.64 for the fourth objective.

Together with the fact that before the experiment there were no statistically significant differences in the control groups, and after the experiment such statistically significant differences appeared, we can claim that with a probability of 99% statistically significant differences in the students' training after the experiment were established for the categories: knowledge, comprehension and application, analysis, and with a probability of 95% statistically significant differences in the students' training after the experiment were established for the category – synthesis and evaluation.

4. CONCLUSION

The present study showed that the development of algorithmic competence of future teachers of Computer Science is contributed by:

- the content presented in the modular structure and implemented in a mixed form,
- classes of problems in Computer Science and Methods of its Teaching focused on students' achieving of the pedagogic objectives in B. Bloom's taxonomy,
- the system of electronic learning resources, which structure and content correspond to the selected classes of problems in Computer Science.

The directions of the research development are possible with the transfer of the proposed approach to other modules of Computer Science teachers training as well as to Computer Science training of specialists of other spheres.

REFERENCES

Baranova E. V., Elizarova I. K., 2014. Svidelel'stvo o gosudarstvennoj registratsii programmy dlja EVM «Sintaksicheskij analizator» ot 9 ijunja 2014 g.

Baranova E.V. & Simonova I.V., 2018. The development of professional competencies in the bachelor-level pedagogical training through digital learning in the field of informatics. *Izvestia: Herzen University Journal of Humanities & Sciences,* 190, PP. 116-124

Bloom, B. S.; Engelhart, M. D.; Furst, E. J.; Hill, W. H.; Krathwohl, D. R., 1956. *Taxonomy of educational objectives: The classification of educational goals.* Handbook I: Cognitive domain. New York: David McKay Company.

Harin Sellahewa. 2015. Using an Online Student Response System in Small Group Teaching: A Pilot Study. *Innovation in Teaching and Learning in Information and Computer Sciences* 10: 38-23.

Jansen B., Booth D., Smith B., 2009. Using the taxonomy of cognitive learning to model online searching, *Information Processing & Management* 45 (6), 643-663

Phil Maguire, Rebecca Maguire & Robert Kelly, 2017. Using automatic machine assessment to teach computer programming 27: 197-214.

Thoma, J., Hutchison, A., Johnson, D., Johnson, K., Stromer, E., 2017. Planning for Technology Integration in a Professional Learning Community. *Reading Teacher, 71(2),* 167-175.

Simonova I., Ustiugova T., Yakovleva O., 2017. The Impact of Online Services on Developing Students' Media Competence. *International Journal of Research in E-learning*, Vol. 3 (2), 2017. – PP.35-48

Zylka, J., Christoph, G., Kroehne, U., Hartig, J., Goldhammer, F., 2015. Moving beyond cognitive elements of ICT literacy: First evidence on the structure of ICT engagement. *Computers in Human Behavior, 53,* 149-160.

INVESTIGATING K-2 STUDENTS' COMPUTATIONAL THINKING SKILLS DURING A PROBLEM-SOLVING ACTIVITY ABOUT THE WATER CYCLE USING EDUCATIONAL ROBOTICS

Charoula Angeli, Eftychia Xerou and Maria Nicolaou
University of Cyprus, Cyprus

ABSTRACT

The main purpose of the study was to investigate K-2 children's development of computational thinking skills through an activity with Blue-Bot, a floor programmable robot. Twenty children between six and seven years old participated in the study. Children were engaged in problem-solving activities with the Blue-Bot to learn how to program it and about the water cycle. The results of the study reported statistically significant learning gains between the initial and final assessment of children's computational thinking skills as they were measured holistically with a rubric that was developed for the purposes of this study. In addition, the results showed that learning with robotics activities was an effective way to teach children about the water cycle.

KEYWORDS

Computational Thinking, Robotics, Blue-Bot, Science, Young Children

1. INTRODUCTION

Despite the fact that currently there is not one unanimous definition of computational thinking, after a systematic examination of what is currently known in the literature, Grover and Pea (2013) concluded that researchers have come to accept that computational thinking is a thought process that utilizes the elements of abstraction, generalization, decomposition, algorithmic thinking, and debugging (detection and correction of errors). Abstraction is the skill of removing characteristics or attributes from an object or entity in order to reduce it to a set of fundamental characteristics (Wing, 2011). While abstraction reduces complexity by hiding irrelevant detail, generalization reduces complexity by replacing multiple entities which perform similar functions with a single construct (Selby, 2012). For example, programming languages provide generalization through variables and parameterization. Abstraction and generalization are often used together as abstracts are generalized through parameterization to provide greater utility. Decomposition is the skill of breaking complex problems into simpler ones (Wing, 2008; National Research Council, 2010). Algorithmic thinking is a problem-solving skill related to devising a step-by-step solution to a problem and differs from coding (i.e., the technical skills required to be able to write code in a programming language) (Selby, 2012). Additionally, algorithmic notions of sequencing (i.e., planning an algorithm, which involves putting actions in the correct sequence), and algorithmic notions of flow of control (i.e., the order in which individual instructions or steps in an algorithm are evaluated) are also considered important elements of computational thinking (Lu & Fletcher, 2009). Debugging is the skill to recognize when actions do not correspond to instructions, and the skill to fix errors (Bers et al., 2014). For the purposes of the study reported herein, the elements of algorithmic thinking, sequencing, decomposition, and debugging are of particular interest and constitute the main areas of the authors' research investigation.

In regards to teaching computational thinking skills during the last decade, the research community has embraced educational robotics with genuine enthusiasm as an approach for teaching computational thinking to young students (Stoeckelmayr et al., 2011; Bers, 2010; Bers et al., 2014; Kazakoff, Sullivan, & Bers, 2013; Alimisis & Kynigos, 2009; Benitti, 2012; Bredenfeld, Hofmann, & Steinbauer, 2010; Johnson, 2003; Botički, Pivalica, & Seow, 2018). In this study, the authors used the Blue-Bot, shown in Figure 1, to teach children computational thinking skills.

Figure 1. Blue-Bot

Specifically, the study herein sought to investigate the effects of learning with the Blue-Bot on young children's computational thinking skills within the context of two problem-solving scenarios which engaged the children in rich problem-solving activities. The first problem-solving scenario was exploratory in nature in order for the children to learn how to program the Blue-Bot, while the second one was about the water cycle. For this reason, the researchers also examined the effects of learning with the Blue-Bot on children's understanding of the stages of the water cycle. All in all, the researchers sought to answer the following two research questions: (1) Are there any learning gains related to children's understanding of the water cycle? (2) Are there any learning gains related to children's development of computational thinking measured on two different occasions?

The research contributes to the body of knowledge that can be used to inform the teaching of computational thinking skills, and responds directly to calls for more research into how to teach young children computational thinking (Grover & Pea, 2013, 2018; Guzdial, 2008; Lye & Koh, 2014).

2. METHODOLOGY

2.1 Participants

Twenty young children between 6 and 7.5 years old participated in the study. The average age of the participants was 6.68 years (*SD* = .47). Of the 20 participants, 13 were girls and seven were boys. Students were randomly selected from different private and public schools located in urban and rural areas in a southern Mediterranean country. The majority of the students (13) were bilingual and a small number of students (4) were trilingual. Prior to participating in the study, the researchers obtained written consent from the children's parents or guardians. All children had no previous experience with either computers or robotic devices.

2.2 Blue-Bot

The Blue-Bot is a robotic programmable floor device in the shape of a bee. It is transparent and when is working a blue light turns on. Students can program the Blue-Bot by using the directional buttons located on its back or through Bluetooth from a tablet or a mobile phone. For the purposes of the current study students programmed the robotic device by using the directional buttons. The directional buttons can move the Blue-Bot in four different directions, namely, backward (15 cm), forward (15 cm), left (90 degrees), and right (90 degrees). The execution of a command or a sequence of commands starts with the push of the GO button.

The CLEAR button is used to clear the Blue-Bot's memory, which can hold up to 40 commands at a time. It has also a PAUSE button which can pause the function of the robotic device for one second. Blue-Bot can be charged through a USB cable. The Blue-Bot blinks and beeps at the conclusion of each sequence of commands.

2.3 Knowledge Test about the Water Cycle

A knowledge test was developed by the researchers to assess students' conceptual knowledge about the water cycle. The test was used both as a pretest and a posttest. The test consisted of two questions. The first question was a matching question asking the children to match the six words on the first column with the six pictures on the second column. The second question instructed the students to number from one to five the pictures provided so that they represented in the correct order the five stages of the water cycle. Each correct answer was given a score of 1 point, thus the maximum possible score on the first exercise was 6 points. The second question instructed the students to number from one to five the pictures provided so that they represented in the correct order the five stages of the water cycle. The correct placing of all stages was given 1 point to the students. The maximum possible score on the test was 7 points for both questions. The test was administered individually in 5 minutes.

2.4 Problem-Solving Scenarios and Mats

Research participants were engaged in problem-solving tasks using two scenarios and two mats, one mat for each scenario. The mats are shown in Figures 2 and 3. Both scenarios requested children to program the Blue-Bot to perform a certain route on a mat. Sometimes the route involved a number of obstacles that the children needed to find a way to bypass by programming the Blue-Bot to take an alternate route. The first scenario aimed at familiarizing the children with the Blue-Bot by asking them to program it in order to follow certain paths on the first mat to collect different items suitable for a journey, such as, a bag-pack, a bottle of water, a boat, sunglasses and several others in order to prepare the Blue-Bot for his journey on the second mat.

Figure 2. First mat

The second scenario made use of the second mat, shown in Figure 2, and aimed at teaching children about the water cycle by completing a journey through the sun, the clouds etc. This was done through programming the Blue-Bot to undertake a journey consisting of several paths in order to learn about the water cycle.

2.5 The Assessment of Computational Thinking

There is currently a dearth of research instruments in the literature for assessing young children's computational thinking. In this study, the researchers developed inductively a rubric for assessing children's computational thinking in a holistic way. The rubric is presented in the results section.

Figure 3. Second mat

2.6 Research Procedure

The research data for this study were collected in two 45-min sessions. Students worked individually in both sessions. There was a two-day elapsed time between the sessions. During the first five minutes of the first session, participants answered the pretest knowledge test about the water cycle. For the remaining 40 minutes, they followed the instructions on the first problem-solving scenario in order to learn how to program the Blue-Bot. Two days later, the children were engaged in the second problem-solving task. During the first 40 min of the second session, they programmed the Blue-Bot to execute a number of paths in order to learn about the water cycle. At the last five minutes of the session, students answered the posttest knowledge test about the water cycle.

3. RESULTS

3.1 Rubric for Assessing Children's Computational Thinking

Children's computational thinking was assessed based on the correctness of their sequences of instructions expressed in Blue-Bot's command language, such as, MOVE FORWARD, TURN LEFT, MOVE BACKWARD, and TURN RIGHT for each problem-solving subtask. In effect, the children were assessed on their sequencing skills taking into consideration previous attempts before succeeding. The rubric also provided a way to evaluate how many failed attempts the children made before succeeding, and whether they used decomposition as a computational thinking strategy. A complete example follows:

X's first attempt (unsuccessful): MOVE BACKWARD-TURN RIGHT-GO

X's second attempt (unsuccessful): MOVE BACKWARD-TURN RIGHT-MOVE FORWARD-GO

X's third attempt (successful): MOVE BACKWARD-TURN RIGHT-TURN RIGHT-MOVE FORWARD-GO

The researchers collected all possible answers for all subtasks over the two problem-solving scenarios and developed a rubric as shown in Table 1. Table 1 shows a holistic assessment of computational thinking taking into consideration the number of attempts students made, and, if decomposition was used as a problem-solving strategy. An interrater reliability for the rubric was calculated between two independent raters and a 100% of agreement was established.

Table 1. Computational Thinking Scoring Rubric

Code	Description	Score
1	Success on 1st attempt without decomposition	22
2	Decomposition in two parts - Success on 1st attempt	21
3	Decomposition in three parts - Success on 1st attempt	20
4	Decomposition in four parts - Success on 1st attempt	19
5	Decomposition in five parts – Success on 1st attempt	18
6	Decomposition in six parts – Success on 1st attempt	17
7	Decomposition in seven parts – Success on 1st attempt	16
8	Decomposition in eight parts – Success on 1st attempt	15
9	Decomposition in nine parts – Success on 1st attempt	14
10	Decomposition in ten parts - Success on 1st attempt	13
11	Success on 2nd attempt without decomposition	12
12	Decomposition in two parts – Success on 2nd attempt	11
13	Decomposition in three parts - Success on 2nd attempt	10
14	Decomposition in four parts - Success on 2nd attempt	9
15	Decomposition in five parts - Success on 2nd attempt	8
16	Decomposition in six parts - Success on 2nd attempt	7
17	Decomposition in eleven parts - Success on 2nd attempt	6
18	Decomposition in four parts – Success on 3rd attempt	5
19	Decomposition in five parts - Success on 3rd attempt	4
20	Decomposition in six parts - Success on 3rd attempt	3
21	Decomposition in 3 parts – Success on 4th attempt	2
22	Decomposition in 2 parts – Success on 5th attempt	1

3.2 Performance on the Knowledge Test

Students' descriptive statistics in regards to their performance on the pretest and posttest knowledge tests about the water cycle were computed. The descriptive statistics showed an average performance on the pretest knowledge test of 5.7 (SD = 1.03), and an average performance on the posttest knowledge test of 6.75 (SD = .72). A paired samples t-test was subsequently performed showing statistically significant differences between pre and posttest knowledge scores, $t\,(19) = 3.68$, $p < 0.01$.

3.3 Holistic Computational Thinking Performance

Descriptive statistics in regards to students' performance on the computational thinking tasks were computed. Students' mean computational thinking performance on the first problem-solving task was found to be 132.23 (SD = 17.85) while students' mean computational thinking performance on the second problem-solving task was found to be 144.90 (SD = 10.41). A paired samples t-test was then computed showing statistically significant learning gains between the first and second assessment of students' computational thinking skills, $t(19) = 3.57$, $p < 0.01$.

4. DISCUSSION AND IMPLICATIONS

In this study, it was hypothesized that the use of robotics activities with the use of a small programmable floor robot named Blue-Bot would be an effective way for developing young children's computational thinking. The hypothesis was confirmed based on the results of the study reporting statistically significant learning gains between the initial and final assessment of children's computational thinking skills. In addition, the authors hypothesized that learning with robotics activities would be an effective way to teach children about the water cycle. This hypothesis was also confirmed as the findings showed statistically significant within-subjects learning gains between the initial and final assessment of children's understanding of the water cycle. The implications of these findings are important, as they provide a robust support for the integration of robotic devices in the curriculum of young children's education. It represents a great initial tool in the hands of the teachers for the use of the specific robotic devices in class. Furthermore, the robotic activities mentioned above provides a strong foundation for additional efforts for the creation of a complete curriculum of teaching computational thinking through robotics and programming for K12. In essence, robotics can be used as an educational technology to reform and enhance the traditional school curriculum so that children can be taught about computational thinking skills that are so much needed for surviving in the 21st century. In addition, these findings show that robotics can be used to teach young students about the water cycle, which constitutes an important component of the science curriculum in the pre-primary and primary education in an alternative way of teaching, through technology. The use of the specific floor robotic device in this lesson transformed completely a traditional method of teaching a specific subject through a technology enhanced lesson that inspired the students to discover and evolve their computational thinking skills. The results of this study can serve as baseline data for future research studies with larger sample sizes. Moreover, the authors explain that due to the fact that this was a one-sample only study no comparisons with other methods can be made at this point. Thus, it is highly recommended that researchers undertake future studies with more than one group of participants so that comparisons with a control group and other approaches can be made.

REFERENCES

Alimisis, D., & Kynigos, C. (2009). Constructionism and robotics in education. *Teacher Education on Robotic-Enhanced Constructivist Pedagogical Methods*, 11-26.

Benitti, F. B. V. (2012). Exploring the educational potential of robotics in schools: A systematic review. *Computers & Education, 58*(3), 978-988.

Bers, M. U. (2010). The TangibleK robotics program: Applied computational thinking for young children. *Early Childhood Research & Practice, 12*(2), 1-20.

Bers, M. U., Flannery, L., Kazakoff, E. R., & Sullivan, A. (2014). Computational thinking and tinkering: Exploration of an early childhood robotics curriculum. *Computers & Education, 72*, 145-157.

Botički, I., Pivalica, D., & Seow, P. (2018). The use of computational thinking concepts in early primary school. In *Proceedings of the International Conference of Computational Thinking Education 2018 (CTE2018).*

Bredenfeld, A., Hofmann, A., & Steinbauer, G. (2010). Robotics in education initiatives in Europe-status, shortcomings and open questions. In *Workshop Proceedings of International Conference on Simulation, Modeling and Programming for Autonomous Robots* (pp. 568-574). Darmstadt: Germany.

Grover, S., & Pea, R. (2013). Computational thinking in K–12: A review of the state of the field. *Educational Researcher, 42*(1), 38-43.

Grover, S., & Pea, R. (2018). Computational thinking: A competency whose time has come. *Computer Science Education: Perspectives on Teaching and Learning in School*, 19.

Guzdial, M. (2008). Education: Paving the way for computational thinking. *Communications of the ACM, 51*(8), 25-27.

Johnson, J. (2003). Children, robotics, and education. *Artificial Life and Robotics, 7*(1-2), 16-21.

Kazakoff, E. R., Sullivan, A., & Bers, M. U. (2013). The effect of a classroom-based intensive robotics and programming workshop on sequencing ability in early childhood. *Early Childhood Education Journal, 41*(4), 245-255.

Lu, J. J., & Fletcher, G. H. (2009). Thinking about computational thinking. In *ACM SIGCSE Bulletin, 41*(1), 260-264. Chattanooga, TN: ACM. Retrieved 24 June, 2015 from URL http://portal.acm.org/citation.cfm?id=1508959&dl=ACM&coll=portal

Lye, S. Y., & Koh, J. H. L. (2014). Review on teaching and learning of computational thinking through programming: What is next for K-12? *Computers in Human Behavior*, *41*, 51-61.

National Research Council. (2010). *Report of a workshop on the scope and nature of computational thinking.* Washington, DC: The National Academies Press.

Selby, C. C. (2012). Promoting computational thinking with programming. In *Proceedings of the 7th Workshop in Primary and Secondary Computing Education* (pp. 74-77). New York: ACM.

Stoeckelmayr, K., Tesar, M., & Hofmann, A. (2011). Pre-primary children programming robots: A first attempt. In *Proceedings of 2nd International Conference on Robotics in Education* (pp. 185-192). Vienna, Austria: INNOC - Austrian Society for Innovative Computer Sciences.

Wing, J. M. (2008). Computational thinking and thinking about computing. Philosophical transactions of the royal society of London A: mathematical, physical and engineering sciences, 366(1881), 3717-3725.

Wing, J. (2011). Research notebook: Computational thinking - What and why? Retrieved 3 March, 2015 from URL http://www.cs.cmu.edu/link/research-notebook-computational-thinking-what-and-why

STUDENT PERCEPTIONS OF VIRTUAL REALITY IN HIGHER EDUCATION

Tebogo John Matome[1] and Mmaki E. Jantjies[2]
[1]*Master Student*
[2]*Associate Professor*
Department of Information Systems
University of the Western Cape, South Africa

ABSTRACT

Continuous advancements in technology provide an opportunity for higher educational institutions to enhance the electronic learning experiences of students. Following a review of literature, this research explored student perceptions on the possible uses of virtual reality in their universities, as a way of easing their access to learning material. The research was conducted with the aim of answering the question of how virtual reality can be used to enhance learning, for higher learning institutions. Using a mixed-method research method, online surveys were distributed to registered university students in South Africa, using a simple random sampling strategy, to obtain a diverse and non-biased data set. The quantitative and qualitative responses were analyzed separately, before being triangulated, and used to inform the discussion and conclusion. Ultimately, the research found that although there are various benefits associated with the introduction of Virtual Reality - in South African Higher Education Institutions - the diverse population of participating students, and the varying differences in their socioeconomic statuses, would result in the inequitable distribution and usage of its resultant advantages.

KEYWORDS

Augmented Reality, e-Learning, Higher Education, Immersive Technologies, Online University Resources, Virtual Reality

1. INTRODUCTION

In recent years, higher education has been viewed as the key to influencing holistic development (both economic and social), in emerging markets. Matherly, Amin & Al Nahyan (2017) highlight the positive correlation, between the level of investment put into improving the quality of higher education, and the resultant increase in a nation's economic growth; insinuating that the higher the quality of a country's education system, the better the life of the inhabitants of the said country. Lane & Johnstone (2012) also makes mention of the ongoing "great brain race" between various countries. They accredit the intensity of the race to the different nations' realization of the role played by higher education, and the level of skilled human capital it produced, when attempting to influence innovation, and economic development.

It is undeniable that the introduction, and evolution of technology, has changed the way in which all industries operate. Accordingly, the education system has not been overlooked by the effects of digitization and globalization. Many have researched the integration of different advanced learning technologies within the higher education sector. These include the study of challenges and prospects of attaining an online higher education within a South African university (Letseka & Pitsoe, 2014), the study of student perceptions regarding the implementation and use of virtual classrooms (Çakýroðlu, 2014), and using artificial intelligence techniques, to influence interactive and adaptive, online education systems (Almohammadi, Hagras, Alghazzawi & Aldabbagh, 2017). Resultantly, the addition of technology, to education, has resulted in positive outcomes on various issues faced by the sector, over the years. Furthermore, Passig (2015) mentions how advanced educational technologies, with their advanced interfaces, generate an accelerated enhancement in a wide range of skills that the natural educational environment alone cannot account for.

However, it has also been found that the implementation of online learning technologies, are not easily always accessible to different demographic groups. Cohen, Bancilhon & Grace (2017) stress that the realization of a digitally connected society is highly dependent on, and cannot be disassociated from, the need for social and economic inclusion. Thus, introducing advanced technologies requires an understanding of the student body context, especially if the electronic learning requirements will extend beyond the campus environment.

In terms of the study's population, South African higher education institutions can be viewed as the perfect research population for the implementation of new technologies. This is as a result of the nation rich historic background, socio-economic characteristics, and the presence of a digital divide within the country's different races and groupings. For that reason, the University of the Western Cape (UWC), was deemed an appropriate sample frame. Banda & Peck (2015) describe UWC as a previously disadvantaged university, which was initially introduced for the 'Coloured' population in apartheid South Africa, but challenged the apartheid system; ultimately admitting students from a variety of races and ethnicities. The university has since made various strides in the learning and equitable education landscape, and is today a world-recognized institution. In 2016, UWC had a registered student population of 21796 pupils, with a diverse representation from different socio-economic and demographic backgrounds. When comparing UWC to other universities in South Africa, Banda & Peck (2018) further highlight the existing demographic differences of the institution. They state this diversity in demographics as the reason for UWC being currently regarded as a "multiplex research site".

Nyahodza & Higgs (2017) use statistics from a 2016 World Bank survey (which concludes that the lower half of South Africa's population account for a mere 8% of the country's income) – to support their argument that a majority of these individuals are unable to afford educational resources, which also include computers and an Internet access. Furthermore, a study by Hersh & Mouroutsou (2015) identifies income and language as the primary factors, defining the access to learning technologies. This is important to note, in the context of South Africa, where the apartheid era has resulted in a long-lasting influence on economic disparity. Nevertheless, when considering the different technologies that can be used in higher education, Virtual Reality, amongst other emerging technologies, provides an opportunity to bridge the resource gap for students allowing them to gain experience in their learning outcome using technology. This can be especially useful in resource constrained environments. Lu, Li, Chen, Kim & Serikawa (2018) describe virtual reality as a computer system-generated simulation, which creates a virtual environment that can be interacted with, in a realistic manner. Taking into account that traditional learning takes place in the form of real-time interactions between learners and facilitators, Çakýroðlu (2014) makes mention of the implementation of VR-created simulations and assessments, allowing facilitators (teachers and lecturers) to test a learner's ability to react to real-life scenarios, based on their course of learning. This also allows students in high-risk fields (such as surgeons and engineers) to immerse themselves in realistic simulations, without the risks associated with making mistakes during real life operations, as well as without having physical access to such resources. It is, nonetheless, also important to acknowledge the advantages and developments that may arise from the introduction of VR within education. For example, the growth in the popularity of Virtual Reality may be the driving force, facilitating an increase in access to local higher education, across the different socio-economic groups, of South Africa. These possible advantages provide a rational reasoning for the necessity of investigating a possible solution, to a better interaction with learning content, for registered students of South African higher education institutions.

1.1 Research Questions & Objectives

Unterhalter et al. (2017) acknowledge that although the recent student protests in South Africa shine a light on access and funding problems, these protests are not isolated events. Furthermore, they expand on the notion that these events uncover deep-rooted challenges within the higher education system, stemming from an unresolved colonial legacy. One must therefore consider that, due to the large economic disparity amongst the different socio-economic brackets of South Africa, some students find it more difficult than others to access the higher education system as well as related resources. This research therefore aimed to investigate the main research question of, *how can Virtual Reality be used, to enable access to learning resources for higher education students, in South Africa?* This was supported by four research sub-questions, giving direction to the research, and ultimately satisfying predetermined objectives. The research delved into *what the main factors, contributing to the lack of access to Higher Education in South Africa*, are, before a further reviewing past literature to answer the question of *what Virtual Reality solutions have already been implemented, in higher education, across the world.* Thirdly, the research investigated *How a VR-augmented higher education system, affects a diverse student population*, before the final research question aimed to *identify the different ways in which VR can be used to support students' equitable access to higher education learning content.*

The sub-questions will help to satisfy the following objectives, and ultimately answer the primary research. The first objective being *to identify the main forms of virtual reality, which have been used to support education in universities*. Secondly, the research aimed to *determine how VR can be used to support students, in order to adequately and less-effortlessly interacting with their institution's learning content*. The final objective was *to analyze the effects, as well as other advantages, of introducing a VR-augmented higher education system, within a diverse student population*.

2. LITERATURE REVIEW

2.1 Technology in Higher Education

With the advent of technology, higher education qualifications have become more revered than in before. So much so that various countries have invested heavily in improving the quality of higher education, as it directly correlates to a nation's economic development (Matherly, Amin & Nahyan, 2017). Matherly, Amin & Nahyan (2017) identified an increase in salaries, enhanced employment opportunities, better mobility, a longer life expectancy, and an improved quality of life as some of the direct benefits of higher education qualifications. This supports to the notion that the importance of university or higher education is ever increasing, in an increasingly competitive global economy. Winters (2011) further notes that the main indicators and influence on a nation's human capital capability, is the presence of HE institutions in the area of dwelling.

However, in order to gauge the success of implementing technology in higher education, one must understand the knowledge and associated challenges of the technologies' primary users. These users include higher education students, as well as the teachers (and lecturers) of institutions. Jantjies & Joy (2016) highlight the cultural and linguistic diversity of students, as a pivotal factor in the introduction of technology, in education system of South Africa. This is a result of the relatively large number of official languages and cultures recognized in the country, compared to other nations. It is, also important to consider the readiness and willingness of students, to accept the introduction of technology-aided learning. Chaka & Govender (2017) found that Nigerian higher education learners were receptive to the idea of a technology-aided learning systems, with their perceptions of technology driving this acceptance rate. One can therefore assume that, should South African learners have similar perceptions of technology, the adoption of a blended learning system would result in a successful implementation. A Western Cape based study, by Chigona, Chigona & Davids (2014), investigated the factors motivating educators to use ICTs in the province's disadvantaged areas. These factors were identified as the individual expectations of, the resultant feeling of achievement from, and the responsibilities associated with the use of ICTs in the aforementioned areas. As a result, this clarifies the need to motivate, inspire, and train educators on the use of ICTs in South African institutions.

2.2 Introducing Virtual Reality in Higher Education

Virtual reality enables the simulation of virtual environments through software applications to mimic the real-world environment. Hardware enabling users to gain access to virtual reality applications are either head mounted gear such as the oculus rift and the HTC Vive, or mobile devices supported through a head mounted casing. As VR hardware becomes more affordable, educational institutions are finding ways to enhance learning by supporting the immersive learning experience afforded by VR (Duta et al., 2011; Freina and Ott, 2015). Furthermore, a CAVE (Cave Automatic Virtual Environment) which is a 4 or 5 screened cube "room" can be used to allow between 2 to 8 participants to get an immersive 3D experience of a learning task.

A CAVE projects on the surrounding screens allowing surrounding 3D visuals of the content being projected. It is also supported by surround sound (Leder et al., 2019). While CAVES usually entail high implementation costs, they in turn provide simultaneous access to multiple students, as more than two students can use a CAVE at once. While there is a growing number of accessible VR hardware, there is a need for more developments of contextual and multilingual applications for various study fields. Many of the existing learning applications such as DentSim designed to support restorative dentistry education and The Geneva System developed to teach dental anatomy (Duta et al., 2011) were developed for a specific context. This provides an opportunity for African universities to develop applications which are specific to their fields as well considering contextual issues such as availability of content in multiple languages.

However, it is also important to acknowledge that with the advances in technology, there are various high-powered applications of virtual reality, which have been implemented within the modern-day higher education curricula. For example, Al Awadhi, et al. (2018) make mention of the Titan of Spare application, which immerses students into a virtual realm of the solar system, allowing them to discover and better study the solar system's planets, from the comfort of their lecture halls. King, Tee, Falconer, Angell, Holly & Mills (2018) also elaborate on the CILVRS (Collaborative Immersive Learning Virtual Reality Series) project of Bournemouth University, in the United Kingdom. This simulation, in which medical students take on the role of a medical practitioner, awaiting the arrival of their patient, provides students with the opportunity to learn from their mistakes (virtually) without jeopardizing the wellbeing of real patients.

3. RESEARCH METHODOLOGY

3.1 Design & Methodology

A mixed method survey, which is described by Creswell & Plano Clark (2007) as the use of both qualitative and quantitative data sourcing, in a single study, was used to conduct this study. A self-administered questionnaire, which was development and loosely guided by the 13 principles of questionnaire construction, was made available to the student population, using a simple random sampling approach. Responses from eighty-one (N = 81) registered students, completed the survey. The data was analyzed using a thematic approach, described by Clarke & Braun (2016) as the identification and analysis of responses, in order to deduce substantial patterns within a qualitative data set, ultimately classifying them as themes. The formulation of themes from the data, gave the researcher an opportunity to identify patterns and similarities in the students' responses, by finding commonalities in the problems identified, as well as the suggestions provided.

The identified themes, discussed in the research findings are: - 1) Student Access to Different content platforms, provided by the institution, 2) Student Usage and Knowledge of Technologies in Higher Education, and 3) Students' perceptions of a Virtual Reality Augmented in Higher Education System.

The first two themes allowed the for a better understanding of the third research sub-question, regarding How a VR-augmented higher education system would affect a diverse student population. In the first theme, we sought to understand the current experiences of online learning for students. Furthermore, the third theme was formulated to unpack the fourth research sub-question, which aimed to elaborate on the different ways in which VR can be used to support students' equitable access to higher education learning content.

The use and analysis of both qualitative and quantitative methods also allowed for the neutralizing of the weaknesses in one method, by using the strengths of the other method. However, a mixed method analysis also allows a researcher to enhance the strengths of one method, with the strengths of the other (Creswell, 2009). Furthermore, Tobergte (2013) describes triangulation as the effort of combining both types of data that have been used within the mixed method process, in the attempt to use one set to corroborate the other. As a result of the triangulation, the trends found within the qualitative analysis were used to try and provide a sense of justification/context to the trends found within the different themes of the qualitative data.

4. FINDINGS

4.1 Access to Different Content Platforms, Provided by the Institution

In this the theme, the study sought to understand the current digital learning devices and resources, which the students' access, and can be used to support VR. While the university provided full Internet access to students and staff, 26% of participants stated that the main issue they faced with Internet access, was the challenges of a periodic slow Internet connection. Other reasons stated included the lack of access to substantive online journal article portals, with nine percent highlighting this as a challenge to them. 16% of the participants reflected on the inability to access the institution's online student portal (Learning Management Systems) and learning platform, at certain times of the day, due to high usage. Almost half of the students at displayed in Figure 1 did not experience problems when accessing current online learning resources, as the campus had a good network support as well as technician and e-learning walk-in support centers. To understand how VR will be accessed by the student population, the research investigated the types of devices used, to access learning content. Table 1 reflects that almost two-thirds of the students accessed technology on campus and relied on the university computer labs. This provides a reflection on the type of VR applications, as well as tasks, that could be given to students.

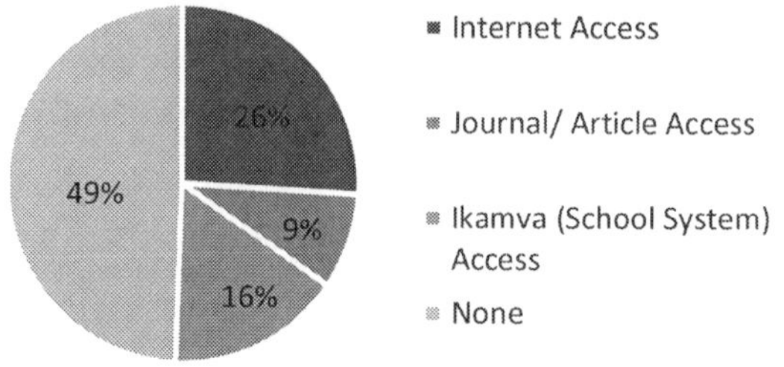

Figure 1. Problems faced when accessing online learning content

Table 1. Access to learning platforms on and off campus

		Desktop	Mobile	Tablet	Total
Residence	Off Campus	14	6	2	22
	On Campus	47	11	1	59
Total		61	17	3	**81**

4.2 Student Usage and Knowledge of Technologies in Higher Education

This theme sought to understand the different platforms used by students to interact with their course content. In Figure 2, 16% of participants stated that their most used applications were Microsoft Office Suite or similar software. Further followed by a 20% use of Email, the institution's Online Library, and the university student Learning Management System services, respectively. Furthermore, 20% of students reflected not having had any use of technology in their learning process. Contrastingly, 8% of students perceived the current technology infrastructure in the institution as being either unsatisfactory or mediocre. In aiming to understand student's current knowledge and use of virtual reality technology, the study also found that more than 60% of the students have neither knowledge of, nor experience with, virtual reality. However, 12% of the students did state that they had experienced virtual reality, with participants highlighting their knowledge for its use in gaming. Additionally, 26% of the students also stated that they only had some knowledge of virtual reality, but had no previous interaction with it. The students reflected that this knowledge of Virtual Reality was gained from either self-study, or first year Information Systems lectures. The results in the study reflected on the student population's lack of previous interaction with any VR applications, especially in the learning context. VR was often known to them as a gaming tool. The results also reflected the importance of students' training support for virtual reality, as a small percentage of them were currently not expected to use technology in their tasks.

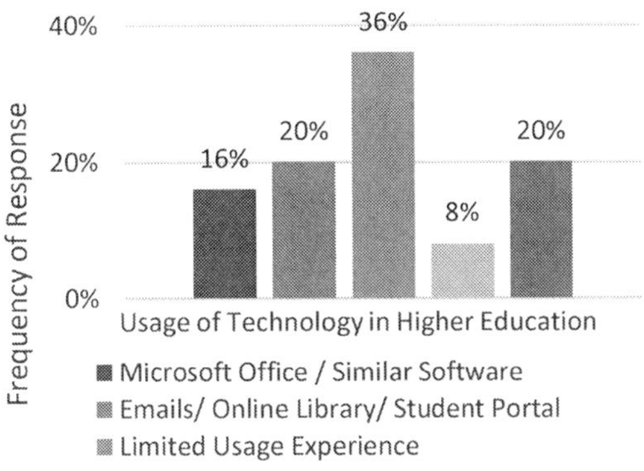

Figure 2. Participant usage of Technology in Higher Education

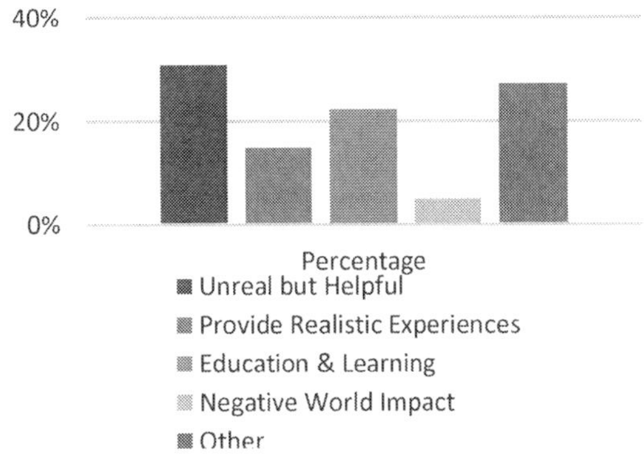

Figure 3. Student expectations of the introduction of virtual reality

4.3 Students Expectations of a VR-Augmented Higher Education System

Regarding what students would expect from a VR supported digital learning system, the results in Figure 3 reflect that 15% of students expected VR to provide them with realistic experiences of learning. Examples of these realistic experiences included visiting nature reserves or foreign destinations, from the comfort of their home. Five percent of the students expect that a VR supported learning experience will have a negative impact on their learning experience. Just over a fifth of the students expect VR to aid in education and learning capabilities of the population, both in formal institutions as well as through private/individual use.

Regarding students' perceptions on the advantages of integrating VR within Higher education, as reflected in Figure 4 below, the study found that while 22% of the respondents were unable to find any advantages of VR in their education, 20% of the students stated that it would afford them the opportunity of practical experience, as opposed to relying solely on the theory they are taught. A further 19% identified a possible increase in their learning and knowledge retention process, with 15% perceiving this innovation as one that will increase interaction between students, as well as lecturers. 10% of the students believe that the ability to access and better interact with course content, when not on the university campus will be the greatest advantage of implementing VR. Additionally, the remaining 16% of respondents highlight an increased interaction with course content as the main advantage associated with a VR-augmented Higher Education system.

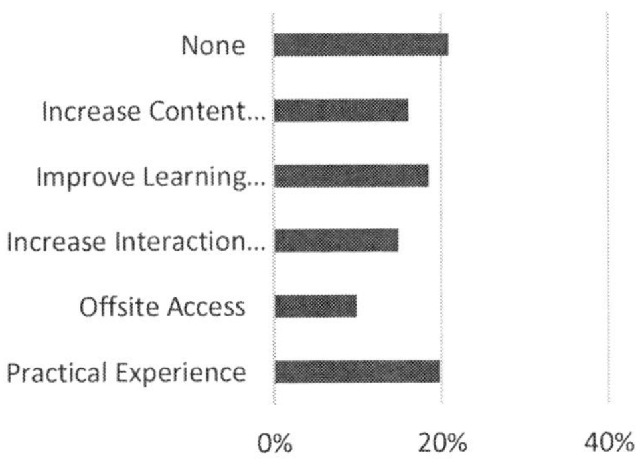

Figure 4. Student's perceived advantages of Virtual Reality in Higher Education

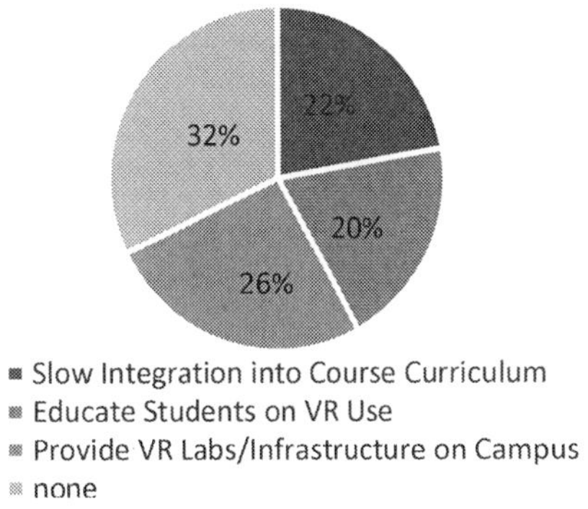

Figure 5. Student Suggestions on How to Make VR implementation Inclusive to All Students

In terms of the different ways that students believe the implementation of VR can be made inclusive, the following findings were recorded. In Figure 5, 22% of student believe that slowly integrating the technology into their curriculum, would be the best way to influence equitable use of the technology. However, while a fifth of the respondents highlight the necessity of educating students on the effective use of VR in higher education, a quarter of the respondents felt that the best way to promote equitable access to the technology is through the building and provision of VR-dedicated labs (and infrastructure), on their campus.

5. DISCUSSION

One aspect of the research aimed to find the main issues faced by students, when interacting with the different online platforms, of their institution. This was analyzed within the theme of Student Access to Different content platforms, provided by the institution. The most prevalent issues were the lack of access to a stable internet connection, as well as the inability to access their online learning management system during certain periods of the day. Resultantly, with institutions having a limited number of computer labs (and computers), compared to the overall student population, most students would be required to use personal computers and laptops to interact with their online content. If taken in the context of Nyahodza & Higgs (2017) - who stated that a large fraction of South African students are unable to afford educational resources, such as personal computers - this lack of access to a workspace, and adequate internet connection poses a challenge to VR, within higher education learning. In cases where students do not own smart phones, the lecturers would be expected to provide VR platforms or provide alternative solutions, which consider the resources that students have access to. Dedicated VR supportive labs or access to mobile devices, smart phones or a CAVE would be important in ensuring that students can effectively access and use VR in their education. The results also reflected the importance of the existing e-learning center to support VR systems training support which was currently effective in supporting other e-learning training services.

Regarding the theme of "Student Usage and Knowledge of Technologies in Higher Education" the study reflected that many of the students residing on-campus make use of the institution's Wi-Fi services, and thus mainly relied on the university network services. Furthermore, students residing off-campus would be required to carry the cost of an increase in the bandwidth required to efficiently use VR. The role of free Wi-Fi in supporting current e-learning activities reflected the importance of VR software which was also available offline. The study further reflected that academics using VR should be considerate of the role of the Internet in the e-learning process, and thus cannot solely rely on VR applications requiring access to the Internet, especially with tasks required beyond the lecturer room (Blignaut, Els & Howie, 2010). Furthermore, with a combined total of 56% of students having reported that they had either limited, or no, experience with technology usage in higher education, this reflected on literature by Walker & Mkwananzi (2015), highlighting that students that are enrolled in higher education institutions, filter in from positions of extreme inequality. When discussed in conjunction with other findings, where 60% of the students reported that they had no knowledge or experience of virtual reality, extensive training and education on the usage of the VR technology was found to be important in its successful implementation.

When investigating the theme of "Students' expectations of a Virtual Reality-Augmented Higher Education System", many of the participants had no prior knowledge of VR and its use in education. With regards to the advantages expected from a VR-augmented Higher Education, a combined 26% of the respondents cited perceived advantages in possible interaction and collaboration between students, as well as with lectures, as a result of better accessibility and interaction with course content. This realization correlated with Viberg & Grönlund (2013), who stated that the introduction of VR would change the traditional delivery of, and access to, learning content; by overcoming the spatial-temporal characteristic of modern-day formal education. Furthermore, Viberg & Grönlund (2013) also made mention of the advancements afforded by VR, resulting in habitual online meetings and classrooms, as well as the opportunity to integrate mobile learning into curricula, to further overcome these spatial-temporal factors. Considering the increase in mobile technology adoption (relative to that of personal computers) in developing countries, with mobiles being identified as the second largest platform usage for accessing online learning content – tailoring the introduction of VR to a more mobile-based platform would deliver the most benefits, and a greater realization of the aforementioned advantages.

In terms of promoting inclusivity of, and equitable access to, virtual reality in the higher education system, the findings identified the need for dedicated virtual reality labs and infrastructure (provided by the institution) as being the most imperative factor to widespread adoption and usage. In reference to Letseka & Pitsoe (2014) who stated that education delivery models of global institutions is moving towards one that is cost-effective, while not foregoing service quality, this finding would highlight the need for South African institutions to transition towards integrating and procuring emerging technologies, within their respective campuses. The findings reflect on the notion of Hersh & Mouroutsou (2015) who state the main hindrances of access to these emerging technologies include the cost off lack of funding for maintenance of emerging technologies, as well as a need for training and support for academics. Future use of VR application in higher education could thus enhance learning effectively through both infrastructure and human resource support to ensure its success.

6. CONCLUSION

Conclusively, although there has been an increase in the implementation of virtual reality technologies, within the global education system; it is important to note that this increase is predominantly in the institutions of developed nations. This may be due to cost of infrastructure associated with VR technology being relatively high, in comparison to other technologies that are currently being used in institutions. Furthermore, with the financial, procurement and quality-related challenges – faced by the South Africa government, as well as some higher education institutions – the introduction of Virtual Reality, in the nation's current economic climate, would more of a burden, than an advantage to all parties with a vested interest. However, even with the challenges of introducing this technology, there is indeed a plethora of benefits that can be realized.

In addition to increasing the accessibility of online interaction with an institution's learning content, as well as providing practical experience and knowledge of one's respective field of study; a relationship between VR and higher education will provide facilitators with increased avenues of disseminating and assessing course-related content, in a way that will be easier to remember, for the students. Nevertheless, the training of VR-usage for such a diverse student population, from various backgrounds, may be further complicated by other technology adoption factors. With the data and internet, prices of South Africa being identified as one the most expensive in the world (in comparison to other developing countries) the bandwidth-heavy nature of VR usage would limit the holistic adoption of the technology across the entire student population. Another notable aspect of the study would be the consideration of the limitations surrounding the study. These limitations, in one way or another, may have had an influence on the outcome of the study; and could be mitigated in future research.

The first limitation is the duration of the study, which was conducted over a period of seven months. Another limitation would be the location of the study. With the study being conducted solely in the University of the Western Cape, it would be difficult to generalize the study to the rest of South Africa's higher learning institutions, as they each have a different demographic profile, respectively. This study, with consideration of the above limitations, has served as an investigation of the effects of VR in a higher education institution, in the Western Cape. Furthermore, the results of the study can be further researched, on a larger scale, and over a longer time period; to better investigate the trends suggested within this article. Overall, although the benefits associated with the introduction of VR within the South African higher education system will provide new and enhanced opportunities, when accessing and interacting with one's online course material, the financial requirements of such an implementation for both institutions, and students, would not promote an equitable distribution and adoption of the technology. Resultantly, the access to VR augmented online learning content will only be beneficial to primarily those of the upper socioeconomic brackets of the nation.

REFERENCES

Almohammadi, Khalid, Hani Hagras, and Daniyal Alghazzawi. 2017. "A Survey of Artificial Intelligence Techniques Employed for Adaptive Educational Systems within E-Learning Platforms." Journal of Artificial Intelligence and Soft Computing Research 7 (1): 47–64. https://doi.org/10.1515/jaiscr-2017-0004.

Awadhi, Shouq Al, Noor Al Habib, Dalal Al-Murad, Fajer Al deei, Mariam Al Houti, Taha Beyrouthy, and Samer Al-kork. 2018. "Interactive Virtual Reality Educational Application" 3 (4): 72–82.

Banda, Felix, and Amiena Peck. 2016. "Diversity and Contested Social Identities in Multilingual and Multicultural Contexts of the University of the Western Cape, South Africa." Journal of Multilingual and Multicultural Development 37 (6): 576–88. https://doi.org/10.1080/01434632.2015.1106547.

Blignaut, Seugnet, Christo Els, and Sarah Howie. 2010. "Contextualizing South Africa's Participation in the SITES 2006 Module." South African Journal of Education 30 (October 2004): 555–70.

Cakiroglu, Unal. 2014. "Evaluating Students' Perspectives about Virtual Classrooms with Regard to Seven Principles of Good Practice." South African Journal of Education 34 (2): 1–19. https://doi.org/10.15700/201412071201.

Chaka, John Gyang, and Irene Govender. 2017. "Students' Perceptions and Readiness towards Mobile Learning in Colleges of Education: A Nigerian Perspective." South African Journal of Education 37 (1): 1–12.

Chigona, Agnes, Wallace Chigona, and Zane Davids. 2014. "Educators' Motivation on Integration of ICTs into Pedagogy: Case of Disadvantaged Areas." South African Journal of Education 34 (3): 1–8. https://doi.org/10.15700/201409161051.

Clarke, Victoria, and Virginia Braun. 2017. "Thematic Analysis." Journal of Positive Psychology. https://doi.org/10.1080/17439760.2016.1262613.

Cohen, Jason, Jean Marie Bancilhon, and Thomas Grace. 2018. "Digitally Connected Living and Quality of Life: An Analysis of the Gauteng City-Region, South Africa." Electronic Journal of Information Systems in Developing Countries 84 (1): 1–12. https://doi.org/10.1002/isd2.12010.

Creswell, J.W., & Plano Clark, V.L. (2007). Designing and conducting Mixed Methods Research. USA. Sage Publications.

Creswell, John W. 2009. Research Design: Qualitative, Quantitative, and Mixed Methods Approaches. 4th ed. California: Sage. http://www.ceil-conicet.gov.ar/wp-content/uploads/2015/10/Creswell-Cap-10.pdf.

Dută, Mihaela, Corneliu I Amariei, Crenguta M Bogdan, Dorin M Popovici, Nicolae Ionescu, and Cristina I Nuca. 2011. "An Overview of Virtual and Augmented Reality in Dental Education." Journal of Oral Health and Dental Management 10 (1): 42–49. http://scholar.google.co.za/scholar_url?url=https://pdfs.semanticscholar.org/0ca2/e4b2aa03f327ec58f496e56116ed27bfedc9.pdf&hl=en&sa=X&scisig=AAGBfm14jb5sJYvMpVkNBlcPwMC4XdF7nw&nossl=1&oi=scholarr.

Freina, Laura, and Michela Ott. 2015. "A Literature Review on Immersive Virtual Reality in Education: State of The Art and Perspectives." In ELearning and Software for Education (ELSE). Romania. https://www.researchgate.net/publication/280566372_A_Literature_Review_on_Immersive_Virtual_Reality_in_Education_State_Of_The_Art_and_Perspectives.

Hersh, M. A., and S. Mouroutsou. 2015. "Learning Technology and Disability: Overcoming Barriers to Inclusion: Evidence from a Multi-Country Study." IFAC-PapersOnLine 48 (24): 83–88. https://doi.org/10.1016/j.ifacol.2015.12.061.

Jantjies, Mmaki, and Mike Joy. 2016. "Lessons Learnt from Teachers' Perspectives on Mobile Learning in South Africa with Cultural and Linguistic Constraints." South African Journal of Education 36 (3): 1–10. https://doi.org/10.15700/saje.v36n3a1274.

King, Denyse, Stephen Tee, Liz Falconer, Catherine Angell, Debbie Holley, and Anne Mills. 2018. "Virtual Health Education: Scaling Practice to Transform Student Learning." Nurse Education Today 71 (December): 7–9. https://doi.org/10.1016/j.nedt.2018.08.002.

Lane, J.E., Johnstone, D.B. (Eds.). (2012). Universities and Colleges as Economic Drivers: Measuring Higher Education's Role in Economic Development. State University of New York Press.

Leder, J., Horlitz, T., Puschmann, P., Wittstock, V. and Schütz, A., (2019). Comparing immersive virtual reality and powerpoint as methods for delivering safety training: impacts on risk perception, learning, and decision making. Safety science, 111, pp.271-286.

Letseka, Moeketsi, and Victor Pitsoe. 2014. "The Challenges and Prospects of Access to Higher Education at UNISA." Studies in Higher Education 39 (10): 1942–54. https://doi.org/10.1080/03075079.2013.823933.

Lu, Huimin, Yujie Li, Min Chen, Hyoungseop Kim, and Seiichi Serikawa. 2018. "Brain Intelligence: Go beyond Artificial Intelligence." Mobile Networks and Applications 23 (2): 368–75. https://doi.org/10.1007/s11036-017-0932-8.

Matherly, Laura L., Nadia Amin, and Shamma Sultan Khalifa Al Nahyan. 2017. "The Impact of Generation and Socioeconomic Status on the Value of Higher Education in the UAE: A Longitudinal Study." International Journal of Educational Development 55 (May): 1–10. https://doi.org/10.1016/j.ijedudev.2017.04.002.

Nyahodza, Lena, and Richard Higgs. 2017. "Towards Bridging the Digital Divide in Post-Apartheid South Africa: A Case of a Historically Disadvantaged University in Cape Town." South African Journal of Libraries and Information Science 83 (1): 39–48. https://doi.org/10.7553/83-1-1645.

Passig, David. 2015. "Revisiting the Flynn Effect through 3D Immersive Virtual Reality (IVR)." Computers and Education 88: 327–42. https://doi.org/10.1016/j.compedu.2015.05.008.

Tobergte, David R., and Shirley Curtis. 2013. "Social Research Methods." Journal of Chemical Information and Modelling 53 (9): 1689–99. https://doi.org/10.1017/CBO9781107415324.004.

Unterhalter, Elaine, Stephanie Allais, Colleen Howell, Tristan McCowan, Louise Morley, Ibrahim Oanda, and Moses Oketch. 2018. "Conceptualising Higher Education and the Public Good in Ghana, Kenya, Nigeria, and South Africa." Conference: Comparative and International Education Society (CIES), no. March: 1–32. http://discovery.ucl.ac.uk/10050089/.

Viberg, Olga, and Åke Grönlund. 2013. "Computers & Education Cross-Cultural Analysis of Users' Attitudes toward the Use of Mobile Devices in Second and Foreign Language Learning in Higher Education: A Case from Sweden and China." Computers & Education 69: 169–80. https://doi.org/10.1016/j.compedu.2013.07.014 .

Walker, Melanie, and Faith Mkwananzi. 2015. "Challenges in Accessing Higher Education: A Case Study of Marginalised Young People in One South African Informal Settlement." International Journal of Educational Development 40: 40–49. https://doi.org/10.1016/j.ijedudev.2014.11.010.

Winters, John V. 2011. "Human Capital, Higher Education Institutions, and Quality of Life." Regional Science and Urban Economics 41 (5): 446–54. https://doi.org/10.1016/j.regsciurbeco.2011.03.001.

Youngblut, Christine. 1998. "Educational Uses of Virtual Reality Technology." Institute for Defense Analysis, no. January. http://papers.cumincad.org/data/works/att/94ea.content.pdf.

DEVELOPING PRESCHOOL CHILDREN'S COMPUTATIONAL THINKING WITH EDUCATIONAL ROBOTICS: THE ROLE OF COGNITIVE DIFFERENCES AND SCAFFOLDING

Kyriakoula Georgiou and Charoula Angeli
Department of Education, University of Cyprus, Dramas 11-13, 1678, Nicosia, Cyprus

ABSTRACT

The development of computational thinking is as important as writing, reading and arithmetic, and, it should start as early as kindergarten (Wing, 2008). However, little has been done in terms of investigating the factors influencing the development of computational thinking in preschool education (Bers et al., 2014; Ching et al., 2018; Kazakoff et al., 2013; Sullivan et al., 2013). Accordingly, the study herein investigated how young children's computational thinking could be developed using the Bee-Bot and two scaffolding techniques, while children's field-dependence/independence (FDI) was taken into consideration. The study has practical significance for classroom teachers, as they can use the results of this research to integrate the teaching of computational thinking skills in their lessons.

KEYWORDS

Computational Thinking, Cognitive Types, Scaffolding, Educational Robotics, Young Children

1. INTRODUCTION

The development of computational thinking is as important as writing, reading and arithmetic, and, it should start as early as kindergarten (Wing, 2008). However, little has been done in terms of investigating the factors influencing the development of computational thinking in preschool education (Bers et al., 2014; Ching et al., 2018; Kazakoff et al., 2013; Sullivan et al., 2013).

Accordingly, the study herein investigated how young children's computational thinking could be developed using the Bee-Bot and two scaffolding techniques, while children's field-dependence/independence (FDI) was taken into consideration. The study has practical significance for classroom teachers, as they can use the results of this research to integrate the teaching of computational thinking skills in their lessons.

2. THEORETICAL FRAMEWORK

2.1 Field-Dependence/Independence (FDI)

FDI reflects the ways in which individuals perceive and process information from their surrounding environment (Evans, Richardson, & Waring, 2013; Witkin, Moore, Goodenough, & Cox, 1977). FDI is differentiated from learning styles in that learning styles are self-reported accounts of individuals' instructional preferences across specific domains and tasks (Messick, 1987). Witkin et al. (1977) conceptualized FDI as a bipolar construct with two distinct modes of perception, namely, field-dependence (FD) and field-independence (FI). FI learners have been characterized as analytical, and visually perceptive, while FD learners have been referred to as global and not visually perceptive (Hall, 2000). FDI is a relevant construct to consider in this study, because there is systematic evidence showing that it plays a significant role in students' learning during problem-solving activities with various technological tools (Angeli, 2013; Angeli & Valanides, 2004a, 2009, 2013; Chen & Macredie, 2004).

2.2 Computational Thinking

Grover and Pea (2013) concluded that researchers have come to accept that computational thinking is a thought process that utilizes the elements of abstraction, generalization, decomposition, algorithmic thinking and debugging (detection and correction of errors). Of particular interest to this study are the skills of algorithmic thinking and debugging. Sequencing (i.e., planning an algorithm, which involves putting actions in the correct sequence), and flow of control (i.e., the order in which individual instructions or steps in an algorithm are evaluated) are considered important elements of algorithmic thinking. Debugging is the skill to recognize when actions do not correspond to instructions, and the skill to fix errors (Bers et al., 2014).

3. RESEARCH PURPOSE AND HYPOTHESIS

While the Bee-Bot constitutes an easy to use tool with young children, at the same time, it does not provide a visual representation of the commands that children use to program it, debilitating this way their ability to remember and reflect on their algorithm. This weakness of Bee-Bot creates a need for finding effective ways in order to appropriately scaffold children's learning with the Bee-Bot. To this end, the authors developed and investigated the effectiveness of two scaffolding techniques on FD and FI children's computational thinking skills during problem-solving activities with the Bee-Bot, and, hypothesized that scaffolding and FDI will both play a significant role in children's problem-solving performance.

4. METHOD

4.1 Participants

The participants were 180 children, 82 females and 98 males, from nine public preschools. The children were five to six years old, and permission was granted from their parents who signed consent forms prior to their children's participation in the study. All children who participated in the study had no previous experience with the Bee-Bot or robotics in general. Children were first classified into FD or FI learners, and, subsequently, each group of FD and FI learners was randomly clustered into two experimental groups that used two different scaffolding strategies (type A and B) and, a control group. As a consequence six equivalent groups were formed since children were categorized based on their cognitive style (FI and FD) and different scaffolding systems (External memory system A, External memory system B and Control Group) with thirty participants in each group as Table 1 shows.

Table 1. Synthesis of the three groups of participants based on the number of the students; their gender and individual characteristics

Groups	Participants		
Control Group	60	Boys	Girls
		37	23
Scaffolding type A	60	Boys	Girls
		35	25
Scaffolding type B	60	Boys	Girls
		26	34
Total	180	96	82

4.2 Research Instruments

4.2.1 Children's Embedded Figures Test (CEFT)

The CEFT (Karp & Konstadt, 1971) has an internal credibility of Cronbach's $\alpha = 0.87$. It is specially designed to identify the cognitive type of children aged from five to nine years old. It includes 38 shapes in which smaller shapes like a triangle (△) and a small house () are hidden in them. Participants are instructed to discover the hidden shapes in the more complex ones having at their disposal thirty seconds for each shape. The total administration time for the test is 20 min. One point is given for each shape correctly recognized. The maximum score on the test is 20 points.

4.3 Research Materials

4.3.1 Problem-solving Tasks

Children were engaged in a series of problem-solving tasks in order to program the Bee-Bot to move from one place to another. The first problem-solving task consisted of thirteen subtasks while the other two problem-solving tasks consisted of five subtasks. The subtasks were designed and presented to each child in increasing levels of complexity (Armoni & Gal-Ezer, 2014). Children were allowed twenty minutes for each problem-solving task. The tasks were developed by the researchers of this study and were checked for internal validity by two experts in computational thinking who discussed and resolved all disagreements.

4.3.2 Bee-Bot

The Bee-Bot is a programmable floor robot suitable for children of three to eight years old. The Bee-Bot can store a maximum of forty commands in its memory. It consists of seven keys that enable the Bee-Bot to move forward and backward, to turn left or right by 90 degrees, to clear its memory, to pause, and to GO, that is to execute a sequence of commands.

4.3.3 Bee-Bot Mats

Bee-Bot mats are surfaces, as shown in Figure 1, made of durable plastic. Each surface is organized into squares of 15cm x 15cm because the Bee-Bot can move only in 15cm increments. For the purposes of this study, the researchers designed and created three different mats, one for Phase 2, another for Phase 3, and one for Phase 4 (see Figure 1).

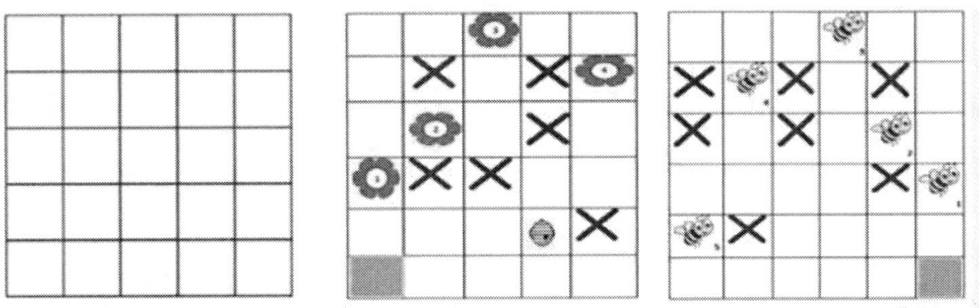

Mat 1 for Phase 2 **Mat 2 for Phase 3** **Mat 3 for Phase 4**

Figure 1. The three mats used in the research

4.3.4 Scaffolding Strategies

Type A scaffolding used a model (a representation of the real mat in reduced size) of the mat and the actual Bee-Bot in order to better facilitate the formation of mental rotations that are so essential for children younger than seven years old. The child thought about the algorithm and with the help of the researcher noted down in a matrix all commands. The matrix was then used as an external memory system that the child used to program the Bee-Bot to run on the real mat. Type B scaffolding provided each child with 5cm x 5cm laminated cards of all Bee-Bot commands and each child was asked to use the cards to form a sequence of commands for each problem-solving subtask. Then, the child used this external memory system to program the Bee-Bot and test the algorithm on the real mat.

4.4 Research Procedures

During the first phase, the CEFT was administered individually to classify the children to FD or FI participants. On the following day, during Phase 2, the researcher worked with each child individually to demonstrate the Bee-Bot commands. Phase 3 took place a day after Phase 2. During the third phase, the children, in the two scaffolding groups and the Control group, worked with the researcher individually to solve the second problem-solving task. A day after Phase 3, during the fourth phase, the external memory systems were removed and children's performance was assessed with the third problem-solving task.

5. RESULTS

5.1 Computational Thinking Evaluation Rubrics

The researchers developed inductively, based on students' answers (i.e., sequences of commands) two rubrics for measuring computational thinking. The first rubric assessed children's computational thinking holistically, and the second rubric assessed children's sequencing skills. Regarding the first rubric, the authors first wrote down all attempts the children made for a problem-solving task. For example, X's performance for Subtask2 in Phase 3 was recorded as follows:

X's first attempt (unsuccessful): MOVE BACKWARD-TURN RIGHT
X's second attempt (unsuccessful): MOVE BACKWARD-TURN RIGHT-MOVE FORWARD
X's third attempt (successful): MOVE BACKWARD-TURN RIGHT-TURN RIGHT-MOVE FORWARD

Then, the researchers collected all possible answers from all 180 students for Subtask2 and created a table as follows. Table 2 shows the number of possible attempts children made to solve the task. If for example, the maximum number of attempts made to find the correct answer was 3, then the max score is 3 for finding the correct answer during the first attempt, two if it took two attempts and one if it took three attempts.

Table 2. Subtask2: Holistic measurement of computational thinking

Code	Description	Score
3	Attempt 1- Success	3
2	Attempt 2 - Success	2
1	Attempt 3 - Success	1

Similarly, for sequencing, the researchers first wrote down all sequences of commands the learners executed for each attempt made. For Subtask2, as it was presented above, Table 3 was prepared.

Table 3. Subtask2: Measuring the skill of sequencing

Code	Description	Points received (one point per correct command in correct sequence)
1	Attempt 1 - MOVE BACKWARD-TURN RIGHT	2
2	Attempt 2 - MOVE BACKWARD-TURN RIGHT-MOVE FORWARD	2
3	Attempt 3 - MOVE BACKWARD-TURN RIGHT-TURN RIGHT-MOVE FORWARD	4

The total score for sequencing was then calculated as follows: Total_Sequencing_Subtask2 = Sequencing_Subtask2_Attempt1 + Sequencing_Subtask2 _Attempt2 + Sequencing_Subtask2_Attempt3 = 2 + 2 + 4 = 8.

5.2 Holistic Computational Thinking and the Skill of Sequencing

Table 4 presents children's holistic computational thinking scores in Phase 3 for each scaffolding type and FDI. As it is shown, FD and FI children in Scaffolding Type A tended to score higher on the holistic computational thinking assessment than FD and FI children in Scaffolding Type B and the Control group. Also FI learners scored higher in all groups. A 2 X 3 analysis of variance was performed and found that both main effects of FDI ($F(1, 174) = 4.54$, $p < 0.05$) and type of scaffolding ($F(2, 174) = 52.60$, $p < 0.01$) were found to be statistically significant in favor of FI children and Scaffolding Type A, respectively. Post-hoc comparisons showed that both Scaffolding Type A and Scaffolding Type B outperformed the Control group. After removing the external memory systems in Phase 4, as Table 4 shows, FI learners outperformed all other learners in all groups. FD learners in Scaffolding Type A scored higher than the FD children in Scaffolding Type B. In order to examine whether these descriptive differences were statistically significant, a 2 X 3 analysis of variance was again performed. It was found that only FDI was a significant main effect ($F(1, 174) = 19.38$, $p < 0.01$) in favor of the FI children.

Table 4. Descriptive statistics of children's holistic computational thinking in Phase 3 and Phase 4 for each scaffolding type and cognitive type

Phase 3			
	Mean	SD	N
		Scaffolding Type A	
FD	234.93	48.31	30
FI	249.43	9.8	30
Total	241.18	35.33	60
		Scaffolding Type B	
FD	224.40	38.48	30
FI	231.83	27.44	30
Total	228.12	33.35	60
		Control Group	
FD	163.00	55.31	30
FI	179.33	44.20	30
Total	171.17	50.32	60
Phase 4			
	Mean	SD	N
		Scaffolding Type A	
FD	165.77	63.95	30
FI	207.17	34.57	30
Total	186.47	55.08	60
		Scaffolding Type B	
FD	159.13	59.88	30
FI	201.63	46.36	30
Total	180.38	57.26	60
		Control Group	
FD	185.77	56.69	30
FI	203.87	43.30	30
Total	194.82	50.84	60

Table 5 presents children's scores on the skill of sequencing in Phase 3 for each scaffolding type and FDI. As it is shown, FD and FI children in Scaffolding Type A outperformed all other learners. Also, the scores between the FD and FI learners in Scaffolding Type A were almost the same. A 2 X 3 analysis of variance was performed and found that only the main effect of scaffolding technique was found to be statistically significant ($F(2, 174) = 19.38$, $p < 0.01$) in favor of Scaffolding Type A. Post-hoc comparisons showed that both Scaffolding Type A and Scaffolding Type B outperformed the Control group. After removing the external memory systems in Phase 4 FI learners outperformed all other learners in all groups. A 2 X 3 analysis of variance was again performed and found that only FDI was a significant main effect ($F(1, 174) = 20.16$, $p < 0.01$) in favor of the FI children.

Table 5. Descriptive statistics of children's performance on the sequencing skill in Phase 3 and Phase 4 for each scaffolding type and cognitive type

Phase 3			
	Mean	SD	N
		Scaffolding Type A	
FD	494.60	48.79	30
FI	494.27	40.67	30
Total	494.43	44.53	60
		Scaffolding Type B	
FD	487.20	48.79	30
FI	471.77	81.49	30
Total	479.48	68.25	60
		Control Group	
FD	360.87	112.64	30
FI	383.93	90.26	30
Total	372.40	101.86	60
Phase 4			
	Mean	SD	N
		Scaffolding Type A	
FD	301.33	88.40	30
FI	370.63	55.97	30
Total	335.98	81.25	60
		Scaffolding Type B	
FD	299.50	85.75	30
FI	348.83	79.77	30
Total	324.17	85.79	60
		Control Group	
FD	318.43	77.42	30
FI	354.30	69.75	30
Total	336.37	75.26	60

6. DISCUSSION

The findings showed that in Phase 3 children in both scaffolding groups outperformed the children in the Control group on the holistic measurement of computational thinking and the skill of sequencing. These results are consistent with previous work by Jonassen (1992) and more contemporary work by Angeli and Valanides (2004b) that showed the necessity of using scaffolding techniques, such as, external memory systems, to facilitate young students' learning with technological tools. However, when the external memory systems were withdrawn during Phase 4, no significant differences were detected between the scaffolding groups and the Control group on the holistic measurement of computational thinking and the skill of sequencing. Only FDI was found to be a statistically significant main effect in Phase 4, indicating that FI children were better in computational thinking than FD learners. This finding is consistent with previous research, which showed that FI learners outperformed the FD learners in self-directed problem-solving tasks and that FD learners needed support and scaffolding to succeed (Angeli & Valanides, 2004a, 2004b). In conclusion, the findings of this study strongly indicate that FD learners need scaffolding to succeed in problem-solving tasks with robotics and that teachers need to consider learners' cognitive type to ensure that all learners can learn with robots during classroom activities.

REFERENCES

Armoni, M., and Gal-Ezer, J. 2014. Early computing education: why? what? when? who?. *ACM Inroads*, Vol. 5, No. 4, pp 54-59.

Angeli, C., and Valanides, N. 2004a. Examining the effects of text-only and textvisual instructional materials on the achievement of field-dependent and field independent learners during problem-solving with modeling software. *Educational Technology Research and Development*, Vol. 52, No. 4, pp 23–36.

Angeli, C., and Valanides, N. 2004b. The effect of electronic scaffolding for technology integration on perceived task effort and confidence of primary student teachers. *Journal of Research on Technology in Education*, Vol. 37, No. 1, pp 29-43.

Angeli, C. 2013. Examining the effects of field dependence–independence on learners' problem-solving performance and interaction with a computer modeling tool: Implications for the design of joint cognitive systems. *Computers & Education*, Vol.62, pp 221-230.

Angeli, C., and Valanides, N. 2013. Using educational data mining methods to assess field-dependent and field-independent learners' complex problem solving. *Educational Technology Research & Development*, Vol.61, No.3, pp 521-548.

Bers, M. U., et al, 2014. Computational thinking and tinkering: Exploration of an early childhood robotics curriculum. *Computers & Education*, Vol. 72, pp 145-157.

Chen, S., and Macredie, R. D. 2004. Cognitive modeling of student learning in webbased instructional programs. *International Journal of Human-Computer Interaction*, Vol.17, No.3, pp 375–402.

Ching, Y. H. et al, 2018. Developing Computational Thinking with Educational Technologies for Young Learners. *TechTrends*,Vol. 62, pp 1-11.

Evans, C. et al, 2013. Field independence: Reviewing the evidence. British Journal of Educational Psychology,Vol. 83, No.2, pp 210-224.

Grover, S., and Pea, R. 2013. Computational Thinking in K–12: A Review of the State of the Field. *Educational Researcher*, Vol.42, No. 1, pp 38-43.

Hall, J. K. 2000. *Field dependence–independence and computer-based instruction in geography*. Unpublished doctoral dissertation, Virginia Polytechnic Institute and State University, Blacksburg, VA.

Jonassen, D. H. 1992. What are cognitive tools?. *Cognitive tools for learning* pp 1-6. Berlin: Springer.

Karp, S. A., and Konstadt, M. 1971. *Children's embedded figures test*. Washington: Consulting Psychologists Press.

Kazakoff, E. R. et al,2013. The effect of a classroom-based intensive robotics and programming workshop on sequencing ability in early childhood. *Early Childhood Education Journal*, Vol. 41, No.4, pp 245-255.

Messick, S. 1987. Structural relationships across cognition, personality, and style. *Aptitude, Learning, and Instruction*, Vol. 3, pp 35-75.

Shute, R., and Miksad, J. 1997. Computer Assisted Instruction and Cognitive Development in Preschoolers. *Child Study Journal*, Vol.27, No.3, pp 237-53.

Sullivan, A. et al, 2013. The wheels on the bot go round and round: Robotics curriculum in pre-kindergarten. *Journal of Information Technology Education*, Vol.12, pp 203-219.

Wing, J. 2006. Computational thinking. *Communications of the ACM*, Vol.49, No. 3, pp 33–36.

Wing, J. M. 2008. Computational thinking and thinking about computing. *Philosophical Transactions of the Royal Society A: Mathematical, Physical and Engineering Sciences*, Vol. 366, No.1881, pp 3717-3725.

Witkin, H. A. et al, 1977. Field-dependent and field-independent cognitive styles and their educational implications. *ETS Research Bulletin Series*, Vol.1975, No.2, pp 1-64.

REGION-WISE PAGE DIFFICULTY ANALYSIS USING EYE MOVEMENTS

Tsubasa Minematsu
Kyushu University
744, Motooka, Nishi-ku, Fukuoka, 819-0395, Japan

ABSTRACT

In this study, we investigated which section of a page was difficult for students to read, based on eye movement data and subjective impressions of the page's difficulty, with the aim of helping teachers revise teaching materials. It is problematic to manually model relationships between eye movements and subjective impressions of the page's difficulty. Therefore, in this study, we used a neural network to model the relationships automatically. Our method generated relevance maps representing locations where students found difficulty, in order to visualize region-wise page difficulty. To evaluate the quality of the relevance maps, we compared them with a distribution of gaze points and highlights added by the students. In addition, we administered a questionnaire to evaluate whether the relevance maps were useful to teachers when revising teaching materials. Results imply that our method can provide useful information for teachers making revisions to teaching materials.

KEYWORDS

Learning Analytics, Eye Movement, Machine Learning, Neural Network

1. INTRODUCTION

Improvement of learning supports is vital for enhancing education. Knowing what students find difficult is useful for improving learning supports. If teachers know what students are not able to understand in their lectures, it is easier for them to revise their teaching materials and thus teach difficult contents more carefully. In addition, this information can help to improve the summarization of current teaching materials (Shimada, et al., 2015) and inform recommendations for supplemental materials (Shiino, et al., 2019) provided by e-learning systems.

Several researchers have focused on relationships between learning behaviors and students' subjective impressions of difficulty. Nakamura et al. predicted subjective impressions of difficulty of English word tests by combining features such as eye movements and head poses (Nakamura, et al., 2008). Ohkawauchi et al. (Ohkawauchi, et al., 2012) and Shiino et al. (Shiino, et al., 2019) focused on more complex teaching materials, such as textbooks containing figures, tables, text, formulations, and images. Ohkawauchi et al. asked students to rate the degrees of difficulty in specific sections of teaching materials. The difficulty ratings were shown to teachers as evidence of students' understanding. Shiino et al. estimated the difficulty of each page of certain teaching materials by using students' clickstream data recorded from an e-learning system M2B (Ogata, et al., 2015).

These previous studies did not consider where on the page students found difficulty. The location information is more useful than teaching material-wise information and page-wise information. However, it is difficult to collect the location information by using questionnaires. To solve this problem, eye movement data can be used. The analysis of eye movement data can be helpful in understanding learning behaviors within pages. In previous works using eye movement data, findings have been shown related to effective attention guidance techniques (De Koning, et al., 2010); effectiveness of using both text and pictures in teaching materials (Mason, et al., 2013); and relationships between students' scan paths and performance (The & Mavrikis, 2016) (Jian & Ko, 2017). We believe that eye movement data can be helpful in representing how students comprehend the contents of different teaching materials.

In this study, we investigated which section of a page was difficult for students to comprehend based on the students' eye movements while studying by themselves. The research reported in this paper attempted to model relationships between subjective impressions of difficulty and eye movement data. We then visualized page regions related to the difficulty reported. We used a neural network for modeling such relationships because it is difficult to manually design features for representing eye movements. Visualization of a difficult page was performed based on finding the network's neurons related to the difficulty. In our experiment, we evaluated sections of a page students found difficult, with the aim of supporting teachers when they revise their materials in the future.

Our research questions are summarized as follows:

R1. Can we model relationships between subjective impressions of difficulty and eye movement data?

R2. Is our visualization of the page regions where students find difficulty useful for teachers when they revise textbooks?

2. DATA COLLECTION

We performed all procedures in accordance with the approved guidelines of the ethics committee of Kyushu University. In addition, we received prior written informed consent from participants in accordance with the Declaration of Helsinki.

We focused on analyzing reading patterns within pages of teaching materials from the eye movements of students. The eye movement data were collected from 15 university students engaged in an e-learning system. The 15 participants were undergraduate students in Kyushu University (seven females) with a mean age of 20.2 years (SD=1.6). Before our experiment, we confirmed that all participants had little knowledge or experience regarding information science and the statistical mathematics presented in our experiment. In this study, we used a Tobii eye tracker (Tobii pro spectrum 150 Hz) which was attached to a monitor. The monitor displayed teaching materials; the distance between the monitor and the eyes of the students was 57 cm. We measured their eye movements in a dark room with each student individually in order to reduce the effects of ambient noise. In our data collection, the sampling rate was set to 150 Hz.

Before the measurement, we calibrated the eye tracker device for each student. After completing the calibration, students viewed teaching materials in the e-learning system, consisting of a statistical test and correlation. The contents included figures, tables, text, formulations, and images. In addition, the content alignment was free.

We asked all the students to give their subjective impressions of a page's difficulty. Students used a slider interface to provide an impression score on a scale of zero to ten after finishing each page. The higher the score, the more difficult the page. To initialize eye movements, a black page was displayed for one second before the students started to read the next page. In addition, students could read previous pages freely.

Students were made to participate in an examination after they finished reading all the pages. In order to enhance their motivation, we informed the students about the examination before the measurement. In addition, the students added highlights on each page where they found difficult contents. Finally, our measurement covered the students' eye movements, subjective impressions of page difficulty, and highlights.

2.1 Preliminary Analysis

We show distributions of subjective impressions of page difficulty for each student. As shown in Figure 1, subjective impressions of the page difficulty were distributed, and the means and variances were different between the students. As we know, it is difficult to analyze such subjective impressions based on absolute values. In this study, we normalized subjective impressions of page difficulty for each student between zero and one. The normalized values were binarized using a threshold value. If the normalized value of the student was more than the threshold value, it was classified as a difficult page. We set the threshold value to 0.75 experimentally.

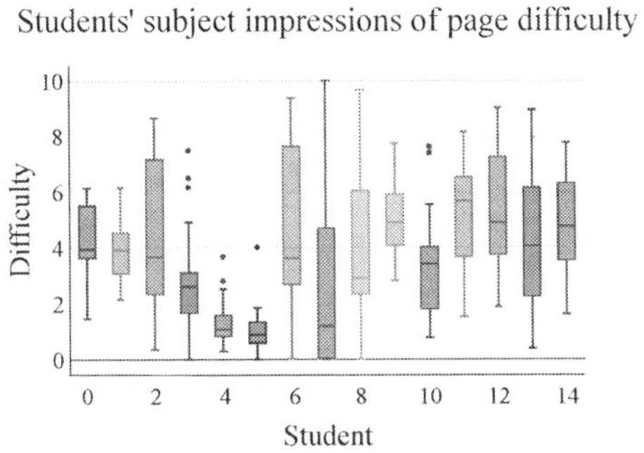

Figure 1. Distribution of subjective impression of page difficulty

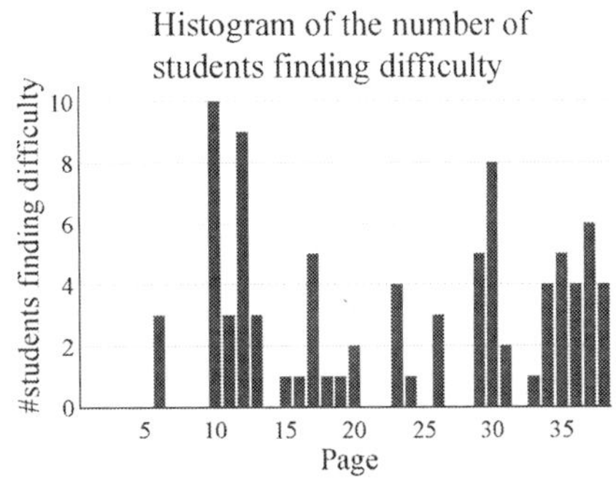

Figure 2. Distribution of the number of students finding difficulty in each page

Figure 2 shows the distribution of the number of students finding difficulty in each page. We could confirm that more than half of the students felt some specific pages to be difficult, such as pages 10, 12, and 30. These pages contained explanations about the definition of correlation coefficient and an example of a t-test. Based on this preliminary analysis, we observed that some students found the contents of the teaching materials difficult.

3. READING PATTERN ANALYSIS BASED ON A NEURAL NETWORK

3.1 Modeling Relationship between Students' Eye Movement and Difficulty

We used a neural network to investigate the relationship between students' eye movements and subjective impressions of a page's difficulty. The neural network used in this study accepted eye movement data and then classified whether the data were related to difficult pages. The advantage of neural networks is that they obtain effective features for classification automatically based on input data. In other machine learning approaches, we have had to design effective features manually. However, it was difficult to design manually in our study because we focused on page difficulty and student's eye movements, which represented both temporal and spatial information. Therefore, we chose to use a neural network.

Our neural network accepted a three-dimensional tensor as the input and provided a probability of page difficulty. The probability of page difficulty represented whether a tensor generated from eye movement data belonged to a difficult page. The tensor represented a student's eye movement and was generated based on reading pattern codes proposed by Minematsu et al. (Minematsu, et al., 2019). We encoded a sequence of eye movement data to three-dimensional tensors, which represented temporal and spatial information. First, the sequence was divided into T time slots. Then, we computed a density map of gaze points at each time slot based on a kernel density estimation. The size of the density map was $H \times W$. Therefore, we obtained a $H \times W \times T$ tensor from the sequence of eye movements on the page. The first and second axes represent spatial information, and the third axis represents temporal information. We did not form a one-dimensional vector because convolution layers can accept high dimensional tensors. H, W, and T were set to 20 experimentally.

Our neural network architecture is described in Table 1. Our neural network contained five convolution layers, two fully connected layers, and three max-pooling layers. In all convolution layers and fully connected layers, the kernel size was 3×3, and the stride was 1×1. In all max-pooling layers, the kernel size was 2×2, and the stride was 2×2. We used rectified linear units (ReLUs) as activation functions, with the exception of the output layer. In the output layer, a sigmoid function was used to provide a probability of difficult pages. We used cross entropy cost function to train our neural network. Our neural network was optimized using the Adam optimizer based on backpropagation. The learning rate was set to 0.0001. The other parameters were set to the default values described in (Kingma & Ba, 2015). After training, our neural network was able to model relationships between eye movements and difficult pages.

Table 1. Neural network architecture

Layer	Input shape (height × width × channel)	Output shape (height × width × channel)
Input	$20 \times 20 \times 20$	$20 \times 20 \times 20$
Convolution	$20 \times 20 \times 20$	$20 \times 20 \times 32$
Convolution	$20 \times 20 \times 32$	$20 \times 20 \times 32$
Max-pooling	$20 \times 20 \times 32$	$10 \times 10 \times 32$
Convolution	$10 \times 10 \times 32$	$10 \times 10 \times 64$
Max-pooling	$10 \times 10 \times 64$	$5 \times 5 \times 64$
Convolution	$5 \times 5 \times 64$	$5 \times 5 \times 64$
Max-pooling	$5 \times 5 \times 64$	$3 \times 3 \times 64$
Convolution	$3 \times 3 \times 64$	$1 \times 1 \times 64$
Fully connected	$1 \times 1 \times 64$	$1 \times 1 \times 64$
Fully connected	$1 \times 1 \times 64$	$1 \times 1 \times 1$

3.2 Interpretation of the Model

We used layer-wise relevance propagation (LRP) (Lapuschkin, et al., 2016) to visualize page areas where students found difficulty. LRP can provide a relevance score in each element of an input tensor of eye movements. The relevance score represents the contribution to the decision by our neural network at each element of the input tensor. When a relevance score in an element is positive, it means that the element supports the decision. Therefore, we focused on positive relevance scores in each input tensor to analyze which part of eye movement was related to the subjective impression of page difficulty. The details are referred to in (Lapuschkin, et al., 2016).

To summarize difficult areas on each page, we integrated the relevance scores of all students. First, relevance scores in each input tensor were normalized between -1 and 1. The normalization was performed by dividing each relevance score by the maximum value of the absolute value. Second, we summed the relevance tensors along the third axis, which represented temporal information, and then summed the relevance maps of all students. After the summation, we obtained relevance maps for each page. The size of the relevance maps were $H \times W$. The relevance maps were normalized again between -1 and 1. Finally, we extracted positive values, and applied the following function to extract values, in order to clarify the magnitude of relevance scores. The function is follows:

$$f(x) = \frac{\mathbf{1.0}}{(\mathbf{1} + \mathbf{exp}(-\mathbf{10}(x - \mathbf{0.5})))} \tag{1}$$

where x is a relevance score. In the relevance map, a region with a large score contributes to classifying the page as a difficult page. In other words, the region can be related to difficult contents within the page.

4. EXPERIMENT

We obtained relevance maps by applying the method described in Section 3. The relevance maps were used to understand where students found difficulty on the page. We also visualized a distribution of gaze points for each page, in order to understand where students were looking. This distribution was called a gaze map in this study. The gaze map of the page was generated from all of the input tensors of eye movements on the page by following the same procedure as that used to generate relevance maps. In the gaze maps, when many students looked at a region for a long time, the region had a large value. In addition, the highlights added to the pages by students were available. We used the highlight maps to represent location and number. To obtain the highlight maps, we counted the number of highlights added on the same location of each page, which was then divided by the maximum value in all pages. We evaluated the relevance maps using the gaze maps and the highlight maps.

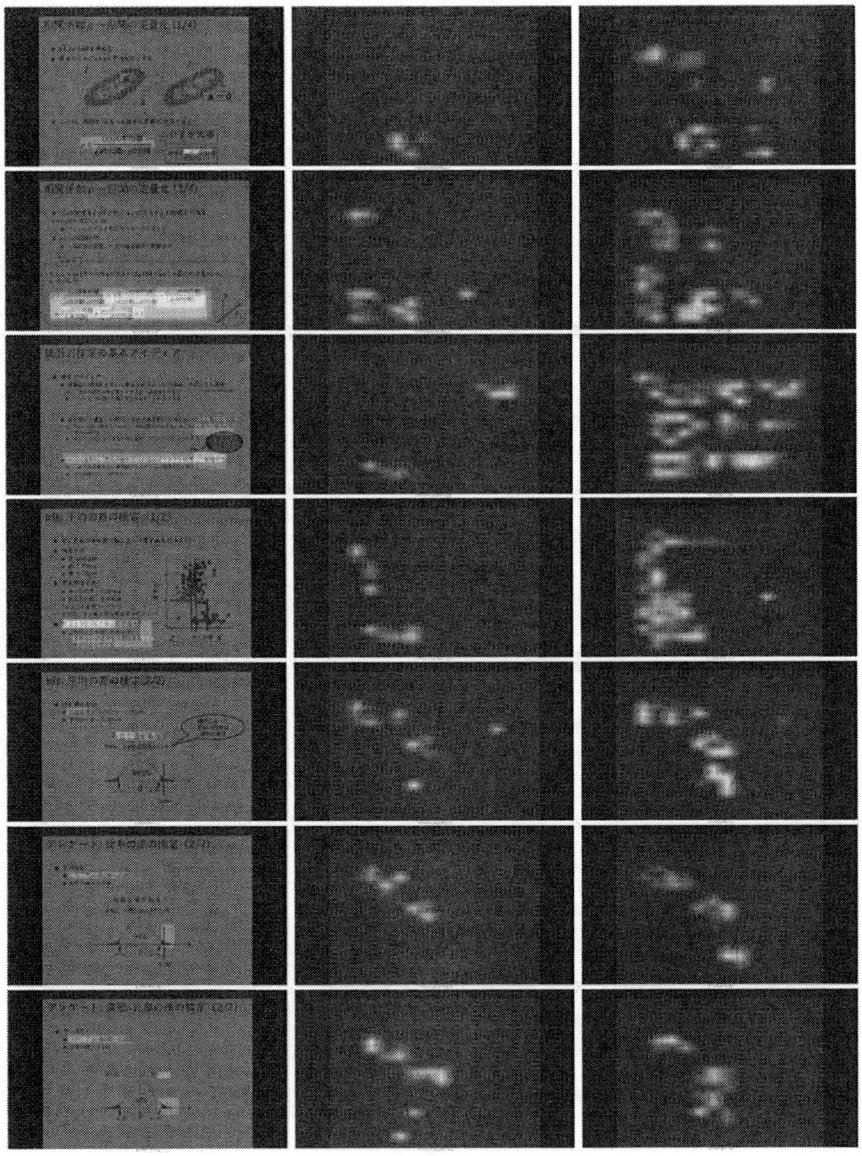

Highlight Relevance Gaze

Figure 3. Visualization of highlight maps, relevance maps, and gaze maps in pages with more than five students who found difficulty on those pages

4.1 Qualitative Evaluation

We compared the relevance maps with the gaze maps and the highlight maps. Figures 3 and 4 show the highlight maps, the relevance maps, and the gaze maps superimposed on the corresponding pages. Figure 3 only includes those with more than five students who found difficulty on those pages, while Figure 4 shows the remainder. A figure in red has a larger value than a figure in blue.

According to the highlight maps in Figures 3 and 4, we could roughly confirm where some students found difficulty. The relevance maps in Figure 3 support this conclusion more than those in Figure 4. For example, the relevance maps and the highlight maps focus on equations in the first and the second row of Figure 3. We believe that it is easy for the neural network to model the eye movements and subjective impressions of the pages with contents the students found difficult.

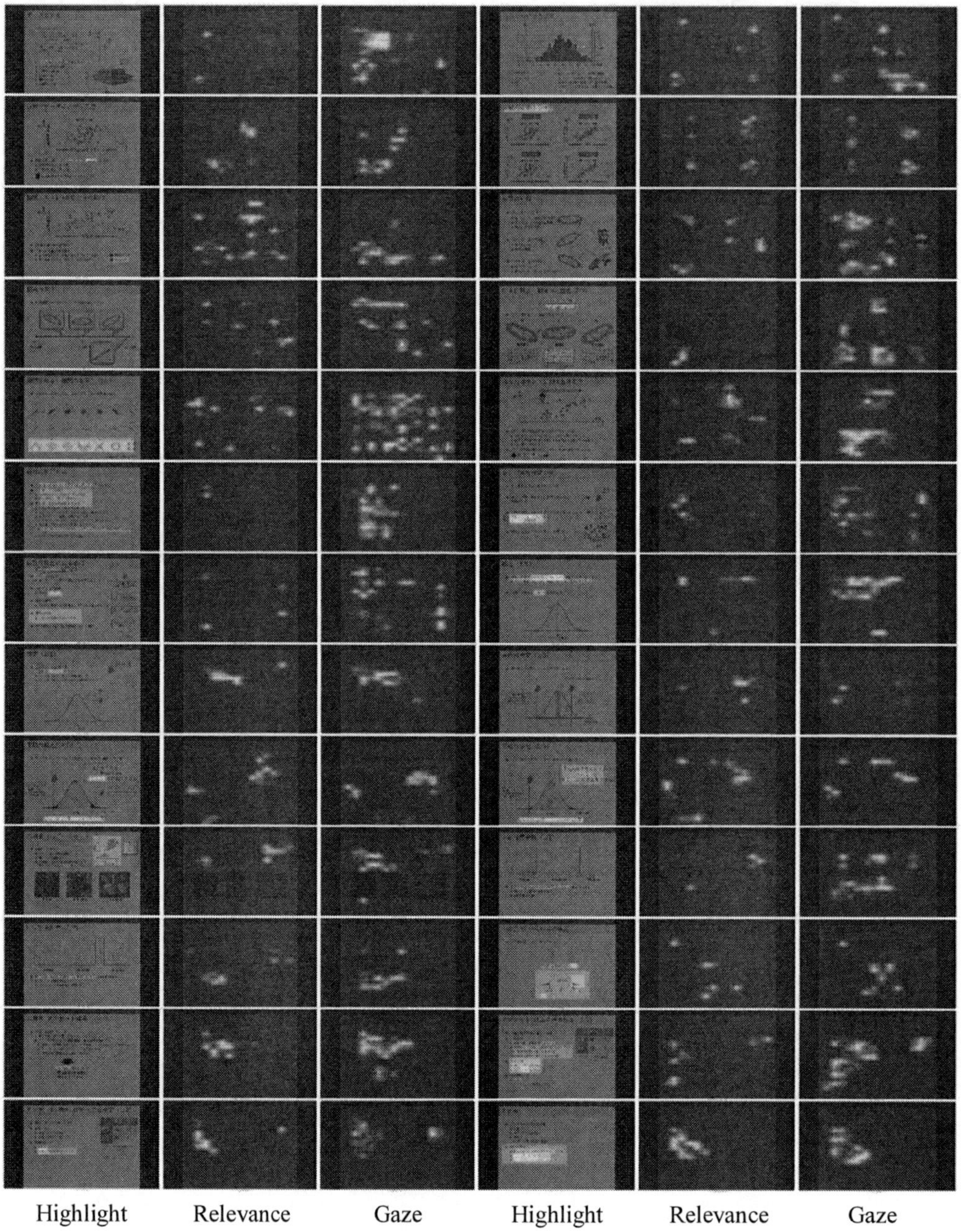

Figure 4. Visualization of highlight maps, relevance maps, and gaze maps in pages with less than four students who found difficulty on those pages

The gaze maps showed where students looked most frequently. Comparing the relevance maps with the gaze maps, the relevance maps showed more specific regions than the gaze maps. The neural network accepted tensors of eye movements as the input. Some relevance scores in the tensors became negative when performing LRP. Therefore, scores in the relevance maps were more limited than scores in the gaze maps.

4.2 Evaluation for Modification of Teaching Materials

We administered a questionnaire to the creator of the teaching materials in order to evaluate the quality of the relevance map from the point of view of a teacher. In Section 4.1, we confirmed that the relevance maps could be similar to the results in the highlight maps. However, the relevance maps may not always help teachers revise teaching materials. To investigate whether the relevance maps support teachers, we showed the relevance maps and the gaze maps to the creator of the teaching materials. Note that we did not explain how the maps were generated; only that they were generated by two different systems. In fact, system A generated the gaze maps, and system B generated the relevance maps.

Table 2 shows the questionnaire about the relevance maps and the gaze maps, and the responses. Q1 asked what the creator found to be difficult for the students. Q2 asked whether the creator would refer to the maps when modifying teaching materials. The creator answered the questions for each page.

According to the answer to Q1, the creator believed that the gaze maps represented page difficulty more accurately than the relevance maps. However, the answer to Q2 showed that the creator did not choose both the gaze maps and the relevance maps for every page. We believed the result was related to the page difficulty. To confirm, we focused on more difficult pages. If the number of students finding difficulty in a page is less than the threshold values, we ignore the page when computing the weighted average. Table 3 shows some weighted averages when easier pages were removed. In Q2, we confirmed that almost all weighted averages increased. This meant that the creator tended to refer to the relevance maps in difficult pages. Therefore, the relevance maps were more useful for the creator than the gaze maps in the modification of teaching materials.

Table 2. Questionnaire about the relevance maps and the gaze maps

Question		Evaluation					
		Agree A (1)	Agree A a little (2)	Neither agree nor disagree (3)	Agree B a little (4)	Agree B (5)	Weighted Average (n =33)
Q1	Which of the systems present similar results to what you find difficult for the students?	11	6	8	6	2	2.45
Q2	Which system do you want to refer to when modifying teaching materials?	1	4	22	3	3	3.09

Table 3. Weighted average varying threshold values about the number of difficult pages. n is the number of pages used for computing their weighted average

Question	Threshold values							
	≥ 0 (n =33)	≥ 1 (n =23)	≥ 2 (n =17)	≥ 3 (n =15)	≥ 4 (n =11)	≥ 5 (n =7)	≥ 6 (n =4)	≥ 7 (n =3)
Q1	2.45	2.26	2.35	2.47	2.55	2.57	2.00	2.00
Q2	3.09	3.13	3.18	3.27	3.36	**3.57**	3.25	3.33

5. DISCUSSION

In this study, we visualized the locations of difficult contents on the relevance maps by modeling relationships between students' eye movements and their subjective impressions of the page's difficulty. Therefore, in research question R1, we believed that such a relationship could be modeled.

In R2, our visualization method is useful for a teacher when pages are difficult for students, according to Table 3. In addition, the relevance maps may help teachers revise teaching materials. Even if teachers use the gaze maps, the maps may not be able to help them because they are redundant. Teachers have to extract useful information from the gaze map. However, the relevance maps focused on some specific regions in our experiment. Note that our visualization method may not be useful for teachers when pages are not difficult. We can provide more useful information for teachers by removing easy pages in advance.

We believed the highlight maps accurately represented where students found difficulty. However, students did not always add highlights. The relevance maps could localize difficult contents even if students forgot to add highlights, because they were generated automatically from eye movements.

The major limitation of this study was that we did not consider explanations on each page, or the types of content (such as figures, text, and equations). We believe that such information can strongly affect students' reading behaviors and their subjective impressions of difficulty. To further investigate these details, analysis of the multimodal information will be needed, including images of pages and types of contents.

6. CONCLUSION

In this study, we proposed a method to model relationships between students' eye movements and their subjective impressions of the difficulty of pages. Our method generated relevance maps representing locations where students found difficulty, automatically based on their eye movements. Our experiment implied that the relevance maps could provide useful information for teachers when revising teaching materials, as the system suggests where to revise on each page based on the relevance maps.

We only used eye movement data for modeling the relationships. However, eye movement data alone cannot completely represent the contexts of teaching materials, such as the contents of each page. We believe that information could improve the quality of the relevance maps. For example, we may be able to use prior materials that were difficult for students to better understand equations, and much longer texts. In the future, we will combine eye movement data and additional information, such as the types of content on each page.

ACKNOWLEDGEMENTS

We are grateful to Dr. Kaori Tamura for helping with data collection. This work was supported by JSPS KAKENHI Grant Number JP19K20421.

REFERENCES

De Koning, B. B. et al., 2010. Attention guidance in learning from a complex animation: Seeing is understanding? *Learning and instruction*, Vol. *20, Issue* 2, pp. 111-122.

Jian, Y.-C., and Ko, H.-W., 2017. Influences of text difficulty and reading ability on learning illustrated science texts for children: An eye movement study. *Computers & Education* Vol. 113, pp. 263-279.

Kingma, D. P., and Ba, J., 2015. Adam: A Method for Stochastic Optimization. *Proceedings of the 3rd International Conference for Learning Representations*. San Diego, US, pp. 7-9.

Lapuschkin, S. et al., 2016. The LRP Toolbox for Artificial Neural Networks. *The Journal of Machine Learning Research*, Vol. *17*, pp. 3938-3942.

Mason, L. et al., 2013. An eye-tracking study of learning from science text with concrete and abstract illustrations. *The Journal of Experimental Education,* Vol. 81, Issue 3, pp. 356-384.

Minematsu, T. et al., 2019. Analytics of Reading Patterns Based on Eye Movements in an e-Learning System. *Society for Information Technology & Teacher Education International Conference,* Las Vegas, NV, U.S., pp. 744-749.

Nakamura, K. et al., 2008. Estimating learners' subjective impressions of the difficulty of course materials in e-learning environments. *APRU 9th Distance Learning and the Internet Conference*, Tokyo, Japan, pp. 199-206.

Ogata, H. et al., 2015. E-book-based learning analytics in University education. *International Conference on Computer in Education (ICCE 2015)*, Hangzhou, China, pp. 401-406.

Ohkawauchi, T. et al., 2012. Study of a Teacher Support Method For Improving Lectures for E-Learning on Demand. *Proceedings of the iieej transactions on image electronics and visual computing workshop 2012*, Kuching, Malaysia, pp. 1-4.

Shiino, T. et al., 2019. Page-wise Difficulty Level Estimation using e-Book Operation Logs. *Proceedings of the 9th International Learning Analytics and Knowledge Conference.* Tempe, U.S.

Shimada, A. et al, 2015. Automatic Summarization of Lecture Slides for Enhanced Student Preview. *International Conference on Computer in Education (ICCE 2015)*, Hangzhou, China, pp. 218-227.

The, B. and Mavrikis, M., 2016. A Study on Eye Fixation Patterns of Students in Higher Education Using an Online Learning System. *Proceedings of the Sixth International Conference on Learning Analytics & Knowledge.* Edinburgh, United Kingdom, pp. 408-416.

TOWARDS GENERATING EXERCISE QUESTIONS WITH LOD FOR WEB-BASED INVESTIGATIVE LEARNING

Rei Saito[1], Yoshiki Sato[1], Miki Hagiwara[1], Koichi Ota[2] and Akihiro Kashihara[1]
[1]*The University of Electro-Communications, 1-5-1, Chofugaoka, Chofu, Tokyo,1828585, Japan*
[2]*Japan Advanced Institute of Science and Technology, 1-1, Asahidai, Nomi, Ishikawa, 9231292, Japan*

ABSTRACT

Web allows learners to investigate any question to learn with a large number of Web resources. In such investigative learning, leaners are expected to investigate the question by navigating Web resources/pages to construct their knowledge and decomposing the question into sub-questions. In acquiring skills in such investigative learning, learners need to practice with exercise questions. However, it is hard to define correct knowledge to be constructed for the questions since Web-based investigative learning could result in diverse knowledge as correct one for the same question. Towards this issue, this paper proposes the method with Linked Open Data (LOD) for generating exercise questions, which includes an initial question and sub-questions to be decomposed from an initial question. These sub-questions are extracted and selected as keywords with LOD and Word2vec. This paper also reports a case study with the generation method. The results suggest that it is effective as scaffolding particularly for novice learners.

KEYWORDS

Web-Based Investigative Learning, Linked Open Data, Exercise Questions

1. INTRODUCTION

On the Web, learners are expected to investigate any question to learn from a huge number of Web resources. Such learning process involves navigating Web resources/pages and constructing wider and deeper knowledge from their points of view (Henze and Nejdl, 2001). However, they tend to search a limited number of Web resources/pages for investigating a question. As a result, they would construct limited knowledge. In elaborately investigating an initial question, learners are expected to deepen and widen the question, which requires them to identify related questions to be further investigated during navigation and knowledge construction with Web resources (Hill and Hannafin, 1997). This corresponds to decomposing the initial question into related ones as sub-questions.

In addition, Web resources do not usually provide learners with learning scenario implying questions to be investigated and their sequence. Learners could not accordingly follow it to construct their knowledge. They need to decompose a question into the sub-questions by themselves for elaborate investigation. Such question decomposition corresponds to creating a learning scenario, which could play a crucial role in self-regulating navigation and knowledge construction process with Web resources (Azevedo and Cromley, 2004).

On the other hand, it is not easy for learners to create their own scenario in concurrence with navigation and knowledge construction (Zumbach and Mohraz, 2007). In our previous work, we have proposed a model of Web-based investigative learning, and developed a tool named interactive Learning Scenario Builder (iLSB) as a model-based learning environment (Kashihara and Akiyama, 2017). iLSB provides scaffolding for conducting investigative learning process as modeled. We have also confirmed the effectiveness of iLSB from a case study whose results suggest iLSB makes learning scenario created by learners wider and deeper.

In this paper, we address the issue how to improve skills in Web-based investigative learning particularly for novice learners who could not create appropriate scenario by themselves. In acquiring cognitive skills, it is necessary for learners to practice repeatedly (Azevedo and Cromley, 2004; Azevedo et al., 2015). Our approach to this issue is to provide learners with exercise questions for Web-based investigative learning. In general, it is necessary to define correct knowledge/scenario to be constructed/created for such exercise questions. However, Web-based investigative learning could result in diverse knowledge and scenario as correct ones for the same question. It is accordingly hard to prepare exercise questions with correct results (knowledge/scenario to be constructed).

Toward this issue, we propose a method for generating exercise questions with Linked Open Data (LOD). This method extracts and selects keywords representing sub-questions to be decomposed from an initial question by means of LOD and Word2vec. It then generates an exercise question, which includes the initial and sub-questions. Learners are expected to investigate the exercise question with iLSB and to create a learning scenario including the initial and sub-questions.

In this paper, we also report a case study whose purpose was to evaluate the appropriateness and effectiveness of exercise questions generated. The results suggest that these could appropriately and effectively function particularly for novice learners.

2. WEB-BASED INVESTIGATIVE LERNING

2.1 Difficulties in Web-Based Investigative Learning

In Web-based investigative learning, it is important for learners to construct deeper and wider knowledge as to an initial question by gathering and navigating Web resources, associating the contents learned in the resources, and decomposing the initial question into sub-questions in a self-directed way. In addition, most Web resources do not have any learning scenario such as table of contents in instructional textbook, which implies questions to be investigated and their sequence. Learners accordingly need to create their own scenario during navigation and knowledge construction, which results in individual learning.

On the other hand, it is difficult for learners to concurrently navigate Web resources, construct their knowledge, and create their own scenario. This could prevent them from creating more appropriate, wider, and deeper learning scenario. In order to address this problem, we have modeled the process of Web-based investigative learning, and developed iLSB to provide scaffolds for conducting Web-based investigative learning as modeled in our previous work.

2.2 Model of Web-Based Investigative Learning

This model consists of three cyclic phases: (a) search for Web resources, (b) navigational learning, and (c) question decomposition. In phase (a), learners are expected to use a search engine with a keyword representing an initial question to select Web resources suitable for investigating the question. In phase (b), they are expected to navigate Web pages in the selected resources and to construct their knowledge by extracting keywords representing the contents learned in the pages and associating them. In phase (c), they are expected to find out some related sub-questions to be further investigated about the initial question, which could be obtained from the keywords extracted in phase (b). They are expected to investigate each sub-question in the same way. We assume that these three phases are repeated until they do not decompose into sub-questions anymore.

The question decomposition results in a tree called question tree. In this tree, each node corresponds to a question that is represented by a keyword (called q-keyword). In this work, q-keyword is used as a substitute for question investigated. This tree includes part of relationships between a question and sub-questions whose root represents initial question. This tree also corresponds to learning scenario.

2.3 Interactive Learning Scenario Builder (iLSB)

We have developed iLSB as an add-on to Firefox to scaffold investigative learning process as modeled. iLSB provides a search engine for selecting Web resources, a keywords repository for knowledge construction, and a question tree viewer for question decomposition as scaffolding for each phase of the model. Figure 1 shows the interface of iLSB.

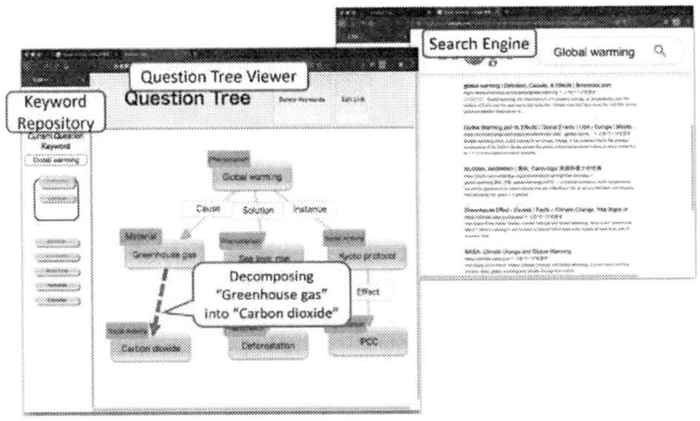

Figure 1. User Interface of iLSB

Let us demonstrate how iLSB scaffolds investigative learning process with an example of initial question "What is global warming?". Learners are first expected to input "global warming" as q-keyword into a search engine and to gather Web resources related to "global warming". Next, they are expected to store keywords such as "Greenhouse gas", and "Kyoto Protocol" in the keyword repository while navigating the Web resources/pages, which represent the contents learned about the initial question. They are then expected to associate the keywords to construct their knowledge. After that, they are expected to find out sub q-keywords such as "Greenhouse gas" to be further investigated from the stored keywords, and to add the sub q-keywords to the question tree viewer. They are next expected to investigate these sub q-keywords in the same way. They are finally expected to create a question tree, whose root is "global warming".

2.4 Issue and Purpose

Even with iLSB, some learners still have difficulties in creating their own scenario, which tends to be insufficient. It is necessary for such learners to do exercises to acquire skills in Web-based investigative learning. For exercises in Web-based investigative learning, it is an important issue how to define exercise questions. We have provided learners only with an initial question as exercise one so far. However, they often have difficulties in finding out sub-questions to be decomposed from the contents learned. In order to improve skills in question decomposition, we define an exercise question as the one including an initial question and related sub-question candidates, which expects learners to select proper sub-questions.

In this paper, we propose a method for extracting keywords (called c-keywords) as q-keyword candidates to be included in an exercise question from LOD, which are related to an initial question. This method then generates an exercise question to be presented to learners, which is composed of the initial question and extracted c-keywords. This exercise question intends to improve learners' skill for appropriate question decomposition. c-keywords are divided into positive c-keywords that have strong relationship with the initial question and negative c-keywords that have weak or less proper relationship with the initial question. In creating a learning scenario, learners are expected to select positive c-keywords and to avoid selecting negative ones. Such selection allows learners to enhance their skills in question decomposition.

3. GENERATING EXERCISE QUESTIONS

3.1 Linked Open Data (LOD)

LOD is a set of structured data interlinking with related ones on the Web. In this work, we use DBpedia Japanese as LOD (DBpedia Japanese, 2016) whose data are extracted from Japanese Wikipedia. The data of DBpedia Japanese are stored in RDF format, which is described with triplet such as subject, predicate and object. A collection of RDF data is viewed as a network structure. These data are obtained using query language SPARQL. By sending SPARQL query to DBpedia Japanese, it is possible to obtain keywords (c-keywords) related to q-keyword representing an initial question.

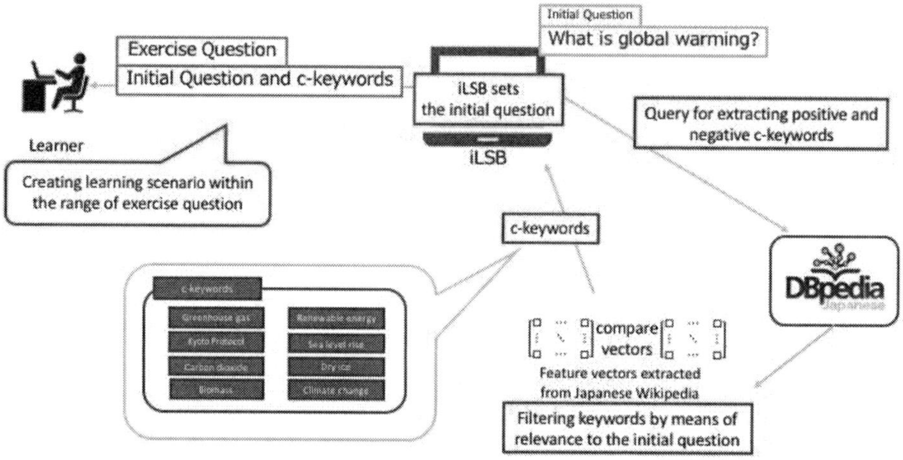

Figure 2. Framework of Generating Exercise Question

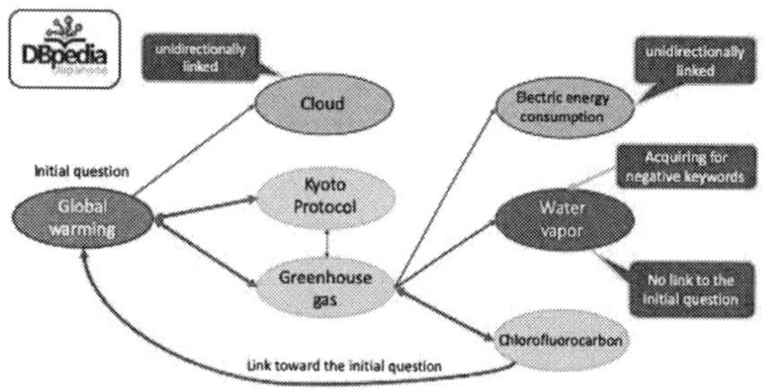

Figure 3. Links between Initial Question and Positive and Negative c-keywords

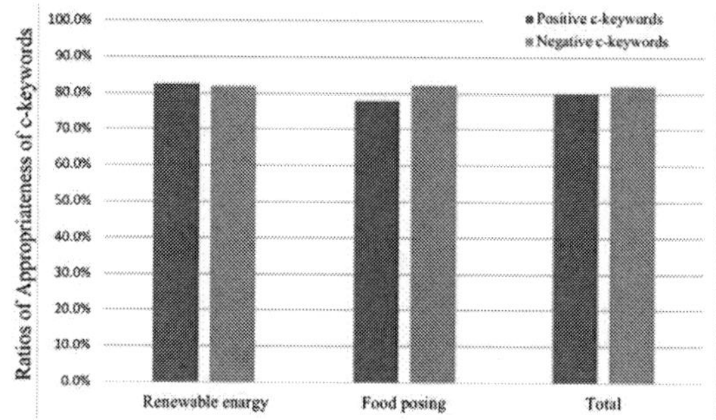

Figure 4. Ratios of Appropriateness of c-keywords

3.2 Word2vec

Word2vec is an algorithm that analyzes words in documents to generate word vectors including words and their adjacent words. It learns weights of adjacent relations between words by means of neural network from a large number of documents as input.

In order to generate word vectors from Japanese Wikipedia, we use MeCab (Kudo, 2013) to extract words from the sentences, which are inputted to Word2vec. The extracted vectors are used to calculate cosine similarity between the initial question and c-keywords to be obtained from DBpedia Japanese.

3.3 Framework of Exercise Questions

Figure 2 shows the framework for generating an exercise question for Web-based investigative learning. In the proposed method, the exercise questions are generated by means of DBpedia Japanese and Word2vec, which include positive c-keywords highly related to the initial question and negative c-keywords less related to the initial question.

First of all, this method sets up an initial question, and sends SPARQL queries for extracting c-keywords to DBpedia Japanese. As for all the extracted keywords, it calculates cosine similarity with q-keyword representing the initial question by means of word vectors extracted with Word2vec in advance. This method extracts keywords with higher similarity as positive c-keywords, and also extracts keywords with lower similarity as negative c-keywords. An exercise question is then generated. Learners are expected to investigate the initial question with iLSB and to obtain sub-questions from these c-keywords particularly from the positive ones to create proper learning scenario. Such exercise question intends to help learners select sub q-keywords for scenario creation. In addition, it is possible to adjust difficulty of exercise question by changing the amount and ratio of positive and negative c-keywords to be provided to learners. Such adjustment allows learners to improve their skills in creating proper learning scenario.

3.4 Extracting c-keywords with SPARQL Query

Both positive and negative c-keywords are extracted with SPARQL query in consideration of the links with the initial question on DBpedia Japanese. Figure 3 shows the links between an initial question ("Global warming" as the q-keyword) and its positive/negative c-keywords on DBpedia Japanese. In Figure 3, positive c-keywords are expressed as yellow nodes, and negative c-keywords are expressed as red nodes.

Since positive c-keywords should be highly related to the initial question, it is necessary to extract keywords closely related to the initial question on DBpedia Japanese. This method accordingly searches and extracts keywords such as Kyoto Protocol in Figure 3 that are bidirectionally linked with the initial question on DBpedia Japanese. The method moreover searches keywords such as Chlorofluorocarbon and Water vapor that are bidirectionally linked with the extracted positive c-keywords. However, the method does not extract the searched keywords such as Water Vapor that have no link to the initial question.

On the other hand, negative c-keywords should not be far from the initial question so that learners could not immediately understand these are not necessary for question decomposition. This method accordingly searches keywords as negative ones like "Water vapor" that are bidirectionally linked with positive c-keywords and that have no link with the initial question.

4. CASE STUDIES

4.1 Appropriateness of c-keywords

4.1.1 Purpose and Procedure

We conducted a case study whose purpose was to ascertain whether c-keywords extracted by the proposed method were appropriate as positive and negative q-keywords as to initial question. In this study, three of the authors evaluated each c-keyword as "appropriate" or "inappropriate" by referring to reliable Web resources related to initial question. The appropriateness was decided by majority of three authors. In this study, we prepared two initial questions, "What is renewable energy?" and "What is foodborne illness?".

The appropriateness of positive c-keywords was calculated as the ratio of positive c-keywords evaluated as "appropriate" to all positive ones. The appropriateness of negative c-keywords was calculated as the ratio of negative c-keywords evaluated as "inappropriate" to all negative ones.

4.1.2 Results

Figure 4 shows the results of appropriateness of positive and negative c-keywords for each initial question and for total. As shown in this figure, "appropriate" ratings of both positive and negative c-keywords were about 80% for each initial question. This suggests that positive and negative c-keywords extracted by the proposed method are almost appropriate.

4.1.3 Discussion

Let us discuss inappropriate c-keywords. According to Figure 4, about 20% of c-keywords were considered as inappropriate keywords. Most of positive c-keywords evaluated as inappropriate represent extremely subdivided examples and company names. Although these c-keywords are highly related to the initial question on DBpedia Japanese, these are not appropriate as sub-questions for the initial questions. As for the negative c-keywords evaluated as inappropriate, there was a negative keyword mackerel that often causes food poisoning, for example. However, this is considered to be a negative c-keyword because there is no link to the initial question foodborne illness. How to remove these inappropriate c-keywords is one of our future work.

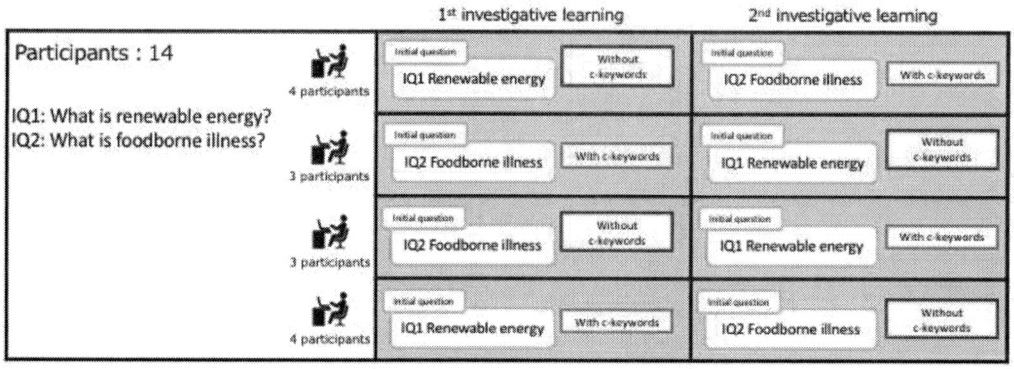

Figure 5. Procedure

4.2 Effectiveness of Exercise Question

4.2.1 Purpose and Procedure

We conducted a case study whose purpose was to ascertain whether exercise questions generated were effective in creating appropriate learning scenario. Participants were 14 graduate and undergraduate students in science and technology. They conducted Web-based investigative learning twice only with initial question and with exercise question including initial question and c-keywords. The initial questions provided were "IQ1: What is renewable energy?" and "IQ2: What is foodborne illness?" IQ1 was represented as renewable energy, and IQ2 was also represented as foodborne illness. The procedure of this study is shown in Figure 5. The participants were divided into the following four groups in order to remove the order effects of presenting the initial questions and c-keywords:

(a) Investigating IQ1, then investigating IQ2 with c-keywords,
(b) Investigating IQ2 with c-keywords, then investigating IQ1,
(c) Investigating IQ2, then investigating IQ1 with c-keywords, and
(d) Investigating IQ1 with c-keywords, then investigating IQ2.

The participants first practiced using iLSB for 30 minutes. Then, they conducted Web-based investigative learning for each initial question from 30 to 60 minutes with iLSB. In investigative learning with c-keywords, the list of c-keywords was provided on paper. The participants were asked to obtain sub-questions from the c-keywords to create learning scenario.

After their investigative learning, three of the authors manually evaluated each question decomposition in their scenarios with three ratings, "appropriate", "weak appropriate" and "inappropriate" by referring to reliable Web resources about the initial questions. The evaluation was decided by majority vote of three raters. When the three ratings did not match with each other, it was determined as "weak appropriate".

In order to ascertain the effectiveness of exercise questions, in addition, the participants were divided into high rating group and low rating group according to the ratio of "appropriate" ratings for question decomposition in learning scenario created without c-keywords. The high rating group had 6 participants. Three of them investigated IQ1, and the others investigated IQ2. The remaining 8 participants were classified into the low rating group. In evaluating the effectiveness of the exercise questions, we set the following hypothesis:

Hypothesis: Presenting c-keywords to learners promotes appropriate question decomposition.

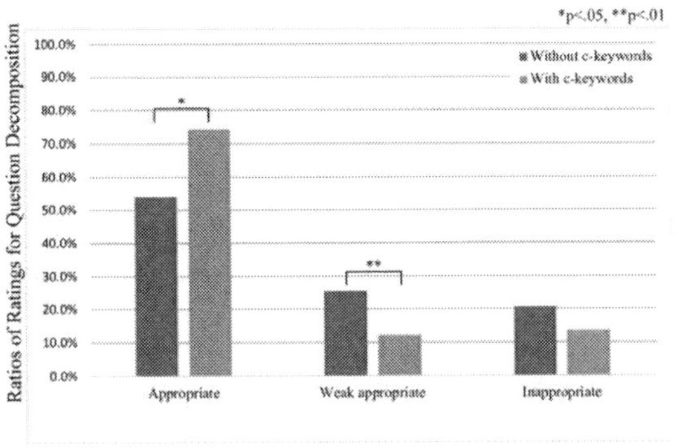

Figure 6. Ratios of Ratings for Question Decomposition in All Participants

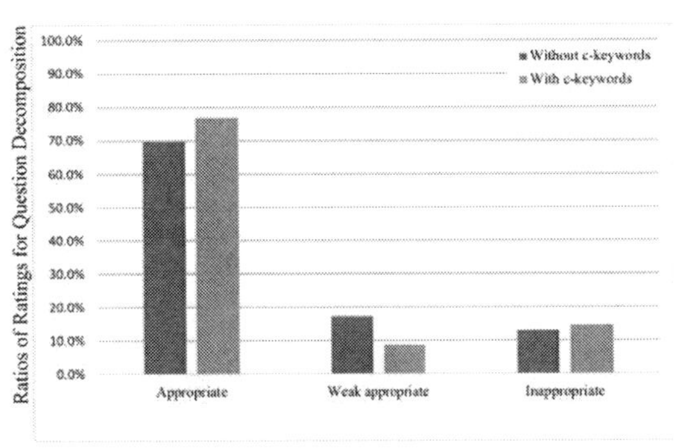

Figure 7. Ratios of Ratings for Question Decomposition in High Rating Group

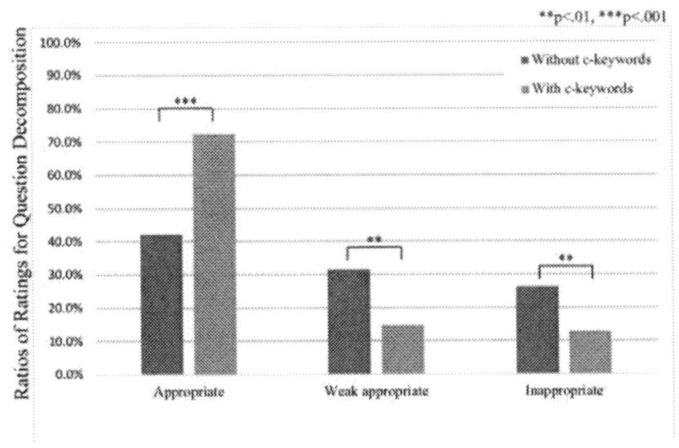

Figure 8. Ratios of Ratings for Question Decomposition in Low Rating Group

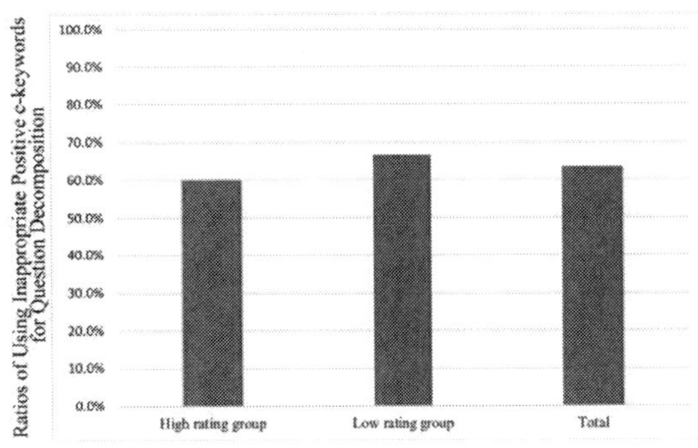

Figure 9. Ratios of Using Inappropriate Positive c-keywords for Question Decomposition

4.2.2 Results

Figure 6 shows the ratio of ratings for question decomposition (QD for short) across all participants. In order to confirm whether the proposed method supports the hypothesis, we compared the ratio of ratings for QD in learning scenarios created with and without c-keywords. As for QD evaluated as "appropriate", the ratio of ratings for QD with c-keywords was significantly higher than the one without c-keywords from the results of the one-sided t-test ($t(26)=-2.34$, $p<.05$). As for the ratios of QD evaluated as "weak appropriate" and "inappropriate", on the other hand, the ratios of ratings for QD with c-keywords decreased compared to the ones without c-keywords. In particular, the ratio of QD evaluated as "weak appropriate" decreased significantly ($t(26)=2.56$, $p<.01$).

Figure 7 shows the ratios of ratings for QD in the high rating group. From the results of one-sided t-test, there were no significant differences between with c-keywords and without c-keywords. These results suggest that the hypothesis is not supported in the high rating group. On the other hand, Figure 8 shows the ratios of ratings for QD in the low rating group. From the results of one-sided t-test, the ratio of "appropriate" ratings for QD with c-keywords significantly increased compared to the one without c-keywords ($t(14)=-4.39$, $p<.001$). In addition, the ratios of "weak appropriate" and "inappropriate" ratings for QD with c-keywords also significantly decreased (Weak appropriate: $t(14)=2.75$, $p<.01$, Inappropriate: $t(14)=2.72$, $p<.01$). From these results, the hypothesis is supported for the low rating group.

Figure 9 shows the ratios of question decomposition rated as "inappropriate" and involving positive c-keywords evaluated as inappropriate in 4.1. From these results, about 60-65% of such question decomposition used inappropriate positive c-keywords in both groups.

4.2.3 Discussion

Let us first discuss question decomposition conducted by all participants shown in Figure 6. Overall, presenting c-keywords significantly contributes to increasing the "appropriate" rating for QD and to decreasing the "weak appropriate" rating for QD. Although the "inappropriate" rating did not significantly decrease, the results suggest c-keywords could promote appropriate question decomposition.

As for the high rating group, secondly, the results shown in Figure 7 suggest presentation of c-keywords was not effective for their question decomposition. In investigative learning without c-keywords, they could conduct appropriate question decomposition as shown in this Figure. This seems the main reason why c-keywords did not contribute. In addition, the ratio of the "inappropriate" rating for QD with c-keywords slightly increased. As shown in Figure 9, this suggests that inappropriate positive c-keywords prevented them from appropriate question decomposition. We accordingly need to improve the accuracy of extracting positive c-keywords by means of LOD and Word2vec.

Let me next discuss about the low rating group. The results shown in Figure 8 suggest that presenting c-keywords promotes their appropriate question decomposition, and that exercise questions could be effective scaffolding for novice learners. In addition, the ratio of the "appropriate" rating for QD with c-keywords in Figure 8 was higher than the one for QD without c-keywords in the high rating group in Figure 7. This result suggests that c-keywords allow the low rating group to conduct appropriate decomposition in the same way as the high rating group.

5. CONCLUSION

This paper has addressed the issue of how to generate exercise questions for self-directed investigative learning on the Web. Toward this issue, we have proposed a method of extracting and selecting keywords related to an initial question as c-keywords by means of LOD and Word2vec to present as exercise question. We have also conducted case studies to ascertain the appropriateness and effectiveness of the proposed method. The results suggest that the proposed method provides appropriate exercise questions, and promotes appropriate question decomposition particularly for novice learners. On the other hand, we have found out the necessity of improving the accuracy of c-keywords.

In future, we will address the issue how to generate exercise questions according to learners' skills by changing the number and the ratio of positive and negative c-keywords to be included.

ACKNOWLEDGEMENT

The work is supported in part by JSPS KAKENHI Grant Number 17H01992.

REFERENCES

Azevedo, R. and Cromley, J. G., 2004. Does training on self-regulated learning facilitate students' learning with hypermedia?. *Journal of Educational Psychology*, Vol.96, No.3, pp.523-535.

Azevedo, R., Johonson, A. and Burkett, C., 2015. Does Training of Cognitive and Metacognitive Regulatory Processes EnhanceLearning and Deployment of Processes with Hypermedia?. *Proceedings of the 37th Annual Meeting of the Cognitive Science Society*, pp.136-141.

DBpedia Japanese, 2016, http://ja.dbpedia.org/

Henze, N. and Nejdl, W., 2001. Adaptaion in open corpus hypermedia. *In International Journal of Artificail Intelligence in Education.* Vol. 12, No. 4, pp.325-350.

Hill, J. R. and Hannafin, M. J., 1997. Cognitive strategies and learning from the world wide web. *Educational Technology Research and Development.* Vol. 45, No. 4, pp.37-64.

Kashihara, A. and Akiyama, N., 2017. Learning scenario creation for promoting investigative learning on the Web. *Journal of Information and System in Education*, Vol.15, No.1, pp.62-72.

Kudo, T., 2013, MeCab, https://taku910.github.io/mecab/

Zumbach, J. and Mohraz, M., 2008. Cognitive load in hypermedia reading comprehension: Influence of text type and linearity. *Computers in Humman Behavior.* Vol. 24, No. 3, pp.875-887.

EXPLORING THE TEACHING EXPERIENCES OF TEACHERS USING COMPUTER-BASED ASSESSMENTS WHEN TEACHING INTERACTIVE MULTIMEDIA CLASSES

Nafeth Al Hashlamoun and Lina Daouk
Computer and Information Science Department, Higher Colleges of Technology, Abu Dhabi, UAE

ABSTRACT

This research explores the experiences of using Computer-based Assessments (CBA) in teaching an introductory level class called Introduction to multimedia (CIS 1503). This course is the first multimedia course in the Computer and Information Systems (CIS) department that is running at a Higher Education Institute in the Middle East (HEIME). It introduces students to various multimedia components such as 2D graphics, audio and video. The core objective of this course is to provide students with practical experience in various stages involved in the design, development and delivery of interactive multimedia content.
A phenomenological approach has been chosen to help understand and explore the participants' awareness of the phenomenon under investigation and that is "Using CBA in teaching interactive multimedia classes". Three specific questions were considered. These questions were investigated from the teachers' point of view.
The data explicitation process (as defined and used by (Giorgi, 2009)) resulted in forming four central themes representing the essence of the original ones. The central themes were: (1) to manage the teachers' marking load; (2) to enhance student satisfaction and attentiveness; (3) to support the management of assessments; and (4) to provide an effective archiving system for assessments and students' work. This was followed by a discussion of the opportunities and challenges arising from using CBAs in teaching this particular course. A description of the limitations within this research was also listed at the end of the study.

KEYWORDS

Computer-Based Assessments, Phenomenology, Assessments, Phenomenological Research

1. INTRODUCTION

The fast evolution of Information and Communication Technology (ICT) in the field of teaching and learning opened up new possibilities for delivering learning contents and examination. This has encouraged educational institutions to change from paper-based to computer-based assessments (Clariana and Wallace, 2002; Deutsch et al., 2012). In agreement with this and in accordance with their strategic planning, the HEIME has reviewed all its programmes with the aim of providing a learning environment of the highest standards. This was done by incorporating the latest teaching methodologies and learning technologies. In turn, teachers were encouraged to use proper technologies in order to meet the new challenges of designing and implementing assessment methods that go beyond the conventional practices.

Consequently, teachers teaching the CIS 1503 course shifted from using paper-based to computer-based assessments. The online tool that the CIS 1503 teachers used for their assessments was a Blackboard Learn tool called 'Tests and Surveys'. This tool was used to measure student knowledge, gauge their progress, and gather information from them.).

2. THEORETICAL FRAMEWORK

The theoretical framework used in this study is phenomenology, a theoretical framework that focuses on exploring how human beings make sense of their experiences and transfer these experiences into consciousness, both in isolation and as shared meaning (Patton, 2002). Phenomenology aims to clarify the structure and meaning of a phenomenon via the person's description. It is used to determine thorough descriptions of participants' experiences. These descriptions are used to conduct a "structural analysis which portrays the general meaning or essence of experiences" (Moustaka, 1994, p. 13).

3. METHODOLOGY

As defined by Maypole and Davies (2001), a phenomenological research is a descriptive method that tries to understand the lived experiences of the people who were involved with the issue that is being researched. The phenomenological approach must be clearly distinguished from the phenomenographic approach. They are related in that each is based on the term "phenomenon", which means "to bring to light". However, although phenomenography and phenomenology have much in common, they have different aims, methods and goals, and therefore different results. Phenomenography refers to a research approach aiming at describing the different ways a group of people understand a phenomenon (Larsson and Holmström, 2007). Likewise, it aims to document the range and variety of experiences informants bring to the topic of interest, whereas phenomenological approach aims to clarify the structure and meaning of a phenomenon. Following the same line of thought, a phenomenological study captures what the German philosopher, Husserl (1931) referred to as the "essential character" of the experience through the eyes of the participants (who are the "teachers" in this study). Hence, Phenomenology is an appropriate research method to discover what Husserl would call the teachers' lived experiences.

This study followed a phenomenological approach, with the aim of answering three different research questions. The first was about the range of teachers' experiences in using online CBA in teaching Interactive Multimedia classes; the second was about the values derived from using online CBA in teaching this particular course, and the third was about the changes that teachers have seen in students' day-to-day practices.

The phenomenological interviews were designed to bring forth the interviewees' awareness of the phenomenon under investigation (Marton & Booth, 1997, Moustaka, 1994, Prosser et al., 1994). Interviewees were provided with information about the aim of the study prior to participating in the interviews. Interviews lasted 40 to 50 minutes each. At the beginning of each interview, interviewees were asked 'seed' questions related to their previous experiences and the number of times they had used computer-based assessments while teaching the CIS 1503 course. Interviewees started by talking about their experiences in terms of the phenomenon under study (which is using CBAs in teaching this course). This semester, three CIS teachers are teaching the Interactive Multimedia course in Khalifa City campus, which is one of seventeen campuses that make up the HEIME. All of these teachers were asked to participate in the study. They all had taught the course before without using any computer-based assessment tool. The characteristics of the interviewees are presented in Table 1 below.

Table 1. Demographics of the Interviewees

	Teaching Experience	Number of times teaching the course without using computer-based assessments	Number of times teaching the course using computer-based assessments (including this semester)
Interviewee-1	9 years	4 times	2 time
Interviewee-2	17 years	1 time	1 time
Interviewee-3	10 years	3 times	2 times

4. THE EXPLICITATION OF THE DATA

According to Hycner (1985), an explicitation of data versus an analysis is necessary in a phenomenological research. The reason being that the word analysis implies breaking something into parts and consequently a loss of the whole phenomena, while explicitation looks at all the constituents of the phenomena, keeping the whole in context. In view of that, five explicitation steps were applied

4.1 Bracketing and Phenomenological Reduction

As stated by Gearing (2004), bracketing is a "scientific process in which a researcher suspends or holds in abeyance his or her presuppositions, biases, assumptions, theories, or previous experiences to see and describe the phenomenon". Similarly, Tufford and Newman (2012) define bracketing as a method used to mitigate the potential negative effects of the researcher's presumptions that are related to the study, and as a result, increase the rigor of the project. Moustaka (1994) has also suggested that the researcher should not make any presumptions and concentrate on a particular issue "freshly and naively". These recommendations were used to avoid improper subjective judgment and to allow the phenomena to emerge fully and holistically from the interviews. For instance, the researchers started the analysis of data by specifying what they thought they might find (such as: "both teachers and students believe that computer-based assessments are very good"). Then they put these expectations aside in order to hear what emerges from the data. This helped the researchers to extract the "pure" phenomena from the participants' viewpoint.

4.2 Listening to the Interview Recordings Repeatedly

As advised by Hycner (1985) and Creswell (2012, p. 273), the interviews in this research were listened to repeatedly to allow the researchers to develop a holistic sense of the phenomenon. Besides, Creswell (2012) stated that there is a need to read through the data in order to obtain an overall sense of the material. Hence, the transcripts were examined thoroughly more than once. Special attention was given to the non-verbal and para-linguistic levels of communication. For instance, two of the interviewees kept changing their voice levels and pitch along with the changes in the topics of discussions. One of them spoke softly and slowly when she was hesitant to discuss a sensitive issue. Oppositely, the other interviewee used an increased volume when she was happy about some issues.

4.3 Delineating the Codes (Units of Meaning)

At this stage, the researchers started to investigate the data carefully. They tried to make sense out of the text data by picking up the essence of the meaning expressed in words, phrases, sentences, paragraphs, and non-verbal or para-linguistic cues during the interview (Hycner, 1985). Further to that and based on Creswell's recommendation, the entire transcript was coded. "Coding is the process of segmenting and labelling text to form descriptions and broad themes in the data" (Creswell, 2012, p. 243). Hence, the interview data was analyzed for noteworthy statements, sayings, or quotes that help the researchers comprehend how the participants experienced the phenomenon. A list of codes (units of relevant meaning) was created, and redundant ones were recognized. This resulted in a smaller and more manageable number of codes. These codes are shown in the left column of Table 2.

4.4 Clustering of Codes (the Units of Relevant Meaning) to Form Themes

At this stage of the process, similar codes were clustered together to form the themes. To achieve that, the researchers tried to identify and group the codes that seem to "fit together" to describe a major idea. For example, as is illustrated in the second row in Table 2, the following codes: "Marking essays can't be automatic", "Marking the essay questions is an issue", "Not easy", and "Takes the same time" seem to fit together to describe the major idea "Difficulty in marking essay questions".

Upon the analysis of the themes that appear in the second column of Table 2, clusters of themes were gathered together creating what Hycner (1985) terms as "central themes" that express the essence of these themes. The clusters, the themes, and the developed central themes are presented in Figure 1. In this figure, the dark boxes at the top of the diagram contain the central themes, the bolded headings at the top of each white box represent the themes, and the points listed in the white boxes represent the codes (unites of relevant meaning).

4.5 Distinguishing Common and Unique Themes

Following Hycner's recommended list of steps describing the phenomenological analysis of interview data, themes that are common to most or all the interviews were identified. Subsequently, themes that are unique to a single interview were also distinguished. Finally, general and unique themes were placed back into the overall context from which they emerged (Hycner, 1985). The resulted general and unique themes for the interviews are discussed on the next pages. They are also shown in Figure 2.

Table 2. Codes (Units of Relevant Meaning) & the Developed Clusters (Themes)

Units of Relevant Meaning (Codes)	Clusters of Units of Relevant Meaning (Themes)
• "Automatic marking" • "Easy grading" • "Creating MCQ questions on papers needs more work" • "Reusing is an advantage" • "Collaborating and sharing resources"	**1) Reduced marking load**
• "Quiz every session" • "More quizzes prepares them slowly to achieve" • "The use of computers made it possible"	**2) Increased rate of occurrence of assessments**
• "Marking essays can't be automatic" • "Marking the essay questions is an issue" • "Not easy" • "Takes the same time"	**3) Difficulty in marking essay questions**
• "takes a long time to get used to the system" • "not so easy at the beginning" • "was not used to it" • "Faced some technical problems"	**4) Time consuming at the beginning**
• "instant feedback" • "Allows students to see their marks immediately after submission" • "Students know where they stand" • "they can get their results instantly" • "get the marks very quickly"	**5) Increased opportunity for timely feedback**
• "Used assessments to control attendance" • "Made them more participative" • "Progress in the students' performance" • "They are the digital generation. They can use these things easily"	**6) Encourages student participation**
• "Have to be very strong in using computers and sometimes in typing" • "Some students still prefer paper-and-pencil test" • "Resisted using it at the beginning"	**7) Requires specific computer skills**
• "they normally highlight what they believe is important" • "some students feel that using keyboards is very noisy" • "are used to writing notes and highlighting text"	**8) Some students still prefer traditional tests**
• "Randomizing questions" • "Nice features like randomizing" • "One Question at a time" • "Showing the exam question by question" • "Providing different sets of questions"	**9) Helps to reduce cheating in assessments**
• "students like it when they see their marks right away after submission even if they get low marks" • "Absorbs lots of students' shock in relation to the assessment" • "Reducing the number of complaints"	**10) Minimizes student complaints about marks**
• "Problems with technology" • "Lockdown browser may rise some technical issues" • "Lockdown browser froze on students"	**11) A possibility of facing technical issues**

• "A need for physical separators to eliminate the cheating incidents" • "There is a scope of cheating" • "Tendency of looking at each other's work" • "Taking pictures"	**12) Requires using cheating prevention techniques**
• "Archiving is easier to handle" • "less steps are required to archive. It became faster" • "a couple of clicks to get your files stored in a safe place"	**13) Students' work is archived securely**
• "Depends on how you set the system" • "the test must be downloaded first" • "There have been issues and we needed to call the educational technology specialist"	**14) Teachers need good technical skills to manage course contents**

5. THE STUDY RESULTS

As a result of following the steps in the data collection and explicitation process, the qualitatively different central themes below emerged:

1) Online CBA as a workload management tool
2) Online CBA as an instrument that enhances student satisfaction and attentiveness
3) Online CBA as a way to facilitate the management of assessments
4) Online CBA as an effective archiving system for assessments and Students' work

These central themes are described in more details below

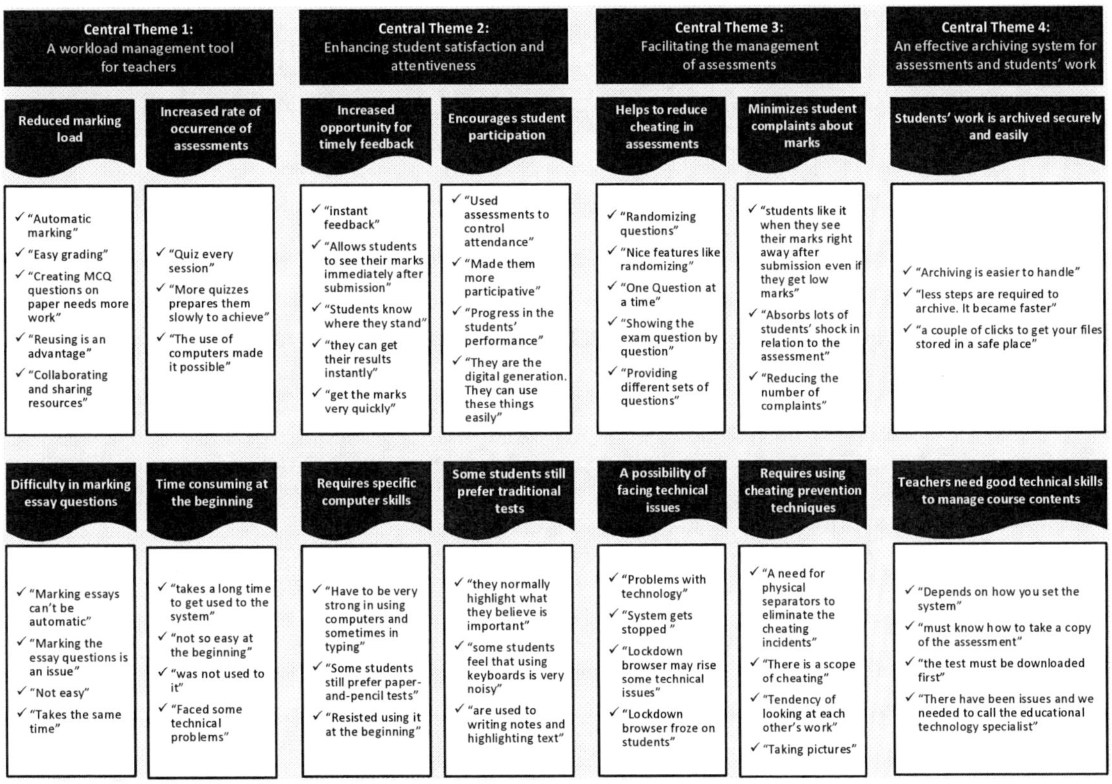

Figure 1. Central Themes, Themes, and Codes (Units of Relevant Meaning)

5.1 CBA as a Workload Management Tool

The data collected during the interviews indicated that using online CBA helped teachers reduce the time needed for marking, allowing them to spend their time in dealing with other critical work. This permitted them to spend extra time in creating and putting into operation higher quality assessments, and recycle the core concepts through other activities. This was demonstrated by the following comments made by the interviewees:

"It saved a lot of my time." ...(Interviewee-1)

"BB Learn gave me what I call easy grading. [...] I see it way easier" ...(Interviewee-2)

"we can utilize our time in doing other things." ...(Interviewee-3)

Additionally, some teachers believe that using online CBA allows them to increase the rate of occurrence of assessments. This was evident by the following comments made in the interviews.

"I am giving a quiz every session. More quizzes prepares them slowly to achieve" ...(Interviewee-1)

"it made it possible to give more quizzes" ...(Interviewee-2)

Although there seems to be concrete evidence that online CBA allows teachers to manage their marking load, the data gathered shows that teachers faced some difficulty in designing essay questions that can be marked automatically. As a result, some teachers had to mark some of the essay questions manually. This was evident by many comments such as the following:

"We tried to do that by providing the system with some acceptable phrases or sentences [...] I believe that marking essays can't be automatic." ...(Interviewee-1)

"There is always a possibility that the system marks it wrongly. I always double check the mark" ...(Interviewee-3)

In addition, one interviewee stated that she had to invest a great amount of time at the beginning to get used to the new system. Following is one of the comments she made in the interview:

"Most of us needed training on how to write questions and use available functionalities" ...(Interviewee-3)

5.2 CBA as an Instrument that Enhances Student Satisfaction and Attentiveness

This theme considers the likelihood of using online CBA as an instrument that encourages student satisfaction and attentiveness. The collected data indicates that online CBA increased the opportunity for timely and detailed feedback. This had a very positive effect on the students' satisfaction level as is clear in the following comments that are made by two of the interviewees:

"the feature that my students like the most is the instant feedback" ...(Interviewee-1)

"It allows students to see their marks immediately after submission. They love that!" ...(Interviewee-1)

"This helped them to get the mark very quickly." ...(Interviewee-3)

Interviewees also commented on how using CBA had encouraged students' participation. Two of the interviewees stated that they used computer-based assessments to control attendance by holding early morning assessments in class. This guaranteed that students came on time and participated for the rest of the class since they knew that they are likely to have another assessment at the beginning of the next class. This was evident by the following comments made in the interviews.

"In general, when students know they have a quiz at the beginning of the lesson, they make sure that they are in class on time. [...] this also made them more participative"... (Interviewee-1)

"Having these quizzes resulted in a good progress in the students' performance." ... (Interviewee-2)

Conversely, interviewees also believe that using online CBA will not be effective unless students already have acquired good technical skills. This was obvious in the following comments:

"Students have to be very strong in using computers and sometimes in typing. [...]was complaining that the time was not enough. The reason for is related to her typing speed." ...(Interviewee-1)

"Some students still prefer paper-based tests. They feel that it's not easy to use computers to provide their answers. [...] they resisted using it at the beginning. "...(Interviewee-2)

Furthermore, one interviewee indicated that some of her students still prefer pencil-and-paper assessments rather than computer-based assessments. She stated that these students felt more comfortable when taking the test on papers than on computers. They found it easier to read the text on papers, especially that they could highlight what they believe is important and add notes when needed. This was obvious in the comments of interviewee-2:

"Some of them may possibly feel happy with using pen and paper. [...]"...(Interviewee-2)

5.3 Online CBA as a Way to Facilitate the Management of Assessments

Some of the interviewees pointed out that online CBA facilitated the management of their assessments. They believe that using online CBA helped them to reduce cheating incidents. For instance, it enabled them to use a feature called 'random blocks' to help ensure that students see their own sets of questions. Random blocks select questions at random to be presented each time the test is taken. This was evident in the comments of two interviewees':

"Randomising questions was a good solution. It reduced the chances of cheating" ...(Interviewee-1)

"It is better to show them one question at a time."...(Interviewee-3)

Additionally, the data collected shows that using computer-based assessments helped the interactive multimedia teachers minimise the number of students' complaints about their marks. Interviewee-3 gave the following comment:

"the most important thing for many of our students is their marks [...]As you know, the number of students visiting the faculty room increases in the exam period."...(Interviewee-3)

"students like it when they see their marks right away after submission even if they get low marks. This doesn't only please them. It also reduces the number of complaints. They trust that computers don't make mistakes." ...(Interviewee-3)

In contrast, the gathered data shows that all interviewees are concerned about the possibility that students might experience technical problem during the exam. One of the interviewees even believe that at least one computer support specialist must be present at all computer-based exams. Following are some of the comments made by the interviewees:

"Lockdown browser froze on students. I had to ask for help from both the Ed Tech and the TSD guys. I had to stop the exam [...]"...(Interviewee-1)

"Lockdown browser may rise some issues."...(Interviewee-3)

Besides, another interviewee stressed that there is a chance that students cheat in a CBA. She recommends the installation of physical separators between the computers units used for testing at the college. She believes that this helps eliminate the cheating incidents. Following is one of her comments related to this point:

"Some students have the tendency of looking at each other's work. [...] Not having these physical separators increases the chances of cheating."...(Interviewee-1)

5.4 Online CBA as an Effective Archiving System for Assessments and Students' Work

This theme reflects on the possibility of using online CBA as an effective archiving system. The data investigation shows that two of the interviewees saw online CBA as an effective archiving system where they can store both the assessments and samples of students' work in a secure place. This was evident in the following comments:

"I personally prefer dealing with softcopies rather than physical ones. Now, it doesn't take more than a couple of clicks to get your files from a safe place" ...(Interviewee-1)

"less steps are required to archive. It became faster" ...(Interviewee-2)

On the other hand, some interviewees also believe that using online CBA as an archiving system will not be effective unless teachers already have been trained on how to store their files on Bb Learn and have learned to take full advantage of the system. Interviewees have all stated that they have attended a number of training sessions to be able to use this feature effectively. This was evident in the comments of two interviewees':

"We needed some training on the system to know about how and where we can store these files." ...(Interviewee-1)

"it was difficult to start with. [...] There have been issues and we needed to call the educational technology specialist. " ...(Interviewee -3)

6. COMMON AND UNIQUE THEMES

In order to understand and explore the participants' awareness of the phenomenon under investigation and that is "Using CBA in teaching interactive multimedia classes", the researchers started by identifying the similarities and differences between the experiences of the teachers who participated in this research. They looked for the themes that were common for most or all of the interviews, and then the themes that were exclusive to a single interviewee were noted. The outcomes of this phase of the analysis are depicted in Figure 2.

6.1 Common Themes (All or Most of the Interviewees)

Not all the emerged themes were common amongst all interviewees. The common themes amongst all interviewees were centered on *the reduced marking load*, the *possibility of facing technical issues,* and *the need for teachers to have good technical skills to be able to manage course contents effectively.* Additionally, Interviewee-1 and Interviewee-2 believed that using online CBAs allowed for an *increased rate of occurrence of assessments*. They also pointed out that this kind of automation of assessments *encouraged student participation and attentiveness*. Additionally, they both believe that *using online CBAs requires students to have specific* computer *skills.* They also claimed that using this tool allowed them to *archive the assessments and students' work easily and securely*.

Furthermore, Interviewee-1 and Interviewee-3 believed that using online CBA does not necessarily automate the marking of all types of questions. They declared that there is a *difficulty in marking essay questions.* They also pointed out that there is an *increased opportunity for timely feedback.* The last theme that was common between these two interviewees is that CBAs *helped them reduce cheating in assessments.* These themes (the ones shared between Interviewee-1 and Interviewee-2, and the ones shared between Interviewee-1 and Interviewee-3) are considered as common themes since the number of interviewees represents the majority that is two thirds of the sample.

6.2 Unique Themes (Individual Interviewees)

The analysis of collected data shows that some of the emerged themes were discussed by one interviewee only. For example, the theme focusing on how *some students still prefer traditional tests* was expressed by interviewee-2 only. Likewise, the themes related to *minimizing students complaints about marks,* the *great amount of time required at the* initial *stage of using online CBAs,* and *the need for using cheating prevention techniques* was only expressed by interviewee-3, and these themes are considered unique themes.

As argued by Tesch (1944), identifying the common themes is one way of recognizing the "invariants", the shared experiences that do not vary across the interviewees, and therefore, can be seen as the essence of the phenomenon or the phenomenon's constituents. However, the minority voices or unique themes cannot be neglected. They are as important as commonalities with regard to the phenomenon researched. These unique themes are seen as individual ways in which the phenomenon reveals itself. They can make us aware of the range of distinctiveness in the shared experience (Groenewald, 2004; Hycner, 1985; Tesch, 1944). Hence, both the common and the unique themes have been analyzed carefully.

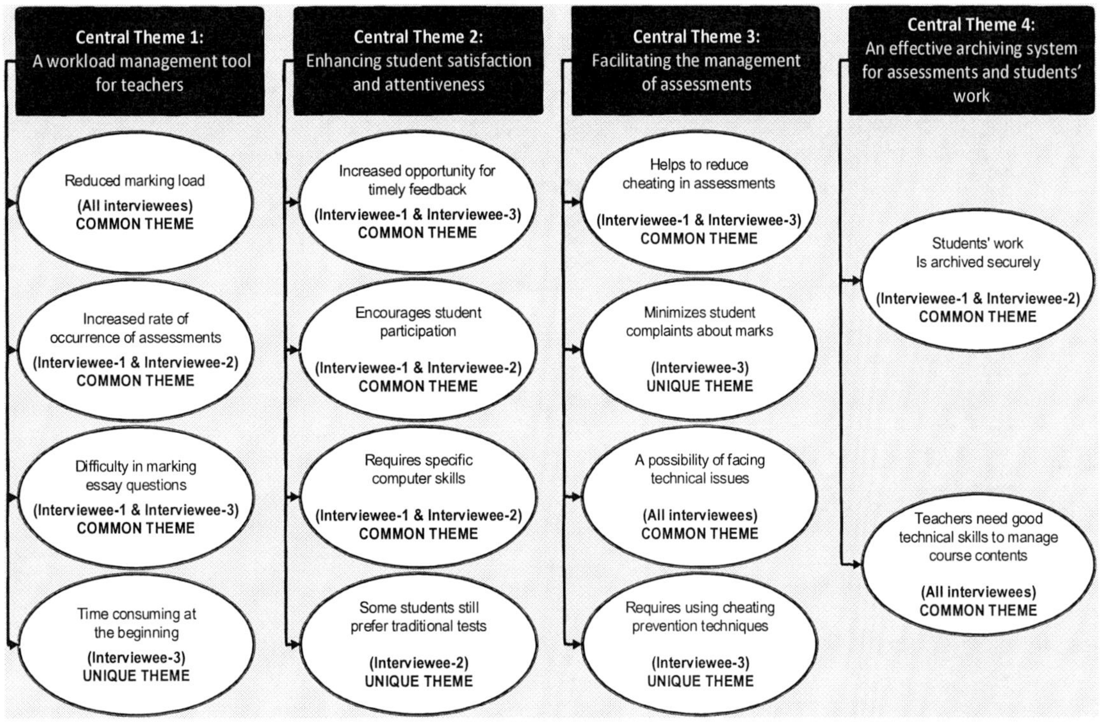

Figure 2. Common and Unique Themes

7. DISCUSSION

At the end of the study, the researchers rated their findings for a degree of match with the earlier specified expectations. Their findings are different from their expectations in that some expectations remained unconfirmed and some findings were not anticipated. For example, it became evident from the analysis of the emerged central themes that the use of online CBA is perceived as presenting both values and challenges. These are presented in Table-3 below.

All interviewees were able to identify one value of using online CBA in their Interactive Multimedia classes. This value is *the reduced marking load.* This value is consistent with the findings of Peat (2002) and Ricketts and Wilks (2001) who listed the 'reduction of marking load for staff' as one of the main benefits of using computer-based assessments. They believe that the time taken for marking and giving back the results compromises the time that can be utilized for general help and guidance. Similarly, Terzis, Moridis, and Economides (2012) listed time reduction as one of the advantages of using CBA.

Other values of using online CBA mentioned by most of the interviewees were related to: first, *the increased rate of occurrence of assessments*; second, *the increased opportunity for timely feedback*; third, *encouraging students' participation*; fourth, *reducing cheating in assessments*; and fifth, *the ability to archive assessments and student's work easily and securely*. The first and third values are in harmony with the findings of Bull and McKenna (2004) who indicated that one of the reasons academics may wish to use CBA is to increase the frequency of assessments, thereby encouraging students to learn, participate, and practice skills. The second value is in line with the findings of many previous studies. For example, Thelwall (2000) asserted that "the most obvious way in which computerization of assessment can be a virtue is through instant marking and feedback". He believed that instant feedback is often more effective than when given after a delay; the fourth value is consistent with the recommendation of Csapó et al. (2012) who studied a range of security issues in Computer-Based Assessment. This is due to the fact that randomization of items may pose other justice problems which might disadvantage or advantage some students; and finally, the fifth value is in harmony with the findings of Amelung et al. (2011) who assured that storing assignments and students' work centrally is very helpful, especially if they can be accessed quickly and easily.

Table 3. Values and Challenges as Percieved by the Interviewees

		A workload management tool for teachers	**Enhancing student satisfaction and attentiveness**	**Facilitating the management of assessments**	**An effective archiving system for assessments and students' work**
THEMES SHOWING VALUES	**Common Themes**	Reduced marking load **(All interviewees)**	Increased opportunity for timely feedback **Interviewee-1** **Interviewee-3**	Helps to reduce cheating in assessments **Interviewee-1** **Interviewee-3**	Students' work is archived securely **Interviewee-1** **Interviewee-2**
		Increased rate of occurrence of assessments **Interviewee-1** **Interviewee-2**	Encourages student participation **Interviewee-1** **Interviewee-2**		
	Unique Themes			Minimises student complaints about marks **Interviewee-3**	
THEMES SHOWING CHALLENGES	**Common Themes**	Difficulty in marking essay questions **Interviewee-1** **Interviewee-3**	Requires specific computer skills **Interviewee-1** **Interviewee-2**	A possibility of facing technical issues **(All interviewees)**	Teachers need good technical skills to manage course contents **(All interviewees)**
	Unique Themes	Time consuming at the beginning **Interviewee-3**	Some students still prefer traditional tests **Interviewee-2**	Requires using cheating prevention techniques **Interviewee-3**	

The value that was mentioned by only one interviewee *was minimizing students' complaints about marks*. This is seen as an obvious result of the immediate presentation of different types of feedback that provides students with an analysis and explanation of their marks.

Like any other educational technology, there are yet challenges to be addressed when it comes to the use of online CBA. The first challenge that all interviewees considered was *the possibility of facing technical issues.* Concerns about technical issues or discomfort with computer technology are acknowledged in the existing international literature. The second challenge is *the need for teachers to have good technical skills to manage the course contents*. That is, they have to know not only how to create and manage assessments, but also how to store assessments and related files and, ultimately, to organize the contents. Participants showed that a training session on how to manage the course contents is highly needed to be able to get the best out of using CBAs.

Other challenges of using online CBA mentioned by most of the interviewees were related to: first, *the difficulty teachers may encounter in marking essay questions.* Participants believe that writing essay questions may require providing many criteria per question, and even this does not guarantee a good level of automation. They stated that they always depend on manual grading; and second, *the need for specific computer skills*. Some studies have revealed that for a successful implementation of CBA, students require some degree of computer literacy (Alderson, 2000). Difficulties for students lacking computer skills and other technical issues are acknowledged in the existing international literature.

On the other hand, *the time required in the initial stage of implementation, the preference of using traditional tests,* and *the need to use cheating prevention techniques* were conceived as unique challenges. The reason why they are considered unique is that they have been mentioned by one interviewee only. The first challenge can be possibly alleviated by enrolling teachers in extensive BB Learn training courses upon starting the use of CBA; whereas the second challenge can be addressed by providing students with some help about using CBA in the classroom before introducing computer-based assessments. The researched finds the third challenge logical. It can be addressed by designing at least one assessment lab that has these physical separators installed. This lab can be used by different assessments related to different courses.

8. LIMITATIONS AND CONCLUSION

In this section, it is important to admit that the time constraint of this study has restricted the amount of data that could be collected and analyzed. This is seen as a limitation of this study as it constrained the researchers to conduct only three interviews, the minimum number recommended by Giorgi (2009), who stated that in phenomenological method in human science, it is recommended that one uses at least three participants. While the collected data were adequate to enable a phenomenological exploration of the range of experiences expressed by the teachers, having more time would allow for conducting more interviews, and therefore, provide sufficient opportunities for the full range of experiences communicated by the Interactive Multimedia teachers. Additionally, the applicability of the results of this study to a general population is questionable as the researchers explored the experiences of only teachers using CBA when teaching an interactive multimedia course.

To conclude, as shown in Table 3, the investigation of data has shown that the implementation of online CBA is perceived by the interviewees as presenting both values and challenges. This conclusion is not only based on the themes that are common to most or all of the interviewees. It is also based on the individual variations or unique themes since they are as important as commonalities with regard to the phenomenon researched (Groenewald, 2004). Additionally, this study has confirmed that some changes were seen in the students' day-to-day practices. For instance, the use of CBA has enhanced their satisfaction and attentiveness, and encouraged them to participate more.

On the other hand, as it is common with other research studies, this research has uncovered new research questions like: How do students feel about the use of online CBA? What factors affect male and female students' perceptions towards the use of CBA? Why there might be common or unique themes amongst the interviewees? In addition, how this particular implementation of CBA can be enhanced?

REFERENCES

Alderson, J. C. 2000. Technology in testing: The present and the future. *System,* 28, 593-603.

Amelung, M., Krieger, K. & Rosner, D. 2011. E-Assessment as a Service. *Learning Technologies, IEEE Transactions on,* 4, 162-174.

Bull, J. & Mckenna, C. 2004. *Blueprint for Computer-assisted Assessment*, Psychology Press.

Clariana, R. & Wallace, P. 2002. Paper–based versus computer–based assessment: key factors associated with the test mode effect. *British Journal of Educational Technology,* 33, 593-602.

Creswell, J. W. 2012. *Educational Research: Planning, Conducting, and Evaluating Quantitative and Qualitative Research,* Boston, MA, London, Pearson.

Csapó, B., Ainley, J., Bennett, R., Latour, T. & Law, N. 2012. Technological Issues for Computer-Based Assessment. *In:* Griffin, P., Mcgaw, B. & Care, E. (eds.) *Assessment and Teaching of 21st Century Skills.* Springer Netherlands.

Deutsch, T., Herrmann, K., Frese, T. & Sandholzer, H. 2012. Implementing computer-based assessment – A web-based mock examination changes attitudes. *Computers & Education,* 58, 1068-1075.

Gearing, R. E. 2004. Bracketing in Research: A Typology. *Qualitative Health Research,* 14, 1429-1452.

Giorgi, A. 2009. The descriptive phenomenological method in psychology; a modified Husserlian approach. *Reference and Research Book News,* 24.

Groenewald, T. 2004. A phenomenological research design illustrated. *International Journal of Qualitative Methods, 3,* Article 4.

Husserl, E. 1931. *Ideas: general introduction to pure phenomenology,* London : New York, London : Allen & Unwin New York : Humanities Press.

Hycner, R. H. 1985. Some guidelines for the phenomenological analysis of interview data. *Human Studies,* 8, 279-303.

Larsson, J. & Holmström, I. 2007. Phenomenographic or phenomenological analysis: does it matter? Examples from a study on anaesthesiologists' work. *International Journal of Qualitative Studies on Health & Well-Being,* 2, 55-64.

Marton, F. & Booth, S. 1997. *Learning and Awareness,* New yourk, Routledge.

Maypole, J. & Davies, T. G. 2001. Students' Perceptions of Constructivist Learning in a Community College American History 11 Survey Course. *Community College Review,* 29, 54-79.

Moustaka, C. 1994. *Phenomenological research methods. Phenomenological research methods. SAGE Publications, Inc,* Thousand Oaks, CA, SAGE Publications, Inc.

Patton, M. 2002. *Qualitative Research & Evaluation Methods,* Thousand Oaks, CA, Sage Publications:.

Peat, M. & Franklin, S. 2002. Supporting student learning: the use of computer–based formative assessment modules. *British Journal of Educational Technology,* 33, 515-523.

Prosser, M., Trigwell, K. & Taylor, P. 1994. A phenomenographic study of academics' conceptions of science learning and teaching. *Learning and Instruction,* 4, 217-231.

Ricketts, C. & Wilks, S. 2002. Improving student performance through computer-based assessment: Insights from recent research. *Assessment & evaluation in higher education,* 27, 475-479.

Terzis, V., Moridis, C. N. & Economides, A. A. 2012. How student's personality traits affect Computer Based Assessment Acceptance: Integrating BFI with CBAAM. *Computers in Human Behavior,* 28, 1985-1996.

Tesch, R. 1944. Emerging themes: The researcher's experience. *Phenomenology+ Pedagogy,* 5, 230-241.

Thelwall, M. 2000. Computer-based assessment: a versatile educational tool. *Computers & Education,* 34, 37-49.

Tufford, L. & Newman, P. 2012. Bracketing in Qualitative Research. *Qualitative Social Work,* 11, 80-96.

USING ACTOR NETWORK THEORY FOR DATA ANALYSIS

Suna Ryu
Korea National University of Education
250 Taeseontopyeonro, Cheongjusi, Chungbuk 28173, Korea

ABSTRACT

The present study explores how the visualization of an actor network enables researchers to understand mediating processes better by investigating relationships and effects among elements and entities other than human-actor accounts. In particular, the study presents how visualization may facilitate an understanding of the dynamics and structures of an ecological classroom and thus provide insightful reflections for analyzing data and for drawing conclusions. In doing so, the study explores the possibility that object-oriented thinking guided by actor–network theory (ANT) may allow researchers to understand what data means when the initial design/theoretical conjecture does not work.

KEYWORDS

Visualization, Actor Network Theory, Data Analysis, Classroom Research

1. INTRODUCTION

When conducting classroom research, researchers must deal with complicated data and understand what is happening at a given moment(Stainback and Stainback, 1988; Cobb and Whitenack, 1996). One of the advantages of conducting classroom research is the possibility of uncovering new findings outside of the planned scope through retrospective analysis. However, it remains difficult for researchers to deal with the complex data involved, particularly when trying to decide what to do when the known data points not do what the researcher wants them to do.

The difficulty increases as the definition of *learning* is shifting from the acquisition of knowledge to changes in disciplinary practices. The interpretation of these changes in practice requires researchers to consider many things, rather than simply, for example, a test outcome. To handle this complexity, the understanding of the mediation process from a sociocultural perspective has received increasing attention. For example, the analytical triangle of cultural-historical activity theory has been used to understand several kinds of mediation processes among subjects, objects, rules, and divisions of labor. Typically, human actors are centralized to provide a kind of cause–effect explanation. Any kind of mediating process is, thus, delineated to suggest or direct what/why/how humans think, talk, and behave for connotating certain social and cultural meanings. Consequently, our awareness and consciousness of taking the social and cultural meanings of mediation artifacts into consideration from a given cultural frame may restrict our ability to observe and interpret other hidden meanings that may arise through the data.

In this context, this study suggests that a visualized actor network may help researchers understand the mediating process better by allowing them to expand different possibilities of relationships and effects among elements/entities beyond human actors. In particular, this study illustrates how object-oriented thinking for the mediating process helps researchers to understand what data mean.

2. BODY OF PAPER

The basic premise of actor–network theory (ANT) is to examine what makes and sustains links. Any element of the material and social world can be an actor in ANT. The role of mediation is to maintain or restore links among actors. ANT explores and describes how any elements (e.g., human, nature, technology, and social rules) come and hold together to describe forces and ties within a network. While researchers usually investigate how members in a group influence each other or struggle for power, ANT treats other interactions the same as human–human interactions (Latour, 2005). The establishment of a network (typically, either in a small group or in a classroom for educational research) is described as *translation* and consists of four phases: *problematization, interessement, enrollment*, and *mobilization*. Problematization is the phase in which a problem is defined. In this phase, there is an obligatory passage point that actors must perform to obtain their solution. The interessement and enrollment phases are those in which the actors recognize the solution and become part of the network. Finally, the mobilization phase is the moment at which the network works stably and as expected.

Pragmatically, when ANT is applied in a small group or in a classroom, researchers identify the elements of a network to examine how connections are established, which enables them to understand what sustains/mobilizes the connections. For example, the inclusion of all entities as part of mediation processes helps us to move away from a typical, holistic approach of the teacher-blamed or student-matter frames for the success/failure of argumentation. When innovative scientific argumentation-centered curriculum or a new technology (e.g., talking and writing [TW] maps) were introduced to classrooms, some groups/classrooms functioned better/worse than did others. In most cases, a presumption held by researchers was that there would be competence/ability differences among teachers and students, and this would be the main reason for the differences shown. In the following sections, this is explicated in more detail through a case in which something unexpected occurred beyond the teacher-blamed, student-matter frame in the mediating process.

2.1 Data Sources, Analysis, and Interpretation: Different Uses of Post-Its (Using ANT for Uncovering Data)

During two consecutive academic years (2017–2018), high school students in the ninth and tenth grade participated in a scientific argumentation design-experiment by dealing with five science-oriented issues, five socio-scientific issues, and two science experiment topics for each year (Table 1).

Table 1. Topics of TW activity and scientific argumentation

Subject	Topic	Questions
Chemistry and Biology Integrated	Regularity of matter Combination of matter "Natural or synthetic vitamin?"	1. The iron and calcium around us are metal or ionic compounds. What does iron or calcium in vitamins look like? Do they exist in metallic or ionic form? 2. Can you design a scientific experiment testing your idea from 1? Let us describe your experimental steps to find the answer to 1 3. There are synthetic nutrients and natural nutrients. Investigate the differences between these two. Which is better? Please explain your choice (either natural or synthetic) based on scientific evidence
Physics and Life science	Interactive system "Design a ride that is both thrilling and safe"	1. Investigate and introduce one of the world famous rides and explain the amount of momentum and impact applied to it 2. Investigate two or more safety issues related to the rides introduced in 1. Think about possible solutions to resolve these safety issues

		3. Assume that you're a world-renowned creator of play equipment. Design a ride that is both thrilling and safe. What aspects of your ride make it more thrilling and safer than other rides? Please explain why
Physics and Earth Science	Earth as system "Propose a new government policy to prepare for an unusual natural phenomenon"	1. Can you think of an unusual natural phenomenon? What causes this phenomenon? Please explain the causes of this natural phenomenon scientifically 2. Interpret your answer to 1 in terms of the interactions of the components of the Earth system 3. Propose a new government policy to prepare for the unusual natural phenomenon selected in 1
Physics	Mechanics and energy "Design a ride that is both thrilling and safe"	1. Investigate and introduce one world famous rollercoaster. Explain the mechanical energy conversion 2. Explain how the following are related to the safety of roller coasters: (1) Why does the roller coaster not fall off the rail during rotation? (2) Why does a person on a roller coaster not fall off the rail while rotating? (3) What is the role of the safety bar? Why should one wear a safety bar? (4) Why do you think an accident would happen despite wearing a safety bar? 3. Assume that you're a world renowned creator of play equipment. Design a ride that is both thrilling and safe. What aspects of your ride make it more thrilling and safer than other rides? Please explain why.
Chemistry	Language of chemistry "Design an experiment to test whether 90% of eggshell is made of calcium carbonate"	1. Design an experiment to test the hypothesis that 90% of eggshell is made of calcium carbonate. Include the chemical reactions related to this experiment 2. Conduct your experiment. How does your result compared to your hypothesis? 3. Compare your group's experiment with the experiments of other groups. (If the result is different, please explain why.)
Earth Science	Changes in the earth's surface "What should we do when an earthquake happens and why?"	1. In 2016, an earthquake with a magnitude of 5.8 and of intensity scale VII occurred in Gyeongju City. In 2017, an earthquake with a magnitude of 5.4 and of intensity scale IX occurred in Pohang. While these two earthquakes shared the same Richter scale magnitude, the intensity scale was greater in Pohang. Why do you think the intensity scale was greater in Pohang than it was in Gyeongju?

		2. When an earthquake occurs, the Korea Meteorological Administration sends out emergency disaster letters. Compare the emergency disaster systems of Korea and Japan. Improve the current emergency disaster system 3. Refer to our school's manual on what to do when a disaster occurs. What should we do when an earthquake happens and why?
Physics	Electromagnetism	Some people say that the electromagnetic waves generated from electric blankets are harmful to the human body. However, some people think that these electric waves are not harmful 1. Design an experiment to verify whether electromagnetic waves are generated by electric blankets 2. Discuss the effects of magnetic fields and electromagnetic waves on the human body as caused by electric blankets 3. As a scientist, what do you think about the use of electric blankets? What is your conclusion?
Earth Science	Air pollution	1. What causes fine dust? Explain the reasons scientifically 2. How does fine dust affect the lives of young people? 3. Design a manual that minimizes the adverse effects of fine dust on students' health
Physics	Sound and light	1. Describe the principles of making sound from an electric speaker 2. Design a speaker that considers both performance and design
Chemistry	Structure of various molecules	1. Although water and ammonia have similar molecular weights, their boiling points are different. The boiling point of ammonia is -33.4°C, whereas the boiling point of water is 100°C. Explain the reason for this difference with regard to molecular structure 2. If the structure of a water molecule were not curved, what phenomena would happen in the natural environment? What kinds of changes would happen in our lives?
Physics	Electrical energy	1. Explain the principles of generating various kinds of electric energy 2. Discuss the most suitable energy generation method for our country. Consider various factors such as power generation, sustainability, the environment, and economic matters

Students used a modeling tool, TW maps (Figure 1), in which they came together to talk and then write down their arguments to develop a collective model. Our design conjecture was that group argumentation would occur if they were forced to write down their argument. After the completion of the group's TW map, a member stayed in the group as a representative to explain the group's map, whereas the other students in the group visited other groups. Students began to call this activity a *gallery talk*. By using 360° virtual reality cameras for each small group, verbal and nonverbal interactions were captured and observed. Interesting episodes (20% of all videos) were selected and fully transcribed.

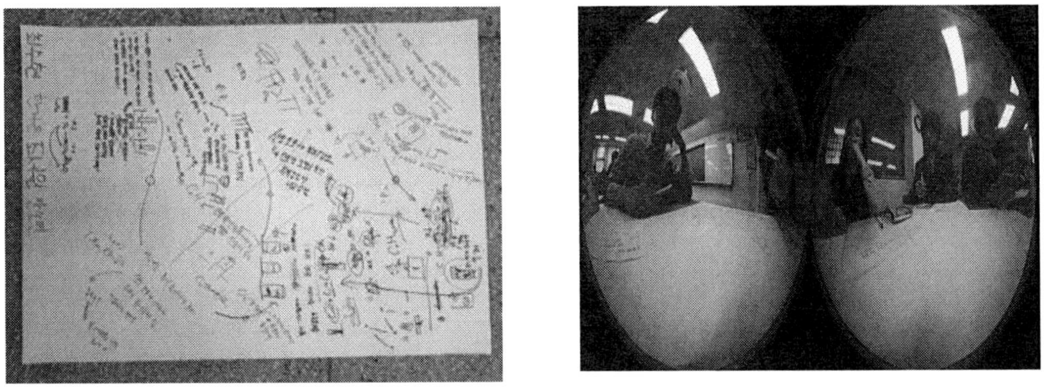

Figure 1. TW activity and 360 VR camera

After two months, a noticeable change in developing arguments was observed in one classroom across all small groups but not in other science classrooms. The change was that the classroom attempted to predict questions and reflections from other groups' members and prepared them ahead of time, which helped students develop arguments of better quality. Originally, our theoretical conjecture was that developing a TW map followed by a gallery talk would mediate students in such a way that they would demand evidence and justifications and discuss rules for good arguments more often to improve their argument quality. The gallery talks seemed to serve as a mediation process that produced better arguments by having students prepare questions and reflections from visitors.

However, an issue we faced from this data was why this occurred in only one classroom but not in the other four classrooms. The same science teacher taught all the science classes, and the classroom in which the students prepared questions was not a superior class. Using ANT, we examined the relationships between the tools and humans and their effects. In particular, we wanted to move beyond the typical expectation that some students are better participants than are others.

We first identified more actors in the network. While we were able to identify four actors at the beginning of this process (i.e., *students*, *TW map*, *small group discussion*, and *gallery talk*), we were able to add more actors as we began to include non-human elements, including *information resources*, *science practice experience*, *peer acceptance*, *experiment equipment*, *argumentation topics*, *assessment sensitivity*, and *communication competence*. Next, we described the relationships between the links among these actors. We traced how the claim was linked to the actors and found focal factors as well as obligatory passage points. When we analyzed students' work on the question "How can you design an experiment to determine whether the eggshell consists of 90% calcium carbonate?", we found a noticeable difference from the question-predicted classroom: post-it notes. While *post-it note* was not included as an actor in other classrooms, it was identified as one of the main actors in this classroom and was related to other actors, including *experiment equipment*, *argumentation topics*, and *peer relationships*.

A retrospective analysis was then performed. We traced how students in this classroom used post-it notes, and we compared this with the use of other classrooms. We also interviewed a few students and asked how they used post-it notes. Post-it notes were not an element used in the original design, which is the reason for our ignorance of their use during the initial observation. Students spontaneously began to use post-it notes because the space on the white paper was often limited, particularly during the gallery talk. To address this, the science teacher prepared and distributed post-it notes to each group. Students in this classroom took notes from the gallery talk, and the main part of the notes were composed of questions and reflections. Thus, when students visited other groups and received similar types of questions and reflections from others, they generated several more questions and reflections. Cumulatively, students became accustomed to asking and answering questions as well as giving and receiving reflections, all of which students had to prepare. It must be noted that post-it note-taking was also used in other classrooms; however, it was not identified as a main actor. The students used post-it notes in different ways. For example, students in one classroom used post-it note-taking as a way to summarize other groups' key claims. After taking notes from other groups, they came back to their own groups with these notes, enabling them to compare the differences and similarities between their writings and the claims of the other groups. In this way, the students scrutinized the accuracy of relevant science content knowledge by having the opportunity to compare arguments but did not necessarily reflect on and prepare questions in their argumentation practice.

2.2 Visualization of the Actor Network

While ANT provides core ideas and principles useful for analyzing messy and complicated data, ANT does not necessarily suggest specific ways in which to visualize a network. We came to think that a correlation measurement used in social network analysis can be useful in showing the relationships among actors within ANT. Thus, we applied some visualization techniques of SNA to identify the focal actors, the obligatory passage points, and the mediating processes in which actors interact with each other to produce effects. As the inter-node link in SNA represents social interactions, the line in ANT can be an intermediate currency in the network. Thus, in this way, the number, length, and intensity of lines correlate with the relationships between actors. The measurements of in- and out-degree lines and betweenness can be used to identify key actors and mediators in the network. The identification of in-degree lines for actors can be used to identify obligatory passage points. The map below (Figure 2) shows how *student-generated arguments* (A_number) related to other actors, such as *peer acceptance*, *science experiment*, *pre-existing knowledge*, *beliefs on claims*, *class topics*, and *TW tool*. The map shows obligatory passage points including *science experiments*, *peer acceptance*, *information resources*, *post-it note-taking*, and *task-proceeding remarks*.

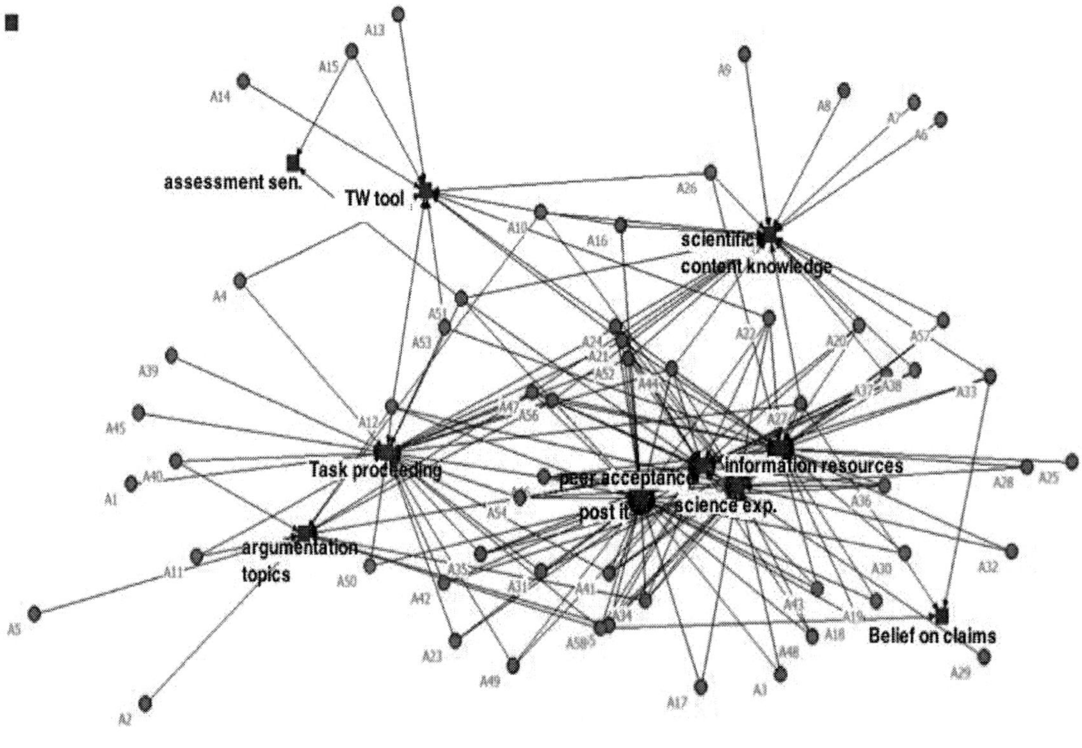

Figure 2. Key actors in student argumentation

It is quite interesting that *science experiments*, *peer acceptance*, *information resources*, and *post-it note-taking* are closely tied together, thereby increasing the eigenvector centrality, a measure of relative influence. For example, if two nodes have the same number of connections, a node connected to another node with many links maintains a higher eigenvector centrality than does one with fewer links. Although a more detailed explanation is required, the network suggested that the four actors were likely to be addressed simultaneously when argued.

3. CONCLUSION

A larger set of unexpected messy data is a common phenomenon in DBR. To handle this, we propose that using ANT with the visual technique of SNA may help researchers uncover the meaning of such messy data. In particular, focusing on ontological entities allows researchers to interpret the mediation process from other lenses, without adhering to the original theoretical conjectures, which often merely emphasizes human actors. The visualization of ANT enabled us to understand the structure and dynamics of classroom interactions. As a cultural resource, *post-it note-taking*—a way to record and provide questions and reflections, uniquely seen in one classroom—was identified as a mediator, which led to active feedback and discussion. If we did not use ANT, it would not have been easy to identify the role of post-it note-taking.

ANT provides fluid and complex—but extremely detailed—interpretations of the interactions between objects. From this multiplicity perspective, knowledge, learning, or practice is continuously produced and modified within webs of actors, which is consonant with the principles of DBR. Therefore, the flexibility and adaptability of ANT can be useful when conducting DBR for creating and modifying research plans as well as for data interpretation.

REFERENCES

Cobb, P. and Whitenack, J. W. 1996 'A method for conducting longitudinal analyses of classroom videorecordings and transcripts', *Educational Studies in Mathematics*, 30(3), pp. 213–228.

Latour, B. 2005. *Reassembling the social: An introduction to actor-network-theory*. Oxford university press.

Ponti, M., 2011, Uncovering causality in narratives of collaboration: Actor-network theory and event structure analysis. In *Forum Qualitative Sozialforschung/Forum: Qualitative Social Research* (Vol. 13, No. 1).

Stainback, S. B. and Stainback, W. C. 1988 *Understanding & conducting qualitative research*. Council for Exceptional Children.

Yaneva, A. 2016. *Mapping controversies in architecture*. Routledge.

USING KAHOOT TO IMPROVE STUDENTS' ACHIEVEMENT AND CRITICAL THINKING IN UNDERGRADUATE OF PSYCHOLOGY STUDENTS

Jaka Warsihna[1], Zulmi Ramdani[2] and Bagus Hary Prakoso[3]
[1]*Institute of Research and Community Service (LPPM), Indonesia Open University, Indonesia*
[2] *Faculty of Psychology, UIN Sunan Gunung Djati Bandung, Indonesia*
[3] *Centre for Educational Assessment, Ministry of Education and Culture, Indonesia*

ABSTRACT

Kahoot is one of the most popular evaluation methods used as an effective instrument in the learning process. As a platform of digital-based media, there are many advantages that can be gotten by using it, such as making easier and faster for teacher and lecturer in getting assessment results, reducing of the cost in making and duplicating a couple of questions, and psychologically improving students' attention in understanding material actively and openly. This is a preliminary study which is conducted using experimental design toward 60 of psychology students who attended the research methodology and psychometric courses. The purposes of this study are to explore the psychological factors that might happen during learning Kahoot media and to identify the effect of Kahoot learning in improving student achievement and creating a critical thinking character. The results of this study show that there is a significant difference between pretest and posttest score during the experimental period. Therefore, this preliminary study gives important information about the effectiveness of using Kahoot in the learning process.

KEYWORDS

Critical Thinking, Digital Platform, Kahoot, Psychology Students, Students' Achievement

1. INTRODUCTION

Globalization era and the growth of technology has been brought everyone to a deep attachment in all of human life and contexts. That situation also makes a change toward using of learning media and instrument which is more adaptive, especially in giving the accessibility of the information that was gotten (Esteves, Pereira, Veiga, & Vasco, 2018). The use of technology-based learning media in this digital era allows everyone to get optimal results by simply issuing simple efforts such as online-based media in evaluating student academic performance in the classroom (Boticki, Baksa, Seow, & Looi, 2015; West, 2013). The use of online learning media will further facilitate and accelerate the implementation of various activities or evaluations in learning.

Much of the research has been done shows the same information, where the use of online-based media in an innovative and certainly efficient media in organizing the educational process (Gómez-Peña, Sifuentes, & Finch, 2015). One of the platforms that are widely used today is Kahoot's media as an instrument in assessing learning outcomes. With various conveniences and benefits obtained by using this media, it allows each teacher to use it whenever and wherever as long as various facilities and situations around it support the existence of the use of Kahoot (Dellos, 2015; Lin, Ganapathy, & Kaur, 2018). On the other hand, the use of online-based media such as Kahoot is an alternative media that can be used to foster curiosity and the psychological state of students to be better (Plump & LaRosa, 2017). Among them are being able to increase psychological factors such as school engagement, intrinsic motivation, student achievement, and other related personal factors (Dellos, 2015).

The results obtained from Kahoot are not much different in terms of accuracy with the classical-based method the paper test (Ramdani, Widyastuti, & Ferdian, 2018). So that the media can be used directly to get teaching with more interesting methods and the results obtained are probably not much different. There has been a lot of previous research focusing on the use of Kahoot and its effect on student achievement in the classroom or in order to improve their various positive personal attributes in school (Dellos, 2015; Ismail & Mohammad, 2017; Lin et al., 2018; Yapıcı & Karakoyun, 2017). The use of Kahoot allows students to get more interesting learning method so that they not only increase their awareness of the importance of the material but also increase their efforts to actively learn and enjoy each learning activity. However, not many studies have tried to explore the use of Kahoot's media toward students' critical thinking attributes in schools, even though these psychological attributes are very important as part of higher-order thinking students and also how they continue their plans and lives in society (Amrullah, Tae, Ramdani, Irawan, & Prakoso, 2018).

Critical thinking is one of the important abilities that students must have in their learning process (Facione et al., 1995). One of these critical thinking skills can be developed using technology-based media such as Kahoot. The existing scheme in using Kahoot allows each student to prepare themselves as well as possible to determine the most appropriate choice they will face in the matter (Lin, Ganapathy, & Kaur, 2018). As a media with accessibility that is easily accessible to everyone, Kahoot can be one of the online media which then requires its users to think carefully with the answers they will choose because they are faced with limited time and accuracy in choosing answers (Lin et al., 2018). There are not many studies that try to see Kahoot's use of increasing critical thinking, especially in psychology learning. Whereas psychological material has a lot to do with concepts and theories that must be mastered specifically (Ramdani et al., 2018). So the use of online media such as Kahoot can make it easier to memorize and increase students' curiosity about deeper psychological material (Plump & LaRosa, 2017). This study tries to see the effect of Kahoot's media usage on improving student achievement and their critical thinking processes and how these factors interact in creating a better quality of education.

2. THEORETICAL FRAMEWORK

2.1 Kahoot as Digital Platform

Kahoot is an online media platform that used to evaluate the results of the learning process. It provides many interesting and useful feature, especially in doing an activity such as quiz, survey, and group discussion about learning (Dellos, 2015). The use of this media is very easy because the teacher practically only moves various questions and related cases that must be completed by students within a certain period of time (Lin et al., 2018). The implementation of activities using Kahoot is certainly very efficient to use in the classroom because the examination can be done together. This platform also provides an attractive display because it contains a collection of visualizations and music that are useful for stimulating not only the student's kinetic body but also to increase their curiosity about the material to be tested (Pede, 2017). One of the challenges that might be faced is related to external factors such as noise and the air temperature around it. In addition, the effectiveness of Kahoot's use can run optimally if it is equipped and supported by adequate of internet facilities.

Figure 1. Kahoot platform

2.2 Students' Achievement

Learning achievement is often the main indicator in seeing whether the learning process runs optimally or not. This learning achievement is manifested in various forms and activities all of which stem from the ability of students to understand and learn a material (Dunn & Kennedy, 2019). As one of the important factors in the learning process, learning achievement is highly related and determined by other factors that only appear personally, but also the influence of other extrinsic factors (An & Carr, 2017). Learning achievement determines whether can graduate at the next higher stage. The optimal or not a person's learning outcomes depend on how he prepares himself to get the best results. This also determined by the personal students who interact with the environment in which they grow and develop (Liao, Chen, & Shih, 2019). The use of appropriate media will result in more active and collaborative learning, especially if the learning is designed with technological progress and adapted to the dynamics that occur in the classroom.

2.3 Critical Thinking

Critical thinking is an intellectual and structural process which is actively related to the ability in conceptualizing, applying, analyzing, constructing, and evaluating information which is gotten through the process of observation, experience, reflection, reason, and communication (Boa, Wattanatorn, & Tagong, 2018). According to Sasson, Yehuda and Malkinson (2018), critical thinking is an important part of human life in understanding the complexity of the phenomenon. Critical thinking emphasis the students feel on the problem, having a strong and a clear perspective about the future life, full of consideration in doing tasks, and good at problem-solving and making a decision (Facione, Facione, Sanchez, & Gainen, 1995). This psychological aspect is closely related to various other aspects of life, such as in filtering information received by individuals, clarifying conflicts that arise, solving a difficult problem, even correcting a decision that might be wrong.

Critical thinking is important to be trained in daily life, especially when individuals get information related to uncertain rumours and issues (Sasson et al., 2018). The theoretical framework of the critical thinking starts from The Delphi Panel (Facione, 1990) by doing identification toward the key elements that might happen in the reasoning process while the critical thinking disposition refers to the human' tendency in dealing with the problem which is based on logical reasoning (Facione et al., 1995). Critical thinking encompasses various aspects that are not only in the form of the critical nature that is created within but also includes a set of abilities that are trained and developed to deal with various difficult and confusing situations. With critical thinking, students are expected to be able to develop themselves better in accordance with the demands of the environment.

2.4 Kahoot, Students' Achievement and Critical Thinking

The learning process which is based on critical thinking is needed, especially in getting the goals of learning (Amrullah et al., 2018). Students who have higher critical thinking criteria tend to have better academic performance, as well as those with average and lower critical thinking (Fong, Kim, Davis, Hoang, & Kim, 2017). The ability to analyze and interpret is the part of the planning process while the ability to evaluate, inference, and to make deduction are the part of making a decision process (D'Alessio, Avolio, & Charles, 2019). Critical thinking disposition is also able to increase the effectiveness of student learning in the classroom (Fung, 2017).

According to Pitt et al., (2015), critical thinking is useful for preparing everything needed by students in the learning process. Other research shows that there is a significant result between score, which is gotten from students with their academic performance (Pitt et al., 2015). Students' achievement and critical thinking are two psychological aspects which have been proven to get a lot of improvement when processed using online-based media (Esteves et al., 2018). The use of online-based media such as Kahoot allows students to prepare themselves as well as possible in the face of an exam that will be given (Licorish, Owen, & Daniel, 2017). This continues to their ability to prepare themselves, put themselves in the right situation, choose the best choice according to what they understand and try themselves to be prepared and always active in dealing with various severe social and environmental stimuli (Plump & LaRosa, 2017).

3. METHOD

This preliminary study is conducted using experimental pretest-posttest one group only design (Stephens, Matzke, & Hayes, 2018; Weger & Wagemann, 2015). The aim of this method is to see the effect of using Kahoot as an evaluation method based digital which is hopeful to improve students' achievement and their critical thinking dispositions. Samples were chosen by using a purposive sampling method where a researcher can select the subjects based on the criteria which were decided before the time sampling (Azwar, 2007, 2016). Samples who are in listed as a student in research methodology and psychometric courses in February until June 2019 period. All subjects who were participating in the research got the informed consents as a form of their willingness to follow the research.

The experimental study was done for 4 weeks, where the first week, subjects will be getting the material according to the courses guideline. The second week, they are given a set of multiple questions with using a paper-based test examination. In the third week, they get knowledge about how to use Kahoot as an evaluation method in their learning process and in the last week, subjects were given the same and parallel a set of questions using Kahoot media. After that, they also are given an additional questionnaire that measures critical thinking disposition as a form of validated criteria of learning achievement. Further qualitative analysis was carried out to get students' personal understanding of whether Kahoot's use was able to improve critical thinking indicators experienced by students before and after learning using Kahoot.

This preliminary study uses two measurements which were made by the researcher that measure students' learning achievement and critical thinking disposition. The learning achievement measurement tool is made by the method of preparing a cognitive test according to the material to be tested (Ramdani, 2018). The results are two forms of a set of questions that measure the learning achievement, each of which consists of 20 multiple choice questions with 4 answer choices. While the second measuring instrument is a critical thinking disposition scale that is made by modifying the theory of critical thinking (Facione et al., 1995; Facione, 1990). Analysis of the data used in this preliminary study was a Spearman correlation for the relationship of two scores, while for the test using Kahoot using a different test paired sample test.

4. RESULTS AND DISCUSSION

The preliminary study was carried out by looking at the differences in the pretest and posttest scores in 60 psychology students involved during the experimental period. Subjects consisted of 14 men (23%) and 46 women (77%) who were divided into two classes proportionally. But before a different test, is carried out, all the scores will be tested for normality test.

Table 1. One-sample kolmogorov-smirnov test

Variable	Sig.	Test Distribution
Pretest	.730	Normal
Posttest	.659	Normal
Total Score	.828	Normal
Critical Thinking	.923	Normal

Based on the results of the normality test in table 1, all the scores tested were normally distributed because the significance values produced to meet the statistical normality standard (>.05) where if the significance value of the score was above .05 then the data were normally distributed. All the data are correlated to see the relationship with the data being tested (see table 2).

Table 2. Correlations

Variable	Pretest	Posttest	Total Score	Critical Thinking
Pretest	1	.138	.063	.153
Posttest	.138	1	-.052	-.067
Total Score	.063	-.052	1	.231
Critical Thinking	.153	-0.67	.231	1

The information in table 2 explains the very weak relationship between pretest and posttest score (.138) so that with this result, further analysis can be done to find out the difference in scores in the experimental group. Other data also explain the moderate correlation between student achievement scores and their critical thinking characters with a correlation coefficient of .231 (see table 2).

Table 3. Paired samples test

	T	df	Sig.
Pretest – Posttest	-3.063	59	.003

The difference in pretest and posttest scores with paired sample test analysis produces a significance of .003 (see table 3). This shows that if the significance value is less than 0.05, then the significant difference in the pretest and posttest scores is significant, which means that the form of treatment used is able to improve learning achievement.

The use of the Kahoot platform is one of the alternative media that can be done by teachers in utilizing technological progress in a positive direction. Learning activities that are made with interesting and not boring conditions will increase the motivation to instil students to take part in the activity (Licorish et al., 2017). Research conducted by Plump & LaRosa (2017) shows that Kahoot's media contributes to improving student engagement and learning experience. In addition, this media is also able to make students more focused on facing all the forms of questions they receive (Plump & LaRosa, 2017). Psychologically, the use of Kahoot is able to provide a pleasant feeling for students because of it occurs a biological process that is received by the body by listening and seeing the display presented in the media (Licorish et al., 2017). Specifically, several related studies also provide information about the benefits of using this media. Explaining Kahoot is very helpful for students in testing their abilities in memorizing terms in science (Pede, 2017).

Research on Kahoot's media is very much related to various psychological aspects that not only affect the prestige of student learning, these media are also very closely related to the dynamics of critical thinking possessed by someone (Fong et al., 2017). The use of media that involves kinetic responses and raises curiosity about the object to be learned is closely related to the critical thinking character possessed (Plump & LaRosa, 2017). The more critical someone is about the things that will be learned, it will increase the effort involved to get the best results (Dehghani, Mirdoraghi, & Pakmehr, 2011). The results showed that moderate correlations between critical thinking and the restoration of learning meant that there was a significant correlation between these two variables. Although not yet tested for the effect of Kahoot on increasing critical thinking of students in this study, but from the initial assumptions of the researcher and strengthened by the results of the related literature analysis it can be predicted that Kahoot might also have an impact on increasing students' critical thinking. The use of Kahoot's media, which is consistent and directed, equipped with adequate technological quality, is considered to determine the success of the learning process of students in the classroom.

Additional interviews were conducted to find out how students feel and experience when using Kahoot as an evaluation instrument for their learning. The results of the interview support previous research that using Kahoot allows students to be able to think critically about the situation they are facing in relation to the subject matter being tested. In addition to being able to increase their interest and seriousness in learning and working on problems. Kahoot also plays a role in providing a new and more pleasant atmosphere. Although the results of the correlation between Kahoot and critical thinking have not been explored further, this research proves that the use of fun and challenging media can increase students' seriousness in facing lessons.

5. CONCLUSION

The preliminary study shows the informative description about the importance of using Kahoot as an innovative, attractive, and an effective media platform in the learning process. Some things that must be considered in the future include the quality of the material that will be applied in Kahoot must be clearly and properly validated, the use of quality internet and Kahoot' supporting media must be adequate, and the experimental procedure mode must clearly measure various other related psychological attributes. Further studies will also look at the psychological factors that occur during the administration of the Kahoot instrument by using a deep qualitative approach.

ACKNOWLEDGEMENT

This research is a longitudinal collaboration which is conducted by the Faculty of Psychology UIN Sunan Gunung Djati Bandung with the Center for Educational Assessment (PUSPENDIK), Agency of Research and Development, Ministry of Education and Culture of Indonesia.

REFERENCES

Amrullah, S., Tae, L. F., Ramdani, Z., Irawan, F. I., & Prakoso, B. H. (2018). Studi sistematik aspek kreativitas dalam konteks pendidikan. *Psympathic : Jurnal Ilmiah Psikologi*, *5*(2), 187–200. doi.org/10.15575/psy.v5i2.3533

An, D., & Carr, M. (2017). Learning styles theory fails to explain learning and achievement: Recommendations for alternative approaches. *Personality and Individual Differences*, *116*, 410–416. doi.org/10.1016/j.paid.2017.04.050

Azwar, S. (2007). *Metode penelitian*. Yogyakarta: Pustaka Pelajar.

Azwar, S. (2016). *Konstruksi tes kemampuan kognitif* (Edisi 1, C). Yogyakarta: Pustaka Belajar.

Boa, E. A., Wattanatorn, A., & Tagong, K. (2018). The development and validation of the Blended Socratic Method of Teaching (BSMT): An instructional model to enhance the critical thinking skills of undergraduate business students. *Kasetsart Journal of Social Sciences*, *39*(1), 81–89. doi.org/10.1016/j.kjss.2018.01.001

Boticki, I., Baksa, J., Seow, P., & Looi, C. K. (2015). Usage of a mobile social learning platform with virtual badges in a primary school. *Computers and Education*, *86*, 120–136. doi.org/10.1016/j.compedu.2015.02.015

D'Alessio, F. A., Avolio, B. E., & Charles, V. (2019). Studying the impact of critical thinking on the academic performance of executive MBA students. *Thinking Skills and Creativity*, *31*, 275–283. doi.org/10.1016/j.tsc.2019.02.002

Dehghani, M., Mirdoraghi, F., & Pakmehr, H. (2011). The role of graduate students' achievement goals in their critical thinking disposition. *Procedia - Social and Behavioral Sciences*, *15*, 2426–2430. doi.org/10.1016/j.sbspro.2011.04.121

Dellos, R. (2015). Kahoot! A digital game resource for learning. *International Journal of Instructional Technology and Distance Learning*, *12*(4), 49–52. Retrieved from http://citeseerx.ist.psu.edu/viewdoc/download?doi=10.1.1.694.5955&rep=rep1&type=pdf#page=53

Dunn, T. J., & Kennedy, M. (2019). Technology-enhanced learning in higher education; motivations, engagement and academic achievement. *Computers and Education*, *137*, 104–113. doi.org/10.1016/j.compedu.2019.04.004

Esteves, M., Pereira, A., Veiga, N., & Vasco, R. (2018). Teaching and learning in a digital world. *Advances in Intelligent Systems and Computing*, *715*, 499–506. doi.org/10.1007/978-3-319-73210-7

Facione, N. C., Facione, P. A., Sanchez, G., & Gainen, J. (1995). The disposition toward critical thinking. *Journal of General Education*, *44*(1), 1–125. doi.org/10.2307/27797240

Facione, P. A. (1990). *Critical thinking- A statement of expert consensus for purposes of educational assessment and instruction (The Delphi Report)*. California State University.

Fong, C. J., Kim, Y., Davis, C. W., Hoang, T., & Kim, Y. W. (2017). A meta-analysis on critical thinking and community college student achievement. *Thinking Skills and Creativity*, *26*, 71–83. doi.org/10.1016/j.tsc.2017.06.002

Fung, D. (2017). The pedagogical impacts on students' development of critical thinking dispositions: Experience from Hong Kong secondary schools. *Thinking Skills and Creativity*, *26*(November 2016), 128–139. doi.org/10.1016/j.tsc.2017.10.005

Gómez-Peña, G., Sifuentes, R., & Finch, M. (2015). Technology: Learning can be fun and games. *Gifted Child Today*, *60*(1), 33–39. doi.org/10.1080/00043249.2001.10792048

Ismail, M. A.-A., & Mohammad, J. A.-M. (2017). Kahoot: A promising tool for formative assessment in medical education. *Education in Medicine Journal*, *9*(2), 19–26. doi.org/10.21315/eimj2017.9.2.2

Liao, C. W., Chen, C. H., & Shih, S. J. (2019). The interactivity of video and collaboration for learning achievement, intrinsic motivation, cognitive load, and behaviour patterns in a digital game-based learning environment. *Computers and Education*, *133*, 43–55. doi.org/10.1016/j.compedu.2019.01.013

Licorish, S. A., Owen, H., & Daniel, B. K. (2017). "Go kahoot!" Enriching classroom engagement, motivation and learning experience with games. *Proceedings of the 25th International Conference on Computers in Education. New Zealand: Asia-Pacific Society for Computers in Education*, 755–764. Retrieved from https://www.researchgate.net/publication/322150947

Lin, D. T. A., Ganapathy, M., & Kaur, M. (2018). Kahoot! It: Gamification in higher education. *Pertanika Journal of Social Sciences and Humanities*, *26*(1), 565–582.

Pede, J. (2017). *The effects of the online game Kahoot on science vocabulary acquisition Part of the Science and Mathematics Education Commons, and the Special Education and Teaching Commons*. Retrieved from http://rdw.rowan.edu/etdhttp://rdw.rowan.edu/etd/2405

Pitt, V., Powis, D., Levett-Jones, T., & Hunter, S. (2015). The influence of critical thinking skills on performance and progression in a pre-registration nursing program. *Nurse Education Today*, *35*(1), 125–131. doi.org/10.1016/j.nedt.2014.08.006

Plump, C. M., & LaRosa, J. (2017). Using Kahoot! in the Classroom to Create Engagement and Active Learning: A Game-Based Technology Solution for eLearning Novices. *Management Teaching Review*, *2*(2), 151–158. doi.org/10.1177/2379298116689783

Ramdani, Z. (2018). Construction of academic integrity scale. *International Journal of Research Studies in Psychology*, *7*, 87–97. doi.org/10.5861/ijrsp.2018.3003

Ramdani, Z., Widyastuti, T., & Ferdian, F. R. (2018). Penerapan analisis teori klasik, model rasch, dan computer based test moodle : Sebuah pilot studi. *Indonesian Journal of Educational Assessment P-ISSN*, *2*(1), 21–30.

Sasson, I., Yehuda, I., & Malkinson, N. (2018). Fostering the skills of critical thinking and question-posing in a project-based learning environment. *Thinking Skills and Creativity*, *29*, 203–212. doi.org/10.1016/j.tsc.2018.08.001

Stephens, R. G., Matzke, D., & Hayes, B. K. (2018). Disappearing dissociations in experimental psychology: Using state-trace analysis to test for multiple processes. *Journal of Mathematical Psychology*, (XXXX). doi.org/10.1016/j.jmp.2018.11.003

Weger, U., & Wagemann, J. (2015). The challenges and opportunities of first-person inquiry in experimental psychology. *New Ideas in Psychology*, *36*, 38–49. doi.org/10.1016/j.newideapsych.2014.09.001

West, D. M. (2013). Mobile learning : Transforming education, engaging student, and improving outcomes. *Center for Technology Innovation at Brookings*, (September).

Yapıcı, İ. Ü., & Karakoyun, F. (2017). Gamification in biology teaching: A sample of Kahoot application. *Turkish Online Journal of Qualitative Inquiry*, *8*(4), 396–414. doi.org/10.17569/tojqi.335956

EXPLORING THE EFFECTS OF STRUCTURAL TRANSPARENCY AND EXPLORATORY GUIDANCE IN SIMULATION-BASED LEARNING ENVIRONMENTS

Carlos Capelo[1] and Ana Lorga[2]
[1]*Universidade Europeia, Estrada da Correia, 53, 1500-210 Lisboa – Portugal*
[2]*Universidade Lusófona de Humanidades e Tecnologias, Campo Grande, 376, 1749-024 Lisboa – Portugal*

ABSTRACT

Simulation-based learning environments are used extensively to support learning on complex business systems. Nevertheless, there exist studies that identify problems and limitations due to cognitive processing difficulties. Particularly, previous research addressed some aspects of model transparency and instructional strategy and produced inconclusive results about their impact on learning effectiveness. This study investigates the learning effects of using transparent simulations (that is, showing users the internal structure of models), and exploratory guidance (that is, guiding learners so they are able to explore the simulation by themselves, supported by specific cognitive aids). We present a set of hypotheses about the influence of the degree of simulator transparency and the degree of exploratory guidance on participants' model comprehension which is assessed in terms of mental model structure and behaviour similarities. A test based on a simulation experiment with a system dynamics model, representing a supply chain system, was performed. Participants are required to use the simulator to investigate on some issues related to the bullwhip effect and other supply chain coordination concepts. Participants provided with the more transparent strategy and offered the more exploratory guidance demonstrated better understanding of the structure and behaviour of the underlying model. However, our results suggest that while exploratory guidance is a beneficial method for both model structure and behaviour understanding, making solely the model transparent is more limited in its effect.

KEYWORDS

Management Education, Simulation-Based Learning, System Dynamics, Model Transparency, Instructional Guidance, Supply Chain Management, Bullwhip Effect

1. INTRODUCTION

1.1 Simulation-Based Learning in Management Education

Research has suggested that the use of SBLEs frequently induces active learner behaviour, scientific reasoning and constructive learning processes (de Jong and van Joolingen 1998). Particularly, studies have shown that (SBL) with system dynamics (SD) can support and enhance learning. SD is a scientific approach for (computer-based) modelling and simulation developed to facilitate our understanding and management of complex, dynamic systems (Davidsen and Spector, 2015). The models are expressed graphically so as to facilitate effective description about the systems they intend to represent.

From a mental models perspective, students can use the simulation program to support the construction and improvement of their mental models. They form an initial mental model and develop into a target conceptual model (the same one underlying the simulation model). Moreover, SBL facilitates improving the learner's mental models by engaging in inquiry that is otherwise impractical or even impossible.

Simulators are promising tools for teaching in the management domain. Studies have shown that students perceive simulation as a more effective method than text-based case study and lecture (Farashahi and Tajeddin, 2018). However, evidence regarding the impact of their utilization remains limited (Lean at al., 2015). Therefore, a need exists for more research addressing how the learning potential of such environments might be enhanced (Davidsen and Spector, 2015). According to the literature, the effectiveness of SBLEs depends on many factors related to the learning context. The present study focusses on two aspects: simulator transparency and instructional strategy.

1.2 Simulator Transparency and Instructional Guidance

Simulator transparency refers to what extent the structure of the underlying computational model is shown to students using the simulation. In black-box model simulations, students can explore a system's behaviour, but the underlying computational models remain hidden and can only be inferred by what appears on the screen. Studies have suggested that this type of ''black-box'' situation could lead students to form wrong mental models, interfering with proper learning. "Glass-box model'' or ''transparent'' simulations have alternatively been proposed to obviate the above-described problems, as their relations among variables are accessible by the students. Transparent simulators have been used in SD learning environments, which provide their stocks-and-flows diagram (SFD) detailing the causal structure of the underlying system. By using this approach, students may trace the cause and effect structure and understand the relationships between structure and behaviour (Milrad et al., 2003), and they have the potential to understand even counterintuitive system behaviours (Groesser, 2012).

Research shows that structural knowledge provided by transparent simulations has the potential to improve leaning and task performance (Größler et al., 2000; Qudrat-Ullah, 2007). Kopainsky and Alessi (2015) found that participants provided with the more transparent strategy demonstrated better understanding of the underlying model, but their performance, however, was the equivalent to those in the less transparent condition. The implication of previous study is that the students must not only identify the structure of the simulator model, but will also have to recognize the relationship between structure and behaviour (Davidsen and Spector, 2015).

Instructional guidance refers to the support provided to students during simulation in the form of questions, hints, procedures, steps, or materials. The associated issue is about how much and what type of instructional guidance needs to be offered in order to optimize the learning potential of simulations. In SBL, direct instruction occurs when detailed instructions are given, and students must learn the underlying concepts through a sequence of programmed steps. In inquiry learning method, general questions or learning goals are presented, and students are free to explore the SBLE. Studies have found that students achieve deeper understanding of subject matter when developing scientific reasoning (Clement, 2008), as they formulate hypotheses, define actions and scenarios, conduct experiments, interpret simulation results, and draw conclusions. However, research on inquiry learning with computer simulations (for example: de Jong, 2006) found evidences that students operating in complex simulation environments generally have difficulty in all phases of the inquiry process. Cognitive load theory (Sweller et al., 2011) provides an explanation for those problems. In a simulation task, the complexity of the model may exceed the working memory limits of participants. To obviate these "cognitive load" problems and increase the effectiveness of simulation, de Jong (2006) suggests that instructional method be integrated with ''cognitive tools'' aimed at guiding and supporting the students' activities. Van Borkulo et al. (2012) argue that, to enhance model-based learning, students need to be walked through each element of the model (approach known as model progression), allowing participants to incrementally build their mental models. Mulder et al. (2015) examined how model progression and worked examples can promote inquiry learning and found positive effects due to both increasing model complexity and providing worked examples.

2. RESEARCH HYPOTHESES

This research focuses on the issue of which model transparency and instructional guidance conditions are the most suited for optimizing the learning potential of simulation for teaching the bullwhip effect and SCC, leading to enhanced student understanding of their main concepts. The analysis of the students' understanding of the simulation model considers two components: the comprehension of model structure and the comprehension of model behaviour. The expected relations and hypotheses are based on the following variables:

(i) Level of Model Transparency (LMT) – this variable represents the transparency level of the simulator. LMT indicates to what extent students have access to the variables and relations included in the model.

(ii) Level of Exploratory Guidance (LEG) – this variable represents the exploratory level of the instructional method used to guide students throughout the simulation task. LEG indicates to what extent students may choose methods and activities to explore the SBLE.

(iii) Comprehension of the model structure (CMS) - this variable indicates to what extent students understand the structure of the simulation model. CMS measures the similarity between the structure of the external representation of the students' mental models and the structure of the simulation model.

(iv) Comprehension of the model behaviour (CMB) - this variable indicates to what extent students are able to understand and infer the dynamical behaviour of the SCC simulator. CMB measures the similarity between the student's expectation on model behaviour (inference of student's mental models) and the actual behaviour of the simulation model.

The following hypotheses are defined: H1- LMT positively influences CMS, H2- LMT positively influences CMB, H3- LEG positively influences CMS, H4- LEG positively influences CMB, and H5- CMS positively influences CMB.

3. METHOD

3.1 Simulator, Participants, Procedure, and Facilitation

The SD model incorporated in the simulator represents a supply chain of a beer distribution system. It is based on the famous board game (the beer game) first developed in the 1960s at the Massachusetts Institute of Technology. The simulator interface includes three screens. The first screen is separated into three sections: (i) one section allows participants to adjust simulation parameters, (ii) a second section include three graphics that present the historical behaviour over time for inventory, supply flows, and order backlog for each of the supply chain stages, and (iii) a third section with a table presenting performance measures. A second screen provides a description of each of the variables in use. A third screen, when available, shows the SFD of the simulator model.

The participants define the experiment scenario, adjust the parameters accordingly and run the supply chain simulator for a period of six months. Then, they observe the graphics to analyse the behaviour over time and appreciate the overall performance indicators.

In order to test the model of hypotheses, a 2x2 experimental design with four treatment groups was defined: two groups (A and C) of participants who interact with an opaque simulator (low LMT), two groups (B and D) who use a transparent simulator (high LMT), two groups (A and B) who receive step by step instructions (low LEG), and two groups (C and D) who receive exploratory guidance (high LEG).

This research was conducted at Universidade Europeia in Lisbon. The experiment involved four classes of supply chain management courses (with 93 students in total). Each one of the four different experimental treatments was assigned randomly to one of the four classes. As participants from group A are submitted to the basic conditions (low LMT and low LEG), the present quasi-experiment design considers groups B, C, and D as experimental groups, while group A assumes the role of control group.

All the participants, from both experimental and control groups, were familiar with the concepts included in the simulator, as they attended lecture classes on supply chain coordination and bullwhip effect. The experiment was carried out individually in class with a participant per computer. All students were given a full experimental guide including: presentation of the simulator, objectives, instructions for accessing, starting, and running the simulator, instructions for performing the simulation task, SFD of the simulator model (only for treatment groups B and D), and sheets for recording scenarios and results.

In the simulation experiment, the participants were asked to investigate the impact of some factors on supply chain performance. The following five factors were considered: demand irregularity, demand information sharing, supply line control, order fraction, and inventory cover. Past research found that students operating in complex simulation environments generally have considerable difficulty in all phases of the inquiry process (de Jong 2006). To obviate these problems, previous studies (van Borkulo et al.,2012; Elsawah et al., 2017; Mulder et al., 2015) suggest that participants need to be guided through the simulation model, gradually increasing the task complexity (model progression). And according to Mulder et al. (2015), complementing model progression with worked examples enhances students' inquiry performance and learning. Consequently, the students from groups C and D (submitted to exploratory guidance) address the five factors sequentially and one at a time. And they are also guided to firstly analyse performance effects caused by the factor being addressed and then to look at potential interactions with other factors previously analysed. Additionally, the students (from groups C and D) receive a demonstration on how to investigate the supply chain effects of the first factor (demand irregularity) by defining hypotheses and scenarios, adjusting the parameters, running the simulator, and interpreting the results.

Treatment		Experimental Procedure								
		a) Lecture on SFDs	b) Description of the model SFD	c) Objectives and task description	d) Instructions about simulator	e) Simulation according to step-by-step guidance	e) Simulation according to exploratory guidance (*)	e) SFD visible during simulation	f) Instructions on causal diagramming	g) Final questionnaire
A	Low LMT, low LEG			●	●	●			●	●
B	High LMT, low LEG	●	●	●	●	●		●	●	●
C	Low LMT, high LEG			●	●		●		●	●
D	High LMT, high LEG	●	●	●	●		●	●	●	●

(*) Including work examples in the inquiry process and model progression approach

Figure 1. Experimental procedure

The experiment procedure involved three sessions and had the following steps (figure 1).

Session 1: This session involved only the participants from experimental groups B and D. (a) The students received a lecture on SFDs, so that they were able to read and interpret the SFD representing the simulator model. Then, (b) the instructor described the SFD to the students in a form of a guided tour.

Session 2: In this session, the students performed the simulation task. (c) The students read the introduction with the overall description and the objectives of the simulation task. (d) The participants read the instructions for accessing, starting and running the simulator. Some simulation runs were conducted to familiarise participants with the game interfaces and commands. (e) The participants performed the simulation task, following the instructions included in the experimental guide. Students from experimental groups A and B adjusted the parameters and run the simulator according to step-by-step instructions that guide them to discover the performance effects of those parameters. Students from experimental groups C and D were free to explore the simulator. They analysed the questions to be addressed, defined hypotheses and scenarios, adjusted the selected parameters, run the simulator, interpreted the results, defined new hypotheses scenarios, and repeated the process. As mentioned before, the students from groups C and D were guided through work examples on how to perform this inquiry process and according to model progression approach. During the simulation task, the participants from experimental groups B and D were encouraged to read the SFD. The students were also instructed to ask for support if they found any difficulties in reading the SFD (groups B and D) or in any stage of the inquiry process (groups C and D).

Session 3: (f) Firstly, the students received instruction in how to read and draw a causal-loop diagram (CLD). (g) Then, they individually answered a questionnaire to measure learning on the simulator model, which consists of two parts. In the first part, they were asked to complete a CLD representing the simulator model. Students had to fill in the empty boxes writing the corresponding concepts, which they selected from a list of eleven missing concepts. They also had to identify eight missing links between the concepts and draw the corresponding arrows and signs that indicated the cause-and-effect relationships. In the second part the students responded to twenty multiple-choice questions related to the behaviour of the model. No pre-test was given (before the simulation task) because the topic tested (simulator model) was new material for all the students. And they did not previously know about the questionnaire that they would be required to answer.

3.2 Research Variables

This section summarises the use of the variables that were defined in the research model.

Level of Model Transparency (LMT) – This variable features two degrees. In the low degree (low LMT), the students perform the simulation task without accessing the SFD of the simulator model (treatment groups A and C). In the high degree (high LMT), the students, during simulation task, have access to the SFD representing the simulator model (treatment groups B and D).

Level of Exploratory Guidance (LEG) – This variable features two degrees. In the low degree (low LEG - treatment groups A and B), the students perform the simulation task by strictly following the "step-by-step" instructions provided. For each issue being addressed, they replace the parameters with the values given, run the simulator and observe the results. The students are not encouraged to reason scientifically. In the high degree (high LEG - treatment groups C and D), the students are free to explore the simulator, performing all the simulation runs they need. This experiment condition is designed in order to foster scientific reasoning and promote inquiry learning with appropriate aids. They are asked to investigate the supply chain performance effects of the selected factors. The students reflect on each issue, formulate some hypotheses about model behaviour, and define experimental scenarios in order to test those hypotheses (including the parameters to be adjusted and corresponding values). They run the simulator, interpret the results, test the hypotheses, attempt to explain model behaviour, and determine further steps before the cycle repeats.

Comprehension of the model structure (CMS) - this variable measures the similarity between the structure of the external representation of the students' mental models and the structure of the simulation model. As the structure of the simulation model is known by the researchers in advance, it can be compared with the participants' mental model in order to evaluate how that elicited mental model matched the simulated reality. As described in previous section, the students were asked to complete a causal-loop diagram representing the simulator model by inserting some missing concepts (eleven) and links (eight). This diagram represented the elicited structure of the students' mental model. Each concept or link answered was worth one point. Thus, CMS ranges from 0 to 19.

Comprehension of the model behaviour (CMB) - this variable measures the similarity between the student's expectation on model behaviour (inference of student's mental models) and the actual behaviour of the simulation model. In the second part of the final questionnaire, the students responded to multiple-answer questions related to the dynamical behaviour of the model (20 questions). Each question was worth one point. Thus, CMB ranges from 0 to 20.

4. RESULTS AND DISCUSSION

Table 1 presents the mean values, standard deviations, and sample sizes for the dependent variables CMS and CMB corresponding to the four experimental treatments. Table 2 displays the results of an independent-samples t-test of significance for differences in means between pairs of treatment groups.

Table 1. Means and standard deviations for variables CMS (Comprehension of Model Structure) and CMB (Comprehension of Model Behaviour) for the four experimental groups

			CMS - Comprehension of Model Structure		CMB - Comprehension of Model Behaviour	
Treatment	Description	N	Mean	SD	Mean	SD
A/CG	Low LMT, low LEG	24	6.167	2.761	5.833	1.659
B	High LMT, low LEG	23	9.609	5.408	6.217	2.194
C	Low LMT, high LEG	22	8.000	4.546	7.227	2.581
D	High LMT, high LEG	24	14.292	4.379	8.667	2.929

Variable definitions: LMT - Level of Model Transparency; LEG - Level of Exploratory Guidance

Table 2. Independent-samples t-test of significance for differences in means between pairs of treatment groups

	CMS - Comprehension of Model Structure			CMB - Comprehension of Model Behaviour		
Pair	Mean Difference	SD	Significance p	Mean Difference	SD	Significance p
B-A	3.442**	1.261	0.010	0.384	0.569	0.504
C-A	1.833	1.121	0.111	1.394**	0.646	0.038
D-A	8.125***	1.057	0.000	2.833***	0.687	0.000
D-B	4.683***	1.439	0.002	2.449***	0.753	0.002
D-C	6.292***	1.318	0.000	1.439*	0.813	0.083

***p<0.01, **p<0.05, *p<0.1

The lowest mean values for the variables CMS and CMB were found in participants from group A (control group), which were submitted to the basic conditions (opaque simulation and "step-by-step" guidance). This result may be explained by the lack of essential information concerning the structure of the simulator model. Additionally, the "step-by-step" guidance did not foster scientific reasoning and inquiry learning, and this may have led participants to misinterpret cause-and-effect relationships and model behaviour.

On average, the participants from group D (transparent simulation and exploratory guidance) exhibited the highest values for the variables CMS (mean=14.292) and CMB (mean=8.667). As shown in Table 2, the mean values of CMS and CMB for group D were significantly different from the equivalent values for group A (pair D-A; CMS mean difference=8.125, p<0.001; CMB mean difference=2.833, p<0.001). These results suggest that students learn more effectively on SCC concepts if the SBLE combines transparency and a higher degree of exploratory guidance. These processes combined gave participants from group D a significant cognitive aid that accelerated their learning about the relationships between structure and behaviour of the simulated system.

The students from group A and those from the group B were submitted to equivalent guidance conditions ("step-by-step" instructional guidance). The difference between these treatment groups is that while students from group A used an opaque simulator, students from group B interacted with a transparent simulator. As expected, the comparison between treatment groups A and B presented in Tables 1 and 2 demonstrates that simulator transparency did cause the participants to improve their CMS. The statistical testing presented in Table 2 (pair B-A) provides evidence that the average responses from those groups are significantly different (CMS mean difference = 3.442, p = 0.010). On the other hand, the comparison between group D (transparent simulation and exploratory guidance) and group C (opaque simulation and exploratory guidance) reveals an even stronger difference in means for CMS (mean difference=6.292, p<0.000). Consequently, the variable LEG seems to positively moderate the impact of LMT on CMS. Students demonstrate on average an increasing comprehension of the model structure if they combine transparent simulation with a higher degree of exploratory guidance.

As shown in Table 2, it is clear that the difference in means for CMS between group C (opaque simulation and exploratory guidance) and group A (control group) is not significant (mean difference=1.833, p=0.111). This means that when students are performing the opaque simulation, the mean value of CMS for those students submitted to exploratory guidance is not significantly different from the equivalent value for those submitted to "step-by-step" guidance. However, the difference in means for CMS between group D (transparent simulation and exploratory guidance) and group B (transparent simulator and "step-by-step" guidance) is very significant (mean difference=4.683, p=0.002). Thus, the variable LMT seems to positively moderate the impact of LEG on CMS. These results suggest that by using an exploratory guidance solely, students do not learn more effectively about the model cause-and-effect relationships. In other words, even though students from group C apply a scientific approach (hypothesis formulation and testing) supported by specific cognitive aids, they are not more able to derive structure from behaviour.

There were very few differences between the means of the CMB for the treatment A (CMB mean = 5.833) and treatment B (CMB mean = 6.217). The independent-samples t-test be-tween treatments A and B displayed in Table 2 (pair B-A) does not suggest that by increasing simulator transparency, the participants revealed on average a higher CMB. Although the CMB mean increased with the use of the transparent simulator, as presented in Table 2, it is not significantly different (CMB mean difference=0.384, p=0.504). Therefore, the null hypothesis, that transparent simulations will yield the same results as opaque simulations in foster their comprehension of model behaviour, cannot be rejected. As students from group B were explained the stocks-and-flows diagram of the simulator model, they took advantage of that structural knowledge and were more able to identify and represent the key variables and the feedback processes into a causal-loop diagram. Nevertheless, however, these students (from group B) were not more successful in comprehending the model behaviour. These results seem to evidence a learning difficulty, frequently mentioned in systems dynamics literature (Davidsen and Spector, 2015), that is difficult to develop an understanding of how the behaviour of a complex system emerges from its underlying causal structure. On the other hand, the comparison between group D (transparent simulation and exploratory guidance) and group C (opaque simulation and exploratory guidance) indicates a positive difference in means for CMB (mean difference=1.439, p=0.083). Even though that difference is not very significant, it seems to suggest that the variable LEG also positively moderates the impact of LMT on CMB. Students demonstrate on average an increasing comprehension of the model behaviour if they combine transparent simulation with a higher degree of exploratory guidance.

Table 3. Regression results for all independent variables. Regression CMB (2) is obtained through a stepwise procedure

	Dependent Variables					
	CMS - Comprehension of Model Structure		CMB - Comprehension of Model Behaviour (1)		CMB - Comprehension of Model Behaviour (2)	
Independent Variables	Standardized Beta	Significance p	Standardized Beta	Significance p	Standardized Beta	Significance p
LMT	0.462***	0.000	0.175*	0.071		
LEG	0.312***	0.001	0.373***	0.000	0.221**	0.016
CMS					0.482***	0.000
Adjusted R2	0.305		0.156		0.336	

***p<0.01, **p<0.05, *p<0.1

As seen from Tables 1 and 2, there was a significant difference between the means of the CMB for group C (opaque simulation and exploratory guidance) and group A (mean difference =1.394, p=0.038). Moreover, the difference for CMB between treatments D (transparent simulator and exploratory guidance) and B (transparent simulator and "step-by-step" guidance) displayed in Table 2 (pair D-B: mean difference = 2.449, p=0.002) indicates a stronger significant difference than that found between groups C and A. Consequently, these results seem to suggest that by increasing the level of exploratory guidance, the students demonstrate on average a higher CMB. But they may even learn more effectively about the dynamics of the SCC system if they combine exploratory guidance with transparent simulations. Thus, the findings indicate that LMT also positively moderates the impact of LEG on CMB.

As presented in Table 3, regression analysis for CMS on the independent variables shows a highly significant effect for LMT (β=0.462, p<0.001) and a significant effect for LEG (β=0.312, p=0.001). Regression analysis of CMB (1) show a low effect for LMT (β=0.175, p=0.071), which is not significant (at a 0.05 level), and a highly significant effect for LEG (β=0.373, p<0.001). Regression analysis of CMB (2) on the most significant independent variables (including CMS) shows a strong effect for CMS (β=0.482, p<0.001) and a significant effect for LEG (β=0.221, p=0.016).

5. CONCLUSION

This study is based on an education experiment aimed at testing hypotheses about the impact of simulator transparency and instructional guidance on students' learning. The simulation experience involves a simulator based on SD, designed to foster students' understanding of the bullwhip effect and other SCC concepts. The results from regression analysis confirm four of the five hypotheses. The hypothesis H1 (the level of transparency of the SCC simulation model positively influences the level of comprehension of the model structure) is supported. This finding is consistent with some of the literature on learning from transparent models (Grobler at al., 2000, Kompainsky and Alessi, 2015). However, the hypothesis H2 (the level of transparency of the SCC simulation model positively influences the level of comprehension of the model behaviour) is not full supported, thus suggesting that by using a transparent simulator solely, students do not learn about the model behaviour any more effectively than they would otherwise. This conclusion is in line with a learning difficulty frequently mentioned in systems dynamics literature (Davidsen and Spector, 2015), that is difficult to develop an understanding of how the behaviour of a complex system emerges from its underlying causal structure.

The hypotheses H3 (the level of exploratory guidance of the instructional method positively influences the level of comprehension of the SCC model structure) and H4 (the level of exploratory guidance of the instructional method positively influences the level of comprehension of the SCC model behaviour) are supported. The findings evidence a strong impact of the exploratory instructional process on learning about the SCC concepts. Students achieve a deeper understanding of the model structure and behaviour when they have opportunity to explore the simulation themselves and receive appropriate facilitation, such as worked examples and support on scientific reasoning (hypothesis formulation and testing) and model progression (gradually increasing task complexity). These results reinforce two assumptions already articulated in previous research. (i) The idea of using simulations to foster scientific reasoning and inquiry learning as pointed out by Clement (2008). (ii) And the importance of worked examples and model progression to obviate students' difficulties in all phases of the inquiry process and enhance learning as evidenced, for example, by Elsawah et al., (2017) (model progression) and Mulder et al. (2015) (model progression and worked examples).

Finally, the hypothesis H5 (the level of comprehension of the model structure positively influences the level of comprehension of the model behaviour) is also supported. This hypothesis was derived from the research question of whether or not improved mental models of systems lead to better inference of the systems behaviour. This finding is consistent with previous studies on this topic (Capelo and Dias, 2009).

REFERENCES

Capelo, C., Dias, J. 2009. A Feedback Learning and Mental Models Perspective on Strategic Decision Making. *Educational Technology Research & Development*, 57: 629-644.

Clement, J. J. (2008). Creative model construction in scientists and students. The role of imagery, analogy, and mental simulation. New York: Springer.

Davidsen, P., Spector, J. (2015). Critical Reflections on System Dynamics and Simulation/Gaming. *Simulation & Gaming*, 46, 430-444.

Elsawah, S., McLucas, A., Mazanov, J. (2017). An empirical investigation into the learning effects of management flight simulators: A mental models approach, *European Journal of Operational Research*, 259 (1), 262-272.

Farashahi, M., Tajeddin, M. (2018). Effectiveness of teaching methods in business education: A comparison study on the learning outcomes of lectures, case studies and simulations. *The International Journal of Management Education*, 16, 131–142.

Größler, A., Maier, F. H., & Milling, P. M. (2000). Enhancing learning capabilities by providing transparency in business simulators. *Simulation & Gaming: An International Journal*, 31, 257-278.

Groesser, S. N. (2012). Model-Based Learning with System Dynamics. In N. Seel (Ed.), *Encyclopedia of the sciences of learning*, pp 2303–2307. New York: Springer.

de Jong, T., van Joolingen, W. R. (1998). Scientific discovery learning with computer sim-ulations of conceptual domains. *Review of Educational Research*, 68(2), 179–201.

de Jong, T. (2006). Technological advances in inquiry learning. *Science*, 312, 532–533.

Kopainsky, B., Alessi, S. M. (2015). Effects of Structural Transparency in System Dynamics Simulators on Performance and Understanding. *Systems*, 3, 152-176.

Lean, J., Moizer, J., Warren, M. (2015). The use and impact of simulations in management education. *The International Journal of Management Education*, 13, 349.

Milrad, M., Spector, J. M., & Davidsen, P. I. (2003). Model facilitated learning. In S. Naidu (Ed.), *Learning and teaching with technology: Principles and practices*, pp 13-27. London, England: Kogan Page.

Mulder, Y. G., Lazonder, A. W., de Jong, T. (2015). Simulation-based inquiry learning and computer modeling: Pitfalls and potentials. *Simulation & Gaming*, 46, 322-347.

Qudrat-Ullah, H. (2007). Debriefing can reduce misperceptions of feedback: The case of renewable resource management. *Simulation & Gaming: An International Journal*, 38, 382-397.

Sweller, J., Ayres, P., & Kalyuga, S. (2011). *Cognitive load theory*. New York: Springer.

van Borkulo, S., van Joolingen, W., Savelsbergh, E., Jong, T. (2012). What can be learned from computer modeling? Comparing expository and modeling approaches to teaching dynamic systems behavior. *Journal of Science Education and Technology*, 21 (2), 267–275 2012.

BECOMING STORYTELLERS: IMPROVING ESL STUDENTS' ACADEMIC ENGAGEMENT AND 21ST CENTURY SKILLS THROUGH INTERACTIVE DIGITAL STORYTELLING

Annalisa Raffone and Johanna Monti
"L'Orientale" University of Naples - UNIOR NLP Research Group
Naples, Italy

ABSTRACT

21st Century education is rapidly changing due to the emerging of new media technologies that provide easy access to a great amount of information.
Accordingly, as today's students are immersed in a technological society, they need to be equipped with the skills necessary to interpret, synthesize and produce new information. Thus, today's educators and researchers face the challenge of making students become skillful users of new technologies so to increase their motivation and engagement by also improving their learning outcomes.
In particular, in the context of Second Language Acquisition (SLA), using technology appropriately could be a valuable approach to create a meaningful learning context where the acquisition of language and literacy skills is accompanied by that of digital skills.
To that end, Digital Storytelling (DST) seems to perfectly embody and meet the various educational needs of today's students because due to its dynamic feature of combining traditional storytelling with a variety of digital multimedia it provides opportunities for the improvement of learning skills including cooperative learning, motivation, and engagement.
In the light of CALL (Computer-Assisted Language Learning), Collaborative Learning (CL), and the Constructivist Paradigm (CP), this paper aims at addressing the potential of Interactive Digital Storytelling in enhancing ESL (English as a Second Language) students' academic engagement and 21st Century Skills.
Therefore, this paper describes the implementation of DST at "L'Orientale" University of Naples with 24 ESL students involving qualitative and quantitative methods of collecting data. Results showed that DST enhanced students' engagement with their studies and the reinforcement of their digital skills.

KEYWORDS

Digital Storytelling, CALL, Collaborative Learning, Constructivism, ESL, 21st Century Skills

1. INTRODUCTION

In May 2018 the Council of European Union adopted the "Recommendation on Key Competencies for Lifelong Learning" (2018), a document aiming at promoting the development of a series of skills for personal fulfillment, employability, social inclusion, and active citizenship. Among the eight skills that the Recommendation indicates as essential for today's students to acquire to live and work in today's world, there are Literacy, Multilingual, and Digital Skills.

As a result, the evidence is a need for meaningful technology integration in the curriculum able to help students acquire new and consolidate past knowledge by also transforming it into new information and products.

Actually, in recent years the growing capabilities of technology have turned the emerging CALL approach into a more and more valuable educational setting (Torsani, 2016) where the teaching and learning of languages can benefit from better processing and understanding of the material.

As students are heavy users of new technologies, teachers should be able to appropriately embed technology into the classroom so to make students turn into flexible learners able to adapt to new educational situations, take on different tasks, quickly solve problems, cooperate between them and develop their ideas about different topics.

In effect, researchers (Dexter et al., 1999) have stated that technology can be considered effective in educational settings only when it can engage students in their learning process.

Therefore, the emerging of DST as an instructional tool could be considered as a valuable support in the context of SLA especially when it comes to student motivation and engagement. In fact, despite traditional face-to-face teaching, in which each student communicates only with the teacher, DST helps students develop their personal and academic skills by fostering learning, motivation, and engagement due to its multimodality and peer-to-peer collaboration.

Although there already exist some studies involving the use of DST to foster learning in Italy, to the best of our knowledge, little research has been conducted with ESL students at Italian Universities to enhance their motivation and engagement.

Thus, this paper aims at exploring the use of DST in fostering ESL students' engagement[1] and the development of digital skills. Section 2 and 3 present the literature review and the theoretical framework supporting the study. Section 4, 5 and 6 describe the research questions, objectives and significance of the study. Section 7 states the statement of ethics. Section 8 presents the methodology used in collecting and analyzing data. Section 9 describes the implementation, results, and discussion. Section 10 draws conclusions and future work.

2. LITERATURE REVIEW

DST is usually defined as the art of telling stories with digital multimedia (Robin, 2008) but it is more than that as it involves a complex process of research, elicit of a specific topic, a conscious selection of material and mixing of different multimedia to finally create a powerful digital story.

Researchers (Robin, 2006; 2008) have shown that integrating DST into the curriculum could help teachers in transferring information by enhancing student engagement and providing better educational outcomes.

Moreover, not only storytelling is considered as a powerful tool for the transmission of knowledge since ancient times but, with the advances in new media technologies, it has become even more useful because by using different software to edit and mix a variety of digital multimedia (photos, images, videos, text, music, voice-over) stories can be created and presented in a more engaging way, thus stimulating students' language skills together with what has been defined as "21st Century Skills" that include digital skills, creativity, critical thinking, and motivation.

Also, DST engages students due to its *interactivity* because when students develop their digital stories they actively participate in the learning process thus shifting from teacher-centered to student-centered learning. This aspect is particularly important in enhancing L2 learners' motivation as being the co-constructor of your knowledge represents one of the most important factors in developing language proficiency.

In effect, several researchers (Castañeda, 2013; Pardo, 2014; Razmi et al., 2014) have demonstrated that L2 learners were extremely motivated in developing their language abilities thanks to the dynamism of DST and the fact that they were creating their artifacts.

Furthermore, when students are asked to create their digital stories in groups, even collaborative learning is enhanced as they feel they are working to reach the same goal, and so they help each other and confront themselves by limiting competition.

Actually, in the context of SLA, as the DST process is shared among the students, they can discuss the content and analyze their different points of view, thus enhancing their knowledge and social interaction.

---

[1] The term *engagement* is used in this study to indicate the enthusiasm that Digital Storytelling is able to arise into the students and the consequently commitment they have with their English studies.

3. THEORETICAL FRAMEWORK

This study has been developed by taking into account a series of theoretical paradigms, in particular: the CALL approach, the Cooperative Learning, and the Constructivist Theory.

DST perfectly fits in the context of CALL as it represents powerful instructional support to language teachers and students. In fact, by using DST teachers have the opportunity to explore a new way of teaching so to better engage students with their studies by also making them both active participants of the learning process and in the conditions of acquiring a second language in a meaningful and more interesting way than the one provided by face-to-face learning.

Actually, the CALL approach demands for the use of a student-centered learning that allows learners to work independently (Seljan et al., 2004) and DST seems to respond to this need as the creation of a digital story is a process that, despite being previously accurately explained by the teacher, has to be entirely made by the students that consequently learn how to do research, select material and combine digital and non-digital elements.

Moreover, the interactivity typical of the CALL approach (derived by the interaction between the human and the computer) is also provided by DST as students use different kinds of text, image, video, and audio-editing software to develop their stories.

Also, the Constructivist Theory emphasizes student-centered learning (Bruner, 1990; Ally, 2004) with students constructing their understanding of a given subject due to a series of tasks to accomplish.

To that end, DST helps students foster active learning and critical thinking because when constructing their digital stories they are exposed to different problems (e.g. choosing and selecting appropriate material to convey a specific meaning) and are asked to solve them by stimulating their minds (Harris, 2005).

Furthermore, Constructivism also involves Cooperative Learning which aims at making classroom activities social learning experiences due to peer-to-peer interaction (Gillies, 2016). In this way, DST provides a constructivist learning environment in which students have the opportunity to share and acquire present and new knowledge and confront and help each other by working in groups.

Besides, they enhance not only their academic but also their social skills by providing constructive feedback and supporting each other in the completion of the given tasks.

4. RESEARCH QUESTIONS

This study is based on three major research questions:

1. Are students effectively more engaged when Digital Storytelling is embedded in the classroom?
2. Can Digital Storytelling create an authentic learning environment that enhances student-centered and cooperative learning?
3. Can Digital Storytelling improve students' "21st Century Skills"?

5. OBJECTIVES OF THE STUDY

The main objective of the study was to explore the use of technology in ESL education with University students. In particular, the primary aim was to understand the potential of DST in enhancing ESL students' engagement with their studies together with the development of digital skills.

By enacting a Digital Storytelling Laboratory, students found themselves immersed in a meaningful educational environment in which they got involved mainly due to multimedia collaborative project-based tasks. In this way, they entirely worked with the English language from the perspective of each of the four traditional language skills (i.e. speaking, writing, listening, reading) by also acquiring knowledge of the usage of the different software necessary to create their digital stories.

Moreover, this investigation aims at shedding new light on the impact of DST on student engagement and motivation in the context of SLA.

6. SIGNIFICANCE OF THE STUDY

This study may help in acquiring a better understanding and perspective on the integration of technology into the curriculum, in particular, that of DST in creating a constructivist learning environment that could engage ESL Italian University students with their studies together with the development of digital skills.

7. STATEMENT OF ETHICS

During the Digital Storytelling Laboratory, the whole class has been treated with respect and sensitivity. Indeed, mutual respect has always been demanded to the students between them and with the instructor. Participants were assumed anonymity and were asked to sign an informed consent.

8. METHODOLOGY

Quantitative and Qualitative analyses were used to collect data. Qualitative data were collected through participant observation and oral interviews (cf. sections 9.2 - 9.3). Quantitative data were collected in the form of an online survey (cf. sections 9.1 - 9.2 - 9.3).

8.1 Participants and Context

This study lasted three months and was conducted between March and June 2019 as part of an Innovative Industrial Ph.D. Research Project.

To that end, a Digital Storytelling Laboratory was enacted at "L'Orientale" University of Naples, addressing 24 Bachelor's students (23 females and 1 male) in their second year of the course English Language and Linguistics of the Undergraduate's Degree in Comparative Languages and Literatures.

The Laboratory took place at the "Aula Informatica" of the same University where each student was assigned a computer with Internet access. Nevertheless, the DST process also sometimes required the additional use of students' personal computers.

The activity duration was two hours per week.

8.2 Data Collection and Analysis

Quantitative and Qualitative data were collected from 24 University students attending the Digital Storytelling Laboratory to understand if the production of digital stories could lead to ESL students' engagement and the development of digital skills.

Participant observation was conducted especially during the DST process during which the students had to cooperate between them to complete tasks and managed to do research and mix digital and non-digital material within the time required. In this way, it was possible to elicit whether students were able to execute the intended use of technology explained by the instructor.

Moreover, an online survey was conducted to investigate the influence of DST on ESL students' motivation and acquisition of digital skills that provided a deeper understanding of the integration of DST into the ESL curriculum.

9. IMPLEMENTATION, RESULTS AND DISCUSSION

The project was carried out between March and June 2019 and students attended the Digital Storytelling Laboratory as an additional course to their studies.

Since the beginning of the course, they showed great enthusiasm for a new, different, and more interactive approach to the English language.

The course was structured so that students could acquire the basic skills necessary to embark on the DST process.

Firstly, they were introduced into the field – completely new to them – and the instructor encouraged them to speak their minds to create a comfortable educational environment in which each student could express himself/herself without experiencing feelings of stress and enhance positive feedback.

Then, students were shown some different already existing digital stories so to create a sense of familiarity with the products and make them begin to think about the kind of artifacts they intended to produce.

Students worked in self-selected groups, each of whom were then asked to do accurate research to choose specific topics for the production of the digital stories which were subsequently discussed with the instructor and the other students. The topics of videos were sorted according to students' studies and themes they recognized as important in their lives.

After that, they were introduced to several kinds of text, image and video editing software to edit their stories. Although some students were already accustomed to several kinds of editing software, most of them showed to benefit from learning how to meaningfully introduce technology into their studies. Some others showed enthusiasm to practice their artistic attitude for something academic.

During the whole DST process, discussion about the chosen topics was enhanced. This helped students in developing their ideas about the different topics to increase their critical thinking and learn how to cooperate to reach the same goal.

At the end of the course, each group showed its digital story to the whole class and the instructor helped them to construct valuable feedback around the stories so to effectively underline what was good and what was needed to be better improved.

The digital stories were then released on the web[2] so to make students receive feedback on their work from a wider audience. This gave them a sense of satisfaction and success after working hard to produce their micro-films.

Based on the analysis of data, students enhanced their engagement with the English language together with 21st Century Skills. Students stated that DST was able to foster their engagement with the English language due to the following factors:

a) integration of technology, which helped to promote "21st Century Skills", in particular, Digital Literacy; b) promotion of student-centered and cooperative learning; c) enhanced creativity, knowledge about the chosen subjects and language learning.

9.1 Promotion of 21st Century Skills Through Technology

According to the participants, DST enhanced their motivation with their studies and helped them to develop their digital skills due to a series of different but interconnected factors.

First of all, they were immersed in an educational environment in which they could experience the English language not only from a traditional linguistic point of view but also by exploring different types of language registers as each group chose a different kind of story that required the usage of specific language styles. At the same time, they were more motivated to interact with subjects related to their course studies due to the interactivity of DST. Besides, having the possibility to explore a topic using several types of media directly led to interdisciplinarity so that students independently chose to investigate their topics from different perspectives expressing them by using mixed technologies.

Findings from the survey showed that students improved their ability in using technology with a purpose and not only as a way of entertainment:

Student A: I learned how to use programs to create the video but also improved my drawing skills.

Student B: It rarely happens to learn through the use of digital instruments, but thanks to this course I was able to learn new things through the use of digital tools.

Student C: It was really innovative to create a story through technology.

---

[2] An official YouTube Channel of the Unior Digital Storytelling Lab has been created to share the digital stories on the web. More information at: https://www.youtube.com/channel/UCNgmjdc_EPoGq8mlMdywFiw.

In effect, students were able to quickly learn how to use the needed software to create the stories, and many of them also had the opportunity to enhance their creativity by designing settings and characters by themselves.

Each time they faced a problem with technology, they found their solution online or searched for the help of the instructor during the Lab or beyond the classroom time by email.

The steps required for the creation of digital stories also enhanced students' problem-solving ability and social skills.

9.2 Student-Centered and Cooperative Learning

Students especially liked the idea of controlling their learning process, and the need to complete the tasks within the time required gave them a sense of responsibility which also led to better cooperation within and outside the working groups. Cooperation was experienced both as peer-to-peer and student-instructor interaction as during the whole Digital Storytelling Lab everything was previously explained and clarified by the instructor and students received continuous feedback when needed. On the contrary, cooperation with peers was also enhanced when students had to select the material for their digital stories and create and assembling digital media – which made them develop their critical thinking skills and the ability to research that they had quite never experienced.

Results showed that students benefited from the working-in-group experience, as explained by the following statements:

Student D: The most valuable thing I found in this Lab is the importance given to group work.

Student E: I found this course really helpful because it showed me how to better interact with others and it gave me a wider sense of responsibility.

Cooperation also seems to connect to student-centered learning because, as students affirmed in the oral interviews too, they not only learned about how to collaborate between them but this collaboration fostered their sense of responsibility as each storyteller had to do his/her part in the completion of the work.

In this way, students understood the importance of constructive feedback both in relation with the instructor and with their peers.

9.3 Creativity and Learning

Research findings also showed that doing accurate research on the chosen topics and combining text with media led students to a deeper understanding of the subject matter.

DST motivated students to interact with the chosen topics thanks to its multimodality:

Student F: Since it was a different way of telling a story, I had to think outside the box of my usual stories and find new ideas more fitting for the project.

Student G: I learned a lot because I had to think about a lot of strategies to make our project work.

In effect, creativity was particularly enhanced when students had to research, select and choose the appropriate material for their stories. Some groups decided to create characters and settings on their own, especially those students that already had some experience with graphic design software. During the oral interviews at the end of the course, these students said that this course allowed them to integrate academic content with their artistic attitudes which enhanced their motivation:

Student H: I felt excited about the discussion with the group about the topic of the video, that part was inspiring. I had fun in the making of the digital drawings too.

Also, the development of creativity seems to be connected to enhanced digital literacy and language learning.

Besides, students described the process of writing the story as a fundamental step that helped them not only to improve their knowledge about the chosen topic but also their language proficiency. Actually, everything was realized in English, from researching the topic to creating the digital story:

Student I: DST helped me releasing my creativity especially during the step of writing the script. I felt really stimulated in a way I've never been.

Student J: DST was able to help me learn how to write a script in English which could help me in the future.

Student K: We made researches in English and also we wrote and projected everything in English, not translating. This is a very good method to improve a language.

According to the findings, the choice of using DST improved students' motivation in handling the project which allows claiming that this practice could be a valuable resource for enhancing ESL students' engagement with their studies if appropriately integrated into the classroom.

Today's students are heavy users of new technologies and the ability to purposefully use them is essential for their social, learning and professional outcomes.

10. CONCLUSIONS AND FUTURE WORK

In our 21st Century technology-immersed society, today's educators face the challenge of engaging and motivating their students by giving them appropriate resources to express and construct meaning.

Thus, especially in the context of SLA, the need for enhancing student engagement and motivation has led many researchers to state the importance of integrating technology into the classroom (Jacobsen, 2001).

To that end, DST seems to be a powerful vehicle to make students construct their knowledge and develop the skills necessary to respond to today's educational needs.

This study explored the use of DST with ESL students at "L'Orientale" University of Naples whose results allow stating that if appropriately used, DST could be meaningful technological support to foster student engagement and motivation.

The research findings help to claim that DST is effectively powerful in fostering ESL students' motivation with their studies by enhancing student-centered and cooperative learning, in addition to the development of digital, social and learning skills. These skills fall into the recognized "21st Century Skills" that are considered fundamental to make students able to live and work in today's world and DST seems to help in constructing an authentic learning environment in which collaboration, communication, problem-solving, and language learning are actively interconnected.

Nevertheless, even though the findings show the positive impact of DST on ESL students' levels of engagement and acquisition of technology skills, further research needs to be carried out to understand if DST could also improve ESL students' academic performance.

ACKNOWLEDGEMENT

This work is supported by the Italian Ministry of University and Research under the PON Research and Innovation Program "Innovative Industrial Doctorates" (2014-2020).

REFERENCES

Ally, M., 2004. Foundations of educational theory for online learning. In T. Anderson & Ellomi, F. (Eds.). *Theory and Practice of online learning*. Athabasca, Canada, pp. 3-31.

Bruner, J. E., 1990. *Acts of meaning*. Harvard University Press, Cambridge.

Castañeda, M. E., 2013. "I am proud that I did it and it's a piece of me". In *CALICO Journal*, Vol. 30, No. 1, pp. 44-62.

Dexter, S., et al., 1999. Teachers' views of computers as catalysts for changes in their teaching practice. In *Journal of Research on Computing in Education*, Vol. 31, No. 3, pp. 221-239.

Gillies, R. M., 2016. Cooperative Learning: Review of Research and Practice. In *Australian Journal of Teacher Education*, Vol. 41, No. 3, pp. 39-54.

Harris, J., 2005. Our Agenda for Technology Integration: It's Time to Choose. In *Contemporary Issues in Technology and Teacher Education*, Vol. 5, No. 2, pp. 116-122.

Jacobsen, M., 2001. Building different bridges: Technology integration, engaged student learning, and new approaches to professional development. *The 82nd Annual Meeting of the American Educational Research Association*. Seattle, USA.

Pardo, B. S., 2014. Digital Storytelling: A case study of the creation, and narration of a story by EFL Learners. In *Digital Education Review*, No. 26, pp. 74-84.

Razmi, M., et al., 2014. Digital Storytelling in EFL Classroom (Oral Presentation of the Story): A Pathway to Improve Oral Production. In *Procedia - Social and Behavioral Sciences*, Vol. 98, pp. 1541-1544.

Robin, B. R., 2006. The Educational Uses of Digital Storytelling. *Proceedings of SITE 2006*. Orlando, USA, pp. 709-716.

Robin, B. R., 2008. Digital Storytelling: A Powerful Technology Tool for the 21st Century Classroom. In *Theory into Practice*, Vol. 47, pp. 220-228.

Seljan, S., et al., 2004. Computer-Assisted Language Learning (CALL). *Proceedings of the 27th International Convention MIPRO 2004: MEET+HGS*. Rijeka, Croatia, pp. 262-266.

The Council of the European Union, 2018. Council Recommendation of 22 May 2018 on Key Competencies for Lifelong learning. In *Official Journal of the European Union*, Vol. 61, pp. 1-32.

Torsani, S., 2016. *CALL Teacher Education: Language Teachers and Technology Integration*. Sense Publishers, Rotterdam.

VISUALIZATION OF LEARNING LOG OF WEB-BASED APPLICATION FOR UNDERSTANDING THE STRUCTURE OF GEOMETRIC PROOFS

Satomi Hamada[1] and Masanori Yamada[2]
[1]*Graduate School of Human-Environment Studies, Kyushu University*
[2]*Faculty of Arts and Science, Kyushu University*
744, Motooka, Nishi-ku, Fukuoka 819-0395, Japan

ABSTRACT

Many students are not good at geometric proofs. One reason for this is that it is possible to memorize the proof procedure explained by the teacher without understanding the structure of a geometric proof. So far, we have developed a web-based application that supports the understanding of the "structure of geometric proofs" in junior high school mathematics and have verified its effectiveness. Although the results of the evaluation experiments have indicated the usefulness of this web-based application, it was not possible to identify the factors that brought about its usefulness. In addition, because the web-based application was not equipped with a log analysis function, it was not possible to grasp the aspects that students struggle with during a proof in the web-based application. In this paper, we present the results and problems of the evaluation experiment of the web-based application so far and discuss the newly added log analysis function.

KEYWORDS

Mathematics, Geometric Proof, Visualization of Proof Structure, Visualization of Learning Log, Learning Analytics

1. INTRODUCTION

1.1 Challenges of Geometric Proofs in Junior High School Mathematics

In eight grade mathematical geometry in Japan, according to the Ministry of Education, Culture, Sports, Science, and Technology (MEXT, 2008), the purpose of geometric proofs is "to understand the congruence of the figure, deepen the view of the figure, check the nature of the figure based on the congruence conditions of the triangle and logical considerations, and cultivate the ability to express the word". To understand the needs and meaning of a proof which makes this logical rationality and deductive reasoning and its method, geometry can visualize the reasoning process (MEXT, 2008). In the second grade of junior high school, students are taught the assumptions and conclusions of geometric proofs at first. After understanding how to proceed with the proof based on the underlying evidence, students complete "fill-in-the-blank questions" and "short-answer questions". A "fill-in-the-blank question" presents a completed proof with blank spaces that must be filled with the correct information. A "short-answer question" is a question where students must write proof sentences without using hints. In Japanese junior high school mathematics, learning instructions are being reported in order to try to understand geometric proofs using these two question types (Sekiguchi 1994, Fujita 2014, Kurayama 2015).

Looking at the national academic ability and learning situation survey over the past ten years conducted by the National Institute for Education Policy (2007-2016), the average correct answer rate for "fill-in-the-blank questions" is approximately 75%, while the average correct answer rate for "short-answer questions" is approximately 30%. The factors that cause this large difference in correct answer rate between the two question types are discussed with reference to the following two prior studies.

First, Moore (1994) classified the cognitive difficulties of proofs into seven categories, with one of them being "not understanding how to use definitions to capture the overall structure of a proof". Next, according to an analysis by Koseki et al. (1987), among the students who could not prove the "short-answer questions", approximately 40% understood that the three sides and corners of a triangle can be used to prove geometric joint. It was thought that although 40% of the students understood that the three sides and corners of a triangle can be used to prove a geometric joint that would lead to a correct answer, they were incorrect because they could not assemble them. In subsequent research, Kunimune et al. (2000) conducted the same survey for public secondary schools in an area close to the target area of the previous survey in order to clarify the situation after 12 years has passed. As a result, although a slight increase in comprehension was seen, approximately one quarter of students did not understand the mechanism of a geometric proof at the end of learning in junior high school. They continued to point out that it must be considered as a teaching issue. That is, based on the points of Moore (1994) and Koseki et al. (1987), the students' understanding of the proof did not change over 12 years, and the students who could not answer the "short-answer question" correctly could not do so due to a lack of understanding of proof structure.

An effective theory for this factor is the theory of multi-step formation of intellectual activity (Gal'perin 2012). The multi-step formation theory of intellectual activity refers to idea that intellectual behavior is acquired through four stages: (1) explanation and presentation of intellectual activity, (2) activity using a specific object, (3) activity described in language, and (4) activity internalization. Based on these steps, this research developed and evaluated a learning support system that supports the structural understanding of geometric proofs. The structure visualization of the proof question is performed as the method of support.

Based on this multi-step formation theory of intellectual activity, Hirashima (2015) reported the results of an "information structure-oriented approach to operating the logical structure itself" for Japanese question-and-answer learning. Based on this, from the viewpoint of promoting the structural understanding of geometric proofs, it seems that the structuring of the learning content and its visualization are equally effective for different kinds of logical proof structures. However, although "fill-in-the-blank questions" used in conventional proof learning include the structure of the geometric proof, the student can complete the proof by focusing mainly on one sentence including blank spaces. Therefore, "fill-in-the-blank questions" are not sufficient for a proper understanding of geometric proof structure. Accordingly, proof learning that visualizes the structure of a geometric proof and includes a process that can actually be manipulated, i.e., somewhere between the "fill-in-the-blank question" and "short-answer question", is considered to be effective.

1.2 Positioning of this Research

Kurayama (2015) researched geometric proofs and said "If a student who answers a fill-in-the-blank question immediately answers a short-answer question, they must consider the whole from only a part." Therefore, she has developed a system where students can use a card selection method to think about proof structure from its parts to learn it effectively. In her system, each element of a structured proof problem is provided as an "assumption card" and "condition card". In this system, the student assembles while examining a simple sentence given as a card. It is thought that this system will be more focused on the "construction of proof" than the "structure of proof". Further, Funaoi et al. (2009) developed a system where a proof is constructed in the form of a flow chart and errors are visualized after a correctness judgment. This system is designed to express "the flow of proofs" from the condition of the blank and to "recognize the error of the student" by visualizing it. To effectively learn a proof, it is important to consciously understand it through visualization of its structure and flow. It is difficult to understand the structure of a proof in terms of its components and what kind of relations they have. Therefore, it is considered that students can use the proof activity to imagine proof structure through a proof activity that applies proof pieces like a jigsaw.

Based on the above, this research aims to design, develop, and evaluate a web-based application focusing on the structure of proofs, and an appropriate usage is suggested. This paper presents the results and problems of a previous evaluation experiment and discusses the newly added log analytics function.

2. OUTLINE OF THE WEB-BASED APPLICATION

A web-based application was developed that enables the student to acquire an image of the "structure of a proof" while visualizing it and that embeds elements in each area of the hypothesis part.
In this research, the development language was JavaScript. The structures of geometric proofs were set based on previous research, such as that by Kurayama (2015). The developed application can be implemented on both iOS and Windows devices. Figure 1 illustrates the configuration of the system.

The web-based application has three steps for studying. The student-side user interface of step 1 is shown in Figure 2. The "proof structure board" that visualizes the "structure of geometric proof" on the left of the figure has an assumption part, intermediate joint proof part, and conclusion. Each area on this "proof structure board" is a figure-related piece arranged at the right side of the screen (e.g.,$\angle$AED=$\angle$CEB) or a figure property piece (e.g., the apex angle is equal); these pieces can be dragged around to assemble proofs. The right of Figure 2 is the screen after dragging the pieces. In addition, a "reason" is selected from the reason list in the joint proof section. If the piece cannot be placed, the piece will be returned to the first position. Once the proof has been assembled, the user receives a decision of correct or incorrect. If the proof was incorrect, the incorrect parts are highlighted as a basis for the student to answer again.

The student-side user interface of step 2 is shown in Figure 3. In step 2, a function is provided for learning with consideration of the relationship between each element of the "proof structure". In this step, the student constructs the "proof structure" themselves from five elements (assumption, reason, establishment items, triangle joint conditions, and conclusions) that constitute the proof, which are provided as pieces to the student. In this manner, from step 1 of acquiring an image of the whole proof structure, it becomes possible to be aware of the relation of each element, and it is predicted that the understanding of "proof structure" is promoted. The student-side user interface of step 3 is shown in Figure 4. In step 3, based on the "proof structure" created in steps 1 and 2, an activity of converting into "proof text" is performed. Specifically, "proof text" is provided as a piece for each word, such as "what if", "because", and "AB = CD". Then, while referring to the "proof structure" presented on the left of the screen (see Figure 4), a "proof sentence" is assembled.

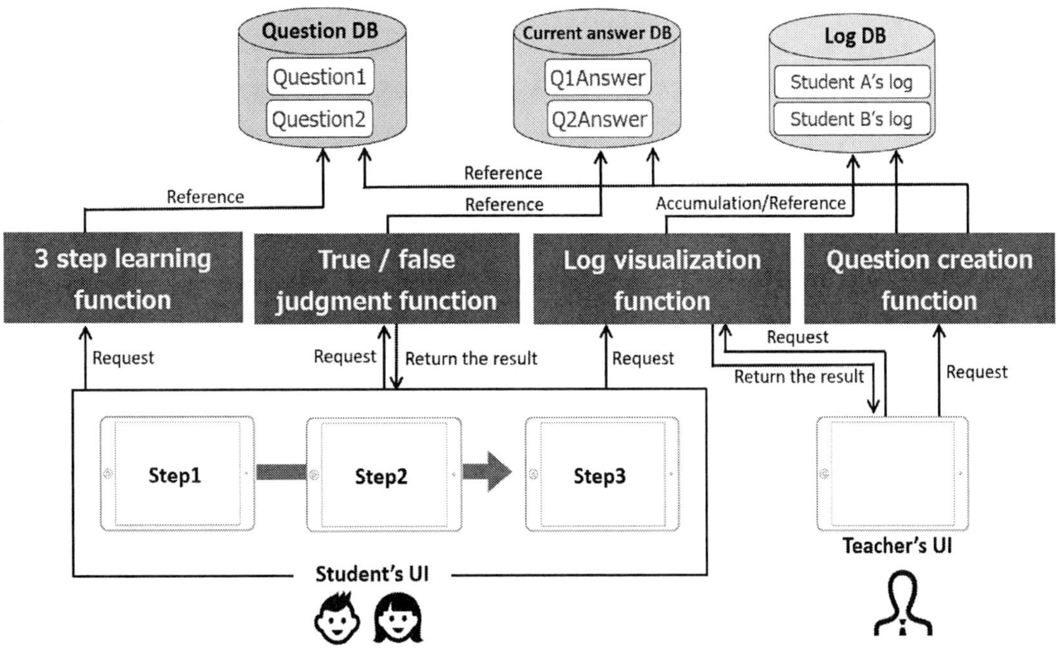

Figure 1. System configuration diagram

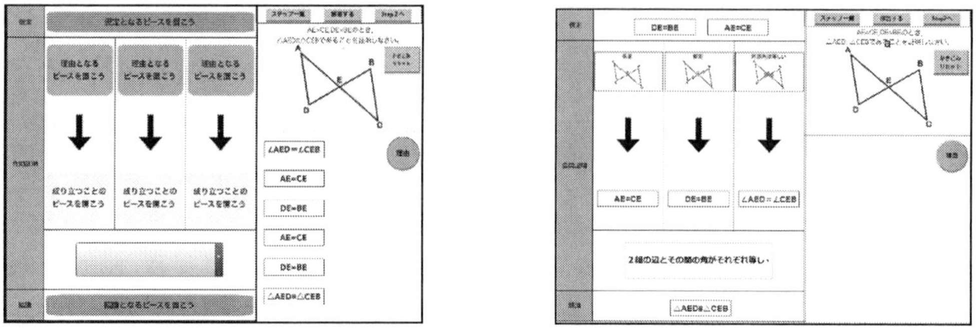

Figure 2. The student-side user interface of step 1

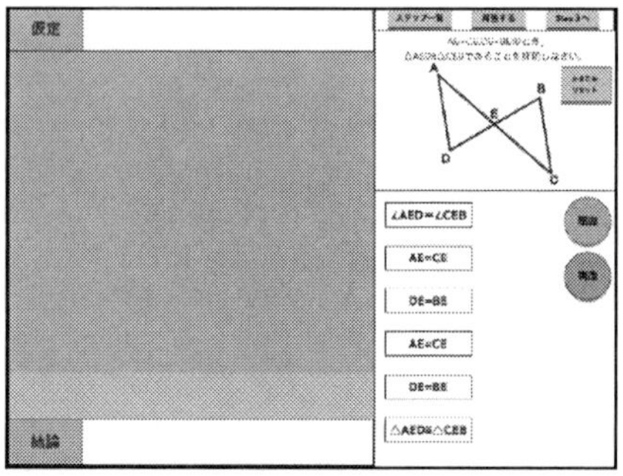

Figure 3. The student-side user interface of step 2

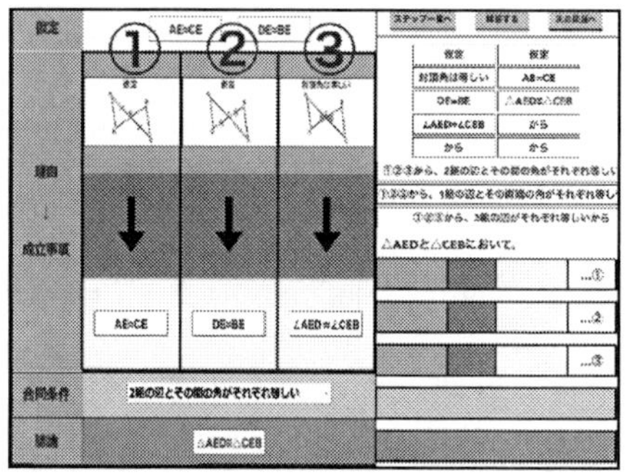

Figure 4. The student-side user interface of step 3

3. EVALUATION OF THE WEB-BASED APPLICATION

3.1 Results of Evaluation Experiment

The evaluation experiment used the web-based application equipped with only step 1. The evaluation was performed with the cooperation of 33 junior high school students in the eighth grade. It was conducted according to three procedures: (1) pre-questionnaire and pre-test, (2) implementation of the task using the web-based application, and (3) post-questionnaire and post-test. In the pre-test, an awareness survey for simple proof questions and short-answer questions were given. In the implementation of the task using the application, we worked on the task while talking with multiple people around one tablet. Later, in the post-test, a "short-answer question" and an answer form on the "structure of proofs" were prepared at the same level as the pre-test.

Five of the nine students who answered the proof question incorrectly in the pre-test answered the short-answer question correctly, and two answered correctly on the "structure of geometric proofs". However, one student made a mistake in the writing part.

3.2 Challenges for the Web-Based Application: Learning Analytics

Based on the above, as a result of verifying this web-based application, it was found that the understanding of "the structure of proofs" was promoted. However, it can be understood that there are students who cannot write the "text of proofs" even if they can understand the "structure of proofs", and it became apparent that this web application requires a further scaffolding function. Also, in the evaluation experiment, analysis was performed using performance tests and questionnaires, but the data obtained from the web-based application cannot be taken into consideration.

In this regard, one of the effective approaches is learning analytics. Learning analytics is defined as "the use of intellectual data, learner-generated data, and analytical models to discover information and social connections, and to predict and advise learning" (Siemens 2010). Learning analytics also contribute to improve learning environments, and examine learning effectiveness in students by collecting and analyzing data to assess learning behavior and performance (Pechenizkiy et al. 2014; Ogata et al, 2015). Yin et al (2019) investigate the successful learning patterns based on eBook reading logs. Shimada et al (2015) also investigated the successful learning pattern using eBook logs outside class. Learning analytics allow teachers to understand learning process that improve learning performance. Yamada et al (2018) developed and evaluated the effects of concept map system using eBook log, and indicated the successful learners tended to flip forward the pages and made a concept map that contains more nodes. Onoue et al (2019) developed concept map categorization system for teachers to improve instructional design. Thus, learning analytics is one of the most helpful perspectives for the improvement of learning environments.

In this research, based on the concept of learning analytics, it is necessary to consider the data obtained from the web application and to conduct a detailed analysis in addition to the questionnaires and tests. This web-based application is intended to be used in classes. Therefore, there is a need for a function that enables the teacher to confirm what the student in question is finding difficult in the middle of a proof. Also, to consider appropriate usage patterns, including data during the use of the web-based application, analysis is also required. Therefore, in this paper, the log analysis function of the newly developed web-based application is considered.

4. LOG ANALYTICS FUNCTION

A function was added to visualize the log of the student in the application, as shown in Figure 5. This function accumulates the learning log in MongoDB in JSON format, and an interface was developed using JavaScript frameworks Vue.js and D3.js. On the left side of the screen, student IDs using this web-based application are arranged. On the right side of the screen, the operation history of each student is displayed in chronological order. A circle represents an operation of placing one piece. See Figure 6 for the location of each area described below. A red circle means placed in the assumed area, a blue circle means placed in the reason part of the joint certification area, a yellow circle means placed in the establishment area of the joint certification area, and a green circle means that a combination of conditions is selected from the three. The letters in these circles refer to the contents of the pieces placed in the area. Taking Figure 5 as an example, it can be seen that hamada placed the piece "AB = CE" in the assumed area at 17:52:47.

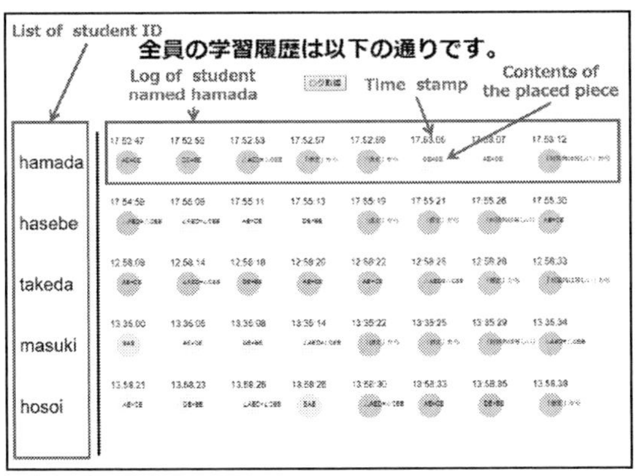

Figure 5. Log analysis function screen

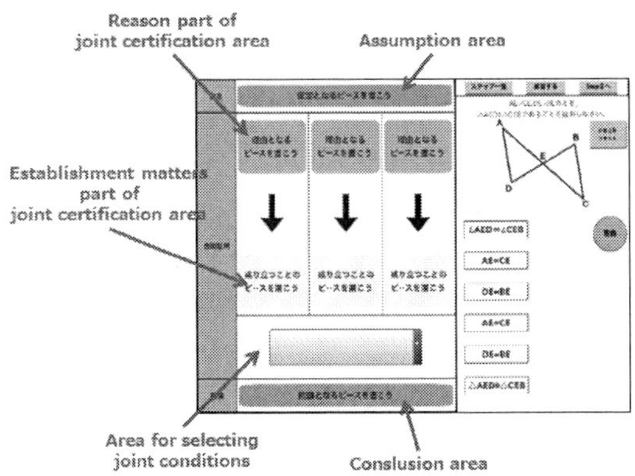

Figure 6. The location of each area

Such visualization of the operation history allows the teacher to confirm what difficulties the student had in the process of making a proof. For example, in Figure 5, because Takeda placed various pieces in the assumption and conclusion areas, it can be understood that the assumption and conclusion cannot be extracted from the problem sentence. Also, by visualizing the studnt's operation history, it is possible to grasp how to proceed with the proof of the student who is good at the proof. Taking Figure 5 as an example again, Masuki and Hosoi clarify the relationship of figures that can be used from problem sentences and what should be shown to prove that they select the congruence conditions that can be used on them. It turns out that they can think of things paradoxically. Then, by displaying the behavior history of all students in a list, it becomes possible to compare the students with each other, making it easy for the teacher to grasp the characteristics of the students. In the future, in addition to the functions presented here, additional functions are planned to calculate and visualize the operation time and error rate for each question for all students. This will allow teachers to provide efficient instructions that focus on the problems faced as they teach their assigned classes.

4.1 Log Accumulation Method

The method of accumulating logs is described here. As shown in Figure 7, each time a piece is placed on the student's screen, information is stored in a log array and sent to a database called MongoDB in JSON format. Here, a unique ID is assigned to each piece and area placed. Note that this web-based application has a function that allows the student to annotate figures displayed on the screen. This function is used with the library called fabric.js, and the drawing record can be converted to the json format by a command, so the drawing record is also saved in the JSON format. Therefore, each time a piece is placed, student ID, problem ID being worked on, area where piece is dropped, content of dropped piece, server time, device time, and drawing content are arranged in an array. The array is then saved in the database in JSON format.

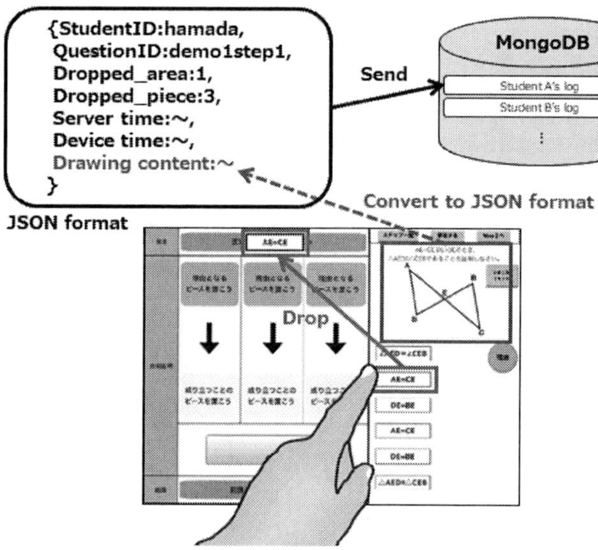

Figure 7. Log accumulation method

4.2 Log Visualization Method

Here, how logs are visualized is described. As shown in Figure 8, data is extracted for each student ID from the stored data, converted to a character string, and a graphic is created using the d3.js library. In addition, the color at the time of producing a figure was made to be the same as the color of each area, as shown in Figure 6. It was predicted that the teacher would be able to grasp the order in which students consider proofs.

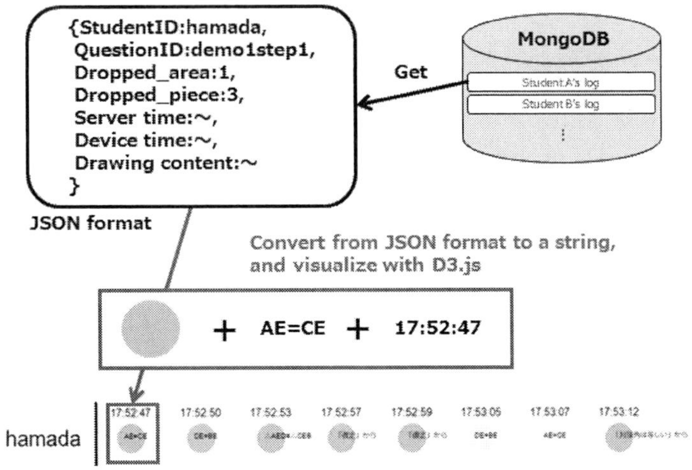

Figure 8. Log visualization method

5. CONCLUSION AND FUTURE WORK

In this paper, the evaluation results of a web-based application that supports the understanding of the "structure of geometric proofs" in junior high school mathematics were presented, and the newly added log analysis function was examined. In the future, we will evaluate the web-based application with the improved log analysis function and clarify the following two questions:

"1. How did students use this web-based application effectively?"

"2. What is the difference between students who are good and bad at proofs?"

The following two points are proposed as proposals for solutions at this stage. For 1, it will compare the pre-test and post-test, and use the log analysis function to clarify the usage of students who have improved proof ability. As a result, it will continue to consider what kind of usage should be proposed in the future. For 2 as well, the log analysis function is also used to refer to the history of students who are not good at proof and clarify where the problem is. And it is going to consider what kind of approach should be provided by the web-based application for the problem, and plan to provide a new function. Based on the above, the method of appropriate class use of this web-based application will also be discussed.

ACKNOWLEDGEMENT

We would like to thank everyone at T junior high school for their cooperation in the evaluation experiment of this research. This research was supported in part by JSPS KAKENHI JP 19H01716 and JP 18K18657.

REFERENCES

Fujita, T. and Jones, K., 2014. Reasoning-and-proving in geometry in school mathematics textbooks in Japan, *International Journal of Educational Research*, Vol. 64, pp 81-91.

Funaoi, H., Kameda, T., and Hirashima, T., 2009. Kikasyoumeimondai no Kaiketu ni okeru Suiron no Ayamari no Intarakuthibu na Kashika (Visualization of an Error in Solution of Geometry Proof Problems), *Japan Journal of Educational Technology*, Vol. 32, No. 4, pp 425-433.

Gal'perin, P. la., 2012, *Readings in Educational Psychology*. Routledge Press, England, pp. 142-154.

Hamada, S., Yokoyama, M., and Takaoka, R., 2018. Tyugakkousuugakukagoudousyoumei wo Taisyoutosita SyoumeikouzourikaisienWebapuri no Kaihatu to Yuuyouseikentou (Development of a Web based Application for Understanding Structure of Geometric Proof in Junior high School), *Japan Journal of Educational Technology*, Vol. 42 (Suppl.), pp 169-172.

Hirashima, T., 2015. Gakusyukadai Thushin no Gakushukenkyu – Jouhoukouzou toshiteno Gakushukadai no Saiteigi toKouzousousa toshiteno Gakushukatudou no Sekkei (Learning Objects Oriented Approach: Redefinition of Learning Objects as Information Structure and Design of Learning Activity as Structure Manipulation), *Transactions of the Japanese Society for Artificial Intelligence*, Vol. 39, No. 3, pp 277-280.

Kitamura, T., Hase, H., Maeda, K., Hayashi, Y., and Hirashima, T., 2016. Ronri no SankakuModeru wo motiita Sanhoukouronrikumitatekatudou no Sekkei to Enshusisutemu no Kaihatu･Hyouka (Development and evaluation of exercises system of a three-way logic assembly activities using the triangle logic model), *SIG on Advanced Learning Science and Technology*, Vol 78, pp 6-11.

Koseki, K., 1987. Sansuu･suugakukyouikuzensyo2 Zukei no Ronsyousidou (Complete book of math and math education 2 Proof instruction of figure), MEIJITOSYO Press, Japan.

Kunimune, S., 2000. Zukei no Rnsyou ni Kansuru Rikaido no Henka (Changes in the level of understanding of geometric proof), *Journal of Japan Society of Mathematical Education*, Vol. 82, No. 3, pp 66-76.

Kurayam, M., 2015, Ka-dosentaku wo Riyoushita Syoumeimondaikaiketusiensisutemu (Development of Interactive Environment for Proof Questions by Choosing Cards), *The 29th Annual Conference of the Japanese Society for Artificial Intelligence*, Hakodate, Japan, pp. 1-2.

Moore, R. C., 1994. Making the Transition to Formal Proof, *Educational Studies in Mathematics*, Vol. 27, pp 249-266.

National Institute for Educational Policy Research, 2018, National Assessment of Academic Ability, 2007-2016.

Ogata, H., Yin C., Oi, M., Okubo, F., Shimada, A., Kojima, K. and Yamada, M.(2015). e-Book-based Learning Analytics in University Education, Ogata, H et al (Eds.). *Proceedings of the 23th International Conference on Computers in Education*, pp.401-406.

Onoue, A., Yamada, M., Shimada, A., and Taniguchi, R. (2019). The Integrated Knowledge Map for Surveying Students' Learning, *Proceedings of SITE 2019*, pp.838-846

Pechenizkiy, M. and Gašević, D., 2014. Introduction into sparks of the learning analytics future, *Journal of Learning Analytics*, Vol. 1, No. 3, pp 145-149.

Sears D. A. and Reagin JM., 2013. Individual versus collaborative problem solving: divergent outcomes depending on task complexity, *Instructional Science*, Vol. 41, No. 6, pp 1153–1172.

Sekiguchi, Y., 1994, Suugaku no Kyouju･Gakusyuukatei ni okeru Scaffolding ni tuite (Teaching of mathematics About scaffolding in the learning process), *Proceedings of the 27th Mathematical Education Conference*. City, Country, pp. 203-208.

Shimada, A., Okubo, F., Yin, C., Kojima, K., Yamada, M., and Ogata, H. (2015). Informal learning behavior analysis using action logs and slide features in e-textbooks, *Proceedings of 2015 IEEE ICALT*, pp.116-117

Siemens, G. 2010. What are learning analytics? Available: http://www.elearnspace.org/blog/2010/08/25/what-are-learninganalytics/

Yamada, M., Shimada, A., Oi, M., Taniguchi, Y., and Konomi, S. (2018). BR-Map: Concept map system using e-book logs, *Proceedings of CELDA 2018*, pp.248-254

Yin, C., Yamada, M., Oi, M., Shimada, A., Okubo, F., Kojima, K., and Ogata H. (2019). Exploring the Relationships between Reading Behavior Patterns and Learning Outcomes Based on Log Data from E-Books: A Human Factor Approach, *International Journal of Human-Computer Interaction*, 35(4-5), pp.313-322.

DESIGN OF LEARNING ANALYTICS DASHBOARD SUPPORTING METACOGNITION

Li Chen[1], Min Lu[2], Yoshiko Goda[3] and Masanori Yamada[2]
[1]Graduate School of Human-Environment Studies, Kyushu University
744, Motooka, Nishi-ku, Fukuoka 819-0395, Japan
[2]Faculty of Arts and Science, Kyushu University
744, Motooka, Nishi-ku, Fukuoka 819-0395, Japan
[3]Research Center for Instructional Systems, Kumamoto University
2-39-1, Kurokami, Chuo-ku, Kumamoto, 8600862 Japan

ABSTRACT

Metacognition is an aspect in self-regulated learning and is necessary to achieve such learning in an effective and efficient manner. However, it is not always easy and accurate for learners to monitor or assess their own metacognition. In this study, we designed a learning analytics dashboard to improve self-regulated learning in online environments through the collection and analysis of learning log data. There are two separate dashboards used in our system: a knowledge monitoring dashboard and a strategy use dashboard. The knowledge monitoring dashboard is designed to support the knowledge monitoring skills of learners, allowing them to monitor their prior knowledge, whereas the strategy use dashboard is designed to help learners develop metacognitive skills of planning, monitoring, and regulation.

KEYWORDS

Metacognition, Self-Regulated Learning, Dashboard, Learning Analytics

1. INTRODUCTION

Self-regulated learning (SRL) is considered an effective way to achieve academic goals such as test grades and academic skills in school, or even the capacity to self-instruct in the future (Zimmerman, 2002). SRL is considered to be a self-directive process, through which SRL learners transform their mental abilities or intelligences into academic skills (Zimmerman, 1998). SRL is closely linked to the concept of self-generated thoughts, feelings, and behaviors, particular in terms of metacognition and motivation (Tobias and Everson, 2009; Zimmerman, 1998; Zimmerman, 2002). Considering the metacognition in SRL, it is necessary to allow learners to make sense of their own learning process and take responsibility for their own learning.

As information and communication technologies advance, various types of data can be collected, not only test scores and psychometric data, but also learning logs to allow learning behaviors to be analyzed through a learning analytics (LA) approach. This new approach provides a new direction for recording and monitoring learning and for supporting learners in developing their metacognitive skills through SRL.

This paper aims to design a learning analytics dashboard to support the metacognition skills of learners by visualizing their log data during the SRL process.

2. THEORETICAL BACKGROUND

2.1 Metacognition and SRL

SRL strategies are defined as “actions and processes directed at acquiring information or skill that involve agency, purpose, and instrumentality perceptions by learners” (Zimmerman, 1989). Self-regulation is an important construct of learning that includes both metacognition and motivation dimensions (Tobias and Everson, 2009).

Metacognition, which refers to the ability to set goals or plans, monitor and evaluate one's own learning (Tobias and Everson, 2002), is one aspect of SRL and is necessary in regulating learning in an effective and efficient manner (Tobias and Everson, 2009). Many models of metacognitive strategies concerning SRL include three general scales, namely, planning, monitoring, and regulating (Hofer et al., 1998; Pintrich et al., 1993; Pintrich, 1999).

Planning activities contain the usage plan of several cognitive strategies, such as setting goals and criteria or standards for evaluation, clarifying the aim of the learning activities, and conducting task analyses of problems (Belfiore and Hornyak, 1998; Hofer et al., 1998; Zimmerman, 1989). By planning activities, learners are expected to develop a cognitive strategy utilization, activate their relevant prior knowledge and experience, and improve their organization and understanding of the learning content (Hofer et al., 1998).

Monitoring activities include tracking one's attention during the learning processes, checking the degree of understanding, and use of learning or examination strategies (Hofer et al., 1998; Lan, 1998) by observing or recording one's own learning behaviors or performance (Belfiore and Hornyak, 1998; Zimmerman, 1989). Monitoring one's own learning behaviors and processes is an important aspect in SRL because it helps learners to be aware of their weaknesses or deficiencies in their learning processes and regulates their learning strategies or academic behaviors during the next phase (Hofer et al., 1998; Winne and Stockley, 1998).

Regulation strategies are related to and based upon monitoring strategies, and they aim at improving the learning behaviors of learners and repairing deficits in their comprehension (Hofer et al., 1998). For example, learners focus on one part of a text, summarize what they have read, and reread the texts based on their comprehension, adjusting their learning/reading pace according to their learning ability, or choosing course-related materials (Hofer et al., 1998; Thiede et al., 2009).

However, it has been shown that metacognitive skills are required to monitor one's own prior knowledge for effective and efficient learning (Tobias and Everson, 2002, 2009). The lack of an ability to distinguish correctly what learners know or have learned, from what they do not know or need to learn, will lead to a failure to engage in more advanced metacognition strategies (Tobias and Everson, 2009; Yen et al., 2018). This is because metacognition strategies are highly ordered processes used to monitor and coordinate basic or complex cognitive processes. However, learners with low or underdeveloped knowledge monitoring skills are considered to be inefficient at reading the learning materials, leading to a failure to apply a reasonable time allocation and sequence management. Thus, Tobias and Everson (2009) emphasized the importance of knowledge monitoring (KM), which is the metacognitive ability to monitor one's prior knowledge, and placed monitoring knowledge at the bottom of all metacognitive phases, indicating that it is the fundamental component of metacognition.

Therefore, in our study, a dashboard for supporting the metacognition of learners was designed based on the dimensions of knowledge monitoring, planning, monitoring, and regulation.

2.2 Metacognition and Learning Analytics

Although metacognition is an important and effective way for learners to monitor and regulate other cognitive strategies, metacognition measurements are facing considerable challenges. When observing the performance of learners, or assessing their metacognition through self-reported inventories, the validity of the inferences of these evidence-based approaches, as well as the accuracy and candor of a self-assessment, are problems and issues to be overcome (Tobias and Everson, 2009; Winne and Nesbit, 2009). For example, learners cannot observe or remember all events or their learning behaviors during their learning activities. In addition, their perception will be influenced by their previous experience, the pace of events, biases, their memory, and other factors.

Concerning these issues in measuring metacognition, information and communication technology (ICT) has shown significant potential in collecting learning log data. As ICT advances, the types of log data and the methods of data collection vary. For example, the interaction between or across learners, or between learners and computers, can be collected to show the software or system features the learner uses (Tobias and Everson, 2009). In addition, the system operations during the entire learning process can also be collected, such as copying or highlighting texts, or adding annotations, to present the learning behaviors of learners (Tobias and

Everson, 2009; Yamada et al., 2017; Yen et al., 2018).

In Yamada et al.'s (2017) study, the correlations between SRL awareness, learning performance, and behaviors, such as the duration of the slide pages read, the adding of markers, and annotations, were analyzed. As the results indicate, the slide pages that the learners read for a certain duration (from 240 to 299 s) have positive effect on their annotation utilization and learning performance improvement.

2.3 Visualization

Yen et al. (2018b) pointed out that visualization is useful for learners to be aware of what they have been doing and what they should do by making such information salient for them. For example, in online inquiry activities, the visualization of driving questions, a set of goals, or the structure and sequence and associations of tasks, could help learners conduct such activities more smoothly, such as planning, monitoring, and evaluating during SRL (Manlove et al., 2006; Zhang and Quintana, 2012).

However, such visualization tools have been used in domain-specific systems. Considering the utilization of visualization to support the general skills and metacognition of learners, visualization tools should be applied in domain-general systems.

Learning analytics has many advantages including the continuous and automatic collection of the learners' data in ubiquitous learning environments, which are not interfered with by the learners' engagement or intervention of external instructors (Yamada et al., 2016; Yin et al, 2015). Teachers can understand learner's learning behaviors out of class and informal learning settings (Shimada et al, 2015). Integrating these advantages into a dashboard, learning analytics can be provided through a visual display of the data information, informing the learners regarding undetectable patterns of their progress and behaviors (Teasley, 2017) by collecting and analyzing the data generated from online learning platforms, primarily a learning management system (LMS). As Verbert et al. (2014) reviewed in their research, various types of data can be collected and visualized which are relevant with learners' behaviors, including learners' social interaction with other learners or systems, resource use which is used in examples of recommender systems, to estimate learners' knowledge levels, time spent which is visualized for instructors and learners to help them understand learners' time and efforts spent on specific learning sessions, and also the test and self-assessment results that capture knowledge and self-awareness levels.

Kim et al. (2016) examined the effects of a learning analytics dashboard, which presents students with frequency data of certain activities in a college online course. As the results indicate, students who receive a dashboard treatment achieve a higher final score than those who do not; however, the dashboard usage frequency does not have a significant impact on the learning achievement.

Roberts et al. (2017) emphasized student involvement in the dashboard development process and analyzed the students' attitudes toward learning analytic dashboards. As their results indicate, students want access to additional resources easily or general links to an assessment or unit, numerical (class mean/median/max/min) or graphical statistics, and an anonymous comparison with their peers, among other information.

Based on a review of previous studies, and taking the good features pointed out above into account, we designed a dashboard to support learners' KM, learning process monitoring, and regulation during SRL.

3. DESIGN OF LA DASHBOARD FOR METACOGNITION

Our learning-analytics based dashboard consists of two parts: knowledge monitoring and use strategies. In the use strategy phase, three dimensions, namely, planning, monitoring, and regulating, are included.

The learning analytics dashboard was designed based on the BookRoll system (see Figure 1), and the data collection is conducted using this system. BookRoll is an e-book system applied to distribute digital versions of course materials. Students can highlight the contents or add annotations within the digital materials. Furthermore, the accumulated data on the students' use of the BookRoll system functions can be collected and used to visually represent their processes in viewing the materials (Ogata et al., 2017).

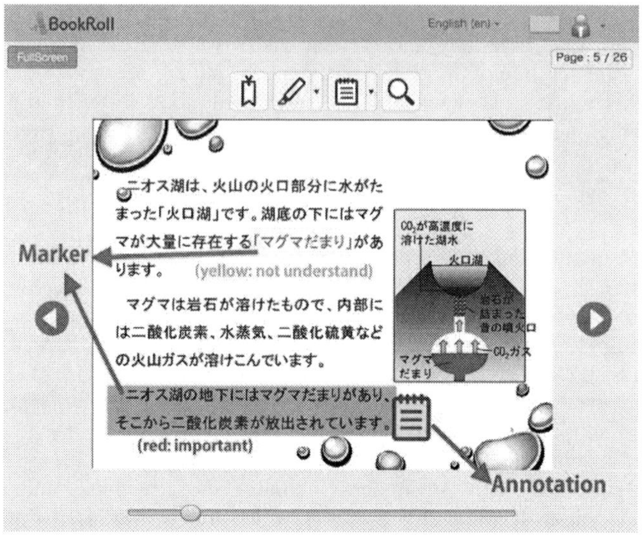

Figure 1. Interface of BookRoll system

3.1 Knowledge Monitoring

Based on the "hierarchy of metacognitive processes" proposed by Tobias and Everson (2009), in which knowledge monitoring is placed in the fundamental phase of the metacognitive processes, one component of our dashboard is to support the knowledge monitoring of learners.

With metacognitive skills used to monitor one's own prior knowledge, learners can adopt more appropriate learning strategies. For example, they can decide to skip parts of the learning materials that they are familiar with or have already mastered or focus on the parts they do not yet understand and seek help from others based on their recognition that their knowledge needs to be improved or supplemented (Tobias and Everson, 2009). Thus, in our study, we designed a dashboard to support learners in knowledge acquisition by providing them access to recommended learning materials related to the knowledge they do not know or are not familiar with.

To assess the monitoring of prior knowledge of the learners, Tobias and Everson (2002) developed a knowledge monitoring assessment (KMA). With KMA, learners are required to estimate whether they can solve each problem, and then take a test on the same content; the accuracy of KM of the learners can be inferred through a comparison of the accuracy between the metacognitive estimation and their test performance.

In addition, using a KMA, the knowledge monitoring of the learners can be divided into four types: (1) estimated as known and with a correct answer on the test (+ +), (2) estimated as known but with an incorrect answer on the test (+ -), (3) estimated as unknown but with a correct answer (- +), and (4) estimated as unknown and with an incorrect answer (- -) (Tobias and Everson, 2002).

The first (+ +) and fourth (- -) types of learners show consistency between their KM and the actual knowledge acquisition, whereas there is a difference in that the fourth type needs greater effort in the learning content and knowledge. By contrast, the second (+ -) and third (- +) types of learners show a discrepancy in estimating and utilizing their knowledge and indicate an insufficient KM skill of metacognition. On our designed dashboard, the estimation and actual results of the tests, as well as the pattern of the KM, are presented to learners, who are divided into one of four KM categories according to the most frequent pattern they demonstrate. All of these categories are presented to the learners through a graph, with the test scores shown along the x-axis, and the numbers of their "correct" and "incorrect" judgements shown along the y-axis.

In Figure 2, the design of the "knowledge monitoring dashboard" is shown. On this dashboard, the results of the tests and their knowledge estimation, as well as the KM pattern according to such data, are provided to learners. For learners who have difficulties in knowledge acquisition, the link between the contents they do not understand with the related digital learning materials will also be provided. When learners make a mistake on the test, the "link to the related materials" icon is presented next to the answer. In addition, when they click the icon, learners can access the recommended materials on the BookRoll system through the link.

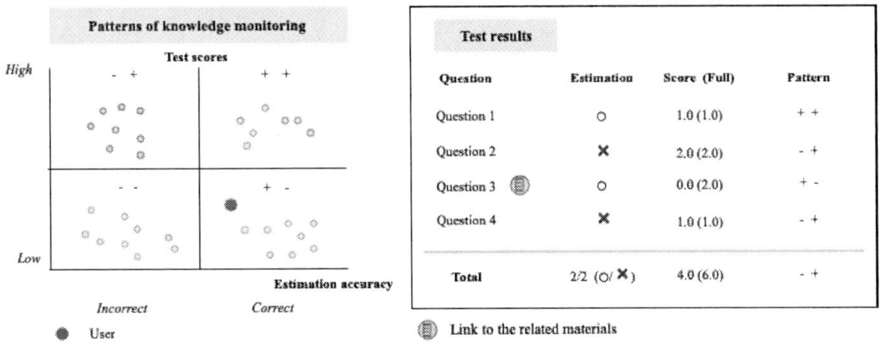

Figure 2. Design of knowledge monitoring dashboard

3.2 Planning

As we reviewed in the theoretical background section, the aim of planning is the development of cognitive strategies through activities such as organizing the contents and activating prior knowledge (Hofer et al., 1998). In our study, we considered designing our dashboard in a way that does not support the planning process, but applies a preplanning phase to help learners organize their learning content and compared it with that of other learners.

Thiede and Anderson (2003) proposed that, after reading a text, it is effective to improve the learner's understanding and comprehension by summarizing the contents using keywords and then rereading the text that the learner is unfamiliar with. Considering the effectiveness of a summarization approach, we designed the dashboard to support the metacognition of knowledge organization by showing learners how to utilize BR-Map.

BR-Map is a concept map tool using logs stored on the BookRoll system (see Figure 3). BR-Map can read and list all logs of highlights and annotations from the BookRoll database (the operations applied when learners read e-learning materials) and display them as objects on the left-side pane. Learners click an object on the left-side pane, and drag-and-drop it into the right-side pane, namely, the "concept map area," and create concept map(s) by connecting the objects using an "arrow" (Yamada et al., 2018).

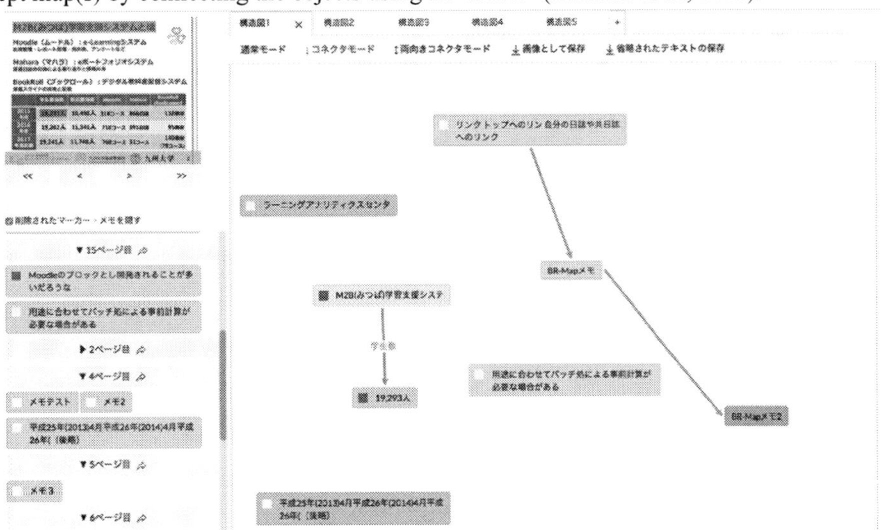

Figure 3. Interface of BR-Map

With our dashboard, to improve the learner's perception of the knowledge organization and construction, we designed a function for presenting the slide pages applied when making the user's own BR-Map, or for adding highlights or annotations to these pages; the details of BR-Map of the learner or other students are presented when clicking on the slide pages icon (Figure 4).

3.3 Monitoring and Regulation

Monitoring strategies alert learners to concentrate on and understand their learning processes to regulate learning. During the monitoring phase, learners are expected to focus on the processes rather than the outcome only (Zimmerman, 1998). Many activities can be conducted to support self-monitoring, such as tracking the learner's attention to the learning materials, determining how well the learner reads a text, or checking for the learner's understanding of a particular lecture.

Therefore, in our design, how learners read a learning text, and the time they spend on each page, is shown on the dashboard (in Figure 4). A thicker arrow means more learners are reading on the same path, and the intensity of the color indicates the time they spend on each page; the darker the color, the more time the learners required.

Because the point of a self-evaluation is a comparison of one's own performance or behaviors based on certain criteria or standards (Belfiore and Hornyak, 1998), it is necessary to provide learners with the criteria or standards to make a judgement regarding whether they finished the work well. However, it is difficult to generate standard learning behaviors, and considering the class average information and an anonymous comparison to the learner's peers, which is information sought out by students, we provide both the individual utilization of BookRoll system tools, and a class average utilization. Learners can switch the frame by clicking the "Me" and "Class" icons.

In addition, when learners click the slide page, the detailed information will be provided on the dashboard, including the numbers and contents of the markers (highlighting), the numbers of annotations, and the time they spent on each page (Figure 5). By checking the information of the learning materials and comparing the information with other students, learners are expected to become aware of their insufficient understanding of the materials, as well as the contents they should concentrate on, and thus finally improve their selection of cognitive strategies and learning behaviors.

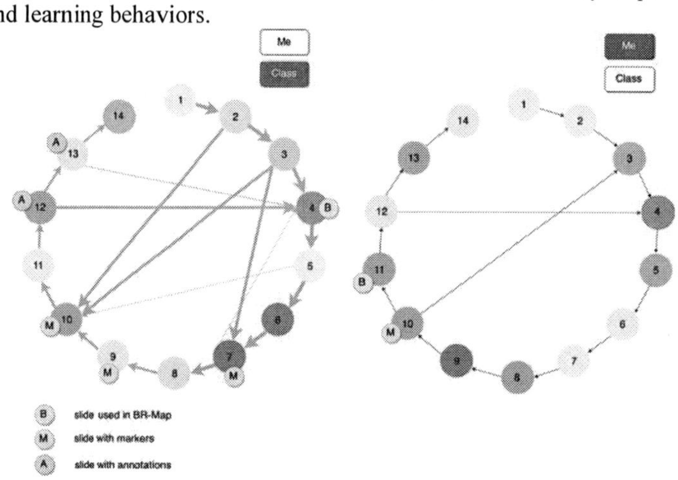

Figure 4. Design of strategy using dashboard 1 - slide reading path and time

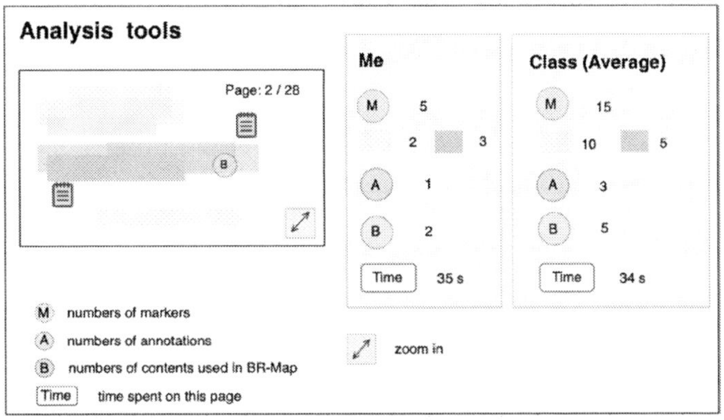

Figure 5. Design of strategy using dashboard 2 - analysis tools

4. CONCLUSION AND FUTURE STUDIES

In the present study, we designed a learning analytics dashboard to support the metacognition of learners regarding the dimensions of knowledge, planning, monitoring, and regulation. However, we have yet to develop this dashboard fully, and we were unable to clarify whether it achieves the expected level of effectiveness. Therefore, in a future study, we will develop this dashboard further and evaluate the dashboard especially in the dimension of effectiveness, efficiency, usefulness, and usability (Verbert et al. 2014) through a practical experiment.

ACKNOWLEDGEMENT

This work was supported by a JST AIP, Grant No. JPMJCR19U1, Japan.

REFERENCES

Belfiore, P. J. and Hornyak, R. S., 1998. Operant theory and application to self-monitoring in adolescents. In: Schunk, D. H., and Zimmerman, B. J. (eds.), *Self-Regulated Learning: From Teaching to Self-Reflective Practice*, Guilford Press, New York.

Hofer, B. et al., 1998. Teaching college students to be self-regulated learners. In: Schunk, D. H., and Zimmerman, B. J. (eds.), *Self-Regulated Learning: From Teaching to Self-Reflective Practice*, Guilford Press, New York.

Kim, J. et al, 2016. Effects of Learning Analytics Dashboard: Analyzing the Relations among Dashboard Utilization, Satisfaction, and Learning Achievement, *Asia Pacific Education Review*, Vol. 17, No. 1, pp. 13-24.

Lan, W, Y., 1998. Teaching self-monitoring skills in statistics. In: Schunk, D. H., and Zimmerman, B. J. (eds.), *Self-Regulated Learning: From Teaching to Self-Reflective Practice*, Guilford Press, New York.

Manlove, S. et al, 2006. Regulative Support for Collaborative Scientific Inquiry Learning, *Journal of Computer Assisted Learning*, Vol. 22, No. 2, pp. 87-98.

Ogata, H. et al, 2017. M2B System: A Digital Learning Platform for Traditional Classrooms in University. *Practitioner Track Proceedings of the Seventh International Learning Analytics & Knowledge Conference (LAK 2017)*. Paper presented at Simon Fraser University, Vancouver, Canada, pp. 155-162.

Pintrich, P. R. et al, 1993. Reliability and Predictive Validity of the Motivated Strategies for Learning Questionnaire (MSLQ), *Educational and Psychological Measurement*, Vol. 53, No. 3, pp. 801-813.

Pintrich, P. R., 1999. The Role of Motivation in Promoting and Sustaining Self - Regulated Learning, *International Journal of Educational Research*, Vol. 31, No. 6, pp. 459-470.

Roberts, L. D. et al, 2017. Give Me a Customizable Dashboard: Personalized Learning Analytics Dashboards in Higher Education, *Technology, Knowledge and Learning*, Vol. 22, No. 3, pp. 317-333.

Shimada, A. et al, 2015. Informal learning behavior analysis using action logs and slide features in e-textbooks, *Proceedings of IEEE ICALT 2015*, pp.116-117.

Teasley, S. D., 2017. Student Facing Dashboards: One Size Fits All? *Technology, Knowledge and Learning*, Vol. 22, No. 3, pp. 377-384.

Thiede, K. W. et al., 2009. Metacognitive monitoring during and after reading. In: *Handbook of Metacognition in Education*, Routledge.

Thiede, K. W. and Anderson, M. C., 2003. Summarizing Can Improve Metacomprehension Accuracy. *Contemporary Educational Psychology*, Vol. 28, No. 2, pp. 129-160.

Tobias, S. and Everson, H. T., 2002. Knowing What You Know and What You Don't: Further Research on Metacognitive Knowledge Monitoring, Research Report No. 2002-3. College Entrance Examination Board.

Tobias, S. and Everson, H. T., 2009. The importance of knowing what you know: A knowledge monitoring framework for studying metacognition in education. In: *Handbook of Metacognition in Education*, Routledge.

Verbert, K. et al, 2014. Learning dashboards: an overview and future research opportunities. *Personal and Ubiquitous Computing*, Vol. 18, No. 6, pp. 1499-1514.

Winne, P. H. and Nesbit, J. C., 2009. Supporting Self-Regulated Learning with Cognitive Tools. In: *Handbook of Metacognition in Education*, Routledge.

Winne, P. H. and Stockley, D. B., 1998. Computing technologies as sites for developing self-regulated learning. In: Schunk, D. H., and Zimmerman, B. J. (eds.), *Self-Regulated Learning: From Teaching to Self-Reflective Practice*, Guilford Press, New York.

Yamada, M. et al, 2016. Learning Analytics in Ubiquitous Learning Environments: Self-Regulated Learning Perspective. *Proceedings of International Conference on Computers in Education 2016 (ICCE 2016)*, pp. 306-314.

Yamada, M. et al, 2018. BR-MAP: Concept Map System using e-Book Logs. *In 15th International Conference on Cognition and Exploratory Learning in the Digital Age (CELDA 2018)*, pp. 248-254.

Yamada, M. et al, 2017. Learning Analytics of the Relationships among Self-Regulated Learning, Learning Behaviors, and Learning Performance, *Research and Practice in Technology Enhanced Learning*, Vol. 12, No. 1, p. 13.

Yen, M. H. et al, 2018. Assessing Metacognitive Components in Self-Regulated Reading of Science Texts in E-Based Environments, *International Journal of Science and Mathematics Education*, Vol. 16, No. 5, pp. 797-816.

Yen, M. H. et al, 2018(b). A Framework for Self-Regulated Digital Learning (SRDL), *Journal of Computer Assisted Learning*, Vol. 34, No. 5, pp. 580-589.

Yin, C. et al, 2015. Analyzing the Features of Learning Behaviors of Students using e-Books, *Proceedings of International Conference on Computers in Education 2015 (ICCE 2015)*, pp.617-626

Zhang, M. L. and Quintana, C., 2012. Scaffolding Strategies for Supporting Middle School Students' Online Inquiry Processes, *Computers & Education*, Vol. 58, No. 1, pp. 181-196.

Zimmerman, B. J., 1998. Developing self-fulfilling cycles of academic regulation: An analysis of exemplary instructional models. In: Schunk, D. H., and Zimmerman, B. J. (eds.), *Self-Regulated Learning: From Teaching to Self-Reflective Practice*, Guilford Press, New York.

Zimmerman, B. J., 1989. A social cognitive view of self-regulated academic learning, *Journal of Educational Psychology*, Vol. 81, No. 3, 329.

Zimmerman, B. J., 2002. Becoming a Self-Regulated Learner: An Overview, *Theory into Practice*, Vol. 41, No. 2, 64-70.

MEASURING COMPUTATIONAL THINKING – ADAPTING A PERFORMANCE TEST AND A SELF-ASSESSMENT INSTRUMENT FOR GERMAN-SPEAKING COUNTRIES

Josef Guggemos[1], Sabine Seufert[1] and Marcos Román-González[2]
[1]*University of St.Gallen, Guisanstr 1a, 9010 St.Gallen, Switzerland*
[2]*Universidad Nacional de Educación a Distancia, C/ Juan del Rosal 14, C.P. 28040, Madrid, Spain*

ABSTRACT

Far-reaching technological changes are shaping our society and the ways in which we work. A key 21st-century skill for taking advantage of those changes may be computational thinking (CT). CT aims at enabling humans to carry out more effective problem solving by utilizing concepts of computing and computer technology. For a successful integration of CT into curricula, however, it is important to take assessment into account. We review two instruments that capture CT: the Computational Thinkig Test (CTt), a performance test, and the Computational Thinking Scales (CTS), that relies on self-assessment. We have adapted both instruments from English to German. Using a sample of 202 upper-secondary students from Switzerland, we provide further evidence on the validity of both instruments. To this end, we apply item response theory and confirmatory factor analysis. Furthermore, we evaluate the relationship between CTt and CTS. Both instruments show good properties and may be suitable for assessing CT in German-speaking countries at the secondary level.

KEYWORDS

Computational Thinking, Rasch-Scaling, Performance Test, Self-Assessment

1. INTRODUCTION

Tremendous technological changes are shaping our society and ways of working (Weng, 2015). A key driver for these changes are advances in the field of computing (Wing, 2008). From an educational point of view, it is vital to determine skills that are necessary for being successful in such an environment. Among others, computational thinking (CT) is regarded as a key 21st-century skill (Voogt, Fisser, Good, Mishra, & Yadav, 2015; Wing, 2006).

Already used in the 1980s, the term CT experienced a revival in 2006 due to Wing's seminal article. Wing conceptualized CT as "solving problems, designing systems, and understanding human behavior, by drawing on the concepts fundamental to computer science" (2006, p. 33). Research activity on CT has experienced a sharp increase in recent years. Using Scopus as the database, Hsu et al. (2018) reviewed 120 CT studies published from 2006 to 2017. Of these studies, 65 were published in 2016 and 2017. None of the 120 articles relate to German-speaking countries. However, CT is also a construct of interest in such countries (for Germany, e.g., Delcker & Ifenthaler, 2017; for Switzerland, e.g., Repenning, 2018). Moreover, CT was part of the 2018 'International Computer and Information Literacy Study' (ICILS) in Germany (Eickelmann, 2019).

On behalf of the European Commission, Bocconi et al. (2016) reviewed the curricular integration of CT in European countries. Concerning the German-speaking countries, they provide the following evidence: In Austria, elements of CT are part of 'Informatics' in secondary schools. In the German-speaking part of Switzerland, the curricula for primary and lower-secondary schools comprise elements of CT. Furthermore, depending on the canton, CT may also be part of upper-secondary schools (e.g., Canton of St.Gallen, 2018). In Germany, curricula are managed on a regional level; hence, it is difficult to come to an overall conclusion. Examples of federal states where CT is part of the curriculum are Bavaria and North-Rhine Westphalia. On an abstract level, CT might be a curricular goal in German-speaking countries. However, as Grover and Pea (2013, p. 41) concluded: "Without attention to assessment, CT can have little hope of making its way successfully into any K–12 curriculum." Recently, two literature reviews on CT stressed the importance of valid tools for measuring CT (Hsu et al., 2018; Shute, Sun, & Asbell-Clarke, 2017). Against this background, we raise the following research question: *How can CT of secondary students be assessed in German-speaking countries?*

We do not aim at large-scale assessment, like the ICILS study, but instead focus on instruments that researchers and educators can use to measure CT at the secondary level. Due to the need for CT interventional studies (Lye & Koh, 2014), instruments should be suitable for pre-post or longitudinal designs.

For a valid measurement, curriculum, instruction, and assessment have to be in alignment (Pellegrino, 2010). Hence, we will structure our review of the literature in line with the curriculum-instruction-assessment triad.

2. STATE OF THE ART

2.1 Curriculum

The basis for a curriculum may be a robust and agreed definition of CT (Selby & Woollard, 2013). Although such a definition is (and will be) not available, a core set of CT facets might be identified (Bocconi et al., 2016). Table 1 summarizes this core set. Since the core facets presented by Bocconi et al. (2016) are consistent with CT curricula in European countries, we expect a curricular-valid test to be in line with those facets.

Table 1. Core facets of CT

Abstraction	"simplifying from the concrete to the general as solutions are developed" (Barr & Stephenson, 2011, p. 52)
Algorithmic thinking	using "a step-by-step procedure for taking input and producing some desired output" (Wing, 2008, p. 3718)
Automation	"process in which a computer is instructed to execute a set of repetitive tasks quickly and efficiently compared to the processing power of a human" (Lee et al., 2011, p. 33)
Decomposition	"breaking problems down into smaller parts that may be more easily solved" (Barr & Stephenson, 2011, p. 52)
Debugging	"find your own mistakes and fix them" (Hsu et al., 2018, p. 299)
Generalization	"move from specific to broader applicability" (Selby & Woollard, 2013, p. 4)

2.2 Instruction

The crucial question regarding CT instruction is whether coding is necessary to foster CT. Buitrago Flórez et al. (2017) concluded that teaching programming might be a suitable approach for fostering CT. However, using professional programming languages like Java can be extremely difficult for secondary students due to complex syntax. It may be preferable to use visual programming languages (Lye & Koh, 2014; Repenning, 2017). Scratch, developed by the MIT Media lab (https://scratch.mit.edu), is such a visual programming language and is freely available in a German version. Scratch reduces cognitive load because it relies on visual blocks to build code and therefore prevents syntax errors. Students arrange the blocks via drag and drop.

In terms of instructional practice, Hsu et al. (2018) found that in 52% of all cases, a programming language is used to foster CT (other approaches are experiments and computer games). Scratch accounts for 41%, by far the highest share. The professional programming language with the highest share is MATLAB (4%). Overall, professional programming languages play only a minor role (15%).

2.3 Assessment

Román-González, Moreno-León, and Robles (2019) presented a classification for CT assessment tools. In line with this classification, two kind of assessment tools may be suitable for a pre-post design: Diagnostic tools address the "CT aptitudinal level"; perceptions-attitudes scales capture "the perceptions (e.g., self-efficacy perceptions) and attitudes of the subjects not only about CT, but also about related issues such as computers, computer science, computer programming, or even digital literacy" (Román-González et al., 2019, pp. 81-83).

Román-González et al. (2017, 2018a, 2018b) have developed and validated a *diagnostic tool* for secondary students: the Computational Thinking Test (CTt). Figure 1 shows a sample item. The authors rely on the CT framework of Brennan and Resnick (2012). It is consistent with the core CT facets. 'Abstraction' is covered as visual code blocks represent the problems, including conditionals and variables. 'Algorithmic thinking' is necessary because all tasks require sequencing steps to come to a solution. 'Automation' is captured by means of loops. 'Decomposition' manifests itself in the use of functions to split up the problems into more manageable elements. 'Debugging' is required because students have to identify mistakes in provided sequences of code blocks. 'Generalization', however, is not directly addressed by CTt. For assembling visual code blocks, the authors utilize the 'code.org' platform (https://code.org/), which is similar to Scratch (Hsu et al., 2018, p. 302). This might be favorable in terms of alignment with instruction. The test comprises 28 selected response items and can be taken online; secondary students should be able to process CTt in less than 45 minutes. No programming experience is necessary, which makes CTt a very flexible instrument. Since 'code.org' is licensed under Creative Commons, new items could be constructed with reasonable effort. The authors validated CTt using a sample of 1,251 Spanish secondary (5th to 10th grade) students and classical test theory. The reliability of the test is sufficiently high (Cronbach's alpha = .79). Concerning criterion validity, the authors investigated the nomological net of CT (Román-González et al., 2017; Román-González et al., 2018b). They report high correlations with problem-solving ability (r = .67) and moderate correlation with reasoning ability (r = .44), spatial ability (r = .44), and CT self-efficacy (r = .41). Moreover, there is evidence for instructional sensitivity of CTt (Brackmann et al., 2017; Rose, Habgood, & Jay, 2019). This means that responses of students to the items change due to instruction (Naumann, Rieser, Musow, Hochweber, & Hartig, 2019).

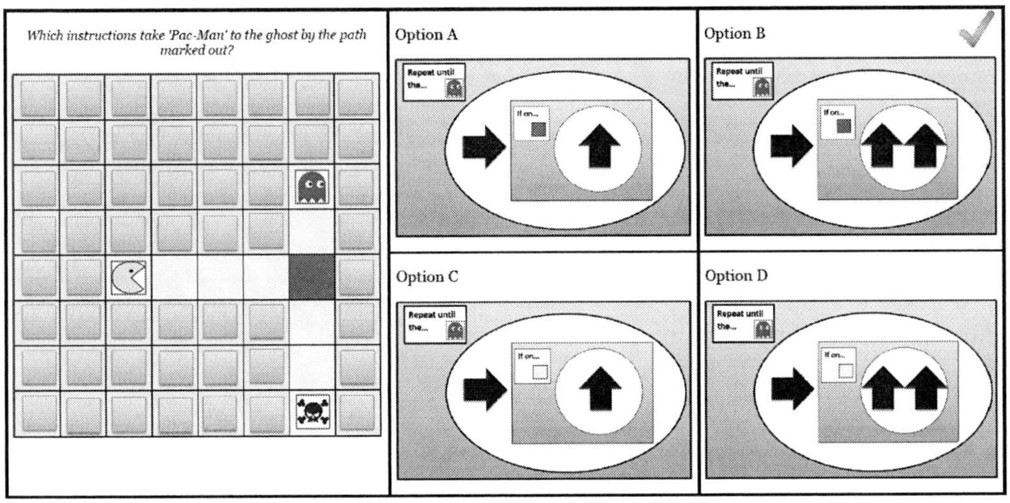

Figure 1. Item 6 of CTt

In sum, we regard CTt as a suitable instrument for measuring the CT of secondary students. As the authors acknowledge (Román-González et al., 2018b), the focus of CTt is narrow. However, it covers core CT facets and therefore might be a good trade-off between curricular validity, reliability, and required test time. Currently, CTt has only been validated using classical test theory. Using item response theory (IRT) may allow further insights. In principal, CTt should be suitable for IRT methods because all items can be solved independently from each other; local stochastic independence of the items might be fulfilled.

As the focus of CTt is narrow, a *perceptions-attitudes scale* may complement CTt. The Computational Thinking Scales (CTS) are such an instrument (Korkmaz, Çakir, & Özden, 2017). The authors draw on the 'International Society for Technology in Education' (ISTE, 2015) framework of computational thinking that comprises five dimensions: 'Creativity', 'Algorithmic thinking', 'Cooperativity', 'Critical thinking', and 'Problem solving'. CTS consists of 29 self-assessment questions. It has been validated by means of confirmatory factor analysis using a sample of 580 Turkish undergraduate students. Fit-values are decent (Korkmaz et al., 2017, p. 565): CFI = 0.95, RMSEA = 0.06. Overall, we regard CTS as an appropriate instrument for capturing CT. Cost efficiency is high, because it requires only about five minutes test time.

3. METHOD

3.1 Adaption of CTt and CTS

Since CTt and CTS show promising results in validation studies and are suitable for capturing CT in longitudinal designs, we have adapted them to German. In terms of CTt, we utilized 'code.org' to create the visual code blocks in German. We also replaced the five easiest items by five more difficult items. This is possible because the original version of CTt comprises 40 items. An online version of CTt in German is available for Unipark from the authors upon request. A short version of CTS can be found in the appendix.

3.2 Psychometric Test Validation of CTt

We go beyond the work of the test developers and rely on probabilistic test theory. Due to the favorable characteristic of specific objectivity, we aim at Rasch modeling. The main advantage is that students (proficiency) and items (difficulty) can be located on a common (logit) scale that allows for a criterion-referenced test interpretation (Hartig & Frey, 2013). For assessing Rasch scalability of CTt, we draw on the framework of Bühner (2011, p. 547). First, we carry out Andersen's likelihood ratio test (LRT) (Andersen, 1973) using the R package 'eRm 0.16-2' (Mair & Hatzinger, 2007). In order to perform the LRT, the persons in the sample are split up into subgroups. Then, it is tested if the items as a whole work in the same way in these subgroups, i.e., the same parameter estimations are obtained. The median of the CTt raw score, gender, age (above and below average), and computer literacy (above and below average) act as split criteria. Computer literacy is measured with the dimension 'practical computer knowledge' of the INCOBI-R (Richter, Naumann, & Horz, 2010). Based on DIF-analyses, we may exclude items that discriminate specific groups.

To check for item homogeneity (unidimensionality), we conduct confirmatory factor analysis ('lavaan' 0.6-3 package in R, Rosseel, 2012) with CT as a single factor. Since the data are binary (correct/wrong), we use a 'WLSMV' estimator. A chi-square test acts as a global fit test. Furthermore, we rely on CFI, TLI, RMSEA, and SRMR as fit measures. Cutoff values for a decent fit may be: CFI and TLI > .95, RMSEA < .08, and SRMR < .11 (Bühner, 2011, pp. 425–427). Moreover, we analyze the correlation of the residuals by means of principal component analysis (PCA). This approach would also indicate violations of local stochastic independence of the items (OECD, 2017, pp. 169–170). For assessing person homogeneity, we perform a mixed Rasch analysis ('mixRasch' 1.1 package in R, Willse, 2011).

After having checked Rasch scalability, we examine if the items meet the cut-off values applied in the PISA studies (OECD, 2017, pp. 131–134) using the R package 'TAM 3.1-45' (Robitzsch, Kiefer, & Wu, 2019). The deviance from the item discrimination implied by the Rasch model is evaluated by means of weighted mean square error (wMNSQ = Infit). It should lie between 0.8 and 1.2. The point-biserial correlation should be above 0.30. The percentage of correct answers should fall between 20 and 90%. Not more than 10% of missing data should be present. Finally, we provide EAP/PV- and WLE-reliability as a measure for overall test reliability. These measures are comparable with Cronbach's alpha.

3.3 Psychometric Test Validation of CTS

CTS items are measured on a 7-point scale of rating. Hence, we use confirmatory factor analysis with a 'MLR' estimator for test validation ('lavaan' package 0.6-3 in R, Rosseel, 2012). A chi-square test acts as a global fit test. Furthermore, we rely on CFI, TLI, RMSEA, and SRMR as fit measures. Convergent validity is assessed by means of the average variance extracted (AVE). An AVE of greater than 0.5 may be evidence for convergent validity (Hair, Ringle, & Sarstedt, 2011, p. 145). Discriminant validity may be ensured if the square root of the AVE of every construct is higher than all correlations with other constructs (Fornell-Larcker criterion). To assess the reliability of the measures, we use composite reliability in conjunction with Cronbach's alpha. They should be higher than 0.7 (Hair et al., 2011, p. 147). Since the five facets are, as the name implies, facets of CT, we also checked if a second-order model (Bagozzi & Yi, 2012) with CT operationalized by the five facets yields a decent fit.

3.4 Sample

Two hundred and two upper-secondary students from German-speaking Switzerland act as a sample. They all attended the 11th (second last) grade at a 'Kantonsschule' (high school). On average, they were 17.23 years old (SD = 0.85 years) and 56% are female. CTt, CTS, and context questions were administered using Unipark at the beginning of the school year 2018/19. Teachers supervised the students and ensured an adequate test environment, e.g., preventing copying from their neighbor. The intended test time was 45 minutes. Ninety-five percent of the students were able to finish the instrument within this time; teachers allowed every student to complete the work.

4. RESULTS

4.1 Psychometric Validity of CTt

Of the 28 items, the students in the sample answered on average 18.45 items correctly (SD = 5.71, median = 19, min = 6, max = 28). Concerning Rasch-scalability, the LRT yielded mixed results. We did not find significant DIF-effects in terms of gender ($\chi^2 = 36$, df = 27, p = .11), age ($\chi^2 = 16$, df = 26, p = .94), and computer literacy ($\chi^2 = 30$, df = 26, p = .26). However, utilizing the median of the CTt test score as split criterion yielded significant DIF ($\chi^2 = 77$, df = 27, p < .01). Three items caused this overall DIF-effect. Item 1 was far too easy for the students in our sample (-4.80 Logits). Item 10 may have caused problems due to a different response format. The provided answer 'Option A and C are correct' might have confused students. For item 20, we could not find a reason on the content level. Moreover, the DIF-effect was only light to moderate (Penfield & Algina, 2006): Logit = 0.51. Against this background and because content validity was not impaired, we decided to exclude items 1 and 10 from the test and retain item 20. All further analysis was carried out without these two items.

The assumption of item homogeneity (unidimensionality) of CTt is justified: $\chi^2(199) = 341$ (p = .05), CFI = 0.964, TLI = 0.961, RMSEA = 0.026, SRMR = 0.063. Moreover, the PCA of the residual correlations yielded a percentage of variance for the first principal component of only 7%. This finding might also indicate local stochastic independence of the items. Our mixed Rasch analysis revealed a one-class solution; the AIC is lower in comparison to any multiclass solution (Bühner, 2011, p. 547). Hence, deviant problem-solving patterns among the students may be unlikely.

Concerning the cut-off values from the PISA studies, in general, all items show good values. The wMNSQ lies between 0.89 and 1.15 with the exception of item 18. This item has a wMNSQ of 1.22, which is slightly above the cut-off value of 1.2. However, wMNSQ values up to 1.33 might be acceptable (Wilson, 2005, p. 129). All point-biseral correlations are higher than 0.30. The percentage of correct answers for all items lies between .90 and .25. Every student fully processed the items; missing values are not present. Table 2 summarizes the item characteristics. EAP/PV-reliability equals 0.85, WLE-reliability 0.81, which may be sufficiently high for research purposes.

4.2 Psychometric Validity of CTS

In our sample, the fit-values of the published version of CTS with 29 questions indicated room for improvement ($\chi^2(340) = 657$ ($p < .001$), CFI = 0.881, TLI = 0.868, RMSEA = 0.073, SRMR = 0.095). The reasons are mainly cross loadings. For instance, the first item of 'Algorithmic thinking' also loads significantly on 'Critical thinking' and 'Creativity'. Discriminant validity is not ensured. Based on a content review, we selected three items for each of the five facets. This approach yielded a decent fit: $\chi^2(80) = 85$ ($p = .34$), CFI = 0.997, TLI = 0.996, RMSEA = 0.018, SRMR = 0.040. Convergent and discriminant validity are fulfilled: AVE is greater than .543 in every case, the Fornell-Larcker criterion is met. The five facets are reliably measured. The key characteristics of our short version of CTS can be found in Table 3. A second-order model with an overall CT factor yielded a 'Heywood case', i.e., the variance of 'critical thinking' is (non-significant) negative. Applying (meaningful) model restrictions did not solve this problem. Against this backdrop and overall small correlations between the five facets, e.g., between 'Algorithmic thinking' and 'Cooperative thinking', a second-order model might not be justified (Bagozzi & Yi, 2012).

Table 2. Item difficulty, fit, and DIF-effects of CTt (n = 202)

	Item difficulty and discrimination					DIF in Logit			
Item	θ	s.e. θ	wMNSQ	Pt.bis.	P+	Ability	Gender	Age	CL
ct_2	-2.42	0.23	0.99	0.34	87%	-0.04	-0.09	-0.01	-0.13
ct_3	-2.75	0.25	0.99	0.30	90%	-0.06	0.41	0.18	-0.30
ct_4	-0.32	0.16	1.14	0.42	55%	-0.37	0.18	-0.17	0.07
ct_5	-0.45	0.16	1.08	0.45	58%	-0.20	-0.13	0.03	-0.04
ct_6	-2.22	0.21	1.07	0.33	85%	-0.07	0.17	0.09	-0.09
ct_7	-0.18	0.16	0.97	0.54	53%	0.23	0.15	0.21	-0.25
ct_8	-1.24	0.18	1.15	0.34	72%	-0.45	-0.37	-0.01	-0.06
ct_9	-1.63	0.19	0.97	0.44	78%	-0.11	0.10	0.26	-0.41
ct_11	-0.72	0.17	0.92	0.56	63%	0.33	0.43	0.02	-0.06
ct_12	-0.80	0.17	1.09	0.41	64%	-0.23	-0.22	-0.10	-0.07
ct_13	-1.40	0.18	1.05	0.39	74%	-0.25	-0.37	0.41	-0.25
ct_14	-0.94	0.17	1.07	0.42	67%	-0.23	-0.03	0.03	0.17
ct_15	-2.01	0.20	0.91	0.45	83%	0.38	0.10	-0.04	0.32
ct_16	-1.53	0.18	0.98	0.46	76%	0.05	0.35	-0.33	0.21
ct_17	-0.18	0.16	0.94	0.57	53%	0.05	0.26	-0.16	0.18
ct_18	1.45	0.19	1.22	0.30	25%	-0.58	-0.13	0.33	0.08
ct_19	-1.85	0.20	0.92	0.47	81%	0.16	0.03	-0.03	0.16
ct_20	-0.69	0.17	0.89	0.58	62%	0.51	0.32	-0.06	0.02
ct_21	-0.94	0.17	0.94	0.53	67%	0.38	-0.25	-0.11	0.26
ct_22	-0.91	0.17	1.04	0.46	66%	0.04	-0.17	0.04	0.00
ct_23	-1.40	0.18	1.01	0.45	74%	-0.18	-0.31	-0.18	0.02
ct_24	-0.50	0.16	0.89	0.59	59%	0.14	-0.12	-0.19	0.33
ct_25	-1.46	0.18	0.91	0.52	75%	0.29	-0.29	-0.18	0.08
ct_26	-0.26	0.16	0.93	0.57	54%	0.20	-0.03	0.12	-0.17
ct_27	0.51	0.17	0.96	0.56	40%	0.00	0.05	-0.12	0.09
ct_28	-0.10	0.16	0.97	0.55	51%	0.03	-0.01	-0.02	-0.16

Note. θ = difficulty, s.e. = standard error, wMNSQ = weighted mean square error, Pt.bis. = point biserial correlation, P+ = correct responses, Ability = median of CTt raw score, CL = computer literacy (INCOBI-R).

4.3 Comparison CTt and CTS

The latent correlations between CTt and the five facets of CTS are with 'Creativity' .271 ($p = .002$), 'Algorithmic thinking' .309 ($p < .001$), 'Cooperativity' -.003 ($p = .956$), 'Critical thinking' .408 ($p < .001$), and 'Problem solving' .154 ($p = .085$). Considering all CTS facets (latent scores) as independent variables and CTt as a dependent variable in a latent regression, only algorithmic thinking is statistically significant ($b = 0.319$, $p < .001$).

Table 3. Characteristics of used CTS items and constructs (n = 202)

	Construct	Item	Mean (SD)	λ	α	ρc	AVE	Latent correlations, square root of AVE on diagonal				
								(1)	(2)	(3)	(4)	(5)
(1)	Creativity	cr_3	5.6 (1.5)	.75								
		cr_4	5.6 (1.3)	.86	.87	.94	.75	.87				
		cr_5	5.3 (1.3)	.89								
(2)	Algorithmic thinking	al_3	4.0 (1.9)	.90								
		al_4	3.7 (1.8)	.86	.90	.94	.73	**.32**	.85			
		al_5	4.0 (1.8)	.83								
(3)	Cooperativity	co_1	4.6 (1.8)	.85								
		co_2	4.2 (1.8)	.90	.89	.93	.70	**.22**	.15	.84		
		co_3	4.8 (1.7)	.82								
(4)	Critical thinking	cr_1	5.1 (1.4)	.74								
		cr_2	4.9 (1.4)	.75	.80	.88	.57	**.71**	**.62**	**.22**	.75	
		cr_3	4.6 (1.4)	.78								
(5)	Problem solving	pr_1	5.5 (1.5)	.79								
		pr_2	5.4 (1.7)	.68	.78	.86	.54	.20	-.03	-.20	.15	.73
		pr_4	5.1 (1.5)	.74								

Note. Items measured on a 7-point rating scale. λ = standardized loading, α = Cronbach's alpha, ρc = composite reliability, AVE = average variance extracted. Figures in bold indicate significant correlations at the 5% level.

5. CONCLUSION

Recent literature reviews have stressed the theoretical and practical importance of CT. Moreover, CT is a curricular goal in German-speaking countries. The current shortage of quantitative research on CT in German speaking countries may be attributed to the lack of instruments for measuring CT. To tackle this issue, we have adapted two internationally accepted (Shute et al., 2017) instruments for assessing CT and evaluated them using a sample of 202 upper-secondary students from German-speaking Switzerland. CTt, as a diagnostic tool, covers core CT facets addressed in curricula. Against this background, curricular validity might be ensured. Secondary students should be able to perform CTt in less than 45 minutes. CTt relies on dichotomous constructed response items. This allows an objective and very cost-efficient scoring. On the downside, CTt may not be able to capture higher-level cognitive processes.

In terms of psychometric validity, we were able to demonstrate Rasch scalability. The overall EAP/PV- and WLE-reliability of the test is good with values of 0.85 and 0.81, respectively. In sum, CTt may be adequate for summative CT assessment of secondary students in German-speaking countries, e.g., for research purposes, especially because it relies on visual code blocks that most of the applied instructional means also utilize. Since instructional sensitivity of CTt has been demonstrated in other studies, it may be appropriate for measuring CT changes in (quasi-)experimental designs.

In contrast to CTt, the perceptions-attitudes scale CTS covers CT on a broad scale as it relies on the ISTE (2015) framework. 'Creativity' and 'Cooperativity', two of the five facets of CTS, might be constructs related to, but not parts of, CT. The overall low and even negative latent correlations among the five facets, and the convergence problems in case of a second-order model, might be evidence for this assertion. Furthermore, the original version of CTS showed a lack of discriminant validity. We addressed this issue by removing items while considering content validity. In this light, we may have contributed to the psychometric validity of CTS. Overall, we regard CTS as a suitable approach for capturing CT in a longitudinal design. The main advantage is the small amount of time necessary for our short version, with only 15 questions. Students should be able to perform it in less than three minutes. This makes CTS also an attractive option for considering CT as a control variable. The main disadvantage of CTS lies in the nature of self-assessments – it is questionable whether students are able and willing to evaluate themselves accurately. Overall, we agree with Román-González et al. (2019) that only a combination of instruments may yield a comprehensive picture of CT. Since CTt and CTS both are suitable for longitudinal studies, they might be used for capturing CT in a pre-post design in German speaking countries.

REFERENCES

Andersen, E. B. (1973). A goodness of fit test for the Rasch model. *Psychometrika, 38*(1), 123–140.

Bagozzi, R. P. & Yi, Y. (2012). Specification, evaluation, and interpretation of structural equation models. *Journal of the Academy of Marketing Science, 40*(1), 8–34.

Barr, V., & Stephenson, C. (2011). Bringing computational thinking to K-12. *ACM Inroads, 2*(1), 48–54.

Bocconi, S., Chioccariello, A., Dettori, G., Ferrari, A., & Engelhardt, K. (2016). *Developing computational thinking in compulsory education*. Luxembourg: Publications Office of the European Union.

Brackmann, C. P., Román-González, M., Robles, G., Moreno-León, J., Casali, A., & Barone, D. (2017). Development of Computational Thinking Skills through Unplugged Activities in Primary School. In E. Barendsen (Ed.), *Proceedings of the 12th Workshop on Primary and Secondary Computing Education* (pp. 65–72). New York, NY: ACM.

Brennan, K., & Resnick, M. (2012). New frameworks for studying and assessing the development of computational thinking. *American Educational Research Association Meeting, Vancouver, BC, Canada*, 1–25.

Bühner, M. (2011). *Einführung in die Test- und Fragebogenkonstruktion* (3rd ed.). Munich: Pearson Studium.

Buitrago Flórez, F., Casallas, R., Hernández, M., Reyes, A., Restrepo, S., & Danies, G. (2017). Changing a Generation's Way of Thinking: Teaching Computational Thinking Through Programming. *Review of Educational Research, 87*(4), 834–860.

Canton of St.Gallen. (2018). *Lehrplan Informatik*. St. Gallen: Amt für Mittelschulen.

Delcker, J. & Ifenthaler, D. (2017). Computational Thinking as an Interdisciplinary Approach to Computer Science School Curricula: A German Perspective. In P. J. Rich & C. B. Hodges (Eds.), *Emerging Research, Practice, and Policy on Computational Thinking* (pp. 49–62). Cham: Springer International Publishing.

Eickelmann, B. (2019). Measuring Secondary School Students' Competence in Computational Thinking in ICILS 2018—Challenges, Concepts, and Potential Implications for School Systems Around the World. In S.-C. Kong & H. Abelson (Eds.), *Computational thinking education* (pp. 53–64). Singapore: Springer.

Grover, S., & Pea, R. (2013). Computational thinking in K-12: A review of the state of the field. *Educational Researcher, 42*(1), 38–43.

Hair, J. F., Ringle, C. M., & Sarstedt, M. (2011). PLS-SEM: Indeed a silver bullet. *The Journal of Marketing Theory and Practice, 19*(2), 139–152.

Hartig, J., & Frey, A. (2013). Sind Modelle der Item-Response-Theorie (IRT) das „Mittel der Wahl" für die Modellierung von Kompetenzen? *Zeitschrift für Erziehungswissenschaft, 16*, 47–51.

Hsu, T.-C., Chang, S.-C., & Hung, Y.-T. (2018). How to learn and how to teach computational thinking: Suggestions based on a review of the literature. *Computers & Education, 126*, 296–310.

ISTE. (2015). Computational thinking: leadership toolkit. Retrieved from www.iste.org/computational-thinking

Korkmaz, Ö., Çakir, R., & Özden, M. Y. (2017). A validity and reliability study of the computational thinking scales (CTS). *Computers in Human Behavior, 72*, 558–569.

Lee, I., Martin, F., Denner, J., Coulter, B., Allan, W., Erickson, J., . . . Werner, L. (2011). Computational thinking for youth in practice. *ACM Inroads, 2*(1), 32.

Lye, S. Y. & Koh, J. H. L. (2014). Review on teaching and learning of computational thinking through programming: What is next for K-12? *Computers in Human Behavior, 41*, 51–61.

Mair, P., & Hatzinger, R. (2007). Extended Rasch modeling: The eRm package for the application of IRT models in R. *Journal of Statistical Software, 20*(9), 1–20.

Naumann, A., Rieser, S., Musow, S., Hochweber, J., & Hartig, J. (2019). Sensitivity of test items to teaching quality. *Learning and Instruction, 60*, 41–53.

OECD. (2017). *PISA 2015 Technical Report*. Paris: OECD Publishing. Retrieved from http://www.oecd.org/pisa/sitedocument/PISA-2015-technical-report-final.pdf

Pellegrino, J. W. (2010). *The design of an assessment system for the race to the top: A learning sciences perspective on issues of growth and measurement*. Princeton: Educational Testing Service.

Penfield, R. D. & Algina, J. (2006). A generalized DIF effect variance estimator for measuring unsigned differential test functioning in mixed format tests. *Journal of Educational Measurement, 43*(4), 295–312.

Repenning, A. (2017). Moving beyond syntax: Lessons from 20 years of blocks programing in AgentSheets. *Journal of Visual Languages and Sentient Systems, 3*(1), 68–91.

Repenning, A. (2018). Scale or fail: Moving beyond self-selected computer science education in Switzerland. *Communications of the ACM, 61*(5), 40–42.

Richter, T., Naumann, J., & Horz, H. (2010). Eine revidierte Fassung des Inventars zur Computerbildung (INCOBI-R). *Zeitschrift Für Pädagogische Psychologie, 24*(1), 23–37.

Robitzsch, A., Kiefer, T., & Wu, M. (2019). Package 'TAM'. https://cran.r-project.org/web/packages/TAM/ TAM.pdf

Román-González, M., Moreno-León, J., & Robles, G. (2019). Combining assessment tools for a comprehensive evaluation of computational thinking interventions. In S.-C. Kong & H. Abelson (Eds.), *Computational thinking education* (pp. 79–98). Singapore: Springer.

Román-González, M., Pérez-González, J.-C., & Jiménez-Fernández, C. (2017). Which cognitive abilities underlie computational thinking? Criterion validity of the Computational Thinking Test. *Computers in Human Behavior, 72*, 678–691.

Román-González, M., Pérez-González, J.-C., Moreno-León, J., & Robles, G. (2018a). Can computational talent be detected? Predictive validity of the Computational Thinking Test. *International Journal of Child-Computer Interaction, 18*, 47–58.

Román-González, M., Pérez-González, J.-C., Moreno-León, J., & Robles, G. (2018b). Extending the nomological network of computational thinking with non-cognitive factors. *Computers in Human Behavior, 80*, 441–459.

Rose, S. P., Habgood, M. J., & Jay, T. (2019). Using Pirate Plunder to Develop Children's Abstraction Skills in Scratch. In R. Mandryk, M. Hancock, M. Perry, & A. Cox (Eds.), *Extended Abstracts of the 2019 CHI Conference on Human Factors in Computing Systems* (pp. 1–6). New York, New York, USA: ACM Press.

Rosseel, Y. (2012). lavaan: An R package for structural equation modeling. *Journal of Statistical Software, 48*(2), 1–36.

Selby, C. C. & Woollard, J. (2013). *Computational thinking: The developing definition*. University of Southampton.

Shute, V. J., Sun, C., & Asbell-Clarke, J. (2017). Demystifying computational thinking. *Educational Research Review, 22*, 142–158.

Voogt, J., Fisser, P., Good, J., Mishra, P., & Yadav, A. (2015). Computational thinking in compulsory education: Towards an agenda for research and practice. *Education and Information Technologies, 20*(4), 715–728.

Weng, W. (2015). Eight skills in future work. *Education, 135*(4), 419–422.

Willse, J. T. (2011). Mixture Rasch models with joint maximum likelihood estimation. *Educational and Psychological Measurement, 71*(1), 5–19.

Wilson, M. (2005). *Constructing measures: An item response modeling approach*. New York: Psychology Press.

Wing, J. M. (2006). Computational thinking. *Communications of the ACM, 49*(3), 33–35.

Wing, J. M. (2008). Computational thinking and thinking about computing. *Philosophical Transactions. Series A, Mathematical, Physical, and Engineering Sciences, 366*(1881), 3717–3725.

APPENDIX

Short version of CTS (Korkmaz et al., 2017)

Creativity	"I believe that I can solve most of the problems I face if I have sufficient amount of time and if I show effort."
	"I have a belief that I can solve the problems possible to occur when I encounter with a new situation."
	"I trust that I can apply the plan while making it to solve a problem of mine."
Algorithmic thinking	"I think that I learn better the instructions made with the help of mathematical symbols and concepts."
	"I can mathematically express the solution ways of the problems I face in the daily life."
	"I can digitize a mathematical problem expressed verbally."
Cooperativit y	"I like experiencing cooperative learning together with my group friends."
	"In the cooperative learning, I think that I attain/will attain more successful results because I am working in a group."
	"I like solving problems related to group project together with my friends in cooperative learning."
Critical thinking	"I am willing to learn challenging things."
	"I am proud of being able to think with a great precision."
	"I make use of a systematic method while comparing the options at my hand and while reaching a decision."
Problem solving	"I have problems in the demonstration of the solution of a problem in my mind." (R)
	"I have problems in the issue of where and how I should use the variables such as X and Y in the solution of a problem." (R)
	"I cannot apply the solution ways I plan respectively and gradually." (R)

Note. Selection of 15 out of 29 items (Korkmaz et al., 2017, p. 565). Measured on a 7-point rating-scale ranging from 'not true at all' to 'entirely true'. R = reverse coding.

DIGITAL STORYTELLING: STUDENT VULNERABILITY DURING THE PROCESS AND ITS IMPACT ON TEACHING AND LEARNING ONE YEAR LATER

Heather N. Phillips, Janet Condy and Chantyclaire Tiba
Cape Peninsula University of Technology
P O Box 652, Cape Town 8000, South Africa

ABSTRACT

Digital storytelling (DST) is described as 'the modern expression of the ancient art of storytelling' with one of its categories focusing on personal narratives in which authors tell their own personal stories about significant experiences in their lives. The imperative to tap into our students' social-emotional learning through DST and creating a trauma-sensitive school culture is at the forefront of pedagogical conversations today. The DST process allowed pre-service teachers to take risks, risks of self-disclosure, risks of change, risks of not knowing, all of which rendered them vulnerable, resulting in deepened learning. The findings indicate that the process motivated newly qualified teachers to reflect on their own development, their practice and student learning through the lens of human connections, lived curriculum, self-reflection. They learnt the true value of social interaction and student engagement.

KEYWORDS

Digital Storytelling, Vulnerability, Pedagogy, Re-Humanization, Lived Experience, Reflection

1. INTRODUCTION

'Stop moments' in our lives describe not only the 'emerging openings' we experience that shape and shift the direction of our lives but also allow ourselves to be shaped by it. It includes being prepared to 'labour, risk, learn and play with possibilities that could interrupt the normative ways of doing things' (Rodricks: 2018).

Digital storytelling (DST) provides those 'stop moments' where a 'voice' is given to students as an opportunity for self-expression. Xu, et al. (2011) describes storytelling to be a natural method of communicating with others in our daily social interactions. DST, however, is described by The Digital storytelling Association (2002) as 'the modern expression of the ancient art of storytelling' with one of its categories focusing on personal narratives in which authors tell their own personal stories about significant experiences in their lives (Robin, 2008: 224).

These personal stories can overstep boundaries which can render teachers vulnerable in their daily task of teaching. The emotional dimension of vulnerability can develop, within teachers, feelings of negativity, frustration, guilt, anger and even fear which will impact the teaching and learning situation since education has and always will be powered by human connection. However, this emotional dimension can also be both a strength and an essential pillar of learning.

2. LITERATURE REVIEW AND THEORETICAL FRAMWORK

2.1 A Pedagogy of Vulnerability

This study is nestled within a theoretical framework of a pedagogy of vulnerability. Pedagogy of vulnerability is, according to Brantmeier (2013: 3), 'an approach to education that invites vulnerability and deepened learning through a process of self and mutual disclosure on the part of co-learners in a classroom'.

A dictionary description of being vulnerable is: capable of being wounded or injured; open to attack; and sensitive to or affected by certain influences (Turner, 2006). To further conceptualize vulnerability we draw on definitions provided by Hooks, Brown and Kelchtermans. Brown (2015:34) defines vulnerability as 'uncertainty, risk and emotional exposure'. These descriptions conjure up images of negativity and weakness.

Brown (2015) however, affirms that being vulnerable is not about winning or losing; it's being courageous enough to show up and be seen when we are unsure and have no control over the outcome. 'Vulnerability is not weakness; it's our greatest measure of courage'. Hooks (2010) outlines vulnerability to be a process of empowerment, a place of mutual openness where learners are encouraged to take risks. Kelchtermans (2009), however, argues that when referring to vulnerability we are not making reference to a mood or emotion but rather to understand vulnerability as structural and, therefore, as an inherent condition of the teaching profession. The pedagogy of vulnerability allows for voices to be heard and validated in formal school settings. It is a pedagogy that is relevant, especially for teachers who want to contribute to current school climates positively.

The pedagogy of vulnerability 'is guided by a willingness to meet our students where they are. This is a process that does not happen overnight, but one that involves building trust over the course of the semester by taking the time to learn what matters to our students, both inside and outside the classroom' (Mershon, 2018), bearing in mind that being vulnerable means that you are capable of being hurt.

2.2 Digital Storytelling and Pedagogy

'The imperative to tap into our students' social-emotional learning and create a trauma-sensitive school culture is at the forefront of pedagogical conversations' (Dukes, 2018). The DST technique is one mode that can be used to create a platform for students to journey through their own social-emotional arena. Gachago (2015) contends that the DST 'originates directly from participants lived experiences'. This technique allows students to 'combine the art of telling stories with multimedia objects such as images, audio, video, text, graphics and music' (Rossier & Garcia, 2010:37b). Robin (2008:224-228) discusses one category of DST as the opportunity to create and share personal narratives of significant experiences from various episodes in their lives, hence the process can be extremely emotional.

Zembylas (2011) argues that in teaching and learning emotions are regarded as being 'internal states of being' and should remain individual and private so that sentimentality can be avoided. This sentimentality or newly found sensitivity taught pre-service teachers that whether you were a teacher or a learner, whether your backgrounds were diverse, all the stories were similar (Condy, 2015). Ultimately the DST process allowed pre-service teachers to take risks, 'risks of self-disclosure, risks of change, risks of not knowing', all of which rendered them vulnerable, resulting in deepened learning (Brantmeier, 2013).

Robin (2008: 224-228)) continues to discuss the benefits of DST to include:

- It supports learner-centred activites;
- Promotes multiple skills in learners;
- Gives a voice to struggling learners; and
- Encourages deep reflection.

Similarly, Barret (2005) makes reference to the convergence of four learner-centred strategies that are enhanced through DST.

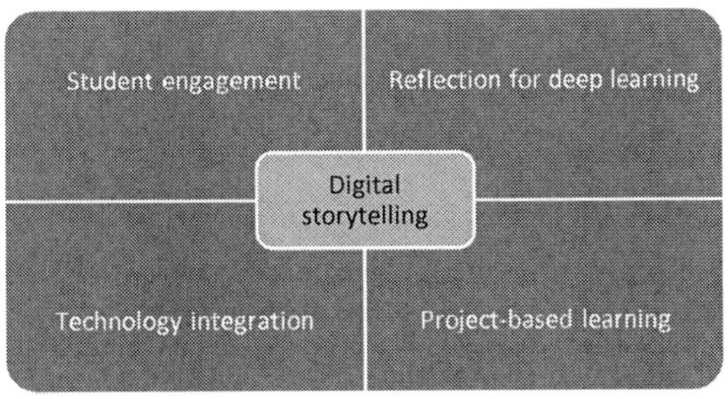

Figure 1. Convergence of four learner-centred strategies (Source: Barret, 2005)

Both Robin (2008) and Barret (2005) purport the significance of using DST as a pedagogical tool, 'to define and explore the 'promise and the pain of a pedagogy of vulnerability, exploring how and when sharing their stories can deepen learning' (Brantmeier, 2013; 2). This deepened learning, Brantmeier (2013) explains, is learning that 'allows for flexibility and responsiveness and it is learning that endures over time'.

2.3 Overstepping the Boundaries

Vulnerability has for many been seen as a sign of weakness. People work hard to hide their vulnerability behind a mask – if you are embarrassed or hurt, you show aggravation; if you are scared or disappointed, you show indifference, if you secretly really like someone, you show contempt...otherwise you are regarded as desperate and pathetic. We buy into the notion that hostility proves strength and vulnerability weakness, and that 'independence and invulnerability are synonymous with power and success' (Straka, 2018). However, to be vulnerable is to be courageous since the focus is on facing your imperfections, facing your authentic self rather than hiding behind a mask.

In accepting our authentic selves we are able to face others and we are able to work from a 'place of mutual openness rather than from an attitude of defensiveness'. Hooks (1994) argues that 'a holistic model of learning will also be a place where teachers grow, and are empowered by the process. That empowerment cannot happen if we refuse to be vulnerable while encouraging students to take risks…'. Lasky (2005) agrees and views this vulnerability as the 'chosen behaviour' for teachers.

Mershon (2018), however stresses that we cannot overstep the boundaries and we need to 'hold ourselves to the same standards we hold our students'. Through the pedagogy of vulnerability we must develop a strong sense of trust (Brown, 2015) between teacher and student, for this trust is not only the 'lubricant of thriving societies (Delhey, et al. 2011:787), but also 'the keystone of successful personal relations' (Forsyth, et al. 2011:3). However, Brown (2015) argues that this vulnerability must be based on mutuality and must respect boundaries. She further relates that 'imperfections are not inadequacies; they are reminders that we're all in this together'.

2.4 The Power of Human Connection

In overstepping our boundaries and creating safe spaces for teaching and learning through the development of strong bonds of trust and respect, we can generate 'deep meaningful connections with self and others' (Straka, 2018). She further stresses that these connections are paramount, both in our development as human beings and in teaching and learning where it is especially critical.

Palmer (1998:17) states that teaching 'is a daily exercise in vulnerability' for it is the way 'teachers live in their jobs'. This translates into a lived curriculum which refers to the content of our lives and our past life experiences which, according to Straka (2018) is the basis of all new learnings. She explains that great learning benefits can be derived from classrooms where lived experience is as important as academic curriculum. These, nestled in a framework of vulnerability, becomes engagement of learning about life itself.

Connecting with vulnerability is a humanizing pedagogy which is 'directed by compassion, care, respect and love for students and teachers, and their identities, histories and experiences' (Keet, Zinn & Porteus, 2009). However it is argued that 'there is an art to disclosure' (Keet, et al, 2009:11) which requires careful judgement. Considering learners and their experiences of possible past trauma and emotional pain is paramount if we do not want them to experience further rejection in the classroom. Re-humanizing vulnerability requires a greater awareness on the part of the teacher and the student in order to eliminate these possible risks.

To protect learners from the pain of rejection or relived trauma during disclosure, and keep their learning space safe, there is a need for constant self-reflection on the part of teachers. Self-reflection is a process of self-examination and self-assessment deliberately effected to improve professional practice (Shandamo, 2010). Brookfield (2004) argues that without reflection, teachers run the continual risk of making poor decisions and bad judgments. This is substantiated by Squires (1999: 16):

Most professional problems are messy and inchoate… they require a continuous process of reflection on what is happening and what has happened (reflection in action and reflection on action). Such a process can improve the quality of decisions and is contrasted with unreflective, unthinking routine, or habit driven behavior.

In many learning contexts, the pedagogy of vulnerability becomes very relevant to teachers for the practice of co-learning. Within this practice we need to build trust and promote critical self-reflection where the assumptions of one's views, values and behavior can be questioned. Brantmeier (2013:4) refers to this critical self-reflection as a 'contemplative practice of examining the origination of one's own worldview and gently, kindly scrutinizing that worldview with comparative and contrasting frames of reference'.

2.5 Vulnerability and Teaching and Learning

Kelchtermans (2009) promotes teachers to consider, more seriously, teaching with vulnerability since it could lead to greater teacher resilience. Greater teacher resilience translates into 'better equipped teachers to be in connection with themselves and their students, creating the necessary conditions for meaningful learning to take place'. Kohan and Turpin (2014) illustrates the link between Kegan's (1982, 1995) concept of disequilibrium and Dewey's (1993, 1989) concept of 'felt difficulty' and argues that 'in order for transformative learning to occur, one may have to "lose balance" or experience disequilibrium. One can surely argue that vulnerability does not automatically lead to deep learning but undergoes many reflective processes in which a 'disequilibrium' or 'felt difficulty' is experienced before transformation can take place.

For deep learning to occur it is important to develop strategies that will foster a resilient mindset to eliminate the possibility of students putting up barriers to positive development of teacher-student interactions. The following strategies will reinforce a positive mindset within the framework of a pedagogy of vulnerability. Teachers should

• Understand the lifelong impact they have on students, including instilling a sense of hope and resilience;

• Believe that the learning that occurs in the classroom and the behavior exhibited by students has as much, if not more, to do with the influence of teachers than what students might bring into the situation;

• Believe that attending to the social-emotional needs of students is not an "extra curriculum" that draws time away from teaching academic subjects;

• Recognize that if educators are to effectively relate to students, they must be empathic, always attempting to perceive the world through the eyes of the student;

• Appreciate that the foundation for successful learning and a safe and secure classroom climate is the relationship that teachers forge with students; and

• Realize that one of the greatest obstacles to learning is the fear of making mistakes and feeling embarrassed or humiliated

Brantmeier (2013:3) refers to the pedagogy of vulnerability as a transformative pedagogy which assists in the actualization of goals for a higher education. Transformative pedagogies are the vehicles to deeper learning and 'holds the potential for self-transformation, self-growth and social change.

Unless we are able to embrace our vulnerability we will not reach our full potential. All we will do is to build walls that will constantly prevent us from understanding or being understood.

3. METHODOLOGY

An interpretivist, qualitative research approach was followed in this study. Data was collected through:

- Digital stories conducted in 2017 and 2018 and
- Focus group interviews, based on the digital stories, conducted in 2019.

Four newly qualified teachers (NQT's), purposively sampled, took part in the 90 minute focus group interview in order to elicit how they experienced the process of creating their digital stories as pre-service students as well as how this experience impacted their teaching one year later. Since the engagement was one of sharing and listening to each other's digital stories, it was thought best to keep the group small to allow a safe space for participants to reflect on their emotional experiences. Focus group interviews were selected as a method to collect data in an attempt to ensure that the process was not intimidating and that a stimulating space could be created for this emotional engagement, rather than one-on-one interviews (Madriz, 2003:365). Participant responses were allowed to dictate the flow of the conversation. Cohen, Manion and Morrison (2008:376) explain that the participant rather than the researcher's agenda should predominate because the interaction from the group during the interview will yield insights that 'might not otherwise have been available in a straightforward interview'. An audio recording was made of the focus group interview data and it was transcribed verbatim.

The data was inductively analysed. The transcripts were read and repeatedly examined. Conceptual themes and issues emerging from the data were identified. The technique of clustering, making comparisons and contrasts was applied (Miles &Huberman, 1994).

Permission was obtained from the institution before the study commenced. Verbal as well as written consent to participate in the study was sought from all participants. Consent was also sought to have the focus group interview recorded. In service teachers were assured of confidentiality and anonymity.

3.1 Findings and Discussion

In an attempt to reflect on the DST process four NQT's experienced one year ago, a focus group interview was conducted to deliberate the process and its impact on their current teaching as well as their students' learning. While engaging in discussions using the pedagogy of vulnerability, NQT's understood that they would need to overstep boundaries which would render them vulnerable within their classroom community and with student engagement.

In the analysis of the data four themes became evident. They are:

- The teacher: facing our imperfections;
- Re-humanizing vulnerability;
- The lived curriculum and self-reflection; and
- Teaching and learning in the face of vulnerability

3.1.1 The Teacher: Facing our Imperfections

Excerpt 1

A discreet and cautious attitude started arousing my personality and character, such that I avoided to be seen by people. I had to deal with the assumptions people concluded about my life. No one had an idea what I was going through and no one showed interest as to why I was discreet and shy. I felt very vulnerable, even today as a young adult there are times I feel small and intimidated; I learnt to be independent at an early age because I knew that one day I will conquer the trial of poverty.

Facing our imperfections means letting go of who we think we should be and embracing who we really are. All four NQT's found it difficult to face their own imperfections during the DST process. Facing your imperfections translates into being vulnerable and this is very often coupled with feelings of fear, anxiety and frustration and has almost become synonymous with being weak. The pre-conceived thoughts are that in vulnerability you open yourself up to a host of criticism, to assumptions, to harm, to negative consequences. 'Walking into our stories of hurt', according to Brown (2017), 'can feel dangerous'. This is evident in the responses by all NQT's:

...she started the course, a lot of people... when they heard about the digital storytelling, I think that caused the most chaos in our class. Because I will say 85% of the people didn't want to do it at all and most of the times, I would speak to them, why don't you want to do it? For most of them it was fear...

I think the fear was from the judgement of peers...

... like you're scared because she tells us prior to the screening that your digital story will be watched by your fellow classmates, so now you're like, oh my God, now people are going to see my struggles...

However, it is in the midst of these struggles of facing our imperfections that we rise up, become courageous and regain our footing. These struggles may differ in magnitude, but as Brown (2017) articulates, 'We reckon with our emotions and get curious about what we're feeling; we rumble with our stories until we get to a place of truth; and we live this process, every day, until it becomes a practice and creates nothing short of a revolution in our lives'.

One NQT shared her revolutionised experience as:

'You get to look at yourself and look at the stereotypes..., the biases and the expectations that you have... it taught me to accept people as they come, so more especially when I started teaching... I can never judge the learner ... I don't know their situation... what the underlining issues are...'

Being vulnerable requires us to be brave and to trust. This results in reciprocity, giving birth to genuine connections being formed; connections which open doors to learning, learning in a safe space.

3.1.2 Re-Humanizing our Vulnerability

Excerpt 2

> Alcoholics supported my behavior because in my culture men must drink and marry. I was following the footsteps of my forefathers, and I should not be ashamed. Other relatives were against the strategy that I used to deal with my mother's death. Some had stereotypes about orphans; they believed that orphans end up being alcoholics and failures.
>
> As days passed I realized my life was falling apart. I lost almost everything that my mother had left behind. Eventually I gave up alcohol and drugs and decided to go back to school. I managed to work for one year to get registered in tertiary education.
>
> Now I'm doing my final year in Bachelor of education, and I'm going to be a teacher.

Another important theme that emerged from DST was that this experience became the tool with which students could critically engage with their own emotional trauma leaving most of them with the determination to succeed. 'Initial trauma and devastation…unites human beings… if we're allowed to talk openly about our collective grief and fear – if we turn to one another in a loving and vulnerable way, while at the same time seeking justice and accountability – it can be the start of the healing process' (Brown, 2017: 57).

However, in the absence of this opportunity to unite, because of vulnerability presenting itself in the form of 'stifling fear' as in the case below,

… how do I tell people that I was raped?... and she wrote a story… her digital story was on something that was not real, the real thing that she wanted to share with the class she never managed to say because the lecturer said, if you don't feel comfortable sharing your story, don't.

'We experience an emotional diversion away from the unravelling that's really happening in our homes and our communities' (Brown, 2017:57). Straka (2018) agrees and states that 'experiences of vulnerability are characterized by passivity, sensitivity and fragility', qualities that 'conjure up images of deficit'. These feelings of negativity respond to the 'dehumanizing circumstances' which result in 'low expectation'. However, vulnerability is a 'fundamental component of human experience' which contributes to further development in teacher resilience (Straka, 2018: 3).

For most of the NQT's their vulnerability became their greatest strength. Faced with opportunity to share emotional trauma gave the NQT in excerpt 2 the license to heal:

'it helped me to change the way I view the world because now I believe that every individual has something to tell…'.

Other NQT responses further justified:

'I think the process of the digital story telling makes you vulnerable but it also gives you strength because it's part of the healing process, ja.'

I gained a voice to share my experience … OF ALL- I LEARNT THAT IT IS OKAY TO BE VULNERABLE FOR I KNOW I AM ENOUGH.

Re-humanizing vulnerability reveals strength and human capacity, leading ourselves and our learners to develop greater resilience and deeper learning.

3.1.3 Lived Curriculum and Self-Reflection

Excerpt 3

> Personally I would say it is has changed the way that I view my learners. When I was starting with my teaching I would go on teaching practice and I used to have these expectations about children. But then I knew that they were different … and I used to think but then if so and so can do it, why can't this child do it. It has taught me to be aware not everyone is cut from the same cloth. We are all different, we do things differently.
>
> And I've managed to look at the child in a more holistic way …

Findings in this study showed that reflecting on their own vulnerabilities translated into NQT's making their lived curriculum part of their classrooms. An almost natural part of the process for all NQT's was to reflect on their experiences, understanding how this translates into the lived curriculum and how the latter impacts their daily engagement with their colleagues and students. When reflecting on our own vulnerabilities we see, more vividly, the vulnerability of others. This is evident in the following responses:

It is an empowering process I would say because you get to, to question things.

I think digital storytelling has taught me to be confident enough to educate my learners… that we are different we are all coming from different backgrounds. But we must not let our backgrounds be the barrier to our teaching and learning… So each person in the classroom has something that is bothering them… we are all human at the end of the day.

I think the process of the digital story telling gave me the confidence like to do self-introspection - so I reflect on whatever I do, like in my working environment, in the classroom, so I reflect and I try to treat people in a way that I would like to be treated, so I just tell myself, maybe that person is going through some stuff, so…

It is this DST experience that sowed the seeds of self-reflection, where 'learning becomes more relevant, has value beyond the classroom, and new meaning is constructed in the process' (Brantmeier, 2013). His substantiation reads: 'Share your story. If the educator opens her/his identity and life up for examination as part of the lived curriculum of the classroom, students will model that self-examination and go deeper in their learning'.

3.1.4 Teaching and Learning in the Face of Vulnerability

Excerpt 4

I think one thing that it has taught me is, to not judge my learners. The school that I'm at - most of the teachers say - oh but these children don't listen, don't even bother about them, … but I opened up my classroom, not only for the learners that I teach, for the learners that are also coming from other classes. My class is always full, whether it's after school, … we chat … so at one stage one of the HOD's asked the learners, what do you like about being here? They said when we come to this class, we feel at home… They are not shy to come to talk to me about things, they come to me and they tell me about these things but when they talk to their own teachers, they are judged … so I've got a lot of children in my class who come and sit, they just want to talk…

It was clear that all NQT's gained new insights around their learners and how they learn. It is evident from excerpt 4 that the DST process brought forth the realization that learning is more than just acquiring academic knowledge, it strengthens social engagement. Dunleavy & Milton (2009) indicates that the literature connects social engagement and intellectual engagement and purports that

'When students have opportunities to connect with adults who approach these relationships with a spirit of caring, empathy, generosity, respect, reciprocity and a genuine desire to know students personally, they can make a unique contribution to young peoples' emerging adaptive capacity, self-sufficiency, resiliency, confidence, and knowledge of themselves as learners' (Dunleavy & Milton, 2009: 15).

It was found that all NQT's appreciated the value of their lived experience and became more aware of the importance of the social interactions with their learners and how it impacted teaching and learning positively. Their responses below bears the evidence of this:

… it teaches us to understand others, when you transfer that understanding of the role of the digital story … it teaches us to understand our own learners.

… the digital story … prepared me for my teaching profession,… a sort of awareness, I must be aware of my surroundings, ja. Secondly, looking at the staff… it prepares me that when you are looking at someone like you see the inner part of that particular person and the outer part …

…when we were doing digital stories, we did not know that the guy that always likes to put on his headphones at the back of the classroom, is going through serious traumatic things, so it actually helped me to understand that people and even children go through a lot and that could be a barrier to teaching and learning.

'Just as teachers need safe spaces to process their vulnerability' (Straka, 2018) so too their learners need safe spaces to process theirs. Without strong social interaction between teachers and students, this vulnerability can 'prove to be a barrier to the creation of effective teacher-students interactions' (Brooks, 2008) – impacting learning negatively.

4. CONCLUSION

The objective of this study was to explore how the DST process impacted teacher vulnerability and consequently how it impacted teaching and learning in classroom settings. This study, set in a framework of a pedagogy of vulnerability, commenced with four NQT's experiencing the creation of their own personal stories which spoke to two themes viz: 'being human today' and 'colliding worldviews'. Limitations in the study include the following: a small sample of four NQT's provided the data and all the participants had completed their degrees at the same site/university. Access to literature, particularly around the concept of vulnerability also posed a limitation to this study.

While vulnerability is part of teaching, teachers manage it differently, and these differences have profound importance for:

- Teachers and their development

The experience of NQT's creating their own digital story forced them to accept their own imperfections, face their fears and anxieties, exposing themselves to critique and assumptions, yet emerging as stronger beings. Straka (2018:4) contends that our vulnerability is transformed into our strength and when we are ready to navigate those vulnerable episodes, those experiences will lead us to developing 'deep, meaningful connection with self and others. It is this connection that is central to our development as human beings'. The implementation of developing these deep meaningful connections will enhance teacher development and their pedagogy.

- Students and their learning

Overstepping the boundaries of vulnerability through personal disclosure led NQT's to understand the value of sharing and thus the importance of reciprocal exchanges with their students. They report that they now view their students through a different lens, a lens which re-humanizes vulnerability and understands that all students are vulnerable and should not be judged with assumption. Brooks (2008) purports that 'the assumptions teachers possess of themselves, their role as teachers and their students capabilities play a significant role in determining expectations, teaching practices and ultimately student success and happiness'.

- Teacher educators and their practice.

The DST process gave birth to a new appreciation of lived experience and self-reflection. NQT's questioned their perceptions of 'why', 'what' and 'how' they teach. They learnt the true value of social interaction and student engagement. The lesson: 'everyone experiences some challenges in life, and most have a story of their own journey through the tough times of life. The puzzle is that two people, who have experienced the same amount and intensity of adversity, and even the same exact event, can emerge differently' (Taylor & Parsons, 2011).

Brinkmann (2010:83) contends 'one of the most important things a human being can learn is to see through acts of dehumanization and recognize vulnerable human beings as human beings'. The vulnerabilities experienced by all those who participate in the process of education are inherently threaded and becomes a powerful resource in the process of learning and connecting to ideas and to one another (Loveless, D.J. et al, 2016).

REFERENCES

Barret, H.C. 2005. Researching and evaluating digital storytelling as a deep learning tool. http://electronicportfolios.com/portfolios/SITEStorytelling2006.pdf. [20 June 2019].

Brantmeier, E.J. 2013. Pedagogy of vulnerability: definitions, assumptions and applications. In Lin, J. et al, Re-envisioning Higher Education: Embodied Pathways to Wisdom and Transformation. Information age forthcoming.

Brinkmann, S. 2010. Human vulnerabilities: Toward a theory of rights for qualitative researchers. Qualitative Inquiry and Human Rights, 82–99.

Brooks, R. and Goldstein, S., 2008. The mindset of teachers capable of fostering resilience in students. Canadian Journal of School Psychology, Vol. 23, No.1, pp 114-126.

Brown, B. 2017. Braving the wilderness: The quest for true belonging and the courage to stand alone. Penguin Random House, UK.

Brown, B. 2015. Daring greatly: How the courage to be vulnerable transforms the way we live, love, parent, and lead. Penguin Random House, UK.

Brookfield, S. 2004. The getting of wisdom: What critically reflective teaching is and why it's important. Retrieved from http://nlu.nl.edu/academics/cas/ace/facultypapters/StephenBrookfield.cfm. [21 June 2019].

Bullough, R. 2005. Teacher vulnerability and teachability: A case study of a mentor and two interns. Teacher Education Quartely, Vol. 32, No. 2, pp 23-29.

Cohen, L. et al, 2008. Research methods in education. (7th ed.). Routledge Falmer, London.

Condy, J. 2015. The construction and transformation of pre-service teacher's individual, social and professional identities during a Digital Storytelling module. In Condy, J. (ed). Telling stories differently: Engaging 21st century students through digital storytelling. SUN MeDIA, Stellenbosch.

Delhey, J. et al, 2011. How general is trust in ''most people''? Solving the radius of trust problem. American Sociological Review, Vol. 76, No. 5, pp 786– 807.

Dewey, J. 1933. How we think: A restatement of the relation of reflective thinking to the educative process. Heath, Boston.

Dewey, J. 1989. The Later Works, vol. Boydston. University Press, Southern Illinois.

Digital Storytelling Association, 2002. The centre for digital storytelling. http://www.dsaweb.org/01associate/ds.html. [18 June 2019].

Dunleavy, J. & Milton, P. 2009. What did you do in school today? Exploring the concept of Student Engagement and its implications for Teaching and Learning in Canada. Canadian Education Association (CEA), Toronto.

Forsyth, P. et al, 2011. Collective Trust: Why Schools Can't Improve Without It. Teachers College Press, New York.

Gachago, D. 2015. Seeing the world through somebody else's eyes: developing capabilities for a socially just education. In Condy, J. (ed).Telling stories differently: Engaging 21st century students through digital storytelling. SUN MeDIA, Stellenbosch.

Hooks, B. 1994. Teaching to Transgress: Education as the Practice of Freedom. Routledge, New York.

Hooks, B. 2010.Teaching Critical Thinking: Practical Wisdom. Routledge, New York.

Kegan, R. 1982. The evolving self. Harvard University Press, Cambridge.

Kegan, R. 1995. In over our heads. Harvard University Press, Cambridge.

Keet, A. et al, 2009. Mutual vulnerability: a key principle in a humanizing pedagogy in post-conflict societies. Perspectives in Education, Vol. 27, pp 5-6.

Kelchtermans, G. 2009. Who I am in how I teach is the message: self-understanding, vulnerability and reflection. Teachers and Teaching: theory and practice, Vol. 15, No. 2, pp 257-272.

Lasky, S. 2005. A sociocultural approach to understanding teacher identity, agency and professional vulnerability in a context of secondary school reform. Teaching and Teacher Education, Vol. 21, No. 8, pp 899-916.

Loveless, D. J. et al, 2016. The vulnerability of teaching and learning in a selfie society. Sense Publishers, Rotterdam, Netherlands.

Madriz, E. 2003. Focus Groups in Feminist Research. Collecting and Interpreting Qualitative Materials. Sage, Thousand Oakes, California.

Mershon, K. 2018. A Pedagogy of Vulnerability: The Craft of Teaching in the Academic Study of Religion. https://craftofteachingreligion.wordpress.com/2018/10/22/a-pedagogy-of-vulnerability [23 June 2019].

Miles, M.G. and Hubermann, A.M. 1994. Qualitative data analysis. 2nd ed. Sage, Thousand Oaks, California.

Palmer, P. 1998. The courage to teach: Exploring the inner landscape of a teacher's life. Jossey-Bass, San Fransisco.

Robin, B. R. 2008. Digital storytelling: a powerful technology tool for the 21st century classroom. Theory in practice, Vol. 47, pp 220-228.

Rodricks, D. 2018. Methodology as a Pedagogy of Vulnerability: Doctoral Research With/in/From the Borderlands. Qualitative Inquiry. 24. 107780041878810. 10.1177/1077800418788106

Rossiter, M. and Garcia, P.A. 2010. Digital Storytelling: A New Player on the Narrative Field. New Directions for Adult and Continuing Education, Vol. 126, pp 37-48.

Shandomo, H.M. 2010. The role of critical reflection in teacher education. School-University Partnerships, Vol. 4, No.1, pp 101–113.

Straka, A.L. 2018. Perception, permission and purpose: Portraits of vulnerability and resilience in teaching. Unpublished PhD thesis, University of Cincinnati, Cincinnati.

Squires, G. 1999.Teaching as a professional discipline. Falmer press, London, UK.

Taylor, L. & Parsons, J. 2011. Improving Student Engagement. Current Issues in Education, Vol.14 No.1. Retrieved from http://cie.asu.edu/ [15 June 2019].

Turner, L. 2006. Renewing our genuineness in the classroom: Ways to become vulnerable again. Atlantic Universities Teaching Showcase 2005.

Xu, Y. et al, 2011. A new approach toward digital storytelling: an activity focused on writing self-efficacy in a virtual learning environment. Educational Technology and Society, Vol.14, No.4 pp 181-191.

Zembylas, M. 2011. The politics of trauma in education. Palgrave Macmillan, New York.

USING DIGITAL STORIES TO EXPLORE FOUR FINAL-YEAR STUDENT'S COLLIDING WORLDVIEWS AND HOW THIS IMPACTED THEIR CLASSROOM PEDAGOGY

Janet Condy, Heather Phillips and Chantyclaire Tiba
Cape Peninsula University of Technology, South Africa

ABSTRACT

As contexts in schools and higher education become increasingly more diverse, engagement with human differences and different knowledges becomes essential. Institutions need to change their practices to respond to the different needs of learners, as well as valuing their knowledges and prospective teachers need to better equipped for these experiences. Hence, the purpose of this paper is to explore the intersectionality of four final-year students colliding worldviews within a digital story project and how, this experience supported, or not, their own classroom pedagogies. Through the use of the pedagogy of discomfort, we argue that this intentionally initiated module of using digital storytelling influenced these four learners to confront their colliding worldviews, identify their strengths and challenges. They all reflected on how this process had encouraged them to become more self-reflective thinkers in their own lives, those of their peers and their learners.

KEYWORDS

Classroom Pedagogy, Colliding Worldviews, Digital Storytelling, Pedagogy of Discomfort, 21st Century Classroom, Higher Education Institution

1. INTRODUCTION

The purpose of this paper is to explore the intersectionality of four final-year students colliding worldviews within a digital story project and how, this experience supported, or not, their own classroom pedagogies. In this way, the convergence of both these advances in educational psychology and computing, impacted the educational arena and especially the students in this final-year course of a Higher Educational Institution (HEI) that prepares teachers in South Africa.

This innovative research project was anchored in a compulsory subject called Professional Studies for final-year students, in 2017 and 2018 with 106 and 86 students respectively. The majority of students came from working class backgrounds and would have been classified by the Apartheid government as Coloured and African. Although these terms are rejected by the authors, they are used normatively by the student population (Gachago, Clowes & Condy, 2016).

This module was developed in response to the Department of Education's policy to prepare future teachers for diverse classrooms, to provide competent and responsible qualified beginner teachers (Department of Education, 2001). The Minimum Requirements for Teacher Education Qualifications (Department of Higher Education and Training 2011, pp 4) stress that teaching is a complex activity that requires teachers to integrate and apply knowledge and respond to different contexts. Condy, Green and Gachago (2019) state that as contexts in schools and higher education become increasingly more diverse, engagement with human differences and different knowledges becomes essential. Prospective teachers need to be well equipped for these experiences. This is confirmed by Bozalek and Zembylas (2019, pp 9) who state that institutions need to "change their practices to respond to the different needs of learners, as well as valuing the subjugated knowledges that students bring with them."

The main aim of this research project was to create a constructivist learning environment where the students would be challenged to teach a decolonised curriculum, by foregrounding disrupting colliding worldviews and understanding stereotypical views of difference. The researcher considered the 21st century deep learning competencies necessary for the Fourth Industrial Revolution; to live and survive in a rapidly changing world and how to deal with the complexities and ambiguities found in many South African classrooms (Gravett, 2019). Hence the research question became: How did the digital storytelling project, with the focus on colliding worldviews, impact four students pedagogical classroom practices?

2. BACKGROUND AND LITERATURE REVIEW

In South Africa 78% of our Grade 4 children are not able to reading for meaning (Howie, Combrinck, Roux, Tshele, Mokoena & Mcleod Palane, 2016). It is stated in the 2016 PIRLS that our learners could not retrieve basic information from the text to answer the simplest questions. When these learners arrive at HEI's, together with the present technological world, they lack the motivation to read stories and improve their own reading and writing skills, despite signing up to be trained as teachers. Stories are fundamental to develop human communication, learning by analogy rather than direct learning and higher order thinking (Ribeiro, Moreira & Pinto da Silva, 2016, pp 182). Hence the idea of developing a multi-modal approach to this course by integrating a digital storytelling module with mixed groups, a trained facilitator, taught the students how to share their valuable stories, write, organise, cooperate and collaborate their colliding worldviews. Graham (2002) would call these experiences of students coming together to help and support each other a relational worldview.

3. DIGITAL STORYTELLING

For generations, the oral storytelling tradition has been used as a tool for the transmission and exchange of values and knowledge because it is a powerful and a natural form of communication (Smeda, Dakich, & Sharda, 2014). Over the last decade, with the increased use of hardware and software systems available today, the dissemination of stories have changed. Today digital stories can be seen as the merging of traditional stories with the more modern use of multimodal technology used more widely as a pedagogical tool in higher education.

Typically a digital story is a short, personal, narrative of only 3-5 minutes long (Lambert, 2009) combing voice, image and music (Benmayor, 2008), integrating different literacies to engage and motivate students (Ribeiro, Moreira & Pinto da Silva, 2016, pp 183). Technology is more effective when used as part of a broad educational improvement agenda (Pitler, 2006). In this particular research project the digital stories were purposefully used to disrupt students uncritical approach when reflecting on dominant worldviews (Gachago, Clowes & Condy, 2018). Coventry (2008, pp 207) observes, that "Working in multimedia brings something to the student's learning that would otherwise not be possible: speaking and explaining through relatively unfamiliar modes of communication helps enforce a deeper engagement with ideas".

During the two-month teaching module, the researcher took the students through a carefully structured approach of constructing their own digital stories (Kajder, Bull & Albaugh, 2005), using all the elements of digital storytelling to reflect on their colliding worldviews. Students worked in purposively arranged groups so that they shared with people with whom they would not normally have collaborated. This constructivist approach of learning through using authentic contexts, including the social paradigm is one of the most influential educational contexts in the 21st century (Smeda, Dakich, Sharda, 2014).

4. WORLDVIEWS

Politicians, educationists and economists in South Africa are constantly struggling to find out why our literacy and numeracy rates are consistently low in both international and national assessments. One aspect that has not been researched is the fact that as human beings we need to make sense of our lives, our biases, stereotypes and prejudices which gives rise to our worldviews (Tiburt, 2010). Education does not occur in a vacuum. In a 21st century classroom, a teacher may expect to find many worldviews being expressed and encountered, it is essential that teachers need to be aware of and knowledgeable about a range of worldviews. In any society there will be dominant worldviews held by the majority of the community. Alternative worldviews do exist that may be different, unconventional, marginal or complementary to the dominant worldview. Some may provide a purpose and a direction in life, provide values, inform decision making and suggest standards of conduct, and some may even be in conflict to each other. Hence, Tiburt (2010, pp 180) suggests that in the "health profession, as challenging worldviews may be, educators must learn to acknowledge their complexity so that trainees can more effectively communicate with patients and populations who may not share their own worldview."

Tiburt (2010) believes worldviews are metanarratives or sets of beliefs and assumptions that are deeply embedded and largely implicit in how cultures interpret and explain their experience. Hart (2010) extends this belief by saying that worldviews are described as mental lenses that are entrenched ways of perceiving the world. They are intuitively, unconsciously and uncritically developed over time throughout a person's life through socialising and social interaction, and are often taken for granted. Worldviews can be cognitive, perceptual and affective maps that people continuously use to make sense of the social landscape and to find their way to whatever goals they seek (Hart, 2010).

Children are not born with a worldview. Parents or significant others, society and culture, together are important facilitators in developing a child's emergent worldview. A worldview can be either communal as well as personal (Fisher, 2012) as shared vision often promotes community, where there is a strong sense of community, tied together by familial relations and the families commitment to it (Graham 2002). Individuals enjoy freedom in self-expression because it is recognised by the community that individuals take into consideration and act on the needs of the community as opposed to acting alone.

A counter argument exists which suggests there is growing concern that it is not necessary to have a worldview which includes a systematic codified belief system. Fisher (2012) claims that disparate and eclectic presuppositions from a variety of worldviews can fit together, despite apparent contradictions, and may be able to answer life's questions. When systematised and codified worldviews become extreme they move towards fundamentalism. Where this type of worldview refuses to entertain and evidence contrary to his or her worldview.

5. THE PEDAGOGY OF DISCOMFORT

Boler (1999) in her book, Feeling Power: Education and Emotions, first introduced the concept of the 'pedagogy of discomfort'. She explained how students, during the Persian Gulf war, disengaged with media, denying the war took place, with the resulting emotions of powerlessness and numbness. To survive these injustices, and an inability to effect change, students became desensitized, which reinforced their numbness. The students were silenced, which lead to self-hatred and distanced them from human connections, increasing their sense of isolation. This sense of self-imposed isolation not only occurs at an individual level but to the broader societal level, which manifests as identity politics, power relations and fear. Taleb (2010, pp 4) posits that when individuals face knowledge that is fragile and contradicts the beliefs they hold as true "... they may experience discomforting emotions such as guilt, fear, anger, anxiety and deep emotion."

Bheekie and van Huyssten (2015) explain how a dominant culture reinforces emotions that are either acceptable or unacceptable and how HEIs accept these biased viewpoints as normative. Twenty-five years after South Africa's transition to democracy, the constitution provides for a more social just society where issues of diversity such as; race, language, gender, religion, culture and socio-economic status, are still very much alive amongst the student population at the HEI where this research project took place. This project encouraged the participants to engage in critical thinking that explored issues of power in dominant worldviews, habits, practices and knowledge. A classroom environment was created whereby the students explored the messiness of power relations and "to stay away from neat unquestioned stereotypes" (Condy, 2015, pp 145).

6. RESEARCH APPROACH

A case study approach was used within a critical interpretive research paradigm for the researcher to explore four final-year student's colliding worldviews and how this impacted their classroom pedagogy. This design helped describe and explain their real-life phenomena and to develop a true reflection of what was happening by considering the context within which it occurred (Yin, 2003, pp 1).

Qualitative data were collected from two sources: in the form of digital stories in 2017 and 2018 and a focus group interview in 2019. The information gathered from these stories and the one focus group interview helped the researcher to gain insights through "... subjective understanding ..." of how these students and managed their colliding worldviews and how these experiences helped them in their own teaching experiences (Henning et al., 2007, pp 3).

The four students who were purposively selected to be part of this study were involved with postgraduate studies and were available to be interviewed. At the time of the interviews, two students had been teaching for 6 months and two had been teaching for 18 months. The students' names will be kept anonymous: named as NK, SM, MN and LT. All students and the university signed ethical clearance for this research.

7. FINDINGS

Four vignettes present four students' colliding worldviews and how they rose above their circumstances. A short discussion on each vignette follows. To conclude this section, the results of the interviews and how this project influenced their teaching will be discussed.

Vignette 1

Debt almost killed me, my being, and my values. It almost destroyed my future.
Between the period of my matric year and my first year of varsity, I found myself in adjacent walls tall enough to suffocate me, ending my dreams. A corner that was subconsciously built by my parents due to their bad financial decisions.

Deep down in my heart I knew a parent would never intentionally kill their children's dreams or life desires but by allowing debt into our lives, they simultaneously allowed poverty to creep in like darkness tangling innocent light, with no hope of escaping the torture and pain of poverty in our lives.

The void and smell of poverty impregnated my heart with anger, the un-intentional knife caused by the people I loved so dearly had slit through my being and bought pain in my comfort zone, with tears racing down my cheeks each time the thought of the situation at home crossed my mind with unanswered questions
Was it necessary to sacrifice our happiness?
If only my mother never built that house in Eastern Cape...
If only my father never took that loan...

She concluded her digital story by stating that:

> Wearing a smile and confidence was my key to success, my vulnerability fed my hunger to success because through the series of unintentional poverty I had three choices, to give in, to give up or to give it all I got. And I chose giving it all I have...

Discussion

NK grew up strangled by her parents relational worldview culture; who consciously made decisions, probably influenced by the community, putting her family into deep poverty, torture and pain. She knew she had to act alone to rise above her and her families colliding worldviews.

Vignette 2

Days came and passed as I wondered when that day will come, where my long waited for expectation will be fulfilled. I was young and vulnerable but at the same time, I was socialised that I will grow up and be a woman and have my own home and children. I had a view that even though I was younger and uneducated my mother would respect my choices. However, she had a single story about what it meant to be a mother. I was at the age of 19 when I got engaged. Our relationship turned sour when I fell pregnant and had a baby.

She abandoned me because she did not approve of my relationship. Regardless of all her promises to love us unconditionally, she did not keep the promise. Was it a collision of world views? My mother expected me to stay out of school and get a job and further my studies but I thought marriage was the right thing for me at that time. My view was it is okay to get married first and then go back to school later. She wanted what she thought was best for me but it was my choice to make a decision.

SM completed her digital story by stating:

> I grew from this experience and learnt how to forgive, be open minded, allow people around me to be imperfect and build relationships that are none power based. I gained a voice to share my experience with my mother and love her more, show her compassion. Of all I learnt that it is okay to be vulnerable for I know I AM ENOUGH!

Discussion

SM lived in a community that shared a deeply embedded implicit worldview, often taken for granted, that mothers helped their daughters with their children. She intuitively believed that although she was to have a baby before being educated, her mother would support her child. In this case the mother chose consciously not to abide by this codified belief system which developed into a clash of ideologies.

Vignette 3

Life without my mum was not easy. I thought I will be with her for the rest of my life. Her passing away changed everything in my life. I became rebellious and opted to drink alcohol and do drugs. I thought this route would work for me, but it didn't work at all. The consequences of doing drugs were divisions within the family. Our family views collided. Alcoholics supported my behaviour because in my culture men must drink and marry. I was following the footsteps of my forefathers, and I should not be ashamed. Other relatives were against the strategy that I used to deal with my mother's death.

Some had stereotypes about orphans; they believed that orphans end up being alcoholics and failures. Some of my family members lose hope on me especial in the side of education, assuming that I won't be successful without my mother.

As days passed I realized my life was falling apart. I lost almost everything that my mother had left behind. My siblings were angry with me. Eventually I gave up alcohol and drugs and decided to go back to school.

MN completed his digital story by declaring:

> Fortunately, I got a part-time job in the university in order to get something to eat and books. I told myself that the death of my mother is not the end of my future and dreams. Now I am doing my final year Bachelor in Education, and I'm going to be a teacher.

Discussion

Although in MN's culture there was a strong sense of community where men must drink and marry, he, personally, experienced a colliding worldview when he chose drugs to mourn the death of his mother. He was not acting on the needs of the community: rather he chose to act alone against his cultural deeply rooted worldviews. After hearing they believed he was a failure, he consciously and critically decided to change his worldview and worked hard at changing his landscape to find his way to achieve his goals.

Vignette 4

Born and bred in the valleys of the Eastern Cape residing with my mother, father and siblings. Our mother was our pillar of strength, as she 45 was the breadwinner, there was no one to support her in raising us. She was however, not a single mother.

In the outside world I felt isolated and small, my ego was bruised my self-esteem was crushed. I sometimes wished I wasn't born, regretting to be part of my own family and friends. I felt worthless in society, since we had nothing and we were underestimated.

School was a knotty experience and obscure to society. I was never present in school excursions due to financial problems that we had. In class, I felt continuously anxious; the only thought that I pondered is "I can't wait for lunch time so that I can get a slice of that delicious jam sandwich."

A discreet and cautious attitude started arousing my personality and character, such that I avoided to be seen by people. I had to deal with the assumptions people concluded about my life. No one had an idea what I was going through and no one showed interest as to why I was discreet and shy.

LT narrated at the end of her digital story that:

> My vulnerability and persevering through my trials and tribulations made me believe that poverty and my background will never determine my future. Instead I will keep rising above my circumstances to be the human I am today, because I believe that I am like a lighthouse that has never been shaken by heavy storms

Discussion

In LTs family, poverty was the commonly held worldview, but this differed from the community in which she lived and where she was educated. Within her community the core worldview held a belief that learners should be able to attend excursions and be socially involved – this was her colliding worldview when she found herself alone.

8. INTERVIEWS

When analysing the focus group interview data about how the digital storytelling project explored the students colliding worldviews, and how this experience impacted their classroom pedagogy, it became evident that the main theme was that they gained a greater awareness. They became more self-reflective within their own thinking and their own lives; they were more aware of how to deal with their learners, and how to be aware of working with their staff members.

The students reflected that this digital storytelling process provided them with a greater sense of awareness to themselves, their learners and their teaching environment. One student narrated that this process of exploring ones colliding worldviews was an empowering process because you have got to question things: "it helped me to change the way I view the world because now I believe every individual has a story to tell … that we can be different as people but we have the same circumstances that we go through ..." Another student added that: You get to look at yourself and look at the stereotypes that you've got, the biases… the expectations you have. However, one student cautioned: "I must be aware of those stumbling blocks you see, there are difficulties that I'm going through at work – it's a sort of an awareness thing …"

One student confronted the idea of a worldview as a given construct saying: "I want to disagree with the fact that it [a worldview] is a given … views actually mutate … It is given at a certain age perhaps when you are still growing up. What your parents teach you is what you take. But then as you grow older you start making your own decisions – like you can change those views, you can question them, critique them … I think views change based on circumstances or situations and the moment you start realising them you start being aware of them you will constantly critique the way you view your thinking…. You realise you have a right to confront people when there's biases and stereotypes…"

One student shared that: "it gave me strength like to be the person I am, that will stick to my morals and values because I feel like I am the role model to my learners, so I have to be true to myself."

Not only were the students more self-aware but this process encouraged a more awareness of working with their learners:

> like its personal issue so we don't have to judge or punish. You must just speak with the learner asking why are you behaving like this. So that you can get more information so you can be aware of what is happening to that particular learner.
>
> I use it a lot with my children because when we teach, we expect children to respond in a certain way and at the same time, you find the school has got expectations about the learners. I look at my learners and then I'm like, I don't know what this child is going through, … but then I can never judge the learner … so that has taught me a lot.
>
> I think one thing that it has taught me is, to not judge my learners.
>
> it actually helped me to understand that people and even children go through a lot of things … seriously traumatic things… and that could be a barrier to teaching and learning.

One student explained that this process helped her to constantly motivate her learners: "it has also transferred in a sense that, you as a teacher like you need to constantly motivate … So now you need to constantly tell children that they are the ones being educated. So it also helped in that sense."

For the one student whose parents made the decision to put the family into financial stress, she shared that this process: "empowered me in a sense that … I'm more aware of my financial expenditures, so for me to learn from that … in providing a stable future for my child and for myself. I know that I need to be careful with a lot of things because otherwise I will find myself back in that situation. In the classroom – yes – because for instance with casual money you find that some children cannot pay casual money." She proceeds to provide options of payment to her learners so "that you do not have to stress. That's how I apply my learning."

Now that these teachers are teaching in schools, this process has taught them to be more aware of their teaching environment:

> I must be aware of my surroundings, looking at the staff, that I'm working with, it prepares me … it is very important to understand people, you see, even their behaviour. Academically or like here at work, it prepares me that it gives me strength … because there are stumbling blocks …
>
> … it has a sense of greater awareness not only for yourself but for what's happening around you because from that digital story, you were able to see that people have burdens within and they're not just going to show you, so in the teaching profession that also happens because yes in varsity it was peers but now it is your colleagues …
>
> The whole process has taught me to be confident enough to educate my learners that we are different – we must not let our backgrounds become the barriers to our teaching and learning – we are all human at the end of the day.

9. CONCLUSION

Through the intentionally initiated influences of this module, framed within the pedagogy of discomfort, which set out to address evolving learning processes with supporting pedagogical applications, these four students developed socially, emotionally and professionally. As a result of collaboration, reflection and interpersonal communication skills, these students have been motivated to use multimedia to confront their own biases and stereotypical worldviews and to consequently, improve their own pedagogical practices.

Teachers today require more complex and different skills to be prepared to engage, address and challenge the critical and dominant worldviews, in our educational arena facing our diverse learners. They need to be aware of the interconnectedness between fast-changing different knowledges and professional practices that will result in transforming our learners in the 21st century. The researcher agrees with Tiburt (2010, pp 180) who suggests that educators should learn to acknowledge the complexity of student and learner's worldviews so that we can more efficiently communicate with them. The pedagogy of discomfort created a safe space for this transformation to occur where all four students agreed that this process of writing and reflecting on a particular colliding worldview and putting it into a digital story, was an uncomfortable experience. Yet six months to a year later, they shared how much they had learnt from sharing their vulnerabilities and that they have been able to inculcate these learnings into their own personal lives as well as their pedagogical practices.

All four students willingly shared their taken-for-granted, unconscious personal and community worldviews and the discomfort of these traumatic experiences. At the time of these ideological clashes none of the students were able to change anything. However a few years later, when reflecting on this experience, during the making of their authentic digital stories, they shared how this experience created many different personal and pedagogical opportunities and how much stronger they had all become to rise above their circumstances.

The findings of the focus-group interviews suggest that this project, heightened the students awareness of their own colliding worldviews which in-turn encouraged them to become more metacognitively aware of their own worldviews as well as learning valuable pedagogical approaches of how to manage their peers, learners and be a role model in their communities. Some students reflected on how they could now identify their own 'stumbling blocks' and those found in their peers in the staffroom and now know they have to be approached with caution and care. The researcher argues that these students now hold strong views on listening to their learners, motivating them, exploring their worldviews and how not to judge. They have become more passionate about confronting people who hold unconvincing biases and stereotypical worldviews.

REFERENCES

Benmayor, R. (2008). Digital storytelling as a signature pedagogy for the new humanities. Arts and Humanities in Higher Education, 7(2): 188-204.

Bheekie, A. & van Huyssteen, M. (2015). Be mindful of your discomfort: An approach to contextualized learning. International Journal of Research on Service-Learning and Community Engagement, 3(1) Retrieved from http://journals.sfu.ca/iarslce.

Boler, M. (Ed.). (1999). Feeling power. Emotions and education. New York: Routledge.

Condy, J. (2015). The constructions and transformation of pre-service teacher's individual, social and professional identities during a digital storytelling module. In J. Condy, (Ed.). Telling stories differently: Engaging 21st Century students through digital storytelling (pp. 141-151). Cape Town: SUN Media.

Condy, J., Green, L. & Gachago, D. (2019). Exploring being human today: a journey to equip prospective teachers in South Africa to engage critically with diversity. In G. Maré (Ed.), Race in education (pp. 41-68). Cape Town: Sun Press. ISBN: 978-1-928357-84-1.

Fisher, B. J. (2012). Exploring worldviews: A framework. The TEACH Journal of Christian Education, 6(1): Retrieved from https://research.avondale.edu.au/teach/vol6/iss1/11.

Gachago, D., Clowes, L. & Condy, J. (2018). 'Family comes in all forms, blood or not': disrupting dominant narratives around the patriarchal nuclear family. Gender and Education, 30(8): 966-981. Retrieved from https://doi.org/10.1080/09540253.2016.1259464.

Gravett, S. (2019). Industry 4.0 is being taken seriously. Mail & Guardian: 18 January 2019.

Hart, M. A. (2010). Indigenous worldviews, knowledge, and research: The development of an indigenous research paradigm. Journal of Indigenous Voices in Social Work, 1(1):1-16.

Henning, E., van Rensburg, W. & Smith, B. (2007). Finding your way in qualitative research. Pretoria: Van Schaik.

Howie, S., Combrinck, C., Roux, L., Tshele, M., Mokoena, G. & Mcleod Palane, N. (2017). Progress in international reading literacy study 2016: South African children's reading literacy achievement. Pretoria. Centre for Evaluation and Assessment.

Kajder, S., Bull, G., & Albaugh, S. (2005). Constructing digital stories. Learning & Leading with Technology, 32(5), 40–42.

Lambert, J. (2009). Where it all started: The centre for digital storytelling in California. Story circle: Digital storytelling around the world, California: Wiley-Blackwell, pp 79-90. https://www.google.co.za/url?sa=t&rct=j&q=&esrc=s&source=web&cd=2&cad=rja&uact=8&ved=2ahUKEwiwrdGTmILjAhWVSBUIHQ1NC

Pitler, H. J. (2006). Viewing technology through three lenses. Principal, 85(5):38-42.

Prebel, J. (2016). Engaging a "Pedagogy of Discomfort": Emotion as critical inquiry in community-based writing courses. Composition Forum, 34 Retrieved from http://files.eric.ed.gov/fullte4xt/EJ1113429.pdf.

Ribeiro, S., Moreira, A. & Pinto da Silva, C. (2016). Digital storytelling: Emotions in higher education. In Competencies in teaching, learning and educational leadership in the digital age. Retrieved from https://www.research gate.net/publication.288434000. ISBN: 978-989-8533-23-4.

Smeda, N., Dakich, E. & Sharda, N. (2014). The effectiveness of digital storytelling in the classrooms: A comprehensive study. Smart Learning Environments, 1(6) doi 10.1186/s40561-014-0006-3.

South Africa. National Department of Higher Education and Training. (2015). The Revised Minimum Requirements for Teacher Education Qualifications (MRTEQ). Pretoria: Government Gazette 553 (38487).

Taleb, N. N. (2010). The black swan: The impact of the highly improbably. London: Penguin Books.

Tiburt, J. C. (2010). The role of worldviews in health disparities education. Journal of General Internal Medicine, 25(2):178-181.

Yin, R. K. (2003). Case study research: Design and methods. Thousand Oaks, CA: Sage

DIVERSITY AS AN ADVANTAGE: AN ANALYSIS OF CAREER COMPETENCIES FOR IT STUDENTS

Patricia Brockmann[1], Heidi Schuhbauer[1] and Annika Hinze[2]
[1]*Technische Hochschule Nuernberg Georg Simon Ohm, Postfach 120320, D-90121 Nuremberg, Germany*
[2]*University of Waikato, Private Bag 3105, Hamilton 3240, New Zealand*

ABSTRACT

Due to increasing digitization in all aspects of life, the demand for qualified software development professionals continues to increase. Students from underrepresented groups, such as first generation students from non-academic families, minorities, single parents and women represent an underutilized pool of untapped potential talent. The question arises as to which unique perspectives computer science graduates from underrepresented groups can bring to software development companies. In addition to programming skills, non-technical competencies, such as foreign language abilities, intercultural communication, creativity, conflict management, team-building and organizational skills are vital for success in diverse, international project teams. A large job market database for new graduates, developed for a consortium of universities in Bavaria, Germany, is analyzed using machine learning tools. Career competencies desired by recruiting companies are compared to potential advantages offered by computer science graduates from underrepresented groups.

KEYWORDS

Education, Diversity, Competencies, Computer Science, Machine Learning

1. INTRODUCTION

The rise of digitization rapidly permeates through all aspects of modern life. As a result, the demand for qualified software development professionals continues to increase. This growing demand, accompanied by a simultaneous shortage of available software developers, widens the skills gap between job openings and qualified applicants. Traditionally, a number of groups have remained underrepresented among computer science students: first generation students, people who come from a migration background, single parents and women. People from these hitherto underrepresented groups offer an untapped source of potential talent.

In Germany, the proportion of people who come from a migration background (23%) is significantly higher than the proportion of migrants at universities (11%) (BAM 2011). At the Technical University of Applied Sciences in Nuremberg, 65% of the students are from non-academic families, approximately 5% have children, 10% are international students and 5% do not have a high school diploma (THN 2018). The number of female students in the Computer Science Department has actually been declining. In the Winter Semester of 2018/2019, only 17% of newly enrolled students were female (IN THN 2018).

Graduates from underrepresented groups can bring unique advantages to software development teams. They can help to increase the diversity of perspectives examined. Ilumoka (Ilumoka2012) discusses the importance of diversity in engineering teams. Especially during the requirements engineering phase, non-technical skills, such as intercultural communication and foreign language abilities, can be of exceptional value for multi-national teams or for stakeholders in foreign countries. During the software development and testing phases, cooperation, team-building and conflict management skills can prove vital for the success of a software project.

This work considers two research questions:

1. Which career competencies do students need to master for future careers as IT professionals?
2. Can machine learning methods help to gain information about the job market to help computer science students plan their future careers?

Section 2 Related Work discusses literature related to career competencies which are important in IT. Section 3 Methodology describes the machine learning methods used in this investigation. Section 4 Results presents the findings of the analysis. Section 5 Conclusions discusses the implications of the results, their relevance for IT graduates from diverse backgrounds and describes plans for further research.

2. RELATED WORK

This section discusses work related to the career goals and motivation of computer science students as well as the competencies students need to learn for their future careers as software developers. International, cultural and gender aspects are presented.

Liebenberg and Pietersee (Liebenberg 2016) investigated the career goals of software development students and professionals in South Africa. They found that both students and professionals valued stability and work/life balance most highly. Professionals additionally expressed the value of creativity. They assert that knowing people's motivation can help to improve recruitment and retention of software developers.

The intercultural competencies necessary to work in global software development teams have been investigated by a number of authors. Beecham, et al., (Beecham 2017) conducted a wide-scale literature review of distributed global software engineering courses. They identified a number of difficulties inherent to working in international software teams, which students need to learn to address: distance, teamwork, soft issues, stakeholders from industry, infrastructure and distributed software development processes. They categorized various types of distances, such as physical (geographic), time zones, cultural, language and institutional distances. Other authors, such as Hoda et al., (Hoda 2016) concentrated on the socio-cultural capabilities which students need to learn to work effectively in global software development teams. They pointed out the importance of overcoming language barriers, different perspectives regarding time, attitudes towards achievement, differences in autonomy and work habits as well as assumptions about national culture. They underline the importance of cross-cultural training. One example of the importance of cultural sensitivity in requirements engineering was reported by Hinze, et al. (Hinze 2018). To develop a medical app aimed at improving the health of migrant communities, sensitive personal data needed to be collected. With such a multi-cultural stakeholders, they stressed the importance of establishing personal relationships in order to create a trusting environment. Ideally, they recommend that one member of the research team should come from the cultural community studied, in order to help build bridges between the two worlds.

A number of authors have analyzed the effect of gender on computational thinking in schools and in the work place. Budinska and Mayerova (Budinska 2017) investigated the relationship between computer science concepts and computational thinking, in this case graph tasks. They found that boys were comparatively better at tasks with simple, relatively abstract representation and a larger amount of text, with the goal defined to identify a problem. They found that girls were better at tasks with less text, but with a relatively more complicated representation of structure, with a focus on simple operations on graphs. They concluded that because boys and girls have different methods of acquiring mechanical and abstract thinking, they each need different types of assignments to increase their motivation. Cheryan, et al. (Cheryan 2011) examined whether role models have an effect on self-confidence. They found that women who interacted with non-stereotypical role models believed they would be more successful in computer science than those who interacted with stereotypical role models. Faulkner (Faulkner 2009) discusses the subtle dynamics which can contribute to a feeling of 'belonging' in work relationships. She discusses the importance of informal conversation topics among colleagues, which can make women and other underrepresented groups feel like outsiders. Branz, et al. (Branz 2019) used Sentiment Analysis to evaluate how male and female team members interact on software engineering projects. They used statistical and machine learning methods to analyze a large data set from an incident management system to investigate the emotional content of project communication. They found that the types and intensities of sentiments expressed differed considerably between male and female developers.

The literature discussed here illustrate some of the challenges which computer science students will face upon graduation. The question arises as to whether students from underrepresented groups can leverage their backgrounds to make unique contributions to increase the diversity of ideas contributed to software development teams.

3. METHODOLOGY

In order to test the two questions proposed in Section 1 Introduction, an initial experiment was conducted using machine learning. To approximate the professional competencies required for future IT careers, a large database of job openings for new graduates was analyzed. The Job-Boerse (Jobboerse 2004) was developed in 2004 by the Computer Science Department at the Technical University of Nuremberg Georg Simon Ohm in Germany. Currently, 15 universities are participating in the project. For this experiment, a total of 30,792 job ads spanning over 3 years (2016 - 2018) were analyzed.

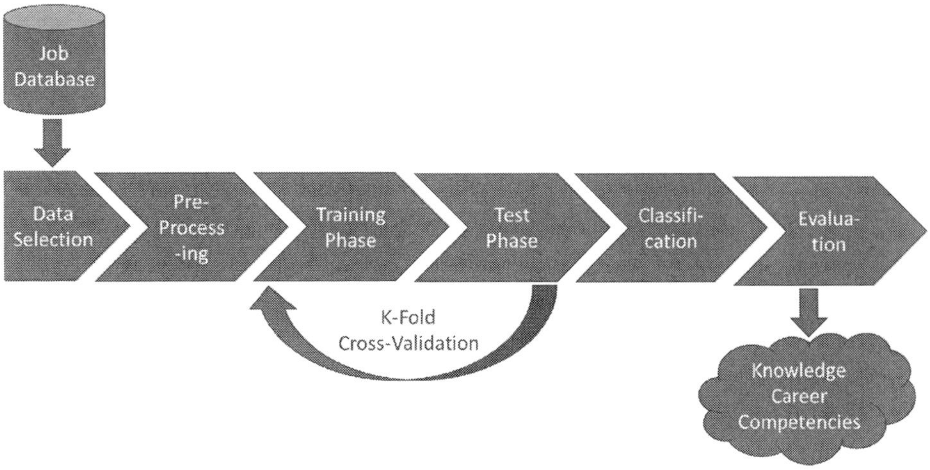

Figure 1. Machine Learning Process

First, data was extracted from the job database. Unlike highly structured database entries, individual job offers are stored as unstructured text. The first challenge was to extract the information relevant for this analysis, such as the job title and necessary qualifications, from free-form text. Next, the extracted data was cleaned in a pre-processing phase. Text errors in the database were corrected using a pre-processor written in Python, based on the FTFY library (Speer 2019). The analysis was performed using a machine learning system named Weka. The Weka system is a research project of the Machine Learning group at the University of Waikato in Hamilton, New Zealand (Frank 2016).

Three competing algorithms were tested to classify job offers:

1. Naive Bayes Classifier (NBC)
2. K-Nearest Neighbors (KNN)
3. Support Vector Machine (SVM)

A Bayes statistical classifier algorithm was used as a baseline to test whether machine learning algorithms are actually better than classical statistical methods. Bayes classifiers are based on the Bayesian statistical theorem. Data points are assigned to a given class using a set of features, called a feature vector. A naive Bayes classifier (NBC) simplifies this process by making the 'naive' assumption that all feature variables are independent of class (Rish 2001). The naive Bayes algorithm has proved effective in text classification in a number of applications (Chen 2009).

The K-Nearest Neighbors algorithm (K-NN) is an instance-based learning algorithm which is based on similarity measures between data points. K-NN is a supervised learning method which uses data from the past, with known output values, to predict an unknown output value for new data (Korde 2012). It has also been called a non-parametric, 'lazy' machine learning algorithm, because the algorithm makes no assumptions about the form of the problem. Any new generalization beyond the initial training data is first performed when each new query is encountered (Sebastiani 2002).

A Support Vector Machine (SVM) is a supervised machine learning algorithm which classifies data into groups by constructing hyperplanes. In a two dimensional space, this hyperplane would be represented by a line dividing the data points into two groups. Non-linear classification can be performed by mapping inputs to higher dimensional hyperplanes (Tong 2001). Support vector machines have been shown to be highly effective to classify text (Basu 2003).

During the initial training phase, a randomly selected subset of the job ads was used to train each of the three algorithms to classify job descriptions into groups. These groups were defined as specific job titles, such as 'developer', 'consultant', 'engineer', 'analyst' and 'project manager'. This was followed by a test phase, during which a different subset job ads, those not used during the training phase, were tested. This test data set of new, unseen job ads was input into the trained algorithms to see whether the job titles in the new job ads could be correctly recognized by each of the three algorithms.

To estimate the effectiveness of the competing algorithms, a K-fold Cross Validation Test was performed. Each of these training and test phases were repeated for 10 cycles for each of the machine learning algorithms tested. During each test cycle, a different subset of the jobs data was used for the training phase and the remaining data for the test phase (Wong2015).

Finally, the career competencies were grouped into clusters using the K-means algorithm. The K-means algorithm partitions data objects into a specified number of groups, 'K'. Each data object is assigned to the cluster with the nearest mean value (Jain 2010). The K-means algorithm has been shown to be effective to group large text document data sets (Huang 2008). The premise here is that the competencies associated with job titles are those desired by companies recruiting new graduates.

4. RESULTS

As described in Section 3 Methodology, records were first extracted from the job database, then cleaned with a pre-processing routine written in Python to remove data entry errors, misspellings and inconsistencies. Next, each of the three algorithms were implemented using the Weka machine learning system: Naive Bayes Classifier (NBC), K-Nearest Neighbor (KNN) and Support Vector Machine (SVM). During the supervised training phase, each algorithm was trained to associate correct pairs of input text (job descriptions) and output results (job titles). After that, for each algorithm, a test phase with a different subset of job ads were tested to see how well each algorithm had learned to recognize job descriptions associated with specific job titles. These cycles of training and test phases were repeated 10 times, with different subsets of test and training sets for the job ads for each cycle to perform a K-fold Cross Validation.

Accuracy is defined as the number of correctly predicted results (true positives and true negatives) in proportion to the total observations. Precision is a measure of positive predictive value, while recall calculates the proportion of relevant instances that have been retrieved in relation to the total number of relevant instances. F1 is the weighted average of precision and recall, and thus takes both false positives and false negatives into account (Powers 2011). The classification accuracy and f1-scores of each of the three algorithms are shown below in Table 1.

Table 1. Accuracy and F1 of classifier algorithms

Algorithm	Accuracy	F1
Naïve Bayes Classifier	0.78	0.77
K-Nearest Neighbor	0.72	0.71
Support Vector Machine	0.91	0.91

Although the naive Bayes algorithm would be considered a relatively simple statistical method, it performed slightly better than the K-Nearest Neighbor algorithm, which performed poorest. The performance of the Support Vector Machine was the best of all three algorithms. These findings are similar to the results reported by Elnahrawy (Elnahrawy 2002). He found the naive Bayes classifier simple and fast, both in learning as well as in classification. Significantly, the naive Bayes classifier outperformed the K-Nearest Neighbor in both speed and accuracy. The Support Vector Machine delivered excellent results with respect to accuracy. The disadvantage was that it was very slow to learn and thus computationally expensive. Based on these findings Support Vector Machine (SVM) was selected to perform the classification of the job ads.

The next step was to classify job ads according to job titles. The most frequently identified job titles found during the test phase are shown in Figure 2.

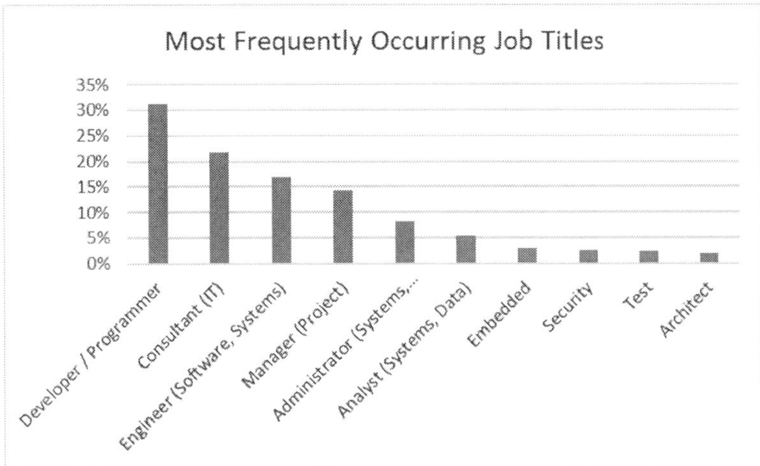

Figure 2. Most frequently identified job titles

These results provide an initial starting point to identify the most promising career opportunities for IT graduates. As expected, technically-oriented job titles, such as developers, programmers and software engineers appeared quite frequently. Interesting to note is that a significant number of highly sought job titles, such as consultant, analyst and project manager, are fields which are not limited to programming.

The next step was to identify the key competencies desired by prospective employers. Here, an unsupervised K-means clustering algorithm, as described in Section 3 Methodology, was used to group similar terms. Terms were grouped together in to a number "K" of clusters. Some of the clusters which formed were not very helpful. For example, one of the clusters formed included the words 'status', 'gender', religion', 'race' and 'disability'. It can be inferred that these terms are part of standard non-discrimination clauses. Especially of interest here are the clusters related to technical and non-technical skills. The most common clusters are displayed in Figure 3, along with the percentage of job ads which contained these terms.

As expected, job offers contained a number of specifications defining desired technical competencies. Computer programming skills and knowledge of software engineering, from initial requirements engineering, design, development, test and integration of software systems remain core competencies of any computer science degree program.

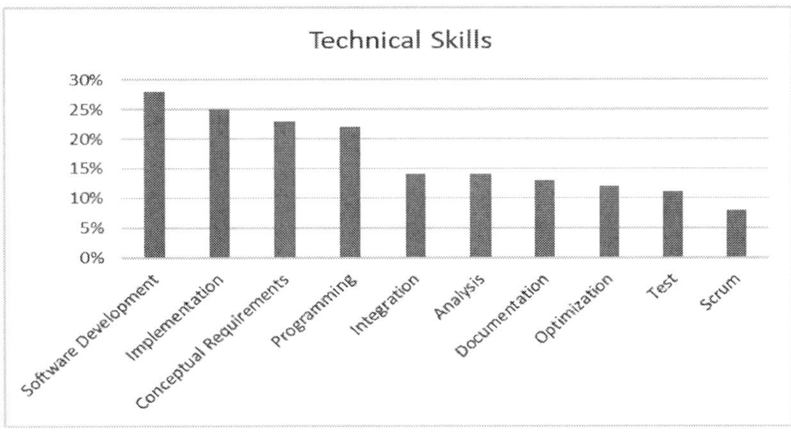

Figure 3. Most commonly sought technical skills

Significant for this research is that a number of non-technical skills were also specified as highly desirable by prospective employers.

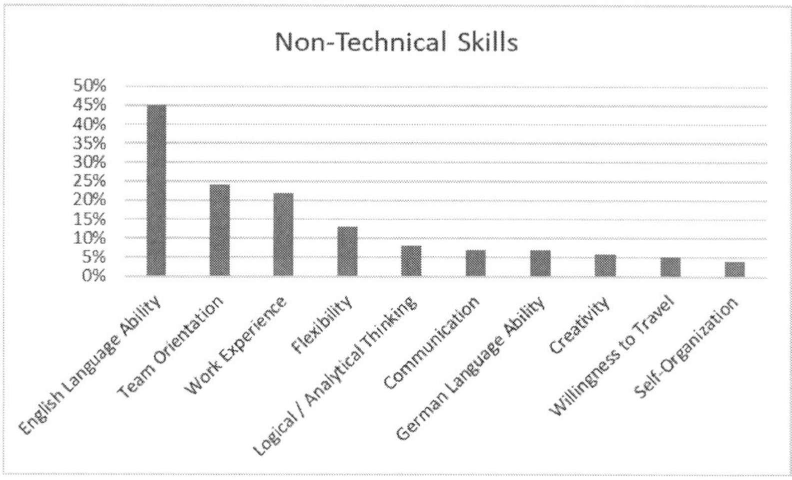

Figure 4. Most commonly sought non-technical skills

The ability to communicate effectively, both in the native language (German) but especially in English, were the most common non-technical skills sought. Working effectively in teams, flexibility, logical and analytical thinking, creativity and self-organization highlight abilities which would be considered soft skills. The willingness to travel was also specified as desirable for some careers.

5. CONCLUSIONS AND FUTURE WORK

In conclusion, the most commonly advertised job titles, technical and non-technical competencies for computer science graduates have been identified in a university career database. Machine learning methods proved effective in extracting useful information from large amounts of unstructured data. The ramifications of the knowledge gained, as presented in Section 4 Results, have consequences for underrepresented students and for the computer science curriculum at universities. It has been demonstrated that employers value both technical skills as well as personal characteristics when recruiting IT graduates. Although project management is often a mandatory course, the development of soft skills tends to be overlooked. Team training and conflict management are rarely taught explicitly in undergraduate computer science programs.

Students from underrepresented groups may be able to contribute unique soft skills, which traditional students may lack. For example, the ability to plan and organize multiple competing tasks can be vital for the success of large software development projects. Working together in teams often requires learning to resolve conflicts between team members. The ability to communicate both verbally as well as in written form is often not taught explicitly as part of the curriculum in computer science. Women tend to score higher in verbal ability, while men tend to score higher in spatial ability (Lewin 2001). This could imply that women may have an inherent advantage in communication skills. For students from migration and non-academic backgrounds, however, written skills may prove especially challenging. Extra support in learning how to improve their written skills, especially in their non-native language, may be necessary. Growing up bilingual and bi-cultural enables someone to build bridges between stakeholders and team members from different countries. The importance of bi-cultural proxies as bridge builders is discussed in MacGregor, et al. (MacGregor 2005). Bi-coded individuals are defined as people, who due to their life history, are able to operate equally well in two different cultures. Such bi-coded individuals can help serve as an intercultural translators between two cultures.

As opposed to concentrating on the disadvantages underrepresented students have, diversity can contribute unique advantages. Woolley, et al. (Woolley 2010) examined the role of collective intelligence performance. They found that diversity within teams tends to increase the collective intelligence of the entire team significantly (Woolley 2015). Bear, et al. (Bear 2011) found that diverse teams showed increased participation and collaboration, which led to a higher perception of efficacy among team members.

Especially groups performing creative or innovative tasks tend to benefit more from diversity (Williams1998).

In conclusion, students from underrepresented groups represent a potential source of untapped talent and could contribute to a diversity of perspectives in computer science. Future research will focus on evaluating in detail how the specific non-technical soft skills desired by prospective employers can be fulfilled by students from underrepresented groups. Interviews, surveys and machine learning analysis of text communication artifacts will be conducted with students from a migration background, first generation students, single parents and female students, to ascertain which unique advantages they can bring, especially in soft skills gained during their life history. This work is part of a larger research project to recruit, support and retain students from underrepresented groups in STEM subjects, as described in (Schuhbauer 2019).

ACKNOWLEDGEMENT

This research was supported in part by a grant from the Staedtler Trust for the research project "DiaMINT".

REFERENCES

BAM 2011, Bundesanstalt fuer Migraiton und Fluechtlinge, Bestandsaufnahme und Vernetzung, *Vernetzungsworkshop: Integration von Studierenden mit Migrationshintergrund an deutschen Hochschulen*.

Basu, A., Walters, C. and Shepard, M., 2003, Support vector machines for text categorization, *HICSS 2003 Proceedings of the 36th Hawaii International Conference on System Sciences*, Big Island, HI, U.S.A.

Bear, J. B. and Woolley, A. W., 2011, The role of gender in team collaboration and performance, *Interdisciplinary Science Reviews*, Volume 36, Number 2, pp. 146-153.

Beecham, S., Clear, T., Barr, J., Daniels, M., Oudshoorn, M. and Noll, J., 2017, Preparing Tomorrow's Software Engineers for Work in a Global Environment, *IEEE Software*, Number 1, Vol. 34, pp. 9-12.

Branz, L., Pastran Reina, L., Richter, J., Waizmann, B. and Brockmann, P., 2019, Sentiment Analysis of Male and Female Developer Comments: Exploring Gender Influence on Emotinal Expressions in Software Engineering Projects, *GE@ICSE19 Second Workshop on Gender Equality in Software Engineering,* Montreal, Canada.

Budinska, L. and Mayerova, K., 2017, Graph Tasks in Bebras Contest - What does it have to do with gender*?, CSERC 17 Computer Science Education Research Conference*, Helsinki, Finland.

Chen, J., Huang, H., Tian, S. and Qu, Y., 2009, Feature Selection for text classification with Naive Bayes, *Expert Systems with Applications*, Number 36, pp. 5432-5435.

Cheryan, S., Siy, J., Vichayapai, M., Drury, B. and Kim, S., 2011, Do Female and Male Role Models Who Embody STEM Stereotypes Hinder Women's Anticipated Success in STEM?, *Social Psychological and Personality Science*, Volume 2, Number 6, pp. 656-664.

Elnahrawy, E., 2002, Log-Based Chat Room Monitoring Using Text Categorization: A Comparative Study, *Proceedings of the International Association of Science and Technology for Development Conference on Information and Knowledge Sharing*, St. Thomas, U.S. Virgin Islands.

Faulkner, W., 2009, Doing gender in engineering workplace cultures. Observations from the field, *Engineering Studies*, Volume 1, Number 1, pp. 3-18.

Hinze, A., Timpany, C., Bowen, J., Chang, C., Starkey, N., and Elder, H., 2018, Collecting Sensitive Personal Data in a Multi-Cultural Environment, *HCI 2018 Proceedings of the International Human Computer Interaction Conference*, Las Vegas, Nevada, U.S.A.

Hoda, R., Ali Babar, M., Shastri, Y., Yaqoob, H., 2016, Socio-Cultural Challenges in Global Software Engineering Education, *IEEE Transactions on Education*, Number 3, Volume 60, pp. 173-182.

Huang, A., 2008, Similarity Measure for Text Document Clustering, *New Zealand Computer Science Research Student Conference,* Christ Church, New Zealand

Ilumoka, A. 2012, Strategies for overcoming barriers to women and minorities in STEM, *IEEE 2nd Integrated STEM Education Conference (ISEC)*, Ewing, New Jersey, U.S.A., pp. 1-4.

Inthn 2018, Technical University of Applied Sciences Nuernberg Computer Science Department, Lehrbericht 2018.

Jain, A., 2010, Data Clustering 50 Years Beyond K-Means *Pattern Recognition Letters*, Number 31, pp. 651-666.

Korde, V., 2012, Text Classification and Classifiers: A Survey, *International Journal of Artificial Intelligence and Applications*, Number 2, Volume 3, pp. 85-94.

Lewin, C., Wolgers, G., Herlitz, A., 2001, Sex differences favoring women in verbal but not in visuospatial episodic memory, *Neuropsychology*, Volume 15, Number 2, pp. 165-173.

Liebenberg, J. And Pieterse, V., 2016, Career Goals of Software Development Professionals and Software Development Students, *CSERC 16 Computer Science Education Research Conference*, Pretoria, South Africa, pp.22-28.

MacGregor, E., Hsieh, Y. and Kruchten, P., 2005, Cultural Patterns in Software Process Mishaps: Incidents in Global Projects, *HSSE 05 Proceedings of the 2005 workshop on Human and social factors of software engineering*, St. Louis, Missouri, U.S.A.

Powers, D. M. W., 2011, Precision, Recall and F-measure to ROC, Informedness, Markedness and Correlation, *Journal of Machine Learning Technologies*, Volume 2, Number 1, pp. 33-37.

Rish, I., 2001, An empirical study of the naive Bayes classifier, *IJCAI 2001 Workshop on Empirical Methods in Artificial Intelligence*, Seattle, Washington, U.S.A., pp. 41-46.

Schuhbauer, H. 2019, Evaluation of an E-Learning Course in Moodle in Comparison to a Traditional Lesson, ICICTE2019 Proceedings, 19th International Conference on Information Communication Technologies in Education, http://icicte.org/assets/icicte2019proceedings.pdf, pp. 44-53.

Sebastiani, F., 2002, Machine Learning in Automated Text Categorization, *ACM Computing Surveys*, Volume 34, Number 1, pp. 1-47.

Speer, R.,2019,ftfy, Version 5.5, doi = 10.5281/zenodo.2591652, https://doi.org/10.5281/zenodo.2591652.

Technical University of Applied Sciences Nuernberg, 2004, Job-Boerse, https://www.hochschuljobboerse.de, lastaccessed April 26, 2019.

Technical University of Applied Sciences Nuernberg, 2018, Diversity an der Hochschule, https://www.th-nuernberg.de/hochschule-region/strategie-und-profil/hochschule-der-vielfalt, lastaccessed = April 26, 2019.

Tong, S., Koller, D., 2001, Support Vector Machine Active Learning with Applications to Text Classification, *Journal of Machine Learning Research*, Volume 2, pp.45-66.

Williams Woolley, A., Aggarwal, I. and Malone, T. W., 2015, Collective Intelligence and Group Performance, *Current Directions in Psychological Science*, Volume 24, Number 6, pp. 420-424.

Williams Woolley, A., Chabris, C. F., Pentland, A., Hashmi, N., and Malone, T. W., 2010, Evidence for a collective intelligence factor in the performance of human groups, *Science*, Volume 330, Number 6004, pp. 686-688.

Williams, K. and O'Reilly, C., 1998, Demography and diversity in organizations: A review of 40 years of research, *Research in Organizational Behavior*, Volume 20, pp. 77-140. bb

Williams, K. Y., & O'Reilly, C. A. I. 1998, Demography and diversity in organizations: A review of 40 years of research, In L. L. Cummings (Ed.), *Research in organizational behavior,* Vol. 20, pp. 77–140.

Wong, T., 2015, Performance evaluation of classification algorithms by k-fold and leave-one-out cross validation, *Pattern Recognition*, Volume 48, pp. 2839-2846.

RELATIONSHIP BETWEEN LEARNING TIME AND DIMENSIONS OF A LEARNING ORGANISATION

Vaclav Zubr
University of Hradec Kralove, Faculty of Informatics and Management
Rokitanskeho 62, 50003 Hradec Kralove, Czech Republic

ABSTRACT

The introduction of a learning organisation model brings many benefits to organisations. To evaluate whether it is a learning organisation, the Marsick and Watkins Dimensions of a Learning Organisation Questionnaire can be used. In the Czech Republic, only a few studies have been conducted using this questionnaire. The aim of this paper is to compare the IT sector and the education sector in terms of learning time and assessment of the individual dimensions of the learning organisation by Marsick and Watkins. In 2018 and 2019, studies with the Dimensions of a Learning Organisation Questionnaire focusing on the IT sector and the education sector (secondary schools) were conducted in the Czech Republic. In total, 201 respondents from the IT sector and 121 respondents from secondary schools participated in the study. When comparing the time spent on self-education in both sectors, it is clear that the employees spend 1 to 20 hours per month with self-education, while in the IT sector common employees dedicate more to self-education, executives dedicate more to self-education in the education system. When comparing the average values of the dimensions of a learning organisation in relation to the time spent on self-education, the results in both sectors are very similar. It can be argued that the assessment of individual dimensions increases with the time spent on self-education up to 20 hours per month. The biggest difference in average values can be seen in Dimension 4, while the smallest difference on average dimension can be seen in Dimension 7.

KEYWORDS

Learning Organisation, Learning Time, Dimensions of a Learning Organisation

1. INTRODUCTION

According to Senge, a learning organisation can be defined as: *"... an organisation where people constantly improve their skills and achieve the results that they really desire, where they find support, new and dynamic models of thinking, where collective thinking and inspiration are welcome and where people still learn how to learn together."* (Senge, 2016). A learning organisation is made up of basic components: organisation, people, knowledge, and technology. Individual components support each other in learning, which is the essence of a learning organisation (Serrat, 2017). Learning becomes an integral part of the whole work process, work and learning are interconnected in the process of continuous improvement. A key aspect of organisational learning is interaction between individuals (Yadav, Agarwal, 2016). Organisational learning is a process where the meaning of information is created, information is collected, interpreted and distributed. Considering the learning support level of the learning organisation, several learning organisation action requirements can be identified, such as: providing strategic guidance for learning, supporting employees in sharing visions, building systems to capture and share learning, fostering collaboration and team learning and to support dialogue and create opportunities for continuous learning (Jamali et al., 2009). Organisational learning has a positive impact on gaining a long-term competitive advantage, improving performance, strengthening human resources, creativity and innovation, and accelerating the process of change to a learning organisation (Saadat, Saadat, 2016).

After 2010, the concept of a learning organisation has become the subject of many studies around the world (Zubr, 2019). In all these studies, the Dimensions of a Learning Organisation Questionnaire (DLOQ) is used to evaluate the learning organisation created by Watkins and Marsick (Watkins, Marsick, 1993). Most often, studies are focused on the education sector and the banking sector (which is close to IT) (Zubr, 2019). Therefore, this study is focused on the IT sector and the education sector in the Czech Republic.

1.1 Dimensions of a Learning Organisation Questionnaire

According to Marsick and Watkins (Marsick, Watkins, 2003), there are seven dimensions of learning organisations that represent organisations' efforts to create learning opportunities for all employees, to create a platform that supports dialogues, responses and experiments among members, as well as team learning, vision sharing or strategic leadership (Norashikin et al., 2016). These seven dimensions include: Create Continuous Learning Opportunities, Promote Inquiry and Dialogue, Encourage Collaboration and Team Learning, Create Systems to Capture and Share Learning, Empower People toward a Collective Vision, Connect the Organization to its Environment and Provide Strategic Leadership for Learning. Based on some studies, it was discovered that only two dimensions of a learning organisation led to higher organisational performance - namely, Promote Inquiry and Dialogue and System Connection. The remaining dimensions have no effect on organisational performance (Norashikin et al., 2016). DLOQ is developed on the basis of a theoretical framework combining four articles: organisational learning, workplace learning, learning climate and learning structure perspective (Kim et al., 2015). For example, this questionnaire can be used to evaluate an organisation as a learning organisation.

In the basic version, the questionnaire contains 42 questions, according to the authors' recommendation, it can be shortened to 21 questions to maintain the validity of the data obtained. To maintain the questionnaire's validity, a reverse translation, expert review and Cronbach's alpha coefficient should be performed to ensure that dimensional reliability is not significantly lower than the actual work validation reliability (Watkins, O'Neil, 2013).

1.2 Small and Medium Enterprises in the Czech Republic

Small and medium-sized enterprises are defined by the number of employees, up to 250 people. Looking closer, they can be divided into tiny enterprises (1-9 employees), small enterprises (10-49 employees) and medium-sized enterprises (50-249 employees) (Czech Statistical Office, 2005) (Czech Statistical Office, 2013). These enterprises are of relatively high importance within the Czech economy, e.g. in 2017 the share of small and medium-sized enterprises in the total number of active business entities was 99.8%. In 2017, the share of employees in small and medium-sized enterprises in the total number of employees in the business sphere was 58.0%. Small and medium-sized enterprises in the Czech Republic represent more than 1 million economic entities as a whole, they are significant employers', a driving force for the business sector, growth, innovation and competitiveness. These enterprises are actively supported by the state, e.g. in the form of projects and various programmes (Ministry of Industry and Trade, 2017). Total IT accounts for 3.6% of the business sector, in IT the tiny enterprises (40,232) and small enterprises (1,463) are the most represented (Czech Statistical Office, 2017).

1.3 Schools as Learning Organisations

Education is an important sector in all countries, producing professionals in various fields. However, the quality of schools across countries varies. The culture of a learning organisation in a secondary school environment is not defined anywhere, but the definition of a learning organisation culture at universities can be applied. Schools characterised by a learning organisation culture support continuous learning for the sustainable improvement of teaching and learning. The knowledge gained leads to the education and support of individual development, teamwork and leadership in order to fulfil the institution's mission (Ponnuswamy, Manohar, 2016). Schools then have the ability to adapt to new environments and, through learning, find their way to carry out their visions. According to OECD-UNICEF paper, the school as a learning organisation, focuses on *"developing and sharing a vision centred on the learning of all students, creating and supporting continuous learning opportunities for all staff, promoting team learning and collaboration among all staff, establishing a culture of inquiry, innovation and exploration, embedding systems for collecting and exchanging knowledge and learning, learning with and from the external environment and the larger learning system and modelling and growing learning leadership."* (OECD, 2016).

2. METHODOLOGY

In total, two studies were conducted in the Czech Republic in 2018 and 2019 using a shortened 21 questionnaire version of the DLOQ, including 7 dimensions in Czech language. To maintain the questionnaire's validity, the questionnaire was translated by two independent translators from English to Czech and then back to English. At the same time, the preservation of the questionnaire's meaning was assessed. The Cronbach reliability coefficient was calculated for each dimension using IBM SPSS Statistics version 24. Total reliability was 0.933 in 2018, in 2019 total reliability was 0.941. Respondents evaluated the individual dimensions on a 6-point Likert scale. The final version of the questionnaire was created using "docs.google.com". The reference to the questionnaire was then sent to respondents' e-mail addresses.

In 2018, a cross-sectional questionnaire was conducted focusing on small and medium-sized enterprises in the IT sector in the Czech Republic, contacts to small and medium-sized enterprises were obtained from the Albertina database for trade and marketing (Albertina for Trade and Marketing, 2019). A total of 2,884 respondents from small and medium-sized enterprises from the Czech Republic were addressed with a focus on IT activities. Approximately 250 e-mails sent were returned as undeliverable after sending due to the absence of the e-mail address, 25 respondents responded to the e-mail with the response that they no longer operate the business.

In 2019, a cross-sectional questionnaire was conducted focusing on secondary schools across the Czech Republic. Altogether 1,304 representatives of secondary schools were addressed, 91 emails were returned due to the absence of the given email address, 1 respondent directly to the survey.

The data obtained was analysed using Microsoft Excel 2016 and IBM SPSS Statistics Version 24 using descriptive statistics, parametric and non-parametric assays at confidence levels $\alpha = 0.01$ and $\alpha = 0.05$.

The main research question of this survey was to determine whether there is a relationship between learning time and the dimensions of the learning organization score.

3. RESULTS

In 2018, 201 respondents from small and medium-sized enterprises in the IT sector in the Czech Republic participated in the study (questionnaire returns were 6.97%). The respondents consisted of 137 men and 64 women. The respondents most frequently reported employment in the organisation within five years (32.8%), followed by 11 - 15 years (21.4%).

In 2019, 121 respondents from secondary schools in the Czech Republic participated in the study (9.28% return). The respondents consisted of 45 men and 76 women. The most frequently reported employment periods were less than 10 years (32.2%), followed by 11-20 years (27.27%). The respondents' demographic profile is showed in Table 1.

Table 1. The respondents´ demographic profile. (own processing)

	Number of respondents	
	2018 (n = 201) n (%)	**2019 (n = 121) n (%)**
Age		
21 – 30 years	30 (14.9)	4 (3.3)
31 – 40 years	76 (37.8)	17 (14.0)
41 – 50 years	57 (28.4)	29 (24.0)
51 – 60 years	32 (15.9)	57 (47.1)
Over 61 years	6 (3.0)	14 (11.6)
Organisation size		
Up to 10 employees	65 (32.3)	0
Up to 50 employees	91 (45.3)	73 (60.3)
Up to 250 employees	45 (22.4)	47 (38.9)
More than 250 employees	0	1 (0.8)

Position in employment		
Staff member	72 (35.8)	34 (28.1)
Executive member	129 (64.2)	87 (71.9)
Learning time		
0 hours per month	9 (4.5)	1 (0.8)
1-10 hours per month	109 (54.2)	40 (33.1)
11-20 hours per month	48 (23.8)	54 (44.6)
21-35 hours per month	15 (7.5)	20 (16.5)
More than 36 hours per month	20 (10.0)	6 (5.0)

When comparing the demographic profile of respondents, it is clear that respondents from organisations employing up to 50 employees were dominantly represented in the survey in both years, similarly to the representation of common employees and executives. From this viewpoint, both surveys can be compared, although they were conducted in different sectors. The respondents' profile in terms of learning time per month is also similar. While the IT sector has the highest number of employees dedicated to learning 1-10 hours per month, teachers spend usually 11-20 hours a month self-educating. Self-education is mostly applied by e-learning focused on current topics related to a particular job.

Table 2. Comparison of respondents´ responses with different education intensity (own processing)

Hours a month	**Average of D1**		**Average of D2**		**Average of D3**		**Average of D4**		**Average of D5**		**Average of D6**		**Average of D7**	
	2018	**2019**	**2018**	**2019**	**2018**	**2019**	**2018**	**2019**	**2018**	**2019**	**2018**	**2019**	**2018**	**2019**
0	2.74	2.67	3.46	1.67	3.78	3.00	3.15	3.33	3.11	4.33	3.37	3.33	3.29	3.00
1 - 10	4.48	4.46	4.35	4.11	4.13	4.18	3.56	3.95	4.34	4.63	3.89	4.19	4.28	4.50
11 - 20	4.39	4.50	4.44	4.32	4.35	4.40	3.49	4.16	4.40	4.79	3.95	4.60	4.46	4.83
21 - 35	4.60	4.18	4.58	3.67	4.44	4.09	3.62	3.72	4.62	4.60	4.08	4.35	4.38	4.22
36 or more	5.10	4.83	4.73	4.50	4.17	4.50	3.55	4.28	3.55	4.50	4.40	4.72	4.67	4.44

When comparing the average values of the two dimensions, it is clear that the results are very similar and there is no statistically significant difference in the t-test at the significance level $\alpha = 0.05$ ($p = 0.06 - 0.96$). The lowest $p = 0.06$ can be seen for dimension 4, while the highest $p = 0.96$ can be seen for dimension 7. Generally speaking, with education up to 20 hours a month, the assessment of dimensions in both sectors is increasing in both years.

When comparing the time spent on learning for IT sector staff and executive members, it is clear that common staff in the IT sector is dedicated to learning for 1-20 hours per month compared to teachers as staff members. However, teachers self-educate for at least an hour a month. For education of executives in the education sector we can see more respondents who spend 11-20 and 21-35 hours per month, while IT sector executives most often devote 1-10 hours per month to learning.

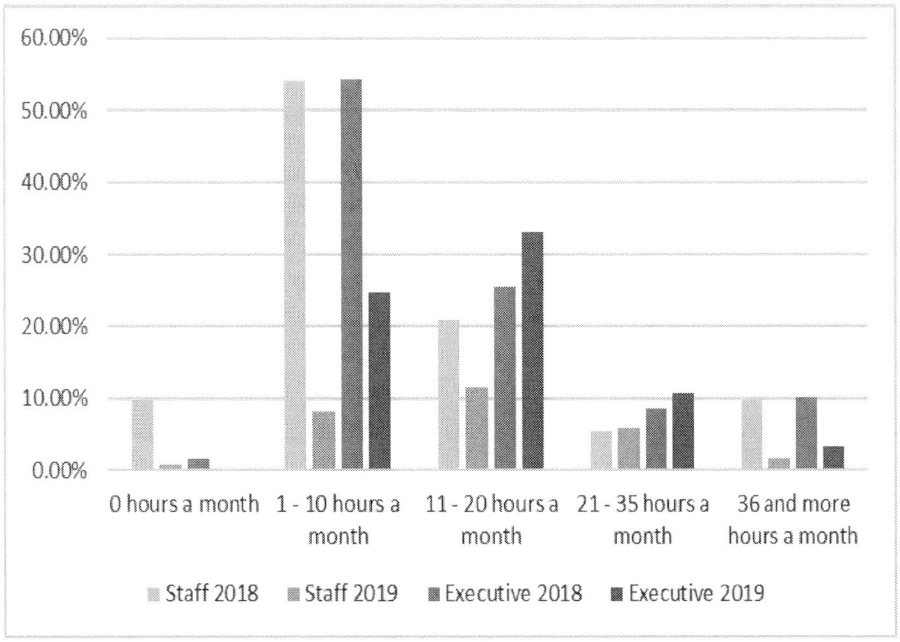

Figure 1. Learning time (per month) by worker´s position (own processing)

4. DISCUSSION

In the Czech Republic, only a few studies of a learning organisation have been performed using DLOQ. (Zubr, 2019) The IT sector and the education sector were selected for this study. The IT sector in the Czech Republic represents an important employer within small and middle-sized enterprises (Ministry of Industry and Trade, 2017), the education sector keeps its significance in all countries thanks to its function of producing quality workers.

A total of 201 respondents participated in the survey in 2018, 121 respondents in 2019. Due to the percentage of the questionnaire return (2018: 6.97% vs. 2019: 9.28%), these surveys can be compared for the number of respondents. Looking at the composition of respondents, the individual years are quite different. In 2018 137 men and 64 women were included in the survey, while in 2019, 45 men and 76 women participated in the survey. Therefore, the gender ratio is reversed in the two years. This is determined by the sectors in which the survey was conducted. While in 2018, there was approximately 3 women for every 10 men in the Czech Republic's the IT sector, in the area of education this ratio is reversed, i.e. for every ten women there is approximately 2.7 men (Czech Statistical Office, 2018).

In both surveys, organisations with less than 50 employees are the most represented, with 45.3% of these enterprises being represented in 2018 and 60.3% of enterprises in 2019. Small and medium-sized enterprises in 2018 are the second most represented group of small firms with less than 10 employees. No school with less than 10 employees participated in the survey and only 1 school said it had more than 250 employees. Given the nature of the schools addressed, it can be assumed that the response from "more than 250 employees" was wrong. Based on available data, a total of 44,993 teachers worked in Czech secondary schools in the 2017/2018 school year and there are currently around 1,400 secondary schools in the Czech Republic (Czech News Agency, 2019) (Ministry of Education, Youth and Sport, 2014) (List of Schools, 2019). Therefore, there is an average of around 32 teachers per school, which is in line with the study's outcome (the dominant representation of schools with less than 50 employees).

Both surveys show that approximately 78% of employees in both sectors spend 1-20 hours a month on self-education. In the education sector, only one respondent stated that they did not spend one hour per month with education. This result is expected in the education sector - in order to ensure the quality of teaching students, it is necessary that educators continue to educate themselves and monitor current changes in the subjects taught. Therefore, it is not surprising that 16.5% of teachers say they spend 21-35 hours a month on self-education. When comparing the time of self-education among ordinary and senior executives, it is clear that ordinary workers in the IT sector educate more often than ordinary staff in the education sector. By contrast, education managers educate more than IT sector workers. This result is surprising in view of the above-mentioned assertion of maintaining a certain quality of student education, which is being looked after by ordinary staff in education.

If we compare the different dimensions of the learning organisation in relation to the time devoted to learning, it is clear that the results are very similar for both years. The biggest difference between the average dimension rating is for Dimension 4: Create Systems to Capture and Share Learning, where p is approaching 0.05 ($p = 0.06$). Dimension 4 is generally assessed by the higher education staff as a higher average score than in the IT sector. This result is expected due to the need for teachers to be constantly educated, a number of training events for teachers and hence systems that make learning easier to share. It should also be noted that non-teaching topics and seminars can also be included in teacher education for secondary school teachers, e.g. in healthcare, a relatively sophisticated network of learning sharing systems can be recorded. It can be argued that the average rating of individual dimensions increases with learning times up to 11-20 hours per month, while in the IT sector, for most dimensions, the average rating for 21-35 hours per month may increase further. The smallest difference between learning time and dimensional assessment for each sector was noted for Dimension 7: Provide Strategic Leadership for Learning. This result indicates that there is an effort to establish a learning organisation in both sectors.

When comparing the average rating of individual dimensions of this study with similar studies abroad from the banking sector, the average rating in IT sector in the Czech Republic in 2018 is higher for employees who are engaged in self-education at least an hour a month (Berberoğlu, Emine, 2011) (Soahib et al., 2014). Compared to other studies abroad, the same result was also achieved in the education sector (Abo Al Ola, 2017). According to Voolaid data, the average score of dimensions of the study from Czech Republic is higher than international average in 2013 (Voolaid, 2013).

5. CONCLUSION

Based on a comparison of the results from individual studies conducted in 2018 and 2019, it can be argued that the introduction of the concept of a learning organisation in both sectors in the Czech Republic is on the right track. The assessment of individual dimensions implies that the time devoted to self-education is directly related to the assessment of individual dimensions, and there is leadership-supporting learning in organisations. Based on the results of this study, we can say that the relationship between learning time and the dimensions of the learning organization score exist. Comparing two different sectors brings the possibility to learn from mistakes and weaknesses in one sector or to use the positive functional approach of the other sector. Sectors could also join together and work together on common weaknesses (e. g. Dimension 4). A change in the approach to evaluating employee education (e. g. setting up systems to measure the difference between actual and expected performance, publishing the evaluation to all employees or balancing the time and resources spent on education) would contribute to improving Dimension 4 evaluation in both sectors. Improving the evaluation of individual dimensions in both sectors would bring many benefits of a learning organization concept (e. g. improving the competitive advantage by engaging with the external community and recognizing employee initiative; improving job satisfaction of employees and thus increasing their performance).

The relatively low number of respondents who participated in both surveys can be considered as a limitation of this study. The low response rate is attributed to a number of other questionnaire surveys that are addressed to respondents by various students and statistical firms. Due to reluctance to respond to another questionnaire survey, respondents in several cases directly refused to participate in the survey and did not complete the questionnaire even after repeatedly addressed. Unfortunately, it is not possible to address each respondent personally due to the inclusion of respondents from the whole Czech Republic.

Although these studies have been carried out in two sectors, it is necessary to map other employment sectors in the Czech Republic in the future, or to compare them to those abroad.

ACKNOWLEDGEMENT

The paper was written with the support of the specific project 2019 grant "Determinants of Cognitive Processes Impacting the Work Performance" granted by the University of Hradec Kralove, Czech Republic and thanks to help of students František Hašek and Jan Petružálek.

REFERENCES

Abo Al Ola, L. M., 2017. The availability of Dimensions of Learning Organizations Ques-tionnaire (DLOQ) in Educational College at Taif University from the Perspective of Employees. *Journal of Educational and Psychological Sciences*, 18(1), 447-487.

Albertina for Trade and Marketing., 2019. http://www.albertina.cz/?gclid=Cj0KCQiAzrTUBRCnARIsAL0mqcz2seJjjxmISfi7QlvHHAwN-ZnZrWpd4Botnujmtq08Zio1vx0BfBMaAu-bEALw_wcB, last accessed 2019/07/15.

Berberoğlu, A., Emine, Ü., 2011. Relation between organizational learning and organizational commitment: Case study of a private bank in North Cyprus. P*roceedings of the European Conference on Intellectual Capital – Nicosia, Cyprus*. University of Nicosia, Cyprus, pp. 87-93.

Czech News Agency - Czech newspaper, 2019. https://www.ceskenoviny.cz/zpravy/ve-skolach-pribyva-ucitelu-podle-reditelu-je-jich-ale-stale-malo/1737874, last accessed 2019/07/20.

Czech Statistical Office (March 2013), 2013. https://www.czso.cz/documents/10180/20534676/116111a.pdf/9c378e0f-d77a-4f21-bf3e-e4ed35cb1122?version=1.0, last accessed 2019/07/18.

Czech Statistical Office, 2005. https://www.czso.cz/csu/czso/cri/male-a-stredni-podniky-jejich-misto-a-role-v-ceske-ekonomice-2005-rhybfgzbj0, last accessed 2019/07/18.

Czech Statistical Office, 2017. https://www.czso.cz/csu/czso/odvetvi-informacni-ekonomiky, last accessed 2019/09/09.

Czech Statistical Office, https://www.czso.cz/documents/10180/91606479/2501321924.pdf/a84d8e9a-6f38-455d-a524-e55ed62d9fde?version=1.1, 2018, last accessed 2019/07/24.

Jamali, D. et al., 2009. The learning organization: tracking progress in a developing country. A comparative analysis using the DLOQ. *The Learning Organization*, 16(2), 103-121.

Kim, J. et al., 2015. Examining the Dimensions of the Learning Organization Questionnaire: A Review and Critique of Research Utilizing the DLOQ. *Human Resource Development Review,* 14(1), 91-112.

List of Schools, 2019. http://www.seznamskol.eu/typ/stredni-skola/, last accessed 2019/07/20.

Marsick, V., Watkins, K., 2003. Demonstrating the Value of an Organization´s Learning Culture: The Dimensions of the Learning Organization Questionnaire. *Advances in Developing Human Resources,* 5(2), 132-151.

Ministry of Education, Youth and Sport, 2014. http://www.msmt.cz/vzdelavani/skolstvi-v-cr/statistika-skolstvi/vykonova-data-o-skolach-a-skolskych-zarizenich-2003-04-2013, last accessed 2019/07/15.

Ministry of Industry and Trade, 2017. https://www.mpo.cz/assets/cz/podnikani/male-a-stredni-podnikani/studie-a-strategicke-dokumenty/2018/10/Zprava_MSP_2017.pdf, last accessed 2019/07/20.

Norashikin, H. et al., 2016. Learning Organization Culture, Organizational Performance and Organizational Innovativeness in a Public Institution of Higher Education in Malaysia: A Preliminary Study. *Procedia Economics and Finance*, 37, 512-519.

OECD, 2016. *What makes a school a learning organisation? A guide for policy makers, school leaders and teachers.* OECD, Paris.

Ponnuswamy, I., Manohar, H. L., 2016. Impact of learning organization culture on performance in higher education institutions. *Studies in Higher Education,* 41(1), 21-36.

Saadat, V., Saadat, Z., 2016. Organizational Learning as a Key Role of Organizational Success. *Procedia - Social and Behavioral Sciences,* 230, 219-225.

Senge, P., 2016. *Fifth Discipline: The art and practice of the learning organization.* Management Press, Praha.

Serrat, O., 2017. *Knowledge Solutions.* Springer, Singapore.

Sohaib, M. et al. 2014. Factors Affecting the Organizational Learning: A Study of Banking Sector of Pakistan. *International Journal of Management and Organizational Studies*, 2(2), 16-22.

Voolaid, K., 2013. *Measurement of Organizational Learning of Business Schools. Thesis on Economics H33.* TUT Press, Tallin.

Watkins, K. E., Marsick, V. J., 1993. *Sculpting the learning organization: Lessons in the art and science of systematic change.* Jossey-Bass, San Francisco, CA.

Watkins, K. E., O´Neil, J., 2013. The Dimensions of the Learning Organization Questionnaire (the DLOQ): A Nontechnical Manual. *Advances in Developing Human Resources,* 15(2), 133-147.

Yadav, S., Agarwal, V., 2016. Benefits and Barriers of Learning Organization and its five Discipline. *IOSR Journal of Business and Management,* 18(12), 18-24.

Zubr, V., 2019. Studies with Dimensions of Learning Organization Questionnaire – Research Study. *Hradec Economic Days 2019*. Hradec Kralove, Czech Republic, pp. 592-600.

FINANCIAL LITERACY AS A PART OF LIFELONG EDUCATION

Hana Mohelska and Vaclav Zubr

University of Hradec Kralove, Faculty of Informatics and Management, Rokitanskeho 62, 500 03 Hradec Kralove, Czech Republic

ABSTRACT

This article is focused on the financial literacy of elementary students as a part of a lifelong education. The introduction covers the concept of financial literacy and the development of financial education in EU countries and in the Czech Republic. It also presents the strategic documents that have been gradually published. It turns out that there is a gap for research in the field of financial education strategy for elementary and school students and its coherence with lifelong education. The national strategic plan focuses mainly on the high school students, but the practice show that it should start with students that are in the compulsory education. The results of the OECD's research called Program for International Student Assessment (PISA) show educators and policy makers the quality and equity of learning outcomes achieved elsewhere and allow them to learn from the policies and practices applied in other countries. The goal of this article is to evaluate the project of financial education and analyze the current situation in the financial literacy of the elementary school students in Czech Republic in comparison with foreign countries. The article searches for the strengths, opportunities and threats using the method of SWOT analysis. Based on the obtained results it formulates conclusions and recommendations.

KEYWORDS

Financial Literacy, Financial Education, SWOT Analysis, Lifelong Education

1. INTRODUCTION

Financial literacy is the education and understanding of various financial areas including topics related to managing personal finance, money and investing. This topic focuses on the ability to manage personal finance matters in an efficient manner, and it includes the knowledge of making appropriate decisions about personal finance such as investing, insurance, real estate, paying for college, budgeting, retirement and tax planning (Kenton, 2019).

National surveys show that young adults have amongst the lowest levels of financial literacy. This is reflected by their general inability to choose the right financial products and often a lack of interest in undertaking sound financial planning. Even from an early age, children need to develop the skills to help choose between different career and education options and manage any discretionary funds they may have, whether from allowances or part time jobs. These funds may entail the use of savings accounts or bank cards. In 2005, the OECD recommended that financial education start as early as possible and be taught in schools. Including financial education as part of the school curriculum is a fair and efficient policy tool. Financial education is a long term process. Building it into curriculums from an early age allows children to acquire the knowledge and skills to build responsible financial behavior throughout each stage of their education. This is especially important as parents may be ill-equipped to teach their children about money: levels of financial literacy are generally low around the world. In 2012, financial literacy is an optional component of the OECD Program for International Student Assessment (PISA). PISA currently tests the attainment of 15-year-olds in mathematics, reading and science across 65 countries. The introduction of a financial literacy assessment will result in a unique international benchmark on the level of financial literacy of young people. The rich data will enable detailed investigations of the main factors associated with financial literacy levels and will help to identify policy measures that can be employed to improve levels in the future (Atkinson et al., 2015).

The OECD's Principles and Good Practices for Financial Education and Awareness recommend that financial education start as early as possible and be taught in schools. Including financial education as part of the school curriculum is a fair and efficient policy tool. Financial education is a long-term process. Building it into curriculums from an early age allows children to acquire the knowledge and skills to build responsible financial behavior throughout each stage of their education. This is especially important as parents may be ill-equipped to teach their children about money and levels of financial literacy are generally low around the world.

The OECD Program for International Student Assessment (PISA) examines not just what students know in science, reading and mathematics, but what they can do with what they know. Results from PISA show educators and policy makers the quality and equity of learning outcomes achieved elsewhere and allow them to learn from the policies and practices applied in other countries. PISA 2015 Results (Volume IV) (OECD, 2017) provide Students' Financial Literacy, is one of five volumes that present the results of the PISA 2015 survey, the sixth round of the triennial assessment. It explores students' experience with and knowledge about money and provides an overall picture of 15-year-olds' ability to apply their accumulated knowledge and skills to real-life situations involving financial issues and decisions. Many young people face financial decisions and are consumers of financial services in this evolving context. As a result, financial literacy is now globally recognized as an essential life skill. Around one in four students in the 15 countries and economies that took part in the latest OECD Program for International Student Assessment (PISA) test of financial literacy are unable to make even simple decisions on everyday spending, while only one in ten can understand complex issues, such as income tax.

Around 48,000 15 years old took part in the test, which evaluated the knowledge and skills of teenagers around money matters and personal finance, such as dealing with bank accounts and debit cards, or understanding interest rates on a loan or mobile payment plan.

1.1 Financial Literacy Components

Financial literacy as the management of personal/family finances includes the three following components:

- **Monetary literacy** represents the competences necessary for the management of cash and non-cash money and the transactions with them, and the management of the instruments intended for that purpose (e.g. current account, payment instruments, etc.).
- **Price Literacy** represents the competences necessary for understanding price mechanisms and inflation.
- **Budget Literacy** provides the competences necessary for the management of the personal/family budget (e.g. ability to work with budget, set financial objectives and decide on the allocation of financial resources) and includes the ability to manage different living situation in financial terms. In addition to the things described above, budget literacy also includes two specialized components:
    - **Management of financial assets** (e.g. deposits, investments and insurance)
    - **Management of financial liabilities** (e.g. loans or leasing).

This requires, in both cases, the orientation in the market of various complicated financial products and services, the ability to compare individual products or services with each other and to choose the most suitable ones with regards to the specific life situation (NSFV, 2018).

1.2 Lifelong Learning in Organizations in the Czech Republic Regarding the Europe 2020 Strategy

The framework of actions for the lifelong development of skills and qualifications, adopted by the European social partners in March 2002, emphasises that, in order to maintain competitiveness, businesses need to adapt their structures more rapidly. The increase in teamwork, alignment of hierarchies, decentralisation of competences and greater need for the ability to multitask contribute to the development of "learning organisations". The ability of organisations to define the abilities, mobilise, recognise and support their development for all employees is the cornerstone of new strategies to increase competitiveness (Zubr, Mohelská, 2017).

The European Union (EU) member states have historically developed different approaches to the financing, management and evaluation of educational activities. The field of education therefore is not among the EU's common policies. Unlike the common monetary and customs policy, the education policy has the status of a so-called 'complementary' policy. This means that EU activity in this area does not directly affect national education policy but is limited to supporting member states. The EU institutions can only grant member states recommendations (Cankaya, et al., 2015). According to the Lifelong Learning Strategy of the Czech Republic (CZ) (MEYS, 20), lifelong learning presents all possibilities for learning (whether in traditional educational institutions inside the education system or otherwise) as a single interconnected unit that facilitates diverse and numerous transitions between education and employment and which provides the same qualifications and competence in various ways and at any time during a person's lifetime (Cheng, 2003;Veteška and Tureckiová, 2008). Based on the above, it can be concluded that the essence of the EU's efforts in education lies in its systematic and large-scale financial support given to individual countries and regions.

2. METHODOLOGY

To obtain the required findings and conclusions of the present study, we conducted a content analysis of national and international strategic documents. We simultaneously used a comparative method to link our findings, or more precisely the students' knowledge of financial literacy subjects with relevant binding documents. As a source of information to perform the analysis of the project, publicly available information was used, as well as information from the ČSOB company's intranet and from the ambassadors themselves.

Internal information

Detailed information about project Financial education ČSOB for schools, which is analyzed in the practical part of the work, were found using the in-house resources. The project does not have a strategic plan, only a tactical plan for the maximum period of one year. The main indicators of this plan, which also form the objectives, are the numbers of the ambassadors involved, the lessons taken, the schools involved and the number of students who have completed the lessons. Unfortunately, not all indicators are determined for each individual year.

SWOT analysis

SWOT analysis is a universal analytical technique for evaluating internal and external factors that influence the success or failure on the market. The core of this analysis is the identification of key factors within, meaning what the organization (or part of it) is good at and what it does wrong. It is equally important to know the key factors of the external environment. The goal is to discover and then reduce weaknesses, promote strengths, look for new opportunities and know the project's threats. The key to success is to exploit opportunities and minimize threats.

3. PROCEDURE FOR THE INTRODUCTION OF THE FINANCIAL EDUCATION IN CZECH REPUBLIC

For the program to be successful in the introduction of financial education, there must be an institution to provide the project, lead, define priorities, take care of its promotion, co-ordinate other stakeholders and much more. Only one institution cannot cope with all these activities. It is therefore desirable to involve other key participants, such as the Ministry of Education, Youth and Sports, representatives of governments, representative of the school system - universities, faculties, elementary schools, high schools, even kindergartens as well as representatives of financial institutions - banks, insurance companies, investment companies, etc. The involvement of other participants is also important in order to increase credibility, increase the number of experts and the amount of resources available. At an imaginary peak, although the authors of the text in the ideal case see the Central bank however in the Czech Republic the position is held by the Ministry of Finance (Fabris, Lubурić, 2016).

3.1 Resolution of the Czech Republic Government

In the Czech Republic everything started on 7. December 2005, when a task for the Deputy Prime Minister and Treasury Secretary was defined at the meeting of the Government of the Czech Republic – to create an expert working group on the financial sector composed of representatives of financial institutions, consumer organizations, Ministry of Finance and Ministry of Industry and Trade. And a common task for ministers of finance, education and industry and trade– to prepare the system of building the financial literacy in elementary schools and high schools. Based on the resolution, the Expert group for financial sector, which included three working groups, was established. For this work, the most important sub-group is the Working Group on Financial Education ("PSFV" – Pracovní skupina finančního vzdělávání), which started its activities in August 2006. The initial goal of PSFV was to propose measures to increase financial literacy and improve the process of financial education, which has fulfilled a later discussion of financial literacy standards and financial education strategy (PSFV, 2010).

3.2 Research of the Financial Literacy Level

In their text Fabris and Luburić (2016) mention that the opening point of the strategy should be to answer the questions: "Where are we now?" and "Where do we want to be in the future?". The answer to the first question can be found by means of a national survey, which will later allow for a simple comparison of the initial state and fulfilment of predetermined targets (2016).

That's why, in 2007, Ministry of Finance commissioned a quantitative research process to the company STEM/MARK to map the basic level of financial literacy based on a subjective assessment of the population and to ascertain the assessment of its own level of education and the need for further training in financial services among consumers. The survey was conducted on the adult population of the Czech Republic through standardized personal interviews with the help of questionnaires (STEM/MARK, 2007).

Research has shown that the adult population of the Czech Republic evaluates the level of its financial literacy by an average mark of 3, about half of them is satisfied with the level of its knowledge and half of them are not or does not know. People with degree, with higher household incomes and private entrepreneurs have evaluated themselves with higher marks. An interesting observation is also that the vast majority (81%) of the respondents noted that they didn't get any knowledge of financial and bank orientation in school and almost all (93%) of them would welcome being able to learn the basic concepts in this area in the high school and less than half would have included this curriculum at the elementary school (STEM/MARK, 2007).

3.3 Financial Education Strategy

Based on the findings of the aforementioned survey, in the second half of the year 2007 the already mentioned financial education strategy was established, aiming to create a coherent system of financial education for increasing the financial literacy level in the Czech Republic. The proposed financial education process has been given a two-pillar structure that should involve the entire population. This structure defines the main target groups in the framework of initial education and further education of the adults (PSFV, 2014).

3.4 System of Building Financial Literacy on Elementary Schools and High Schools

In December 2007, a strategic document System of building financial literacy on elementary schools and high schools was completed, describing the process of implementing financial education in initial education. Its integral part are the financial literacy standards, which set the financial literacy target level for each of the degrees of education, while the financial literacy level set in the standards for the last year of high school is also considered to be the financial literacy level of the adult consumer.

The document further imposes the inclusion of these standards in the framework educational programs (referred to as "the RVP" – Rámcový vzdělávací program), the development of methodological recommendations to schools, the inclusion of financial education topics in education programs under the system of further education of pedagogical workers and the future revision of this document in line with the evolution of financial markets and student's needs. The financial literacy teaching got to "RVP" high schools in 2009 and the "RVP" elementary education in the year 2013. The Czech Republic thus became one of the first countries in which compulsory teaching of this type was introduced (Ministry of Finance of the Czech Republic, 2018).

3.5 National Strategy for Financial Education

The Organization for Economic Co-operation and Development (OECD) and the European Commission recommended the creation of national strategies approved by the governments of the individual states to raise awareness on the need for financial education and the necessity of establishing a single coordinated system. The original strategy was not a government-approved concept, so the Ministry of Finance, in cooperation with the Ministry of Education, Youth and Sports and the Czech National Bank, came up with its updated version. In May 2010, this update was adopted under the name National financial Education Strategy (Ministry of Finance of the Czech Republic, 2018).

4. FINANCIAL EDUCATION ČSOB FOR SCHOOLS PROJECT ANALYSIS

One of the cornerstones of ČSOB's corporate philosophy is socially responsible behavior. It consists of responsible business, philanthropy in the form of various grant programs for non-profit organizations and employee involvement. In accordance with their socially responsible activities, or the Corporate Social Responsibility (CSR), ČSOB's focus is on four main pillars of responsible Business (ČSOB, 2018):

- financial literacy and education,
- longevity,
- business support,
- environmental responsibility.

Financial literacy and financial education are the most natural issues for the bank and within this category the analysed project Financial education ČSOB for elementary schools can be found.

4.1 The Project's Characteristics

Since 2016, the Financial education ČSOB for schools has been offering complementary teaching of financial literacy in elementary and high schools. The content of the teaching is created following the RVP published by the Ministry of Education, Youth and Sports. The intention is to diversify standard financial education with an interactive and entertaining lecture, which is usually conducted by the representatives of the bank from the region. It is also important to mention that this is free of charge for the school, as the project ambassadors are volunteers (ČSOB, 2018).

4.2 Goals of the Project

The goal of the program is to prevent the "threat" of low financial literacy inside the population and promote its development among children and associated communities. In ČSOB, they believe that a higher level of financial literacy and financial education not only enriches the lives of individuals, but also contributes to healthy economic growth in society. Consumers with good financial knowledge and healthy personal finances require better and more efficient products and solutions, which contributes to increasing competition, innovations and quality of products in financial markets.

The target group were the elementary and high school students, who are thought financial literacy in the framework of the standard curriculum. Secondarily, this project offers the possibility of extending knowledge and education to teachers who teach this topic.

5. PROJECT'S SWOT ANALYSIS - RESULTS

5.1 Strengths

A strong aspect of this project is excellent knowledge of the financial environment. Many project's ambassadors meet clients who come to address their financial situation almost daily. As a result, lecturers can identify areas of financial education in which the company has the largest gaps, focusing the lectures on these shortcomings. The bank wants clients who have good financial knowledge and healthy personal finances because such clients can cover their commitments.

This project has a great chance to succeed and endure, as it has a strong partner in the form of a financial institution with a long-term interest in increasing the financial literacy within corporate social responsibility (CSR). The life span of many other projects is limited in time by provided subsidies and grants.

Usually the teaching is realized directly by the representatives of the bank from the region and from the branches who know the environment. Many times, they even have a personal relationship for the given area, the city or the school, which makes a positive impression. And although the emphasis is on regional coverage, they can also cover the teaching centrally.

The involvement of two well-known Czech youtubers to help alert children about cybersecurity. Youtubers are perceived by today's children as celebrities, heroes as they believe, take their views as their own and overall try to imitate them. So, if such a person encourages the right behavior in the digital world and presents deterring cases in his posts, he teaches the children through the form of their daily entertainment. Moreover, these young consumers do not even realize that they are subconsciously learning while watching video.

Schools like to choose this project, because it is offered completely free of charge and has very positive responses and references.

5.2 Weaknesses

The projects use the marketing insufficiently in order to inspire an interest in new people. Almost the only presentations that can be seen are interviews given for articles. While the company's YouTube channel is trying to create videos, they have on average only around 200 views (April 2019).

Another weakness is also related to propagation, but it is not about inspiring an interest in new people, but a general perception of the company by the public. The project should publish its work and achievements more, because thanks to that, the ČSOB can be more perceived as a socially responsible company.

The project does not include any possibility to assess whether the financial literacy of the schooled students has been improved. Ambassadors only subjectively assess the improvement of the overall literacy level compared to the beginning of the year 2016.

It might be also perceived as a weakness that a lot of lecturers have no previous experience with giving lectures and teaching children. Although ČSOB offers the possibility of internal training, it is a one-time issue. The most helpful thing would be giving actual the lectures, which, with the increasing number of given lectures, would lead to gaining the necessary skills and self-esteem.

Since the project was launched only three years ago (in 2016), there is not too much room for evaluating its effectiveness and chosen strategy.

The weakness of the project is also the fact that they do not have a strategic plan developed to determine specific targets for a period longer than one year.

5.3 Opportunities

The originally side topic of cybersecurity is becoming more and more important due to fact that it's a current issue, thus creating a space for the inclusion of another field. This new field could be medial education, which is currently included among the cross-cutting themes.

Cross-cutting topics are a compulsory part of basic education, which represent the current world problem circuits. There are several ways of implementing these topics. In particular, the following options are recommended: integration into thought subjects, introduction of a separate subject, or teaching through projects. Ideally, multiple options should be linked. Therefore, if the school would implement the teaching through the ČSOB's project, it would use the third method – teaching through projects (ČSOB, 2918).

Media education is based on the knowledge that mass and network media (periodical press, radio, television, internet media and social networks) are currently a significant factor in both primary and secondary socialization. In basic education, media education offers basic knowledge and skills related to media communication and work with media. These represent a very important source of experiences and knowledge for an increasingly large audience. It is important to be able to process, evaluate and use the stimuli that come from the outside world to utilize an individual in the society. The stimuli from the media are the most important ones coming from the outside world (Němcová et al., 2011).

The whole project could then become a program to support the most recent problems of the society, which are coming into the cross-cutting themes. The project could include teaching financial literacy, digital literacy (cybersecurity) and medial literacy.

The following opportunity responds to the above-mentioned weakness of project's small amount of views for videos published on its YouTube Channel. Creating videos tends to be a costly thing, so it's a shame not to bring the desired effect. It could help to share the videos to ČSOB's other social networks. Whether it's an official site for the whole business or it's the pages of subsidiary companies or other departments. For example, Facebook and Instagram are the best-known social networks.

We will stay on YouTube channel and outline another option to improve the project. Animated series Filip in school has only four episodes. Other parts such as one the on the subject of a complaint that falls within the topic of consumer protection or the demonstration of the execution process.

Another opportunity is the acquisition of accreditation in the system of continuous education of the pedagogical workers, which is awarded by the Ministry of Education, Youth and Sports. In the updated version of the National financial education strategy, lecturers appear as an additional target group, which could also be reflected in the project's goals. Pedagogical workers can pass on the acquired knowledge and experience in the long term, which will multiply the effect of the project.

Teaching is currently ongoing in the school environment. The lecture at the camp or workshop is only an exception. Other possible places to give lectures at are e.g. children's homes, educational institutes, suburban camps, etc. A large proportion of young people, after leaving a child's home or institute, are getting into an existential problem, which may occur be due to the low level of financial literacy. However, as far as the institutions are concerned, it would be advisable for those ambassadors who already have several hours of teaching and ideally have previous experience working with this vulnerable group of children to attend these places.

Further spreading of awareness not only about this project, but also other CSR activities of the ČSOB group in the form of advertising spot is another opportunity. Advertisement is a very common and popular form of propagation, the length of which usually varies between 20 and 30 seconds. Most often an advertising spot can be seen or heard in audiovisual media, i.e. on television, radio, or on the internet. It can be a short spot played before another video, on servers such as YouTube, Stream.cz or before video on news portals.

If there is mutual satisfaction after the lecture, it would be good for lecturers to try to establish further cooperation, whether of single or long-term nature. It could be a one-time teaching of the same class, with only a different theme. The long-term agreement could consist of an annual meeting, for example, with 5th class of elementary school. The schools could plan ahead, and the lessons of the remaining circuits would be adjusted accordingly. For the project, this would result in a certain minimum number of hours to be taught in the next year, making it easier to make plans.

5.4 Threats

The main threat is the existence of a lot of similar projects.

Another threat is any possible scandal around the ČSOB group. Although it might not have a direct link with the project, it would probably harm it as well. A person who does not know the project could be able to make the connection, because the name of the company is included in the name of the project itself. Unfortunately, any negative reviews and emotions are spreading faster and easier than the positive ones.

6. CONCLUSIONS AND RECOMMENDATIONS

Financial literacy is now an essential part of our lives. The company soon understood that it was necessary to start the financial education as soon as in primary school. As a result, children will learn the correct handling of money and understand, at least the basics of how they work, and what obstacles await them.

The draft of the strategic plan contains recommendations on the implementation of teaching in the area of South Bohemia, Vysočina region and North Moravia and Silesia, as these regions are falling behind on the project map. It is also recommended to establish continuous cooperation with schools already involved throughout the Czech Republic.

Another point of the strategic plan is to reach out to an influencer, which would complement the two colleagues already involved. The main theme to be discussed in the project is cybersecurity, which is directly related to the digital space on which they operate.

In addition, the project must focus on better promotion and marketing. One of the identified options is the sharing the videos previously published on YouTube, the creation of new episodes of the Filip at school series, which is also located on YouTube channel and possibly the creation of a short advertising spot, which could be played as an advertisement before other videos on the Internet or on TV.

An important point in the strategy is the inclusion of a new subject– medial education, which could be as successful as the topic of cybersecurity. Other opportunities are the expansion of target groups on seniors and pedagogical workers and the addition of other places for the realization of the teaching.

ACKNOWLEDGEMENT

The paper was written with the support of the specific project 2019 grant "Determinants of cognitive processes impacting the work performance" granted by the FIM UHK and thanks to help of student František Hašek.

REFERENCES

Atkinson, A., F. Messy, L. Rabinovich and J. Yoong (2015), Research and Literature on Financial Education for Long-term Savings and Investments, OECD Working Papers on Finance, Insurance and Private Pensions, No. 39, OECD Publishing. http://dx.doi.org/10.1787/5jrtgzfl6g9w-en.

Cankaya, S., et al., 2015. The Educational Policy of European Union. Procedia - Social and Behavioral Sciences, 174, 886-893.

ČSOB, 2018, https://www.csob.cz/portal/documents/10710/316999/financni-vzdelavani-csob-pro-skoly.pdf, last accessed 2019/07/22.

Fabris, N., Luburić, R., 2016. Financial Education of Children and Youth. Journal of Central Banking Theory and Practice, 5(2), 65-79.

Cheng, Y. C., 2003. Quality assurance in education: Internal, interface and future. Quality Assurance in Education Journal, 11(4), 202-213.

Kenton, W., 2019. Financial Literacy, https://www.investopedia.com/terms/f/financial-literacy.asp, last accessed 2019/07/23.

NSFV - Národní strategie finančního vzdělávání 2.0: změnou chování k převzetí odpovědnosti za svou finanční prosperitu. 2018. https://www.psfv.cz/assets/cs/media/PSFV_Konzultace_2018-05-15_NSFV-20-draft1.docm, last accessed 2019/01/24.

Ministry of Finance of the Czech Republic, 2018. Návrh revidované Národní strategie finančního vzdělávání, https://www.mfcr.cz/cs/o-ministerstvu/verejne-diskuze/2018/navrh-revidovane-narodni-strategie-finan-31870, last accessed 2019/07/22

Ministry of Finance of the Czech Republic, 2017. Standard finanční gramotnosti, https://www.mfcr.cz/cs/aktualne/aktuality/2017/standard-financni-gramotnosti-29163, last accessed 2019/07/22.

PSFV - Ministry of Finance of the Czech Republic, 2014. Role PSFV a její činnost. https://www.psfv.cz/cs/pro-odborniky/pracovni-skupina-pro-financni-vzdelavani/role-psfv-a-jeji-cinnost, last accessed 2019/07/18.

MEYS – Ministry of Education, Youth and Sports, 2010. ET 2020: a strategic framework of European cooperation in education and training. MEYS, Department for EU affairs EU, Prague.

Němcová, Z., et al., 2011. Issues of Financial Literacy Education. Procedia - social and behavioral sciences, 28, 365-369.

OECD (2017), PISA 2015 Results (Volume IV): Students' Financial Literacy, PISA, OECD Publishing, Paris. http://dx.doi.org/10.1787/9789264270282-en

STEM/MARK, 2007. Research for Ministry of Finance of the Czech Republic. Research final report 2007, https://www.mfcr.cz/assets/cs/media/Odborne-vyzkumy_2007_Zaverecna-zprava-z-vyzkumu-plne-zneni-STEMMARK-2007.pdf, last accessed 2019/07/29.

Veteška, J., Tureckiová, M., 2008. Competencies in education (in Czech). Grada, Prague.

Zubr, V., Mohelská, H., 2017, Selected Factors Supporting the Learning Organization. Emerging Technologies for Education. SETE 2017. Lecture Notes in Computer Science. Springer, Cham, 195-202.

PRESERVICE TEACHERS' ADOPTION OF A MAKERSPACE

Junko Yamamoto
Slippery Rock University of Pennsylvania, United States of America

ABSTRACT

Innovation includes new inventions, new ideas, or new methods. Everett Rogers' Diffusion of Innovations framework, however, suggests not all are willing to adopt innovation. Technology Acceptance Model (TAM) indicates that perceived usefulness and perceived ease of use influence one's choice to use available technology. Since the nature of work is rapidly changing, the future workforce needs to be prepared to innovate or adopt innovation. This means that educators also need to be innovators or early adopters. In this study, education majors in an instructional technology class in the United States were introduced to the idea of a makerspace. When they were given choices, some participants tried new tools or methods without the instructor's assistance, and some tried with the assistance. However, there was also a group of education majors who chose not to try out new tools or methods, even they knew that the help was available. This finding implies that Rogers' theory about people's aptitude of adopting innovation and TAM are applicable to future educators.

KEYWORDS

Teacher Education, Makerspace, Adoption, Diffusion of Innovation, Technology Acceptance Model

1. INTRODUCTION

Teachers are tasked to prepare their students to be successful in the workforce for a lifetime. Since society and the required skills change rapidly, lifelong learning, creativity, innovation, and adaptation of new ideas needs to be embedded in instructional strategies. Learners need to develop an aptitude for dealing with uncertainty, and to make a mental effort to acquire new skills. In order to facilitate classroom activities that stimulate creativity and innovation, teachers need to be prepared and willing to teach themselves as new methods, ideas, and tools are presented to them. Consequently, the International Society for Technology in Education (ISTE) published the 2017 Standards for Educators that expect teachers to be able to facilitate activities that nurture creativity and innovation (International Society for Technology in Education, 2017).

The idea that the education should prepare a future workforce is not new. For example, Trilling and Fadel published a book about 21st Century skills in 2009. In the book, they stated that the nature of work has changed from routine manual or routine cognitive work to being more reliant upon expert thinking. According to Trilling and Fadel (2009), schools need to teach critical thinking, creativity, collaboration, communication, information literacy, media literacy, technology literacy, and flexibility. Routine jobs are more likely to be replaced by artificial intelligence than jobs that require expert thinking and creativity. The Implication being that a future workforce needs to be innovative. Since the book was published in 2009, society has indeed witnessed routine works, such as cash register checkout and highway toll payment, being replaced by machines. Hence, schools need to educate students to be innovative, and also to quickly adopt innovation.

Innovation refer to creating something new, which can be a new idea, designing new ways of completing a task, or making something that no one has made before. Innovation does not have to involve technology (Krueger, 2019). Designing and making something new, using digital or non-digital tools and materials promotes a leaner's innovative ability. Likewise, using a tool in a way that no one has used it before, even if the tool has been available for a long time, qualifies as an innovation.

Working with hands to create something new stimulates brain (McQuinn, 2018) and it promotes creativity and innovation. Because of it, the maker space movement has gained momentum in the United States.

Although 3D printers, cutting machines, and robotics kits are found in a makerspace, digital technology is not required for a maker space. Conventional tools such as a sewing machine (Mann, 2018) and woodworking tools can also be a part of a maker space. The purpose of this paper is to show how future teachers can use a makerspace to convert an abstract concept into a concreate visual product.

2. BODY OF PAPER

2.1 Literature Review

2.1.1 ISTE Standard

Teacher education is often driven by standards. Standards for teacher education function as accountability measures, ensuring that educators are preparing teacher candidates to have the ability to successfully prepare the future generations for their jobs (Chung & Kim, 2010). Aligning instruction to standards in teacher preparation also demonstrates a high quality teacher education (Murray, 2001). ISTE Standards for Educators includes categories such as "Designer: Educators design authentic, learner-driven activities and environments that recognize and accommodate leaner variability," and "Facilitator: Educators facilitate learning with technology to support student achievement of the ISTE Standards for Students" These standards call for creating personalized learning experiences, designing authentic learning activities, encouraging independent learning, challenging learners to use the design process, and modeling creativity (ISTE, 2017).

2.1.2 Makerspace

One of the elements captured in these standards can be facilitating creativity through a utilization of a makerspace. A makerspace is a space that students can create digital or physical objects to express their understanding. Students share materials and collaborate in the space (Trust, Maloy, & Edwards, 2018). Making does not need to involve technology: students can make their mental representation models or prototype of a product using common materials, such as cardboard and duct tape (Maughan, 2018). The concept of maker space is more about the act of making, rather than a physical space (Trust, Maloy, & Edwards, 2018). Technology integration in classrooms has shifted from teacher-centered models to student-centered models (Mulienburg & Berge, 2015; Passehl-Stoddart, Velte, Henrich, & Gaines, 2018), and makerspace is in line with a student-centered approach.

Designing a makerspace does not start with which tools to use, but rather with what is desirable for learners to accomplish. For example, rather than thinking, "we must use a 3D printer," and forcing technology onto an educational setting, the designer should think, "I would like my learners to create a 3D model." When multiple tools are available, and learners choose what they want to use, the technology integration is at the infusion level according to the Technology Integration Matrix (https://fcit.usf.edu/matrix/matrix/). When a teacher sets up the context, and students determine which tools to use, the technology use realizes "resource fluency" (Muilenburg & Berge, 2015). Choosing tools should be left up to a learner. When a teacher assigns students to create a 3D model that moves, students should have a choice to use a variety of tools, such as cardboard with Hummingbird, Lego EV3, or wood combined with metal and rubber.

2.1.3 Theoretical Framework: Diffusion of Innovation and Technology Acceptance Model

Teachers' willingness to try something new is important for creating a learner-driven environment. Unfortunately, the availability of new ideas, resources, or tools does not automatically warrant their use by the majority of the population. Many innovations require a lengthy period from when it becomes available to when they are adopted. In other words, not all people adopt innovations when they become available. Some choose not to use tools at all. In general, 2.5% of a population are innovators. Only about 10%-25% of a population are earlier adopters of an innovation. (Rogers, 1983). Rogers (1983) explain that 13.5% of a population adopt an innovation at early stage. Then next 34% are the early majority. It is followed by the late majority, which make up for 34%. Finally, 16% of the population is the laggards (p.246-247). Although

Rogers published the book decades ago, human nature has not changed. There are some individuals that are interested in learning something new, and there are those who resist changes.

Diffusion is the process in which an innovation is communicated and adopted. Individuals go through an innovation-decision process to decide if they want to adopt or reject new ideas, resources, or technology tools. The innovation-decision process commands mental work. Adopters need to cope with uncertainty and need to have the motivation to seek out innovation. Level of education and social status may affect the attitude to adopt innovation, but age is not an influential factor. In addition, earlier adopters have greater ability to deal with abstraction, and have greater rationality than later adopters (Rogers, 1983).

The Technology Acceptance Model (TAM) explains the diffusion of innovation through the lens of who is willing to adopt the technology. The availability of technology does not automatically result in its adoption. There are two factors of innovation that must be considered for the technology to be adopted: perceived usefulness and perceived ease of use. Self-efficacy, or belief that they can succeed on a task, influences perceived ease of use (Davis, 1989). Self-efficacy involves motivation, cognition, and self-regulation. Those with high self-efficacy tend to be more willing to take risks, and keep trying when they experience difficulties. On the other hand, those who doubt their ability to cope with a task shy away from it (Bandura, 1994). In fact, self-efficacy plays a key role in an educator's decision to adopt technology (Joo, Park, & Lim, 2018).

Perceived usefulness and perceived ease of use increase an educator's willingness to adopt a new technology tool (Flavell et al., 2019; Kukul, Ünal, Karataş, Çakmak, Yılmaz, & Ömeroğlu, 2018; Shittu, Kareem, Objelodan, & Fakomogbon, 2017). Furthermore, those who enjoy challenges may be more willing to try something new (Flavell et al., 2019). Teachers' psychological factors, ranging from a willingness to take risks, fear of failure, a lack of confidence, and general technology anxiety influence perceived usefulness and perceived ease of use (Flavell, Harris, Price, Logan, & Peterson, 2019). Figure 1 shows the Technology Acceptance Model.

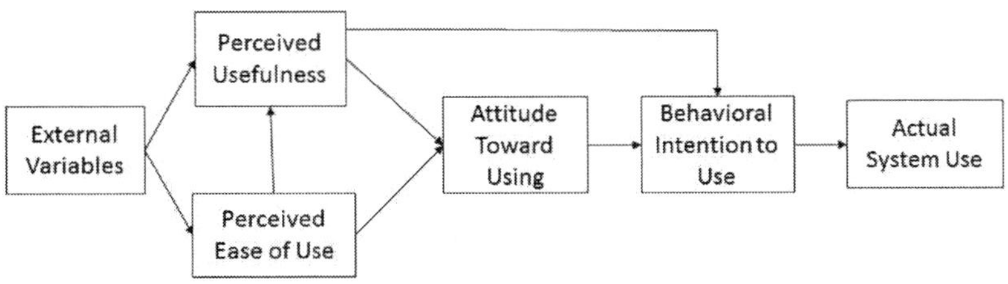

Figure 1. Technology Acceptance Model (TAM) (Davis, Bagozzi, & Warshaw, 1989, p. 985)

2.2 Research Questions

Research questions include:

1. Do education majors increase their knowledge about makerspace after the instruction?
2. What type of tools do research participants choose to use?
3. Will there be research participants who use tools that they have never used without the instructor's assistance?
4. Will there be research participants who use tools that they have never tried with the instructor's assistance?
5. Will there be research participants who does not use tools that they have never used even when assistance is available?
6. Do perceived usefulness and perceived ease of use influence the decision to use new tools?

2.3 Methods

2.3.1 Research Participants

Research participants were preservice teachers who were enrolled in an undergraduate level instructional technology class in a teacher preparation program in the United States of America during the fall 2018 semester. There were 26 who participated in this study. The participants included 4 Middle Level (Grade 4-8) Math Education majors, 3, Middle Level (Grade 4-8) Science Education majors, 2 Middle Level (Grade 4-8) English Education majors, 6 Secondary (Grade 7-12) English Education Majors, 6 Secondary (Grade 7-12) Social Studies Education majors, 2 French Education Majors, 1 double major of Secondary English Education and French Education, 1 Art Education major, and 1 Pre-Math Education major.

There were 10 freshmen, 11 sophomores, 2 juniors, 1 senior, and 2 post baccalaureate students. In this teacher preparation program, students take the instructional technology class before they take a teaching methodology class. Also, a typical semester schedule of a freshman or a sophomore is populated by general education courses, or courses that any majors would take. Hence, they have taken a limited number of content area courses and/or pedagogy courses prior to the study.

2.3.2 Instruments

A Likert-type survey was used with the following statements:

- I know what a makerspace is.
- I know how to design makerspaces.
- I know how to use a makerspace.

Value assigned to the self-evaluation were:

Strongly Agree = 5; Agree = 4; Neither Agree or Disagree = 3; Disagree = 2; Strongly Disagree = 1

A T-test was used to calculate the mean difference between the pre-instructional survey and post-instructional survey. This instrument was used for research question 1.

Moreover, participants wrote reflections with these prompts:

- "Which tools did you choose?" This prompt was used for research question 2.
- "Why did you use the tools?" This question was used to determine participants' beliefs about the usefulness and ease of use.
- "Did you know how to use the tools?" This question was asked to find out participants' levels of self-efficacy regarding new tools.
- "Did you decide to use the tools because you saw it being used during the project explanation?" This question was asked to find out if participants perceived the usefulness of tools when they saw the instructor model the use before the participants decided which tools to use.
- "How do you rate yourself about exploring new tools and learning how to use them? Elaborate your answer." This question examines participants' attitudes about willingness to learn new tools.

Kukul et al. (2018) used an interview form for data collection.

2.3.3 Instruction

The participants were introduced to the concept of makerspace and used a makerspace for two seventy-five-minute class sessions. After they used the makerspace, they presented their products to peers and explained to them what they represented. Idealistically, the future teachers were to create a teaching material in their instructional technology class. However, with 21 out of 26 research participants being freshmen and sophomores, the instruction needed to adjust according to the prior content and pedagogical knowledge of the participants. In the past, the instructor made projects more open-ended by asking preservice teachers to choose something to teach for their certificate area. However, this open-ended assignment overwhelmed freshmen who had very limited content knowledge, especially when they were taking general education classes, instead of their content area classes. Hence, the instructor decided to make the project semi close-ended where students were to select a hero from their subject areas.

The task was to create a presentational material that represents a hero, or someone who made a significant contribution to their area of certification. The instructor chose the task because the research participants would be likely to have some prior knowledge about the person that they would like to present about, and if they chose someone that they have positive emotions about, they would likely be motivated to do further research. The students were asked to determine their heroes of their teaching certificate area, research about their heroes, and make something to present their heroes to the class. Any subject area has someone who made a significant contribution. When each student identifies someone he or she looks up to, he/she is likely to have positive emotion on the topic. Internal motivation facilitates "active engagement, deeper understanding, and a desire to learn more" (Trilling & Fadel, 2009, p.33).

Since the project required the participants to look up new methods and tutorials, a training to ensure that they have this skill was necessary. Hence, they completed Google Fundamentals Training Level 1 (https://teachercenter.withgoogle.com/fundamentals/course) prior to the project. They participated in Unit #1 (Get Ready to Use Technology in Classroom) and Unit #2 (Expand Your Access to Help and Learning). When an open-ended task is assigned, it is important to show sample products in the beginning of the project. The instructor presented heroes in different subject areas using a variety of technology tools. At this stage, the concept of the makerspace was introduced to the students. The instructor showed two examples:

The first example was made for world language education. The instructor visited a native speaker of Spanish with her iPhone, and recorded a brief biography of Roberto Clemente. Clemente was a Puerto Rican baseball player who played for the Pittsburgh Pirates. He not only overcame racism to become a popular baseball player in the United States, but also made an impact on Puerto Rican Society. The instructor uploaded the biography recording to Dropbox, and set the audio file to be publically accessible. She then used Cricut, a cutting machine, to create 3-D model of Roberto Clemente, representing a baseball player bearing number 21, a Puerto Rican flag, and a bridge. The instructor then created a QR code to access the Clemente's biography recording and the Spanish language biography from Smithsonian Institution Traveling Exhibition Service (http://www.robertoclemente.si.edu/spanish/virtual_legacy.htm). She pasted the QR codes to the 3-D model.

The second example was made for social studies education majors. The process of creating the example started with a story about Marcus Tullius Cicero attempting to defend the ideal of the Republic when the climate of Roman politics was moving towards dictatorship. The story ended with Cicero's assassination by Mark Anthony. The instructor made the story into a digital movie using Windows Movie Maker, and uploaded it to YouTube.

As the instructor showed two examples, she explained that research on the content was the driving force for making both. She advised the students to spend time on increasing content knowledge before selecting which tools to use. She also explained that since the objective is to explore innovation and creativity, everyone would be free to choose materials that they want to use. Students were also invited to seek out help in adding an audio recording, a video, and a QR code to their work. The instructor also informed the students that they will have access to a Cricut cutting machine, cardstock, vinyl, scissors, glue, color pencil, s paper cutter, and s laminator. Students reported to two class sessions where the instructor set up the makerspace. They then presented their heroes to the class.

2.3.4 Data Analysis

Research question 1: Do education majors increase their knowledge about makerspace after the instruction?

Paired sample t-tests were calculated in order to compare values between pre-instructional time and post-instructional time. Table 1 shows the result of the t-tests.

Table 1. Mean comparisons between pre-instructional and post-instructional self-assessments

	n	Mean Pre (SD)	Mean Post (SD)	Mean Post- Mean Pre	t	Sig. (2 tailed)
I know what a makerspace is.	26	2.4231 (1.30)	4.6923 (.68)	2.2692	8.092	.000
I know how to design a makerspace.	26	2.1538 (1.19)	4.5769 (.70)	2.4231	9.726	.000
I know how to use a makerspace.	26	2.3462 (1.16)	4.6538 (.69)	2.3076	9.129	.000

The result of the t-tests indicate that the concept of makerspace was a new idea to the research participants. All names that are used in this manuscript are pseudonyms. Mary stated,

"Before this assignment, I was unaware of makerspace and how it works. This tool essentially brings ideas to life, encourages collaborations, and promotes creativity. I am now more familiar with this kind of environment and it is something I would implement into my own classroom. Reading and exploring the makerspace website to find ideas heled to enhance my understanding."

Research question 2: What type of tools do research participants choose to use?

In this study, the participants freely chose to use tools that they wanted to use. Table 2 shows tools and materials that the participants chose to use to create their hero presentation.

Table 2. Tools and materials used

Tools used	Frequency
Internet search for content	12
Construction paper	5
Glue	4
Google Docs	3
Scissors	3
Microsoft word	2
iMovie	2
Cricut Design Space	2
Laminator	2
Popsicle sticks	1
Paper trimmer	1
Paint	1
Styrofoam balls	1
Drawing supplies	1
PowerPoint (to create a digital movie)	1
QR code maker	1

The data indicates that 12 out of 26 students said that they used the Internet to search for content. The total number exceeds 26, the number of research participants, because one person used multiple items to complete his or her project.

Research question 3: Will there be research participants who use tools that they have never used without the instructor's assistance?

This group represent early adopters. Reflective writing was used to answer this question. Students' statements in this section represent the research participants who tried new tools or methods. Linsey made a movie using PowerPoint. Although she knew how to use PowerPoint, she did not know how to create a movie and published it on YouTube. She decided that she wanted to create a video about Sir Isaac Newton when she saw the instructor's sample movie about Marcus Tullius Cicero. However, while the instructor told the class that she made her movie with Windows Movie Maker, it was Linsey's initiative to turn PowerPoint slides into a movie. She wrote, "I knew how to upload videos to YouTube prior to this project. However, I did not know how to turn a PowerPoint into a slide show and create voice narrations. I had to turn to the Internet to find instructions on how to do so. ....I am always open to new and exciting technologies or tools."

Janet also taught herself how to make a movie, but she chose iMovie. She "was not very familiar with it. This project gave me the opportunity to really learn how to use iMovie effectively and efficiently and I now know how to use it better than I did." Jackson also used iMovie for the first time. He stated, "Using iMover was a totally new experience. I had never uploaded a video to YouTuble. Lastly, I had never had the need to record audio on my laptop, so I was unfamiliar with how to use the laptop microphone. ....While learning how to use iMovie was a slight struggle at times, I was able to learn enough to create a decent finished product."

Beth and Amber stated that they used Google search, YouTube video, and Pinterest to look for ideas prior to deciding which tools they wanted to use. Amber said, "I had to research and look up tutorials on how to create the project that I was working on."

Melinda, a French Education Major, took the idea of combining Cricut and a QR code from the instructor's Roberto Clemente presentation. She created a graphic representation that was structured similar to the one that the instructor presented, but chose to present about Charles Aznavour, a French Armenian singer. She created 2 QR codes that allow the audience to access Charles Aznavour's 2 famous songs. She said she regularly used YouTube and Pinterest when she needs to learn something new, and successfully completed the project without the instructor's assistance.

Elaine, a French and English Education Major, decided that she wanted to create something about Antoine de Saint-Exupéry, a French writer. She wanted to create a planet mobile to represent scenes from *Le Petit Prince*, Saint-Exupéry's famous book. She stated, "Although I did not use any tool out of the ordinary, I did have to research and look up tutorials on how to create the project that I was working on. I never made a planet mobile: therefore, this project created a new experience for me."

Research question 4: Will there be research participants who use tools that they have never tried with the instructor's assistance?

This group belong ether in early majority, according to Rogers' framework. Mary stated, "Because I became familiar with makerspace in class and motivated to take advantage of this workspace since I knew what I was getting into. If I was unaware of how this tool worked, I many have been hesitant to utilize it and may have missed out on a great, creative opportunity."

Jillian, a math education major, became interested in using Cricut Design Space when she saw the instructor's sample during the project explanation. She is a math education major, and decided to create a display on Pythagoras. She stated,

"I did not know how to use the Cricut Design Space or the laminator, but through this project I was able to learn how to use two different tools that I would have never had the chance to learn. I really liked Dr. XXX's Roberto Clemente example presentation. She also explained how she used a Cricut for the images. Knowing what a Cricut was, but now how to use it I knew would be a challenge. I wanted to challenge myself and use something that I have never used before. I also wanted to use the laminator because I saw how nice Dr. XXX's project looked, and I knew in the future I would be using a laminator in my class. ...The Cricut took a few moments of trial and error, but I believe I learned a lot from that experience. I was able to use my problem-solving skills to discover how to use the program, and how to troubleshoot."

David, who is "open to learning about new tools" decided to use Circuit after instructor suggested it. He made a visual presentation of Joshua Chamberlain, capturing his leadership during the Battle of Gettysburg in the American Civil War. The instructor recommended that he add an eagle shaped cut out of gold vinyl and helped him use Cricut. He stated,

"I used this tool because it helped me to create a nice eye-catching piece for my project. The precise cuts and glossy sheen of the vinyl material make it stand out among the other parts of the project, and crated a wonderful centerpiece for the project that other methods may not have achieved. I honestly say that it helped immensely."

Research question 5: Will there be research participants who do not use tools that they have never used even when assistance is available?

Statements in this group showed the characteristics of late majority or laggards. Late majority can be someone who did not try to do something new during the project, but wished they had tried after they saw peers' successes. Heather wrote,

"I wanted to spend time on the small details of the project instead of trying to learn something brand new and get caught up in the process. With that being said, after walking around and seeing everyone else's project I have learned so much and cannot wait to try out some of their ideas… after seeing all of the other projects I am inspired in so many ways."

Kim said,

"I feel like I could have done better by trying to use a tool like Cricut. Cricut is something I have never used before and wish I would have tried it." Megan said, "I could have been a little more creative and gone out of my comfort zone to create this project."

On the other hand, laggards are the ones who refuse to try new tools or methods even after they see peers' successes. Geoff explained he choose to use the material because "they were familiar to me … 'and are very convenient." Mike said, "I tend to stay away from exploring new tools because of trying to learn how to use it is sometimes difficult and I would rather use that I know and works best for me. Makes it easier on me and being able to get things done efficiently without the headache of trying to learn how to use something new."

Research Question 6: Do perceived usefulness and perceived ease of use influence the decision to use new tools?

Comments about perceived usefulness included (the author italicized relevant text):

- "I used the laminator for the finishing touches and *to enhance the quality* of my work."
- "*I thought that QR code will be useful*. If I had not seen the model of Roberto Clemente that was presented to the class I would have had no idea that I could have done that and I would have not used it in my project."

- Comments by Jillian and David in Research Question 4 indicate that they decided to use Cricut because they saw the use of the cutting machine improve the quality of a finished product.

Comments about perceived ease of use included (the author italicized relevant text):

- "I was able to work out how to use the QR Code Maker *with ease*."
- "I tend to stay away from exploring new tools because trying to learn how to use it is sometimes *difficult*."
- "Cricut *seems complicated* [hence, I did not use it]; I would like to become more familiar with it. A fellow student taught me how to use the laminating machine. *I liked this tool because it is simple*, yet it makes a project appear professional."

However, some strived to keep trying when they encountered difficulties. For example, Janet's quote in Research Question 3 shows, "...While learning how to use iMovie was a slight struggle at times, I was able to learn enough to create a decent finished product."

3. CONCLUSION

3.1 Implications

This research used Diffusion of Innovation theory and Technology Acceptance Model as frameworks. According to Rogers, the decision making process requires mental work. The framework also implies that adopters tend to have some tolerance to uncertainty. Although Rogers suggested the framework decades ago, his work is still applicable because human nature has not changed. There are those who enjoy the challenge of learning something new, and those who avoid the mental work. Likewise, some have higher tolerance to uncertainty. In this study, two participants saw that the instructor used Movie Maker to create Marcus Tullius Cicero's biography movie, and decided to make a digital movie. One used iMovie, and the other turned PowerPoint into a movie. Both had never created a digital movie before, but they searched for tutorials from YouTube and Pinterest and taught themselves how to create a digital movie. One participant used Cricut and QR code creator for the first time, and completed the project without the instructor's assistance. They represent the research participants who were willing to seek out new ideas and teach themselves.

Two participants reflected that they decided to used Cricut after they saw the Roberto Clemente 3D model. They had access to a laptop with Cricut Design Space, machine, and a variety of cardstock paper and vinyl to cut with the machine. They completed their project with instructor's help to use the machine. They represent the population that is willing to adopt innovation when assistance is available.

The third group decided not to try anything new, but wished they had tried after they saw peers' successful adoption. statements from this group has the characteristics of late adopters. They did want to spend the time to learn Cricut while they used a makerspace. However, after they viewed peer's finished products, they wished they had used the tool. Finally, the fourth group self-reflected that they prefer to stay in their comfort zone, and would like to avoid, the "headache of trying to learn how to use something new." The fourth group has the characteristics of laggards. The research participants' comments support the conclusion that perceived usefulness and perceived ease of use influence the decision to adopt a new technology tool. However, attitudes about the perceived ease of use differs among those who are willing to learn on their own, those who learned to use a tool with assistance, and the who avoided using new tools.

3.2 Limitations

This research used Diffusion of Innovation theory as a framework. According to Rogers, the decision making process require mental work. The framework also imply that adopters tend to have some tolerance to uncertainty, and the motivation to seek innovation (Rogers, 1983). This research showed that not all are willing to try new tools or methods when they become available. However, the research did not measure personal attributes, such as the willingness to make cognitive effort, tolerance to uncertainty, and the motivation to seek out new tools or methods. It is suggested, therefore, these personal attributes should be measured in future studies.

This research also used the Technology Acceptance Model, which suggests that the perceived usefulness and perceived ease of use of technology influence the decision to adopt a new technology tool. While some studies, such as Çakiroglu, Gökoglu, & Öztürk (2017) and Joo, Park, & Lim (2018) use surveys to measure perceived usefulness and perceived ease of use, the present study did not because the participants were encouraged to freely choose materials and tools. Collecting data on perceived usefulness and perceived ease of use of specific maker space tools, and examining how self-efficacy influences perceived ease of use, is a meaningful area of future study.

REFERENCES

Bandura, A. 1994. Self-efficacy. In V. S. Ramachaudran (Ed.), Encyclopedia of human behavior (Vol. 4, pp. 71-81). New York: Academic Press.

Çakiroglu, Ü. Gökoglu, S., & Öztürk, M. 2017. Pre-service computer teachers' tendencies towards the use of mobile technologies: A technology acceptance model perspective. *European Journal of Open, Distance and E-Learning, 20* (1). 175-190.

Chung, H. and Kim, H., 2010. Implementing professional standards in teacher preparation programs in the United States: Preservice teachers' understanding of teaching standards. *KEDI Journal of Educational Policy,* Vol. 7, No. 2, pp.355-377.

Davis, F. D. 1989. Perceived usefulness, perceived ease of use, and user acceptance of information technology. MIS Quarterly, 13(3), 319-339.

Flavell, H., Harris, C., Price, C., Logan, E., & Peterson, S. 2019. Empowering academics to be adaptive with eLerning technologies: An exploratory case study. *Australasian Journal of Educational Technology, 35*(1), 1-15.

International Society for Technology in education., 2017. ISTE Standards for Educators. Retrieved from https://www.iste.org/standards/for-educators

Joo, Y J., Park, S., Lim, E. 2018. Factors influencing preservice teachers' intention to use technology: TPACK, teacher self-efficacy, and technology acceptance model. *Educational Technology & Society, 21*(3), 48-59.

Krueger, N., April 2019. Innovate, iterate, educate: Sometimes teachers' small ideas make the biggest difference. *Empowered Learner*, Vol. 2, No. 4. Pp/ 17-21.

Kukul,V., Ünal, M., Karataş, S., Kılıç Çakmak, E., Yılmaz, A. and Ömeroğlu, E. 2018. Analysis of teachers'opinions in the context of acceptance of technology, *Journal of Kırşehir Education Faculty*, 19(3), 2055-2067.

Mann, L., 2018, Making a place for makerspaces in information literacy. *Reference & User Services Quarterly*, Vol. 58, No. 2. pp.82-86.

Maughan, S., Dec. 14, 2018. School & library spotlight fall 2018: Q & A with Nicholas Provenzano. *Publishers Weekly*, Retrieved from https://www.publishersweekly.com/pw/by-topic/childrens/childrens-authors/article/78847-school-library-spotlight-fall-2018-q-a-with-nicholas-provenzano.html

McQuinn. C., 2018, The brain science of making. *School Library Journal.* Retrieved from https://www.slj.com/?detailStory=brain-science-of-making

Muilenburg, L. Y., and Berge, Z. L., 2015. Revisiting teacher preparation: Responding to technology transience in the educational setting. *The Quarterly Review of Distance Education,* Vol. 16, No. 2, pp 93-105.

Murray, F. B., 2001. From consensus standards to evidence of claims: Assessment and accreditation in the case of teacher education. *New Directions for Higher Education,* Vol. 113, pp. 49-66.

Passehl-Stoddart, E., Velte, A., Henrich, K. J. and Gaines, A. M., 2018. History in the making: Outreach and collaboration between special collections and makerspaces. *Collaborative Librarianship*, Vol. 10, No. 2, pp. 133-149.

Rogers, E. M., 1983. *Diffusion of Innovations* (3rd Ed.). The Free Press, New York, USA.

Shittu, A. T., Kareem, B. W., Obielodan, O. O., & Fakomogbon. 2017. Investigating predictors of pre-service science teachers' behavioral intention toward e-resources for teaching. *Contemporary Educational Technology, 8*(2), 142-157.

Trilling, B. and Fadel, C., 2009. *21st century skills. Learning for life in our times*. Jossey-Bass, San Francisco, USA.

Trust, T. Maloy, R. W., and Edwards, S., 2018. Learning through making: Emerging and expanding design for college classes. *TechTrends,* Vol. 62, pp.19-28. doi: 10.1007/s11528-017-0214-0

INTEGRATED CONTEXTUAL LEARNING ENVIRONMENTS WITH SENSOR NETWORK FOR CROP CULTIVATION EDUCATION: CONCEPT AND DESIGN

Rin-Ichiro Taniguchi[1], Daisaku Arita[2], Atsushi Shimada[1], Masanori Yamada[1], Yoshiko Goda[3], Ryota Yamamoto[4] and Takashi Okayasu[1]

[1]*Kyushu University, Japan*

[2]*The University of Nagasaki, Japan*

[3]*Kumamoto University, Japan*

[4]*The University of Tokyo, Japan*

ABSTRACT

This paper presents an outline of our project, in which we develop an observation framework for integrating lecture and contextual learning in the field of crop cultivation. Specifically, we will use multi sensing of learners' activities in classrooms, and contextual learning in fieldwork, farm planting, and farming environments. The motivation for our project is twofold: First, crop cultivation provides a powerful illustration of educational technology. It requires both explicit knowledge (from lectures) and implicit knowledge (from contextual learning outside of class). Second, from a practical viewpoint, the number of Japanese farmers is shrinking due to low income and to aging population. Thus, in order to maintain crop yields, farming skills must be transferred efficiently to novice farm workers. Herein, the major features of our framework will be described.

KEYWORDS

Crop Cultivation Education, Learning Support, Sensing System, Learning Analytics

1. INTRODUCTION

Recently, information and communication technology (ICT)-supported learning has become increasingly popular. This sort of instruction utilizes several types of information systems, including e-book systems, learning management systems, e-portfolios etc. It is becoming clear that these systems are quite useful, especially for textbook-based learning (i.e., understanding and memorizing facts described in textbooks). This lecture style focuses on acquiring declarative knowledge; that is, explicit knowledge. However, the lecture style is insufficient, especially for acquiring procedural knowledge in specific professional fields/subjects (Byrnes and Wasik, 1991). For example, those in the fields of crop cultivation, musical instrument playing, caregiving, etc., require practical training to acquire procedural knowledge. In professional contexts, people are required to perform well in real settings, using not only declarative knowledge, but also procedural knowledge activation. This includes skills (i.e. the "know-how" for cognitive activities) (Anderson, 1995) implicit to their fields. It takes a long time to acquire practical professional skills, implicit knowledge, or specialized cognitive processes necessary for expertise in each field (Ericsson, et al. 2018). Thus, development and implementation of learning environments which foster practical and professional skills is desirable. Our aim is to develop an ICT-based framework to accelerate or to optimize the contextual learning process. Particularly, our area of study is the field of crop cultivation. The goal is combining declarative knowledge (acquired in lectures) with procedural knowledge (mastered in a field). Procedural knowledge (required to be a professional), is related to declarative knowledge (such as concepts in a subject) (Rittle-Johnson, 2019). This point is a fundamental motive for integration of classroom learning environments with crop-cultivation learning outside of class.

The motivation for our project is twofold: First, crop cultivation provides a powerful illustration of educational technology. It requires both explicit knowledge (from lectures) the implicit knowledge (from contextual learning outside of class. We investigate the essential point of learning, and the framework we build can be applied to many types of subjects which require explicit and implicit knowledge. Second, from a practical viewpoint, the number of Japanese farmers is shrinking due to a decreasing birthrate and an aging population. Thus, in order to maintain crop yields, farming skills must be transferred efficiently to novice farm workers.

As illustrated in Figure 1, our project will develop an observation framework for integrating lecture and contextual learning within the field of crop cultivation. We will use multi sensing of learners' activities, farm planting, and farming environments. The goal will be realized by combining the following three major elements:

1. Formalizing a mechanism to create a knowledge map of crop cultivation activities.
2. Analyzing the learning process, with reference to both learners' knowledge maps, and the data acquired by multi sensing of their learning/training processes.
3. Instructional design-based analysis of the processes above.

In this paper, we outline a system integrating learning environments for the acquirement of knowledge (both declarative and procedural) in the fields of crop cultivation education. Finally, we suggest directions for future research.

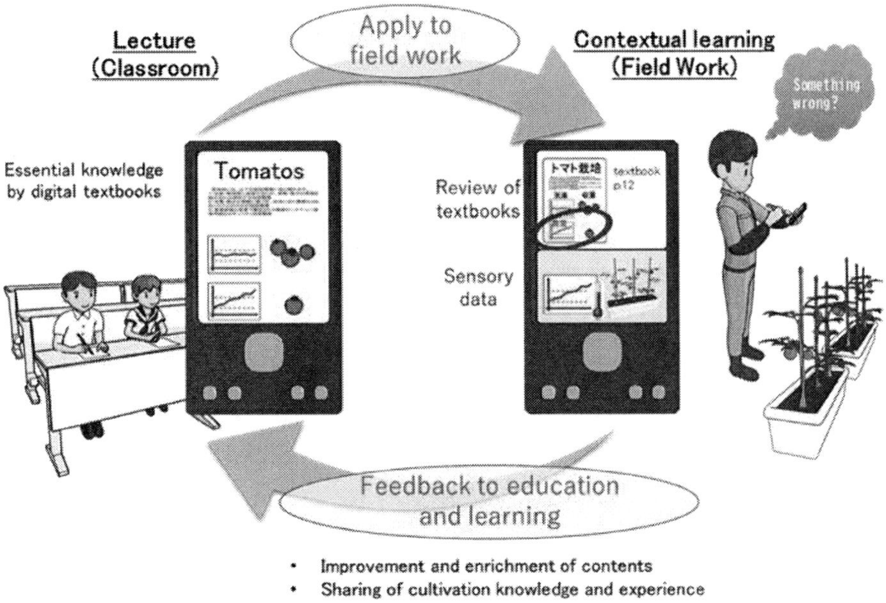

Figure 1. Project overview: seamless collaboration of lecture and contextual learning

2. PROPOSED SYSTEM

2.1 System Overview

Figure 2 shows the overview of our educational system. The Moodle system provides lecture schedule and outlines, and manages user accounts, as well as attendance information and reports submitted by students. There are three major subsystems connected to the Learning Tools Interoperability (LTI) protocol, enabling transfer of user information between systems. The subsystems consist of an e-book viewer system (BookRoll), a knowledge management system, (BR-MAP) and the sensory information visualizer (SALATA). SALATA collects sensory information (such as temperature, humidity, wind direction, and solar radiation) from the MIHARAS system. Additionally, SALATA collects user-generated contents such as photos, voices, text memos. In the following subsections, we explain the details of these subsystems.

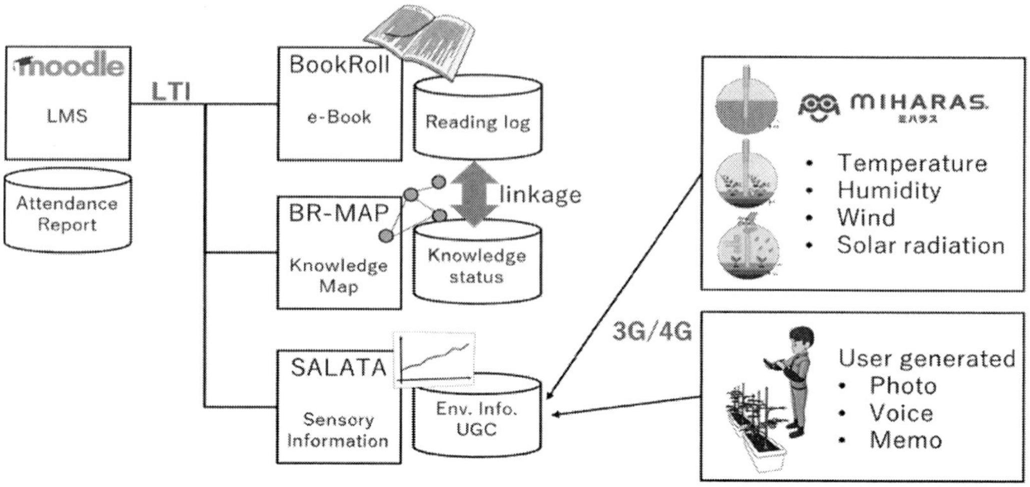

Figure 2. System overview

2.2 Learning Management System

The Moodle is a well-known learning management system used worldwide. In our project, we collect course attendance and daily reports from students using plugins on the Moodle (see Figure 3). A clicker is one of the most useful plugins for collecting answers on students' quizzes and questionnaires (see Figure 4). Additionally, the Moodle provides several links to the related subsystems (i.e., BookRoll, SALATA, and BR-Map).

Teachers used Moodle to manage student attendance, provide quizzes, and receive reports. Data and access logs are also collected in the Moodle database. This information is utilized for analytics of teaching and learning activities. The main role of Moodle is platform for the connection between other systems.

Figure 3. Example of course settings in Moodle

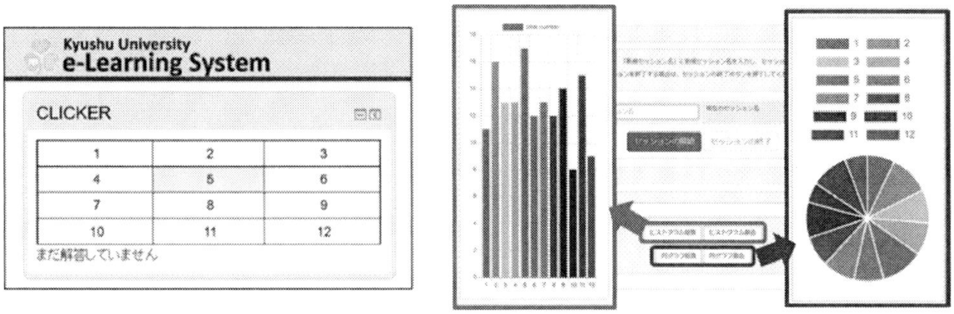

Figure 4. Clicker plugin on Moodle. Web UI for students (left), Aggregation results for teachers (right)

2.3 e-Book Viewer

BookRoll (Figure 5) is an e-book viewer system, developed by Kyushu University and Kyoto University (Ogata et al. 2017). Main role of the BookRoll is to promote input by reading. It provides digital textbooks to students, and collects precise reading logs (such as when a student opens material, or turns a page in in that material. Many types of operations are recorded as the logs. For example, OPEN means that the student opened the e-book file, whereas NEXT means that the student clicked the next button to move to the subsequent page. The browsing duration for each page can be easily calculated by the timestamps.

BookRoll provides useful functions, such as bookmarking, highlighting, and text memos. Students can freely and directly bookmark pages in lecture materials, highlight keywords or sentences, and write text memos reflecting their thoughts. These operations' logs are also collected into BookRoll's system database, and utilized to analyze learning activities. BookRoll is core learning support system in this project. Other learning support systems use BookRoll log, in order to collect the data that indicated learning process data. BR-Map is one of the learning support systems that use BookRoll logs.

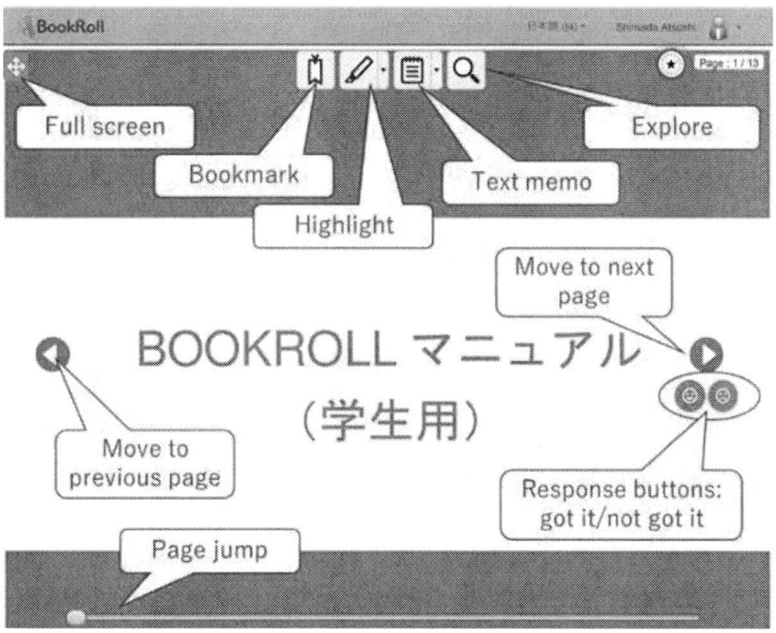

Figure 5. e-Book viewer

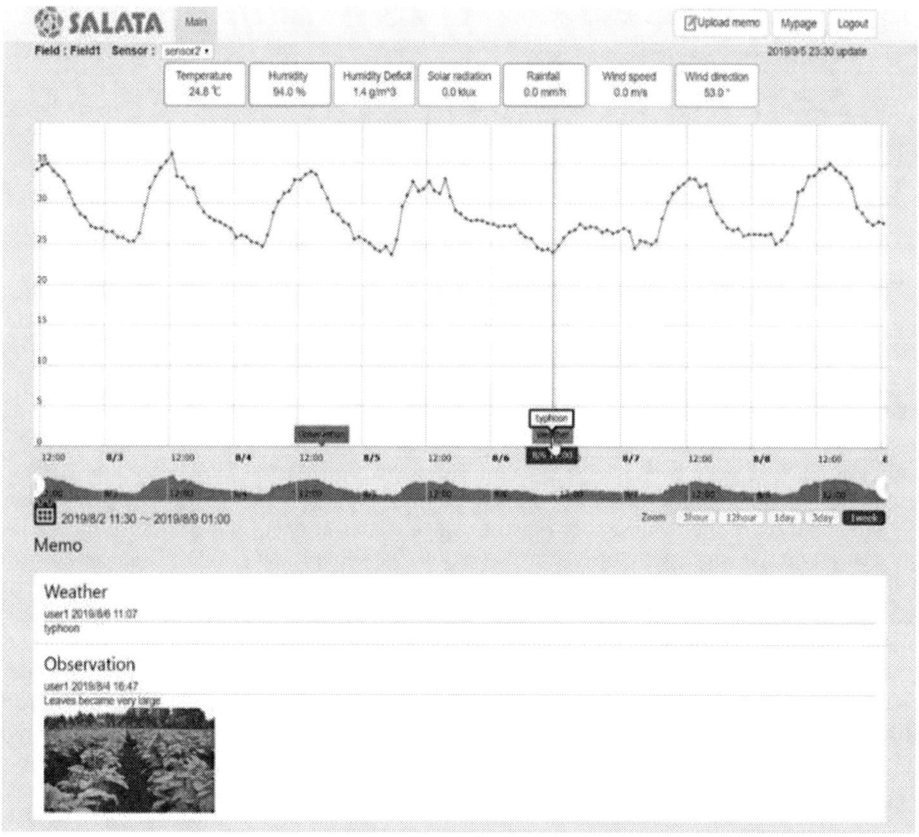

Figure 6. Temperature view in SALATA

2.4 Sensory Information Monitoring System

SALATA is a sensory information monitoring system for the contextual learning of crop cultivation. It was developed by Kyushu University. It has a database which stores environmental information on farm fields, to be used in contextual learning. Environmental information is measured using sensing devices. Currently, we employ MIHARAS (MIHARAS Web site), developed by Nishimu Electronics Industries Co., Ltd. It is capable of measuring: 1) temperature; 2) humidity; 3) humidity deficits; 4) solar radiation; 5) rainfall; 6) wind speed; 7) wind direction; 8) soil temperature; 9) soil moisture; and 10) soil electrical conductivity. The SALATA provides a graphical interface displaying graphs of this information. Figure 6: Temperature view in SALATA, for example, shows the temperature graph over the course of one week.

Each student brings a tablet to the farm field, examines the crops in reference to the environmental information provided by the SALATA, adding text memos and photos to the graph. These reports capture what students observe, notice and think. In Figure 6, there are two memos: the left memo's "observation" has a text "Leaves became very large" with a photo taken by a student after several fine-weather days. The right memo with a category "weather" has a text "typhoon" and is highlighted because the student taps the memo to select.

The SALATA collects not only environmental information and students' memos, but also students' operation logs. The SALATA analyzes these data sets to judge whether students understand the knowledge in the BR-Map. In this case, the BR-Map is based on the relationship between crops and the environment. For example, a student who understands that too-high humidity causes some crop diseases can write a memo regarding high- humidity-related crop diseases. In addition, the SALATA can provide hints to students in a farm field who lack understanding of the relationship between humidity and crop diseases.

2.5 Connecting Declarative Knowledge with Procedural Knowledge: Knowledge Map as Knowledge Connection Tool

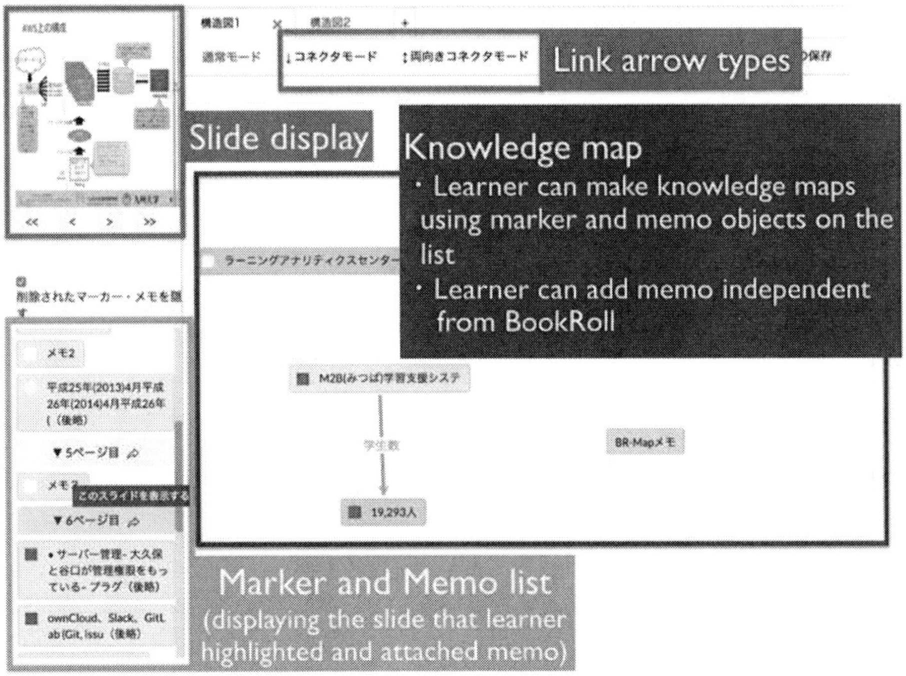

Figure 7. The interface of BR-Map (Yamada et al, 2018)

Using e-textbooks and sub-learning materials on BookRoll, students are able to absorb learning contents (such as terminology and rules of agriculture). Learners mainly gain declarative knowledge from e-textbooks. However, knowledge absorbed in class is insufficient for them to perform cultivation well in the field. Learners are required to master not only declarative knowledge (such as crop features and generally suitable weather conditions for crops) but also procedural knowledge (such as treatment in bad weather conditions, adjustment of field drainage, and real-world weather situations).

In order to effectively gain information and skills, a knowledge management platform which connects declarative knowledge with procedural knowledge is required. BR-Map (Yamada et al, 2018), a knowledge map, can connect with learning logs on BookRoll. Thus, it can serve as a knowledge management platform, allowing learners to connect declarative knowledge with procedural knowledge. Figure 7 shows the interface of BR-Map.

BR-Map uses the marker and memo logs from BookRoll. First, learners read e-textbooks on BookRoll, adding markers on parts and memos. When a learner opens BR-Map, it reads the marker and memo logs from BookRoll database, and lists them on left pane. Learners click the object on the left pane, and drag-and-drop it on the right pane's "knowledge map" area. Learners can add independent memo(s) from BookRoll to the knowledge map area. Therefore, learners connect objects using arrows, and create a knowledge map. Learners can download the knowledge map as png file.

BR-Map can serve as a knowledge management platform for the connection of declarative knowledge from lectures with procedural knowledge from fields. In order to promote the connection, BR-Map will be modified as follows: 1) read the data and action logs from SALATA; and 2) develop functions which allow learners to connect this data on knowledge map area. This process is based on Rittle-Johnson's (2019) viewpoint on the relationship between declarative and procedural knowledge. BR-Map can be effective seamless learning environment connected classroom and crop field. It allows learners to connect the knowledge learned in the class and the one learned in crop field. Learners seem to be aware of procedural knowledge in expertise process. Thus, it is expected that modified BR-Map enhances retention and interest of crop cultivation.

3. CONCLUSION

In this paper, we created a design for an ICT-based educational system for crop cultivation education. This framework aims at supproting both lecture and contextual learning in the field of crop cultivation. Our proposed system will be implemented by cooperation between digital learning environments and multi sensing systems. In our future work, we plan to begin an experiment in an agricultural high school starting mid-September. The target course aims to teach cultivation of of leaf and root vegetables using classroom lectures and practical fieldwork in. Approximately forty students will participate in the experiment. We will begin collecting and analyzing learning logs from the students, and will investigate the effectiveness, usability, and usefulness of the proposed system.

ACKNOWLEDGEMENT

This work was supported by JSPS KAKENHI Grand Number JP18H04117, JP18H04125 and JP16H03080, Japan.

REFERENCES

Abiteboul, S. et al, 2000. *Data on the Web: From Relations to Semistructured Data and XML*. Morgan Kaufmann Publishers, San Francisco, USA.

Anderson, J.R, 1995. Cognitive Psychology and its implications, 4th edition, W. H. Freeman and Company, New York, USA

Beck, K. and Ralph, J., 1994. Patterns Generates Architectures. *Proceedings of European Conference of Object-Oriented Programming.* Bologna, Italy, pp. 139-149.

Bodorik P. et al, 1991. Deciding to Correct Distributed Query Processing. *In IEEE Transactions on Data and Knowledge Engineering*, Vol. 4, No. 3, pp 253-265.

Byrnes, J. P and Wasik, B.A., 1991. Role of conceptual knowledge in mathematics procedural learning, Developmental Psychology, 27, pp.777-786.

Ericsson, K.A, Hoffman, R.R., Kozbelt, A, and Williams, A.M., 2018, The Cambridge Handbook of Expertise and Expert Performance, second edition, The Cambridge University Press, Cambridge, UK.

MIHARAS: https://www.nishimu-products.jp/miharas

Ogata, H., Oi,M., Mohri, K., Okubo, F., Shimada, A., Yamada, M., Wang, J., and Hirokawa, S, 2017. Learning Analytics for E-book-Based Educational Big Data in Higher Education, In H.Yasuura, C.-M.Kyung, Y.Liu, Y.-L.Lin. (Eds.) *Smart Sensor at the IoT Frontier*, Springer, pp.327-350

Rittle-Johnson, B., 2019. Iterative Development of Conceptual and Procedural Knowledge in Mathematics Learning and Instruction, In J.Dunlosky and K.A. Rawson (Eds.) The Cambridge Handbook of Cognition and Education, The Cambridge University Press, pp.124-147.

Yamada, M. Shimada, A., Oi, M., Taniguchi, Y., and Konomi, S., 2018. BR-MAP: Concept Map System using e-Book Logs. *In 15th International Conference on Cognition and Exploratory Learning in the Digital Age (CELDA 2018)*, pp. 248-254.

DIGITIZATION OF THE STUDENT LIFE CYCLE TO PROMOTE UNDER-REPRESENTED GROUPS IN STEM SUBJECTS

Heidi Schuhbauer and Patricia Brockmann
Technische Hochschule Nürnberg Georg Simon Ohm
Postfach 120320, D-90121 Nürnberg, Germany

ABSTRACT

A project to support underrepresented groups in STEM (Science, Technology, Engineering and Math) subjects is being carried out at the Department of Computer Science at the Technical University of Nuremberg Georg Simon Ohm (TH GSO). This project intends to counteract the shortage of specialists in the STEM occupations by supporting underrepresented student groups (i.e. students with a migration background, from non-academic households, female students, and single parents) before, during and after their studies. To this end, digitization measures in STEM studies should be evaluated and carried out at the TH GSO Nuremberg. The entire life cycle plays a decisive role in this, starting with the choice of the students' course of study, through their university or college studies, to entry into the labor market, and is included in this research project. Specific digital prototypes will be developed as supporting measures. The identification of underrepresented groups of students in STEM subjects is the starting point of this project. At the beginning of the student life cycle, the identified groups should be provided with information about STEM fields to support their choices of study subjects. For this purpose, some digital advisory tools will be developed. To prevent them from breaking-off their studies, influencing factors have to be identified. Knowing these factors, an early-warning system will be developed. This system should identify students who are at risk of failing and propose supporting measures to them at an early stage. At the end of their studies, they should be assisted in their choice of a suitable job and in applying for jobs with digital tools.

KEYWORDS

Computer Science, Digital Measures, Diversity, Shortage of Specialists, Education

1. MOTIVATION

In a society shaped by science and technology, the STEM labor market has attracted a lot of attention for years. Digital networking is increasing. Digitalization is changing how and where we work and the way we act in society. Rapidly increasing digitalization increases the importance of STEM (Science, Technology, Engineering and Math) education. Overall, there is a growing demand for STEM professions [Bundesagentur für Arbeit 2018]. Carnevale et al. state that "there is added pressure to find more STEM workers due to baby boomer retirements" [Carnevale et al. 2011, p. 53]. They note that more women and minorities in STEM jobs are necessary [Carnevale et al., p. 69].

Due to the continuing high demand for qualified personnel in STEM professions, one of the most important preconditions is a sufficient number of graduates in STEM subjects. More than ever before, we are challenged to qualify as many suitable candidates as possible for the job market in technical studies. Therefore, we must consider how we can acquire applicants for STEM studies from groups that are currently underrepresented among our students. These include students with a migration background or young people from non-academic households. Of course, we aim to increase the proportion of women in technical professions. According to Cohoon [Cohoon 2003], although the proportion of women in mathematics, biology and physics has increased, the proportion of women in computer science has remained low. Blum et al. [Blum et al. 2007] postulate that women often do not enter the field of computer science due to influences from their environment and culture as well as their perception of the field. They recommend appropriate public relations work, education and methods to improve micro culture in order to increase the participation of women in computer science. Ilmuoka [Ilmuoka 2012] discusses the importance of diversity in the workplace to generate a creative variety of thinking styles that promotes problem solving and innovation. She recommends a comprehensive STEM immersion program that starts at school to overcome obstacles for disadvantaged groups in the classroom. Convincing and supporting potential students from underprivileged groups increases the pool of qualified STEM graduates.

The aim of the project that is described in this article is to support students from underrepresented groups in all phases of their studies. This support should be target group oriented. To this aim, digitization opportunities should be uncovered and digital solutions should be implemented at the Technical University Georg Simon Ohm in Nuremberg, Germany. According to Gartner's IT Glossary, "Digitization is the process of changing from analog to digital form, also known as digital enablement" [Garnter] whereas digitalization means the use of digital technology to change business models. The aim of this research project is to investigate, introduce and evaluate digitization procedures in STEM studies with the intention of attracting and supporting new candidates for STEM studies from underrepresented groups before, during, and after their studies. Schuhbauer [Schuhbauer 2018] describes a framework for digitalization in education. This is used as a basis for developing digitized courses of action.

In the next chapter, this article describes related works, followed by the methodology of the project. After that, the article defines the different elements that are part of the research project. At the end, it shows how the evaluation should be done.

2. RELATED WORKS

Several related works discuss the topic of minority students in higher education. Swail [Swail 2003] states that pre-college preparation, admission policies, affirmative action, and financial aid are important factors, but campus-wide support, from the chancellor's office to the classroom, is critical to success. Rendón et al. [Rendón et al. 2000] deal with different models for minority student retention in higher education. They note that students elect to stay or leave college because "college and university faculty and administrators have made transformative shifts in governance, curriculum development, in- and out-of-class teaching and learning, student programming, and other institutional dimensions that effect students on a daily basis." [Rendón et al. 2000, p.152] They propose that retention research should include collaborative relationships and mutual learning experiences [Rendón et al. 2000, p. 152]. Birnbaum [Birnbaum 1983] declares that diversity in higher education is important for different types of students. Limiting the field to minority students in STEM subjects, there are also a number of studies. Anderson and Kim [Anderson & Kim 2006] address different dimensions of ensuring the success of students of color in science and technology in the United States. They emphasize the need for academic and financial support. They identified the working hours of students as one negative predictor of obtaining a bachelor's degree. They write: "The key is for higher education institutions to know how to better identify those students who need support - and what type of support, both academic and financial, would be most helpful - in order to be successful in the STEM fields." [Anderson & Kim 2006, p. 16] Museus and Liverman [Museus & Liverman 2010] focus also on students of color in STEM subjects. They analyze successful institutions to shape future research on students of color in STEM.

The project that is described in this article focuses on digitized solutions. The influence of digitalization in education is discussed in Schuhbauer [Schuhbauer 2018]. She recommends actions that should make education fit for the digital future. These are the recommendations:

- Both teachers and learners must become aware of the extent to which the changes through digitization and networking will influence education. Dynamic and velocity of changes in technology necessitates life-long learning. Education is no longer just a matter of conveying content. Dealing with change must become the subject of qualification procedures.
- Dealing with technology must not be an obstacle. Therefore, teachers and learners should be qualified to handle technology. Using technological equipment has to be taught theoretically and exercised practically. Educational institutions need a modern digital infrastructure.

- Learners should be enabled to learn self-reliantly using electronic media. To provide electronic educational material, teachers should be enabled to utilize online courses, blended learning, gamification, and learn management systems.
- Methods of learning have to be part of the teaching material. The teacher increasingly assumes the role of a guide and shows how and from where learners can acquire knowledge and how they can acquire it. Teaching staff must be qualified to do this.
- These recommendations mean that digitalization and networking require the revision and adaptation of educational guidelines. Educational guidelines for digitalization have to be developed and implemented. Therefore, knowledge about prospective job profiles is necessary.

Dahlström and Doracic [Dahlström & Doracic 2009] describe the aim and challenges of digitization education. They point out the challenges of digitization in education and their way to tackle them. Perry [Perry 2005] examines the characteristics and variety of digitization training initiatives. She "briefly discusses the benefits and challenges associated with the development of digitized library resources, and the need for greater attention to professional development for those working in digitization" [Perry 2005, p. 523].

The research goal for this project is the use of digitization to support underrepresented groups in STEM subjects. This project combines the focus on underrepresented groups with the megatrend digitalization. The research questions are: Which groups of potential students need special support? Which activities of the student life cycle do not match the expectations of these focus groups? Which digital tools can improve the uncovered situations?

3. METHODOLOGY

An adequate phase model of the student life cycle for our research project shall be determined methodically, e.g. by document analyses, with machine learning, observations and surveys. Therefore, existing phase models have to be identified and analyzed. Based on the requirements analysis, a life cycle model suitable for the research purpose is to be designed.

The life cycle of a student begins even before the official enrolment at a university. Before a candidate makes a decision for a STEM degree of study, he tries to find out which university is most suitable for him. A student's life cycle can end when the student has completed his studies. However, there are models in which the cycle continues through the alumni phase or entry into working life.

In the first step, an elemental model for the project was defined which has to be further developed over the course of the project. The aim of the project is to support students of the target group before, during, and after their studies. Therefore, the concept of a student life cycle is an adequate framework for the project. A simplified version that is the basis for our project definition phase is shown in Figure 1.

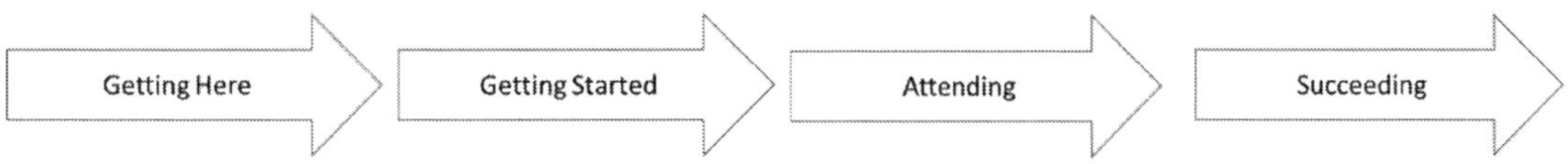

Figure 1. A simplified version of the students' life cycle [Pipitone & Poirer]

"Getting Here" includes services that help students to select a course of studies and to get settled. "Getting Started" includes services that support students' orientation at the university and in their selected courses. "Attending" includes all of the services, which support academic delivery. "Succeeding" includes services which support students to complete their studies and to enter into a career. For this project, the state "Getting Here" is contained in Phase 1 "Before Studies". The two states "Getting Started" and "Attending" are handled in Phase 2 "During Studies". The state "Succeeding" is in project Phase 3 "After Studies". The life cycle of the students (Figure 2), starting with the choice of the course of study of the students, through their studies at the university or college up to their entry into the labor market, plays a decisive role and is included in this research project.

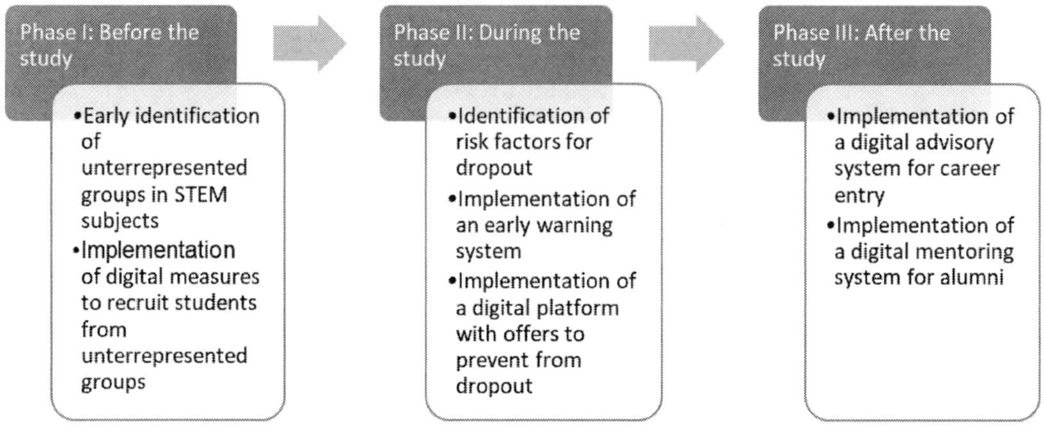

Figure 2. Aim of the project according to the students' life cycle

Subsequently, concepts will be developed for the underrepresented groups of students identified for the respective life cycle phases, which show support possibilities through digitization. The target groups will test the results of the first prototypes developed in the following year at the Technical University of Nuremberg. The results of these initial tests will be used in the further development of prototypes and in the technical implementation of new procedures.

Aim of the research project described is to investigate possibilities to assist persons from underprivileged groups at every phase of the students' life cycle during their studies and to implement some of the ideas as digital tools. The next section describes ideas for this purpose.

4. PHASES OF THE STUDENT LIFE CYCLE

The project consists of several small projects. They refer to the student life cycle and are introduced in this section.

4.1 Before their Studies

At the beginning, it is important to identify the target group. Their decision making process for a STEM study should be influenced positively.The group of disadvantaged students should be identified at an early stage. For this purpose, statistical data from the students' database at the Technical University Georg Simon Ohm can be evaluated. It has already been established for all courses of study at the Technical University of Nuremberg that 65% of students come from non-academic families, about 5% of students have children, 10% are international students and 5% are so-called occupationally qualified persons without classical university entrance qualifications [Technische Hochschule Nürnberg]. Further data analysis, especially for STEM, are part of this project. Based on a first view on the database of the Technical University of Nuremberg and external studies, it is hypothesized that that following groups are underrepresented in STEM studies:

- students with children,
- students with family members in need of care,
- disabled students,
- students with a migration background,
- students from non-academic households,
- students with financial needs,

- students with special social or personal circumstances (e.g. depressed), and
- students with special academic needs (lack of prior knowledge for the course of studies).

These hypotheses have to be tested. Results of related research projects, for example from the social sciences, and studies (e.g. from [Deutsches Zentrum für Hochschul- und Wissenschaftsforschung]) should be integrated. The aim is to clarify which groups are underrepresented in the STEM degree programs.

In the phase where pupils gather information about study possibilities, the specific target groups should be informed about STEM studies. Studies, questionnaires and interviews with the target groups will be carried out, which will form a database for the analysis and evaluation of attitudes, expectations and factors which influence the decision-making process in the selection of the future study program. These results should reveal relevant decision factors.

Potential students should receive structured and comprehensive information about courses of study. Guidance on the choice of studies should be offered to them in order to positively influence the decision factors for selecting a STEM subject. Digital tools should be developed for that purpose. The first step will initially be a prototype for an information and advisory portal. This portal should guide the choice of study subjects by providing information that is especially important for minorities. This portal solution should be tested and evaluated at some schools in Nuremberg.

4.2 During their Studies

Advisory tools and social media can advise students during the enrollment phase.

During the lecture phases, underrepresented groups may require special help or advice. Some students need subject-specific support (e.g. because of language problems or lack of previous knowledge) or flexible learning times (e.g. because of childcare). Learning concepts from literature have to be identified and evaluated in order to assess their suitability for these groups. From this, concepts have to be developed, which support them and enable them to learn in a self-directed way.

A research question is how attendance at lectures, preparation and follow-up of courses, the processing of exercises, etc. can be supported through digital technologies. Initially, the influence of digital measures on students' success has to be analyzed. Based on the evaluation of questionnaires, interviews, experiments, and analyses of social media, students' opinions on the current digital educational measures of the Technical University of Nuremberg are collected and subsequently analyzed with regard to their acceptance and effectiveness. Successful methods should be strengthened.

The examination phases can put students from underrepresented groups under particular pressure. Therefore, the preparation for and taking of examinations should be supported by advisory systems. A portal could help students with questions to find helpful contacts. These students also often require special help in writing papers, e.g. reports, seminar papers and dissertations. Students from non-academic backgrounds and students with a migration background in particular experience difficulties here and are often left alone. For them, offers of help which feature a low inhibition threshold are to be developed.

Dropping out of the university should be prevented. Reasons for dropping out which are specific to underrepresented students should be analyzed more precisely using questionnaires, interviews and study analysis. These results point out where special assistance is needed for these target groups. To prevent dropouts, an early warning and assistance system should be implemented as a web-based portal or mobile app, which informs students about digital educational measures, such as counselling and assistance services. A prototype for an early warning system using machine learning will be developed to identify students who are at risk. The students identified will test a prototype of the digital advisory system based on chatbot technology to obtain information about what types of support are available. Student advisors have reported that students from underrepresented groups often do not have the confidence to ask a professor for help. For these students, chatbots may provide a low-threshold source of information to help them.

4.3 After their Studies

To support the target groups after their studies and help them to enter professional life, a database of career qualifications linked to job profiles should be developed. To prepare this database, job advertisements, labor market reports and labor market forecasts have to be analyzed. A forecast about the necessary skills for STEM graduates for the future is one project aim in this phase.

Since students from underrepresented groups often have few role models in STEM occupations, they are particularly grateful for advice when choosing a career profile. This advice can be provided using social media and digital advisory tools.

Solutions, e.g. in the form of portals, need to be developed for a successful entry into professional life and to provide support in the first work phase, with questions on employment contracts, labor law and also on further training opportunities.

An interesting aspect is the establishment of an alumni network. Particularly successful reports from graduates can be helpful in taking the fear out of studying for new students. Mentoring programs with digital information and communication tools should be implemented.

The process of lifelong learning can be supported with digital advice and e-learning offers.

4.4 Accompany all Phases

Though all of the phases of the student life cycle, the contact points between students and the university should be identified and described. To ensure that the results of this project are tailored to the specific target groups of the students, the points of contact between students and the university must be identified from the students' point of view and described using the modern method of digitization research called the "Customer Journey" [Neonen et al. 2008]. Touch points are defined as points of interaction (e.g. matriculation) and points of contact (e.g. gathering information on studies). All actions that students can take in connection with the university are described with Customer Journeys. The actions are presented in a process-oriented way. The difference to common process descriptions, however, is the perspective: the processes are not described from the point of view of the company or the university, but from the point of view of the customers or the students. These process descriptions form the basis for the discovery of digitization opportunities. Weak points in the processes should be documented and possible suggestions for improvement worked out.

Customer Journey Maps visualize customer processes (Customer Journeys) of an organization. In the context of this work, the university has to be seen as the company and the students as customers. Prospective students and applicants are also regarded as customers, as they are also part of the Customer Journey Analysis. In our project, the processes of students at a university have to be visualized. In order to create a Customer Journey Map, the touchpoints of student processes have to be recorded and evaluated as part of an analysis process (called Customer Journey Mapping). Such touchpoints usually generate internal processes that have to be operated by the organization. If there are changes at the touchpoints, the internal processes must be adapted accordingly. If only the touchpoints of a customer process are optimized and the internal process associated with these contact points is neglected, both process dimensions are desynchronized. Therefore, it is useful to consider the internal process view when analyzing customer journeys. In this way, both process dimensions can be analyzed and optimized simultaneously, taking into account possible interdependencies. The synchronization of the two dimensions takes place on the basis of the recorded touchpoints and internal interfaces as connection points between the process dimensions. [Schötteler 2018, p 19]. Figure 3 shows a template for a process analysis based on Customer Journey Maps.

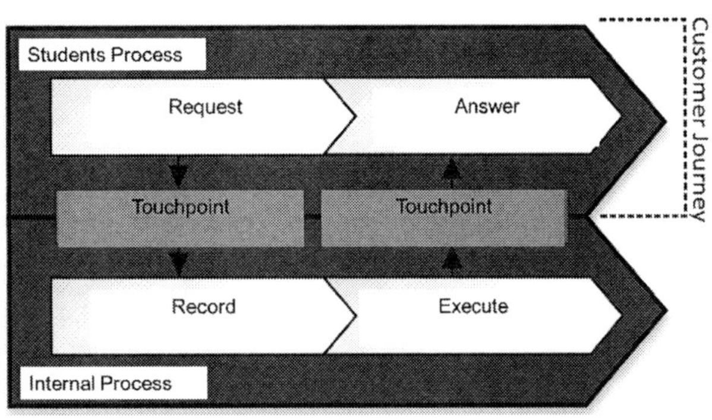

Figure 3. Template for Process Analysis Based on Customer Journey Maps

The touchpoint of students with the university which were identified and the corresponding internal processes reveal the possibilities where students can be contacted und supported by student advisors.

5. COURSE OF PROJECT

The project started in March 2019. A duration of eighteen months is planned. First, the data analysis has to be done. Afterwards, the work tasks of the three phases of the student life cycle start. Based on these results, some tools will be developed and evaluated by students. One prototype is a portal which should guide the choice of study subjects by providing information that is especially important for minorities. Another prototype is an early warning and assistance system to prevent dropping out of the university. It informs students about digital educational measures, such as counselling and assistance services. This tool should identify students who are at risk. The students identified will test a prototype of the digital advisory system and gain information about available help measures. A prototype for the phase “After their Studies” should assist minority students to entry into professional life. It should provide support in the first work phase, with questions on employment contracts, labor law and also on further training opportunities. This prototype has to be tested and evaluated by graduated minority students at the Technische Hochschule Nuremberg. The evaluation results of these prototypes are a valuable basis for further developments and for improvements of the developed solutions.

This project aims to especially support students from underrepresented groups in STEM subjects to increase the number of STEM graduates. Concepts will be developed for the underrepresented groups of students identified for the respective life cycle phases, which show support possibilities through digitization. The target groups will test the results of the initially developed prototypes in the following year at the Technical University of Nuremberg. The results of these initial tests will be used in the further development of prototypes and in the technical implementation of new measures.

ACKNOWLEDGEMENT

This work was supported by a grant from the STAEDLER foundation, as part of the project DIAMINT - Digitization of the student life cycle to support underrepresented students in STEM studies.

REFERENCES

Anderson, E., and Kim, D., 2006. *Increasing the success of minority students in science and technology.*

Birnbaum, R., 1983. *Maintaining diversity in higher education.* Jossey-Bass, Inc., 433 California St., San Francisco, CA 94104.

Blum, L., Frieze, C., Hazzan O., and Dias, M.B., 2007, *A Cultural Perspective on Gender Diversity in Computing.* In: Reconfiguring the Firewall, P. Meszaros, A.K. Peters Eds., CRC Press, p. 109-133.

Bundesagentur für Arbeit, *Blickpunkt Arbeitsmarkt, MINT-Berufe*, September 2018, https://statistik.arbeitsagentur.de/Statischer-Content/Arbeitsmarktberichte/Berufe/generische-Publikationen/Broschuere-MINT.pdf.

Carnevale, A.P., Smith, N., & Melton, M. 2011. *STEM: Science Technology Engineering Mathematics*. Georgetown University Center on Education and the Workforce.

Cohoon, J.M., 2003, *Must there be so few? Including women in CS.* In: 25th International Conference on Software Engineering. Proceedings, p. 668-674.

Dahlström, M., and Doracic, A., 2009. *Digitization Education.* D-Lib Magazine, 15(3/4), 1082-9873.

Deutsches Zentrum für Hochschul- und Wissenschaftsforschung, https://www.dzhw.eu/forschung/.

Gartner, *Gartner IT Glossary Digitization*, https://www.gartner.com/it-glossary/digitization/.

Ilumoka, A., 2012, *Strategies for overcoming barriers to women and minorities in STEM.* IEEE 2nd Integrated STEM Education Conference, Ewing, NJ, pp. 1-4.

Museus, S. D., and Liverman, D., 2010. *High-performing institutions and their implications for studying underrepresented minority students in STEM.* New Directions for Institutional Research, 2010(148), 17-27.

Nenonen, S., Rasila, H., Junnonen, J.M., and Kärnä, S., 2008, *Customer Journey–a method to investigate user experience.* In Proceedings of the Euro FM Conference Manchester, pp. 54-63.Perry, C. A., 2005. Education for digitization: how do we prepare?. The Journal of Academic Librarianship, 31(6), 523-532.

Pipitone B., and Poirer, W., *Student Services Revitalization/Transformation*, http://collegequarterly.ca/2011-vol14-num01-winter/pipitone-poirer-student-life-cycle.html.

Rendón, L.I., Jalomo, R.E., and Nora, A., 2000. *Theoretical considerations in the study of minority student retention in higher education.* Reworking the student departure puzzle, 1, 127-156.

Schötteler, S., 2018. *Entwicklung eines Konzepts zur digitalen Transformation bei der IHK Nürnberg für Mittelfranken*. Master Thesis. Technische Hochschule Nürnberg.

Schuhbauer,H., 2018, *Proposal for a Framework for Digitalization in Education*, ICERI2018 Proceedings, International Conference of Education, Research and Innovation, ISBN: 978-84-09-05948-5, pp. 2720-2726.

Swail, W.S., 2003. *Retaining Minority Students in Higher Education*: A Framework for Success. ASHE-ERIC Higher Education Report. Jossey-Bass Higher and Adult Education Series. Jossey-Bass, 989 Market Street, San Francisco, CA 94103-1741.

Technische Hochschule Nürnberg, *Diversity an der Hochschule*, https://www.th-nuernberg.de/hochschule-region/strategie-und-profil/hochschule-der-vielfalt/.

LEARNING ENGAGEMENT, LEARNING OUTCOMES AND LEARNING GAINS: LESSONS FROM LA

Dirk Tempelaar[1], Bart Rienties[2] and Quan Nguyen[2]
[1]*Maastricht University School of Business and Economics,* Tongersestraat 53, 6211 LM, Maastricht, Netherlands
[2]*Open University UK, Institute of Educational Technology, Walton Hal, Milton Keynes, MK7 6AA, UK*

ABSTRACT

Learning analytic models are built upon traces students leave in technology-enhanced learning platforms as the digital footprints of their learning processes. Learning analytics uses these traces of learning engagement to predict performance and provide learning feedback to students and teachers when these predictions signal the risk of failing a course, or even dropping-out. But not all of these trace variables act as stable and reliable predictors of course performance. In previous research, the authors concluded that trace variables of product type, such as mastery, do a better job than trace variables of process type, such as clicks or time-on-task, in predicting performance. In this study, we extend this analysis by focusing on learning gains rather than learning outcomes as the most important performance dimension. Distinguishing two different levels of initial proficiency, our empirical analysis into the learning of mathematics by first-year university students indicates that the lack of stability of the engagement types of process type is mainly explained by learning pattern found in students of high initial proficiency. For these students, high levels of engagement lead to lower, rather than higher, predicted learning outcomes. Amongst students with lower initial proficiency, higher levels of engagement play a different role.

KEYWORDS

Blended Learning, e-Tutorials, Learning Analytics, Learning Engagement, Learning Traces, Process and Product Data

1. INTRODUCTION

Learning Analytics (LA) has the prime aim to improve the study success of students by collecting data about the way students learn, designing models that can extrapolate observed learning behaviours into predictions of learning outcomes, and provide learning feedback to students and teachers in case those predictions signal a risk of unsuccessful learning, or even drop-out (Ifenthaler, 2015; Ifenthaler, Mah, & Yau, 2019). An important source of data applied in predictive modelling is trace data generated by technology-enhanced learning environments that represent the digital footprints of the learning of students in these learning tools. LA is not without challenges (Ifenthaler et al., 2019): how to define study success, and what trace variables to choose to provide reliable predictions of that study success, are amongst such challenges.

Early applications of LA focussed strongly on signalling the risk of drop-out or more generally: failing the course. Failing is determined by course performance measures as expressed in terms of grades. Best predictors of performance on final exams that are timely enough to allow for educational interventions are typically early, of course, performance measures, such as scores on an intermediate test or quizzes. All of these are outcome measures that characterise the level of proficiency of the students, but not necessarily the amount of learning taking place in the course. And that is actually what course learning objectives are about: to learn new concepts, to increase rather than establish students' levels of proficiency.

This growth objective is best represented by the concept of learning gain (Rogaten and Rienties, 2018; Rogaten et al., 2018). In this learning gain literature, a rich set of learning gains is distinguished, ranging from learning gains of affective type, through behavioural types, to cognitive types. The difficulty in applying these concepts is in the measurement. That is especially true for learning gains of affective and behavioural types, but even if one limits the focus on learning gains of cognitive type only, as we will do in this study, measurement is a challenge. Some empirical studies use indirect measures such as the use of self-report surveys by students asking to quantify how much they learned, while other studies applied objective tests in a pre- and post-test design (Rogaten and Rienties, 2018; Rogaten et al., 2018). But where the use of objective testing is generally to be preferred above self-report surveys, the measurement of cognitive learning gains would require the use of equivalent pre- and post-tests, as in progress testing, which is hardly ever done.

The aim of the current study is to investigate potential differences in typical LA type of models with learning outcomes versus learning gains as response variables and trace variables of student engagement as predictor variables. Research questions in this context are: how do these prediction models differ between the two different response variables? And as a follow-up question: what role do the different trace variables, all representing different facets of student engagement, in these prediction models? This last research question connects to previous research of the authors (Tempelaar et al., 2015, 2017, 2018a), where we found that some measures of engagement, such as time-on-task or the intensity of using worked-out examples, are negatively related to course outcomes in multivariate prediction equations, rather than the positive relationship hypothesized. Does that outcome hold when we predict learning gain rather than learning outcome, is the research question of this contribution, thereby providing an immediate extension of our Tempelaar (2017) study?

2. METHODS

2.1 Context of the Empirical Study

This study takes place in a large-scale introductory mathematics and statistics course for first-year undergraduate students in a business and economics program in the Netherlands. The educational system is best described as 'blended' or 'hybrid' applying the flipped classroom approach. The main component is face-to-face: Problem-Based Learning (PBL), in small groups (14 students), coached by content expert tutors (in 78 parallel tutorial groups). Participation in tutorial groups is required. Optional is the online component of the blend: the use of the two e-tutorials SOWISO (https://sowiso.nl/) and MyStatLab (MSL) (Nguyen et al., 2016; Tempelaar, 2017; Tempelaar et al., 2015; 2017). This design is based on the philosophy of student-centred education, placing the responsibility for making educational choices primarily on the student. Since most of the learning takes place during self-study outside class through the e-tutorials or other learning materials, class time is used to discuss solving advanced problems. Thus, the instructional format shares most characteristics of the flipped-classroom design. Using and achieving good scores in the e-tutorial practice modes is incentivized by providing bonus points for good performance in quizzes that are taken every two weeks and consist of items that are drawn from the same item pools applied in the practising mode. This approach was chosen to encourage students with limited prior knowledge to make intensive use of the e-tutorials.

The subject of this study is the full 2018/2019 cohort of students (1208 students in total, 1055 students included in this study who have full data records). A large diversity of the student population was present: only 20% were educated in the Dutch high school system, against 80% being international students, with 56 nationalities present. A large share of students was of European nationality, with only 3.9% of students from outside Europe. High school systems in Europe differ strongly, most particularly in the teaching of mathematics and statistics. Therefore, it is crucial that this introductory module is flexible and allows for individual learning paths. Students spend on average 28.3 hours in SOWISO and 25.0 hours in MSL, which is 30% to 35% of the available time of 80 hours for learning both topics. This study focuses on learning engagement of students in only one of the two e-tutorials, to know the math related SOWISO tool, for several reasons: the availability of trace data for several types of engagement (see next section), reliable time-on-task data by correction for inactive time, and the availability of prior education data regarding mathematics, but not statistics.

2.2 Instruments and Procedure

Both e-tutorial systems SOWISO and MSL follow test-directed learning and practising approach. Each step in the learning process is initiated by a question, and students are encouraged to (attempt to) answer each question. If a student does not master a question (completely), she/he can either ask for hints to solve the problem step-by-step, or ask for a fully worked example. After receiving feedback, a new version of the problem loads (parameter based) to allow the student to demonstrate his/her newly acquired mastery. Students' revealed preferences for learning strategies are related to their learning dispositions, as we demonstrated in previous research (see Nguyen et al. (2016) and Tempelaar et al. (2017, 2018 a, b) for the use of worked-examples in SOWISO, and (Tempelaar, 2017) for the use of worked-examples in MSL). This study extends Nguyen et al. (2016) and Tempelaar et al. (2018a, b) by investigating three learning strategies in the SOWISO tool: worked examples, and supported and tutored problem-solving.

Figure 1 demonstrates the implementation of the alternative learning strategies students can opt for a sample exercise:

- Check: the untutored problem-solving approach, offering only correctness feedback after problem-solving;
- Hint: the tutored problem-solving approach, offering feedback and hints to assist the student in the several problem-solving steps;
- Solution: the worked-examples approach;
- Theory: asking for a short explanation of the mathematical principle.

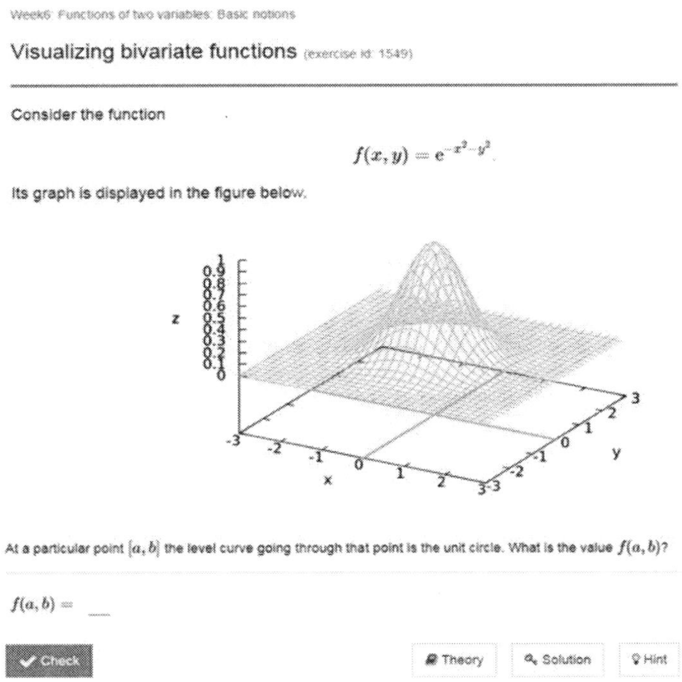

Figure 1. Sample of SOWISO exercise with the options Check, Theory, Solution, and Hint

Our study combines trace data of the SOWISO e-tutorial with prior-education SIS data and course performance data. Clicks in the two e-tutorial systems represent an important part of that trace data, but trace data can include more than click data only. Azevedo (Azevedo et al., 2013) distinguishes between trace data of product and process type, where click data is part of the category of process data. In this study, we will combine both process data, as, e.g. the clicks to initiate the learning supports of Check, Hint, Solution and Theory mentioned above, but also product data, as, e.g. mastery in the tool, as discussed below. SOWISO reporting options of trace data are very broad, requiring making selections from the data. First, all dynamic trace data were aggregated over time, to arrive at static, full course period accounts of trace data. Second, from the large array of trace variables, a selection was made by focusing on process variables most strongly connected to alternative learning strategies.

In total, four trace variables were selected:

- Mastery in the tool, the proportion of exercises successfully solved as product indicator;
- Attempts: the total number of attempts of individual exercises;
- Hints: the total number of Hints called.
- Solutions: the total number of worked-out examples called.

The Attempts variable is cumulative: it is the sum of calls for hints, for worked-out examples, and untutored problem-solving attempts. The system does not trace the number of clicks for the Check option, but that number follows from removing the Solution and Hints activities from the total number of Attempts.

Pass/fail decisions for the course are based on four course outcome measures: performance in the exam, both for mathematics (MathExam) and statistics (StatsExam), and the aggregated performance in the three quizzes for both topics: MathQuiz and StatsQuiz. The exam brings 40 credits, against 6 credits for quizzes, indicating the limited weight of the quizzes (13%). Because of missing adequate trace and prior education data for the statistics part, predictive modelling will be limited to the two mathematical performance variables, indicated as Exam and Quiz.

Prior education measures are based on self-reported accounts of the secondary mathematics program at the secondary level. Most countries distinguish three levels of math teaching in upper-level high school: the highest level, preparing for science university studies, the intermediate level, preparing for social sciences university studies, and the lower level, preparing for humanities. Examples are the levels Hl, SL, and SL studies of the International Baccalaureate (IB) program. To be admissible to the school, at least the intermediate level is required. That allows describing the level of prior education by an indicator variable, labelled as MathMajor, having a value of 1 for students educated in the highest track, and 0 for students educated in the intermediate track. Shares of these two tracks are 37.1% and 62.9%, respectively.

2.3 Learning Gains and Learning Outcomes

Although learning gain, how much students actually learn by taking a course, is obviously the more important aim than the learning outcome, how much students know at the end of the course by combining newly learned knowledge with prior knowledge, most empirical studies in learning analytics focus on learning outcomes. This is best explained by the simple reason that student assessment in any course brings exact measures of learning outcomes in the form of exam and quiz grades, whereas learning gain is defined by the growth in knowledge throughout the course, and thus requires the measurement of the starting level. Such measures are however difficult to operationalize, and for that reason, many empirical studies in learning gains take the step to equate learning gains with learning outcomes. In our context, we collected two measures that may qualify as a proxy of the level cognitive understanding at the start of the course: the outcome of a diagnostic entry test, and self-reported data on prior mathematics education at the secondary level. In a preliminary analysis, we investigated the potential of the diagnostic test score as a measure of starting level of proficiency and concluded that it was less fit to play that role. There are two different aspects to this misfit. First, the diagnostic test is used as an instrument to inform students how well they are prepared to take the course. So there is an issue with coverage: the entry test covers topics at a foundational level, rather than topics taught in the course itself. Second: students administer the diagnostic test outside class, which gives rise to very different response patterns. Some students do not take the test seriously, especially when they know they are well prepared, given their high level of proficiency. Other students, especially at the other end of the continuum of preparedness, tend to take the entry test 'too' seriously and achieve scores that are higher than their ready knowledge. The prior education measure does not share these issues. It is less fine-grained in that it distinguishes only two different levels, but the coverage of the advanced level program overlaps to large extent topics taught in our course, and there are no issues with the administration. Therefore, we opted for the prior education dummy variable to describe two different proficiency levels at the start of the course: one for students of the advanced track, one for students of the intermediate track.

In terms of model design, it is not the initial level of proficiency of the two groups itself that is crucial in the learning gain approach, but the difference between these two levels. We estimate that difference using multivariate regression models, where learning outcome is the response variable, and trace variables together with the prior education dummy variable serve the role of predictor variables. The estimate of the regression coefficient of the prior education dummy represents the difference in prior proficiency between the two groups expressed in units of the learning outcome variable. In that context, the learning gain equals the difference between learning outcome itself, and the estimated effect of prior education.

3. RESULTS

3.1 Learning Outcomes and Traces of Learning

Correlating course outcomes (Exam and Quiz), track of prior education (the dummy MathMajor) with traces of engagement with the e-tutorial, both of product type (Mastery) and of process type (Attempts, Solutions, Hints, Time) produces some unexpected outcomes: see Table 1. As expected, Exam and Quiz are strongly positively related, and both are moderately positively related to having followed math classes at an advanced level in high school. The unexpected outcomes refer to the correlations between Exam, the main course outcome variable, and the several trace variables of process type. Except for Time, these correlations are non-significant or even negative: Attempts, Solutions, Hints. Correlations between the other course outcome variable, Quiz, exhibit a very different pattern: these are all significantly positive.

Table 1. Bivariate correlations of course outcomes, prior education and traces of learning in the e-tutorial; full sample

Variable	1.	2.	3.	4.	5.	6.	7.	8.
1. Exam	1.000							
2. Quiz	.558***	1.000						
3. MathMajor	.381***	.375***	1.000					
4. Mastery	.219***	.545***	.078*	1.000				
5. Attempts	-.037	.356***	-.077*	.778***	1.000			
6. Solutions	-.210***	.108***	-.188***	.557***	.916***	1.000		
7. Hints	-.007	.104***	-.052	.217***	.166***	.056	1.000	
8. Time	.071*	.262***	.009	.423***	.360***	.207***	.202***	1.000

Note: ***p <.001; **p <.01; *p <.05.

Correlations between the several engagement variables of trace type are all positive or non-significant. Number of Attempts and number of Solutions are so strongly related, that they constitute a collinear set. On average, students do 745 Attempts, of which 325 are calls for worked examples: the Solutions. This ratio of 44% of the Attempts being calls for Solutions is rather constant over students, causing a high correlation. This affects the regression in the next step of the analysis: including both Attempts and Solutions gives rise to high variance inflation factors. All regressions have been run with both Attempts and Solutions as a predictor, and in all cases, the fit of the regression model with Solutions is far better than that with Attempts. For that reason, the Attempts variable is excluded from all regression models.

The Hints variable behaves differently: not only is its correlation with Attempts no more than weak, students call on average no more than 29 Hints, what is in only 4% of their Attempts.

The regression equations explaining the two course outcomes variables, Exam and Quiz, out of e-tutorial trace variables is provided in Table 2.

Table 2. Regressions of course outcomes on e-tutorial trace data

	Exam			Quiz		
LA trace predictor	b	SE(b)	β	b	SE(b)	β
Mastery	6.143	0.405	0.526***	1.556	0.066	0.736***
Solutions	-0.006	0.000	-0.496***	-0.001	0.000	-0.329***
Hints	-0.006	0.002	-0.091***	-0.001	0.000	-0.052**
Time	-0.000	0.000	-0.044	-0.000	0.000	-0.005
R^2	0.222			0.370		

Note: ***p <.001; **p <.01; *p <.05.

Trace variables explain 22% of the variation in the Exam outcome and 37% of the variation in Quiz outcome. Since quizzes are taken in the same e-tutorial tool as students practice in, and contain items similar to those students encounter in the practice mode, it is not surprising that the Quiz outcome variable is better explained by the trace variables, than the Exam outcome variable. Remarkably, all trace variables of process type have negative or zero betas. That is: taking the mastery level of the student into account, students who call more Solutions, or who call more Hints, are predicted to achieve lower course outcomes, on average.

3.2 Learning Gains and Traces of Learning

To operationalize learning gains, an estimate of the cognitive abilities of the students before entering the course is required. The best estimate available is the level of prior education in high school: advanced track or intermediate track. The indicator variable MathMajor serves that role: it indicates if a student took the advanced track (MathMajor=1) or the intermediate track (MathMajor=0). Including the MathMajor variable in the regression model implies that regression intercepts and slopes differ between the two groups, based on differences in correlations. These group-specific correlations are contained in Table 3, with correlations of the students of the MathMajor track above the diagonal, and those of the MathIntermediate track below the diagonal.

Table 3. Bivariate correlations of course outcomes, prior education and traces of learning in the e-tutorial; MathMajor sample above the diagonal, MathIntermediate sample below the diagonal

Variable	1.	2.	3.	4.	5.	6.	7.	8.
1. Exam	1.000	.557***		.205***	-.048	-.253***	-.118*	-.037
2. Quiz	.456***	1.000		.505***	.279***	-.003	.038	.148**
3. MathMajor								
4. Mastery	.214***	.574***		1.000	.783***	.527***	.203***	.434***
5. Attempts	.008	.445***		.808***	1.000	.890***	.162***	.355***
6. Solutions	-.128***	.230***		.618***	.927***	1.000	.076	.218***
7. Hints	.082*	.179***		.231***	.165***	.037	1.000	.206***
8. Time	.138***	.334***		.428***	.380***	.224***	.194***	1.000

Note: ***p <.001; **p <.01; *p <.05.

Comparing the first two rows with the first two columns makes clear that large difference exists between the two groups. Correlations between e-tutorial trace data and the two course outcomes Exam and Quiz are more positive everywhere for the students of the intermediate level track than for advanced level track. These differences in correlations show up in different regression equations, as exhibited in Table 4.

Table 4. Regressions of course outcomes on prior education and e-tutorial trace data

	Exam			Quiz		
LA trace predictor	b	SE(b)	β	b	SE(b)	β
MathMajor	3.269	0.339	0.472***	0.533	0.054	0.419***
Mastery	5.560	0.385	0.467***	1.463	0.062	0.684***
Solutions	-0.005	0.000	-0.388***	-0.001	0.000	-0.230***
Hints						
Time						
Mastery*MathMajor						
Solutions*MathMajor	-0.002	0.001	-0.120**	0.000	0.000	-0.126***
Hints*MathMajor	-0.012	0.003	-0.105***			
Time*MathMajor	-0.000	0.000	-0.096*	-0.000	0.000	-0.073*
R^2	0.324			0.455		

Note: ***p <.001; **p <.01; *p <.05.

The regression coefficients of the MathMajor indicator variable are positive, signalling that students from the MathMajor group score on average 23% higher in the Exam and 37% higher in the Quiz. Other differences between the two groups are visible from the estimates of the interaction terms. The negative effects of the trace variables of process type, Solutions, Hints and Time, accounting for the Mastery interaction term and the main effects are much stronger for the MathMajor group than for the MathIntermediate group.

4. DISCUSSION AND CONCLUSION

The MathMajor variable has a strong effect on the two learning outcomes, both directly, as well as indirectly through three of the four interaction terms, as visible from Table 4. The direct effect tells us that students of the advanced track score, on average 3.3 points higher in the final exam (on a range of 0 … 20), and 0.53 points higher in the quiz (on a range of 0 … 3), than students of the intermediate math track. That direct effect is intuitive: the math topics covered in our course have a strong overlap with the curriculum of the advanced track, next to the circumstance, that one can expect the proportion of talented math student to be higher in that track, than the intermediate level track. That direct effect is our proxy of the difference between learning outcome and learning gain. If we bring that direct effect to the left side of the regression equation, the resulting equation describes predicted learning gain as a function of trace variables and interaction terms.

The interesting part of the regressions in Table 4 is the role of the trace variables. The direct effect of the trace variables is statistically non-significant, except for Solutions, telling that when controlling for Mastery level and prior education, calling more Solutions predicts lower performance. That is: the student who needs more worked-out examples to reach the same mastery level as another student needing less worked-out examples, will score less in exam and quiz, on average. There is no significant overall effect for Hints and Time. However, there are significant interaction effects for Hints, Time as well as Solutions, all with negative betas. All are telling the same story: students of the advanced track who, accounting for their mastery level, need more Solutions, Hints or Time, are expected to do less well than students of the advanced track who reached the same mastery level using fewer Solutions, Hints or Time. The effects for Hints and Time are unique to the students of the advanced track: no similar effect is at work in students of the intermediate track. The interaction effect of Solutions related to students of the advanced track, adds to the general effect of Solutions that relates all students.

In our previous research (Tempelaar, 2017; Tempelaar et al., 2017, 2018 a, b), investigating learning processes in the same course but with different year classes, we invariably found that trace variables of process type derived from learning processes in the e-tutorials play a less unambiguous role in prediction models. Their bivariate relationships with course performance variables are generally positive (as in this study, except for Solutions). However, in multivariate prediction equations that include the Mastery trace variable of product type along with the trace variables of process type, these betas of the process type trace variables are generally negative (as in this study). Telling the story that the student who needs a more intensive process to reach the same mastery level as another student, is expected to do less well in the exam and quiz. Where process that is more intensive means: more Solutions, Hints and or Time.

In the current study, we can specialize these effects by focusing on learning gains rather than learning outcomes. We find different regression models for students of the two tracks of prior education. For students educated at the advanced track who learned a substantial part of the course coverage in high school, passing the course does not require large learning gains. For these students, high levels of engagement rather than low levels of engagement represent a risk factor. They require more worked-out examples; more hints and more time on task to reach a certain mastery level signals weaker understanding and predicts lower performance. Student educated at the lower, intermediate track display a different pattern. These students require a large learning gain to pass the course. Spending more time on task and using more hints to reach a certain mastery level represents, in this case, no risk factors; only the frequent use of worked examples does.

This study is based on learning processes of students in a blended learning context, with a one-sided observation of those learning processes: we measure every detail of learning activities in the digital mode, but any learning in the face-to-face mode is left unobserved. Since the balance between these two learning modes will differ from student to student, this is a clear limitation of the context of this study.

REFERENCES

Azevedo, R., Harley, J., Trevors, G., Duffy, M., Feyzi-Behnagh, R., Bouchet, F., et al. (2013). Using trace data to examine the complex roles of cognitive, metacognitive, and emotional self-regulatory processes during learning with multi-agents systems. In R. Azevedo & V. Aleven (Eds.), International handbook of metacognition and learning technologies, pp. 427–449. Amsterdam, The Netherlands: Springer.

Buckingham Shum, S. & Deakin Crick, R. (2012). Learning Dispositions and Transferable Competencies: Pedagogy, Modelling and Learning Analytics. In S. Buckingham Shum, D. Gasevic, & R. Ferguson (Eds.). *Proceedings of the 2nd International Conference on Learning Analytics and Knowledge*, pp. 92-101. ACM, New York, NY, USA.

Ifenthaler, D. (2015). Learning analytics. In J. M. Spector (Ed.), *Encyclopedia of educational technology*, Vol. 2, pp. 447–451. Thousand Oaks, CA: Sage.

Ifenthaler, D., Mah, D.-K. and Yau, J. Y.-K. (2019). Utilising Learning Analytics for Study Success: Reflections on Current Empirical Findings. In D. Ifenthaler et al. (eds.), Utilizing Learning Analytics to Support Study Success, pp. 27-36. Switzerland: Springer Nature.

Nguyen, Q., Tempelaar, D.T., Rienties, B. and Giesbers, B. (2016). What learning analytics based prediction models tell us about feedback preferences of students. In Amirault, R., & Visser, Y., (Eds.). (2016). e-Learners and Their Data, Part 1: Conceptual, Research, and Exploratory Perspectives. *Quarterly Review of Distance Education*. 17(3).

Rogaten, J. and Rienties, B. (2018). Which first-year students are making most learning gains in STEM subjects?. *Higher Education Pedagogies,* 3(1), pp.161-172.

Rogaten, J., Rienties, B., Sharpe, R., Cross, S., Whitelock, D., Lygo-Baker, S. and Littlejohn, A. (2018). Reviewing affective, behavioural and cognitive learning gains in higher education. *Assessment & Evaluation in Higher Education*, 44(3), pp.321-337.

Tempelaar, D. (2017). How dispositional Learning Analytics helps understanding the worked-example principle. In D. G. Sampson, J. M. Spector, D. Ifenthaler, & P. Isaias (Eds.), *Proceedings 14th International Conference on Cognition and Exploratory Learning in Digital Age (CELDA 2017)*, pp. 117-124. International Association for Development of the Information Society, IADIS Press.

Tempelaar, D., Rienties, B. and Giesbers, B. (2015). In search for the most informative data for feedback generation: Learning analytics in a data-rich context. *Computers in Human Behavior*, 47, pp.157-167.

Tempelaar, D., Rienties, B. and Nguyen, Q. (2017). Towards Actionable Learning Analytics Using Dispositions. *IEEE Transactions on Learning Technologies*, 10(1), pp.6-16.

Tempelaar, D., Rienties, B., Mittelmeier, J. and Nguyen, Q. (2018a). Student profiling in a dispositional learning analytics application using formative assessment. *Computers in Human Behavior*, 78, pp.408-420..

Tempelaar, D., Rienties, B. & Nguyen, Q. (2018b). Investigating learning strategies in a dispositional learning analytics context: the case of worked examples. In *Proceedings of the International Conference on Learning Analytics and Knowledge*, Sydney, Australia, March 2018 (LAK'18), p. 201-205.

Williams, A., Sun, Z., Xie, K., Garcia, E., Ashby, I., Exter, M., Largent, D., Lu, P., Szafron, D., Ahmed, S., Onuczko, T., Smith, J., Tempelaar, D. T., Bitting, K. S., Olcott Marshall, A., Christensen, E., Tseng, H., & Walsh, J. (2016). Flipping STEM. In L. Santos Green, J. Banas, R. Perkins (Eds.), *The Flipped College Classroom, Conceptualized and Re-Conceptualized, Part II*, pp. 149-186. Switzerland: Springer International Publishing.

VISUAL MODELING FOR EXPLORATORY PROBLEM SOLVING ON COMPUTER SCIENCE LESSONS

Sergei A. Kostousov and Irina V. Simonova
Herzen State Pedagogical University of Russia
Moika River, 48, St. Petersburg, 191186, Russia

ABSTRACT

The purpose of the article is to identify conditions for the effective use of visual modeling tools that can help reduce the difficulty level of solving problems during the teaching high school students programming. Visual modeling tools are a type of software that allows you to create visual abstractions that reproduce concepts and objects of the real world with their relationships, which can help in solving the problem. In this paper, we focused on preformal models based on intellect- and concept-maps.

The article gives a classification and describes techniques for using various visual modeling tools to solve problem tasks. Formed skills of working with such tools will allow students to produce, represent and express independently their knowledge. In addition, these tools allow structuring the process of solving the problem, optimizing the time for solving each stage of solving a problem task.

The article presents the results of comparing the learning outcomes of the control and experimental groups, which show that the proposed visual modeling tools can help in solving the programming problem tasks.

KEYWORDS

Programming Learning, Problem-Based Learning, Visual Modeling Tools, School IT Education

1. INTRODUCTION

The development of information society demands a high level of information literacy that needs to be formed at school. Preparing future professionals for a wide range of positions requires as well gathering a programming competency. This competency should be improved to the requested level in the university but the formation can be started at school. It is worth noting that programming is a complex activity that requires thoughtful study and independence in the development of knowledge and skills. The analysis of teaching literature and experience of teachers shows that reproductive method prevails for this discipline. This way of learning does not develop creative skills to solve problems independently. The improvement of programming competence can be reached by problem-based learning (Yusri, 2018): the process of problem solving problem correlates with an increase of creativity (Maker, 2004) and problem tasks are closer to real-life problems (Jonassen, 2005). However, problem solving is a less manageable process and its embedding in discipline is not a trivial task.

The aim of our research is an addition of methods for teaching computer science to school students (10-17 y.o.) with tools that may decrease described gap. We focused on deep-learning methods using a problem-based approach enhanced with computer modeling tools for knowledge visualization.

Modern education and teaching methods cannot rest satisfied with the transfer of information from the teacher to the student, since information becomes knowledge only after it is built into the student's internal cognitive schemes (Scardamalia, Bereiter, 2006). Pedagogical studies rise a question how to overcome the passivity of the students and give them opportunity to extract, create and apply new knowledge. Considering the learning process from this point of view, we are challenged by following issues: how to involve the student in the learning process? how can a teacher promote student building of mental models? how can information/communication technologies help?

Since the area of our research is a computer science education, we use computer technology as an object of study and as a learning instrument. It is necessary to create those learning conditions where the use of software tools will help students thoughtfully and critically interpret the concepts they learn while completing training tasks. To achieve it we propose different visual modeling tools. These tools will be considered as a type of software that allows constructing visual abstractions reproducing the concepts and objects of the real world with their relationship that can help to solve a problem (Koznov, 2012). Formed skills of working with such tools will allow students to independently produce, present and express their knowledge (Jonassen, 2005, Brilingaite, 2018). Furthermore, these tools allow you to structure the learning process by allocating time to solve each stage of a problem task.

In order to involve students in the learning process, the reproductive method of teaching can be enhanced by problem-based learning. For example, researches (De Corte, 2004, Yew, Goh, 2016) present the results of the comparison of the learning outcomes of the control group and the group where the problem approach was implemented. The students in the experimental group demonstrated a higher level of academic performance and metacognitive skills. Moreover, authors note that the effect turned out to be stable in the subsequent training, there was also a positive correlation with the skills of adaptation of students in the next stages of training.

However, the review of papers (Dolmans, 2016, Hüttel, 2017) shows that the problem based learning does not always provide an increase and sometimes may cause even a decrease of academic performance: cognitive load, context, learning time and etc. should be considered.

According to those provisions, we try to make the problem solving more manageable (Sawyer, 2018, Ünal, 2017) and propose the method of using visual modeling tools in solving problems on computer science lessons for school students.

2. THE USE OF VISUAL MODELS FOR THE PROBLEM SOLVING

To build a teaching methodology, it is necessary to distinguish terms “a task” and “a problem”. We analyzed a number of definitions of these concepts of different authors (Makhmutov, 1997, Jonassen, 2005, Maker, 2008) and proposed our working definitions.

The task is a situation with some initial conditions, containing in itself such an unknown, overcoming which the target state will be reached. The solution of the problem will be the achievement of the target state, and the process of the solution will be the way to overcome this unknown. We distinguish two criteria for classification: complexity and problematic. The complexity of the task is an indicator of amount of actions necessary to achieve a solution. Problematic determines the degree of uncertainty of the task.

Reproductive tasks (tasks with a very first level of problematic) are tasks in which the initial and target states are precisely defined, and students know the solution method but do not know the solution itself. At the same time, even for a complex task, the student will either know how to solve it, or own universal methods for finding a solution.

A problem task (hereinafter called the problem) is a kind of task where the target state is not defined or the initial conditions are not determined, or the solution process is not known to the student. In this case, the complexity of the task can be either low or high. In real life, problem tasks are more common, and therefore it is important to learn how to solve them. Note that the "problematic" for some tasks may depend on the student’s level of training.

In the classification presented by (Jacob, 1976) and supplemented (Maker, 2008), six types of problems are distinguished. The first type includes those problems both the teacher and the student knew both the initial conditions of the problem and the method for solving it, but only the teacher knew the answer (was described as reproductive tasks). The second type differs from the first one that the problem is known to both participants, only the teacher knows the solution method and the correct answer. The third type has clearly formulated conditions of the problem, but more than one method can be used to find a solution. The fourth type includes problems with known conditions, but there is not the only way to solve it and not the only one correct answer, but not every method and not every solution are admissible. The fifth type has clearly defined conditions, but neither the teacher nor the student knows the method of solving and answering. The sixth type (the maximum level of problematic) assumes that neither the initial conditions of the problem, nor the method of its solution, nor the solution itself are known either to the student or to the teacher. The second and third types will be considered as "well-structured", while the tasks of the following types will be considered as "ill-structured".

Our experience (Kostousov, Kudryavtsev, 2017) shows that the solution of a problem situation by students is more difficult to manage than the solution of reproductive tasks, even quite complex ones. In order to improve the manageability of training, as was already described, we propose the method of using visual modeling tools for working with knowledge on various stages of the solution process.

Table 1 presents the framework of using tools for visual modeling to work with the knowledge on the stages of solving problems of various types, proposed by us in (Kostousov, Kudryavtsev, 2017). Experimental learning has shown that the use of tools allows the students to visualize and structure educational information, which contributes to the formation of skills to reformulate the task, to make the transition from intuitive understanding to formalized description, including algorithmic.

Table 1. Knowledge visualization tools supporting different stages of problem solving

Stage of solution process	Well-Structured	Ill-Structured
1. Identify problem	Mind map	
2. Create problem space (incl. context)	Concept map	
3. Search potential solutions	Decision tree	
	–	Causal model
4. Evaluate and choose solutions	–	Argument map
5. Implement solution	Project diagram, Process diagram	
6. Check and verify	Argument mapping	
7. Reflection	Mind map	

On the other hand, our pedagogical experience shows that the use of all tools at once for schoolchildren's problem is inexpedient: the consistent acquaintance with these tools is necessary, the rationale for choosing a tool depending on the goals and the stage of solving the problem. It should also be noted that the use of the tools listed in Table 1 leads to an increase in the cognitive load on students.

Therefore, we decided to introduce pre-formal visual models that will allow visualizing the elements of the problem in free form. Our hypothesis was that such models would help the student understand the "gap" between the target state and the initial conditions and work out their own solution. We propose the use of *preformal visual models* based on the intellect- and concept-maps (Wang, 2018). I-map can structure brainstorming and c-map can allow to visualize the structure of the application (Kwon, 2019) articulating different possible ways of productions.

3. EXPERIMENT AND DEMONSTRATION

3.1 First Experiment

To test the hypothesis, the pedagogical experiment (Kostousov, Simonova, 2019) was conducted with students (15-17 y.o.), who studied the section of algorithmization and programming. The algorithms for searching and sorting arrays were considered. The purpose of the experiment was to determine whether the visual models help to fix the knowledge obtained as a result of the student's decisions.

To compare the results, 3 groups of students were allocated: the control group (9 people) and two experimental groups: using a table model (9 people) and a visual one (10 people). The students for the groups were randomly selected from 120 people. Since the study examined a small sample, the analysis was performed using the Mann-Whitney test.

It is known that students' learning of the algorithms for searching and sorting arrays causes the students considerable difficulties (Donley, 2018), therefore the algorithms themselves in all three groups were developed together with the teachers, with active discussion with the students. The algorithms for the linear and binary searches, as well as the bubble sorting algorithms, the smallest method and the use of ready-built sorts have been developed.

The problem in this case was not directly in the development of the algorithm, but in the fact that the students needed to understand which algorithms to use in what situations. We focused not so much on the achieving a practical result, but rather on the quality of learning and the students' self-assessment of the results obtained.

At first, both groups were familiar with the algorithms. A discussion of the characteristics of the developed algorithms was conducted with the control group. A comparison table was proposed to the group with a verbal model, in which the algorithms were in one dimension, and the characteristics for comparison were described in another - the students had to fill in the table.

The third group was offered a visual model made in MS Visio. This model can be considered as a pre-formal view of a conceptual map, in which the links are not clearly indicated, but only the attribute structure of search algorithms.

Since the students are not yet familiar with the principles of building models completely independently, they presented a space of problem attributes to support. The task was to build a common visual comparison model: compare the algorithm with its attribute and identify the relationships between the attributes, and also highlight the "positive" and "negative" attributes as possible (Figure 1). The difficulty for the students of the third group was to determine the dependencies between attributes, that is, how some characteristics can influence others, as well as analyzing under what conditions these attributes will help to optimize the operation of the algorithm, and when vice versa.

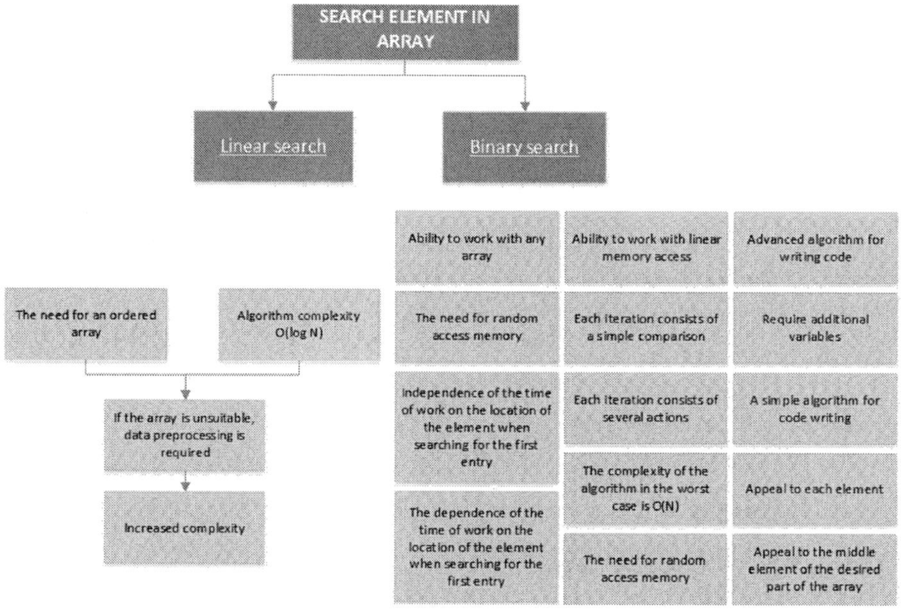

Figure 1. The proposed visual comparison model of the search algorithms for an element in an array where attributes must be associated with one of the search elements

To test the results of the experiment, all the students were offered a test in which there were questions of both theoretical and practical problems: in what situation should the algorithm be used? 10 questions were offered with a description of situations, it was required to choose the correct answer.

Comparison of average scores of test results is presented in Figure 2. As can be seen, the 3rd group showed better results.

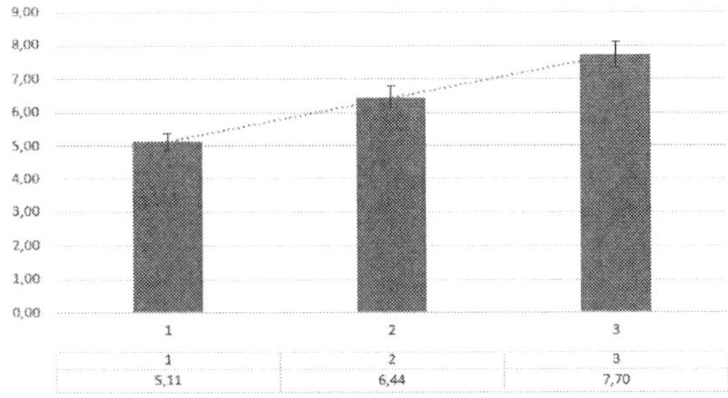

Figure 2. Chart of the average score of the control test in groups

For a more correct comparison of samples, the Mann-Whitney test (1) was used:

$$u_{emp} = n_1 n_2 + \frac{n_x(n_x+1)}{2} - T_x \quad (1)$$

where Tx is the largest sum of ranks, nx is the largest of the sample volumes n1 and n2.

The comparison showed an unreliable difference between the control group and the group where table models were used (the empirical value of the criterion is 36.5, the critical value is 23). The comparison of two experimental groups also turned out to be unreliable (the empirical value of the criterion is 25, the critical value is 23). However, a comparison of the control group and the group where visual models were applied showed a significant difference (the empirical value of the criterion is 11.5, the critical value is 23).

We also conducted a cluster analysis for the test results for three samples. In the calculations, the "nearest neighbor method" was used; the measure of similarity is the ratio of twice the number of common units to the total number of units in the two compared lines. The results showed that the experimental group with visual models had a higher percentage of similarity (average 92%, minimum ~ 85%) than the other two (average value ~ 85, minimum ~ 68%). This can be interpreted as more similar knowledge were gathered by students of the experimental group. Those results encouraged us to provide the advanced experiment.

3.2 Second Experiment

The purpose of this experiment was the clarifying applicability of the proposed method for different types of problems that are appropriate for teaching programming. The advanced experiment was conducted throughout the whole semester for the experimental and control groups.

Preliminary questioning done in both groups showed that the majority of students in each group are studying programming with the aim to continue education in the field of computer science.

At the beginning the "entrance task" was carried out, consisting of 4 standard training tasks with single solutions, to assess the level of students' readiness of using basic algorithmic structures; the visual modeling tools were not used. According to the results (Figure 3) it can be said that the initial level of both groups is quite similar – their compareness can be representative.

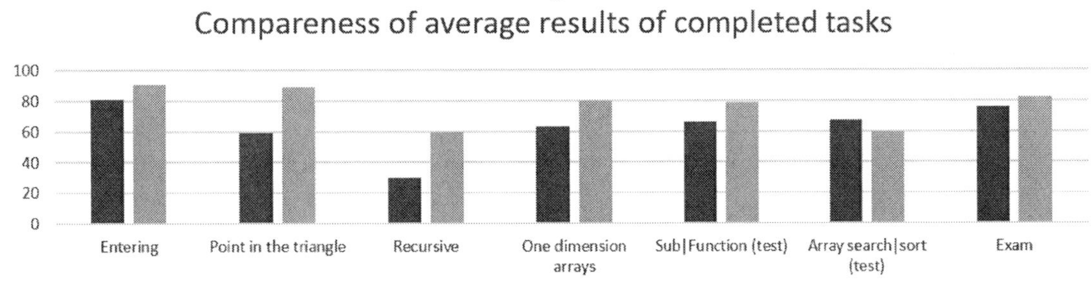

Figure 3. Chart of the average score of the control test in groups

Further task was "point in the triangle": determine whether the point lies inside the triangle according to the coordinates of the point and the vertices of the triangle. The task can be attributed to the different levels of complexity and problematic depending on the condition. For example, it is possible to describe in detail the idea of the algorithm and do not impose strict requirements on the solution, the complexity can be estimated with a rather low rank. The complexity can be increased without increasing the problematic by adding constraints to the condition (we required the use of functions). On the other hand, it is possible to strengthen the problematic without describing the idea of the algorithm, while leaving the requirements for the condition. And finally, it is possible to present this task to the students, without explaining the schema of the solution and specifying the conditions, while raising its problematic and reducing the complexity.

A discussion of the solution method was conducted with the control group, and an experimental constructed a visual model, where the solution methods, data and the structure of the chosen solution method were reflected. The experimental group showed better results (Figure 3).

Next task was "recursive algorithm": "from the rectangle a square of the largest possible area was cut off. From the remaining rectangle, the square of the largest possible area was cut off again, so repeated N times. The result was a rectangle of size A on B. Develop a program that displays all possible sizes of the original rectangle on the screen".

The task can be attributed to the second or third level of problematic depending on the stated conditions. For example, a condition for the mandatory use of a recursive algorithm is introduced, that is, a solution method is indicated, therefore the level of problematic of this task is second, and the level of complexity is higher than that of the previous one.

The development of recursive algorithms causes significant difficulties for the students, so before solving this problem they were offered an additional task, which required to build a visual model of the states of the call stack when finding Fibonacci numbers by the recursive method. The process of building a model allowed each student to understand the main ideas and stages of the recursive algorithm. This technique has reduced the complexity of the problem of cutting squares.

One dimension arrays - a set of tasks for working with one-dimensional arrays: the use of search, sorting, comparisons, etc. Such tasks can be attributed to the second level of problematic (for some even the first), since the solution process only requires the application of the methods studied. However, the level of problematics increased, since in constructing a visual model, it was necessary to correlate the corresponding attributes and characteristics with each of the algorithms, following the relationship between these attributes.

The exam-final task: work with the files, arrays, elements of a windowed application, operators for exception handling. The task had a high level of complexity, because it required the use of many operations to solve, however, the problem was 2 levels, because the exam first required to check operational skills, not creative abilities. Building models for this task was not carried out for any of the groups.

The comparison results are shown in diagram 3. In general, the results are higher for the experimental group. Despite the fact that initially the level of the first group was slightly higher, the increment on subsequent tasks became more noticeable. However, the results of the final exam differed slightly.

Also, comparisons were made of the results of passing tests. With the experimental group, conceptual models were developed for applying subroutines and comparing the characteristics of algorithms for working with arrays. According to the test results, the questions in which checked the knowledge of procedures and functions, the students of the experimental group received higher scores. However, the control group did a better job with the array test questions. Perhaps the abundance of models caused a strong cognitive load, or it was not carried out enough with after action review on the results, or other factors had an impact. This requires an additional research.

We also estimated the time to solve problems in the control and experimental groups. To do this, we tracked the time for completing two tasks: creating a form for registering and entering and setting an exam. A reproductive method was applied with the control group: the code was written on the discussion board. A visual model was built with the experimental group, where possible solutions, the architecture of using subroutines, work with files, etc., are displayed. But the students themselves wrote the application themselves. Comparison with the exam is valid as for both assignments similar work ideas are used, but due to the formulation of the assignment and decontextualization of the exam, these similar features can only be seen by abstracting.

As can be seen from chart 4 (part with the registration and entry form), the experimental group showed a longer working time and a greater spread, in the difference with the control group, where the tasks were handed out almost simultaneously (the difference is less than 5 minutes). However, on the exam, the results were reversed: the experimental students were quicker, the time gap was smaller, and the results were higher.

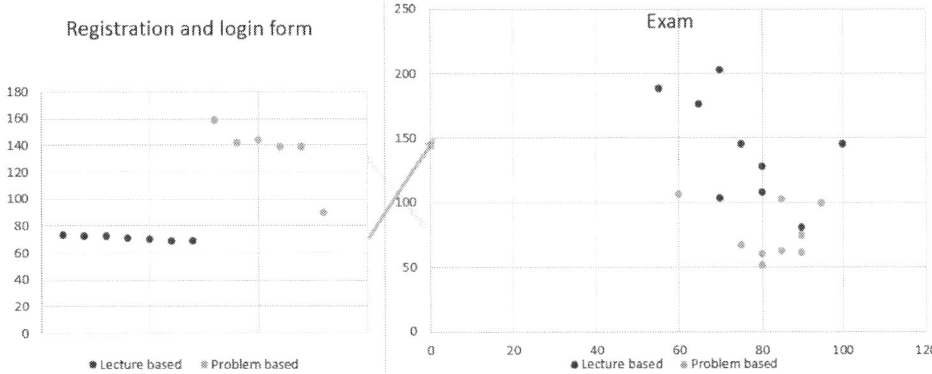

Figure 4. Compareness of time spent (min) and results for two tasks for each group

The calculated values of Wilcoxon signed-rank test show a significant difference for both groups: the control group (2) has a difference in the direction of increasing time, and the experimental one (3) in the direction of decreasing time:

$$\sum x_{ij} = \frac{(1+n)n}{2} = \frac{(1+8)8}{2} = 36_{(2);} \qquad \sum x_{ij} = \frac{(1+n)n}{2} = \frac{(1+6)6}{2} = 21_{(3)}$$

Therefore we can assume that the less manageable independent solution process can lead students to provide more effective solutions in the future.

4. CONCLUSION

Contemporary world requires the use of new techniques in learning process. Education should not only give information but has to provide the methods of knowledge production and information technologies can make this process more efficient. We propose the method of using visual models tool to scaffold gathering knowledge and support the search of different solutions while solving learning problems. Our experiments demonstrate an improvement of academic performance. Visual models can make the solution process more manageable. We can conclude that proposed approach can help in education but further research is needed.

REFERENCES

Brilingaite A., et al, 2018. Competency Assessment in Problem-Based Learning Projects of Information Technologies Students. *Informatics in Education*, 17(1), 21-44.

De Corte E., et al., 2004. The CLIA-model: A framework for designing powerful learning environments for thinking and problem solving. *European Journal of Psychology of Education*, 19(4), 365-384.

Dolmans, D. H., et al., 2016. Deep and surface learning in problem-based learning: a review of the literature. *Advances in health sciences education*, 21(5), 1087-1112.

Donley, K. S., 2018. Coding in the Curriculum: Learning Computational Practices and Concepts, Creative Problem Solving Skills, and Academic Content in Ten to Fourteen-Year-Old Children. *A Dissertation Submitted to the Temple University Graduate Board*, Temple University.

Hüttel, H., & Gnaur, D., 2017. If PBL is the answer, then what is the problem?. *Journal of Problem Based Learning in Higher Education*, 5(2).

Jacob W. et al., 1976. *The creative vision: A longitudinal study of problem finding in art*. New York, NY: Wiley.

Jonassen, D. H., 2005. Tools for representing problems and the knowledge required to solve them. *Knowledge and information visualization*, Springer Berlin Heidelberg, 82-94.

Kivimäki, V. et al, 2018. Supporting understanding of students' learning via visual self-assessment. In EUNIS Annual Congress.

Kostousov S.A., Kudryavtsev D.V., 2017. Towards a framework of using knowledge tools for teaching by solving problems in technology-enhanced learning environment, *Proceedings of the International Association for Development of the Information Society (IADIS) International Conference on Cognition and Exploratory Learning in Digital Age*. Algarve, Portugal. 246-251.

Kostousov S.A., Simonova I.V., 2019. Visual modeling on programming lessons with elements of problem solving in the high school. *Information Innovative Technologies: Materials of the International scientific–practical conference*. /Ed. Uvaysov S. U., Ivanov I.A. – M.: Association of graduates and employees of AFEA named after prof. Zhukovsky, 2019, 348 p.

Koznov D. V., 2012. *Fundamentals of Visual Modeling*. Moscow, BINOM Publ.

Kwon K., Cheon J., 2019. Exploring Problem Decomposition and Program Development through Block-Based Programs. *International Journal of Computer Science Education in Schools*, 3(1), n1.

Maker C. J., et al., 2008. Development of creativity: The influence of varying levels of implementation of the DISCOVER curriculum model, a non-traditional pedagogical approach. Learning and Individual Differences, 18(4), 402-417.

Makhmutov M. I.,1977. *Organizing problem-based learning at school*. Moscow: Prosveshenie. 240p.

Sawyer R., et al, 2018. Filtered Time Series Analyses of Student Problem-Solving Behaviors in Game-Based Learning. *International Educational Data Mining Society*.

Scardamalia M., Bereiter C., 2006. Knowledge building: Theory, pedagogy, and technology. In K. Sawyer (Ed.), *Cambridge Handbook of the Learning Sciences* (pp. 97-118). New York: Cambridge University Press.

Ünal E., Çakir H., 2017. Students' Views about the Problem Based Collaborative Learning Environment Supported by Dynamic Web Technologies. *Malaysian Online Journal of Educational Technology*, 5(2), 1-19.

Wang M., et al, 2018. Using cognitive mapping to foster deeper learning with complex problems in a computer-based environment. *Computers in Human Behavior*, 87, 450-458.

Yew E. H., Goh K., 2016. Problem-based learning: an overview of its process and impact on learning. *Health Professions Education*, 2(2), 75-79.

Yusri, 2018. The Effects of Problem Solving, Project-Based Learning, Linguistic Intelligence and Critical Thinking on the Students' Report Writing. *Advances in Language and Literary Studies*, [Sl], v. 9, n. 6, p. 21-26.

INTERACTION EFFECTS OF TEACHERS' EDUCATIONAL POLICY AND STUDENTS' LEARNING GOAL ORIENTATION ON STUDENTS' LEARNING-AS-DUTY CONCEPTION

Mai Yokoyama and Kazuhisa Miwa
Nagoya University, Japan

ABSTRACT

In order to clarify the effects of teachers' Educational Policy on students' Learning-as-duty Conception, we examined the effects of interaction between teachers' Educational Policy and students' Learning Goal Orientation on Learning-as-duty Conception of the students. A questionnaire survey was conducted with 50 teachers and 189 undergraduate students at a Japanese public university. The interaction between teachers' Educational Policy and students' Learning Goal Orientation showed a significant or a marginally significant for students' Learning-as-duty Conception in five of twelve cases. The findings suggested that the relationship between teachers' Educational Policy and students' Learning-as-duty Conception may change depending on the level of students' Learning Goal Orientation.

KEYWORDS

Educational Policy, Learning Goal Orientation, Learning-as-duty Conception

1. INTRODUCTION

1.1 Learning-as-duty Conception

There are differences in students' learning behavior, depending on their conception of learning. Van Rossum and Schenk (1984) suggested that students who perceived learning as memorizing adopted superficial learning behavior, whereas those who perceived learning as the abstraction of meaning or interpretative processes aimed at the understanding of reality adopted deep learning behavior. Furthermore, Dart et al. (2000) showed that students who held qualitative conceptions such as personal fulfillment and experiential conceptions not bounded by time were more likely to utilize deep approaches to learning, whereas students who held quantitative conceptions, such as an increase of knowledge, were more likely to rely on superficial approaches.

In this study, we focus particularly on "Learning-as-duty Conception." It is widely known that such a conception negatively affects learning behavior. Peterson et al. (2010) argued that Learning-as-duty Conception has a negative effect on academic achievement. Furthermore, Takayama (2002) revealed that Learning-as-duty Conception is a factor that promotes superficial learning behavior.

1.2 Learning Goal Orientation

The individual characteristics for student goals in learning are called goal orientation. It is known that goal orientation is broadly divided into Learning Goal Orientation and performance goal orientation. In this study we focus on Learning Goal Orientation. The learning goal is the goal to acquire new knowledge and skills through challenging activities, and it has been clarified as promoting positive learning behavior. Students who are oriented toward learning goals tend to persevere even when they encounter failure (Diner & Dweck 1978) and deliberately select challenging tasks (Elliot & Dweck 1988). According to Ames and Archer

(1987, 1988), Learning Goal Orientation has a positive effect on both academic achievement and endogenous motivation.

It has been revealed that there are differences in educational support effects, depending on the level of the students' Learning Goal Orientation. For example, Walter et al. (2005) showed that the effect of teacher feedback on students' learning behavior is contingent on the level of the student's Learning Goal Orientation. Patrick et al. (2011) also suggested that the effect of parental support on students' self-efficacy depends on the level of the students' Learning Goal Orientation.

1.3 Factors that Suppress Learning-as-duty Conception

Yokoyama and Miwa (2018) examined the cause-and-effect relationships of goal orientation, learning conception and learning behavior. The results of the study are consistent with the results of Peterson et al. (2010) and Takayama (2002), suggesting that Learning-as-duty Conception inhibits positive learning behavior. In this context, we have a question of how to suppress Learning-as-duty Conception that negatively affects learning behavior. Yokoyama and Miwa (2018) suggested that Learning Goal Orientation can be a factor in suppressing Learning-as-duty Conception. Although the study revealed students' internal factors, such as Learning Goal Orientation, that suppress Learning-as-duty Conception, external factors, such as teachers' intervention, were not examined. We need further study to examine external factors in order to provide educational support to suppress students' Learning-as-duty Conception. One of the external factors is teachers' intervention, which is guided by teachers' Educational Policy. We assumed that teachers' Educational Policy may change students' Learning-as-duty Conception.

1.4 Purpose

Figure 1 shows the outline of this study. The purpose of this study is to examine the effects of teachers' Educational Policy on students' Learning-as-duty Conception. We assume that the effects may depend on students' Learning Goal Orientation. Yokoyama and Miwa (2018) confirmed the negative correlation between students' Learning Goal Orientation and Learning-as-duty Conception in Figure 1. In this study, in order to clarify the effects of teachers' Educational Policy on students' Learning-as-duty Conception, we examined the interaction effects between teachers' Educational Policy and students' Learning Goal Orientation on Learning-as-duty Conception of the students. It is expected that the effects of teachers' Educational Policy on students' Learning-as-duty Conception will vary depending on the level of the students' Learning Goal Orientation.

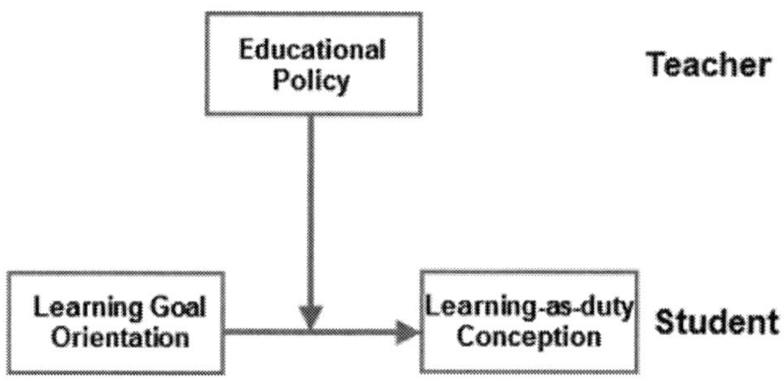

Figure 1. Outline of this study

In this study, we examined such effects in seminar classes consisting of single teacher and a small group of students. The content and methods of seminar classes are usually chosen at the teachers' discretion and thus, each class reflects their Educational Policy. In addition, since the seminar classes are conducted with a small number of students during one or two years through the relatively long term of classes, the teacher-student relationship is expected to become deeper than in general classes. These conditions imply that teachers' Educational Policy of seminars greatly affects students' Learning-as-duty Conception.

2. METHOD

2.1 Method of Survey

The class practice was conducted in the School of Integrated Arts and Sciences of a Japanese public university. A questionnaire survey was conducted with 50 university teachers who had taught in seminar classes for two years, and 189 undergraduate students who had participated in the seminar classes during the third to fourth grade from 2017 to 2018. The seminars were among the compulsory subjects, and took more than 180 minutes a week. The survey was conducted from February to March 2019.

2.2 Measures

For teachers

Educational Policy: The following five categories of items, developed by Fushikida et al. (2014), were used in a comprehensive questionnaire to measure the teachers' Educational Policy of running seminars. (A) Understanding Students' Characteristics (6 items); (B) Educational Goals (7 items); (C) Learning Goals (12 items), (D) Learning Activities (12 items); and (E) Teachers' Instructions (11 items). Each item was rated on a 5-point scale.

For students

Learning-as-duty Conception: Five items from the "Duty and Memorizing" factor in Yokoyama and Miwa (2018), modified from Takayama's (2002) learning conception scale (e.g., "Learning is being forced by parents or teachers." "Learning is being forced to do things that you do not want to do.") were rated on a 5-point scale.

Learning Goal Orientation: Four items from the "Learning Goal" factor in Yokoyama and Miwa (2018), translated from Elliot and Church's (1997) Achievement Goal Scale (e.g., "I hope to have gained a broader and deeper knowledge when I am done with classes." "I want to learn as much as possible from classes.") were rated on a 5-point scale.

2.3 Method of Analysis

The answers from teachers to evaluate their Educational Policy of the seminar are group level (the seminar level) data, while those from students to evaluate Learning-as-duty Conception and Learning Goal Orientation are individual level data. Therefore, hierarchical linear model analysis was performed. The dependent variable was the Learning-as-duty Conception, and the independent variables were the Learning Goal Orientation and the teachers' Educational Policy of the seminar. We calculated the intra-class correlation coefficient (ICC) of Learning Goal Orientation and Learning-as-duty Conception to evaluate intra-group similarity. If the value of ICC indicated .10 or more, it was judged that the answers among students for the same seminar were consistent, and the average value of Learning Goal Orientation for each seminar was able to be utilized for the model as variable. We excluded the data in the seminar consisting of a single student. As a result, the data of 43 seminars, including 43 teachers and 179 students, were analyzed.

3. STRUCTURE OF THE SCALES

3.1 Teachers' Educational Policy of the Seminar

The α coefficients calculated based on the factor structure of Fushikida et al. (2014) were extremely low. Therefore, we performed exploratory factor analysis again (principal factor with promax rotation) for each of the five categories. Items that were loaded at .35 or less and items that were loaded at .35 or more on two or more factors, were excluded. The factor category was decided from the items with high factor loading. An average value of the items was regarded as a representative value of each factor.

As a result of factor analysis of (A) Understanding Students' Characteristics, one factor emerged. The factor and sample items are: (A1) Understanding Students' Characteristics (5 items; α = .61), "Cognitive proficiency" "Interest in learning."

As a result of factor analysis of (B) Educational Goals, two factors emerged. The factors and sample items are: (B1) Goals to Enhance Seminar Activities (4 items; α = .71), "Introduce the latest research development" "Strengthen the relationship between teachers and students, and among students"; and (B2) Goals to Promote Student Growth (2 items; α = .52), "Lead students to growth." Since the α coefficient is small, the second factor was excluded from further analysis.

As a result of factor analysis of (C) Learning Goals, three factors emerged. The factors and sample items are: (C1) Goals to Improve Inquiring Mind (4 items; α = .79),"Improve students' motivation to learn" "Improve students' thinking skills"; (C2) Goals to Acquire Social Skills (3 items; α = .69), "Students are aware of relationship with society" "Students acquire generic skills beyond their major"; and (C3) Achievement Goals of Specialization (3 items; α = .57), "Students utilize acquired knowledge, skills and attitudes" "Students deepen their systematic understanding of learning content."

As a result of factor analysis of (D) Learning Activities, four factors emerged. The factors and sample items are: (D1) Collaborative Learning Outside the University (5 items; α = .88), "Students do fieldwork (observation, survey, etc.) in groups" "Students carry out joint projects with outside parties (other universities, companies, regions, etc.)"; (D2) Students' Presentations (5items; α = .85), "Students give a presentation on the progress of the given task" "Students give a presentation on what they have investigated for a subject"; and (D3) Knowledge Transfer by Teachers (2 items; α = .65), "Teacher gives a lecture"; and (D4) Discussion Between Teachers and Students (2 items; α = .65), "Students discuss among themselves."

As a result of factor analysis of (E) Teachers' Instructions, three factors emerged. The factors and sample items are (E1) Support for Task Execution (5 items; α = .77), "Advise on theme settings" "Show clear goals to be achieved." (E2) Formative Evaluation of Presentation (4 items; α = .75), "Evaluate content of the presentation" "Evaluate skills of the presentation"; and (E3) Teaching on References (2 items; α = .75), "Give advice on reading literature."

3.2 Students' Learning-as-duty Conception and Learning Goal Orientation

The internal consistency was confirmed by calculating α coefficients of five items of "Learning-as-duty Conception" (α = .84) and four items of "Learning Goal Orientation" (α = .74). Since a sufficient α value was confirmed, an average value was regarded as a representative value of each factor.

4. RESULTS

The ICC of Learning Goal Orientation was .12 ($p < .01$), the ICC of Learning-as-duty Conception was .18 ($p < .01$), showing that the responses among students in an individual seminar were consistent. An average value of Learning Goal Orientation in each seminar was treated as a representative variable of Learning Goal Orientation. The hierarchical linear model analysis was performed. Learning-as-duty Conception was defined as a dependent variable, and the teachers' Education Policy of the seminar and Learning Goal Orientation were defined as independent factors. The interaction of two independent factors was analyzed. We conducted 12 analyses, for each of which one of every 12 variables of teachers' Educational Policy of the seminar was used.

In all of the 12 analyses, Learning Goal Orientation showed significant negative effects on Learning-as-duty Conception. This result is consistent with the results of Yokoyama and Miwa (2018). In five analyses among those, the interaction between teachers' Educational Policy of the seminar and Learning Goal Orientation reached a significant or a marginally significant level (Table 1).

In order to examine the relationship between teachers' Educational Policy of the seminar and students' Learning-as-duty Conception, a simple slope test was conducted (Figure 2).

In the relationship between Understanding Students' Characteristics and Learning-as-duty Conception (Figure 2 (a)), in the seminar where the students have low Learning Goal Orientation, the slope was a significant positive value ($\beta = .25$, $p < .01$). This result showed that in the seminar consisting of students with low Learning Goal Orientation, the more the teacher tried to understand the students' characteristics, the higher the students' Learning-as-duty Conception became.

Table 1. Results of Hierarchical Linear Model Analysis

Variable	β	Variable	β	Variable	β	Variable	β	Variable	β
Learning Goal Orientation	−.73**	Learning Goal Orientation	−.81**	Learning Goal Orientation	−.70**	Learning Goal Orientation	−.77**	Learning Goal Orientation	−.68**
Understanding Students' Characteristics	.14+	Goals to Enhance Seminar Activities	−.02	Goals to Acquire Social Skills	−.03	Collaborative Learning Outside the University	−.02	Knowledge Transfer by Teachers	.03
Interaction	−.31+	Interaction	−.75**	Interaction	−.53*	Interaction	−.38**	Interaction	−.23+

** $p < .01$, * $p < .05$, + $p < .10$

In the relationship between Goals to Enhance Seminar Activities and Learning-as-duty Conception (Figure 2 (b)), in the seminar where the students have low Learning Goal Orientation, the slope was a significant positive value (β = .25, p <. 01), while in the seminar where the students have high Learning Goal Orientation, the slope was a marginally significant negative value (β = −. 29, p <.10). This result showed that in the seminar consisting of students with low Learning Goal Orientation, the more the teacher tried to improve seminar activities, the higher the students' Learning-as-duty Conception became. Conversely, in the seminar consisting of students with high Learning Goal Orientation, the more the teacher tried to improve seminar activities, the lower the students' Learning-as-duty Conception became.

In the relationship between Goals to Acquire Social Skills and Learning-as-duty Conception (Figure 2 (c)), in the seminar where the students have high Learning Goal Orientation, the slope was a marginally significant negative value (β = −.22, p < .10). This result showed that in the seminar consisting of high Learning Goal Orientation students, the more the teacher tried to get students to acquire social skills, the higher the students' Learning-as-duty Conception became.

In the relationship between Collaborative Learning Outside the University and Learning-as-duty Conception (Figure 2 (d)), in the seminar where the students have low Learning Goal Orientation, the slope was a marginally significant positive value (β = .12, p < .10), while in the seminar where the students have high Learning Goal Orientation, the slope was a significant negative value (β = −. 16, p < .05). This result showed that in the seminar consisting of students with low Learning Goal Orientation, the more the teacher gave students the opportunity to experience collaborative learning outside the university, the higher the students' Learning-as-duty Conception became. Conversely, in the seminar consisting of students with high Learning Goal Orientation, the more the teacher gave students the opportunity to experience collaborative learning outside the university, the lower the students' Learning-as-duty Conception became.

In the relationship between Knowledge Transfer by Teachers and Learning-as-duty Conception (Figure 2 (e)), in the seminar where the students have low Learning Goal Orientation, the slope was a marginally significant positive value (β = .12, p < .10). This result showed that, in the seminar consisting of students with low Learning Goal Orientation, the more the teacher had the opportunity to transfer knowledge to the students, the higher the students' Learning-as-duty Conception became.

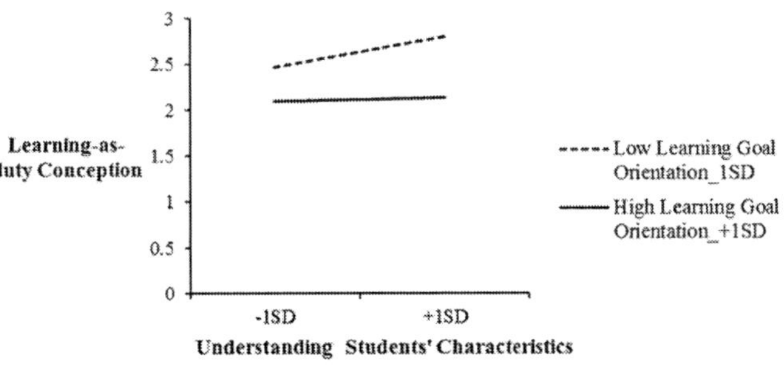

Figure 2(a). Interaction of Understanding Students' Characteristics and Learning Goal Orientation predicting Learning-as-duty Conception

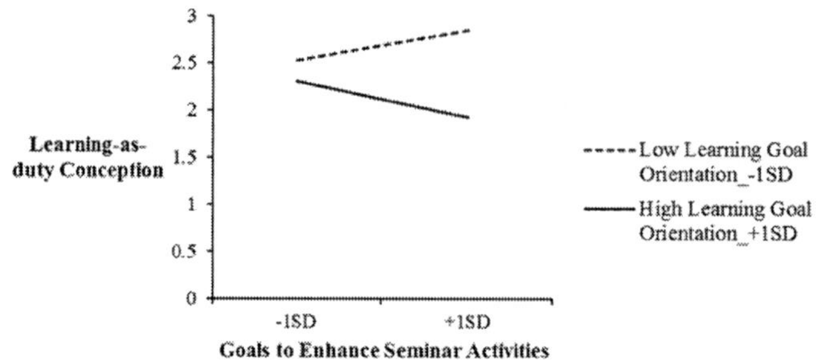

Figure 2(b). Interaction of Goals to Enhance Seminar Activities and Learning Goal Orientation predicting Learning-as-duty Conception

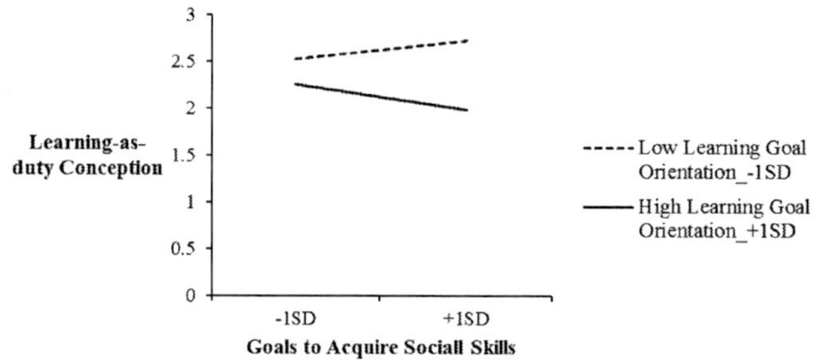

Figure 2(c). Interaction of Goals to Acquire Social Skills and Learning Goal Orientation predicting Learning-as-duty Conception

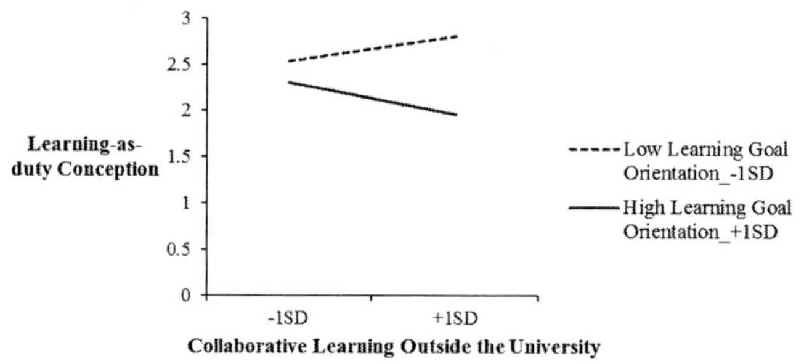

Figure 2(d). Interaction of Collaborative Learning Outside the University and Learning Goal Orientation predicting Learning-as-duty Conception

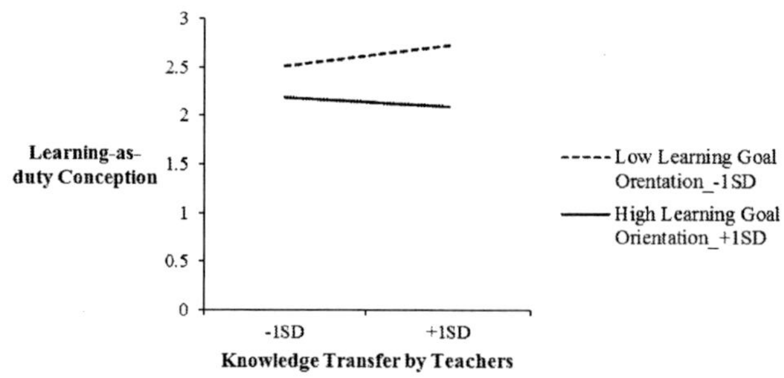

Figure 2(e). Interaction of Knowledge Transfer by Teachers and Learning Goal Orientation predicting Learning-as-duty Conception

5. DISCUSSION

In this study, in order to clarify the effects of teachers' Educational Policy of the seminar on students' Learning-as-duty Conception, we examined the effects of interaction between teachers' Educational Policy and students' Learning Goal Orientation on Learning-as-duty Conception of the students. Since the interaction between teachers' Educational Policy of the seminar and students' Learning Goal Orientation showed a significant or a marginally significant for students' Learning-as-duty Conception in five analyses, in each of the analyses, a simple slope test was performed. The result suggested that the relationship between teachers' Educational Policy of the seminar and students' Learning-as-duty Conception may change depending on the level of students' Learning Goal Orientation. In the following discussion, the effects of teachers' Educational Policy of the seminar on students' Learning-as-duty Conception are discussed, divided into two case i.e., students with higher and lower Learning Goal Orientation.

Case in which the students have high Learning Goal Orientation

As a result of the simple slope test, in the seminar consisting of the students who have high Learning Goal Orientation, Goal to Enhance Seminar Activities, Goals to Acquire Social Skills, and Collaborative Learning Outside the University showed negative relationships with Learning-as-duty Conception. There was a significant positive correlation between Goals to Acquire Social Skills and Collaborative Learning Outside the University ($r = .47$, $p < 01$), meaning that teachers who aim to make students aware of social connections and acquire social skills tend to provide students with opportunities, i.e., they tried to let students experience off-campus collaborative learning. The teachers' Educational Policy, which focuses on emphasizing the acquisition of social skills and considers collaborative learning outside the university as seminar activities, would be effective only for students with high Learning Goal Orientation.

It was indicated that, in the seminar consisting of the students who have high Learning Goal Orientation, the more the teacher gives students the opportunity to experience collaborative learning outside the university, the lower the students' Learning-as-duty Conception becomes. Students who are oriented toward learning goals tend to select challenging tasks (Elliot & Dweck 1988), not fearing taking risks (Printrich 2000), and to seek a challenge in learning. Learning outside the university is often unpredictable as to what will happen, therefore, it is likely to be exciting and challenging for the students. In collaborative learning, teachers are just facilitators, often allowing students to take initiative for classes. It is suggested that students with high Learning Goal Orientation are actively involved in challenging learning and recognize themselves as learners; and as a result, their Learning-as-duty Conception was suppressed.

Case in which the students have low Learning Goal Orientation

As a result of the simple slope test, in the seminar where the students have low Learning Goal Orientation, Understanding Student's Characteristics, Goals to Enhance Seminar Activities, Collaborative Learning Outside the University, and Knowledge Transfer by Teachers showed positive relationships with Learning-as-duty Conception. According to Fushikida et al. (2014), the more the teacher tries to understand the students' characteristics, the more they tend to improve seminar activities. In this study, there was a significant positive correlation between Understanding Students' Characteristics and Enhance Seminar Activities ($r = .55$, $p < 01$). Therefore, if the students have low Learning Goal Orientation, the teachers' Educational Policy, which consciously tries to understand students' characteristics and enhance activities in the seminar, may work as a negative factor as that increases students' Learning-as-duty Conception.

It was indicated that, in the seminar consisting of the students who have low Learning Goal Orientation, the more the teacher has the opportunity to transfer knowledge to the students, the higher students' Learning-as-duty Conception becomes. Students with low Learning Goal Orientation tend not to be interested in learning content (Printrich 2000). It is suggested that students with low Learning Goal Orientation are not interested in the content provided by the teacher in the seminar; therefore, when the teacher frequently intervenes, the students feel that they are being forced, with the result that their Learning-as-duty Conception may increase.

It was indicated that, in the seminar consisting of the students who have low Learning Goal Orientation, the more the teacher gives students the opportunity to experience collaborative learning outside the university, the higher the students' Learning-as-duty Conception becomes. Collaborative learning requires students to participate actively. Students with low Learning Goal Orientation are forced to take part in collaborative learning without their motivation, so their Learning-as-duty Conception may increase.

6. LIMITATION AND FUTURE WORK

The limitation and the future work of this study are summarized as follows; The first is the generalization of the findings in this study. We need to be cautious in generalizing the suggestions obtained in the current study because the analysis is based on the data obtained from questionnaires from only 43 teachers. The second is that we did not take into consideration students' tendencies in the initial stage before the seminars started. It is not clear whether the responses among students in an individual seminar were consistent because the same types of students were gathered in the same seminar, or because they were educated by the same teacher. Perhaps both factors are involved. In future, it will be necessary to conduct a longitudinal survey before students are assigned to the seminars, and to conduct an analysis taking into account students' characteristics and environmental factors. The third is the elucidation of the process of how the students' Learnings-as-duty Conception is suppressed or increased. As shown in the discussion, we mentioned the process of how the students' Learnings-as-duty Conception is suppressed or increased, but it is not empirically evaluated. In order to make use of research findings in educational support, it is important to clarify the process.

ACKNOWLEDGMENT

This work was partially supported by JSPS KAKENHI Grant Number 18H05320.

REFERENCES

Ames, C., & Archer, J. ,1987. Mothers'beliefs about the role of ability and effort in school learning. *Journal of Educational Psychology,* Vol.79, pp.409-414.

Ames, C., & Archer, J. ,1988. Achievement goals in the classroom: Students'learning strategies and motivation process. *Journal of Educational Psychology*, Vol.80, pp.260-267.

Dart, Barry C., Burnett, Paul C., Purdie, Nola M., Boulton-Lewis, Gillian M., Campbell, Jenny, & Smith, David ,2000. Students' conceptions of learning, the classroom environment and approaches to learning. *The Journal of Educational Research*, Vol.93, No.4, pp. 262-270.

Diener, C. I., & Dweck, C. S. 1974. An analysis of learned helplessness: Continuous changes in performance, strategy, and achievement cognition following failure. *Journal of Personality and Social Psychology*, Vol.36, pp.451-462.

Elizabeth R. Peterson., Gavin T. L. Brown., S. Earl Irving, 2010. Secondary school students' conceptions of learning and their relationship to achievement. *Learning and Individual Differences*, Vol. 20, pp.167-176.

Elliot, A. J., & Church, M. A.,1997. A hierarchical model of approach and avoidance achievement motivation. *Journal of Personality and Social Psychology*, Vol.72, pp.218-232.

Elliott, E. S., & Dweck, C. S. ,1988. Goals: An approach to motivation and achievement. *Journal of Personality and Social Psychology*, Vol.54, No.1, pp.5-12.

Fushikida, W., Kitamura, S., & Yamauchi, Y. ,2018. The effects of lesson structures in undergraduate seminars on growth in generic skills studies. *Japan journal of educational technology*, Vol.37, No. 4, pp.419-433.

Patrick Raymund James M. Garcia, Simon Lloyd D. Restubog, Lemuel S. Toledano, Laramie R. Tolentino, & Alannah E. Rafferty, 2011. Differential Moderating Effects of Student- and Parent-Rated Support in the Relationship Between Learning Goal Orientation and Career Decision-Making Self-Efficacy. *Journal of Career Assessment,* Vol. 20, No.1, pp. 22-33.

Pintrich, P. R. ,2000. Multiple goals, multiple pathways: The role of goal orientation in learning and achievement. *Journal of Educational Psychology*, Vo.92, pp.544-555.

Takayama, S., 2002. The relationship between learning conception, it's Determinants and Learning Strategies. Memoirs of the Faculty of Education. *Literature and Social science*, Vol.37, pp.19-26.

Van Rossum, E. J., & Schenk, S. M. ,1984. The relationship between learning conception, study strategy and learning outcome. *British Journal of Educational Psychology*, Vol.54, pp.73-83.

Walter D. Davis., Charles M. Carson., Anthony P. Ammeter., & Darren C. Treadway., 2005. The Interactive Effects of Goal Orientation and Feedback Specificity on Task Performance. *Human Performance*, Vol. 18, No. 4, pp.409-426.

Yokoyama, M., & Miwa, K. ,2018. Relationship between Goal Orientation, Conception of Learning and Learning Behavior. *Proceedings of 15th international conference of cognition and exploratory learning in digital age* (CELDA 2018), pp.233-240.

THE WEIGHT OF EXPECTANCY-VALUE AND ACHIEVEMENT GOALS ON SCIENTIFIC CAREER INTEREST AND MATH ACHIEVEMENT

Laura Francesca Scalas* and Daniela Fadda*
Dipartimento di Pedagogia, Psicologia, Filosofia - Università degli Studi di Cagliari, Italy

ABSTRACT

The study explored a taxonomy of alternative latent models to understand the weight of expectancy-value and approach-related goal orientations in predicting students' achievement behaviors (scientific career interest and math achievement). A full model where all the factors contribute to explaining the total variance of outcomes and two models in which the contribution of expectancy-value and achievement goals factors was evaluated separately within a structural equation modeling framework. Results, among a sample of 812 Italian high school students (486 males and 326 females, *M*age= 18.3), showed that expectancy-value variables explain a substantial portion of math achievement and career interest variance after controlling for the achievement goals. Moreover, when all path coefficients were allowed (full model), global value and its dimensions of opportunity and emotional cost influenced positively student's career aspirations, expectancy resulted the main predictor of math competence, and mastery and performance goals did not show significant effects on the outcomes.

KEYWORDS

Motivation, Expectancy-Value, Achievement Goals, Scientific Career Interest, Math Achievement

1. INTRODUCTION

To understand motivation in several educational domains including math, researchers suggested the importance of two broad constructs: expectancy-value and achievement goal orientations (Eccles and Wigfield, 2002; Pintrich, 2003; Simpkins, Davis-Kean and Eccles, 2006; Wigfield and Cambria, 2010).

Based on expectancy-value theory (EVT; Eccles, 2009; Eccles *et al.*, 1983), expectancy of success in a given task in combination with the value of the task (intrinsic value, attainment value, utility value, and cost) predict academic achievement, effort, engagement and career choices (Eccles, 2009; Guo *et al.*, 2015; Watt *et al.*, 2012). In particular, expectancy typically is the strongest predictor of achievement, whereas value influences career aspirations (Eccles and Wigfield, 2002; Marsh *et al.*, 2013; Simpkins *et al.*, 2006).

Concerning achievement goals, Elliot and colleagues (e.g., Elliot, 1999; Elliot and McGregor, 2001) distinguish between mastery (focused on development of competence) and performance (focused on demonstration of competence) goals. Empirical studies showed that mastery approach goals positively predict students' interest and course enjoyment, whereas performance goals have different effects on learning processes, depending on approach and avoidance orientations, which respectively focus on reaching positive outcomes and on eluding negative outcomes (e.g., Elliot, 1999; Elliot and McGregor, 2001; Elliot and Murayama, 2008; Hulleman *et al.*, 2008).

Although goals and expectancy-value variables are empirically distinct and are independent predictors of achievement-related behaviors (DeBacker and Nelson, 1999; Miller, DeBacker and Greene, 1999; Wigfield, Anderman and Eccles, 2000), several studies in academic domain have investigated associations and causal direction of these factors (Conley, 2012; DeBacker and Nelson, 1999; Miller *et al.*, 1999; Pintrich *et al.*, 1993). Indeed, in line with Eccles's theory (Eccles *et al.*, 1983; Wigfield and Eccles, 1992), longitudinal studies supported the predictive effect of achievement goals on value, considered a motivational construct

*The two authors contributed equally to the present study and should be considered both first author.

subordinated in respect to goals (Harackiewicz *et al.*, 2002, 2008; Hulleman *et al.*, 2008; Pintrich, Ryan and Patrick, 1998; Wolters, Yu and Pintrich, 1996); studies based on a different conception posit, instead, a possible causal influence of expectancy and value on goals (Greene *et al.*, 1999, 2004; Liem, Lau and Nie, 2008; Plante, O'Keefe and Théorêt, 2013), considered as specific orientations towards a domain (Elliot, 2006; Meece, Anderman and Anderman, 2006). As suggested by Wigfield and Cambria's (2010) review about extant research on students' motivation, the exploration of these constructs together is an important way to understand the nature of achievement motivation.

Aim of the present study is to understand the weight of expectancy-value and approach-related goals on individuals' achievement behaviors in mathematical domain (scientific career interest and math achievement). Indeed, although both motivational theories appear to be involved in the determination of academic outcomes, their relationship is still unclear. To overcome this limitation, we compare a taxonomy of models, based on Marsh and Scalas (2018), to understand the weight of each motivational attribute in predicting the outcomes (see Figure 1). In particular, we evaluate the total variance explained by a full model in which the path coefficients of both motivational predictors are freely estimated, and the unique variance explained by only a set of predictor variables after controlling for the other predictors: the expectancy-value prediction model (e.g., Eccles, 2009; Guo *et al.*, 2015) and the achievement goals prediction model (e.g., Harackiewicz *et al.*, 2002; Hulleman *et al.*, 2008). Although an examination of the explained variance is not common practice in structural equation modeling, this approach has been suggested as a relevant criterion in the comparison-model process (e.g., Marsh and Scalas, 2018; Scalas *et al.*, 2014).

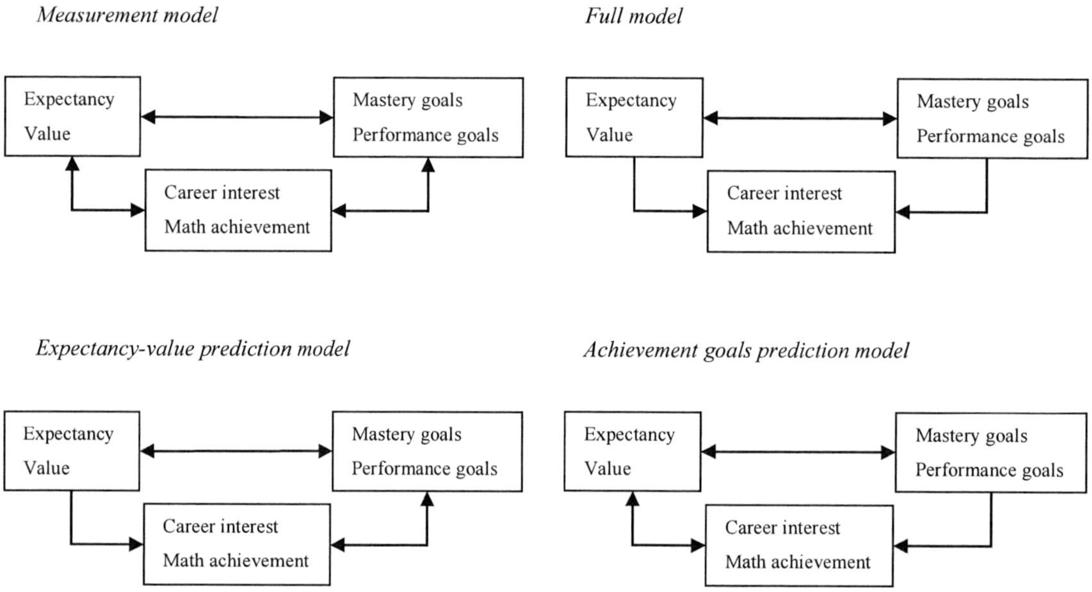

Figure 1. Simplified conceptual representations of estimated models. Two-headed arrows represent latent correlations and one-headed arrows represent regression paths with the outcome variables receiving the arrowhead

2. METHOD

2.1 Participants

This study relies on a convenience sample of 812 Italian high school students (12th and 13th Grades; 486 males and 326 females, *M*age = 18.3, *SD* = .89). Each student received a parental consent form, with information about the study. On the testing date, active consent was sought from the students. The participants anonymously completed the questionnaires in 20-minute group sessions, during school hours. Confidentiality was guaranteed.

2.2 Measures

All participants completed an Italian version of the value scale (Fadda *et al.*, 2018). This version includes 37 items (e.g., *Math is fun to me*) measuring 9 specific factors (intrinsic, ω = .97; importance of achievement, ω = .86; personal importance, ω = .62; utility for school/job, ω = .90; utility for life, ω = .97; social utility, ω = .96; effort required, ω = .93; opportunity cost, ω = .97; emotional cost, ω = .95) and one global value factor (ω = .99). Items were rated on a 6-point Likert scale (1 = *strongly disagree* to 6 = *completely agree*).

Participants also completed the mastery (e.g., *I want to learn as much as possible from this class*; ω = .99) and performance approach (e.g., *My goal in this class is to get a better grade than most of the other students*; ω = .99) scales of the Achievement goals questionnaire (Elliott and McGregor, 2001) applied to mathematics (6 items; 1 = *false* to 6 = *true*).

Expectancy was measured by five items (e.g., *I find many mathematical problems interesting and challenging*; Likert scale from 1 = *false* to 6 = *true*; ω = .99) of the mathematics scale from the Self-Description Questionnaire (SDQ-II; Marsh, 1992). As regards the outcome variables, career aspirations were measured by three items (e.g., *I expect to work in a job uses science*; ω = .99), with a 6-point response scale (from 1 = *strongly disagree* to 6 = *completely agree*), taken from the Program for International Student Assessment (OECD, 2006, 2007). A score of mathematics competence (from 0 to 5) was computed by the sum of the responses to a logical-mathematical test composed of five items, with five-answer options scored as dichotomous (correct/incorrect).

2.3 Analyses

Within a structural equation modeling framework (SEM; Bollen, 1989), we contrasted alternative latent models using Mplus 7.3 (Muthén and Muthén, 2014) with robust maximum likelihood (MLR) estimator and Full Information Maximum Likelihood (FIML; Enders, 2010) to handle missing data present at the item level (0.1% to 1.7%, *M* = 0.7%). A SEM model allows the researcher to examine at the same time several links (correlations or regression paths) among various variables by taking into account the measurement error that in regular analyses based on scale scores could bias the results. In standardized solutions, as the ones reported here, all latent variables are set with a variance equal to 1 and this allows to interpret correlations and betas as in regular analyses based on scale scores. Therefore, for correlations and betas, values close to zero indicate absence of association, whereas values close to one indicate very strong relations, and values around .5 indicate moderate relations among the variables. The ability of the model to fit the data is measured with various indices (e.g., CFI, TLI) and in predictive models it is possible to evaluate how much variance of the outcomes can be explained by the predictors (R2). Comparison between alternative models provides, therefore, an effective way to study relationships between the variables taking into account the measurement error.

Following Marsh and Scalas taxonomy (2008), first, we tested a measurement model in which all factors are merely correlated (model 0). Second, to ensure the same degree of complexity (equivalent number of estimated parameters, degrees of freedom and fit indices), the predictive models were built as follows: 1) the full prediction model includes effects (path coefficients) of expectancy, value, and goals variables on the outcomes; 2) the expectancy-value prediction model includes effects of expectancy-value on the outcomes and correlations between goals and outcomes; 3) the achievement goals prediction model includes effects of goals on the outcomes and correlations between expectancy-value and outcomes (see Table 1). Moreover, to examine the change in fit associated to the release of specific betas, we tested complementary solutions to models 2 and 3. In particular, in relation to model 2, we changed covariances to paths and we fixed the goals paths to be zero (model2a); in relation to model 3, we changed covariances to paths and fixed the expectancy-value paths to be zero (model3a).

We examined the total variance explained by the predictors (R^2) and the following goodness-of-fit indexes: the chi-square (χ^2) test of exact fit, the comparative fit index (CFI), the Tucker–Lewis Index (TLI), and the root mean square error of approximation (RMSEA). CFI and TLI vary from 0 to 1, with values close to 1 indicating a better fit. For RMSEA, values lower than .06 indicate a potentially better fit (Hu and Bentler, 1999), although no golden rules have been established (Marsh, Hau and Wen, 2004). To test differences among nested models (1, 2a, 3a), we computed the Satorra-Bentler scaled chi-square difference test ($\Delta\chi^2$) based on scaling correction factors obtained with the MLR estimator (Satorra and Bentler, 2010).

Table 1. Taxonomy of models used. Each path coefficient is freely estimated (free) or specified as a covariance rather than a regression path (0)

Model	Expectancy	Value	Mastery goals	Performance goals
Measurement	0	0	0	0
Full	free	free	free	free
Expectancy-value	free	free	0	0
Achievement goals	0	0	free	free

3. RESULTS

3.1 Structure of Value and Goals Scales

In line with the Italian validation (Fadda *et al.*, 2018) the value beliefs scale in math was measured including a bifactor component to the exploratory structural equation modeling (ESEM; Morin, Arens and Marsh, 2016). This solution allows items to reflect both a global overarching construct (G-factor) and its specific components. The bifactor-ESEM solution was estimated using a bifactor orthogonal target rotation (Reise, 2012) in which all cross-loadings were "targeted" to be close to zero, whereas all the main loadings were freely estimated as in the CFA model. The model showed adequate fit indices (χ^2= 523.265; *df* = 340; CFI = .988; TLI = .977; RMSEA = .026).

Since the Achievement goals questionnaire (Elliott and McGregor, 2001) applied to mathematics was not validated in the Italian context, we tested the measurement model with CFA procedures. Results showed adequate fit indices (χ^2 = 52.972; *df* = 8; CFI = .972; TLI = .948; RMSEA = .083) and factor loading ranged from .56 to .86 for the mastery approach scale and from .80 to .89 for the performance approach scale. Intercorrelation was r = .50. Finally, a latent model of the logical-mathematical test showed adequate fit indices (χ^2 = 10.114; *df* = 5; CFI = .987; TLI = .974; RMSEA = .036), factor loadings (from .42 to .58) and reliability (ω = .97).

3.2 Models Comparison

In the measurement model all the factors (expectancy-value, achievement goals, scientific career interest, mathematics achievement) are allowed to be correlated without positing causal ordering. Results showed adequate fit indices (CFI = 972; TLI = .959; RMSEA = .030). Correlations among the variables are showed in Table 2.

Table 2. Measurement model correlations. ** p < .01; * p < .05

	Career interest	Math achievement	Mastery goals	Performance goals	Expectancy
Career interest	1				
Math achievement	.354**	1			
Mastery goals	.413**	.183**	1		
Performance goals	.262**	.083*	.501**	1	
Expectancy	.429**	.401**	.461**	.446**	1
Global value	.335**	.083*	.574**	.383**	.463**
intrinsic	.206**	.255**		.148**	.597**
importance of achievement			.118*	.161**	.124**
personal importance			.276**		
utility for school/job			-.132*	-.114*	-.134**
utility for life		-.101*	-.079*	-.101*	
social utility				.387**	
effort required			.168**		-.126**
opportunity cost	.304**	.239**	.304**	.109**	.182**
emotional cost	.241**		.298**	.103*	.135**

Models 1, 2 and 3 present the same number of estimated parameters, degrees of freedom, and fit indices as the measurement model (see Table 3). However, some relations between the predictors and the outcomes are expressed as betas in some models and as correlations in other models. Therefore, it is possible to distinguish between total and unique variance explained by different sets of predictors. The expectancy-value prediction model showed that a substantial amount of variance can be explained by these factors, whereas the variance explained by the achievement goals prediction model is smaller but still statistically significant (see Table 3).

The chi-square difference test based on the difference between the full model and the other nested models (2a and 3a) showed a statistically significant difference for the achievement goals model (model 3a). In this model the effects of expectancy-values variables on outcomes were excluded. On the contrary, no significant chi-square difference was found comparing the full model with for model 2a, where the effects of goals were set to zero (see Table 3).

Table 3. Models fit indices and explained variance of outcomes. Scf is the scaling correction factor for MLR; R^2 is the variance in the outcomes explained by predictor variables; the chi-square difference test ($\Delta\chi^2$) is based on the difference between the full model and each nested model.** p < .01; * p < .05

Model	χ^2	df	scf	CFI	TLI	RMSEA	R^2 Math achievement	R^2 Career interest	$\Delta\chi^2$ (df)
0	1613.238	926	1.186	.972	.959	.030	N/A	N/A	
1	1613.238	926	1.186	.972	.959	.030	.228**	.328**	
2	1613.238	926	1.186	.972	.959	.030	.222**	.326**	
3	1613.238	926	1.186	.972	.959	.030	.034**	.175*	
2a	1618.931	930	1.186	.972	.959	.030			5.692 (4)
3a	1789.257	948	1.191	.965	.951	.033			155.341 (12)**

Concerning effects of predictors on the outcomes, results showed that in the full model, goals did not affect scientific career interest and math achievement of students. Scientific career interest was positively predicted by global value and its dimensions related to cost (opportunity and emotional cost). Math achievement was positively predicted by expectancy and opportunity cost; negatively predicted by utility for life (see Table 4).

The expectancy-value prediction model in which the coefficients of mastery and performance goals were specified as covariances rather than paths, showed pattern of results similar to the full model. Scientific career interest was positively predicted by global value, opportunity and emotional cost. Math achievement was positively predicted by expectancy and opportunity cost; negatively predicted by global value and utility for life (see Table 4). In the achievement goals prediction model, where only goals influences were allowed, scientific career interest and math achievement were predicted by mastery goals (see Table 4).

Table 4. Effects of predictors on the outcomes in the model tested. Model 1: full model; model 2: expectancy-value prediction model; model 3: achievement goals prediction model. Only significant coefficients are reported in this table In bold are path coefficients; non-bold values represent covariances. ** p<.01; *p<.05

	Career interest			Math achievement		
	Model 1	Model 2	Model 3	Model 1	Model 2	Model 3
Mastery goals			**.376****			**.189****
Performance goals					-.067	
Expectancy			.245**	**.447****	**.412****	.324**
Global value	**.224****	**.267****	.100**		**-.107***	
intrinsic			.191**			.250**
importance of achievement						
personal importance						
utility for school/job						
utility for life				**-.088***	**-.078***	-.089*
social utility						
effort required						
opportunity cost	**.256****	**.277****	.200**	**.176****	**.164****	.186**
emotional cost	**.199****	**.221****	.133*			

4. DISCUSSION

Achievement goals theory (e.g., Elliot, 1999) and expectancy-value models (e.g., Eccles *et al.*, 1983) are both important to understand motivation and achievement, but rarely they have been integrated in the same study (e.g., Conley, 2012; Hulleman *et al.*, 2008; Plante *et al.*, 2013), therefore their relationship remains unclear.

Our main aim was to explore alternative models to understand the weight of expectancy-value and goals in predicting career interest and math achievement. Specifically, we contrasted a taxonomy of models to disentangle the role of these factors: 1) a full model where all the factors contribute to the explanation of the outcomes' variance, 2) one model in which we evaluated the specific contribution of expectancy-value, and 3) another model in which we examined the specific contribution of achievement goals factors. Based on Marsh and Scalas (2018) study, we have evaluated the change in the explained variance in each one of the tested models.

Results showed that much of the variance in the outcomes that can be explained by the full model can also be explained by the expectancy-value model alone. This result is inconsistent with Conley (2012) study in a middle school students' sample that supported the importance of considering both goals and value to improve math achievement predictions. In the achievement goals prediction model the variance explained by predictors is considerably smaller, especially with regards to math achievement, and the chi-square difference test showed that this model fits significantly worse than the full model if expectancy-value variables are excluded as predictors. Moreover, in the full model, we did not find any influence of mastery or performance goals on the outcomes. Therefore, results suggested that to understand math competence and scientific career interest outcomes, approach-related achievement goals applied to mathematics do not add much to what can already be explained in terms of expectancy and value.

A possible interpretation comes from the expectancy-value theory (Eccles, 2005; Eccles *et al.*, 1983; Wigfield and Eccles, 1992). According to this conception, task value is a motivational construct subordinated in respect to achievement goals, which should be considered general directions of behaviors (e.g., preference for challenging or competitive tasks; Maehr and Zusho, 2009). In academic domain, longitudinal studies supported the predictive effect of mastery goals on value and the mediation role of intrinsic and utility value on school performance (Harackiewicz *et al.*, 2002, 2008; Hulleman *et al.*, 2008; Pintrich *et al.*, 1998; Wolters *et al.*, 1996). Therefore, goals could act on achievement-related outcomes not directly but via more specific expectancy and value variables.

Consistent with previous literature, where expectancy showed a strong influence on achievement and value influenced choice, effort, and persistence in achievement-related activities (e.g., Eccles and Wigfield, 2002; Marsh *et al.*, 2013), in the present study, a high global value placed on math positively influenced student's career aspirations in science, and expectancy resulted the main predictor of math competence.

Moreover, it should be noted that to perceive high costs in term of time lost for other activities (i.e., opportunity cost) brings students to greater mathematics achievement and scientific career plans. Results showed also, in both models, a negative influence of utility for life on mathematics achievement; this dimension composed of different life domains, from short-term (such as daily routines and leisure time activities) to long term utility (such as unspecified future life activities) has an instrumental nature and it captures the extrinsic motivation for engagement and achievement in a specific task (Ryan and Deci, 2009).

5. CONCLUSION

Our findings based on the comparison of alternative models showed that expectancy-value variables explain a substantial portions of math achievement and career interest variance in respect to achievement goals. Moreover, although caution is required to infer causality from self-reports measures, value and its dimensions resulted the only variables influencing student's career aspiration, and consistent with previous literature expectancy resulted the principal predictor of math competence in the high school context. It should be noted, that we considered students attending the last class of high school, thus it is possible that younger students might have fewer concrete ideas about their future and thus general goals could be more predictive of specific outcomes. Finally, our items were limited to the domain of mathematics and future research might expand model comparison to other academic domains.

Overall, our results suggest that although the study of approach-related achievement goals and their promotion in long-term researches are important for the development of the youth's motivation system, in applied studies, for researchers interested in direct promotion of the high school students' mathematics achievement or future intentions regarding scientific career, it would be more useful to focus interventions on expectancy-value variables.

REFERENCES

Bollen, K.A., 1989. *Structural Equations with Latent Variables*. John Wiley & Sons, New York.

Conley, A. M. (2012). Patterns of motivation beliefs: Combining achievement goal and expectancy-value perspectives. *Journal of Educational Psychology*, Vol. 104, pp.32-47.

DeBacker, T.K. and Nelson, R.M. 1999. Variations on an expectancy-value model of motivation in science. *Contemporary Educational Psychology,* Vol. 24, pp.71-94.

Eccles, J.S., 2005. Subjective task-value and the Eccles et al. model of achievement-related choices. In A.J. Elliot & C.S. Dweck (Eds.), *Handbook of competence and motivation* (pp. 105–121). Guilford, New York, NY.

Eccles, J.S., 2009. Who am I and what am I going to do with my life? Personal and collective identities as motivators of action. *Educational Psychologist,* Vol. 44, pp.78-89.

Eccles, J.S. et al, 1983. Expectancies, values and academic behaviors. In J.T. Spence, (Ed.), *Achievement and achievement motives* (pp.75-146). Freeman, San Francisco.

Eccles, J.S. and Wigfield, A., 2002. Motivational beliefs, values, and goals. *Annual Review of Psychology,* Vol. 53, pp.109-132.

Elliot, A.J., 1999. Approach and avoidance motivation and achievement goals. *Educational Psychologist,* Vol. 34, pp.149-169.

Elliot, A.J., 2006. The hierarchical model of approach-avoidance motivation. *Motivation and Emotion,* Vol. 30, pp. 111-116.

Elliot, A.J. and McGregor, H., 2001. A 2x2 achievement goal framework. *Journal of Personality and Social Psychology,* Vol. 80, pp.501-509.

Elliot, A.J. and Murayama, K., 2008. On the measurement of achievement goals: Critique, illustration, and application. *Journal of Educational Psychology,* Vol. 100, pp. 613-628.

Enders, C., 2010. Applied missing data analysis. Guilford Press, New York.

Fadda, D. et al, 2019. Value beliefs about math: a bifactor-ESEM representation. *European Journal of Psychological Assessment.*

Greene, B.A. et al, 1999. Goals, values, and beliefs as predictors of achievement and effort in high school mathematics classes. *Sex Roles,* Vol. 40, pp. 421-458.

Greene, B.A. et al, 2004. Predicting high school students' cognitive engagement and achievement: Contributions of classroom perceptions and motivation. *Contemporary Educational Psychology,* Vol. 29, pp. 462-482.

Guo, J. et al, 2015. Directionality of the associations of high school expectancy-value, aspirations, and attainment: a longitudinal study. *American Educational Research Journal,* Vol. 52, pp. 371-402.

Harackiewicz, J.M. et al, 2002. Revision of achievement goal theory: Necessary and illuminating. *Journal of Educational Psychology,* Vol. 94, pp. 638-645.

Harackiewicz, J.M. et al, 2008. The role of achievement goals in the development of interest: Reciprocal relations between achievement goals, interest, and performance. *Journal of Educational Psychology,* Vol. 100, pp. 105-122.

Hu, L. and Bentler, P.M., 1999. Cutoff criteria for fit indexes in covariance structure analysis: Conventional criteria versus new alternatives. *Structural Equation Modeling,* Vol. 6, pp. 1-55.

Hulleman, C.S. et al, 2008. Task values, achievement goals, and interest: An integrative analysis. *Journal of Educational Psychology,* Vol. 100, pp. 398-416.

Liem, A.D. et al, 2008. The role of self-efficacy, task value, and achievement goals in predicting learning strategies, task disengagement, peer relationship, and achievement outcome. *Contemporary Educational Psychology,* Vol. 33, pp. 486-512.

Maehr, M.L. and Zusho, A., 2009. Achievement goal theory: The past, present, and future. In K. R. Wentzel & A. Wigfield (Eds.), *Handbook of motivation in school* (pp. 77-104). Taylor Francis, New York.

Marsh, H.W., 1992. *Self-Description Questionnaire III: A theoretical and empirical basis for the measurement of multiple dimensions of adolescent self-concept*: A test manual and research monograph. Macarthur, Australia.

Marsh, H.W. and Scalas, L.F., 2018. Individually weighted-average models: testing a taxonomic sem approach across different multidimensional/global constructs because the weights "Don't make no nevermind". *Structural Equation Modeling: A Multidisciplinary Journal*, Vol. 25, pp. 137-159.

Marsh, H.W. et al, 2004. In search of golden rules: comment on hypothesis-testing approaches to setting cutoff values for fit indexes and dangers in overgeneralizing Hu and Bentler's (1999) findings. *Structural Equation Modeling,* Vol. 11, pp. 320-341.

Marsh, H.W. et al, 2013. Moderation. In T.D. Little (Ed.), *The Oxford handbook of quantitative methods* (pp.361-386). Oxford University Press, Oxford.

Meece, J.L. et al, 2006. Classroom goal structure, student motivation, and academic achievement. *Annual Review of Psychology,* Vol. 57, pp. 487-503.

Miller, R.B. et al, 1999. Perceived instrumentality and academics: The link to task valuing. *Contemporary Educational Psychology,* Vol. 24, p. 250-260.

Morin, A.J.S. et al, 2016. A bifactor exploratory structural equation modeling framework for the identification of distinct sources of construct-relevant psychometric multidimensionality. *Structural Equation Modeling,* Vol. 23, pp. 116-139.

Muthén, L.K. and Muthén, B.O., 2014. *Mplus user's guide*. Muthén & Muthén, Los Angeles.

Organization-for-Economic-Co-operation-and-Development–OECD, 2006. *Evolution of Student Interest in Science and Technology Studies*. Paris: Author.

Organization-for-Economic-Co-operation-and-Development–OECD, 2007. *PISA-2006 science competencies for tomorrow's world.* Paris: Author.

Pintrich, P.R., 2003. A motivational science perspective on the role of student motivation in learning and teaching contexts. *Journal of Educational Psychology*, Vol., 95, pp. 667-686.

Pintrich, P.R. et al, 1998. The differential impact of task value and mastery orientation on males' and females' self-regulated learning. In L. Hoffman, A. Krapp, K.A. Renninger and J. Baumert (Eds.), *Interest and learning: Proceedings of the Seeon conference on interest and gender.* Institute for Science Education Press, Kiel, Germany.

Pintrich, P.R. et al, 1993. Reliability and predictive validity of the motivational strategies for learning questionnaire. *Educational and Psychological Measurement,* Vol., 53, pp. 801-813.

Plante, I. et al, 2013. The relation between achievement goal and expectancy-value theories in predicting achievement-related outcomes: A test of four theoretical conceptions. *Motivation and Emotion,* Vol., 37, pp. 65-78.

Reise, S.P., 2012. The rediscovery of bifactor measurement models. *Multivariate Behavioral Research*, Vol. 47, pp. 667-696.

Ryan, R.M. and Deci, E.L., 2009. Promoting self-determined school engagement: Motivation, learning, and well-being. In K.R. Wentzel & A. Wigfield (Eds.), *Handbook of motivation in school* (pp. 171-196). Taylor Francis, New York.

Satorra, A. and Bentler, P.M., 2010. *Psychometrika*. Vol. 75, pp. 243-248.

Scalas, L.F. et al, 2014. Importance models of the physical self: improved methodology fails to support the Jamesian model and provides support for a normative importance model. *European Journal of Social Psychology,* Vol., 44, pp. 154-174.

Simpkins, S.D. et al, 2006. Math and science motivation: A longitudinal examination of the links between choices and beliefs. *Developmental Psychology,* Vol., 42, pp. 70-83.

Watt, H.M.G. et al, 2012. Gendered motivational processes affecting high school mathematics participation, educational aspirations, and career plans: A comparison of samples from Australia, Canada, and the United States. *Developmental Psychology,* Vol., 48, pp. 1594-1611.

Wigfield, A. et al, 2000. *Relations of children's achievement values and achievement goal orientations.* Paper presented at the annual meeting of the American Educational Research Association, New Orleans.

Wigfield, A. and Cambria J., 2010. Students' achievement values, goal orientations, and interest: definitions, development, and relations to achievement outcomes. *Developmental Review,* Vol. 30, pp. 1-35.

Wigfield, A. and Eccles J., 1992. The development of achievement task values: A theoretical analysis. *Developmental Review,*Vol. 12, pp. 265-310.

Wolters, C.A. et al, 1996. The relation between goal orientation and students' motivational regulation and their use of learning strategies, effort, and classroom performance. *Learning and Individual Differences,* Vol. 8, pp. 211-239.

THE RELATION BETWEEN SELF-DISCLOSURE OF STUDENTS TO THEIR PARENTS AND MATHEMATICS SCORE IN COMPUTER-BASED NATIONAL EXAM (UNBK)

Moch Abduh[1], Bagus Hary Prakoso[1], Dian Rahdiani[1] and Jaka Warsihna[2]
[1]*Centre for Educational Assessment, Ministry of Education and Culture*
Jl. Gunung Sahari Raya No. 4, Jakarta, 10710, Indonesia
[2]*Institute of Research and Community Service (LPPM), Indonesia Open University*
Jl. Cabe Raya Tangerang Selatan, 15418, Indonesia

ABSTRACT

One of non-cognitive factors which has not been optimally explored in supporting academic achievement was self-disclosure. To overcome that problem, the purpose of this study is to examine the relation between students' self-disclosure to their parents and the mathematics score achievement in the Computer-Based National Exam (UNBK) program. This study used descriptive analysis and correlation analysis as a research method. The study used the mathematics score of Junior High School (SMP) and Islamic Junior High School (MTs) students in 2018 UNBK in DKI Jakarta and DI Yogyakarta provinces as samples. The study shows that (1) there is a positive relation between students' self-disclosure to their parents and mathematics score achievement, and (2) students with low self-disclosure had a greater risk of achieving mathematics scores in the low category. The findings of this study are expected to extend the contribution of self-disclosure in enhancing academic achievement, and the development of a self-disclosure instrument for UNBK questionnaire.

KEYWORDS

Self-Disclosure, Mathematics Scores, Computer-Based National Exam

1. INTRODUCTION

The National Exam (UN) is an activity to measure graduates 'competency achievement in certain subjects nationally by referring to Graduates' Competency Standards (SKL). The activities of learning outcomes assessment in education units are carried out by the Ministry of Education and Culture (Kemdikbud) of the Republic of Indonesia every year (Kemdikbud Regulation no. 4 year of 2018).

Since the 2015 school year, the implementation of the National Exam (UN) has applied the Computer Based Test (CBT) mode. In Indonesia program, it is known as the Computer-Based National Examination (UNBK). The implementation of UNBK as a substitute for Paper-Based National Exam (UNKP) which aim to improve efficiency (Sudiyarto, 2018), be more educated and challenging (Belloti, et al (2013), improve the quality of exam (Nizam, 2018), and be more efficient, transparent and has the ability to minimize fraud in cognitive evaluation (Nugroho, et al. 2018).

Indonesia is the largest archipelago with more than 13 thousand islands, has approximately 8.3 million students of secondary school students (formal and non-formal). As of March 11, 2019, the use of UNBK mode has reached 90.0% (http://un.kemdikbud. go.id). In UNBK for Junior High School (SMP) and Islamic Junior High School (MTs), there are 4 subjects tested, namely: Indonesian, English, Science, and Mathematics. The National Exam Results Report 2015-2019 stated that the achievement of mathematics average score is always at the lowest level compared with three other subjects, both for junior and senior high school levels (https://puspendik.kemdikbud.go.id/hasil-un/). This is very exciting and to be the reason for the study linking to the UNBK questionnaire containing self-disclosure items.

The contents of the 2017/2018 UNBK questionnaire seemed to reflect the definition of self-disclosure as verbal communication in private information, individual concepts and emotions conducted by individuals for making the other party understood (Wei et al. 2005). Furthermore, how the non-cognitive questionnaire (self-disclosure) in UNBK becomes pivotal instrument to support academic achievement as Garcia (2014) stated. To explore among mathematics score, questionnaire result, and self-disclosure concepts, furthermore the research findings are included.

The research findings outside Indonesia by Harper, V. B., & Harper, E. J. (2006) connecting with the role of blogging stated that student self-disclosure plays an important role in learning and producing positive learning outcomes. This study provided an indication that blogging encouragement was student self-disclosure. Other research on self-disclosure contribution stated that many authors suggest that self-disclosure plays a critical role in student participation (Goldstein & Benassi, 1994), facilitating student teacher interaction (Fusani, 1994), and achieving learning objectives (Cayanus, 2004 ; Downs, Javidi, & Nussbaum, 1988; Sorenson, 1989).

The research finding in Indonesia connecting to the UNBK mathematics scores by Azis and Sugiman (2015) stated that the cognitive aspects consisting of factual, conceptual, and procedural knowledge have generated indications of varied categories (low, medium, and high). On the affective aspects (personal students in social interaction, manners and respect for teachers) to face the national exam were generally in the low category.

The concept and characteristic of self-disclosure are very varied. According to Devito (2011) in self-disclosure there were five dimensions such as: amount, valence self-disclosure, accuracy/honesty, intention, and intimacy. The type of dimension consists of 6 indicators, namely: attitudes and opinions, tastes and interests, school, finance, personality, and physical (Jourard, 1971). In Indonesia educational practice, the age of junior high school students can be categorized as teenagers with the age range of 12 years to 15 years (Monks & Knoer, 2006). At this period, the child within the developmental period is looking for an identity. They need mentoring parents as a place to share feelings and exchange ideas. Williams & Burden (1997) used a term "mediator" for parent role that will affect children's cognitive development.

Regarding those concepts, research results, and to increase the mathematics score in UNBK, it is necessary to explore and strengthen the concept of self-disclosure through the UNBK questionnaire by verifying and comparing the cases. Based on the background of the problems, the purpose of this study is to examine the relation between self-disclosure of students towards their parents and mathematics scores at UNBK program. The results of this study are expected to be fruitful for policy recommendations about the importance of the self-disclosure role as supporting academic achievement in non-cognitive aspect.

2. RESEARCH METHOD

This study uses description analysis and correlation analysis supported by survey methods, where only a portion of the selected population units is observed (samples), and the unit selection procedure follows scientific method and procedures (Safari, 2018). Questionnaires have been used to reveal and measure the variables of student self-disclosure to parents. The questionnaires were completed on the last day of the UNBK implementation and were filled directly using a computer.

2.1 Population and Sample

The population of this study was the 9th grade junior high school (SMP) students who undertook in the 2018 UNBK in the province (DKI Jakarta and DI Yogyakarta) that has implemented a 100% UNBK program. The UNBK implementation is carried out in its own school or through facility sharing programs (see Figure 1, Figure 2, and Table 1).

Not all the UN participant students can access and fill out the UN questionnaire. Only students who attend UNBK can fill in the questionnaire. Sample determination with Slovin technique (Sugiono, 2011) consisted of representatives of 20 students in each the UNBK participating school. Here is the Slovin formula to determine the sample.

$$n = \frac{N}{1+N(e)^2}$$

Note:
n = number of sample / respondent; N = number of population
E = percentage of accuracy on sampling errors that can still be tolerated; e = 0,1

In the Slovin formula there are provisions as follows: the value of e = 0.1 (10%) for the population in large numbers and the value of e = 0.2 (20%) for the population in small numbers. The sample range that can be taken from Slovin techniques is between 10-20% of the study population. Based on data from UNBK 2017 there were 3.6559.696 students. If using the Slovin formula obtained value n = Population: (N) = 3.6559.696 people assuming the error rate (e) = 10% then the number of samples (n) is n = 99.99 = 100.

The data of participant schools in 2017 UNBK was 11.096. If the sample from each school is 20 questionnaires, then the questionnaire data that will be collected is 20 x 11.096 = 220,192 questionnaires. If all of this data is analyzed, it will be a big sample.

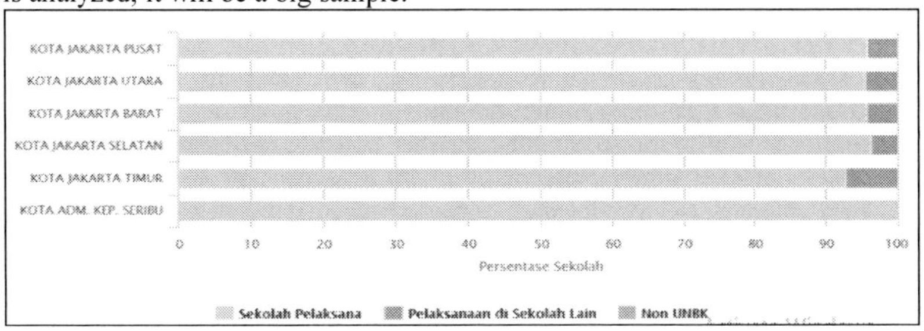

Figure 1. School Percentage in DKI Jakarta that carry outs UNBK

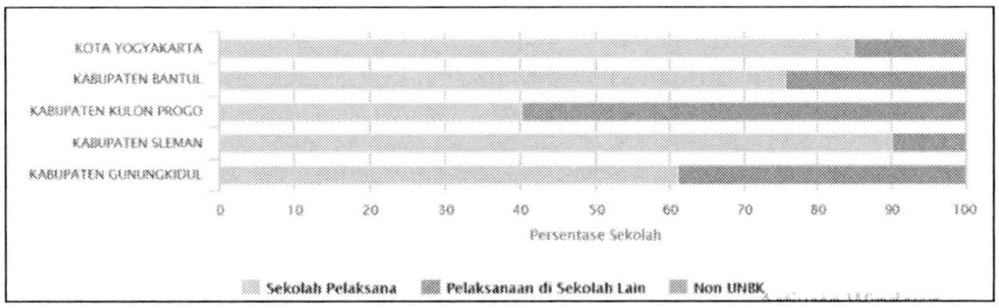

Figure 2. School Percentage in DI Yogyakarta that carry outs UNBK

Table 1. Respondent

Province	Number of Respondent
DKI Jakarta	10.996
DI Yogyakarta	5.854

2.2 Score Category

Table 2. Mathematics Score in UNBK

Score Category	DKI Jakarta		DI Yogyakarta	
	Number of Student	%	Number of Student	%
Less = 0.0 – 55	7009	63.8%	3061	52.4%
Enough = 55.1 – 70	1499	13.6%	1035	17.7%
Good = 70.1 – 85	1331	**12.1%**	852	**14.6%**
Very Good = 85.1 – 100	1157	**10.5%**	897	**15.3%**
Total	10996	100%	5845	100%

2.3 Research Instrument

This study uses instruments applied in the 2017/2018 UNBK questionnaire. The variables used were questions related to students' self-disclosure to their parents, namely:

Table 3. Self-Disclosure Instrument

8a	How often have you done the following things with your parents?	Tell activities with your friends	Always	Often	Rarely	Never
8b		Discuss lessons at school	Always	Often	Rarely	Never
8c		Discuss the tasks from the teacher	Always	Often	Rarely	Never
8d		Tells stories about events at school	Always	Often	Rarely	Never
8e		Discuss about the personal things you feel	Always	Often	Rarely	Never

Source: Ministry of Education and Culture

3. RESULT AND DISCUSSION

3.1 Frequency of Student Response Patterns

Based on table 4 and table 5 can be obtained the most prominent of self-disclosure activities data, namely: (1) telling activities with friends showed that the smallest percentage of **never** answers (5.2% for DKI Jakarta students, and 3.5% for DI Yogyakarta students), (2) discussion of lessons in schools shows that the largest percentage of **rare** answers (43.8% for DKI Jakarta students and 43.6% for DI Yogyakarta students), (3) discuss the tasks from the teacher indicate that the largest percentage of **rare** answers (49% for DKI Jakarta students and 51.8% for DI Yogyakarta students), (4) telling stories about events in schools show that the largest percentage of **often** answers (40.9% for DKI Jakarta students and 43.1% for DI Yogyakarta students), (5) discussion activities about something personal shows that the smallest percentage of **rare** answer (41% for DKI Jakarta never and 45,6% for DI Yogyakarta students), and (6) in general, the comparative tables show that both SMP/MTs students in DKI Jakarta and DI Yogyakarta have **similar pattern** in determining the answers.

Table 4. The frequency table of students' self-disclosure to parents in DKI Jakarta

Instru-ment	Tell activities with your friends		Discuss lessons at school		Discuss the tasks from the teacher		Tells stories about events at school		Discuss about the personal things	
Answer	Respondent	%	Respondent	%	Respondent	%	Respondent	%	Respondent	%
DKI Jakarta Province										
Never	569	**5.2**	658	6	1093	9.9	631	5.7	1755	**16**
Rarely	4085	37.1	4813	**43.8**	5384	**49**	3531	32.1	4509	41
Often	4116	37.5	3969	36	3381	30.8	4492	**40.9**	2884	**26.2**
Always	2226	20.2	1556	14.2	1138	10.3	2342	**21.3**	1848	**16.8**
Total	10996	100	10996	100	10996	100	10996	100	10996	100

Table 5. The frequency table of students' self-disclosure to their in DI Yogyakarta

Instru-ment	Tell activities with your friends		Discuss lessons at school		Discuss the tasks from the teacher		Tells stories about events at school		Discuss about the personal things	
Answer	Respondent	%	Respondent	%	Respondent	%	Respondent	%	Respondent	%
DI Yogyakarta Province										
Never	205	**3.5**	275	4.7	464	7.9	237	4.1	630	**10.8**
Rarely	2247	38.5	2550	**43.6**	3023	**51.8**	2099	35.9	2667	45.6
Often	2481	42.4	2342	40.1	1908	32.6	2523	**43.1**	1755	**30**
Always	912	15.6	678	11.6	450	7.7	986	**16.9**	793	**13.6**
Total	5845	100	5845	100	5845	100	5845	100	5845	100

3.2 Self Disclosure Index

In this study, the self disclosure index is categorized into three categories: high, medium, and low level. In general, the activities of students' self-disclosure to their parents are in the medium category (around 74% for DKI Jakarta SMP/MTS students and around 64.2% for DI Yogyakarta SMP/MTs students).

It is shown that 15.7% of SMP/MTs students in DKI Jakarta and 16.2% of SMP/MTs students in DI Yogyakarta belong to the high category. In the low category, there are 10.3% for SMP/MTS students in DKI Jakarta and 19.7% for SMP/MTs students in DI Yogyakarta. Furthermore, the activities of self-disclosure of SMP/MTs students in DKI Jakarta and DI Yogyakarta towards their parents are fairly transparent generally.

3.3 Correlation Test

Correlation test is applied to examine of how the relation between student self disclosure to parents and the mathematics score achievement in DKI Jakarta and DI Yogyakarta Provinces, by using hypothesis:
H0 = There is no relation between student self disclosure to parents and mathematics score achievement.
H1 = There is relation between student self disclosure to parents and mathematics score achievement.
Criteria: H0 is rejected if the p-value <α (5%).

The analysis results show that between students' self-disclosure to parents and the mathematics score in Yogyakarta has a significant score of 0.000, whereas for DKI Jakarta has a significant score of 0.007. Both provinces have a significant score of <0.05, which means that there is a significant correlation between students' self-disclosure to their parents and the mathematics scores both in DKI Jakarta and in Yogyakarta. The score of the Pearson coefficient correlation is 0.026 for DKI Jakarta and 0.132 for DI Yogyakarta. These results indicate that the high self-disclosure of students to their parents have a positive impact on the mathematics score achievement (see Table 6).

Table 6. Correlation score of between student'self-disclosure to parents and mathematics score

	DKI Jakarta	**DI Yogyakarta**
Correlation	.026 (**)	.132 (**)
Sig. (2-tailed)	.007	.000

** Correlation is significant at the 0.01 level (2-tailed).

3.4 Odds Ratio Test

Table 7. Odds Ratio Index Category on Self Disclosure and Mathematics Score

Mathematics Score Category		Category Index of Self Disclosure for DKI Jakarta			Total	Category Index of Self Disclosure for DI Yogyakarta			Total
		Low	Medium	High		Low	Medium	High	
Less = 0 – 55	Total	750	5206	1053	7009	726	1930	405	3061
	%	66.3%	64.0%	60.9%	63.7%	63.1%	51.5%	42.9%	52.4%
Enough = 55.1 – 70	Total	132	1116	251	1499	171	672	192	1035
	%	11.7%	13.7%	14.5%	13.6%	14.9%	17.9%	20.3%	17.7%
Good = 70.1 – 85	Total	123	989	219	1331	131	552	169	852
	%	10.9%	12.2%	12.7%	12.1%	11.4%	14.7%	17.9%	14.6%
Very Good = 85.1– 100	Total	126	826	205	1157	122	596	179	897
	%	11.1%	10.2%	11.9%	10.5%	10.6%	15.9%	18.9%	15.3%
TOTAL	Total	1131	8137	1728	10996	1150	3750	945	5845
	%	100.0%	100.0%	100.0%	100.0%	100.0%	100.0%	100.0%	100.0%

Table 7 shows that SMP/MTs students in DKI Jakarta with low category index of self-disclosure have the opportunity/risk to obtain mathematics scores in the low category is 6-fold (66.3%: 11.1%) compared to achieve mathematics score in high category. Likewise the SMP/MTs students in DI Yogyakarta with low category index of self-disclosure have the opportunity/risk to achieve mathematics scores in low category is 6-fold compared to achieve mathematics score in high category. Those comparative data indicate that both SMP/MTs students in DKI Jakarta and DI Yogyakarta who have low self-disclosure have a greater risk to achieve mathematics score in low category.

Table 8. Comparison of UNBK mathematics score in self-disclosure activities

Self-Disclosure Statements	Answer	DKI Jakarta			DI Yogyakarta		
		Respondent	Average Score	Standard Deviation	Respondent	Average Score	Standard Deviation
Tell activities with your friends (Linying & Huichang, 2003)	Never	569	42.4692	18.90340	205	50.6585	21.38422
	Rarely	4085	49.7693	21.36575	2247	54.5216	21.10165
	Often	4116	54.7923	22.61838	2481	60.7537	21.82722
	Always	2226	51.3017	22.22039	912	61.1157	22.05941
	Total	10996	51.5819	22.10880	5845	58.0603	21.82672
Discuss lessons at school Dindia and Duck (2000)	Never	658	50.7594	22.89300	275	55.3182	21.23714
	Rarely	4813	52.6449	21.99037	2550	55.8265	21.34206
	Often	3969	51.4766	22.29433	2342	60.3544	22.10991
	Always	1556	47.6560	21.36035	678	59.6497	21.95354
	Total	10996	51.5819	22.10880	5845	58.0603	21.82672
Discuss the tasks from the teacher Dindia and Duck (2000)	Never	1093	43.3281	22.84748	464	56.1853	22.05667
	Rarely	5384	50.6677	21.95500	3023	57.2891	21.62107
	Often	3381	52.9419	22.20465	1908	60.0878	21.95247
	Always	1138	52.5758	21.35867	450	56.5778	21.87761
	Total	10996	51.5819	22.10880	5845	58.0603	21.82672
Tells stories about events at school (Linying & Huichang, 2003)	Never	631	43.3281	19.20281	237	48.5021	20.61740
	Rarely	3531	50.6677	21.95004	2099	54.7642	21.05924
	Often	4492	52.9419	22.33645	2523	60.4459	21.91015
	Always	2342	52.5758	22.10676	986	61.2703	21.92923
	Total	10996	51.5819	22.10880	5845	58.0603	21.82672

Based on table 8, the analysis results and interpretation are presented as follows: **(1)** students who always do activities tell stories about events in schools having higher math scores (around 9 points in DKI Jakarta and 13 points in DI Yogyakarta) compared to students who have never done activities to parents, **(2)** students in DKI Jakarta and DI Yogyakarta who always do activities like discussing personal matters also have higher mathematical values (around 2 points in DKI Jakarta and 5 points in DI Yogyakarta) compared to students who have never done the activity, even though the difference of score is not significant, **(3)** students in DKI Jakarta who always do activities like discussing the assignments from teachers have higher scores (around 9 points) compared to students who never do these activities, **(4)** for students in DI Yogyakarta this activity has no impact anything in mathematics score achievement, because students who always discuss the assignments from teachers and students who never do these activities have relatively similar of mathematics scores, **(5)** activities like discussing lessons in schools actually have a negative impact on mathematics score achievement for DKI Jakarta students. The students who always do activities like discussing lessons in school with their parents have lower mathematics scores (around 3 points) compared to students who never do these activities, **(6)** for DI Yogyakarta students who always do activities like discussing school lessons with their parents have a greater score (around 4 points) compared students who never do so. Thus, this activity has a negative impact on the mathematics score for DKI Jakarta students, but has a positive impact on mathematics scores for DI Yogyakarta students, and **(7)** The students who always tell activities with friends have higher mathematics scores (around 9 points for DKI Jakarta and 11 points for DI Yogyakarta compared to students who are rarely or never doing these activities.

Table 9. Comparison of UNBK mathematics score in self-disclosure activities

Self-Disclosure Statements	Answer	DKI Jakarta			DI Yogyakarta		
		Respondent	Average Score of Math	Standard Deviation	Respondent	Average Score of Math	Standard Deviation
Discuss about the personal things (Jourard and Jaffee, 1970); (Vogel, D. L. & Wester, S. R., 2003)	Never	1755	47.8718	21.38870	630	53.6786	21.43338
	Rarely	4509	53.5207	22.43865	2667	57.7325	21.71685
	Often	2884	52.1663	22.10833	1755	59.8362	22.03040
	Always	1848	49.4629	21.35943	793	58.7137	21.56373
	Total	10996	51.5819	22.10880	5845	58.0603	21.82672

In general, the relation between student self-disclosure and mathematics scores in DI Yogyakarta is slightly higher than that of DKI Jakarta. This presumably occurred because: (1) the number of SMP /MTs students in DKI who participate in UNBK is almost double than that of DI Yogyakarta SMP/MTs students; (2) DI Yogyakarta province often achieves the highest average UNBK score nationally; (3) academic achievements of DI Yogyakarta are in line with the highest achievements of the Good Governance Index (https://kemendagri.go.id/blog/3453-Ini-Hasil-Tata-Kelola-Daerah-Versi-IGI), and the Teacher Competency Test (Jacobson B. N., 2012.), (Umar M. R., 2018), (B.O. Onyilo and I. I. Shamo, 2017), (npd.data. kemdikbud.go.id).

The academic achievements obtained by DI Yogyakarta students hitherto are strengthened by the research finding that in order to improve the UNBK score and education quality in the broadest level, the technical and strategic approaches at each school should be supported by participation among stakeholders and social culture strength (Prakoso, 2018).

4. CONCLUSION

The study shows that (1) there is a positive relation between SMP/MTs students' self-disclosure to their parents and UNBK mathematics score for both DKI Jakarta and DI Yogyakarta provinces, (2) students with low self-disclosure have a greater risk of achieving mathematics scores in less category (<55). The both results indicate that non-cognitive factors in the form of family support, especially in terms of communication between students and their parents have a positive impact on academic achievement.

ACKNOWLEDGEMENT

The authors expresses their utmost gratitudes to the Centre for Educational Assessment (Puspendik) and Puspendik's Management for support and contribution. The second utmost gratitudes are to Dr. Rahmawati for analysis contribution and Haryo Susetyo for UNBK information.

REFERENCES

Azis and Sugiman, 2015. An Analysis of Difficulty on Cognitive and Problem on Affective of SMA Students in Mathematics Learning Facing National Examination. *Jurnal Riset Pendidikan Matematika*, Vol. 2 No. 2, November 2015, 162 - 174. Retrieved from http://Journal.Uny.Ac.Id/Index.Php/Jrpm/Index

B.H. Prakoso., 2018. Promoting Best Practices of Computer Based National Exam (UNBK) Achievement in Indonesia. *Turkish Online Journal of Educational Technology*, Special Issue, Vol.2, 418-425.

B.O. Onyilo and I. I. Shamo, 2017. Teacher Competence as a Tool for Effective and Sustainable Human Capital Development in the Federal Capital Territory: Implications for Career Guidance. *International Journal of Psychology and Counselling*. Vol. 9(3),17-22.

Belloti, Fransesco, 2013. Advances in Human-Computer Interaction. *Journal of Gale Economic Education Humanities Social-Science*. Retrieved from http://infotrac.galegroup.com.

Cayanus, J. L., 2004. Using teacher self-disclosure as an Instructional Tool. *Communication Teacher. 18,* 6-9.

DeVito, J. A., 2011. Communication among People. Karisma Publishing Group. Tangerang, Indonesia.

Dindia, K., & Duck, S. 2000. Communication and Personal Relationships. Wiley. New York, USA.

Downs, V., Javidi, M., & Nussbaum, J., 1988. An Analysis of Teachers' Verbal Communication within the College Classroom: Use of humor, self-disclosure, and narratives. *Communication Education, 37,* 127-141.

Fusani, D. S., 1994. Extra Class Communication: Frequency, Immediacy, Self-Disclosure, and Satisfaction in Student-Faculty Interaction Outside the Classroom. *Journal of Applied Communication Research, 22,* 232-255.

Goldstein, G. S., & Benassi, V. A. 1994. The relation between teacher self-disclosure and student classroom participation. *Teaching of Psychology, 21,* 212-217.

Gutman, L. M., & Schoon, I., 2013. The Impact of Non-Cognitive Skills on Outcomes for Young People. Education Empowerment Foundations. London, UK.

Harper, V. B., & Harper, E. J. 2006. Understanding Student Self-Disclosure Typology through Blogging. *The Qualitative Report, 11*(2), 251-261. Retrieved from https://nsuworks.nova.edu/tqr/vol11/iss2/3

Jacobson B. N., 2012. Teachers' Competence and Students' Academic Performance in Senior Secondary Schools Chemistry: Is there any Relationship? *Global Journal of Educational Research.* Vol 11, No. 1, 15-18.

Jourard, S. M. & Jaffee, P. E., 1970. Influence of an interviewer's disclosure on the self-disclosing behavior of interviewees. *Journal of Counseling Psychology*, 17, 252-257.

Jourard, S. M., 1971. Self-disclosure: An Experimental Analysis of the Transparent Self. Wiley Inter science. New York, USA.

Linying, L., & Huichang, C. 2003. Relation between self-disclosure and personality characteristics, loneliness, mental health. *Chinese Mental Health Journal*, *17*(10), 666-671.

Monks, F.J., Knoers, A.M.P., Haditono, S.R., 2006. Psikologi Perkembangan: Pengantar dalam Berbagai Bagiannya. Gadjah Mada University Press. Yogyakarta, Indonesia.

Nizam, 2018. Biaya UNBK dan UNKP Beda Tipis. Retrieved from http://inilampung.com/biaya-unbk-dan-unkp-beda-tipis

Nugroho, R.A; N.S Kusumawati; O.C Ambarwati, 2018. Students Perception on the Use of Computer Based Test. IOP Conference Series : Materials Science and Engineering, Volume 306 (2018) 012103.

Safari. 2018. Data Analysis with Computer Program. Universitas Negeri Jakarta. Jakarta, Indonesia.

Sorenson, G., 1989. The relationships among teachers' self-disclosive Statements, Students' Perceptions, and Affective Learning. *Communication Education, 38,* 259-276.

Sudiyarto, 2018. UNBK Tekan Anggaran Ujian Nasional Hingga 70 %. Retrieved from https://nasional.tempo.co/read/1069466/kemendikbud-unbk-tekan-anggaran-ujian-nasional-hingga-70-persen/full&view=ok

Sugiyono. 2011. Metode Penelitian Kuantitatif, Kualitatif, dan R & D. Alfabeta. Bandung, Indonesia.

Umar M. R., 2018. Relationship between Teacher Competence, School Climate and Academic Performance of Public Senior Secondary School Students in Sokoto State Nigeria. *International Journal of Humanities and Social Science Invention* (IJHSSI). Vol. 7(1), 34-40.

Vogel, D. L. & Wester, S. R., 2003. To seek help or not to seek help: the risks of self-disclosure. *Journal of Counseling Psychology*, 50(3), pp. 351-361.

Wei, M., Russell, W. D., & Zakalik, R. A. 2005. Adult attachment, social self-efficacy, self-disclosure, loneliness, and subsequent depression for freshman college students: A longitudinal study. *Journal of Counseling Psychology*, *52*(4), 602-614.

Williams, M. & Burden, R. L., 1997. Psychology for language teachers: a social constructivist approach. Cambridge University Press. Cambridge, UK.

https://https://www.kemendagri.go.id/blog/3453-Ini-Hasil-Tata-Kelola-Daerah-Versi-IGI

https://npd.data. kemdikbud.go.id

https://puspendik.kemdikbud.go.id/hasil-un/

https://un.kemdikbud.go.id

SOFTWARE FACTORY PROJECT FOR ENHANCEMENT OF STUDENT EXPERIENTIAL LEARNING

Muhammad Ovais Ahmad[1] and Kari Liukkunen[2]
[1]*M3S Research Unit, University of Oulu, Finland*
Department of Mathematics and Computer Science, Karlstad University, Sweden
Faculty of Electronics, Telecommunications and Informatics, Gdansk University of Technology, Poland
[2]*M3S Research Unit, University of Oulu, Finland*

ABSTRACT

Providing opportunities for students to work on real-world software development projects for real customers is critical to prepare students for the IT industry. Such projects help students to understand what they will face in the industry and experience real customer interaction and challenges in collaborative work. To provide this opportunity in an academic environment and enhance the learning and multicultural teamwork experience, the University of Oulu, Finland offers the software factory (SWF) project. This paper presents the design of the SWF course and the learning environment and assessment techniques, and it discusses the importance of reflective learning diaries and serious games. Additionally, this paper examines factors in the SWF learning environment that affect student learning in the SWF course. Survey data were collected from the last six years of SWF projects. The results show that students consider the SWF to be a good collaborative learning environment that helps them achieve academic triumphs and enhances various professional skills. The learning diaries are effective for increasing students' learning experiences as well as providing an opportunity for teaching staff to monitor students' progress and offer better facilitation. These results are helpful for academic institutions and industry when developing such a learning environment.

KEYWORDS

Collaborative Learning, Project-Based Learning, Software Engineering Curricula, Teamwork, Software Engineering

1. INTRODUCTION

In the last two decades, there has been a significant shift in the information and communication technology (ICT) industry, as highlighted by Marc Andreessen in his essay *Why Software is Eating the World* (Andreessen, 2011). This shift has also pushed educational institutions to train graduates with various skills and competencies. This challenges universities to create software engineering (SE) technology agnostic courses that prepare graduates for the real-world software industry and fulfill industry needs and demand. One way to train SE graduates is to provide project-based learning through capstone courses (Howe, 2010; Walker, 2015). Educational institutions must train students in real-life practical projects where students engage in a collaborative teamwork environment and develop project management skills (Palacin-Silva et al. 2017). Universities around the world already include such capstone courses based on ACM curriculum guidelines (ACM Joint Task Force, 2014). However, various transversal capabilities—leadership, decision making, negotiation, self-reflection, and the infusion of design thinking—receive little or no attention in these courses. To provide such competencies, the University of Oulu established the software factory (SWF) learning environment/laboratory in 2012. The Oulu SWF is an infrastructure platform that serves multiple purposes to support SE research, education, and entrepreneurship.

The SWF is a test bed for SE ideas and a source for original research on the development of basic scientific software (Ahmad et al., 2014). The SWF is an educational vehicle for the university where the artifacts produced in the factory serve to improve learning and provide teaching materials in close collaboration with industry (Ahmad et al., 2014). The Oulu SWF is part of a European Union SWF network (Taibi et al., 2016). The aim of the SWF is for students to share their experiences, learn in a collaborative environment, and grow to compete in the fast-growing ICT domain. The Oulu SWF laboratory is equipped with 17 latest computers, software development tools, a wide range of gadgets for students' i.e. smart phones, tablets, cameras etc.)

This paper describes the SWF course design, assessment techniques, student perception, documentation of teaching experiences, and it discusses the importance of reflective learning diaries. The aim is to identify factors in the SWF laboratory that affect learning, in terms of exploring i) student achievements in term of skills gained, ii) students' perceptions of the SWF learning environment, as measured with the computer laboratory environment inventory (CLEI) (Newby & Fisher, 1997), and iii) students' attitudes toward the SWF project course, as measured with the attitude toward computers and computing courses questionnaire (ACCC) (Newby & Fisher, 1997).

The paper is structured as follows. Section 2 sheds light on related work, and Section 3 discusses the SWF course under the pedagogic lens and presents the SWF course learning objectives, mode of delivery, overall structure, student team formation, mentoring, and student assessment. Section 4 reports students' perceptions, and Section 5 discusses lessons learned from the teacher perspective in the context of teaching and managing such courses. Finally, Section V concludes the paper and sheds light on future research work and improvement to the SWF and similar courses.

2. RELATED WORK

The ACM curriculum guidelines recommend offering project- and problem-based courses to students that prepare them for real work in the industry (ACM Joint Task Force, 2014; Palacin-Silva et al., 2017). It is essential for SE students to have hands-on experience and a glimpse of real software industry work during their education. To prepare students for a profession, universities around the world offer various capstone courses. The concept of the SWF project is also based on capstone course concept.

Since 2010, the SWF and SWF-based courses have been offered at various universities around the world, i.e. University of Helsinki, the University of Oulu, the University of Eastern Finland, the Free University of Bozen-Bolzano, Tampere University of Technology, the Free University of Cagliari, the Technical University of Madrid, Montana State University, the Catholic University of America, and Bowling Green State University (Ahmad et al., 2014; Taibi et al., 2016; Tvedt, et al. 2002). These SWFs aim to provide students with practical experience in software development projects and help the students to gain business experience in a collaborative environment, as well as polish their technical expertise. However, research on SWF projects and course curricula is scarce. Most studies report success stories, students experimenting with processes, and positive experiences of students' motivation in such courses or projects. We did not find any study that reported on SWF course design, mode of delivery nor detailed of students' assessment techniques.

3. SOFTWARE FACTORY PROJECT DESIGN AND EXECUTION

Since 2012, the SWF laboratory has offered a 10 ECTS (290 h of work) advanced-level course for Information Processing Science master's degree program students at the University of Oulu, Finland. The purpose is to expose students to real-life software development projects in a multicultural collaborative environment. The focus is learning by doing—that is, managing authentic, resource-limited project work and integrating the practices of an academic expert in a unique project assigned by a software company. The SWF course is offered every year in the spring semester to 15–20 students.

3.1 SWF under a Pedagogic Lens

When designing a SWF course, various theories or approaches to learning—behaviorism, cognitivism, and constructivism—are taken into consideration (Anderson, 2008). The SWF adopted a blended learning approach to maximize students' learning outcomes as follows:

- From the behaviorism school, we observed how teaching staff behavior affects students' learning, e.g., teacher approval of certain items required by the course. In such cases, the teacher acts proactively to respond quickly. In this way, we avoid unnecessary wait times from the students' perspective.
- Adopting cognitivism approach, the students are encouraged to have a mental map of their project and processes. Such encouragement is important, especially in the context of software development. The students need to have a map for a specific goal, which boosts motivation and reduces stress.
- As constructivists, we do not push students to memorize the concepts taught during the lectures. Various serious games, learning diaries, and discussions enable students to develop their knowledge.

In general, the SWF course is more inclined toward constructivism due to a student-centered model that focuses on learning by doing in a collaborative environment and problem-based learning (Gokhale, 1995). Such a collaborative course and environment have a significant impact on learning (Ahmad et al., 2014; Gokhale, 1995; Khine & Lourdusamy, 2003; Taibi et al., 2016).

3.2 Project Course Learning Outcomes

After completing the course, the students should demonstrate their ability to work on a challenging ICT project. Students learn to acquire and apply professional expertise in the topic of the project. One example of a project is a path finder using the Robot Operating System for an autonomous electric car. Students should be able to:

- Act as independent professional members in an ICT project; a team member collectively produces, monitors, and updates the project plan (a project with a fixed deadline and human resources).
- Search up-to-date scientific literature on the subject matter of the project to build professional expertise in the topic and apply this to the project work.
- Develop analytical and creative skills for successful completion of the project and monitor and communicate the status (time and human resources used) of the project in real time within the team.
- Develop skills to communicate with the customer in a professional context and manage a successful project review with the steering group/project team.
- Report and explain the status (progress, results, and future estimations of the project) to the steering group to support decision making and problem resolution concerning the project's future.
- Work as a project team member with people from different technical and/or cultural backgrounds, produce a realistic outcome in relation to the project deadline and human resources (ok, good, or excellent), and reflect on the relationship between the process model(s) selected for the project (evolutionary, agile, lean, etc.) and the management practices followed in the project.

3.3 Mode of Delivery

The SWF course adopted blended teaching or mixed-mode instruction to boost collaborative learning (Martyn, 2003). This approach has become popular in SE because it helps develop critical thinking and improves understanding of various concepts (Gokhale, 1995; Palacin-Silva et al., 2017). There are four major components of the SWF course: classroom lectures, serious games workshops, weekly customer meetings and monthly progress reports, and individual project work. All SWF project–related communication, materials, and deliverables are stored in the Optima workspace[1].

The course provides traditional introductory lectures (4 × 2 h) and two workshops (2 × 8 h), where the steps for carrying out the course are described with relevant information. The students already have a background in project management and software development tools, processes, and techniques. However, in the first three introductory lectures, these concepts are briefly reviewed. The interesting aspect of these lectures is the participation of software professionals from the local software industry. Oulu is a smart city, and many big ICT companies, such as Nokia, Ericsson, and Bittium, have offices in the city. The invited professionals share their experiences and provide insights into running projects efficiently and adopting a software development and management method or technique based on project needs.

Students are divided into multiple groups during the fourth lecture; each team has three to four members. Additionally, interested software companies are invited to present the project ideas to the student teams.

[1] Optima is a learning management system used at the University of Oulu, Finland. https://www.discendum.com/references/?q=optima

These software companies and entrepreneurs are the real customers of the SWF projects. Such real customer engagement helps students learn more about the dynamics of software projects and enhance their soft skills. The teams select a project based on their interests and present the first draft to teachers and other teams.

The main goal of the workshop is for students to present their initial understanding of the project, problems expected, and possible solutions. The students present their project plan, development process, and management practices. The students break down the customer requirements and needs, as well as discussing the delivery of the project to the customer. In this phase, the teaching staff act as facilitators and guide students to successfully implement the projects. The aim of the workshop is to facilitate students through experiential learning to understand group dynamics and the software development methods, tools, and techniques used in the software industry. Various serious games are played, such as the Marshmallow Challenge, Draw Toast and Scrum Simulation with LEGO. For example, the Marshmallow Challenge is an instructive design exercise that engages students to work in teams. Such activities help students experience the dynamics of collaborative teamwork, the importance of analyzing each other's perspectives, and iteration planning.

The actual software development starts at the end of the first workshop. The students work on their projects for three months. The project team(s) experiment and select development methods, tools, and techniques based on the project requirements and customer demand. Frequent communication inside and outside the team is important. The project team meets the customer based on need, but the course recommends organizing a weekly meeting. Additionally, there are monthly management group meetings, where students present their overall progress, project and team challenges, and the status of the work hours. The students must also write a learning diary once a month. The teaching staff provide feedback in management group meetings.

3.4 Team Formation and Mentoring

We used a team formation tool called CATME (Hrivnak, 2013), which restricts each team to four or five students. The students' characteristics, such as ethnicity, gender, leadership preferences, specific technology skill level, and relevant knowledge, play a critical role in the formation of diverse teams. The teaching staff separately mentor each team and monitor their performance and dynamics. The teaching staff act as facilitators, help students prioritize their tasks, provide feedback on the development process, and discuss the reflective learning diaries to enhance student learning. To track students' progress and facilitate efficiently, teachers use various techniques, such as daily stand-up meetings, agile retrospectives, burn-down charts and Kanban boards (Ahmad et al. 2014; Ahmad et al. 2018).

3.5 Assessment Methods and Criteria

Assessing project work and then grading individual team members is always challenging. It is the teacher's duty to fairly assess each team member and present the criteria clearly and understandably. In the SWF course, we used a rubric-based assessment. It is mandatory for students to attend all the lectures and workshops. The distribution of the SWF course assessment is summarized in Table 1.

Table 1. Software factory (SWF) course evaluation and grading

Criteria	Points	Criteria
Final Software Product (Group Evaluation)	25	Final evaluation by the customer. The product must fulfil the customer requirements and meet functional and non-functional requirements.
Supporting Documents (Group Evaluation)	25	Supporting documents and evidence regarding the entire development process, including planning, management, and the implementation process.
Supervisor Evaluation (Group Evaluation)	10	Supervisor's evaluation of group performance.
Reflective Biweekly Learning Diary (Individual Evaluation)	20	Three reflective reports (3×5 points = 15). Final lesson learned report (5 points).
Peer Evaluation (Individual Evaluation)	20	Peer evaluation of individual performance by other members of the team.
Total	100	Final grade.

The customer evaluates the student project based on the group's communication with the customer, meeting deadlines, the final product, and whether customer got what he or she requested from each team. The customer also considers how each student team member approached them throughout the project.

The students are required to prepare a project plan, which is a live document until the end of the project. The project plan is updated with each sprint, which lasts for two weeks. The students prepare a report at the end of the project, in which the project team describes planning, managing, and implementing the process and the planned and actual work hours. The project report describes the product features and the resources used.

The teaching staff observe each team's progress from the beginning until the final presentation of the project. The teacher provides feedback after every weekly customer meeting and guides the students to improve their preparation for the next steps'. The teachers also consider how the teams prepare their presentations, handle technology during the meetings, and work together internally.

It is mandatory for every student to write four diary entries during the project. Reflective diaries are core elements of self-regulated learning that promote the development of metacognitive strategies (Fulwiler, 1986). Fulwiler described the rationale for introducing reflective diaries: "In the academic world, where we teach students to gain most of their information from reading and listening, we spend too much time telling our students how to see or doing it for them. That's not how I would encourage critical, creative, or independent thinking. Our students have good eyes; let's give them new tools for seeing better: journal writing is, of course, one of those tools."

Peer assessment is a powerful meta-cognitive tool, which has been advocated in various studies (Kaufman, Felder, & Fuller, 2000; Layton & Ohland, 2001; McGourty, Dominick, & Reilly, 1998). According to McGourty et al. (1998): "[i]n a cooperative learning environment, students themselves are often in the best position to provide one another with meaningful feedback regarding both their technical and interpersonal performance." A number of peer assessment tools and advised reducing the possibility of a student intentionally "damaging" his or her peers' scores and ensuring that students do not feel that they are "ratting" on their peers (McGourty et al., 1998; Nicole, Pamela, & Rebecca, 2005). In the SWF course, students are required to fill out a form to report aspects of their team members' contribution and behavior characteristics. The Oulu SWF project peer assessment is based on Sanders (Sanders, Dean, Sanders, & Dean, 1984). Examples of teamwork characteristic statements include attending team meetings, contributing to the discussion at the meetings, completing tasks on time, and the team member's ability to work with the other team members. The students were asked to score the characteristics using the following scale: Always (2 points), Usually (1), Sometimes (0), Rarely (-1), and Never (-2). Furthermore, students have the opportunity to express their feedback in answer to an open-ended question and report their concerns in detail.

4. STUDENT PERCEPTION SURVEY RESEARCH STRATEGY

The students' perceptions of the SWF course and facilities are based on the CLEI and the ACCC (Newby & Fisher, 1997)(see Table 2). Studying the learning environment (i.e. the SWF laboratory) is one way to explore student perception (Kolb & Kolb, 2005; Newby & Fisher, 1997). Newby and Fisher (Newby & Fisher, 1997) developed the CLEI to measure students' perceptions of their learning environment. The CLEI has five constructs: *student cohesion, open-endedness, integration, technology adequacy, and laboratory availability*. In the Oulu SWF context, the laboratory availability construct is not relevant, as the SWF laboratory is assigned to SWF project students 24/7. Furthermore, with the help of the ACCC (Newby & Fisher, 1997), students' attitudes toward computers and computing courses are assessed. The ACCC consists of four constructs: *anxiety, enjoyment, usefulness of computers, and usefulness of course*. In the Oulu SWF context, we removed the usefulness of computers construct because the targeted students are in the final year of the Information Processing Science master's degree program and considered competent in the use of computers.

The teaching staff conduct a voluntary online survey annually at the end of the SWF course from last six years (2012–2018). In six years, 50 of 90 students participated in the survey. The survey first part collect student background information. The second part of survey has variables from CLEI and ACCC which are measured using a five-point Likert-type scale, ranging from 1 (strongly disagree) to 5 (strongly agree). Third part of survey cover competencies gained in the SWF project. Further, in open-ended questions option is provided so that student freely express their SWF experience. The data analysis was conducted through descriptive statistics. Before the analysis, the reliability of the factor construct measurements were analyzed with Cronbach's alpha.

The research strategy also include the students' reflection diaries analysis and teachers' perspective. It is mandatory for each student to write minimum four reflection diaries during SWF project journey. The teaching staff explained their own perspective in light of six years of running SWF projects.

5. STUDENT PERCEPTION SURVEY RESULTS

The Table 2 shows that the reliability of the factor measurement is high; Cronbach's alpha varies between 0.597 and 0.951. These values show that the CLEI and ACCC constructs are internally consistent and reliably measured. Students' perceptions of the SWF laboratory learning environment are measured using the CLEI; their perception is quite positive. Table 2, shows that the highest mean scores are for "student cohesion" and "open-endedness" (mean = 4.24 and 3.84, respectively). "Technology adequacy" had the lowest mean score (mean = 3.28). The students feel confident and support each other in their project work. The students also have a positive response for "open-endedness" (average mean = 3.84), which might be due to the close industrial collaboration. The SWF project allows students to choose and experiment with software development processes and obtain feedback directly from the real software industry. The students collectively work toward the same goal and seek a solution for the given problem. The students are encouraged to use and put their theoretical knowledge into practice in the SWF project. The teaching staff facilitate during the project development. Additionally, the SWF laboratory is fully equipped with the latest technology, which is very important for executing such student projects. For example, the students have access to the latest computers, various types of tablets, smartphones, and smartwatches. This access is why students provide positive responses to the "technology adequacy" construct (mean = 3.28). This positive perception shows that CLEI constructs play an important role in student learning. The existing literature argues that there is a positive association between environmental and such attitudinal constructs (Al-Qahtani, 2012; Saadon & Liong, 2012).

Table 2. Constructs of the student perception survey

Measures	Constructs	M	Std. Deviation	Alpha
Attitude Toward Computers and Computing Courses Questionnaire (ACCC)	Anxiety	2.64	.83	.674
	Enjoyment	3.21	.55	.597
	Usefulness of Course	3.53	.72	.812
Computer Laboratory Environment Inventory (CLEI)	Student Cohesion	4.24	.63	.846
	Open-endedness	3.84	.75	.694
	Integration	3.41	.61	.527
	Technology Adequacy	3.28	1.07	.951

Survey questions use a five-point Likert scale, ranging from 1 (strongly disagree) to 5 (strongly agree).

Student attitudes toward the SWF course are quite positive, as shown in Table 2, the ACCC constructs. The constructs "usefulness of course" and "enjoyment" score the highest (mean = 3.53 and 3.21, respectively). The students found the course useful because they work with a real software company project, develop the product or services based on customers' requirements, and manage and monitor their activities. Furthermore, the usefulness construct shows that the students experience first-hand encounters with a real customer, which helps the students to learn negotiation skills and develop for future jobs. The "anxiety" construct received the lowest mean score (mean = 2.64), which indicates that the SWF course did not bore them, make them nervous, or create bad experiences from the beginning to the end of the project work. Such positive student perception is also reflected in the "enjoyment" construct, which received a mean score of 3.21 on the ACCC scale. Student anxiety can be explained with the students' own words in written responses to an open-ended question:

- *"Groups* [one project assigned to one team] *have huge gaps and differences because some students are very modest, and they felt shy to say that they are good at programming, and it is also hard to say and to evaluate if one person is good at programming. While the course really works, and I learned so many things from this course, and this is more like a practical course."*

- *"Confusion and sense of competition kept me on my toes for the whole length of the project. I like the course concept, but the variety of cultures among students brings variation in multiple aspects of how the projects flow. After understanding how human the students all are, I was able to forgive and work in a way I felt comfortable with."*
- *"Working in a group where people do not listen or understand what you are talking about when discussing web architectures, object-oriented programming makes working in the project really depressing."*
- *"When dividing the team, it is better to do it based on the required technical skills distinction, rather than culture differences. It could involve more interaction of the other teams and customers."*

In a nutshell, the students work collaboratively on the project, which helps them gain or improve various competencies. Students help each other and discuss ideas throughout the project work, which results in building a network that aims for better outcomes of their project. The project also helps students to make new friends and form supportive networks in pursuit of improved outcomes. These results correspond to previous findings (Saadon & Liong, 2012).

5.1 Competencies Gained in SWF

Table 3 shows the competencies gained in the SWF project. The students rate themselves highly against the achievement of various competencies gained during the SWF project. Building positive relationships with multicultural team members received the highest value (M = 4.00), which contributes to developing a shared mental model, managing tasks effectively, solving complex problem, better negotiating inside & outside group.

Table 3. Competencies Gained During the SWF Project Course

Competencies	Strongly disagree	Disagree	Neutral	Agree	Strongly agree	Mean
Effective task management	1	3	7	30	9	3.86
Solving complex problems	1	2	9	29	9	3.86
Usefulness of course	1	5	13	17	14	3.76
Sharing responsibilities	1	5	13	17	14	3.80
Developing a shared group vision	1	2	15	20	12	3.80
Building positive relationships	3	1	6	21	19	4.00
Negotiating with other groups	2	1	10	21	16	3.96
Use of rational argument to persuade others	4	2	13	21	16	3.62
Resolving conflict	4	2	16	17	11	3.58

These positive experiences and competencies gained during the project are also expressed in various students' responses to an open-ended question, as follows:

- *"The* [SWF] *project allowed me to develop my project management skills as a whole, from planning to scheduling, task allocation to having formal meetings, and collaborating with a steering group. I gained a good insight into what duties a project manager has and what kind of personal traits are needed for the successful management of a project."*
- *"I learned about interesting technologies and software tools in usability activities in practice."*
- *"Management has also increased my ability to deal with the different nature of people, how to motivate them and drive or steer them to do the work. Everyone has his own working style to do the work."*
- *"From this course, I found my direction for future work, and I found things that I like to do. Thanks to the teachers, customers, and also my group members!"*

An open SWF environment that emphasizes collaborative work enables students to help each other and generate and discuss ideas throughout the project work. Such a positive environment and experiences helps students to build a network that aims for better outcomes of their project journey. These results are also supported by previous studies. Overall, with these competencies, the students clearly worked collaboratively, which helped them to generate ideas, share their views with each other, and solve complex problems (65%). The benefits of students working collaboratively include opportunities to make new friends and form supportive networks in pursuit of improved outcomes (Saadon & Liong, 2012). These results correspond to previous findings (Baloche, 1994; Jane Burdett, 2003).

6. REFLECTIVE LEARNING DIARY

The reflective diary is a facilitation method, as well as an opportunity for students to reflect on their experiences and practices. Such reflective diaries enable students to see how they can better prepare themselves for the challenging SE profession. Writing reflective diaries is the core element in many medical, nursing and teacher education programs (Tang, 2002). The students write biweekly learning diary entries at the completion of each sprint that answer the main questions (What tasks did you do in this sprint? As a learner, what did you improve or learn compared to the last sprint? What were the issues and challenges you faced in this sprint?).

We expected students to reflect on their individual and group experiences for each sprint. In this way, they can identify their own learning, polish existing skills, and seek improvement opportunities. The teaching staff can also see in which direction the student is heading and make necessary adjustments to assist them. These learning diaries also help students to adapt to individual project needs by understanding software development methods, practices, and tools and their application during software development projects and experiments. We, as teaching staff, observed that in learning diaries, it is evident that students reflect on each sprint practice, seek improvement, and adapt development practices based on their experiences. The following are example statements from the students' learning diaries:

- *"We use Trello* [online tool; www.trello.com] *for task management like Kanban board; our understanding of the Kanban process was minimal. Moving our process to the white board in the Software Factory Lab, we had a deeper course to interact with one another, gather feedback from the supervising teacher, etc. Petty issues, such as missing work-in-progress limits on our board, were quickly raised by the supervising teacher. We thus had to move our work process from Trello to the white board in the Software Factory Lab just to not to repeat ourselves but use a common board and approach."*
- *"Being a multicultural team, it was hard understanding other people, which affected our work output to an extent. We tried to do the best, however, working schedule of team members was quite problematic. While there is no one to blame, we need to work together, find more consensus, interact on Slack more, be as productive as possible during the few minutes we have together, and persevere in the given task."*
- *"We come from different cultures, different languages, and possess different accents; it was quite difficult for team members to understand each other sometimes during conversations. However, when communicating on Slack platform, these issues were not present. This was the reasons why Slack communication was frequent".*

In summary, such reflective diaries are recommended to provide opportunities for students to think critically, look back on the learning activities, help identify what they have learned throughout the practical software development project, and learn how to polish the required skills.

7. TEACHERS' PERSPECTIVE

The teaching staff implement the SWF project in relation to the results and adapt teaching techniques to optimize learning outcomes. In this regard, the following lessons were learned:

- The SWF laboratory involves the local software industry for real projects and customers for the university's SE students. However, non-disclosure agreements must usually be signed. This requirement must be communicated very clearly to students to avoid breaches. Similarly, the message should be communicated to the companies that the students might not be aware of the seriousness of confidentiality, and the companies should be careful when assigning confidential tasks.
- The company and real customers are invited to the final project presentation. However, their evaluation should not focus only on the final product. The evaluation criteria should be clearly communicated to these external stakeholders to avoid confusion and promote fair evaluations.
- The SWF project course design is very effective for motivating students and plays an active role throughout the project. For example, the SWF project has an almost zero dropout rate, despite requiring intense work over one semester. This is why it is important to include serious games and consider the gamification approach to improve students' motivation and active participation and increase collaboration (Glover & Glover, 2013; Sheth, Bell, & Kaiser, 2012).

- The SWF project course is also demanding from the teaching staff perspective due to the frequent communication and mentoring. Each SWF project team requires a teaching assistant to provide technical support, monitor their progress continuously, and facilitate throughout the SWF journey. This technique is very effective in a SE project-based environment (Palacin-Silva et al., 2017; Walker, 2015).
- Creating balanced teams is a challenge with multicultural and heterogenous students. An unbalanced team with inadequate skills or cultural conflicts can create difficult situations during the long and intensive work period. The teaching staff must proactively oversee the teams' work and communication.
- Continues student work assessment and providing frequent feedback improve overall student learning and their ability to execute project efficiently.
- Almost all universities around the world have strong policies regarding the installation of computer laboratory software. Such policies affect students when they need to urgently install software packages. The solution is to install a virtual machine on all students' laboratory computers. This enables students to freely install and update the required software, applications, and tools.

8. CONCLUSION

This paper describes the design of a graduate SE course that uses real projects from software companies with real customers in an SWF laboratory. We documented six teaching experiences, students' perceptions of the SWF laboratory, and the SWF course. Furthermore, this paper provides insight into course delivery, course assessment, peer evaluation, and the use of tool support for forming teams.

The SWF laboratory is an innovative learning environment that offers a graduate-level project-based course. The aim is to bring balance to two aspects: SE processes and building final software development products or solutions. It is very important to maintain a balance because students find it easy to focus on the coding and ignore development processes. Student experimentation with the SE process should be encouraged. Learning and mastering these processes are essential to compete in the competitive job market. The student survey results show that the majority expressed a positive view in two ways: (i) The SWF course is appreciated as an important course in their master's degree curriculum. The SWF project is a good blend of theoretical and practical training that enhances students' enjoyment, and they find the course useful for achieving the required competencies for future jobs; (ii) The SWF laboratory makes it possible to provide opportunities for students to interact with real software industry customers and work collaboratively in a multicultural environment.

Fair assessment is a very important and complex activity for teaching staff in such courses. We developed a matrix that considers various aspects of teamwork. In this way, free riders and hardworking students in the project can be identified easily and treated fairly. In this regard, peer assessment and individual reflective learning diaries play an important role in encouraging and motivating students in this collaborate course. The learning diaries are a good way to promote student engagement and assess their epistemological beliefs and conceptions of learning. This also helps the teaching staff create and update strategies for monitoring and regulating learning. In future work, the SWF course could be run in a geographically distributed context in cooperation with other SWFs and/or other universities. However, this might require much greater technical competency among teaching support staff and strong collaboration between universities. It would be interesting to investigate such courses in different academic and cultural settings.

ACKNOWLEDGEMENT

This research is supported by ITEA3 project VISDOM funded by Business Finland.

REFERENCES

ACM Joint Task Force. (2014). Software Engineering 2014 - Curriculum Guidelines for Undergraduate Degree Programs in Software Engineering. Retrieved from https://www.acm.org/binaries/content/assets/education/se2014.pdf

Ahmad, M. O., Dennehy, D., Conboy, K., & Oivo, M. (2018). Kanban in software engineering: A systematic mapping study. Journal of Systems and Software, 137, 96-113.

Ahmad, M. O., Liukkunen, K., & Markkula, J. (2014). Student perceptions and attitudes towards the software factory as a learning environment. In IEEE Global Engineering Education Conference, EDUCON.

Ahmad, M. O., Markkula, J., & Oivo, M. (2013). Kanban in software development: A systematic literature review. In 2013 39th Euromicro conference on software engineering and advanced applications. 9-16.

Al-Qahtani, M. F. (2012). Students' perception and attitude towards computer laboratory learning environment. Educational Research, 3(4) pp. 402-411.

Anderson, T. (2008). Theory and practice of online learning. Athabasca University Press.

Andreessen, M. (2011). Why Software Is Eating the World. The Wall Street Journal. Retrieved from http://www.djreprints.com.

Anuradha A. Gokhale. (1995). Collaborative Learning Enhances Critical Thinking, Journal of Technology Education. 7(1)

Baloche, L. (1994). Breaking Down the Walls. The Social Studies, 85(1), 25–30.

Fulwiler, T. (1986). Seeing with journals. The English Record, 32(3), 6–9.

Glover, I., & Glover, I. (2013). Proceedings of EdMedia 2013--World Conference on Educational Media and Technology. EdMedia + Innovate Learning. Vol. 2013. AACE.

Howe, S. (2010). Advances in Engineering Education Where Are We Now? Statistics on Capstone Courses Nationwide. Advances in Engineering Education.

Hrivnak, G. A. (2013). CATME Smarter TeamworkCATME Smarter Teamwork (www.CATME.org). Academy of Management Learning & Education, 12(4), 679–681.

Jane Burdett. (2003). Making Groups Work: University Students' Perceptions. International Education Journal, 4(3), 177–191.

Kaufman, D. B., Felder, R. M., & Fuller, H. (2000). Accounting for Individual Effort in Cooperative Learning Teams. Journal of Engineering Education, 89(2), 133–140.

Khine, M. S., & Lourdusamy, A. (2003). Blended learning approach in teacher education: combining face-to-face instruction, multimedia viewing and online discussion. British Journal of Educational Technology, 34(5), 671–675.

Kolb, A. Y., & Kolb, D. A. (2005). Learning Styles and Learning Spaces: Enhancing Experiential Learning in Higher Education. Source: Academy of Management Learning & Education (Vol. 4).

Layton, R. A., & Ohland, M. W. (2001). Peer Ratings Revisited: Focus on Teamwork, Not Ability. In Proceedings of the 2001 American Society for Engineering Education Annual Conference & Exposition.

Martyn, M. (2003). The Hybrid Online Model: Good Practice. Educause Quarterly, 26(1), 18–23.

McGourty, J., Dominick, P., & Reilly, R. R. (1998). Incorporating student peer review and feedback into the assessment process. Frontiers in Education Conference. Moving from "Teacher-Centered" to "Learner-Centered" Education.

Newby, M., & Fisher, D. (1997). An Instrument for Assessing the Learning Environment of a Computer Laboratory. Journal of Educational Computing Research, 16(2), 179–190.

Nicole, C., Pamela, D., & Rebecca, S. (2005). Self and peer assessment in software engineering projects. In Proceedings of the 7th Australasian conference on Computing education - Volume 42 (pp. 91–100). John Garratt Publishing.

Palacin-Silva, M., Khakurel, J., Happonen, A., Hynninen, T., & Porras, J. (2017). Infusing Design Thinking into a Software Engineering Capstone Course. 30th Conference on Software Engineering Education and Training. 212–221.

Saadon, S., & Liong, C.-Y. (2012). Perception of Students on Services at the Computer Laboratory: A Case Study at the School of Mathematical Sciences, Universiti Kebangsaan Malaysia. Procedia Social and Behavioral Sciences, 59, 117–124.

Sanders, D., Dean, Sanders, & Dean. (1984). Managing and evaluating students in a directed project course. ACM SIGCSE Bulletin, 16(1), 15–25.

Sheth, S., Bell, J., & Kaiser, G. (2012). Increasing Student Engagement in Software Engineering with Gamification.

Taibi, D., et al (2016). "Free" Innovation Environments: Lessons learned from the Software Factory Initiatives. ICSEA 2016.

Tang, C. (2002). Reflective diaries as a means of facilitating and assessing reflection. In Proceedings of the 29th HERDSA Annual Conference. pp. 7–10.

Tvedt, J. D., Tesoriero, R., & Gary, K. A. (2002). The Software Factory: An Undergraduate Computer Science Curriculum. Computer Science Education, 12(1–2), 91–117.

Walker, A. Andrew E. (2015). Essential readings in problem-based learning: exploring and extending the legacy of Howard S. Barrows.

A FIELD STUDY ABOUT THE IMPACT OF A VR LEARNING UNIT

Thomas Keller, Fabian Hagen and Elke Brucker-Kley
ZHAW School of Management and Law
St.-Georgen-Platz 2, 8401 Winterthur, Switzerland

ABSTRACT

This paper examines the learning success of the Virtual Reality course unit "So small! - So big!" compared to conventional teaching. In the form of a field experiment and three random sample tests, the learning success of 67 subjects was examined. In the analysis of the collected data, the differences between the educational levels and the sexes were examined in addition to the overall comparison. In addition, the individual questions of the random sample tests were checked for anomalies. The analysis showed that the two learning units are to be regarded as equivalent. The subjects achieved short and medium-term learning success with both teaching methods. However, no differences could be found between the two teaching methods; they must be regarded as equivalent. The only exception is the difference between the educational levels in terms of medium-term learning success.

KEYWORDS

Virtual Reality, Education, Field Experiment

1. INTRODUCTION

The possibilities and benefits of the use of new media in teaching at elementary schools have been discussed for some time. In the context of computer use in schools, the terms media pedagogy and media didactics are often used (cf. (Krauthausen 2012), p. 1). In the context of the present work, however, "new media" primarily means the use of so-called learning or exercise programs. With the use of IT resources, specific knowledge can be imparted in many subjects. New teaching concepts are possible. Especially VR and augmented reality (AR) bring completely new possibilities into the classroom. Simple examples are Google Expeditions and the Google Cardboard. A study by Samsung in Germany in 2017 shows: "More than three-quarters of teachers (79%) agree with the statement that thanks to VR, students have the opportunity to make experiences that they would never otherwise have. [...] In addition, the majority of teachers believe that the use of VR in class can increase the motivation of students (74%) and improve their learning success (62%). According to the teachers (58%), the use of the technology can also help in understanding learning concepts. The greatest potential benefits of VR are attributed to the subjects geography/geography (80%), history (74%) and science (62%)".

Interestingly, however, digital media are only used hesitantly in elementary schools. There may be many reasons for this. On the one hand, on the side of teachers, on the other hand in pedagogy and in very new media such as virtual reality, the lack of pedagogical content for use in the classroom.

What Confucius (551-479 B.C.) already knew still applies to today's school teaching: "Tell me, and I will forget. Show me, and I may remember. Involve me, and I will understand." This guideline is not only perfectly suited to the topic of virtual reality, it is also often quoted in connection with competence-oriented learning in the context of Lehrplan 21 (d-edk 2016) (Swiss curriculum for primary and secondary schools), where the focus is on the actions of learners. The aim of this work is therefore to develop and implement concrete learning units for mathematical learning in VR that exhibit a degree of interaction that comes close to doing in the sense of Confucius.

(Keller and Brucker-Kley 2018a) discuss an immersive VR learning unit and its usability amongst pupils with special needs. This learning unit is now used for further investigations regarding the impact on the learning success. The learning unit itself is not introduced in this paper. Please refer to (Keller and Brucker-Kley 2018b) for that purpose.

2. STATE-OF-THE-ART

In the following, important principles and mathematics didactics are examined in order to subsequently deal with immersive learning in the context of VR.

2.1 Didactics of Mathematics

((Krauthausen 2012), p. 3 f.) criticises the fact that computer-assisted learning programs in mathematics that are well-known and widespread on the market today pay too little attention to the current state of research and knowledge in mathematics didactics. The focus is too much on technology instead of content (the subject-specific content) and the programs thus contribute much to the media competence of learners but little to mathematics skills.

((Burrill 2017), p. 316) mentions mathematical accuracy (fidelity) and user experience as central mathematics didactic principles. The mathematical accuracy means that the software should always be mathematically correct, the user experience should not hinder the work with the mathematical task and should promote mathematical thinking.

Learners need to be able to make decisions to expand their thinking. This possibility is also closely related to the complexity of a task, which does not necessarily require complex mathematical requirements (cf. (Geiger 2017), p. 289). According to ((Joubert 2017), p. 20 ff.), while working on a mathematical task, students use means from the so-called "Modes of Production". These include acting (usually in the sense of indicating a solution), formulating (developing hypotheses, solution strategies, etc.) and validating (checking based on evidence, theorems or explanations). Formulation and validation almost always have to be initiated by the teacher.

For the motivation of learners, mathematics itself should increasingly be presented in a way that makes them exciting and captivating themselves, rather than motivating them with other means in the learning programs (cf. (Krauthausen 2012), p. 20): "Effective learning processes are characterized by a high degree of motivation and joy, which however arise from the matter and not from its packaging" ((Krauthausen 2012), p. 21).

Mathematical learning is an important pedagogical task. Mathematical tasks are intended to encourage learners to do something mathematical and thus experience mathematics in the broadest sense (cf. (Joubert 2017), p. 4). All tasks should always contain pragmatic and epistemological aspects. The epistemological aspects refer to the insights to be conveyed to learners while working on a task (cf. (Sinclair and Zazkis 2017), p. 177), whereby the pragmatic value of a task is almost always equated with solving the task (cf. (Sinclair and Zazkis 2017), p. 190). ((Laborde 2011), p. 82) supplements cognitive aspects (what kind of learning the task triggers in the learner at the current state of knowledge), didactic aspects (with what means the task is set) and instrumental aspects (which instruments the learner needs to solve the task).

2.2 Immersive Learning

Learning in virtual worlds is often called "immersive learning". According to ((Höntzsch et al. 2013), p. 3), immersion describes the degree to which individuals perceive that they interact more with their virtual than with their real environment (individual sense of being there). In a virtual reality, immersion seems to be determined by the degree of representation of the learners, their presence and their possibilities of interaction.

((Höntzsch et al. 2013), p. 3) describe with reference to ((Burdea and Coiffet 2003), p. 3) the three "I" of learning with virtual realities: Imagination, immersion and interaction. "Imagination describes the imaginative power of learners to put themselves in the position of a simulation. Real-time visualizations and reactions of the system provide users with immediate feedback on their inputs (interaction). The information is also recorded multimodally [...], i.e. with several senses. This creates a feeling of immersion, i.e. of being directly involved in the simulated world" ((Höntzsch et al. 2013), p. 3). Imagination, immersion and interaction seem to be important factors for immersive learning.

With regard to pedagogy, ((Geiger 2017), p. 288 f.) points out in the context of mathematics how eminently important it is to select, adapt and implement the tasks in the learning environments. In this context, he points out the importance of cooperation between teachers and researchers in order to anchor well-designed tasks with pedagogically correct approaches in the learning environments and thus improve learning.

A sufficient degree of challenge is important for the learning process (cf. (Geiger 2017), p. 289). ((Höntzsch et al. 2013), p. 4) list the following measures as necessary to avoid overburdening learners in immersive learning environments:

- clear learning objectives, work orders and instructions,
- permanently available background information,
- hints and exercises that stimulate reflection (for example, setting a specific state of the simulation)

((Höntzsch et al. 2013), p. 3) list the possible support of immersion on learning processes in connection with flow and presence experience as a thesis when using three-dimensional virtual worlds. However, with reference to Grunewald (2009), they point out that these effects are also mentioned in the context of computer game addiction. ((Chen 2016), p. 644) also shows a positive effect on the learning (in the context of language learning) of such environments.

According to ((Höntzsch et al. 2013), p. 4), discovering learning leads to an expansion of personal experience space and to the generation and examination of hypotheses, since knowledge in these learning environments is not predetermined but explorative. It is pointed out that the learning environments must be simulated as truthfully as possible in order for the findings to be successfully transferred into reality. It also describes advantages in the depth of information processing, learning success and motivation, the latter not per se resulting in a higher quality or quantity of cognitive processing and skill acquisition.

3. RESEARCH OBJECTIVE

The main objective of this work is to compare the learning success of learning units with VR against those without VR support. In addition, the medium-term learning success is to be researched by making a new survey one month later. Another goal is the question whether there are differences in educational level and gender. In addition, the respondents' opinion of this teaching method is to be questioned and the answers compared with the data collected.

3.1 Research Design – Field Experiment

In this field experiment a slightly modified version of the Pretest-Posttest Control Group Design according to (Campbell and Stanley 1967) is applied. The design provides that a test is performed at the beginning of the field experiment, then the independent variable is changed, and then a test is performed again. In addition to this second test, a new test is performed a month later in this study to measure medium-term learning success.

This research design has a high internal validity, as the pre-test guarantees the equivalence of the test persons. The external validity, on the other hand, is weakened by the fact that it cannot be ruled out that the pre-test influences the subjects in their subsequent behaviour (Campbell & Stanley, 1963, p. 13ff). It could be the case that the pupils then exert themselves more in the following lessons, which would perhaps not have been the case without the pre-test. In the case of the present work, this is attempted to prevent by the students not knowing that they are part of a field experiment.

Four classes from a secondary school in Switzerland serve as comparison groups. These are two classes of level A and two classes of level B. One of the two classes will be in the experimental group (VR unit) and the other one in the control group (regular unit). In total, the comparison groups comprise 87 subjects, 45 of whom were at secondary level A and 42 at secondary level B. The comparison groups are divided into two groups: the first group (VR unit) and the second group (regular unit). Due to failures during the field experiment, 67 subjects were included in the final analysis.

An important factor in the control of interfering variables is the randomisation procedure. The aim is to evenly distribute known and unknown personal factors in order to create a level playing field. In the case of this study, randomization is determined by the class distribution of the schools. Thus, the field experiment must be regarded as quasi-randomized.

A protocol is kept during the execution of the field experiment, which records special features such as assistance or technical problems and contains a short questionnaire for the test persons. The questions will be asked and answered verbally immediately after the course unit has been completed.

4. RESULTS

The following subsections present the findings from the field experiment. A more in-depth discussion of the results can be found here[1].

4.1 Differences Between Experimental and Control Group

The immersive as well as the conventional teaching method have resulted in short and medium-term learning success for the test persons of both comparison groups. The subjects in the experimental group between Test 1 and Test 2 achieved an average learning success of 1.38 points (19.14%). In the control group, the average learning success between the same tests was 1.30 points (18.49%). The medium-term learning success, which is measured by the difference between Test 1 and Test 3, averages 0.64 points (8.88%) for the subjects in the test group. The subjects in the control group recorded an average learning success of 0.45 points (6.40%) between the same tests. The correlation is shown in Figure 1. Average test results of experimental and control group.

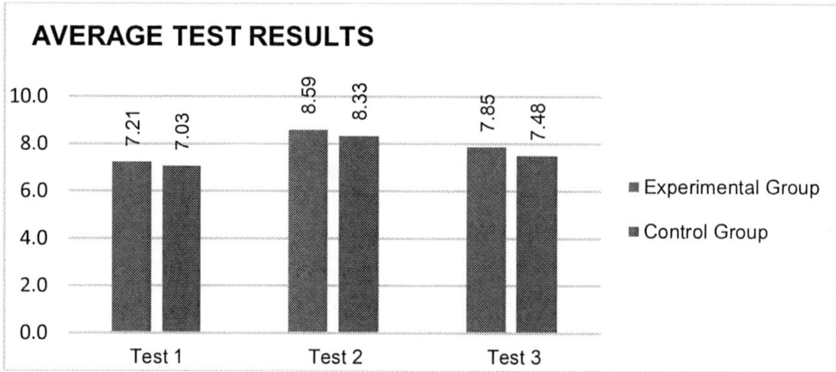

Figure 1. Average test results of experimental and control group

If the average learning outcomes of the subjects in the experimental and control groups are compared, the difference between Test 1 and Test 2 is 0.08 points. The statistical significance is 58.24%, which means that the two teaching methods do not differ. Similar observations can be made for the average learning outcomes between Test 1 and Test 3. There it is a difference of 0.19 points with a statistical significance of 64.71%. These values are illustrated in Table 1.

Table 1. Comparison between experimental with control group

Comparison of Comparative Groups	Experimental Group	Control Group	Difference	Statistical Significance
Learning Success Test 1 to Test 2	1.38	1.30	0.08	58.24%
Learning Success Test 1 to Test 3	0.64	0.45	0.19	64.71%

[1] https://drive.switch.ch/index.php/s/OELriQqJx8mCver

In summary, this means that both immersive and conventional teaching methods have resulted in statistically verifiable learning success for the test persons. If the learning outcomes of the different groups are compared, however, there are no differences. The two teaching methods are to be regarded as equivalent in terms of both short-term and medium-term learning success. However, there are tendencies, if the questions of the random sample tests are considered individually, that the tasks with reference to the linear masses were better solved by the test persons of the experimental group and the tasks with reference to the hollow masses were better solved by the test persons of the control group.

4.2 Difference Between Education Levels

In order to be able to make more precise statements about the learning success of the test persons, the test persons of the comparison groups were additionally divided into secondary level A (Sec A) and secondary level B (Sec B). Their average test results are shown in Figure 2. As can be observed, there are no striking differences in the learning outcomes of the test subjects between Test 1 and Test 2. However, if one looks at Test 3, it is noticeable that the test subjects in Test Group Sec A achieved the highest average score, which was not apparent before.

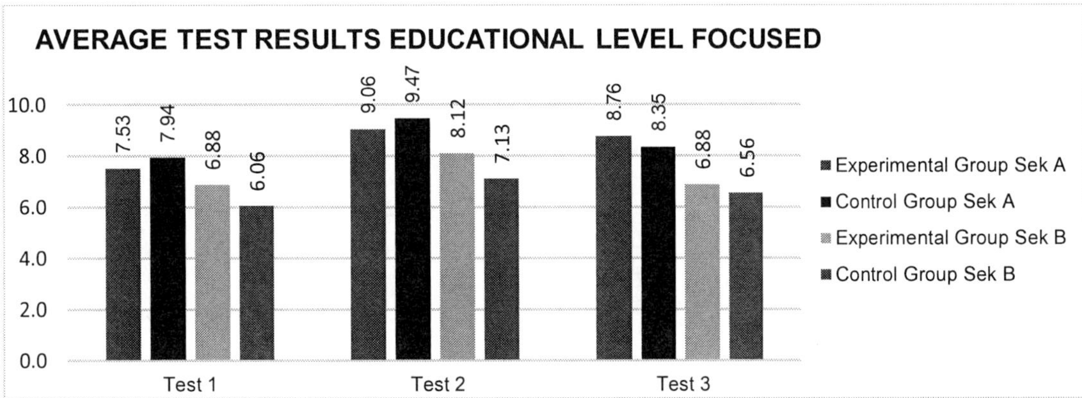

Figure 2. Average test results of different educational levels

The average learning success between Test 1 and Test 3 was 1.53 points (16.33%) for the subjects in the test group's Sec A group. The average learning success achieved by the test subjects in the control group's Sec A was 0.41 points (5.16%), which is considerably lower. If the average learning successes between Test 1 and Test 3 of the subjects in the Sec A of both comparison groups are compared, this leads to the list in Table 1. The difference between the average learning successes is 0.83 points. The statistical significance is 88.50%. This means that the difference is not statistically relevant, but there is a tendency that should be further investigated.

Table 2. Learning success between test 1 and 2

Comparison of Subjects of Sek A	Experimental Group	Control Group	Difference	Statistical Significance
Learning Success Test 1 to Test 3	1.24	0.41	0.83	88.50%

If the average learning success of the subjects in Sec A is compared with that of the subjects in Sec B of the experimental group between Test 1 and Test 3, this leads to a difference of 1.24 points. In addition to the high learning success of the subjects in Sec A, this is mainly due to the fact that the subjects in Sec B did not achieve any learning success in these tests. With a statistical significance of 99.01%, this difference is considered statistically relevant. This correlation can be seen in Table 3.

Table 3. Comparison of learning success between levels

Comparison of Experimental Group	Subjects of Sek A	Subjects of Sek B	Difference	Statistical Significance
Learning Success Test 1 to Test 3	1.24	0.00	1.24	99.01%

In summary, this means that immersive teaching methods led to verifiable short and medium-term learning success in subjects in Sec A. This contrasts with the subjects in Sec B, who only achieved short-term learning success. There is therefore a difference between the educational levels with regard to medium-term learning success with VR learning units.

4.3 Gender Differences

A further possibility of classification is the subdivision by gender. As can be seen in Figure 3, the average test results are similar. The female test subjects in the test group who achieved the highest learning success between Test 1 and Test 2 with 1.77 points (27.06%) are notable. This finding is particularly evident when the focus is placed on the individual questions of the random sample tests. For example, the female respondents in the test group in question 1a, which has a strong relation to the linear measures in the learning unit, have by far the highest average learning success with 225.00% between test 1 and test 2.

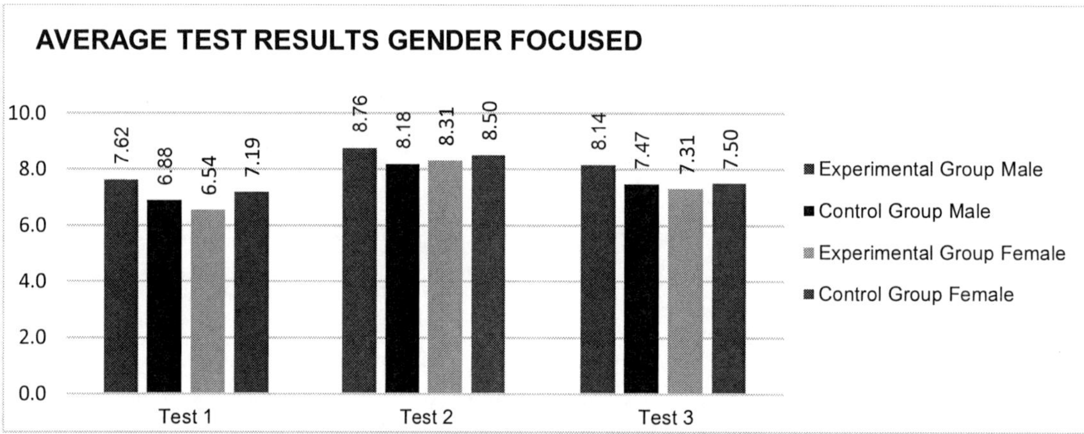

Figure 3. Average test results of genders

As Figure 4 shows, the female respondents in the control group are far below this with an average learning success of 128.57%. The male subjects in the experimental group were also lower with an average learning success of 66.67%. Similar observations can be made for learning success between Test 1 and Test 3. With 125.00% learning success, the female subjects in the experimental group are far ahead of the female subjects in the control group with 57.14% and the male subjects in the experimental group with 66.67%.

The tendency of the female subjects in the experimental group to show high learning progress can also be applied to most other questions, albeit to a lesser extent. In particular, it is the tasks related to the linear measures in which the subjects in the experimental group show greater learning success than the control group.

If, on the other hand, the average learning successes between Test 1 and Test 2 of the female subjects in the test and control groups are compared, the difference is 0.46 points, with the test group being higher. The statistical significance is 78.39%. A similar observation can be made between Test 1 and Test 3, where the difference is also 0.46 points. Here the statistical significance is somewhat lower at 74.82%. This means that both learning units are of equal value for the female subjects.

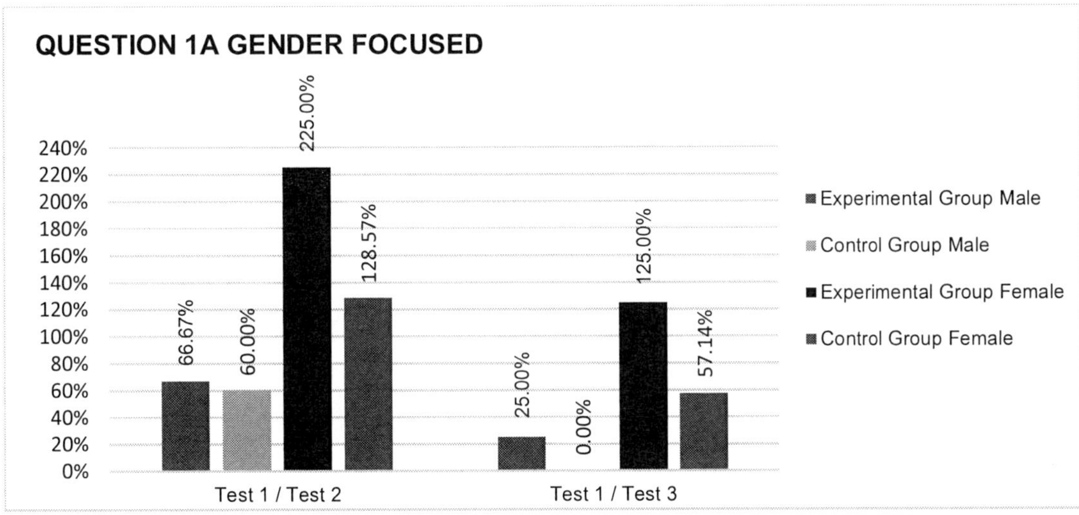

Figure 4. Question 1A visualized according gender

If the average learning successes of the male and female subjects in the comparison group are compared, there is a difference of 0.63 points, with the female subjects being higher.

In summary, this means that there are no differences between the subjects in the experimental and control groups when the focus is on the sexes. The VR and conventional learning units are to be regarded as equivalent. In addition, there are no differences between male and female subjects who used the VR unit. However, there is a tendency that the female subjects benefited more from the VR units than the male subjects.

5. CONCLUSION

The analysis of the data showed that both learning units resulted in short and medium-term learning success for the test persons, but that there were no differences between the two teaching methods. A difference can be observed between the educational levels. Thus, in contrast to the subjects at Sec B, the subjects at Sec A had better learning success in the medium term. Statistically, there are no significant differences between the sexes. However, there are indications that female subjects benefit more than male subjects. This is a finding that would make it possible to provide targeted support for girls, especially in technically related fields.

The above results revealed trends that could not be answered in the present field experiment. They are described in the following and hypotheses for future research are derived from them.

During the data analysis, there were more and more indications that female subjects had greater learning success with the VR course unit than with the conventional course unit. It was also found that they tended to achieve greater learning success than male subjects who did the VR unit. However, this tendency could not be statistically proven in the context of the present study. It concerns both short and medium-term learning success.

The effectiveness of the VR learning unit differs between linear measures and hollow measures. Linear measures performed better than hollow measures. The assumption suggests that the design criteria of the virtual space play a role here.

Furthermore, an important limitation must also be referred to. It cannot be estimated what influence the effect of the new had on the test persons. This can only be avoided if the test persons work with virtual reality over a longer period of time and this technology thus loses the attraction of the new.

Finally, it must be noted that the use of VR learning units does not per se lead to better learning success. As with conventional teaching methods, the quality and design of such VR learning units plays a decisive role.

REFERENCES

Burdea, Grigore C, and Philippe Coiffet 2003 Virtual Reality Technology. 2nd Edition. New Jersey: John Wiley & Sons.

Burrill, Gail 2017 Designing Interactive Dynamic Technology Activities to Support the Development of Conceptual Understanding. *In* Digital Technologies in Designing Mathematics Education Tasks: Potential and Pitfalls. Allen Leung and Anna Baccaglini-Frank, eds. Pp. 303–328. Mathematics Education in the Digital Era. Switzerland: Springer.

Campbell, Donald Thomas, and Julian Cecil Stanley 1967 Experimental and Quasi-Experimental Designs for Research. 2. print. Boston: Houghton Mifflin Comp.

Chen, Yu-Li 2016 The Effects of Virtual Reality Learning Environment on Student Cognitive and Linguistic Development. The Asia-Pacific Education Researcher 25(4): 637–646.

d-edk 2016 Lehrplan 21: Gesamtausgabe. InternetDocument. https://v-ef.lehrplan.ch/lehrplan_printout.php?e=1&k=1.

Geiger, Vince 2017 Designing for Mathematical Applications and Modelling Tasks in Technology Rich Environments. *In* Digital Technologies in Designing Mathematics Education Tasks: Potential and Pitfalls. Allen Leung and Anna Baccaglini-Frank, eds. Pp. 285–302. Mathematics Education in the Digital Era. Switzerland: Springer.

Höntzsch, Susan, Uwe Katzky, Klaus Bredl, Frank Kappe, and Dirk Krause 2013 Simulationen Und Simulierte Welten: Lernen in Immersiven Lernumgebungen. InternetDocument. http://l3t.tugraz.at/index.php/LehrbuchEbner10/article/download/102/108.

Joubert, Marie 2017 Revisiting Theory for the Design of Tasks: Special Considerations for Digital Environments. *In* Digital Technologies in Designing Mathematics Education Tasks: Potential and Pitfalls. Allen Leung and Anna Baccaglini-Frank, eds. Pp. 17–40. Mathematics Education in the Digital Era. Switzerland: Springer.

Keller, Thomas, and Andreas Hebeisen and Elke Brucker-Kley 2018a Integration of Children with Special Needs in Mathematics Through Virtual Reality. *In* Pp. 30–37. http://www.iadisportal.org/digital-library/integration-of-children-with-special-needs-in-mathematics-through-virtual-reality, accessed May 22, 2019.

2018b Integration of Children with Special Needs in Mathematics through Virtual Reality. *In* Pp. 30–37. http://www.iadisportal.org/digital-library/integration-of-children-with-special-needs-in-mathematics-through-virtual-reality, accessed February 22, 2019.

Krauthausen, Günter 2012 Digitale Medien Im Mathematikunterricht Der Grundschule. Heidelberg: Spektrum Akademischer Verlag.

Laborde, Colette 2011 Designing Substantial Tasks to Utilize ICT in Mathematics Lessons. *In* Mathematics Education with Digital Technology. Adrian Oldknow and Carol Knights, eds. Pp. 75–83. New York: Continuum International Publishing Group.

Samsung Studie: Lehrer Sehen Großes Potenzial Für Die Nutzung von Virtual Reality Im Unterricht 2017 PressRelease. Schwalbach/Ts. https://news.samsung.com/de/wp-content/themes/sw_newsroom/download.php?id=NfO684PPbcmccJ0mMOmjsg%3D%3D.

Sinclair, Nathalie, and Rina Zazkis 2017 Everybody Counts: Designing Tasks for TouchCounts. *In* Digital Technologies in Designing Mathematics Education Tasks: Potential and Pitfalls. Allen Leung and Anna Baccaglini-Frank, eds. Pp. 175–192. Mathematics Education in the Digital Era. Switzerland: Springer.

THE LEARNING DESIGN FOR MEDIATION TRAINING THROUGH ONLINE ENVIRONMENTS: GETTING TO THE FIFTH LANGUAGE SKILL

Mª Mercedes Rico Garcia[1], Laura V. Fielden Burns[2] and María José Naranjo Sánchez[1]
University of Extremadura
[1]Centro Universitario de Mérida, Santa Teresa de Jornet, 38, 06800 Mérida, Spain
[2]Faculty of Teacher Traning, Campus Universitario, S/N, Cáceres, Spain

ABSTRACT

From the skills needed to adjust for the current mismatch between labor market demands and higher education training, collaboration and the development of communication strategies stand out. To improve communication as a whole, *The Common European Framework of Reference for Languages (CEFR)*, constitutes a body of reference which adds to the traditional skills new descriptors such as mediation and online interaction. The study constitutes a step towards the identification and design of online training to develop foreign languages mediation competences through virtual environments; that is, the reconstruction of meaning through online production, reception, culture and interaction practices. The contextualization for doing so is a unique one that is relevant to intercultural competences: critical incidents, which will form the basis of the contextualization of learning activities for the proposal. The learning proposal, resulting in the active involvement of students after previous phases of practical experimentation in virtual environments, and the set of parameters guiding the design constitute the main implications of the study.

KEYWORDS

Mediation, CEFR, Online Teaching, Critical Incident

1. INTRODUCTION

The identification of skill gaps between labor market expectations and academic training has forced higher education institutions to reflect on whether universities provide the necessary training to satisfy academic and market demands. The 2018 report 'The Global Graduate Skills Gap in the 21st Century' examining the relationship between graduate skills and employer needs has exposed the skills gap to be a global and worldwide issue. This mismatch in expectations between students and employers needs to be urgently addressed to bridge both sides, making students understand how employers value skills and universities train students in specific areas for successful employment. Among other actions, it has resulted in the adoption of competence-based approaches where students acquire not only specific competences, but master other skills, transferable to a great deal of occupational situations (Rico et al., 2013; Pérez et al., 2010).

In this context, we can raise a question concerning the identification of the skills needed for better employability in the coming years. With the world advancing so fast, it seems to be obvious that the skills needed are also rapidly changing. However, while the digital world and its consequences on the labor market are expanding, soft skills like communication, problem-solving, collaboration, team work, creativity, etc. are becoming as valued as technological knowledge and expertise. In this sense, the World Economic Forum reports that the ten skills needed to thrive in 2020 are:

Table 1. Skills for 2020 according to the World Economic Forum

2020 skills	
• Complex problem solving.	• Emotional intelligence.
• Critical thinking.	• Judgement and decision making.
• Creativity.	• Service orientation.
• People management.	• Negotiation.
• Coordinating with others.	• Cognitive flexibility

In most of these skills, collaboration and communication strategies need to be further trained, which brings us to the need to develop overall communication techniques and other language related skills, both in terms of their development in native languages (L1) and foreign languages (L2). Yet, how can we define these cross curricular abilities so as to improve communicative competences? A description validated internationally in terms of communication from a foreign language learning perspective is The Common European Framework of Reference for Languages (CEFR), a general framework which also includes scales of updated and new descriptors such as mediation and online interaction. Among these, mediation stands out as one of the leading interpersonal skills ("soft skills") of 21st century communication (North and Piccardo, 2016).

Although this framework was created with foreign language learning in mind, it was intended to generally cover the skills needed to communicate successfully, and to be widely applicable to any language, which makes it an appropriate reference for discussing language skills globally, as well. Although mediation has been included in the Common European Framework of Reference for Languages (Council of Europe 2001; 2018) and has been considered an ability users of a given language should possess so that they can participate in today's multicultural contexts, it has not received much attention and has rarely been included in foreign language curricula until recently. This dearth of research supports the need for further investigation.

In this context, the present study constitutes a step towards the identification of descriptors and the design of online training actions to develop foreign languages mediation competences through virtual environments. The research starts by presenting the theoretical framework which supports the study (mediation and online teaching environments). The learning proposal, constituting the main body of the study, consists of a theoretical set of parameters to follow in the design of mediation activities delivered through virtual environments and a set of practical instances to exemplify our teaching proposal.

2. BODY OF PAPER

2.1 Theoretical Background

2.1.1 Mediation

Coste & Cavalli (2015: 12) noted that in terms of the objective of mediation skills, "The aim (...) *is to reduce the gap between two poles that are distant from or in tension with each other*", where mediation is based on the dynamic of the construction of meaning through production, reception, culture and interaction. These relationships are shown in Table 2:

Table 2. Mediation concepts

Mediating communication	Cognitive mediation	
	Mediating concepts	Mediating Texts
Strengthening the effectiveness of communication: • Creating a positive environment • Showing cultural awareness • Facilitating collaborative interaction • Resolving difficult situations	• Collaborating with others to make a decision or to solve a problem	• Transmitting / summarizing / synthesizing information and ideas • Adaptation

Mediation practice is considered to be a key ingredient to intercultural communication, which, among others, focuses on social attributes, thoughts and cultural patterns, factors which are all linked to intercultural understanding, meaning decodification etc. Thus, mediation is defined as a process where users (meditators) are not concerned about expressing their own meanings, but are acting as an intermediary to extract messages from a verbal or visual, spoken or written text in one language, to achieve communicative goals. In this context, intercultural communication has also aroused great interest in the business world, (Moore, May & Wold, 2012) since future professionals must face cultural differences in order to do their jobs successfully. Mediation training is consequently carried out in a variety of contexts and formats in academic and professional settings, emphasizing the suitability of small groups, in-class interaction, and, particularly, the use of role-play and simulations (Walsh, 2015).

2.1.2 Critical Incidents as Context for Mediation

One of the areas where mediation is particularly key is in the managing of what are known as critical incidents in intercultural contact situations, where conflicts of an intercultural nature, such as a misunderstanding about something originating in one's cultural experience, occurs, and is the trigger for a conflict of some kind. These "often derive from mismatches of expectations and are exacerbated by communication and intercultural issues" (Vannini et al, 2017). Previous studies have pointed to these contexts as excellent teaching resources for fomenting greater cultural awareness and understanding in foreign language students (Stakhnevich, 2002; Westwood, & Ishiyama, 1990). What is essentially taught as a resolution to these cultural interactions are the skills of successful mediation, where the host of communicative skills participants utilize to understand one another and create meaning together despite their differences lead to better negotiation and more satisfying outcomes for both parties. We will suggest here that mediation training may use this teaching resource, critical incidents, as a model for contextualizing mediation, following in particular the framework of Brunello (2010; 2015), as adapted by Vannini, et al, 2017), which is based on intercultural communication studies and views the cultural component of critical incidents as fluid and contextually dependent (Vannini et al., 2017, 17).

2.1.3 Critical Incident Analysis (CIA) as a Context for Developing Mediation Skills

The CIA framework by Brunello (2015) notes that cultural incidents, those mismatches of expectations, can have a powerful consequence on relationships and thus outcomes. He gives as an example the bewilderment Belgian project partners experienced to find that their Burundian counterparts were not using the much-requested computer labs funded by their Belgian partners. The first step to analyzing this conflict was to understand what each party was taking for granted: the Belgians assumed that when a hard drive fails it must be fixed, while their counterparts assumed that when a hard drive fails the computer must stop being used, resulting in an empty lab. The CIA framework is based on the situation in which communication occurs, which must take into account "context, culture, history and stakeholders' different interests", such as those exemplified above (Vannini, et al., 2017, 19-20). The CIA framework includes reflection questions which we have organized into the following communicative phases:

Phase 1: Locating and naming expectations
Phase 2: Determining personal responses of mismatched expectations
Phase 3: Assessing level of consequence to mismatches
Phase 4: Reviewing the communicative process

To work these skills in depth, training should be delivered in a variety of contexts and formats where small group teaching, interactive, workshop-style approaches and, particularly, the use of role-play and simulations are emphasized (Walsh, 2015). This type of training must also be considered for a virtual environment, since demand for online learning has been growing, particularly in the higher and professional education sectors, with online enrollments continuing to increase year after year, and showing an increasing focus on teaching job-specific skills online (Friedman, 2018). Online higher education enrollments now outpace ordinary enrollments in university and changing demographics and employer needs are driving a radical shift in how learning is being accessed and consumed (Fong, Schroeder, & Halfond, 2017). However, how can we activate and develop the mediation skills of students in virtual environments across different language proficiency levels when working in a foreign language learning context?

2.1.4 Mediation Tasks through Online Environments

Since geographical barriers are one of the main shortcomings which hinder communicative interaction in many educational settings, with the help of ICT online simulations can be designed to enable users to interact with speakers of other languages and cultures. In agreement with Siegel (2010) and Jauregi & Canto (2012), virtual environments can encourage interaction and facilitate mediation training. Analyzing a set of learning theories, interaction in online environments is also studied by Sadler (2012). The author states the importance of design relevant inputs to achieve successful language acquisition through virtual worlds.

In this line, Iwasaki (2014) claims that cultural competences can be trained by applying the "five Cs" that occur in this virtual world: Communication, Culture, Connections, Comparisons and Communities. Simultaneously, the explosion of online teaching and research in terms of language acquisition, the development of communicative competences and the chances for professional training, has been progressively increasing the demand of blended and /or virtual proposals, mainly in the higher and professional education sectors (Friedman, 2018). In this sense, and in line with our research objectives, efforts should be placed on designing training activities based on solid pedagogic approaches, technologically mediated, to design effective online mediation teaching proposals.

2.2 Learning Design. Proposals to Develop Mediation Skills for Virtual Environments

With the learner at the forefront of the learning process, an effective learning design involves taking decisions around creating pedagogically valuable learning activities where students can take on the role of mediators through teaching practices (role play, simulations, etc.) in appropriate learning scenarios. To reach this end, we can identify a set of considerations which should be taken into account in the design of effective learning proposals.

2.2.1 Pedagogic Considerations

1) The design of learning and teaching activities must be based on appropriate theoretical foundations. Here we turn to experiential learning, which according to Kolb (1984) is seen as a process where learners (1) are exposed to specific experiences, (2) observe and reflect on those situations, (3) create abstract concepts, and (4) test learning in future learning or professional situations.

2) Importance of role-plays to promote mediations (Alexander & Lebaron, 2009; Raines et al.2010). Role play and simulations should provide feedback by tutors and peers which lead students to self-evaluation and reflection.

3) Following learning approaches as experiential learning (experiential learning cycles), the design of tasks (role play, simulations, etc.) broken into stages to maximize its efficiency. In this model, the role-play describes the concrete mediating experience, where the observation and reflection phases may give rise to new concepts that should be evaluated though further practice (a new role play, discussion, etc.)

4) If online training reveals any current and future teaching trend, it is that research and practice should be focused on designing experiential learning activities delivered online, not only by promoting reflection but also by encouraging active skill practice. Unfortunately, much of the content of courses on online mediation seems to consist exclusively of pre-recorded webinars and reading materials without any practical element. Determining what content should be included and how training should be delivered is key (Gonçalves & Rainey, 2018).

5) The usage of quasi-real scenarios such as those presented in immersive platforms, augmented or virtual worlds (Second Life, Fablusi,) is also a good choice to enhance online role-play and simulation activities for a higher education context and professional training (Wills et al., 2011).

6) According to Matz & Ebner (2011), aspects such as transferability should be considered, that is, preparing students for sitting at a real negotiation table; improving human-computer interaction, efficient administration and control, as well as promoting observation and feedback

7) According to Parlamis & Mitchell (2014) in order for online role-play activities to be effective, they must be designed for the online environment, rather than merely replicated from a face-to-face setting. Parlamis & Mitchell explicitly chose replication of an identical face-to-face course online, claiming that this replication may be greatly responsible for making online role-plays less effective.

2.3 Online Practice Proposals

2.3.1 Critical Incident Contextualization

The activities developed follow a critical incident framework according Brunnello (2015), and lean on the Kolb experiential learning model as a methodological guide, whose phases are indicated in the table in italics. What follows is a basic overview of the structuring of the learning proposal in terms of its phasing and progression. It should be noted that prior to these phases students would undergo an introductory lesson on the nature of critical incidents, intercultural competency and mediation that would prepare them to work with these concepts. A general organizing framework for the activities, based on Kolb (1984) is seen is Table 3.

Table 3. Kolb (1984). Experiential learning applied framework for activities

Activity Types	Phase 1 Problem solving & information gap (Exposure to new experience)	Phase 2 Information exchange (Observe and reflect)	Phase 3 Group presentations & discussion (Create abstract concepts)	Phase 4 Active Experimentation (Learning in future learning or professional situations)
Specific skill coverage (reading, speaking, listening, a combinatio n of skills, etc.).	The critical incident is introduced as context for the need for mediation. This can be presented in a variety of formats, including video, audio, and written text. Once the context is presented, students begin to interpret the incident in pairs through follow-up questions, which are created using as a base the reflective questions for pinpointing mismatched expectations (Vanninni, et al., 2017).	Students consider personal aspects that are contributing to the conflict, continuing interaction with their peers in chats and forums. They begin to formulate opinions and present these in media formats such as written texts, video, audio etc. to exchange views with other pairs and get other perspectives.	Developing a scenario projection of the possible consequences of the conflict in terms of best, worst and middle-ground effects that could be expected from the situation. They develop these scenarios as an on-line game format in Second Life, where different paths occur depending on the consequences and mediation developed by the participants, which are presented to their peers in presentations on –line.	In this final stage, students use their Second Life avatars to simulate real-life response to the conflict, using in mediation strategies to engage in role-plays that are realistic and effective.

This framework would then be applied to a series of activities to be developed through a variety of ICT tools, including on-line forums and chats, wikis, blogs, virtual worlds such as Second Life, etc. For an example for how such activities can be designed Tables 4 and 5 show two examples of activity series that would allow students to progress through the phases of experiential learning and mediation strategies while working with critical incidents.

Table 4. From critical incidents to active experimentation, example 1

Mediation Activity 1	
Phase in learning	Information gap: problem presentation
Type	Processing oral speech
Skill coverage	listening, writing
ICT tool	On-line videos
Mediation strategy	Identify and analyze mismatched expectations
Description	Students, in pairs, watch different videos of critical incidents and respond to follow-up questions. They work in pairs to give short answers on what is going on and why, using a guide. Critical incidents include situations where parties from different cultures interact around the following scenarios: arriving late to class, looking at written feedback from someone at work, using exam notes in class, smoking outside, paying for group meals, etc.
Mediation activity 2	
Phase in learning	Mini-presentation and information exchange
Type	Producing texts to construct meaning
Skill coverage	writing
Mediation strategy	Identify and analyze what personal responses occur
ICT tool	Blogs
Description	In pairs, students produce a blog entry on a website called Cultural Perspectives: Wherever You Go, There You Are to describe their particular critical incident to the rest of the class. The objective is to define the critical incident in terms of the mismatched expectations for a lay audience and make the cultural expectations clear. They produce a blog as a class and do follow-up comments to one another's entries with guided questions.
Mediation activity 3	
Phase in learning	Group presentations
Type	Producing scenarios
Skill coverage	writing, reading
ICT tool	Digital presentations
Mediation strategy	Understand consequences of mismatched expectations
Description	In pairs again students create a digital presentation on the possible consequences of the critical incident and explain it in a video to show the variety of consequences the critical incident might have in best case, worst case and a middle-ground scenario.
Mediation activity 4	
Phase in learning	Active experimentation
Type	Role play
Skill coverage	speaking, listening
ICT tool	Second Life avatars
Mediation strategy	Engage in metacommunication
Description	In pairs students do a role play of one of the scenarios with Second Life avatars they have created before-hand, with mediation and communicative strategies in place. These are recoded on-line, and their peers watch their role play and respond through a designated forum with mediation strategy suggestions for improvement. Pairs then return to the avatar role play to repeat with changes taking into account at least one peer suggestion. These are recorded.

3. CONCLUSION

The CEFR pioneered the introduction of mediation as a skill traditionally ignored by other frameworks on reception and production competences. More than merely an additional skill, mediation includes a much- needed social dimension to language learning, the co-construction of meaning and its dynamic nature, including the relationship between the individual and social levels in language learning. Examining this co-construction in the context of critical incidents provides an ideal way for revealing how communication goes awry when factors of cultural relativity are considered. Critical incidents in this sense are an ideal via for mediation skills development since they focus on the reflective process needed for effective communication and the self-and others-awareness key to positive outcomes in difficult circumstances.

The descriptors and the learning design provided are the main implications of this study and may help test designers and item-writers to decide what mediation tasks to design for each level and what aspects of language to focus on. The experimental learning methodology followed in our research (Kolb, 1984), based on a cyclical process that results in active experimentation from previous phases of observation and reflection, can be applied to a great number of interactions in virtual worlds, in which learners can observe language and behavior and interiorize cultural competencies of other virtual word inhabitants. Virtual environments facilitate student-like-avatars' interaction among users and the world around them, affordances which include the facilitation of tasks that lead to enhanced spatial representation, and opportunities for experiential multicultural interaction within an environment where variables such as anxiety minimization, anonymity, and motivation are key for successful language learning. Some of the most important barriers preventing students from using a foreign language effectively are related to inhibitions and fear of negative criticism.

However, practical research must be done on what online learning design frameworks support effective virtual role-plays and how they can best guide the construction and implementation of those activities.

REFERENCES

Alexander, N., Lebaron, M. 2009. Death of the role-play. In C. Honeyman, J. Coben, & G. De Palo (Eds.), *Rethinking negotiation teaching: Innovations for context and culture*. St. Paul, MN: DRI Press, pp. 179–197.

Brunello, P. 2010. ICT for education projects: a look from behind the scenes. Information Technology for Development, Vol. 16, N° 3, pp. 232 – 239.

Brunello, P. 2015. Broken Premises: Towards an Intercultural Understanding of Bilateral Co-operation in ICT for Education in Burundi (Doctoral dissertation). Royal Holloway University of London, London, UK. Retrieved fromhttps://pure.royalholloway.ac.uk/portal/en/publications/broken-premises-towards-an-intercultural-understanding obilateral-cooperation-in-icts-for-education-in-burundi(ed7d06ce-047b-403a342-5500223842ad).html

Common European Framework of Reference for Languages (CEFR): https://www.coe.int/en/web/common-european-framework-reference-languages.

Council of Europe. 2001. *Common European Framework of Reference for Languages: Learning, Teaching, Assessment* (CEFR), CUP, Cambridge. Available on line at www.coe.int/lang-CEFR.

Coste, D and Cavalli, M. 2015. *Education, mobility, otherness - The mediation function of schools*, Council of Europe, Strasbourg, Chapter 3.1.1. www.coe.int/lang

Council of Europe (2018). Common European framework of reference for languages: learning, teaching, assessment – Companion volume with new descriptors. Strasbourg: Council of Europe Publishing. Available at www.coe.int/lang-cefr.

Friedman, J.2018. Expectations for online education in 2018. US News.

Fong, J., Schroeder, R., and Halfond, J. 2017. *The changing landscape for professional and continuing education in the U.S.* Washington, DC: University Professional and Continuing Education Association.

Gonçalves, A. M. and Rainey, D. 2018. Standards, qualifications, and certification for. *International Journal of Online Dispute Resolution*, Vol., Pp. 1–2.

Iwasaki, I. 2014. Exploring Second Life for effective English as a Foreign Language and Culture Learning (竹中暉雄教授退任記念号). 桃山学院大学人間科学, Vol.45, pp. 205-220.

Jauregi, K. and Canto, S. 2012. Enhancing meaningful oral interaction in Second Life. In *Procedia - Social and Behavioral Sciences*, Vol. 3, N° 4, pp. 111 – 115.

Kolb, D. A.1984. *Experiential learning: Experience as the source of learning and development* (Vol. 1). Englewood Cliffs, NJ: Prentice-Hall.

Matz, D., and Ebner, N. 2011. Using role-play in online negotiation teaching. In C. Honeyman, J. Coben, & G. De Palo (Eds.), *Venturing beyond the classroom St Paul, MN: DRI Press, Vol. 2, pp. 293–317.*

Moore, S., May, D., and Wold, K. 2012. Developing cultural competency in engineering through transnational distance learning. *Transnational distance learning and building new markets for universities*, pp. 210-228.

North, B. and Piccardo, E. 2016. Developing illustrative descriptors of aspects of mediation for the Common European Framework of Reference (CEFR). A Council of Europe project. *Language Teaching* Vol. 49, N°3, pp. 1-5

Parlamis, J. D., and Mitchell, L. D. 2014. Teaching negotiations online. *Negotiation Journal*, Vol. *30*, pp. 93–113.

Pérez, J.E. et al., 2010. Active learning and generic competences in an operating systems course. *Engineering Journal of Education,* Vol. 26, pp. 1484-1492.

Raines, S. S., Hedeen, T., and Barton, A. B. 2010. Best practices for mediation training and regulation: Preliminary findings. *Family Court Review*, Vol. 48, Nª483; PP. 541–554.

Rico, M et al. J. 2013. Everything matters: Development of cross-curricular competences in engineering through Web 2.0 social objects, In: D.G. Sampson, P. Isaias, D. Ifenthaler, and J. M. Spector (Eds.), *Ubiquitous and mobile learning in the digital age*, Springer Science & Business Media, New York, NY, pp. 139-157.

Sadler, R. 2012. *Virtual Worlds for Language Learning: From Theory to Practice*, New York, NY: Peter Lang.

Siegel, S. 2010. Gaining Cultural Intelligence through Second Life Learning Interventions. *The International Conference on E-Learning in the Workplace.*

Stakhnevich, J. 2002. Using critical incidents to teach cross-cultural sensitivity. *The Internet TESL Journal*, Vol. 8, Nª 3.

Vannini, S., et al. 2017. Critical Incidents Analysis: mismatching expectations and reconciling visions in intercultural encounters. *The Journal of Community Informatics*, Vol *13*, N° 2.

Walsh, S. 2015. Beyond the role-play—Re-thinking mediator education. *Journal of Mediation & Applied Conflict Analysis*, Vol. *2*, N°2, pp.317–327.

Westwood, M. J. and Ishiyama, F. I. 1990. The communication process as a critical intervention for client change in cross-cultural counseling. *The Journal of Multicultural Counseling and Development, Vol. 18*, N° 4, pp.1-6.

Wills, S., Leigh, E., and I, A. 2011. *The power of role-based e-learning.* New York, NY: Routledge.

GOING BEYOND TECHNOLOGICAL AFFORDANCES - ASSESSING ORGANIZATIONAL AND SOCIO-INTERACTIONAL AFFORDANCES

Kirsi Lainema[1], Timo Lainema[2], Raija Hämäläinen[1] and Kirsi Heinonen[1]
[1] *University of Jyväskylä, Finland*
[2] *University of Turku, Finland*

ABSTRACT

Analysis of the applicability of a learning technology requires evaluating how the affordances of the technology respond to the users' needs. We examine affordances of a digital learning environment. We concentrate on organizational and socio-interactional affordances, which are based on technological affordances. The analysis shows how organizational and socio-interactional affordances emerge from the use of technological affordances. We offer an analytical understanding of the dynamics of various kinds of affordances and how they can be assessed to help educators to better understand how the learning process and the use of affordances can be facilitated and supported.

KEYWORDS

Organizational Affordances, Socio-Interactional Affordances, Computer-Based Learning

1. INTRODUCTION

The use of different learning technologies has rapidly increased on all educational fields, and along it, the study of affordances has gained momentum. The term 'affordance' was first coined by Gibson (1979, cited in Salomon, 1993), who used it to refer to the functional properties that determine the possible *utility* of an object or an environment. Affordances can be defined as action possibilities latent in the object (the learning environment) and dependent on the capabilities of the agent (learners) (Antonenko, Dawson & Sahay, 2017). Affordances are more than just technical properties of an object, as they represent an action potential that needs to be met with respective capabilities of the user. A chair represents an everyday case in point. Chair's affordance is sit-*ability*, and it can be used for that purpose by a person who wants and is able to sit. In the context of a digital learning environment affordances include, e.g. view-*ability*, read-*ability*, and move-*ability*.

It is apparent that the *technological* aspects of digital learning environments dominate the current discussion, and the *socio-interactional* and *organizational* aspects receive less attention. We find, however, that it is mandatory to gauge into the interplay of the three types of affordances in more detail to develop a better understanding on how digital learning environments can be designed and applied to empower students to utilize their full capacity and all available resources. In doing so we also re-consider the notion of affordances as resources for computer-supported collaborative learning (CSCL) (Koschmann, 2012).

Analysis of the applicability and usefulness of a technology requires evaluating how the affordances of the technology respond to the users' needs and abilities (Antonenko, Dawson & Sahay, 2017). Some examples of the affordances of social software tools are, for example, connectivity and social rapport, and collaborative information discovery and sharing (McLoughlin & Lee, 2007). As an example of the first, technology-based environments support networks of people and facilitate connections between them. These kinds of environments are representatives of what Gee (2004) calls affinity spaces, where people acquire both social and communicative skills, and at the same time become engaged in the participatory culture of the environment. In these spaces, learners engage in informal learning, and creative, expressive forms of behavior and identity seeking, while developing a range of digital literacies. One cannot assume that just because social software entails certain affordances, it is all that is required for effective learning. Careful planning and a thorough understanding of the dynamics of these affordances are mandatory (McLoughlin

& Lee, 2007). An explicit approach to identifying technological affordances of e-learning tools and the affordance requirements of e-learning tasks should be used to scaffold the learning design process (Bower, 2008).

Traditionally, socio-culturally oriented research perspective on CSCL is closely associated with affordances (Moeate et. al., 2019). The focus is on group learning and how the social context in which collaboration emerges. This presentation is in line with the notion from Arvaja, Salovaara, Häkkinen and Järvelä (2007), who view collaboration as shared knowledge construction, where participants not only cumulatively share knowledge together, but where the knowledge construction is jointly built on others' ideas and thoughts (see also Mercer, 2010). The aim is that the activities of the collaborative group are not a collection of individual activities, but rather interdependent group processes (e.g. interactions) pursuing a shared conception of a problem (Roschelle & Teasley, 1995). Furthermore, these shared processes are mediated by the community and social context in which the group work takes place (Stahl, 2012).

We argue that the continually increasing amount of resources allocated to the development of educational simulations by educational institutions calls for in-depth studies of affordances. We need to understand how simulations and games can be designed in pedagogically sound ways to empower the users to acknowledge the affordances embedded in these environments. Furthermore, we believe that the use the students make of online learning environments will very much depend on their attitudes towards these environments and on the perceived affordances. This is also the motivation of our study.

2. AFFORDANCES

Research of affordances is interdisciplinary, and while it originates from Ecological Psychology (Gibson, 1979), it has found application in Education (Kirschner, 2002), Information Systems, Organization Studies, and Management disciplines (Pozzi, Pigni & Vitari, 2013). We examine affordances of a digital learning environment perceived and utilized by dispersed student teams. The novelty of our study lies in incorporating not only the technological aspects of affordances in our analysis, but also including the socio-interactional and organizational dimensions to our treatment. The use of socio-interactional and organizational affordances plays a key role in how these technologies can be made to work.

As learners engage in a technology-based learning environment they perceive "affordances" of objects, defined as the acts or behaviors that are afforded or permitted by an object, place, or event (Michaels and Carello, 1981, p. 17). Affordances are, thus, different from properties of objects. Affordances are perceptions on what we can do with the properties of objects. Although affordances can be perceived as preconditions for an activity, they do not imply that a specific activity will occur (Greeno 1994). As affordances are just potentials for action, taking benefit of them requires that they are triggered (Volkoff and Strong 2013) or actualized (Strong et al. 2014). Pozzi, Pigni & Vitari (2013) recognize four steps in the application of affordances: an affordance exists; the user perceives the affordance; the user actualizes the affordance; and finally, the actualization leads to affordance effect. In our study we focus predominantly on affordances as the doings that the actors engage in. In doing so we follow Majchrzak and Markus (2012), who note that affordances are best phrased in terms of action verbs or gerunds, such as "share knowledge" or "information sharing" and involve technological, organizational and social dimensions.

Another novel aspect in our study is that while the overall learning environment is the same for all teams, the team members utilize and combine the various affordances differently and complementarily. Their particular combinations may depend, for example, on the availability and functionality of the technologies, the participants' personal preferences or a mutual team agreement, or the team members' technical skills. Consequently, the teams get organized differently, and utilize and develop different practices to organize the team task and to communicate in the teams. All this has an impact on what is done, when, by whom, and with what kinds of outcomes. This further emphasizes the importance of going beyond the mere technical affordances and assess how the available affordances are organized, taken benefit of, and affect interaction.

2.1 Technological Affordances

The concept of technology affordance refers to an action potential - what an individual or organization with a particular purpose can do with technology (Majchrzak and Markus, 2012). For example, essential for analyzing the potential utility of educational technologies is seen the issue of categorizing technological affordances and aligning them with the abilities they afford the users of the technology (Antonenko, Dawson & Sahay, 2017).

Bower (2008) makes an effort to describe affordances based on their physical characteristics, emphasizing their functionality. He proposes a methodology for matching the affordance requirements of learning tasks with the technological affordances of ICT tools. Bower's affordance classification system includes 11 different areas of technological affordances (see Table 1). In this paper we focus predominantly in the actual action possibilities perceived and utilized by the users (usability). Moreover, we are interested in analyzing the dynamics of technological, organizational and socio-interactional affordances, and their combinations as reported by the learners. Expanding our treatment from predominantly technological view allows for appreciating the interplay between and among the various types of affordances.

2.2 Organizational Affordances

With organizational affordances we refer to the practices of organizing that the actors produce in situ and take advantage of. The organizational dimension of social learning environments is often overlooked and treated as a taken-for-granted element. Our analysis shows, however, that the organizational dimension is, in fact, quite crucial for the team's functioning and the outcomes of the learning exercise. Thus, the way the teamwork is organized has a fundamental influence on what is learned during the exercise.

At first glance, organizational affordances may seem a fuzzy category, as it sometimes is difficult to discern which actions can, in fact, be understood as organizing. In our context organizing is regarded as assembling the available resources to attain order, structure and organizational objectives (BusinessDictionary, 2019). In addition to assembling resources to attain certain objectives, organizational affordances entail also managing the process and the participants. This is accomplished through communication, so organizational and socio-interactional affordances are closely linked and intertwined.

2.3 Socio-Interactional Affordances

Socio-interactional affordances comprise of the various synchronous and asynchronous forms of communicating: emailing, chatting on Skype or Facebook, and on-line talk using VoIP-applications. We found that the participants employed different interactional affordances depending on the situation at hand, and more importantly, depending on their team role.

3. CASE LEARNING ENVIRONMENT, DATA AND ANALYSIS

The study was conducted with higher education business students (N= 207) from 10 universities (2 from Austria, Belgium, China, Estonia, 3 from Finland, New Zealand and USA). These students represented 38 different nationalities (the biggest ones being Finnish 52 students, New Zealandian 52, Austrian 29, Belgian 15, and Chinese 14). Participants were undergraduate students. The simulation game is a clock-driven business simulation, in which the game processes evolve hour by hour. The participants need to make decisions continuously, and not as batches as is the normal case in business simulations. The clock-driven nature of the simulation requires that participants run their simulation companies *in synchronous collaboration*. As the teams of participants were quite big, the teams worked in shifts. It was recommended that during the 14 hour simulation day each team had at least 3-4 participants online all the time. Shift work was natural also from the point of view of the geographical dispersion of the participants - from New Zealand to New York, USA.

The students were placed in teams of 10-13 members (18 teams in total). The teams had a real-time view to their simulation companies through a remote connection. This means that all the team members online saw the same simulation screen on the remote computer, and all the team members were able to make decisions in the simulation. The members used real-time communication in their internal team communication. This was done mostly by using Voice over Internet Protocol (Skype), but some teams also collaborated using chat and email. The students were assigned to write two reflective essays in English: the first directly after the first gaming session, and the second after the final gaming session. We focus on analysing the first essays.

3.1 Data Collection

Out of the 207 participating students, 177 returned the essay after the first simulation session. Students were asked to reflect on teamwork, roles, tasks and virtual collaboration and communication.

3.2 Analysis

Data were analyzed with qualitative content analysis using data-driven analysis (e.g. Krippendorf 2014). The data analysis process was inductive, allowing for the analytical categories to emerge from the data rather than pursuing to fit the data into existing categories. The question that was posed to the data was: what issues/elements in the gaming exercise enabled or hindered the team task? Most students were quite talkative, and wrote lengthy descriptions of their gaming experience. While doing so, they explained how their team got organized, and how they worked as a team. The use of technologies played a key role, and the technology was put in use by means of communication and collaboration.

The analysis entailed careful close reading of the data in iterative rounds. First, two of the authors conducted the qualitative analysis independently. During the reading the observations were summed up and coded in categories of different types of "doings". The findings were mutually discussed, and the analytical categories were further refined to better respond to the aim of the study. Further analyses helped sharpen the focus and yielded in three main categories of action potentials: technological, socio-interactional, and organizational affordances. The analysis details how participants to the learning simulation perceived and seized the various affordances in the learning environment, and how these were intertwined and influenced by each other.

The simulation game exercise consists of different phases and tasks. First, the participants need to familiarize themselves individually with the relevant materials and finalize the course pre-assignments. Then, the team members need to get acquainted with each other, and get the team organized. This is the time point when the team work factually begins, and when the participants start to interact with each other and with the learning environment and its elements. The simulation game is run on two separate days (2 weeks in between), and there are team assignments and individual assignments between the gaming days and after the final gaming day. Our analysis focuses on two sets of activities: activities before the first simulation exercise and activities during the first simulation exercise. This type of an analysis allows for gauging into the specific nature of affordances perceived and employed at each stage. In the next section we present the findings of our analysis.

4. FINDINGS

We report on the preliminary findings of our analysis on a general level. Already this preliminary analysis brings forth important observations. As expected, the three types of affordances seem to be intertwined and co-dependent. Hence, it is arbitrary to forcefully try to separate them from each other. For clarity, we present the findings of our analysis categorized under technological, organizational, and socio-interactional affordances.

4.1 Technological Affordances

Many of the technological affordances were, in fact, related to technological prerequisites. When working in a digital learning environment some basic requirements need to be met before the gaming can take place. For example, in Bower's (2008; see table 1 below) classification, Media affordances and Spatial affordances are normally prerequisites for a functional e-learning system. Teams selected different communication technologies for different purposes and different tasks. E.g., email was found clumsy during gaming, whereas it was deemed an efficient form of disseminating information before gaming. In teams where the members shared more personal information, applications like Facebook were used more often than in teams with less personal information sharing. The choice and use of communication technologies played a key role also in how the teams got organized. In teams with poor audio connection, chat or text messaging was the technology of choice. Some teams moved from audio to chat particularly due to problems with audio. Group discussion in audio were sometimes deemed chaotic due to simultaneous talk and delays in broadcast. On the other hand, some teams were successful in using audio, and found it very useful and convenient. The gaming exercise required simultaneous use of multiple technologies, and some teams quickly saw which combinations were most fruitful. Table 1 illustrates how the different technological affordances (Bower, 2008) show in the essays.

Table 1. Identified Technological affordances (adapted from Bower, 2008)

Technical Affordance	**Explanation**	**Example of how shows in student essays**
Media affordances	Input and output	*Being able to call and interact/discuss with other team members while the game is running was what made the game so alive and exciting* (Team 4).
Spatial affordances	Ability to resize elements, move and place elements.	
Temporal affordances	Access anytime anywhere, synchronous versus asynchronous.	*I decided to join my team in the morning, at 05:00 UTC+0. At this time a few of my team members already worked on...* (Team 12).
Navigation affordances	Capacity to browse to other sections of a resource and move back/forward.	*...a chat with all the team members inside the programme can help us to converse easier because now we had to handle two programmes at the same time* (Team 3).
Emphasis affordances	Capacity to highlight aspects of resources.	*...we started tutoring new people by explaining everything that we were doing loudly and showing it directly in the simulation* (Team 3).
Synthesis affordances	Capacity to combine multiple tools together to create a mixed media environment.	*We mainly discussed by writing but also had Skype call(s)... I prefer not to speak English so writing was ideal for me* (Team 1)
Access-control affordances	Capacity to allow or deny who can operate, capacity to support one–one/many–many contributions.	*I ... expected that production, inventory and sales would've been spread into different pages making it all faster to control and not ... waiting someone to finish their own tasks.*(Team 1).
Technical affordances	Capacity to be used on various platforms, ability to adapt to bandwidth, efficiency of tools.	*In my shift was one girl who had a bad internet connection and therefore she couldn't take part in our Skype-conference* (Team 3).
Usability	Intuitiveness, ease of manipulating a tool.	*The game was easy to get into...* (Team 2).
Aesthetics	Appearance of interface.	
Reliability	Robustness.	*If the game cut out it would automatically re-connect...* (Team 4).

4.2 Organizational Affordances

Much of the organizational work in the simulation gaming exercise was related to securing the availability and timely delivery of resources. Before the simulation exercise the teams needed to get organized. Shift planning was needed to ensure that there were enough team members online, that is, a minimum of 3 people at any given time. Teams also needed to decide how to deal with the responsibilities and roles in the game. It was suggested in the game materials that teams choose designated persons to at least three roles: purchasing raw materials, managing the production, and making sales offers and deliveries to customers. In some teams one of the team members took the initiative to send out a Doodle poll to let the team members indicate when they were available and which role they felt most comfortable with. Others used different excel charts or sent emails to each other. Some teams made plans only for the shifts, and not the roles.

> *In general, I believe our team was overall very unbalanced, as the roles were not clearly defined,...and ultimately everybody had something to say to whatever was to be performed as company activity (production, offers, sales,...).* (Team 12)

However, it appeared that the roles needed not to be very precise and carefully planned for the team to function well.

> *I think we had very clear responsibilities and everyone did their best and we supported each other and helped when needed. Of course, because we didn't have a business strategy at all, everything we did was intuitive, so our functions or ways to do things were built up just in time in the game.* (Team 3)

Communication and organization for the teamwork went hand in hand, and teams with multiple communicative occasions and versatile organizational tools (Doodle, excel charts, explicit goal setting) were better prepared and oriented to the simulation exercise. In some of the teams one or two team members even contacted each team member individually to negotiate a suitable shift and role, which was regarded as a welcomed practice.

> *Firstly, the communication and enthusiasm of my team was beyond impeccable in my opinion. As soon as the team lists were released, I had emails from most of the members in my group by the end of that day.* (Team 3)

Some teams had clear leadership, either by self-selection or by mutual agreement. In these teams the leadership was more established and visible, and acknowledged by most team members. Leadership was partly an issue of controversy, as some participants had reservations for strong leadership. In general, however, teams with clear leadership reported more satisfaction and better results.

> *...I found the team to be relatively effective, although lacking a leader figure. Because of this, I stepped in and created a Facebook group in which we could communicate quicker than that over email. This was effective, and some team members created a roster where it was outlined what hours each individual was online for, and their duty during that given time.* (Team 15)

In the next table, the categories of organizational affordances are presented. Our analysis yielded in three types of organizational affordances or practices, which are partly overlapping. The categories are: organizing, managing, and leading. In the following table we present the activities in each category.

Table 2. Identified Organizational affordances

Organizing	**Managing**	**Leading**
Organizing shifts and tasks (Doodle poll, excel chart)	Managing one's own task	Pointing out critical areas and initiating discussion
Re-organizing shifts and tasks during gaming	"Feeling the pulse"– hearing how others are doing	Setting an agenda for team talks
Gathering information from the team and using it to securing and re-arranging resources	Suggesting what to do next - giving orders	Making projections based on the available data
Ensuring all areas are covered	Compromising through team talk – finding middle ground	Discussing and suggesting strategy
	Managing contacts to collaborative teams	Announcing decisions

The most important organizational work before the gaming exercise was to organize the shifts. Teams with sufficient amount of participants online at any given time were most satisfied with the team work. The teams with too few people online found it stressful and chaotic to try to run the simulation company. Our analysis illustrates how organizational affordances are made possible by employing technological affordances, which, in turn, are prerequisites for the whole learning exercise. It is the dynamics of the various kinds of affordances and their combinations in the digital learning environment that create the potential for learning.

4.3 Socio-Interactional Affordances

Some interactional aspects in the gaming exercise were, similarly to technological affordances, prerequisites of communication. For example, gaining access to the relevant information was imperative as without it the team members could not function properly. Another important aspect was that the needed information was available at the right time. This, in turn, was closely linked with the technology in use. Many teams found email and Skype chat clumsy for rapid communication and chose synchronous VOIP-solutions for talking about pressing issues. The analysis revealed that the socio-interactional affordances fall into four distinctive categories: observing, participating, facilitating, and chairing. Some affordances can be placed in multiple categories, but the main difference between the affordances is the level of input and activity.

In alternating between technologies and channels appropriately, different kinds of communicative contributions are relevant for the team task. However, if everyone was disseminating information and nobody was drawing conclusions, the team task and its accomplishment would be compromised. A balanced participation and contribution brings results and increases the team's satisfaction to the team's functioning.

> *I got so enthusiastic that I watched the game even later in my course because I was so excited about the project. Moreover, I am glad to be a part of such project because it teaches us more than any book about cross- cultural and virtual communication.* (Team 12)

Table 3. Identified Socio-interactional affordances

Observing	Participating	Facilitating	Chairing
Listening to what others are saying	Listening to what others are saying	Listening to what others are saying	Listening to what others are saying
	Acknowledging what others are saying	Encouraging others to speak	Drawing conclusions
	Listening, stepping back	Facilitating the discussion	Making suggestions
	Responding to what others are saying	Repeating what has been said	Announcing decisions
	Disseminating information	Disseminating information	Disseminating information
	Giving feedback	Giving feedback	Giving feedback
		Negotiating, finding middle ground	Negotiating, finding middle ground

When designing learning environments it is important to acknowledge the role of technological affordances as enablers or hindrances to the learning exercise. The technological affordances can be designed in ways that encourage and facilitate team work and interaction, and support the development of organizational skills.

5. CONCLUSION

An abundance of affordances does not mean that they will be perceived or utilized by the actors. As Kaptelinin and Nardi (2006) note, a technology must improve interactions between the individual and the environment to be useful. In the case at hand, operating in the learning environment required coordinated action to accomplish the team task, that is managing the virtual simulation manufacturing companies successfully. In their essays the participants described how they perceived and utilized the various affordances embedded in the learning environment, and to what kinds of outcomes. The participants evaluated their team success not only in terms of how well the team performed, but also how well the team worked together and what they learned. The latter, in our opinion, gives an even better indication of how affordances and their use is connected to learning.

Teams chose partly different combinations of communication technology. Before game most teams resorted to asynchronous communication technologies, such as email, to better control the flow of information and to have a record of all communication. During the simulation game synchronous communication via Skype was found most appropriate by most teams. However, some teams continued to rely on chat and not talk on-line. For some teams this choice was motivated by the team members' reluctance to speak English. Delays in communication lead, however, to misunderstandings, missing information, and confusion. It was apparent that the teams with most self-reported motivation and initial success made changes in their use of technology and communication tool according to what took place in the game. These teams also adapted their organization according to the situation and used appropriate organizational practices to pursue the best possible outcome for the team at any given situation. This is quite an important observation, since flexibility, adaptivity and the accommodation of available resources and affordances to the task at hand are some of the most important skills needed not only in learning activities, but on all areas of life.

Teams with less self-reported motivation and successful outcomes had less occasions of communication before and during the gaming exercise. These teams also resorted more to asynchronous communication during gaming, such as chat and email. Less satisfied teams seemed to be unable to adjust their team effort and to correct the down fall spiral. We assert that student-centered learning requires that the learning environment encourages and empowers the students to search for information, try different tactics and strategies, test ideas and create new knowledge. These potentials need, however, be carefully and purposefully designed and integrated in the learning environment, as they do not miraculously appear there without purposeful planning and effort. Consequently, we find that it is of utmost importance to study affordances in more depth, and to learn how they can be embedded in the learning environments to enhance and empower learning.

> *...this online simulation definitely surpassed by expectation of how much I would learn. Learning how to compromise, learning how to negotiate, learning how to speak up, learning how to manage, and most importantly, learning how to work as a collaborative team through an online virtual world.* (Team 4)

Our study illustrates that while the learning environment contained an abundance of affordances, available for all teams, the teams perceived them differently and employed them differently. Not all affordances were employed by all teams, which lead to varying outcomes and different perceptions of the success of the team work. A more thorough understanding of the dynamics of affordances can to design accessible and learning environments, and to help educators to better understand how the learning process and the use of affordances can be facilitated and supported.

REFERENCES

Arvaja, M., Salovaara, H., Häkkinen, P., & Järvelä, S. (2007). Combining individual and group-level perspectives for studying collaborative knowledge construction in context. *Learning and Instruction*, Vol. 17, No. 4, pp. 448–459.

Antonenko, P., Dawson, K., & Sahay, S. (2017). A framework for aligning needs, abilities and affordances to inform design and practice of educational technologies. *British Journal of Educational Technology*, Vol. 48, No. 4, pp. 916-927.

Bower, M. (2008). Affordance analysis–matching learning tasks with learning technologies. *Educational Media International*, Vol. 45, No. 1, pp. 3-15.

BusinessDirectory (2019). Online: http://www.businessdictionary.com/definition/organizing.html. June 27, 2019.

Gee, J. P. (2004) Situated Language and Learning: a critique of traditional schooling. London: Routledge.

Gibson, J. J. (1979). *The ecological approach to visual perception*. Boston: Houghton Mifflin.

Greeno, J. G. (1994). Gibson's affordances. *Psychological Review*, Vol. 101, No. 2, pp. 336-342.

Kirschner, P. A. (2002). Can we support CCSL? Educational, social and technological affordances. In Kirschner (ed.) *Three worlds of CSCL: Can we support CSCL?* Heerlen: Open Universiteit Nederland, pp. 7-47.

Kaptelinin, V. & Nardi, B. (2006). Acting with technology: activity theory and interaction design. Cambridge: MIT Press.

Koschmann, T. (2012). *CSCL: Theory and practice of an emerging paradigm*. Routledge.

Krippendorff, K. (2004). Content Analysis. An Introduction to Its Methodology. Sage Publications, Thousand Oaks, California. Second Edition

Majchrzak, A., & Markus, M. L. (2012). Technology affordances and constraints in management information systems (MIS). *Encyclopedia of Management Theory*, (Ed: E. Kessler), Sage Publications.

McLoughlin & Lee (2007). Social software and participatory learning: Pedagogical choices with technology affordances in the Web 2.0 era. *Proceedings ascilite,* Singapore. Online: https://researchbank.acu.edu.au/cgi/viewcontent.cgi?article=3049&context=fea_pub

Mercer, N. (2010). The analysis of classroom talk: Methods and methodologies. *The British Journal of Educational Psychology*, Vol. 80, pp. 1–14.

Michaels, C. F. and C. Carello (1981) *Direct Perception*. Englewood Cliffs, NJ: Prentice Hall.

Moate, J., Hulse, B., Jahnke, H., & Owens, A. (2019). Exploring the material mediation of dialogic space—A qualitative analysis of professional learning in initial teacher education based on reflective sketchbooks. *Thinking Skills and Creativity*, Vol. 31, pp. 167-178.

Pozzi, G., Pigni, F., & Vitari, C. (2013). Affordance theory in the IS discipline: A review and synthesis of the literature. *In AMCIS 2014 Proceedings*.

Roschelle, J., & Teasley, S. (1995). The construction of shared knowledge in collaborative problem solving. In C. O'Malley (Ed.), *Computer supported collaborative learning* (pp. 69–97). NATO ASO Series F: Computer and System Sciences, Vol. 128. Berlin: Springer-Verlag.

Salomon, G. (1993). No distribution without individuals' cognition: A dynamic interactional view. *Distributed cognitions: Psychological and educational considerations*, pp. 111-138.

Stahl, G. (2012). Ethnomethodologically informed. *International Journal of Computer-Supported Collaborative Learning*, Vol. 7, No. 1, pp. 1-10.

Strong, D. M., Johnson, S. A., Tulu, B., Trudel, J., Volkoff, O., Pelletier, L. R., Bar-On, I., and Garber, L. (2014). A Theory of Organization-EHR Affordance Actualization, *Journal of the Association for Information Systems*, Vol. 15, No. 2.

Volkoff, O., and Strong, D. M. (2013). Critical Realism and Affordances: Theorizing It-Associated Organizational Change Processes, *MIS Quarterly*, Vol. 37, No. 3, pp. 819–834.

AUTOMATIC ASSESSMENT TO ENHANCE ONLINE DICTIONARIES CONSULTATION SKILLS

Carla Marello, Marina Marchisio, Marta Pulvirenti and Cecilia Fissore
University of Turin, Italy

ABSTRACT

We live in a digital world and our students are surrounded by technologies: it is essential that they learn how to use the digital tools available for education purposes. As for language teaching, among the most recent technologies we can find online dictionaries. They could play a key role to foster language competences, and yet they are not very popular in schools. In order to increase the use of online dictionaries among students, the University of Turin has promoted the nation-wide project 'Esplorare (con) i Dizionari Digitali'. This project makes the most of a Learning Management System (https://esploradizionari.i-learn.unito.it/) that allowed the creation of a student-centered environment. The integration of the platform with an Automatic Assessment System allowed the design and creation of tests to be carried out through the consultation of online dictionaries. In this paper, we analyze the answers given by almost 600 students in 5 different tests on different languages, and we try to understand whether the methodologies and technologies adopted have been influential in making students "meta-linguistic aware" and researchers "meta-design aware". The results obtained show in a statistically significant way that the students who made a larger use of online dictionaries performed better in the tests.

KEYWORDS

Automated Assessment System, Digital Dictionary, Online Digital Lexicography, Reference Skills, Virtual Learning Environment

1. INTRODUCTION

Nowadays, students live in a technology-rich environment and quickly learn how to use different apps and technologies; their way of communicating with teachers and peers, interacting with learning materials, and demonstrating their knowledge have changed over the last years. For what concerns language teaching, among the various technologies that have spread since the advent of internet there are online dictionaries, i.e. monolingual or bilingual dictionaries (free or paid) that can be consulted via any mobile device. Online dictionaries could be a key tool to foster language competences, but they are not popular in schools. How can we motivate our students to use them? Teaching itself is not always enough, except for those languages (e.g. Latin) for which translation is still often practiced in class. The motivation should come directly from the layout of dictionaries, since they are always and easily available on a smartphone. One of the reasons why online dictionaries are not frequently used can be that they still need improvements in some of their search functions. At the same time, Italian lexicography market is not broad enough to justify a significant investment on it. Studying the use of digital dictionaries by students (Marello, 2014), we asked ourselves the following research question: *how to increase the use and the circulation of online dictionaries between students?* To answer to this question, two years ago the University of Turin has developed and promoted the nation-wide research project "Esplorare (con) i Dizionari Digitali", that is 'To Explore (with) Digital Dictionaries', with the goal of helping students understand how online dictionaries are structured so that they can be consulted. The project makes the most of a Virtual Learning Environment (https://esploradizionari.i-learn.unito.it/) that allowed the creation of a student-centered environment, so that students can easily approach online dictionaries and be trained on their use. The integration of the platform with an Automatic Assessment System has allowed the creation of tests with exercises, integrated with the consultation of online dictionaries, grouped by difficulty levels that allow to verify lexical knowledge. The project was made possible thanks to a fruitful cooperation with some high school teachers, who voluntarily chose to participate with their classes. Our research group designed interactive exercises to stimulate the use of online dictionaries. Teachers gave us feedback on how to refine them and chose which way to give the test to their students, whether at home or at school, in a computerized classroom supervised by teachers and researchers.

In this paper, we analyze the answers given by almost 600 students in 5 different tests of different languages to understand whether the methodologies and technologies adopted have been influential in making students "meta-linguistic aware" and researchers "meta-design aware".

2. TECHNOLOGIES AND ONLINE DICTIONARIES TO FOSTER LANGUAGE COMPETENCES

With the succession of new approaches and methods, suggested by the evolution of the psychology of education and theories of linguistic acquisition, but also by changing needs for new political, economic and social conditions, language teaching has resorted to various technological tools. Today, most linguists and language teachers consider unthinkable to teach and learn a language without using any technology (Betti & Garelli, 2010). With the advent of the Internet (1989), computers have definitively been established as an unavoidable tool for teaching and learning languages, as they are able to offer authentic materials of various types that could be far more stimulating than those created ad hoc by teachers and authors that are more interested in grammar rules than in the context of use of the language. In addition to a new way of considering languages, seen as a tool to communicate in the most diverse situations and contexts, other circumstances have favored the use of the computer, such as the theory of social constructivism. According to this theory, a person, in his cognitive, social and affective aspects of behavior, is not a product of the environment, nor the simple result of his internal dispositions, but a personal construction that is produced, day by day, in the interaction of these two factors.

The most significant reflection of constructivism in the teaching and learning of foreign languages is undoubtedly the recognition of the learner as an autonomous individual. The knowledge of a language is defined in terms of ability, of a "know-how", and the learner is considered as an autonomous and self-aware individual who works for the construction of his own future. Since 1976, the European Community has encouraged the use of technology in language teaching, implementing a real linguistic policy that emphasized the need to use multimedia, as recommended in the White Book of Education and Training (1995). More recently, in 2004-2006, the CoE drew up an Action Plan aimed at promoting language learning and linguistic diversity, thus giving everyone the opportunity to learn an L2 during the course of their lives, and improving their teaching through new technologies, as there are still teachers who are struggling to abandon traditional teaching techniques. Both teachers and students need to be taught how to efficiently use existing online resources, and students should be trained to a constant and more proficient autonomous use of such tools through specific tasks, so that they can expand their knowledge.

Online dictionaries are a key tool to learn new languages and to deepen the knowledge of one's mother tongue. Unfortunately, their use is not so widespread, as reports by the researchers cooperating in the European Network of e-Lexicography (ENeL) and in the European survey of dictionary use have shown that, in many countries, dictionaries and dictionary use have even been excluded from the curricula of high schools (Kosem et al., 2019). The cause of it could be seen in their design or their cost, which make them not accessible to everyone. In order to make them an exploited tool by students, it would be important to improve their layout, and to make them so useful, appealing, intuitive and self-explanatory that no training on their use should be necessary (Carr, 1997; De Schryver & Prinsloo, 2001; Klosa & Müller-Spitzer, 2018; Lew, 2011; Lew, 2015; Tarp, 2012).

The English Vocabulary Profile EVP is perhaps one of the closest achievements to this idea. It offers reliable information about which words (and importantly, which meanings of those words) and phrases should be known and used by learners at each level of the Common European Framework (CEF). There are the British and the American English versions, and an audio pronunciation for all entries. It is quite appealing, and it is designed for smartphone. However, experiments performed with university students demonstrate that they tend to use even the best digital dictionaries as if they were traditional dictionaries, which means they choose the first meaning listed, without taking advantage of all the features available within such dictionaries (Dziemianko, 2012).

Freely available Italian online dictionaries might be largely improved; just to mention three easy ways to make them more user-friendly, we might deal with display of homonyms, a 'did-you-mean' function, somewhat like a spellchecker (Lew & Mitton, 2013) and a lemmatizer. The visualization of homonyms should be improved, for example, typing "schifo" in the very good monolingual De Mauro on line it is not immediately clear that this word has two entries, the first one that means 'small rowing boat" and the second one (which is actually the most common one) that means "sense of nausea, disgust". The numbers used to distinguish them are so small that they are difficult to notice. Italian online dictionaries do not feature a 'did-you-mean' function "guessing" the correct spelling of words misspelled by users. In Garzanti, if you type the non existing entry coglio, they suggest ciglio, caglio, cogli; but if you type simbol instead of simbolo (i.e. symbol) no results are shown. Finally, a powerful lemmatizer is important above all in order to forward from inflected forms to the verb in its base form under which it is lemmatized and explained.

The starting point to improve dictionaries is to know which aspects of the dictionary microstructure are the most difficult, according to the different types of users. Eye-tracking studies and log files analysis were carried out to achieve this goal (Lew, 2015; Töpel, 2014; section V in Gouws et al., 2013), but in Italy these techniques are still to be applied in the field of online lexicography. In fact, the Italian dictionary market is not sizeable enough to justify a significant investment by publishing companies to further improve the online layout of dictionaries and to fund experimental research on online testing. The consequence is that Italian university researchers and teachers associations are taking the initiative to address the gap in their skills, to try to make the most of the tools that already exist and to train students to use online dictionaries as they are at present (Marello, 2014).

3. METHODOLOGY OF EXERCISE DELIVERY

The groundwork of the project "Esplorare (con) i Dizionari Digitali" has been influenced by the experience of our research group in the use of an Automatic Assessment System (AAS) in order to develop skills and competences of STEM disciplines (Science, Technology, Engineering, Mathematics). Moodle, a Virtual Learning Environment (VLE), was used, integrated with the AAS Möbius Assessment (Barana et al., 2015). This integration has proven to be effective for the teaching of Mathematics (Barana et al., 2019b) and in open online courses (Marchisio et al., 2019a; Marchisio et al., 2019b) as it exploits the mathematical engine behind it: the Advanced Computing Environment (ACE) Maple. It also allowed the creation of a model of formative automatic assessment and interactive feedback for STEM (Barana et al., 2018). This is why the same technologies and methodologies were adopted, at first, for an experimentation in the creation of new typologies of language questions (Barana et al., 2019a) and then for the realization of the project "Esplorare (con) i Dizionari Digitali". In 2016, a pilot project about the use of online dictionaries started; it used paper questionnaires while the use of computers and smartphones was limited to the consultation of online dictionaries. In 2017, we decided to improve the project with the use of the VLE and the AAS in order to allow the development of more exercises, to reach more students, and to better record their answers. The use of a VLE also allows to take more into consideration attitudes and needs of individuals and to foster the active learning (Felder & Brent, 2009).

The e-learning Moodle platform we opened for the project has a collection of exercises in monolingual and bilingual dictionaries accessible through the AAS, which is available also for tablets and mobile devices. The platform is divided into three area. The first one is open and it can be accessed freely through the credentials of a social network. It contains a demo to learn how monolingual and bilingual online digital dictionaries are structured. The second area is where each teacher has their course dedicated to their class, with tests available for students. The third section is a teacher community where they can exchange best practices, discuss, create materials and receive support from university researchers.

One of the main goals of the project is to train students to access online dictionaries and learn how to get information from them. We focused on maintaining a certain amount of exercises that foster skills and are not merely search options in free online tools, which are severely limited. This was particularly important, as teachers tend to favor lexical or reading comprehension exercises that reveal very little to nothing about the students' practical skills in using and understanding dictionaries and the data they contain. To understand if students used online dictionaries and how they used them, at the beginning of our project we were always asking students at the end of each question which parts of the dictionary, if any, they used in order to solve some tasks we assigned through the platform. We collected many answers to these questions, but some turned out to be inconclusive. In fact, from the execution time recorded it was evident that some students did not use a dictionary at all, but they declared they had, probably only to please the researchers. In some other cases, they affirmed they had not used it in order to impress their school teacher and to show that they already knew the correct answer without consulting the dictionary. After these results, we decided not to ask such metacognitive questions and we prepared other exercises instead, which could not be correctly carried out without knowing how to use dictionary microstructure. In order to increase the use and the circulation of online dictionaries among students, we found some search features that we thought important to make students work on and we designed exercises which make them learn how to overcome them. So far, "Esplorare (con) i Dizionari Digitali" has seen two editions, involving in total more than 600 students, mainly from Piemonte but also from Puglia and Trentino-Alto Adige (Table 1 reports all the numbers of the project). All the classes involved belonged to the upper secondary school, but in the 17/18 edition also undergraduate and postgraduate students were involved. Results present in this paper belong to both edition of the project while the 19/20 edition will start soon.

Table 1. Numbers of "Esplorare (con) i Dizionari Digitali"

	2017/2018 edition	2018/2019 edition
Classes	**9** (+ **3** university courses)	**15**
Students	**207** (+ **305** university students)	**335**
Teachers	**8**	**16**
# exercises carried out	**125**	**200**

Each teacher can select the set of exercises among our collections in order to fit students' needs and choose whether to have them do the exercises in the classroom or at home (according to the "flipped classroom" methodology), entering the activity in the normal school planning. Tests are set in a slightly different way according to this decision. When the test was carried out in class, teachers and researchers were checking on students in order to avoid cheating behavior and try to keep students focused on the test without distractions, without any time or attempts restrictions. When the test was carried out at home, they had an attempt limit (i.e. each student could attempt the test only once) and a time limit; in this way, students could choose when to do the test and hopefully they did it only when they had time to properly focus on it.

The VLE and the AAS allow to record a lot of information about users' logs, as well as the time and attempts for each test, and they automatically compute statistical data about the success rate of each question. Moreover, the AAS records all answers given by students and it allows their automatic evaluation with the exception of open answers (which were rarely used for this project). The AAS provides some tools that are useful after the tests, but also other tools that are quite important for their very creation. AAS gives the possibility to choose among many kinds of response-areas, and to set different options according to the goal of the exercise. Therefore, the AAS allowed to only use automated procedures for both parts of the study (data collection and evaluation). In addition, SPSS, a software package for batched statistical analysis, was used for most part of the analysis of results (explained in the following chapter).

4. RESULTS

4.1 When the Researcher Becomes "Design Aware"

The AAS we used had several advantages: the main one was recording all answers given. This allows the designer to understand what students exactly did and to learn from results. Accessing online dictionaries is facilitated through the AAS: each question that requires the use of a dictionary has a specific pop-up link that directly sends the user to the dictionary entry to be consulted, and this speeds up the process, if compared to having the general dictionary consultation window. In addition, also the pop-up link to the consultation window speeds the process. To use pop-up links through Moodle, it was not possible to use the appropriate option to insert pop-ups designed by the creators of the AAS; it was necessary to design a special way in order to make it possible. Links were inserted as html-type answers to which students must not give an answer: the first time this was tested, the AAS saw the pop-up links as answers left empty, but we solved this problem by inserting the code "function getResponse() { return 1; };". The html solution could still be further improved as the link disappears in the pdf version of the test and the pop-up poses (small) problems in the layout of the exercise, because it tends to create too much space between the parts of the question; these aspects are still under study.

The use of the AAS allows to set some options useful to control the way in which the test is done. Two options we set in every test were the rotation of questions inside the test and the rotation of possible answers to choose from: these decrease the probability of cheating, especially when students take the test in class. In some cases, to reduce the probability of cheating even more, we fully exploited the possibilities of the AAS of using algorithms: thanks to the command "switch", we created three or four equivalent tests with different lemmas. Fig. 1 shows all the features listed above, and it is a pop-up case with the use of both the English dictionary (Collins) and the American one (Heritage). In this question, students have to look up in the online dictionary the plural forms of nouns written in red and select the correct form. For each attempt, nouns in red are different and the related possible answers rotate.

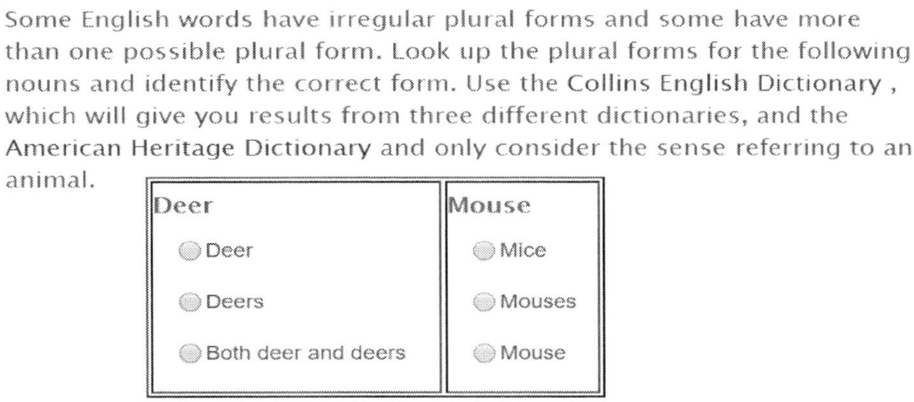

Figure 1. English and American dictionaries pop-up links in AAS question

Each test consisted of 7-10 questions and also had a time limit (usually thirty minutes) and a limit of attempts: these were especially useful in the flipped classroom modality. Despite this, some teachers did not want to adopt the flipped classroom modality because they feared that parents would do the homework instead of their children. Obviously, when students do exercises at home we have less control, but if there is a constructive discussion at home between students and family members for the resolution of the exercises, which is also welcomed. When designing exercises, we tried to create many different types. Not every question has a pop-up link: some suggest students to use the dictionary they want instead. Another typology of exercise did not require the consultation of an online dictionary as we integrated part of the dictionary entry in the body of the question. For example, in one exercise we inserted the modified dictionary entry "campo" from the Italian online dictionary De Mauro where we deleted a part of it and we also deleted the four labels from where they were placed. Students had to reintegrate them properly choosing among the different options proposed in the drop-down menu and associating for each definition the correct label associated to it. Students could choose between the following shortened definitions of four labels: FO fundamental, CO common usage, TS specialistic term, OB obsolete meaning. It is clear that, if we had inserted a pop-up link, students would have easily seen the labels associated with each item and the exercise would have become trivial copying. The goal of the exercise was instead to test sociolinguistic awareness of native speakers and to reach it the consultation of an online dictionary was not required at all.

4.2 Are "Esplora-Students" Really Exploring Online Dictionaries?

Students carried out 581 tests during the two editions of the project (the first one in the school year 17/18 and the second one in 18/19). In detail, 53 students took the "English level B1" test, 25 took the "German" test, 244 took the "Italian: Grammar and Synonyms" test, 199 took the "Italian for the 9th grade" test, 60 took the "Italian for the 10th grade" test. The goal was to understand how much time each student spent consulting the online dictionary and if that influenced the performance of the test. At present, it is not possible for us to automatically track the activity of students while consulting the online dictionary, nor to understand whether the pop-up link has been opened, so we do not know how much time students actually spent consulting the dictionary or what exactly they were looking at. What we did was therefore to analyze data on response times. Students performed tests in a "protected environment" as they did them either at school supervised by teachers and tutors or at home with some automatic restriction of the AAS. For this reason, we assumed that "taking more time in carrying out the test" implies "having spent more time in the consultation of the dictionary" and we tried to understand if there was a correlation between response times and success in the answers given, for each test performed. Data were analyzed with SPSS in order to understand to what extent the use of the AAS (that allowed the use of online dictionaries) helped the students. Statistically results are significant when the bilateral asymptotic significance of the chi-square test (the so-called "p-value") is less than 0.05 and the ETA is greater than 0.3. Table 2 shows some general results regardless of the test done. These are statistically significant as the p-value is lower than 0.001 and ETA is equal to 0.323. Best results were obtained when students spent between 16 and 20 minutes taking the test. In this table (and in the next ones) there will always be the label "U = undefined time" as it is not rare that students start the test but do not close it correctly, losing data about the exact amount of time spent on the test.

Table 2. Correlation between duration and performance of all 581 tests

Duration	Performance	# of students	% of students
between 1 minute and 9 minutes	52.56%	90	15,49%
between 10 minut and 15 minutes	63.05%	99	17,04%
between 16 minut and 20 minutes	71.08%	94	16,18%
between 21 minut and 24 minutes	66.00%	100	17,21%
between 25 minut and 50 minutes	66.05%	91	15,66%
undefined time	26.26%	107	18,42%
Total	**56.93%**	**581**	**100%**

Results of Table 2 do not take into consideration length and difficulty of tests. In order to analyze in a more critical way the data collected, we divided them into two different categories of "classes" according to the time spent in performing the test:

- Table 3 shows results divided in classes A, B, C, D, E, F, G, U where we tried to keep the number of minutes constant (about 5 minutes per class);
- Table 4 shows results divided in classes P, Q, R, S, T, U where we tried to keep the number of students constant (about 97 students per class regardless of the test).

Both tables record for each test which "class of time" performed better and in specific which was the mean of the results of the mentioned class (e.g. in table 3 it is written that 199 students carried out the test "Italian for the 9th grade", the best result was obtained by 38 of them who spent between 16 and 20 minutes to carried it out and on average scored 70.72%).

Table 3. Classes with number of minutes constant

Classes with constant number of minutes: about 5 minutes per class.
A = 1-5 minutes, B = 6-10 minutes, C = 11-15 minutes, D = 16-20 minutes, E = 21-25 minutes, F = 26-35 minutes, G = 36-50 minutes, U = "undefined time"

Test	# of students who carried it out	Class with the best performance	Performance of the mentioned class	# of students in the mentioned class	P value	ETA squared value
English level B1	53	E = 21-25 minutes	80.64%	2	<0.001	0.669
Italian: Grammar and Synonyms	244	D = 16-20 minutes	74.52%	33	<0.001	0.481
Italian for the 9th grade	199	D = 16-20 minutes	70.72%	38	<0.001	0.352
Italian for the 10th grade	60	D = 16-20 minutes	58.83%	7	<0.001	0.702
German	25	D = 16-20 minutes	79.80%	8	0.252	0.226

It turned out that, no matter the category of classes analyzed, the results found were the same. We have not considered results given by the "German" test (as it is not statistically significant) but we want to show it anyway in this paper. All the other results are statistically significant as they all have p-value <0, 001 and ETA value > 0.3. Table 3 shows that students who spent between 21 and 25 minutes had the best performance in the "English level B1" test, although there were only two of them. For all the other Italian tests, the best results were achieved by those students who spent between 16 and 20 minutes.

Table 4. Classes with number of students constant

Classes with constant number of students: about 97 students per class, regardless of the test.
P = 1-9 minutes, Q = 10-15 minutes, R = 16-20 minutes, S = 21-24 minutes, T = 25-50 minutes, U = "undefined time"

Test	# of students who carried it out	Class with the best performance	Performance of the mentioned class	# of students in the mentioned class	P value	ETA squared value
English level B1	53	S = 21-24 minutes	80.64%	2	<0.001	0.624
Italian: Grammar and Synonyms	244	R = 16-20 minutes	74.52%	33	<0.001	0.479
Italian for the 9th grade	199	R = 16-20 minutes	70.72%	38	<0.001	0.343
Italian for the 10th grade	60	R = 16-20 minutes	58.83%	7	<0.001	0.701
German	25	R = 16-20 minutes	79.80%	8	0.252	0.226

Results showed in Table 4 reflect the ones of Table 3 and they both show that:

- for the 3 Italian tests, students who had a better performance were in the D or R class, that means it took them between 16 and 20 minutes to do the test;
- for the English test, students who had a better performance were in the E or S class, that means it took them between 21 and 25 minutes.

We can conclude that, for Italian tests Italian-speaking students were able to have a good performance even without spending too much time consulting the dictionary while for the English test consulting the dictionary made the difference, resulting in better results for those students who consulted it more. Moreover, exercises in these tests were specifically designed in such a way that they could not be correctly carried out without knowing how to use dictionary microstructure: for this reason, we can conclude that it is likely that students who performed better learned more how to use the online dictionary.

5. CONCLUSION AND FURTHER STUDIES

The integration of a VLE with an AAS for the consultation of online dictionaries allowed researchers to become "design aware" and students to become "meta-linguistically aware". In fact, the AAS records all answers given, allowing more studies about how to improve both the content and the layout of exercises. The AAS also records the time spent on each test. Assuming that "taking more time in carrying out the test" implies "having spent more time in the consultation of the dictionary", we concluded that, not surprisingly, for an Italian test Italian-speaking students were able to have a good performance even without spending too much time consulting the dictionary. On the contrary, for the English test, consulting the dictionary made the difference, resulting in better results for Italian speaking students who consulted it more. This also answers our first research question, that is how to increase the use and the circulation of online dictionaries among students: thanks to the project "Esplorare (con) i Dizionari Digitali", students were encouraged to use them and trained on how to, especially when foreign languages tests were involved. However, at present it is not possible for us to automatically track the activity of students while consulting the online dictionary, so a further study would be interesting in order to know whether the pop-up link has been opened or not, and which specific part of the online dictionary has been consulted; the eye-tracking technology could help with this. In addition, we had really positive feedback on the project from students and teachers who took part in it. For further studies, we want to ask them to fill a final questionnaire in order to see the increment of motivation and interest of students and to better measure the meta-cognitive impact of the project. In this way, we could add some qualitative analysis to this purely quantitative one. "Esplorare (con) i Dizionari Digitali" showed us that development of competences for languages and STEM disciplines does not differ as much as it seems; thus, it would be interesting to fully exploit and implement the adaptive formative model of STEM disciplines to the teaching of languages, too.

REFERENCES

Barana, A., Conte, A., Fioravera, M., Marchisio, M. & Rabellino, S. (2018). A model of formative automatic assessment and interactive feedback for STEM. In *Proceedings of 2018 IEEE 42nd Annual Computer Software and Applications Conference, IEEE Computer Society Conference Publishing Services (CPS), pp. 1016–1025.* Tokyo, Japan. Pp. 1016-1025.

Barana, A., Floris, F., Marchisio, M., Marello, C., Pulvirenti, M., Sacchet, M. & Rabellino, S. (2019a). Adapting STEM Automated Assessment System to Enhance Language Skills. In *Proceedings of the 15th International Scientific Conference eLearning and Software for Education - eLSE 2019, pp.403-410.* Bucharest, Romania. 11–12/04/2019.

Barana, A., Marchisio, M. & Sacchet, M. (2019b). Advantages of using automatic formative assessment for learning mathematics. In *Communications in Computer and Information Science*, vol. 1014, pp. 180-198.

Barana, A., Marchisio, M. & Rabellino, S. (2015). Automated Assessment in Mathematics. In *Procedings of 2015 IEEE 39th Annual International Computers, Software & Applications Conference, COMPSAC 2015 (CPS), pp. 670–671.*

Betti, S. & Garelli, P. (2010). *Nuove tecnologie e insegnamento delle lingue straniere*. Milano: FrancoAngeli.

Carr, M. (1997). Internet Dictionaries and Lexicography. *International Journal of Lexicography*, 10(3), pp. 209–230.

Collins English. Accessed at: https://www.collinsdictionary.com/dictionary/english. (5 September 2019).

De Mauro. Accessed at: https://dizionario.internazionale.it/. (5 September 2019).

Commissione Europea. Libro bianco: *Insegnare e apprendere*. Verso la società della conoscenza. 1995.

De Schryver, G.-M. & Prinsloo, D.J. (2001). Fuzzy SF: Towards the ultimate customised dictionary. *Studies in Lexicography*, 11(1), pp. 97–111.

Dziemianko, A. 2012. On the Use(fulness) of Paper and Electronic Dictionaries. In Granger S., Paquot M. (eds.) 2012 *Electronic Lexicography*. Oxford: Oxford U.P.

Felder, R.M. & Brent, R., 2009. Active Learning: An Introduction. *ASQ Higher Education Brief.* Vol. 2, No. 4, pp. 1-5.

Garzanti. Accessed at: http://www.garzantilinguistica.it/. (5 September 2019).

Gouws R. H., Heid, U., Schweickard, W. & Wiegand, H. E. (2013). Dictionaries. An International Encyclopedia of Lexicography. Supplementary Volume: *Recent Developments with Focus on Electronic and Computational Lexicography*. Series: Handbücher zur Sprach- und Kommunikationswissenschaft/Handbooks of Linguistics and Communication science (hsk) 5/4. The Hague, De Gruyter Mouton.

Heritage American. Accessed at: https://www.ahdictionary.com/. (5 September 2019).

Kosem, I., Lew, R., Müller-Spitzer, C., Ribeiro Silveira, M.R. & Wolfer, S. (2019). 'The Image of the Monolingual Dictionaries Across Europe. Results of the European Survey of Dictionary use and Culture'. *International Journal of Lexicography*, Oxford: Oxford University Press. Vol.32, number 1 March 2019, 92-114.

Lew. R. & Mitton, R. (2013) Online English Learners' Dictionaries and Misspellings: One Year On, In *International Journal of Lexicography*, vol. 26-2, 219–233.

Lew, R. (2015). Research into the use of online dictionaries. In *International Journal of Lexicography*, vol. 28-2, pp. 232-253.

Lew, R. (2011). Online dictionaries of English. In P.A. Fuertes-Olivera & H. Bergenholtz (eds.) *e-Lexicography: The Internet, Digital Initiatives and Lexicography*. London/New York: Continuum, pp. 230–250.

Klosa, A. & Müller-Spitzer, C. (eds.) (2018). *Internetlexikografie. Ein Kompendium*. Berlin/Boston, De Gruyter.

Marchisio, M., Operti, L., Rabellino, S., & Sacchet, M. (2019a). Start@unito: Open online courses for improving access and for enhancing success in higher education. In *CSEDU 2019 - Proceedings of the 11th International Conference on Computer Supported Education.* Vol. 1, pp. 639-646.

Marchisio, M., Sacchet, M. & Salusso, D. (2019b). Instructional Design To "Train The Trainers": The Start@Unito Project At The University Of Turin. In *Proceedings of the international conference e-learning 2019.* Pp. 195-202.

Marello, C. (2014). Using Mobile Bilingual Dictionaries in an EFL Class. In A. Abel, C.Vettori, N. Ralli (eds.), *Proceedings of the 16th EURALEX International Congress,* Bolzano: EURAC Research, pp. 63-83.

English Vocabulary Profile. Accessed at: https://www.englishprofile.org/wordlists?. (5 September 2019).

Tarp, S. (2012). Theoretical challenges in the transition from lexicographical p-works to e-tools. In S. Granger & M. Paquot (Eds.), *Electronic lexicography*, Oxford: Oxford University Press, pp. 107-118.

Töpel, A. (2014). Review of research into the Use of Electronic Dictionaries. In Müller-Spitzer C. (ed.)(2014), *Using online dictionaries* (Lexicographica Series Maior 145), Berlin/Boston, De Gruyter, pp. 13-54.

Zingarelli, N. (2019). *Lo Zingarelli 2020. Vocabolario della lingua italiana.* Cannella&Lazzarini(eds.),Bologna: Zanichelli.

VALUE ADDED TEACHERS: THE LEGACY OF EDUCATIONAL TECHNOLOGY COACHES

Gail Drennan

University of the Witwatersrand, Johannesburg, 1 Jan Smuts Avenue, Braamfontein, Johannesburg, 2001, South Africa

ABSTRACT

When helping teachers integrate iPads in their teaching, a grounded theory-based qualitative case study underpinned by the TPACK and SAMR models (Drennan, 2018), found educational technology coaches (ETC) followed an underlying principle of changing teachers' pedagogy. In implementing this principle, ETCs adopted one of four approaches through which teachers' pedagogy could change, depending on teachers' technological competence and confidence. They were: re-imagining change; slowly changing; radically changing; and co-operatively changing. Furthermore, the approaches adopted by the educational technology coaches demonstrated four concomitant behaviours, namely: meeting teachers' needs; knowledge of applications; collegiality; and modelling desired behaviour. The three hallmarks of the legacy of their success were all exhibited by teachers not educational technology coaches. These were posited as teachers' increased iPad integration vision; an escalation in collegial sharing of their improved technological confidence and competence; and a critical mass of "uncoached" teachers asking for help. A figurative model showing this is presented. In conclusion, there are distinct pedagogical advantages to having dedicated ETCs implement iPad integration. These must be balanced against the few disadvantages. Caution is sounded against generalizing these findings to include Android devices, especially with regard to possible non-compatible interfaces of a variety of devices in one classroom.

KEYWORDS

Educational Technology Coach, iPads, Integration, Pedagogy

1. INTRODUCTION

In the decade since the introduction of tablet computers some research has focused on their affordances. Godsk (2013), for example, listed the affordances of iPads. Android tablets, Blackberry Playbooks and HP Touchpads without differentiating between them. Other research has focused on how they were used in the classroom by teachers. Haßler, Major and Hennessy (2015, p. 16) found support for teachers using "transformative pedagogical models" regardless of tablet brand. Many studies considered iPads specifically (See Heinrich, 2012, Lane, 2012, Cochrane, 2013, Karsenti, 2013 and Reed 2013). A Bring-Your-Own-Device (BYOD) classroom, can present teachers and students with multiple incompatible interfaces. Research in these classrooms might obfuscate findings unnecessarily. Classrooms with single brand tablets, such as iPads, would ensure better device management and classroom workflow with few technical issues as all apps work on all devices.

However, Nguyen, Barton and Nguyen (2014) decried the paucity of literature on how teachers' pedagogy changed. Valstad and Rydland (2010) bemoaned leaving the iPad integration decision to individual teachers. Drennan (2018) sought clarity in this under-researched area through a grounded theory-based qualitative case study underpinned by the TPACK and SAMR models. She researched the relationship between ETCs and teachers in five South African private schools all constituted under one brand and sharing one campus: a junior preparatory: a girls' preparatory: a girls' college; a boys' preparatory; and a boy's college. She found single device use, the iPad, ensured better device management and workflow with few technical issues as all apps worked on all ETC, teacher and student devices. She argued that the technological capabilities of the iPad created technological affordances that could lead to new pedagogical affordances. She found ETCs used these to drive pedagogical change.

Teacher pedagogy and classroom power dynamics changed when ETCs helped teachers integrate iPads. Teachers were no longer knowledge and resource gatekeepers. Classroom power dynamics were transformed through more active student engagement. Everything teachers could access or do through the iPad, so could students, making classroom democratisation and learning transparency more possible. Drennan (2018) proposed an emerging model of an ETC to describe their work and its impact on teachers, students and parents, as neither they nor principals may have the time or technological experience to discover, implement or assess new technology or pedagogy. She concluded ETCs used four general approaches when following the underlying principle of changing teacher pedagogy, each dependent on the technological confidence and competence of the teacher. Regardless of approach, ETCs demonstrated four distinct behaviours. Their legacy was revealed through three changes in teacher behaviour.

The title ETC was in use but is misleading. There is no uniformly accepted title, but more appropriate ones include Digital Learning Specialist, Digital Integration Specialist, and Technology Integrator. The ETCs in the study were all teachers with a well-developed interest in educational computer usage, rather than Information Technology (IT) personnel attempting pedagogical relevance. The position of an ETC is a recent one within South African schools. There are no official guidelines as to their qualifications, job description or curriculum. It is hoped the model might give education stakeholders some understanding of the work done by teachers appointed as ETCs, contextualise the work ETCs do with teachers and highlight the role of ETCs as change agents.

2. THE FOUR APPROACHES ETCS USE IN FOLLOWING THE PRINCIPLE OF CHANGING TEACHERS' PEDAGOGY

All the ETCs followed one underlying principle: changing teachers' pedagogy. Drennan (2018) found ETCs adopted one of four approaches to doing so. These are not necessarily progressive as they depend on the ETC-teacher relationship and the teacher's technological confidence and competence. They are: re-imagining changing; slowly changing; radically changing; and co-operatively changing pedagogy.

2.1 Re-Imagining Changing Pedagogy

The approach of re-imagining changing pedagogy was used when ETCs helped teachers integrate iPads in a small way. This was exemplified when a current ETC, then a Grade 2 teacher, helped her first-year intern take her class while she attended an all-day training course. They found a library book, developed questions based on its story and created a Kahoot! quiz. The intern read the story aloud before students completed the quiz on school-owned iPads. Then students physically painted the main character with paint and paper, not digitally on the iPad. The teacher never advocated doing everything on the iPad as her young students are still developing gross and fine motor co-ordination, concluding, *"We just need to do little things but we can integrate effectively"*. She would often make iPads with extension literacy, numeracy or problem solving games, available to students who had completed class work. Unsurprisingly, the intern wanted to continue improving her iPad integration skills and the teacher was redeployed as a full-time ETC.

2.2 Slowly Changing Pedagogy

ETCs worked at a slower pace with new-to-the-iPad teachers, or the technologically resistant or insecure, who might fear appearing incompetent to students. ETCs wanted them to slowly change pedagogy by helping them integrate iPads into one topic or series of lessons. For example, instead of teacher-talk about the voting system with students completing worksheets, an ETC helped a Grade 6 teacher achieve the same end through students using iPads. The students shouldered greater responsibility, within a well-defined rubric, than previously. In groups, some wrote campaign speeches, designed posters, video-interviewed people, or filmed a candidate-promoting advert. Each had a voice and choice. The teacher found this deeper, more authentic student engagement enriched their learning and the final product than was the case previously.

Another ETC showed a highly technologically resistant Grade 5 teacher how to change a disliked topic, rock types, into a more exciting one by creating student buy-in and allowing student development of learning material. The Decide Now! app was used to randomly assign rock types to student groups, satisfying them that the decision was uncoupled from possible teacher favouritism. Students researched their rock type online. They compiled textual and pictorial material in a Book Creator book and videoed themselves singing about their rock type to song lyrics they had adapted. All this material was uploaded into a Book Creator book. Each book was then consolidated into one comprehensive Book Creator book that all students could access as their learning material for the topic. The teacher assessed the work when it was presented, rather than paging through or carrying heavy notebooks. This was a major pedagogic change, as students were active creators of their digital learning material, rather than passive consumers only. Moreover, all students were exposed to everyone else's work and notes were never lost. Increased confidence empowered this teacher to frame challenges as growth, thereafter developing into a confident and competent iPad integrator and later becoming an ETC.

2.3 Radically Changing Pedagogy

ETCs can work quickly with confident and bold teachers. Radically changing pedagogy involved good ETC-teacher co-operation, teacher technological confidence, and an appropriate app. An ETC helped a technologically confident Drama Head of Department (HoD) put her term's work, film study, onto Google Classroom, where her agenda aligned well with iMovie capabilities. It was predicated on 'sweded movies' from the film, "Be Kind, Rewind." Grouped students chose roles, such as director or editor, before shooting two scenes from any film, but without any budget. This authentic task replaced teacher-talk. The HoD confirmed students learnt more about film making than previous classes had and enjoyed themselves. The ETC-teacher co-operation was outstanding, maturing teacher and student competencies.

Another ETC helped a deputy principal create an iTunes U course for a challenging section of Grade 6 Mathematics. For the first time she found students finished the test early and attained excellent results. Students informed her they read the explanations and watched the videos until they understood the concepts. She only teaches it that way now. This might be one way of overcoming the industrial era model of schooling where one teacher in one classroom presents one lesson at one time only. Students who are reluctant to show their lack of understanding in class can review digital material privately until they understand it.

2.4 Co-operatively Changing Pedagogy

Co-operatively changing pedagogy, usually within a department, succeeds irrespective of individual teachers' technological competencies. When all members of a department use an app, teacher learning is expedited through group discussions and self-reflective practices about pedagogic and technical issues. It also helps when extant material is uploaded. For example, the Afrikaans department uploaded their audio-visual presentations of poems and related questions, They added audio of the teachers reading them. Learners were offered a recapitulation of teaching previously limited to one lesson. Now they heard the pronunciation, intonation, cadence, rhythm and stress patterns in their teacher's familiar voice, with text simultaneously available, whenever they chose. This is particularly valuable when lesson time is the only exposure to the language. Learners can repeat access material when and as many times as needed.

ETCs would use the most appropriate approach to changing teachers' pedagogy depending on the technological confidence and competence of the teachers. Regardless of approach, they all exhibited four concomitant behaviours in their interactions.

3. THE FOUR CONCOMITANT BEHAVIOURS ETCS EXHIBIT

ETCs followed the principle of changing teachers' pedagogy by demonstrating four concomitant behaviours in their interactions. These are meeting teachers' needs; knowledge of applications; collegiality; and modelling desired behaviour.

3.1 Meeting Teachers' Needs

ETCs developed respectful and trustworthy relationships with technophobes and technophiles. They let teachers dictate the timing and pace of their interactions. Often this revealed an inverse correlation. The less confident and competent teachers were, the more time ETCs spent with them. The more confident and competent teachers were, the less time ETCs spent with them. All teachers appreciated ETC help as it freed them to concentrate on their students. The subject content knowledge of ETCs facilitated tailor-made solutions to pedagogical needs. One ETC used iMovie to meet three departments' content needs differently: voice-over adverts; make-up tutorials; and meiosis stop-motions. Another demonstrated three apps for flipping classrooms. Also, inter-departmental co-operation allowed one task to meet assessment criteria from both departments. Further, academic support teachers found value in adopting or adapting legal, online material.

Teachers appreciated the benefits of asynchronicity. Assignment time and date stamping strengthened student deadline adherence. Feedback loops with revisions and repeat submissions yielded timeous teacher intervention, deeper feedback, earlier completion and quicker marking turnarounds, especially with voice-recorded comments. Those students who pretended to have lost their work soon learnt responsibility when the history button disproved their claims.

Drennan (2018) categorised teachers into four, broad levels of iPad integration. Progression from the second to third levels seemed to happen when teachers began to use personal devices and not school-owned ones. First level teachers had never used iPads. One twenty-year teaching veteran, but new-to-the-college teacher, allowed observation of his first ETC session. His opening statement, *"I know nothing"*, drew an immediate ETC response, *"Never be afraid of touching."* ETCs focused on how individual teachers wanted to learn, not on how they thought teachers should learn. When teachers were first-time iPad users, ETCs gave, or teachers took, notes, both to reduce the initial cognitive load of learning iPad and app functionality and integration in the first sessions, and to increase their confidence when teaching students or sharing with colleagues. As teachers' experience and experimentation grew, their notes became irrelevant.

Second level teachers had used iPads sporadically, perhaps to email cricket results, but not for teaching purposes. One isiZulu teacher wrote instructions on his PC for students to complete on their iPads, stating, *"I wouldn't use a device for that."* The ETC showed him apps that allowed work to be distributed, submitted and assessed through one device. It also meant he could assess work as soon as students submitted it instead of waiting until all students had submitted work. Furthermore, he could do typed, written or spoken individual feedback quickly and easily.

Third level teachers had used a personal iPad for some years, personally and professionally. One teacher confirmed she always had her iPad with her. She used apps for school email, reading fiction, looking at Pinterest, attending gym and taking school magazine photographs, especially those capturing students' expressions when they were fully involved during her Life Science practicals. These teachers were not dependent on being taught solely by the ETC. Apart from asking colleagues for help, they asked their own eager children, sometimes learning new ways of achieving the same ends. Their students also gave help enthusiastically, often to acclaim from classmates. Teachers do not have to know everything about the technology to integrate it successfully. Regardless of student technological competence, often confined to social media apps, the teacher remains the pedagogical expert. Ironically, when teachers show technological vulnerability student respect often increases.

Fourth level teachers had used an iPad for many years, personally and professionally. One Grade 5 teacher had worked with the ETC for eight years, at two different schools. She used Mail, Keynote, iMovie, iTunes U, Edmodo, Nearpod and Google Classroom. When introduced to Apple Classroom and Clips in the observed session, she grasped their functionality integration immediately. She began to suggest lesson plans for integrating Clips in various subjects. As an experienced teacher she knew where students would struggle and how the app would supersede teacher talk and worksheets. These teachers learn quickly and comprehensively because of their knowledge and experience. They also see integration possibilities in newly demonstrated apps, without necessarily needing ETC elaboration.

3.2 Knowledge of Applications

ETCs need in-depth knowledge of different apps. They must trial and recommend apps, make decisions on purchasing them and be able to demonstrate different app features. This enables them to respond specifically to teachers' needs.

One ETC had trialled over 400 apps. Experience showed a smaller suite of multifunctional or creative apps, rather than content specific apps, were applicable in any subject area with students of any age. A second ETC suggested an isiZulu teacher use a multifunctional, editable Book Creator template to send vocabulary words, with his uploaded pronunciations, to students. They would find and upload appropriate images, then write sentences using the words, finally submitting their work for assessment. This contrasts with a content specific app such as SpellBoard, whose fun and innovative features help students practise spelling only. A third ETC suggested students make short Clips videos of their working out Mathematical problems before sharing them with the teacher. A fourth suggested students combine apps, for instance by making a Clips video on gym equipment usage then linking them to a Quick Response code stuck onto each piece of equipment. These examples show how willing ETCs are to keep up-to-date and how committed they are to investigate thoroughly which apps would be most suitable for particular teachers. It also enables them to offer different solutions to the same problem and to reveal different ways of using one app.

With purchasing decisions, it is best if ETCs give teacher, student and parent stakeholders a list of required apps at the beginning of the year or term. If done extemporaneously, it appears disorganised and unprofessional and can result in a loss of confidence in ETC expertise. Some free apps have the more powerful and productive aspects subject to in-app purchasing. This can frustrate teachers into abandoning their implementation plans. Usually, ETCs can find alternatives to expensive apps. They know that pedagogy trumps technology as, to paraphrase Rockman, it's not what you have, but what you do with it that counts (Cuban, 1993).

Especially when demonstrating to iPad-new teachers, ETCs started with what teachers know and what they want to achieve. They sat next to teachers and demonstrated on their iPad with teachers simultaneously practising on theirs. An ETC showed one teacher the iPad basics and then demonstrated Popplet while linking it to the familiar concepts of mind maps and spider diagrammes. He understood and drew his own Popplet on the economic cycle, asking questions as he did so. She demonstrated how Apple TV would enable him to draw a Popplet facing the class, see immediately when students needed individual attention and could later export the Popplet to student devices. When ETCs explain app features, giving teachers opportunities to practice using them, teachers understand the benefits and implications and are more likely to integrate the app into their teaching. This is important for apps such as iTunes U and Apple Classroom that drive classroom workflow and iPad management.

3.3 Collegiality

Firstly, collegiality involved ETCs teaching or demonstrating to teachers within grades and departments, and across both. They found whole staff teaching ineffective; those who knew nothing got lost and those who knew something got bored. Neither ETCs nor teachers wanted to teach or learn this way. Interacting with groups already professionally constituted worked exceptionally well as teachers were used to sharing readily with close colleagues working in the same grade or subject.

Secondly, ETCs shared with colleagues and teachers outside of school. This is particularly vital for schools with one ETC. The benefits of belonging to a professional learning network should enable them to discuss new trends, share best practices and problem-solve common challenges, or they risk becoming irrelevant. One person can never know everything in their field. Especially in a field that continuously updates itself, ETCs must keep abreast of international trends.

Thirdly, ETCs work symbiotically. There was a high degree of co-operation and support particularly between the two college ETCs. They occasionally team-taught and pooled resources such as their individual cache of small Ozobot robots used to learn coding. Further, one preparatory and one college ETC shared the library office. To the benefits of students from both schools, if one was unavailable, then the other would help teachers, students or parents. This help ranged from pedagogical questions about aspects of app functionality, to asking for different app suggestions about meeting a task's requirements. It also included help in connecting new devices to the network or tracking a misplaced iPad (both IT support jobs).

Fourthly, collegiality extended to ETCs advising parents on boundaries for device security, student safety and schoolwork monitoring. Improved communication resulted in greater parental confidence in teachers. Children occasionally improved their parents' technological skills.

Fifthly, collegiality involved ETCs conducting their own professional development, often learning iteratively with teachers. They shared weekly with all the ETCs in an in-house professional learning network. Additionally, they met fortnightly with the executive principal and IT manager. These meetings had three functions: to give input into the role ETCs play within the school; to give and get support for integration challenges; and to share best practice. One ETC cannot be an ETC and a teacher and an IT support person, as the ETC role will be neglected in favour of the latter, especially in those with strong IT backgrounds. Clear job descriptions and boundaries for each role should be shared with all stakeholders; otherwise ETCs risk combating IT fires instead of stoking pedagogical ones. Further, they learnt from peers outside of school through attending or presenting at workshops, from colleagues on Twitter and through webinars and reflective blogging. Two ETCs were also Apple Distinguished Educators (ADE) whose global community actively shares online and meets yearly to discuss best practice and ideas.

3.4 Modeling Desired Behaviour

ETC behaviour must align with the norms and standards of the school and the teaching profession. It is the role of the principal to see this happens. ETCs model the behaviour they want teachers to model to students. One ETC admitted to a teacher, *"I don't know. I'll get back to you."* They learnt willingly from teachers and students. Seeing this behaviour in practice made it easier for teachers to ask students for help. Another ETC, knowing the importance of all teachers manifesting acceptable academic conduct, always referenced her sources in her presentations. When teachers follow suit, it is easier for referencing to become an embedded student practice and for plagiarism to decrease.

A third ETC had discussed some dangers associated with social media use and given examples of her social media practice, particularly with regard to posting photos of her children. These newly aware students talked to their parents about doing more to keep them safe. Some asked parents to remove certain photos of their children from their timelines. The parents thanked the ETC for modeling legally compliant and ethical behavior professionally and personally.

ETCs challenged teachers to experiment then report back. In turn, they encouraged students to ask peers for help before teachers, knowing well the value of having to understand something before explaining it. Peers also offer an alternative perspective and way of explaining. Moreover, this increased independence, buy-in, flexibility, creativity and metacognition. Teachers further encouraged students to learn-by-doing, for example, by analysing a novel's characters and an app's functionality simultaneously. Then, instead of handwriting diary entries students created Tallagami animated videos of a monologue delivered by one character. Before reading set-works, other students watched pertinent music videos, or interviewed grandparents involved in wars, to give a more textured sense of time and place, strengthening emotional connections to the material. Sometimes students were instructed to decide for themselves what information was important and how to present it. This engendered critical thought, academic responsibility and authentic integration as skills were taught in context. However, sometimes student technological ability outstripped their ethical development, as when they went through Virtual Private Networks to download web material illegally.

4. THE THREE HALLMARKS OF THE LEGACY OF SUCCESSFUL EDUCATIONAL TECHNOLOGY COACHES

The four behaviours discussed above generally manifest within the privacy of an office or classroom, making it difficult to assess ETC success. However, there are three hallmarks of their success. Their legacy is exhibited by the changed behaviour of teachers. They are vision, escalation and critical mass.

4.1 Vision

The first hallmark of ETC success was teacher vision. This arose when teachers saw the possibilities for using the iPad as one tool in their repertoire and discussed their ideas with the ETC. They have caught the vision of changed pedagogy through iPad integration that previously only the ETC held. The iPad never replaces teachers, but, initially under ETC guidance, teachers began to know when the use of an iPad or app would be appropriate.

4.2 Escalation

The second hallmark was escalation. This occurred when a teacher the ETC had helped then helped others, whether teachers, students or parents. As it came from a trusted person it was more easily adopted; it was a targeted intervention that did not waste time; and had the potential to satisfy individual, specific needs. It is unlikely that the ETC would be able to help every teacher or student with every integration query, so peer teaching began to have a multiplier effect. Technological uptake might be uneven across a group of teachers so ETCs value collegial help in raising the standard of iPad integration across subjects or grades. This is especially helpful when teachers resist the approaches of the ETC, especially if there have been failed technological implementations in the past.

4.3 Critical Mass

The third hallmark was critical mass. When "unreached" or "uncoached" teachers asked for ETC help, this increased opportunities for ETC interventions. More importantly, it signalled the reach and impact of ETC work. Furthermore, it was a tacit acknowledgement of the traction iPad implementation was gaining amongst teachers. More teachers were beginning to see iPads as an embedded, ubiquitous technology, not an artificial addenda to their teaching.

In essence, these three hallmarks show that the realisation of the underlying principle of the emerging model of an ETC has been realised: discovering how the teacher wants the iPad or app to change his or her pedagogy for the better. When ETCs based their work on this principle, four concomitant behaviours flowed from it and multiple benefits began to accrue to stakeholders.

5. FIGURATIVE REPRESENTATION OF A MODEL OF AN EDUCATIONAL TECHNOLOGY COACH

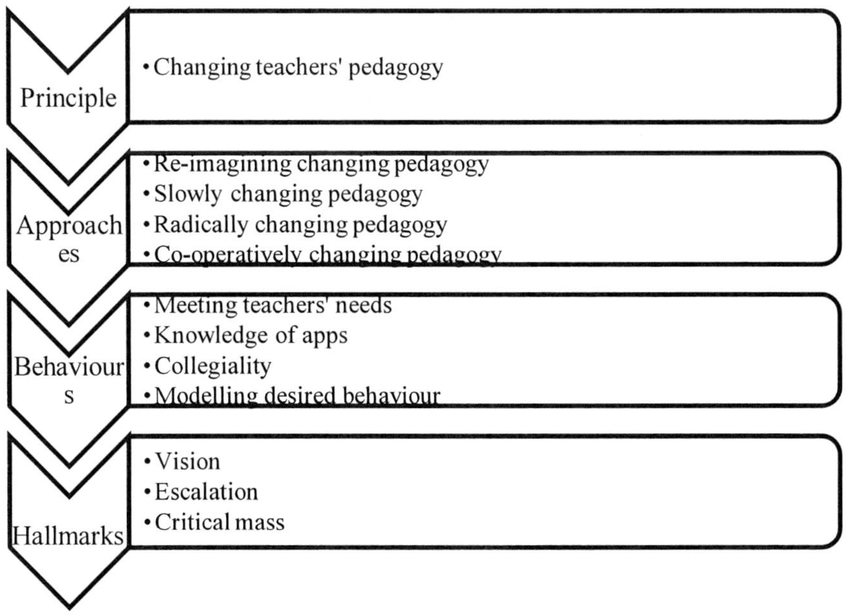

Figure 1. Figurative representation of a model of an educational technology coach

6. CONCLUSION

There are many distinct pedagogical advantages to having dedicated ETCs integrate iPads. However, these must be balanced against the few limitations. It may be possible to apply these findings to include Android devices, but this must be approached with caution.

6.1 Advantages

The first advantage of a dedicated ETC was the quicker, more comprehensive and deeper integration of iPads. This was especially pertinent when schools supplied iPads to teachers, whether or not they recouped some or all of the outlay. Additionally, appropriate, ubiquitous implementation became the norm. This circumvented technology used for its own sake as a checklist add-on to single or principal-observed lessons. Then, increased teacher and student competence and confidence led some to share new apps or ideas for implementation, having done the initial investigation themselves, with ETCs, colleagues or peers. Also, where the iPad was used to distribute, submit and assess work, there was greater teacher-student communication, as many teachers reported students contacting them with queries they were reluctant to voice in class. Moreover, when teachers allowed repeated submissions after ongoing teacher feedback the students adhered to the instructions or rubric more closely, with the final product being of a higher standard. Further, teachers reported students going beyond the brief when they had responsibility for their learning and its demonstration, especially when self-interest led to creative exploration and skill development.

6.2 Limitations

One limitation is the possible loss of a specialist subject or grade teacher to allow the appointment of a dedicated ETC. All schools have budgets with competing demands. Another salary increases the dilemma of using available resources to maximum effect. However, if the school has invested in providing the necessary technological infrastructure, it might be used to best effect when an ETC is appointed to help teachers integrate iPads. Another disadvantage is the initial cost to schools or staff when purchasing devices. This can be mitigated if iPads are distributed over a few years and if teachers contribute towards part of the cost. It is further lessened to a great extent by the pre-loaded suite of iPad apps that make immediate work possible without the need to further purchase and install basic apps.

6.3 Possible Applications

The research under discussion involved iPads. There might be scope to investigate Android devices to see if the same conclusions hold. One of the strengths of using iPads is the seamless co-operation between the operating system and the applications. This might not hold true for android devices where software glitches might frustrate users, as well as slow or stop technological integration and stifle pedagogical change. Moreover, devices from different manufacturers may have non-compatible interfaces, again decreasing opportunities for integration and change, especially if the teacher's device differs from that of any student. A BYOD situation makes the distribution, submission and marking of work near impossible.

REFERENCES

Cochrane, T. et al, 2013. iPadagogy: appropriating the iPad within pedagogical contexts. *International Journal of Mobile Learning and Organisation,* Vol. 7, No. 1. pp.48-65.

Cuban, L. Computer meets classroom: classroom wins. *Teachers' College Record.* Vol. 95, No. 2, pp 185-210.

Drennan, G. 2018. *Affordances of iPads in schools: the role of the educational technology coach.* (Unpublished doctoral thesis, University of the Witwatersrand, Johannesburg).

Drennan, G. and Moll, I., 2018. A conceptual understanding of how educational technology coaches help teachers integrate iPad affordances into their teaching. *The Electronic Journal of e-Learning,* Vol. 16, No. 2,pp 122-133.

Godsk, M. 2013. Tablets for learning in higher education: The top 10 affordances. *E-Learn: World Conference on E-Learning in Corporate, Government, Healthcare, and Higher Education. Association for the Advancement of Computing in Education (AACE).* Las Vegas, Nevada, USA, pp. 1892-1897.

Haßler, B. et al, 2015. Tablet use in schools: a critical review of the evidence for learning outcomes. *Journal of Computer Assisted Learning,* Vol. 32, No. 2.pp139-156.

Karsenti, T. and Fievez, A., 2013. *The iPad in education: uses, benefits, and challenges – A survey of 6,057 students and 302 teachers in Quebec, Canada.* Montreal, QC: CRIFPE.

Lane, J. 2012. TPACK iPad project in schools (TIPS): phase 1. ACEC, Perth, WA.

Nguyen, L. et al, 2014. iPads in higher education-hype and hope. *British Journal of Educational Technology,* Vol. 4, No. 1,pp 190-203.

Reed, A. 2013. iPad's for teaching and learning? "A snapshot of how Iceland is doing it." *Society for Information Technology & Teacher Education International Conference, Association for the Advancement of Computing in Education (AACE).* New Orleans, Louisiana, USA, pp.2927-2931.

Valstad, H. and Rydland, T. 2010. *iPad as a pedagogical device.* (Unpublished master's report, Norwegian University of Science and Technology).

A SMARTPHONE GAME TO PROMOTE SELF-LEARNING IN CHEMISTRY

Krittiya Saksrisathaporn and Patcharaphon Sribunthankul
College of Arts, Media and Technology, Chiang Mai University
Chiang Mai 50200, Thailand

ABSTRACT

In Thailand, for most students in high school, remembering the periodic table is an important part of learning chemistry and to pass a university entrance examination in their scientific program. As many students live in the bigger city areas in Thailand, most of them encounter the same problems such as limitations on lesson time, and their involvement in a wide range of high school and extra-curricular activities which reduces the student's study time. Self-learning is one method that has been proven to be effective, convenient, and fast. Presently, there are few effective resources for students to enjoy self-learning. Game-based learning is one of the approaches that has been suggested, but most of them are too difficult to learn how to play, not attractive and not challenging. In this study, a smartphone-based learning game was designed and developed with better level design, including color emotional theory, and quality graphic design to provide a better user experience. The game consists of three stages, and at each stage, a mini-puzzle game is presented which plays a different style with different goals to be achieved. The first stage of the game is to remember the names and symbols of elements. The second stage is to remember the group and period, while the third stage allows students to apply elements to form chemical compounds. The results from an evaluation showed that 96% of 102 students, enjoyed playing the game, 87% said the game was challenging, and 94% remembered at least 3 elements more than before playing. The satisfaction questionnaire demonstrated the benefits of the game-based learning system on self-learning in chemistry.

KEYWORDS

Game-Based Learning, Serious Game, Chemistry, Periodic Table, Smartphone Game, Android

1. INTRODUCTION

The Periodic Table is one of the topics listed in the science program course for high school and university students in Thailand and is part of the compulsory education curriculum of Thailand. It is considered very important for the Thailand university entrance examination in the scientific program. Moreover, it is a subject that is included in other higher education courses such as Science of Chemistry, Chemical Engineering, Pharmacy, etc. Combined with other lessons that students must learn to prepare themselves for future lessons within the subject make it hard for them to remember. Due to many students in high school living in bigger cities, most of them encounter the same problems with limits on lesson time and being overloaded with additional work from teachers. The student-teacher ratio is also often too high. Furthermore, student's study time is reduced significantly because of the number of activities high school or university students are expected to participate in. Therefore, studying a periodic table, and trying to remember all the elements becomes boring and repetitive, more so when trying to remember from textbooks. If students are unable to learn and remember all the important details of the main topics, essential elements, the periodic table, and chemical compounds, it will continually affect their future learning in chemistry, making it difficult to continue learning, and pass yearly university entrance exams. However, game-based learning has been used as a tool for centuries and is much more attractive and interesting, and results in active learning rather than passive learning through textbooks and theory (Saksrisathaporn & Maneewan, 2012).

Currently, there are only a few other resources that can help students learn chemistry by themselves. Game-based learning is very close in meaning to a serious game, and a serious game has become a hot topic in training and education as shown in the abundant academic research since 2012 (Guillen, V and Aleson-Carbonell, M, 2012). Mostly, the digital game-based learning available in the market does not focus on graphics or level designs. For example, the Kagaku Chemistry Periodic Table of Elements only displays the table on a scrollable screen and includes buttons for explanation and a search window (Freewarepocketpc, 2017). Also, mobile devices have become widely popular devices because they are easy to use, portable and can support a variety of applications.

In this study, a smartphone game named "Chemistry Pop" was designed and developed. The proposed game was designed to help students to learn chemistry with more interest and enthusiasm. This mobile game aims to support science students to learn and remember the essential elements in the periodic table with more interest and enthusiasm and to increase the resources that may help aid students in self-studying. The game is designed with colorful graphics.

The students can play a game and remember the essential elements in the periodic table at the same time. They can also continue growing and improving these memories at a higher level of education. The game consists of three stages, each stage plays differently and has different goals. The first stage is to support the student to remember the names and symbols of elements from the periodic table. The gameplay of this stage is adapted from a "Bubble Shooter" game. The single-player video game Bubble Shooter probably became famous as it is very intuitive and easy to learn. It is a mix of "Tetris" and "Connect Four" (Shooter-bubble (2019). This creates a game addiction feeling similar to the Candy Crush Saga game (Chen, C., 2016). The aim of Bubble Shooter is to collect as many points as possible. To get points you need to destroy the colored bubbles. For the Chemistry pop game, the player must connect and group at least three bubbles of the same property to collect them according to the goal, which is given at each level. Players must shoot the bubbles with given symbols to collect and clear the goal, which uses the elements' names. To pass each level, players must clear all progress bars within the time and moves limits. The second stage is to help students remember the group and period of elements from the periodic table. The bubbles with element symbols will be released randomly and will always be moving. Players must use their fingers to touch, hold and drag to form a circle around bubbles with the same property and need at least three bubbles to collect them and clear the goal, which would be the group or period numbers. The last stage is to help students remember the 5-chemical compounds. The bubbles will be collected if the connection of bubbles is in accordance with a chemical compound. To pass each level, players must clear all progress bars within the time limit. The prototype game was tested and evaluated with a sample student population.

The remainder of this study is structured as follows: Section 2 describes the background and related work. Section 3 presents a flow of the research methodology. Section 4 presents the game design and development. Game testing and evaluation are discussed in Section 5. Lastly, conclusions and future perspectives are discussed in Section 6.

2. BACKGROUND AND RELATED WORK

2.1 Element and Periodic Table

The International Union of Pure and Applied Chemistry (IUPAC) have announced that there are 118 elements, and each element has its own name and symbol, and they are placed on a table by dividing the table into 16 groups and seven periods (IUPAC, 2017). The position of elements on the table is according to the property of each element, which is another important topic for students to learn in chemistry. In addition, the chemical compound is also an important topic because it forms the basic knowledge needed for almost all future lessons within the chemistry subject. Each compound also has its own formula and unique name.

2.2 Game-based Learning and Serious Game

Currently, there are many types of games such as board games, card games, video games, and digital game. These games can be type constructed as an entertainment game, game-based learning, simulation-based games, serious games, etc. According to Lorenz, 2005 (Lorenz et al., 2015) people who play video games have better memory and strategic planning capabilities compared to those who do not play video games. They also have a larger quantity of gray matter, which is the part that sends information to the brain and is an important part of the central nervous system. In 2014, Andre proposed a method of a serious game to test the "Clean world" game. The learning of games occurs within multiple mechanisms, such as mini-games, puzzles, and quizzes played in parallel to the main game environment (Andre et al., 2014).

Game-based learning has been identified as an effective approach to making learning activities playful and engaging (Klopfer et al., 2009). According to Kammardsiri, game-based learning or serious games is one of the assistant systems to improve learning for students in knowledge acquisition, training and learning skills (Kammardsiri et al., 2017). Additionally, the games provide feedback to the student, great improve their motivation and provide enjoy learning outcomes. In 2016, Hsiao and Chen developed a gesture interactive game-based learning (GIGL) approach for improving pre-school children (Hsiao and Chen, 2016). In 2017. Fujimoto presented JobStar Online: Game-Based Learning on Smartphones to Promote Youth Career Education. This game is designed to help youth develop a positive attitude towards career development and prepare for emerging opportunities (Fujimoto et al., 2017). To design digital game-based learning for high school students, many principles are considered to develop these mobile-based educational games. Recently, many researchers focused on game-based learning or serious games to enhance the learning skills of students. As, interactive games can bring intuitive content directly to students through their devices.

Some educational games are traditional games (puzzles, card games, etc.) (Franco et al., 2016). However, most education game-based learning is simple in level design and graphic design. Some of them are puzzle games designed for on PCs or websites (Periodic table Game, 2018). In 2016, Chairs! a mobile game for Organic Chemistry Students to Learn the Ring Flip of Cyclohexane by drawing the Ring Flip of Cyclohexane on the smart phone was developed by Winter (Winter et al, 2016). Also, the simple graphics game named 2048 Periodic Elements is an interesting and very addictive puzzle Game (Google, 2017). Additionally, Chemical Bonding is a learning unit that incorporates an elicitation strategy in the context of chemical bonding for high school students (Rompayom, 2010). This application is run on a mobile device with good quality graphics and plays like a game but is more focused on content than a gameplay feeling.

2.3 A Smartphone Games

According to Granter's global smartphone and tablet survey in 2015, Android has the largest market of smartphones. Besides, InMobi, one of the largest advertising networks in the world, found that Thailand has the highest usage of Android applications through collecting information from the impression count of advertisements. On average, people spend 230 minutes on smartphones daily. According to released data from Thailand's National Statistical Office (NSO) in January 2017, more than 90% of internet users in the country go online via smartphones. More than 50% of mobile phone users use smartphones and it is expected that the percentage will grow (NSO, 2017). In this study, the Chemistry Pop game is made by Unity. The Unity software is a game engine for developing 2-dimensional (2D) and 3-dimensional (3D) games, which can work on two platforms, Windows and OSX. This game-engine can be exported or deployed to 17 different platforms, for example, Windows, Mac, Web, Android, iOS, consoles, etc. The popular 2D game "Gardenarium" by Paloma (2017) and Kyler (2005) with the support of KO-OP (Kiili, 2005) was also made by Unity software.

3. RESEARCH METHODOLOGY

Figure 1. Research methodology

As shown in Figure 1, the research started with a literature review and interviews with four teachers who teach science and Chemistry at Montfort College, a high school in Chiang Mai, Thailand. As mentioned in the introduction section, some problems were listed. Game-based learning was one of the approaches suggested and chemistry was one of the topics that were selected for content to create a prototype game. The smartphone game was designed and developed using Unity software. In this study, a puzzle game was designed and developed. The game is divided into 3 stages creating mini games. The game was tested and evaluated by 102 players (students in the science program).

4. GAME DESIGN AND DEVELOPMENT

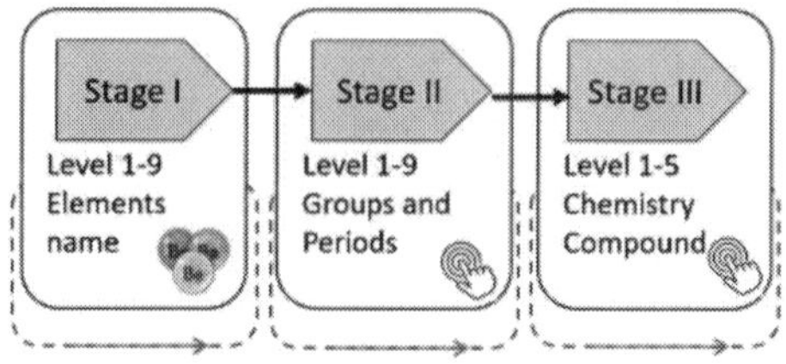

Figure 2. Diagram of 3 stages

As shown in Figure 2, the main game is included with three mini-games in three stages. The first one (stage I) is like a Bubble Shooter game to remember the element's name. The second one (stage II) is a group and period mini game. To play the game, the player must touch, hold and drag their finger to create an area around bubbles of the same group or period to capture them on the screen of the smartphone. The last one (stage III) is a Chemical compound mini game, the gameplay is similar to stage II. The player must collect the compounds according to the goal given. Each game stage is divided into nine levels and each level can be composed of several learning mechanisms. For gameplay, game stage III is influenced by stage II and stage II is influenced by stage I, when the player can remember the element's name and can put them in the right group and period in stage II. The number of atoms depends on groups and periods, which will be the initial compound lesson of Chemistry in stage III. These learning mechanisms aim to embed the knowledge learnt. To design and develop the game with playable quality graphics, it has a detailed graphic design with color sensation. As Figure 3 shows, student name L is a player at all stages, Atom is the fairy of stage I, Group is the fairy of stage II and Compound is the fairy of stage III.

4.1 Character and Scene Design

The short story of the Chemistry Pop game was written. On Friday afternoon in a high school, a student name "L" let all elements in the periodic table escape in a Chemistry laboratory. Fairies "Atom", "Group" and "Compound" ask for responsibility to get them back, so L needs to go and find all escaped elements by playing 3 stages of the game. The game scenes are designed differently regarding time and level design, and the level of difficulty depends on each level in each stage.

(a) Student L (b) Fairy Atom (c) Fairy Group (d) Fairy Compound

Figure 3. Character design

To design and develop a mobile game that has a fine graphic design and provides a playable user experience design. The scene design for stage I and II are different regarding time (Morning, afternoon and night as shown in Figures 4, 5, 6, and 7), and the Kitchen and bathroom scene is designed for stage III (Figures 8 and 9). According to Supawan (Supawan, 2009), colors invoke different emotions thus colors selected in the game design consist of the color red to give sensational feelings, excitement, and challenges. The emerald color provides encouragement, serenity, peace, reduces fatigue and tension, reduces feelings of loneliness but increases communication power. Yellow is the color of happiness, vitality, celebration, involves wisdom, ideas, creativity and encourages optimism. Orange is the color of joy, freedom and provides a liberating feeling. Violet is the color of care and comforting, to help calm the mind and endure, to balance the mind, to recover from depression or sadness, to reduce desperate feelings, and increase cheerfulness and relaxation. Finally, brown is the color of the earth and provides a stable feeling.

4.2 Game Level Design

In this study, the first 20 elements of the periodic table were selected in all stages of the game. They are Hydrogen, Helium, Lithium, Beryllium, Boron, Carbon, Nitrogen, Oxygen, Fluorine, Neon, Sodium, Magnesium, Aluminum, Silicon, Phosphorus, Sulphur, Chlorine, Argon, Potassium, Calcium, and Titanium, but Titanium is only added to the last stage. As shown in Figure 2, stage I and II consists of 9 levels and stage III consist of 5 levels, each stage plays differently and has different goals. The player needs to pass the first until the last stage by unlocking each level. To pass each level, players must clear all bubbles within the time limit. The first level of each stage is easy and will get harder and harder with the new random element from the previous level until the last level. In each level, the player needs to remember the element from the level before they can pass each level until the last level.

The structure of the game level design of all stages is detailed in Table. 1. For example, in stage I, level 1, the possible bubbles are Hydrogen (H) or Helium (He) (total= 2 type elements), In stage I, level 2 the possible bubbles are Lithium (Li) and random element from level 1 (H or He) (total= 2 type elements). The goal of the first stage is to remember the names and symbols of elements from the periodic table. The goal of the second stage is to remember the group and period of elements. The goal of the last stage is to remember the formulas of the 5-chemical compound which consists of laundry detergent (NaOCl), salt (NaCl), bathroom cleaning liquid (HCl), liquid paper (TiO_2+H_2O), and toothpaste (NaF+Al_2O_3).

Table 1. Level design of game stage I II and III

Stage	Level (lv)	H	He	Li	Be	B	C	N	O	F	Ne	Na	Mg	Al	Si	P	S	Cl	Ar	K	Ca	Ti	Random elements lv (num)
1	1	1	1																				
	2			1																			1(2), 2(1)
	3				1	1																	1(1), 2(1)
	4						1																2(2), 3(2)
	5							1															3(2), 4(2)
	6								1	1													5(2)
	7										1	1											6(2)
	8												1										6 (2), 7(2)
	9													1									7 (2), 8(2)
2	1	1	1																				
	2			1	1							1	1										1 (1)
	3					1								1									1 (1), 2(2)
	4						1								1								1 (1), 2(3)
	5							1								1							1 (1), 4(2)
	6								1								1						1 (1), 5(2)
	7									1								1					1 (1), 6(2)
	8										1								1				1 (1), 7(2)
	9																			1	1		1 (1), 2(1), 3(1)
3	NaOCl								1			1						1					
	NaCl																						
	HCl	1																1					
	TiO_2+H_2O	2							3													1	
	NaF+Al_2O_3								3	1		1		2									

Remark: Group **IA**: H, Li, Na, K, **IIA**: Be, Mg, Ca, **IIIA**: B, Al, **IVA**:C, Si, **VA**: N, P, **VIA**:O, S, **VIIA**:F, CI and **VIIIA**: He, Ne, Ar

4.3 Gameplay

For gameplay stage I as presented in Figure 4, the player must shoot the given bubble, which will be at the middle bottom of the screen, to hit the rows of bubbles at the top of the screen. The player must shoot the bubbles with the same element symbol (not the same color as the original bubble shooter game) to connect to each other at least three bubbles to make them pop. The goal is for the players to collect the elements according to the progress bars at the top of the screen, under the score, which will have the complete elements' names on them by popping bubbles with the symbol of the given names. To pass each level, players must clear all bubbles within the time or moves limits. The game will be over if the player cannot reach the goal within the time or moves given. If the last row of bubbles at the top touches the limit line, the game of that level will be over instantly.

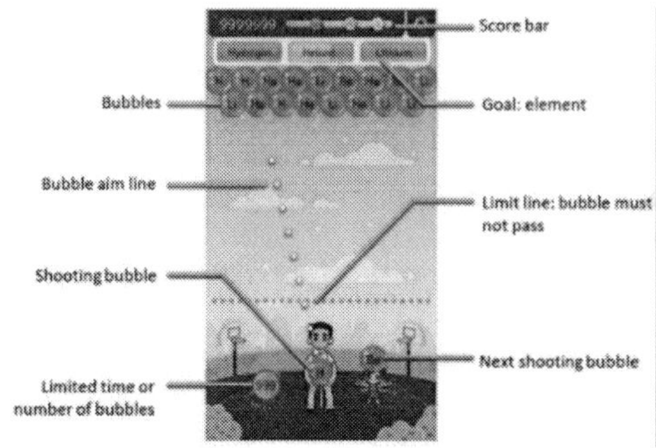

Figure 4. Screenshot of gameplay stage I

Figure 5. Basketball court scene for stage I

For gameplay stage II as presented in Figure 6, the bubbles will be released in random spots of the screen and will always be floating around. The player must touch, hold and drag their finger to create an area around bubbles of the same group or period to capture them. If it is successful, the bubbles are gathered into a bigger bubble. The goal is for the players to capture at least three bubbles of the same property according to the goal given in each level which will give the group or period number to collect them. If the player is unable to group at least three bubbles in a certain time, the big bubble will reduce back to its original form. To pass each level, players must fill all progress bars given (in this case, they are group 1A, 2B and period 1) within the time limit. The game will be over if the player cannot reach the goal within the time given.

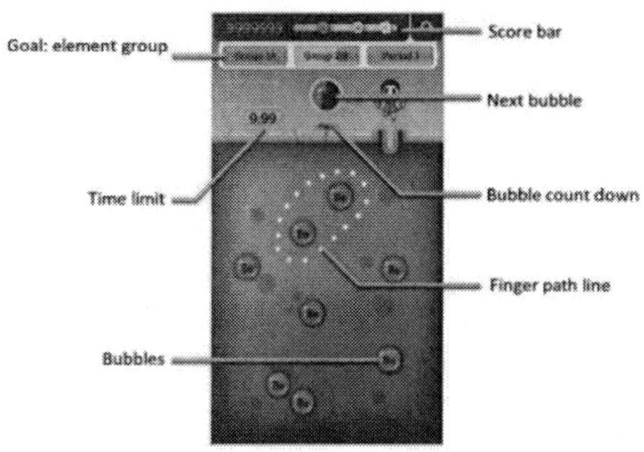

Figure 6. Screenshot of gameplay stage II

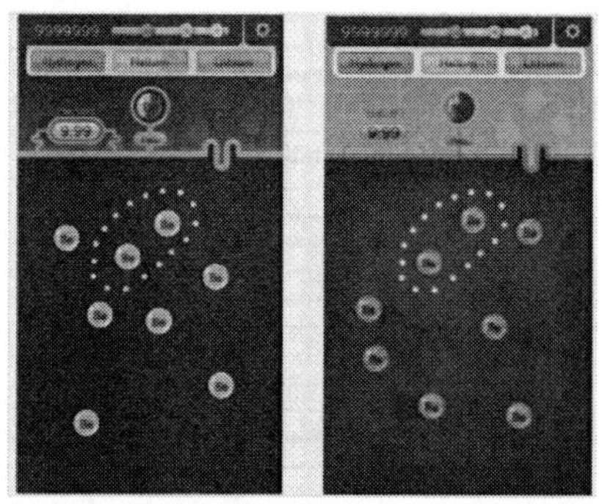

Figure 7. Inside a box scene for stage II

For gameplay stage III as presented in Figure 8. The player must draw around a pair of bubbles to form a connection of a chemical compound on the screen and reach the goal within the time given. Players can add more bubbles to that connection by circling one of the bubbles from the connection to a floating bubble. Also, the player can cut the connection by using their finger to touch, hold and drag a line to cut the connection line between the connected bubbles. The bubbles will be collected if the connection of bubbles is in accordance with a chemical compound. The goal is for the players to collect the compounds according to the goal given, which is the name of the chemical compounds. If the connected bubbles form a compound but it is not the goal the bubble will still be collected as score instead of progress.

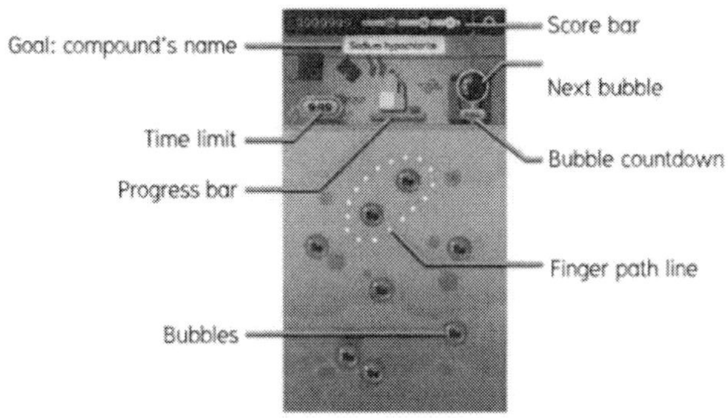

Figure 8. Screenshot of gameplay stage III

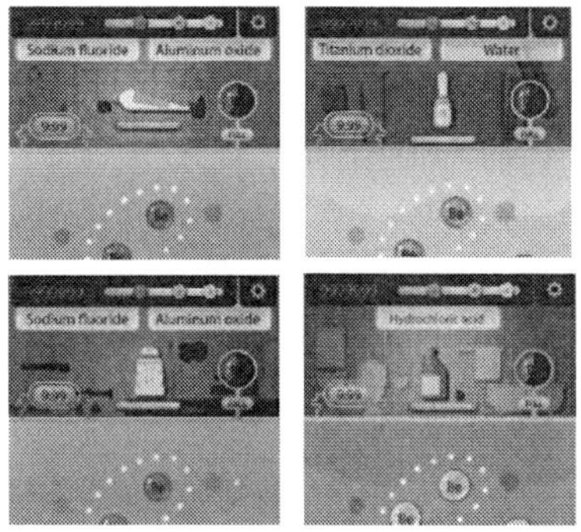

Figure 9. In the room scenes for stage III

5. EVALUATION

The research was conducted by testing the game with the sample group. According to a survey of 102 students in a science program, 63.8% male, 36.2% female, it was found that more than 90% liked to play computer games and more than 85% had played games on smartphones. Most of the sample groups have never experienced using game-based learning before. Moreover, there are more than 80% of the sample group that has experience in playing Bubble Shooter games, 96% enjoyed playing the Chemistry Pop game, 87% said the game is challenging. From inquiring about the knowledge of the periodic table, the survey found that 92.5% of the sample group had studied about the periodic table. In detail about learning techniques, 43% used reading memorization techniques, 20% used music with lyrics about the periodic table to help with memorizing it, 37% use other methods such as images, poems, etc., There are up to 82.5% of the sample that cannot remember the number of elements in the periodic table and up to 55% that cannot remember symbols and names of the first 20 elements in the periodic table. After playing, 96% of 102 students, enjoyed playing the game, 87% said the game was challenging, and 94% remembered at least 3 elements more than before playing.

Assessment of player satisfaction from the sample group after they played the game shows that the opinions of most samples say that the game is interesting and easy to play, the game can help the user to easily memorize, not as boring as normal reading memorization and can motivate the user to be interested in learning. Moreover, users also like the look of the game including characters and scenes. However, some participants found that the prototype game had some application errors occur that should be fixed. Some of them want the game to be further developed. With comments to add and edit certain functions to make the game more complete, including adding a system for introducing new elements that players will encounter in the game, adding extra items or extra points, improving animations of characters in the game to be able to show the emotions differently according to the situation, fixing the reviving duration portion for playing the game, and changing bubble speed.

6. CONCLUSIONS AND FUTURE PERSPECTIVE

This paper has presented the design and development of a smartphone game, a smartphone game to promote self-learning in chemistry, named Chemistry Pop. The game aims to apply the chemistry content of essential element names, the periodic table and chemical compound to players in a more fun and easier way to learn using gaming experiences like bubble shooter games, etc. This game-based learning consists of three stages with the content divided into stage I, learning element names, stage II, learning groups and periods, and stage III, learning chemical compounds. In addition, the user interface is developed and designed for easy usage, with quality graphics details similar to entertainment mobile applications. It allows the player to enjoy learning in a challenging environment without getting bored. The prototype game testing based on student needs proved the effectiveness and importance of game-based learning with education players. The survey results revealed that the players gained more knowledge of elementary chemistry than before playing.

The research perspectives can be done by adding more elements from the periodic table into all three stages and applying other lessons to the game. To compare the game with other approaches used for science subjects. Finally, the Chemistry Pop game can be further developed and enhanced to meet the requirements of the general player and be adapted for a commercial game.

REFERENCES

Andre F. S. Barbosa. et al, 2014. A New Methodology of Design and Development of Serious Games, *International Journal of Computer Games Technology*, Article ID 817167, 8 pages.

Chen, C., and Leung, L, 2016. Are you addicted to Candy Crush Saga? An exploratory study linking psychological factors to mobile social game addiction. *Telematics and Informatics*, Vol 33, No. 4, pp 1155-1166.

Franco-Mariscal, A. J.et al, 2016. A Game-Based Approach to Learning the Idea of Chemical Elements and Their Periodic Classification. *Journal of Chemical Education*, Vol 93, No 7, pp 1173-1190.

Freewarepocketpc., 2017. Kagaku Chemistry Periodic Table of Elements, Retrieved from http://www.freewarepocketpc.net/ppc-download-kagaku-chemistry-periodic-table-of-elements.html

Fujimoto, T. et al, 2017. JobStar Online: Game-Based Learning on Smartphones to Promote Youth Career Education. *Proceedings of the 25th International Conference on Computers in Education.* New Zealand: Asia-Pacific Society for Computers in Education

Google Play., 2017. 2048 Periodic Elements Game. Retrieved from https://play.google.com/store/apps/details?id=com.game.chemistry.

Guillén-Nieto, V., and Aleson-Carbonell, M, 2012. Serious games and learning effectiveness: The case of It's a Deal! *Computers and Education*, Vol 58, No. 1, pp 435-448.

Hsiao, H.S. and Chen, J.C., 2016. Using a gesture interactive game-based learning approach to improve preschool children's learning performance and motor skills, *Computers & Education*, No.95, pp.151-162.

IUPAC, 2017. The International Union of Pure and Applied Chemistry Retrieved from https://iupac.org/.

Kamnardsiri, T. et al, 2017. Designing of a game-based learning framework for training pharmacy students. *The 11th European Conference on Games Based Learning, ECGBL 2017*, pp. 301-310.

Kiili, K. ,2005. Digital game-based learning: Towards an experiential gaming model. *The Internet and higher education*, Vol 8, No. 1, pp. 13-24.

Klopfer, E. et al., 2009. Moving Learning Games Forward: Obstacles, Opportunities and Openness. *MIT The Education Arcade*. Cambridge, MA.

Lorenz, R. C.et al, 2015. Video game training and the reward system. *Frontiers in human neuroscience*, No.9, pp 40.

NSO, 2017. Thailand National Statistical Office. Retrieved from http://www.nso.go.th.

Paloma, 2017. Trippy, Dreamy Exploration: Gardenarium Released, Retrieved from https://www.rockpapershotgun.com/2015/04/03/gardenarium-exploration-game-released.

Periodic table Game. 2018, Retrieved from https://www.funbrain.com/games/periodic-table-game.

Rompayom, P., 2010. Development of Chemical Bonding learning units incorporated with elicitation strategy for high school students. Srinakharinwirot University, Thailand

Saksrisathaporn, K. and Maneewan, T.,2012. A Web-based Traveling Game for the Preservation of Lanna Culture. *2012 IEEE Fourth International Conference on Digital Game and Intelligent Toy Enhanced Learning*, Takamatsu, Japan, pp. 52-56.

Shooter-bubble, 2019. Retrieved from https://www.shooter-bubble.com/

Supawan P., 2009. Color and emotion. *Journal of Rajamangala Pitsanulok.* Vol 3, Issue 11.

Winter, J.et al, 2016. Chairs! A Mobile Game for Organic Chemistry Students To Learn the Ring Flip of Cyclohexane. *Journal of Chemical Education*, v93, n9, pp.1657-1659.

K-TIPS: KNOWLEDGE EXTENSION BASED ON TAILOR-MADE INFORMATION PROVISION SYSTEM

Keita Nakayama, Atsushi Shimada, Tsubasa Minematsu, Yuta Taniguchi and Rin-Ichiro Taniguchi
Kyushu University, Japan

ABSTRACT

Thanks to an increase in the amount of information on the Internet and the spread of ICT-supported educational environments, much attention has been paid to learning support based on "smart" recommendation technologies. In this study, we propose an education improvement model based on the recommender system using the human-in-the-loop design strategy. Our proposed model enhances not only learners via recommendation, but also teachers and the system itself through the interaction between teachers and the system. In this paper, we introduce the details of the proposed model and implementation strategy followed by a report of preliminary experimental results.

KEYWORDS

Education Improvement, Recommendation, Learning Analytics, Learning Log

1. INTRODUCTION

The increasing amount of information on the Internet, that is, the high number of open knowledge objects such as Wikipedia, iTuneU, and repositories managed by universities all over the world seems to be useful for supporting learning. However, learners are often discouraged by the time spent and difficulty in finding suitable and useful knowledge online (e.g., news articles, academic papers, and blogs) from a mass of search results (Chen et al., 2014). To use the information effectively and efficiently, it is necessary to build a system for the appropriate use of this vast knowledge. The recommender system for learning support is a common and useful system in this era of vast information (e.g., Erdt et al., 2015). Thus, a recommender system provides an appropriate learning environment that helps learners find appropriate knowledge targets within the vast amount of information on the Internet.

Researchers have been applying these resources to learning systems to clarify the effects of recommender systems for learning (e.g., Liang et al., 2006; Chen et al., 2007; Yamada et al., 2014). Many techniques for a recommender system have also been proposed. In particular, there are a large number of studies aimed at supporting learners based on student attributes such as learning situation (e.g., Tarus et al., 2018), preference based on learning logs (e.g., Salehi et al., 2014), search queries (e.g., Mbipom et al., 2018), and so on. On the other hand, there are a few studies that try, not only to support learners, but also to improve teaching materials and lectures. In addition, many existing studies unilaterally recommend online resources determined by the system, and do not design a feedback loop to improve the system itself. In order for the system to recommend appropriate resources from an educational viewpoint and for individual learners, it is desirable to involve teachers in the loop of recommendation and improvement of education and learning. In this paper, we propose an education improvement model, which collaborates with the page-wise recommendation method (Nakayama et al., 2019). The page-wise recommendation system provides recommended information for each page as shown in Figure 1. The original recommender system has some drawbacks (see the next section for the details), so our proposed model involves teachers to complement the drawbacks. In addition, the teachers can also get feedback from the system to improve their teaching and teaching materials. Therefore, our proposed model enhances not only learners via recommendation, but also the teachers and the system based on the human-in-the-loop design strategy. In the following section of this paper, we introduce the details of the proposed model and implementation strategy followed by a report of preliminary experimental results.

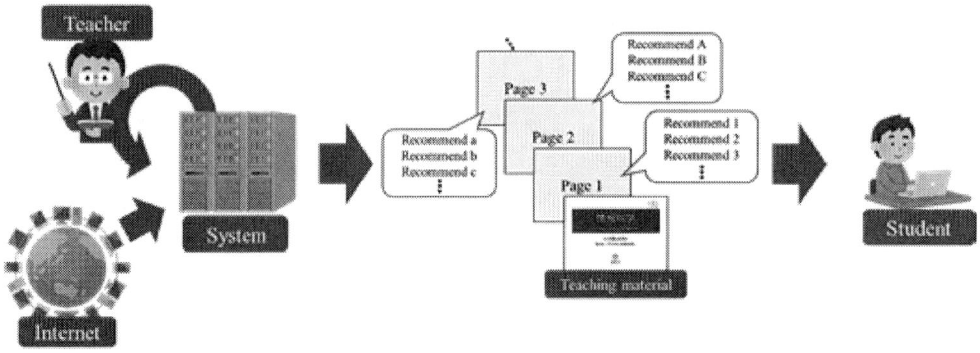

Figure 1. Page-wise recommendation system

2. EDUCATION IMPROVEMENT MODEL BASED ON PAGE-WISE RECOMMENDATION

In this study, we propose an education improvement model based on a system that recommends supplementary materials related to teaching materials used in lectures. The overview of the system configuration is shown in Figure 2. The proposed model improves education and learning by cycling through the following process:

(1) A teacher prepares a lecture plan and teaching material in preparation for a lecture and registers the teaching material in an e-Book system.

(2) The proposed system selects recommended information related to the teaching material from the Internet.

(3) The e-Book system provides the recommendation to the students during the lecture or self-study.

(4) The system analyzes the learning activity logs and gives feedback to the teacher.

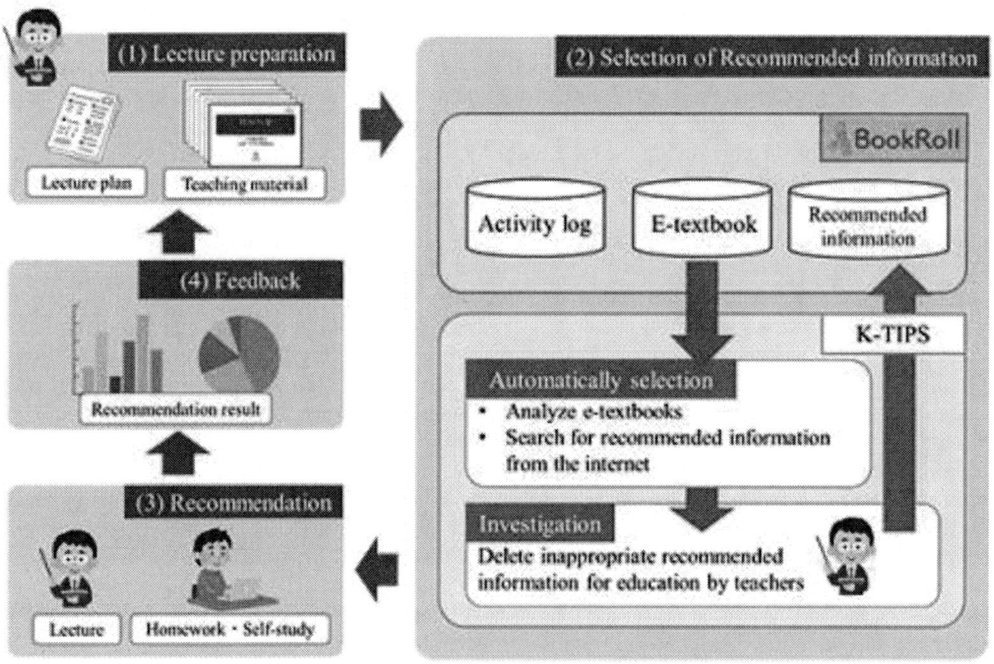

Figure 2. Overview of education improvement model

A method to calculate recommended pieces of information in (2) is inspired by an existing study proposed by Nakayama et al (2019). According to the survey in the paper, the recommended items were mostly suitable for the content in the lecture materials. However, it sometimes contained inappropriate information for learning because the recommended items were automatically retrieved from the Internet and unilaterally provided to students. The problem is that it is not possible to know whether the recommended information is appropriate from an educational viewpoint or for individual learners. Therefore, it is necessary to have a mechanism for acquiring feedback from each user including the teachers and students. In order to solve this problem, in this study, a teacher intervenes in the selection of recommended information in (2). The system provides a list of candidates for recommended items on a web page, and the teacher investigates and decides whether each one is suitable for recommendation or not. We believe that teachers' intervention in selecting recommended information has several advantages for students and teachers, as listed below:

- We can prevent undesirable situations in which inappropriate or unnecessary information is recommended to students.
- The selection results by the teacher are helpful for the system to improve the automatic suggestion of recommended information.

The recommendation results for students are analyzed in (4) based on the student learning activity log (click on the link to the recommended information) in the e-Book system. The analysis results are feedback to teachers, students, and the system itself. Recommending information corresponding to each page of teaching material not only facilitates students' learning, but also allows teachers to understand the students' reaction to teaching materials used in lectures and proceed with a lecture. Therefore, teachers can use the analysis results as feedback from students to improve teaching materials and proceed with a lecture. The responses from students are also meaningful data that can be used to investigate whether recommended information was useful or not. The operation logs of clicking the recommended information indicates whether the student has interest in the recommended information. By collecting the access information of recommended information from each student, it will become possible to provide personalized recommended information according to the individual's learning level in the future. In this way, by examining and evaluating the recommended information from both teachers and students, it is possible to make high-quality recommendations, and further education improvement can be achieved. We will describe the system to realize this education improvement model in the following section.

3. IMPLEMENTATION

3.1 System Configuration

We use two systems to recommend information related to the teaching materials treated in lectures. One is an e-Book system called BookRoll (Ogata, 2015, 2017), the other is Knowledge extension based on Tailor-made Information Provision System (K-TIPS).

BookRoll is an e-Book viewer which has three databases. In each database, teaching materials that are e-textbook used in lectures, recommended information for each piece of teaching materials, and student's activity logs to e-Book system are stored. A teacher conducts a lecture using an e-textbook stored in the e-Book system and students learn by using it during and outside a lecture. Various functions are implemented in the e-Book system, and a recommendation function is one of them. Figure 3 shows the user interface of the e-Book viewer. Students can access the recommended items by clicking the upper right button of the viewer as necessary. In addition, each student can submit a response about whether he/she could understand the contents on the page or not, by clicking the green (understood) or red (not understood) button. When a student uses any of the functions of the e-Book system (such as *open an e-textbook*, *go to the next page*, *highlight*, *click a link to a recommended article*, etc.), learning activity logs are automatically recorded in the database.

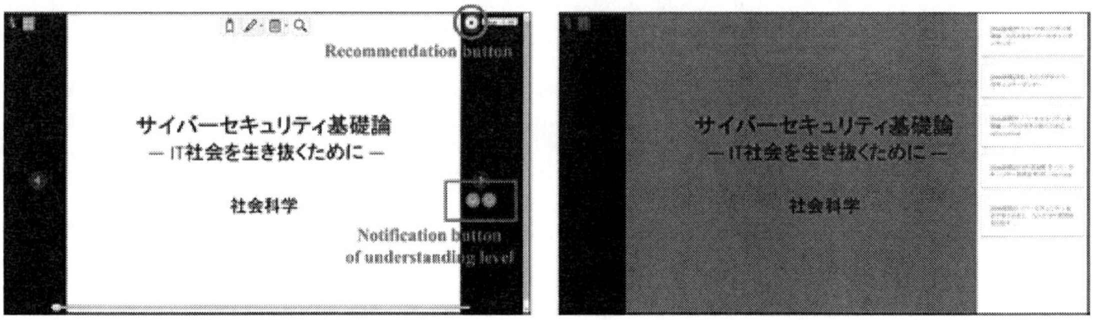

(A) Material viewer (B) Recommendation viewer

Figure 3. Viewer of e-Book system

The K-TIPS is a web application that displays candidates for recommended information, and allows teachers to select recommended information related to each page of teaching material. In this system, the teaching material designated by the teacher is analyzed, and the recommended information is automatically selected from the Internet and presented to the teacher. Then, the teacher investigates the candidates of recommended information and decides the information to be recommended to the student. Finally, it is registered in the e-Book system by the K-TIPS. The details of the web application are explained in the following sections.

3.2 K-TIPS

3.2.1 Overview of K-TIPS

In this research, as mentioned in section 2, we believe that there are various advantages regarding the teacher's intervention in selecting recommended information. Therefore, we developed a web application for teachers to investigate the automatically selected recommended information from the Internet. The interface of the K-TIPS is shown in Figure 4.

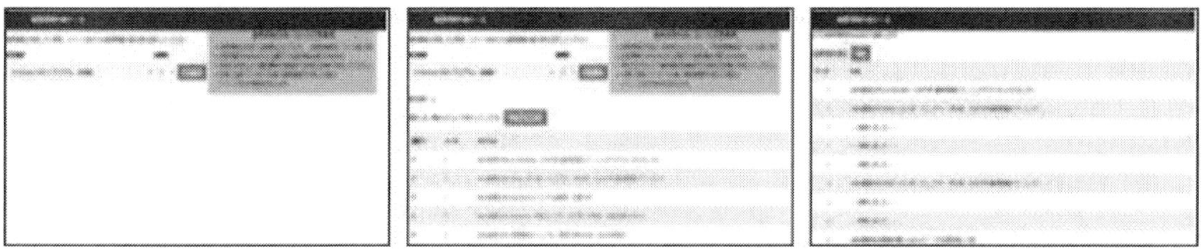

(A) Selection screen (B) Investigation screen (C) Confirmation screen

Figure 4. Interface of K-TIPS

Figure 4-(A) is a web page for selecting lecture materials to be analyzed for calculating recommended information. In this page, the teacher specifies the maximum number of recommended items per page. When the specification is complete, they click a green button. Then, the recommended information for the teaching material is automatically selected from the Internet and displayed on the screen. The automatic selection method of recommended information is described in the next section.

Figure 4-(B) is a web page for investigation. On this page, two details about each recommended item are displayed in a table format: the page number recommended in the e-Book system and the title of the recommended item. In addition, a check box is displayed at the left end of the table. A link to the recommended information is attached to the displayed title, and the teacher can confirm the content of the recommended item by clicking the title. If the teacher judges that the content of the recommended information is not appropriate, they can uncheck the box. After completing the investigation of all candidates, they click the green registration confirmation button to proceed to the confirmation page.

Figure 4-(C) is a web page to confirm the recommended information registered in the e-Book system. In this page, recommended items with boxes that are still checked after investigation are displayed, and recommended items with boxes that are unchecked are displayed as "deleted." The teacher verifies whether the recommended information to be registered is correct, and if there is some mistake, they can return to the investigation page again by clicking the return button. If there are no mistakes, the recommended information is registered in the e-Book system by clicking the registration button, and it is then recommended to the student.

This system stores a list of recommended items automatically selected from the Internet before investigation. Therefore, it is possible to analyze the recommended items deleted by teachers by comparing them with a list of recommended items registered in the e-Book system after investigation. The analysis results can be used to improve the accuracy of the automatic selection method of recommended information, and it is possible to support education and learning by providing recommendations that are more suitable for learning.

3.2.2 Automatic Selection Method of Recommended Information

In this section, we give an overview of the automatic selection method of recommended information for each page of a teaching material (Nakayama et al., 2019). In this method, to select recommended information, the method takes three analytical steps, as follows:

1. Word extraction from teaching material;
2. Calculation of the importance of extracted words;
3. Retrieval of recommended information from the Internet based on important words.

First, nouns in the teaching material are extracted. In the e-Book system, teaching materials are stored as PDFs, and text information about sentences in registered teaching materials is extracted from the PDFs automatically. Therefore, the text information can be utilized to extract sentences and words from the teaching material. In this research, we focus on Japanese teaching materials. In contrast to languages segmented by spaces such as English, Japanese is a non-segmented language. Therefore, it is necessary to divide the sentences to extract words. In this study, we apply MeCab morphological analysis (Kudo et al., 2004). Morphological analysis is the technique of dividing natural language into morphemes, the smallest units of words. In this method, proper nouns are extracted from a sentence through morphological analysis.

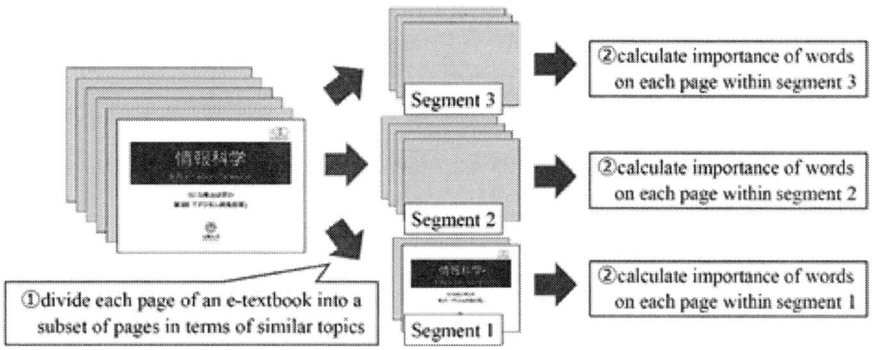

Figure 5. Overview of calculating importance of extracted words

Second, the importance of the extracted words on each page are estimated to select recommended information for each page of the teaching material. The estimation procedure involves two steps: 1) dividing each page of a teaching material into a subset of pages (refer to them as "segments") in terms of similar topics, and 2) calculating the importance of the words on each page within each segment. Figure 5 shows an overview of the process flow to estimate the importance of extracted words. In this method, whole pages of teaching material are divided into segments according to the topic of the contents because it may be considered that there is a difference in importance depending on the topic, even for the same word. After dividing into subsets of pages, the importance of each word is calculated for each segment. The importance of words in each segment is estimated using the TF-IDF method (Salton & Buckley., 1988). The TF-IDF method is a method for evaluating the importance of words in a document using two indicators: term frequency (TF) and inverse document frequency (IDF). Teaching materials are divided into the title area and the body area. The title represents the contents of each page, and words in the title area seem to be important. Therefore, the importance of each word is calculated by weighing words in the title area to the importance of the TF-IDF method.

Third, recommended information is retrieved from the Internet based on the importance of the word. First, let the top *n* words of importance in each page be the important words representing the content of the page. Next, the top *n* words are used as the search query to retrieve related websites. Then, the top *m* of the search results are selected to be the recommended items of information.

3.3 Student Activity Log

An analysis of recommendation results in (4) in section 2 is performed by analyzing student activity logs collected by the e-Book system. As mentioned above, various functions are implemented in the e-Book system. For example, adding a memo or a marker to a current page, evaluating whether a student understands the current page, accessing the current page's recommended information, etc. As shown in Figure 6, various activity logs of students using such functions can be collected.

An analysis of recommendation results uses logs for recommended information (a log with the operation name "CLICK_RECOMMENDATION" in Figure 6). From the log data of recommendations, it is possible to identify the user who accessed the recommended information, the page number of a teaching material, and which recommended information is accessed. Utilization of these learning activity logs has the possibility to improve education and learning in terms of following aspects:

- Update the teaching material by analyzing the number of clicks in each page of the teaching material.
- Determine the demand of each student for recommended information.
- Realize personalized recommendation.

Moreover, we believe that it is possible to analyze from other various viewpoints by utilizing the log data other than the recommendation. For example, it is possible to analyze the relationship between the reaction to the recommendation and the student's level of understanding by using the log indicating whether the student could understand the content of the current page (a log with the operation name "GETIT" or "NOTGETIT" in Figure 6). As a result, we believe that the recommendation results can be used to further improve education.

User ID	e-book ID	e-book title	Page	Operation	Description	...	Time
xxxxxxxxxxxx	ooooooooo	D-06-画像	14	CLICK_RECOMMENDATION	https://***********	...	2019-07-01 11:26:15
xxxxxxxxxxxx	ooooooooo	D-06-画像	13	NEXT		...	2019-07-01 11:26:17
xxxxxxxxxxxx	ooooooooo	D-06-画像	15	NOTGETIT		...	2019-07-01 11:26:20
xxxxxxxxxxxx	ooooooooo	D-06-画像	16	CLICK_RECOMMENDATION	https://***********	...	2019-07-01 11:26:25
xxxxxxxxxxxx	ooooooooo	D-06-画像	17	GETIT		...	2019-07-01 11:26:31

Figure 6. Samples of student activity logs stored in the e-Book system

4. EXPERIMENTS

We have been conducting experiments using the proposed system in multiple lectures for first- and second-year college students using the proposed system since April 2019. A total of 98 teaching materials used in 16 courses in the first semester of the 2019 school year at Kyushu University were used for the experiments and recommended information was provided to students by the end of July 2019. As a result of the recommendations, 1061 activity log data for recommendations were collected from 247 students. In this study, we have developed a web application for teachers to confirm the usage status of recommended information. Figure 7 is the display screen of the recommendation result. The teacher can confirm how many times the recommended items were clicked by students in each page. In the graph displayed, the x-axis is the page number of the teaching material, and the y-axis is the number of clicks for the recommended items of information. In addition, if the teacher moves the mouse cursor to the bar chart, its corresponding page is displayed below the graph. If the number of clicks for the recommended items is extremely high compared to other pages, it is taken into consideration that there may be a problem with the contents of the teaching materials or lectures. It has shown that the number of clicks on the relevant page may increase if the content of the teaching material is difficult or if there is a problem with the style of the lecture (Nakayama et al., 2019). In this way, utilizing the recommendation results can be used to improve education.

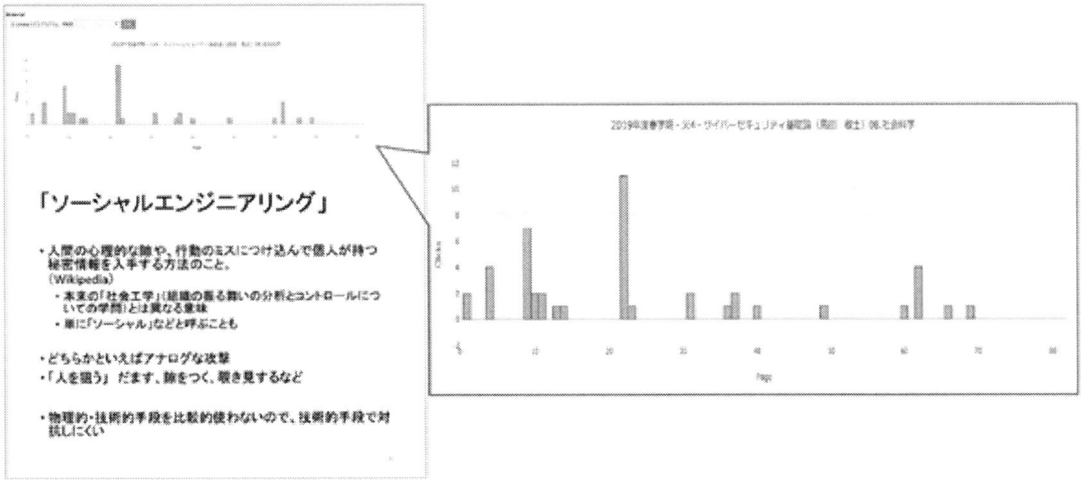

Figure 7. The display screen of the recommendation results

Also, investigation by teachers has been implemented since July 2019. By the end of July 2019, investigation was conducted by a total of four teachers for the recommended information on 42 teaching materials. As a result of the investigation, 1.4% of the recommended information selected automatically was judged as inappropriate or unnecessary for learning and was deleted by the teacher. We analyzed the titles and URLs of recommended information deleted by investigation. As a result, we saw that there were many words related to games (such as "games," "gamer," "game design," etc.) and words related to products (such as "Amazon," "product," and "shohin," which in Japanese means product, etc.) in the recommended information. The reason why the recommended information about the game was presented to the students is that an educational information engineering course included a class about game-based learning. In addition to this, many keywords such as "syllabus" and "yahoo" that were considered unnecessary for learning were confirmed. Based on the results of these investigations, we can implement high-quality recommendations for learning by designing a mechanism for automatically excluding information inappropriate for learning. In addition, we confirmed cases where all recommended items on some pages were deleted by investigation. It can be inferred that these were pages that did not require a recommendation (such as a page with notes about the lecture, etc.). It may be possible to identify pages that do not require a recommendation by using the investigation result.

5. CONCLUSION

In this paper, we proposed an education improvement model based on a system that recommends supplementary teaching materials related to teaching materials used in lectures. Then, we described the system for realizing the proposed education improvement and reported on the current status of recommendation experiments conducted in the university environment. We believe that the proposed system enables both teachers and students to improve their teaching and learning experiences through interaction with recommended information. A page in which many students used the recommended information suggests the possibility that the contents of the material are difficult to understand, so that a teacher will consider an update of the contents.

In future work, as mentioned above, we will work on the development of the method to calculate recommended information using the investigation result by the teachers and the learning support by the individual recommendation from the recommendation result to the student. In addition to these, we will also examine information recommendation for summarized teaching materials. The summarized teaching material is a collection of pages containing important content extracted from the teaching material (Shimada et al., 2017). The contents of the teaching material are automatically summarized to a small number of pages, so that only the essential points are given to learners. The combination of summarization technique and our recommender system will help learners understand the summary of lecture contents and present an opportunity for knowledge extension by using recommended information. We are sure that the collaboration with other digital technologies will support learning and teaching in a new digital educational era.

ACKNOWLEDGEMENT

This work was supported by JST AIP Grant Number JPMJCR19U1 and JSPS KAKENHI Grand Number JP18H04125, Japan.

REFERENCES

Chen, G. D. et al, 2007. Extending e-book with Contextual Knowledge Recommender for Reading Support on a Web-Based Learning System. *International Journal on E-Learning*, Vol. 6, No. 4, pp.605-622.

Chen, W. et al, 2014. A hybrid recommendation algorithm adapted in e-learning environments. *World Wide Web*, Vol. 17, No. 2, pp. 271-284.

Erdt, M. et al, 2015. Evaluating Recommender Systems for Technology Enhanced Learning: A Quantitative Survey, *IEEE Transaction of Learning Technologies*, Vol. 8, No. 4, pp. 326-344.

Flanagan, B. and Ogata, H., 2017. Integration of Learning Analytics Research and Production Systems While Protecting Privacy. In *International Conference on Computers in Education (ICCE2017)*, pp. 333-338.

Kudo, T. et al, 2004. Applying conditional random fields to Japanese morphological analysis. In *Proceedings of the 2004 conference on empirical methods in natural language processing.*

Liang, G. et al, 2006. Courseware recommendation in e-learning system. *In International Conference on Web-based Learning 2006*, pp. 10-24.

Mbipom, B. et al, 2018. An e-learning recommender that helps learners find the right materials. *The Eighth AAAI Symposium on Educational Advances in Artificial Intelligence 2018 (EAAI-18).*

Nakayama, K. et al, 2019. Learning support system for providing page-wise recommendation in e-textbooks. *In Society for Information Technology & Teacher Education International Conference (SITE 2019)*, pp. 824-831.

Ogata, H. et al, 2015. E-Book-based learning analytics in university education. *In International Conference on Computer in Education (ICCE 2015)*, pp. 401-406.

Salehi, M. et al, 2014. Personalized recommendation of learning material using sequential pattern mining and attribute based collaborative filtering. *Education and Information Technologies*, Vol. 19, No. 4, pp. 713-735.

Salton, G. and Buckley, C., 1988. Term-weighting approaches in automatic text retrieval. *Information processing & management*, Vol. 24, No. 5, pp. 513-523.

Shimada, A. et al, 2017. Automatic Summarization of Lecture Slides for Enhanced Student Preview -Technical Report and User Study-. *IEEE Transactions on Learning Technologies*, Vol. 11, No. 2, pp. 165-178.

Tarus, J. K. et al, 2018. A hybrid recommender system for e-learning based on context awareness and sequential pattern mining. *Soft Computing*, Vol. 22, No. 8, pp. 2449-2461.

Yamada, M. et al, 2014. Collaborative filtering for expansion of learner's background knowledge in online language learning: does "top-down" processing improve vocabulary proficiency?. *Educational Technology Research and Development*, Vol. 62, No. 5, pp. 529-553.

CLUSTERING OF LEARNERS BASED ON KNOWLEDGE MAPS

Akira Onoue, Atsushi Shimada, Tsubasa Minematsu and Rin-Ichiro Taniguchi
Kyushu University, Japan

ABSTRACT

This study aimed to cluster learners based on the structures of the knowledge maps they created. Learners drew their own knowledge maps to reflect their learning activities. Our system collected individual knowledge maps from many learners and clustered them to generate an integrated version of the knowledge maps of each cluster. We applied the graph analysis method to extract important keywords from the knowledge map. The results of the analysis showed that the utilization of the knowledge map helped to improve lectures and grasp the learners' level of understanding. We conducted surveys asking course managers to evaluate the effectiveness of the integrated knowledge maps of learners included in the cluster and received both positive and negative responses.

KEYWORDS

Knowledge Map, Similarity, Pagerank, Netsimile, Clustering, Infinite Relational Model

1. INTRODUCTION

Research on the cognitive perspective of learning has been conducted for a long time in the educational psychology field. Cognitive learning in a learning process is one of the most important perspectives for successful learning performances. One of the effective cognitive learning support tools is a concept map, which allows learners to make a map connecting important concepts and their ideas. It enhances the use of cognitive learning strategies (e.g., Fiorella and Mayer, 2017) and productive discussions in collaborative learning settings (Yamada et al., 2016).

In the highly advanced information technology era, a concept map can play an additional significant role in learning. Log data from a digital concept map tool allows researchers and teachers to track the learning process using log data visualizations such as the concept map construction process (Hsiao and Brusilovsky, 2012). As a similar cognitive tool, a knowledge map can be an effective cognitive learning tool. Knowledge maps focus on the construction of knowledge relationships, such as the linkages among information (Crampes et al., 2006; Balaid et al., 2016); this suggests that a knowledge map is effective at granting access to knowledge in a timely manner, identifying knowledge flow, allowing organizational restructuring, and so on. However, categorization and visualization, such as clustering, are required in order to confirm the knowledge construction process and elucidate the knowledge gap between high and low performers. For example, clustering of both learning process data and learning performance data allows teachers to comprehend effective learning styles (Yin et al., 2019). Clustering data seems to help teachers consider instructional designs and support learners.

This research focuses on knowledge map construction and clustering and aims to develop a teaching support system using knowledge map clustering data.

2. RECONSTRUCTION OF A KNOWLEDGE MAP

A knowledge map is a network in which learned keywords are arranged as nodes, and the relationships between the nodes are indicated using arrows. This section discusses how to reconstruct the individual knowledge maps created by many learners.

First, we will introduce the e-book system and BR-Map tool (Yamada et al., 2018), followed by the reconstruction and analytical strategy of knowledge maps. Each learner creates his/her own knowledge map using the BR-Map tool. The words in the nodes of the BR-Map are automatically extracted from the e-book system by referring to the areas highlighted by the learner. The highlighted words or sentences become candidates for nodes in the BR-Map system. Finally, the learners create their own knowledge map by arranging nodes and drawing link nodes.

Second, we executed node and link processing. By using the BR-Map tool, we acquired the knowledge maps created by learners. These knowledge maps contain some nodes corresponding to a single word, sentence, number, symbol, and so on. Ideally, each node should have one word (keyword) to represent a knowledge point. Therefore, we adopted a text mining process to identify the same keywords in sentences proposed by Onoue et al. (2019). There were two steps in determining the nodes in the integrated knowledge map:

1. Morphological analysis by MeCab (Kudo, 2006) with mecab-ipadic-NEologd (Sato et al., 2016).
2. Integration of nodes with similar words based on the normalized Levenshtein distance.

As a result of node processing, each node had one word. In the next step, we analyzed the links between nodes, and separated or integrated them according to the condition of the connected nodes. After node and link processing, we acquired the individual knowledge map of each learner (refer to Onoue et al. [2019] for details about node and link processing).

Third, we made clusters of the learners based on their individual knowledge maps. The clustering algorithm is introduced in detail in section 3.

Lastly, we integrated the knowledge maps of learners included in each cluster. We used a method to create the integrated knowledge maps based on Onoue et al. (2019). The integrated knowledge maps show how course contents are organized and remembered by learners. This information is important for both teachers and learners to reflect their teaching and learning activities, respectively. On the integrated knowledge map, a link between nodes is represented as a weighted link. If two or more learners establish the same link between a certain combination of words, the weight of the link is increased based on the number of learners. The centrality algorithm provides helpful information for understanding the relationships between words that have strong connections with each other.

3. CLUSTERING OF KNOWLEDGE MAPS

A knowledge map is a network portraying how a learner organizes and understands what they have learned. The purpose of this study is to cluster learners based on knowledge maps. Clustering results are useful for helping teachers to understand the patterns of learners' understanding. Providing appropriate information for each learner based on a clustering result can improve learner understanding.

3.1 Similarity between Learners' Individual Knowledge Maps

We calculated the similarity between the individual knowledge maps created by learners using a method based on NetSimile (Berlingerio et al., 2013). The knowledge maps were directed graphs with labeled nodes. Therefore, we needed to take into account the direction of the links and the meaning of the nodes when the similarity between learners' individual knowledge maps was calculated; however, NetSimile was developed for undirected graphs with unlabeled nodes. Therefore, we extended NetSimile so that it could be used to make comparisons of the knowledge maps.

3.1.1 NetSimile

NetSimile is a method for calculating the similarity between two graphs. The similarity of these graphs is defined as the similarity of their "signature" feature vectors. NetSimile has three steps: feature extraction, feature aggregation, and comparison.

During feature extraction, we generated a set of structural features for each node based on its local and egonet features. An egonet is a subgraph consisting of a focus node, and the nodes have a link with a focus node. The original NetSimile algorithm had the following seven features:

$d_i = |N(i)|$: degree of node i, $N(i)$ denotes the neighbors of node i.

c_i: clustering coefficient of node i defined as the number of triangles connected to node i over the number of connected triples centered on node i.

$\bar{d}_{N(i)} = \frac{1}{d_i}\sum_{\forall j \in N(i)} d_j$: the average number of node i's two-hops-away neighbors.

$\bar{c}_{N(i)} = \frac{1}{d_i}\sum_{\forall j \in N(i)} c_j$: the average clustering coefficient of $N(i)$

$|E_{ego(i)}|$: the number of edges in node i's egonet $ego(i)$.

$|E^{o}_{ego(i)}|$: the number of links between $ego(i)$'s nodes and the outside nodes of $ego(i)$.

$|N(ego(i))|$: the number of neighbors of $ego(i)$.

During feature aggregation, NetSimile generates a $nodes \times features$ matrix F_{g_j}, for each graph $g_j \in G = \{g_1, g_2, \ldots, g_k\}$. Then, NetSimile calculates the following five values in each feature (i.e., each column of F_{g_j}) to produce "signature" feature vectors $\boldsymbol{s}_{g_j}$: median, mean, standard deviation, skewness, and kurtosis. Therefore, each graph g_j is represented by five parameters.

Lastly, during the comparison step, we calculated the Canberra distance $d_{Can}(P,Q) = \sum_{i=1}^{d} \frac{|P_i - Q_i|}{P_i + Q_i}$ between the feature vectors P and Q.

3.1.2 NetSimile for Directed Graphs

To cluster the individual knowledge maps created by each learner, we calculated the similarity between the directed graphs with labeled nodes. As mentioned above, NetSimile is a method for calculating the similarity between two undirected graphs with unlabeled nodes. However, we needed to distinguish similarly structured graphs if the nodes had different labels. Therefore, we extended NetSimile to handle directed graphs with labeled nodes. The similarity of these graphs was defined based on the similarity of their "signature" feature vectors. The algorithm has three steps: feature extraction, vectorization, and comparison.

During feature extraction, we took the links' direction into account. Since the learners were instructed to draw links from the upper concept to the lower concept on their individual knowledge map, not only the existence of the link but also its direction was important information. We defined the following 10 features:

$d_i^{in} = |N_{in}(i)|$: income degree of node i, $N_{in}(i)$ denotes the neighbors with incoming links to node i.

$d_i^{out} = |N_{out}(i)|$: outgoing degree of node i, $N_{out}(i)$ denotes the neighbors with outgoing links from node i.

c_i: clustering coefficient of node i defined as the number of triangles connected to node i over the number of connected triples centered on node i.

$\bar{d}_{N_{in}(i)} = \frac{1}{d_i}\sum_{\forall j \in N_{in}(i)} d_j$: the average number of node i's two-hops-away neighbors with incoming links to neighbors of node i.

$\bar{d}_{N_{out}(i)} = \frac{1}{d_i}\sum_{\forall j \in N_{out}(i)} d_j$: the average number of node i's two-hops-away neighbors with outgoing links from neighbors of node i.

$\bar{c}_{N(i)} = \frac{1}{d_i}\sum_{\forall j \in N(i)} c_j$: the average clustering coefficient of $N(i)$

$|E_{ego(i)}|$: the number of links in node i's egonet $ego(i)$.

$|E^{in}_{ego(i)}|$: the number of income links to $ego(i)$'s nodes from outside nodes of $ego(i)$.

$|E^{out}_{ego(i)}|$: the number of outgoing links from $ego(i)$'s nodes to outside nodes of $ego(i)$.

$|N(ego(i))|$: the number of neighbors of $ego(i)$.

During the vectorizing step, we generated the "signature" feature vector $\boldsymbol{s'}_{g_j}$. $\boldsymbol{s'}_{g_j}$ by vectorizing (arranging in a row) the feature matrix F_{g_j}. Both the original and our proposed methods needed to match the number of dimensions of the feature vectors for calculating the feature vector distance. In the original NetSimile algorithm, the number of rows of each feature matrix F_{g_j} is different for each graph because each graph has a different number of nodes. In order to make it possible to calculate the distance between the feature vectors, the number of dimensions was aligned in the feature aggregation step. On the other hand, the aggregation step cannot handle word information on the nodes. Therefore, we avoided the aggregation strategy and took the other approach to consider the word information on each node in our proposed method.

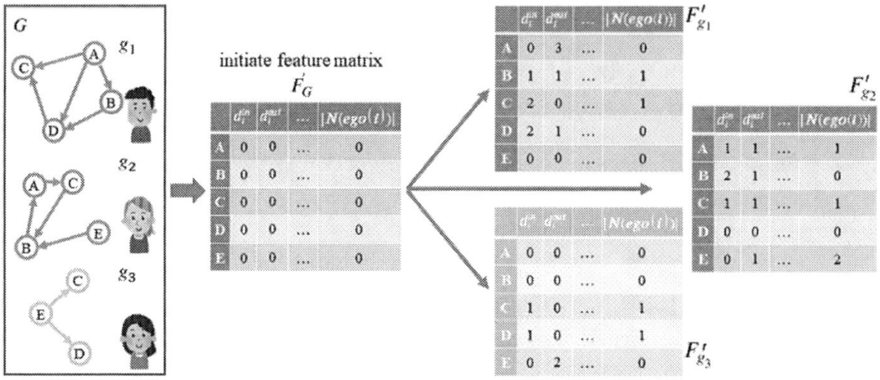

Figure 1. Example of creating a feature matrix

We made a dictionary vector , which contained all of the words in $\boldsymbol{G}$ without duplicates. As a result, the number of rows of feature matrix F'_G became a list of all words, as shown in Figure 1 (A, B, C, D, and E are the lists of words extracted from all graphs without duplication). We gave a score of zero to all features corresponding to a word when a graph did not contain the word in the nodes. For instance, g_1 did not have a node with the word "E," so the scores in the fifth row in F'_{g_1} were all zero. This approach enabled the alignment of the length of rows for all graphs, resulting in generating the same dimensional feature vectors. The feature vector of each graph was represented by the concatenation of row vectors.

Lastly, in the comparison step, we calculated the cosine distance $d_{Cos}(P,Q) = \frac{\sum_{i=1}^{|V|} P_i Q_i}{\sqrt{\sum_{i=1}^{|V|} P_i^2}\sqrt{\sum_{i=1}^{|V|} Q_i^2}}$.

3.2 Clustering Learners using the Infinite Relational Model

After calculating the similarity between each learner's knowledge map, we created a relation matrix $\boldsymbol{R} = (r_{ij})_{i,j=1}^{l}$ so that $r_{ij} = 1$ if the similarity between learner i's knowledge map and learner j's knowledge map is over the threshold (th). In the other case, we set it so that $r_{ij} = 0$. l denoted the number of learners. $\boldsymbol{R}$ is a symmetric matrix indicating whether each learner's knowledge map has strong relationships.

Lastly, the infinite relational model (IRM) (Kemp et al., 2006) was applied to $\boldsymbol{R}$ in order to classify learners based on their knowledge maps. IRM, which is based on a nonparametric Bayesian model, can estimate the number of hidden clusters from binary relational data (refer to Kemp et al. [2006] for the detailed algorithm of the IRM).

4. EXPERIMENT

4.1 Subjects and Course

We conducted the experiments during the university education course. The main themes of the course were basic skills, laws, and ethics related to cybersecurity. The course was conducted over eight weeks from April to June 2018. In total, 98 first-year students created an individual knowledge map for this course. After the final lecture, we asked the learners to create knowledge maps for the purpose of reflecting what they had learned over the eight weeks.

4.2 Evaluation of the Sub-Maps

After calculating the similarity between each learner's knowledge map, we created a relation matrix $\boldsymbol{R}$ shown in Figure 2. In this research, we set the threshold of similarity (th) to be 0.3 when creating a relation matrix. The yellow part in Figure 2 corresponds to the combination of learners who obtained similarities larger than th. The red and blue lines represent the boundaries of clusters in the row and column directions. The learners were classified into seven clusters in the row direction and six clusters in the column direction. In the rectangular area surrounded by blue and red lines, the larger the proportion of yellow elements, the stronger the connection between the learners corresponding to the rows and columns. Although there were some clusters with strong similarities, such as the right block of cluster "A" in Figure 2, we focused only on the clusters that contained the same learners in both the rows and columns as much as possible. As a result, we selected four clusters (A, B, C, and D in Figure 2 to evaluate the result of the clustering. To analyze the characteristics of each cluster, we made an integrated knowledge map for each cluster.

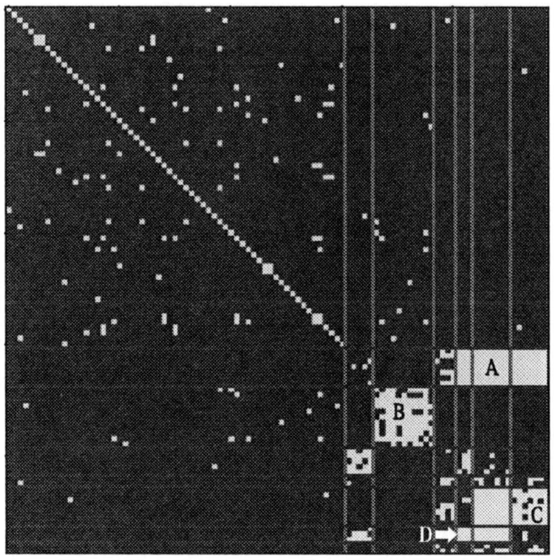

Figure 2. Relation matrix sorted by the IRM

Figure 3. Correspondence between lecture themes and node colors

We administered a questionnaire to the course managers who designed the course and provided the lecture materials, in order to evaluate the effectiveness of sub-map k, which is the integrated knowledge map of learners included in the cluster. A larger-sized node represented an important node, which means that many learners drew links to/from the node. Additionally, the node's color corresponded to the lecture that had learning materials in which the word was frequently used (shown in Figure 3). In order to evaluate the clustering result, we constructed the whole integrated knowledge map shown in Figure 4, and sub-maps $k_A \sim k_D$ shown in Figure 5. The whole integrated knowledge map is a combination of the individual knowledge maps of all learners. Each sub-map had structural features. k_A mainly consisted of nodes about copyright, and there weren't almost links between nodes of different lectures. k_B consisted of individual knowledge maps of the most learners. There were mainly nodes of introduction and cryptography. k_C mainly consisted of nodes of introduction, ethics and copyright. k_D consisted only of nodes about copyright. There were links between the nodes of introduction and the nodes of other lectures. After presenting the integrated knowledge map and sub-maps to the course manager, we asked them to fill out the questionnaire.

Table 1 shows the questionnaire about the integrated knowledge maps and the responses. Each course manager answered each question according to a five-grade evaluation system. Q1–Q3 asked about the readability of $k_A \sim k_D$. Q4–Q6 asked whether $k_A \sim k_D$ matched the course managers' aim for the course. Q4 and Q5 asked them to consider whether it would help to improve classes in terms of supporting education. Q7–Q9 asked about how to use sub-maps. In particular, we investigated whether the course managers wanted to compare sub-maps or the whole integrated knowledge map with the sub-maps. Q10 and Q11 asked whether utilizing the knowledge map would be useful for improving the content of the lectures, and for grasping the learners' level of understanding. Q12 asked whether the course managers wanted to use sub-maps in their educational activities.

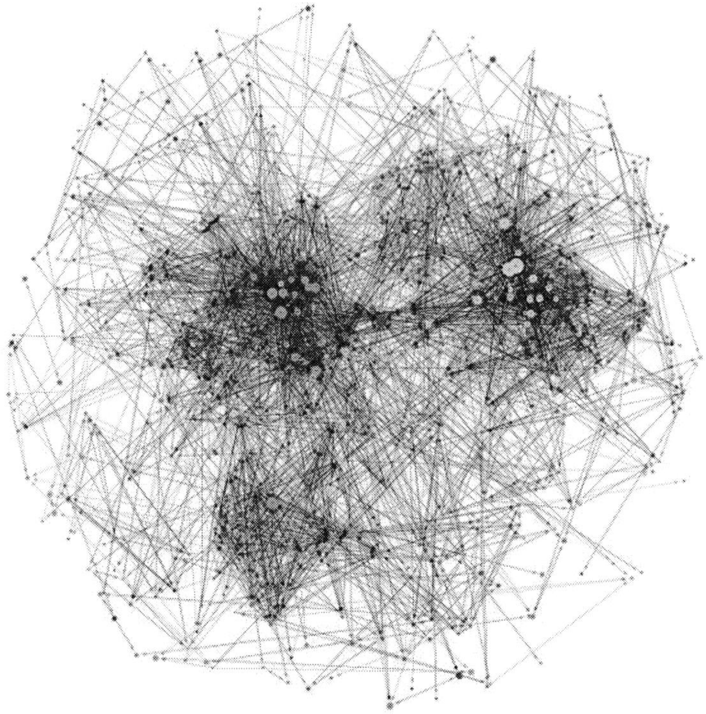

Figure 4. The whole integrated knowledge map

Table 1. Results of the questionnaire about the clustered integrated knowledge map

	Question	Evaluation				
		Strongly agree	Agree a little	Neither agree nor disagree	Disagree a little	Strongly disagree
1	From the sub-maps, it is possible to grasp which part of the lecture contents the learners understand.	0	4	0	0	0
2	It is easier to recognize the understanding of each learner than the whole knowledge map.	2	2	0	0	0
3	I can identify the relationships between the contents of each lecture.	0	2	1	1	0
4	It is supposed to be divided into the clusters.	0	0	3	1	0
5	The result of the sub-map matches the purpose of this class.	0	0	4	0	0
6	The nodes I consider to be important are larger than others.	0	0	1	3	0
7	I want to know the same part between sub-maps.	0	1	1	2	0
8	I want to know the different parts of sub-maps.	0	1	1	2	0
9	I want to know which part the sub-maps constitute in the whole knowledge map.	1	2	0	1	0
10	The sub-map can be used effectively for lecture improvement.	0	3	1	0	0
11	It is useful for grasping the students' understanding.	0	4	0	0	0
12	I want to use the sub-map.	0	3	1	0	0

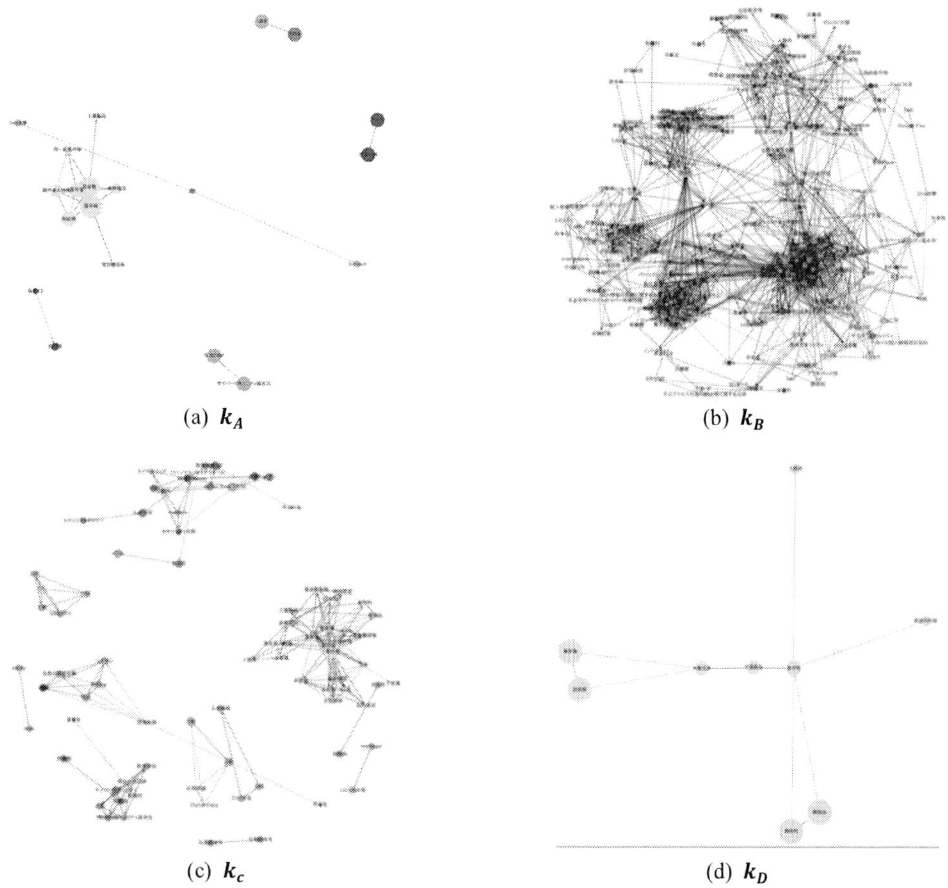

Figure 5. Sub-maps of clusters A, B, C, and D

We received both positive and negative responses. The question on the importance values of each node and the comparison between sub-maps mainly received negative responses. The answers to Q6 showed that the nodes with high importance were not considered as important by the course managers. We guess that the course managers had difficulty in comparing the importance of the sub-maps because the sizes of the nodes were not regulated among the sub-maps. Besides, the answers to Q7 and Q8 suggested that comparisons among the sub-maps are not necessary for the course managers. In our future work, based on the answers to Q6–Q9, we are going to improve the visualization strategy to emphasize the sub-maps on the whole knowledge map. We expect that this strategy will help course managers to grasp the relationships not only between the whole map and sub-maps, but also among the sub-maps.

On the other hand, the positive results were mainly about the readability of the sub-maps (k_A~k_D). The answers to Q1 and Q3 suggested that the course managers could grasp the students' situations, i.e., which contents the students had interest in from the lectures. Additionally, from the answers to Q2, we found that the sub-maps were more useful than the whole integrated knowledge map used on its own. It turned out that the course managers wanted a summary of the knowledge map rather than all of the information. Moreover, the answers to Q10–Q12 suggested that the course managers thought that utilizing the knowledge map would help to improve the lectures and grasp the learners' level of understanding. Furthermore, the course managers wanted to use sub-maps in their educational activities. We received the following comments regarding improving the sub-maps:

- Sharing the comments of the course managers reading the sub-maps.
- Annotations on the structural features of the sub-maps.

In comparison with the results of the questionnaire mentioned above, the answers to Q4 and Q5 were neither positive nor negative. We will continue with additional interviews to clarify how the course managers interpreted the knowledge maps and the purpose of reading the knowledge maps in our future work.

5. CONCLUSION

This study aimed to cluster learners based on knowledge maps and to develop a teaching support system using knowledge map clustering data. A knowledge map is a network showing how a learner organizes and understands what they have learned. We calculated the similarity between the individual knowledge maps based on NetSimile and classified learners based on their knowledge maps using the IRM. We administered a questionnaire to the course managers who designed the course and provided the lecture materials in order to evaluate the effectiveness of the sub-maps. We received both positive and negative responses. The importance values of each node and comparisons among the sub-maps received negative responses. In contrast, the positive responses were mainly related to the readability of the sub-maps and utilizing the knowledge map.

In future research, we intend to continue developing the analyzation method of the knowledge map. First, it was difficult for the course managers to compare the importance values among the sub-maps because the sizes of the nodes were not regulated among the sub-maps. In addition, the course managers wanted to compare the whole map and sub-maps. Therefore, we are going to improve the visualization system to emphasize the sub-maps on the whole knowledge map. Second, the course managers asked for an explanation of what the sub-maps represented. Therefore, we will consider adding functions such as the automatic generation of annotations to make it easier for users of knowledge maps to understand their structural features. In this study, we manually selected clusters to be visualized as sub-maps. However, when there is a lot of data to be analyzed, manual cluster selection is not desirable. In order to promote the use of knowledge maps for the improvement of teaching methods, we will develop an automatic selection method for the clusters to be visualized.

ACKNOWLEDGEMENT

This work was supported by JST AIP Grant Number JPMJCR19U1 and JSPS KAKENHI Grand Number JP18H04125, Japan.

REFERENCES

Balaid, A. et al., 2016. Knowledge maps: A systematic literature review and direction for future research, *International Journal of Information Management*, 36, pp.451-475

Berlingerio, M. et al., 2013. Network similarity via multiple social theories. *In Proceedings of the 2013 IEEE/ACM International Conference on Advances in Social Networks Analysis and Mining*, Niagara Falls, Ontario, Canada, pp. 1439-1440.

Crampes, M. et al., 2006. Concept Maps for Designing Adaptive Knowledge Maps, *Information Visualization*, 5(3), pp.211-224.

Fiorella, L., & Mayer, R.E. 2017. Spontaneous spatial strategy use in learning from scientific text, *Contemporary Educational Psychology*, 49, pp.66-79.

Hsiao, I. H., & Brusilovsky, P. 2012. Motivational social visualizations for personalized e-learning. *In European Conference on Technology Enhanced Learning*, Springer, Berlin, Heidelberg, pp. 153-165

Kemp, C. et al., 2006. Learning systems of concepts with an infinite relational model. *In AAAI*, Vol. 3, pp. 5

Kudo, T. 2006. *Mecab: Yet another part-of-speech and morphological analyzer.* [online] Available at: http://mecab. sourceforge.jp. [Accessed 17 Jul. 2019].

Onoue, A. et al., 2019. The Integrated Knowledge Map for Surveying Students' Learning. *In Society for Information Technology & Teacher Education International Conference*, Las Vegas, NV, United States, pp. 838-846.

Page, L., et al., 1999. *The PageRank citation ranking: Bringing order to the web*. Stanford InfoLab.

Sato, T. et al., 2017. Implementation of a word segmentation dictionary called mecab-ipadic-NEologd and study on how to use it effectively for information retrieval. *In Proceedings of the Twenty-three Annual Meeting of the Association for Natural Language Processing*. The Association for Natural Language Processing.

Yamada, M. et al., 2016. A computer-supported collaborative learning design for quality interaction. *IEEE Multimedia*, 23(1), pp.48-59.

Yamada, M. et al., 2018. BR-Map: Concept Map System Using E-Book Logs, *Proceedings of 15th International Conference of Cognition and Exploratory Learning in Digital Age*, Budapest, Hungary, pp. 248-254.

Yin, C. et al., 2019. Exploring the Relationships between Reading Behavior Patterns and Learning Outcomes based on Log Data from e-books: A Human Factor Approach, *International Journal of Human-Computer Interaction*, pp.313-322.

DO CHILDREN REPRESENT VIRTUAL SPATIAL-TEMPORAL QUALITIES DIFFERENT THAN ADULTS?

Selma Dündar-Coecke
Centre for Educational Neuroscience, Department of Psychology and Human Development, UCL Institute of Education, University College London, UK

ABSTRACT

Decades-old research has demonstrated the effects of virtual space on perception mostly with adult samples. Little is known about children's ability to utilize spatial-temporal qualities from computerized settings. Past research with primary school children suggested that the ability to utilize spatial-temporal information is crucial for inferring cause-effect relationships of natural phenomena. However, children's performance lagged behind when spatial-temporal qualities were presented on a computer screen. To investigate this matter further, 16 adults, 17 nursery, and 19 reception age children were tested individually (N=52) across three tasks –virtual, virtual with less intense, and actual spatial-temporal tasks-. The results showed that: (1) young children performed poorly on virtual tasks. (2) Children's ability to process spatial-temporal information varied largely depending on the characteristics of the task. (3) Spatial-temporal analysis in a virtual space required extra support from widely distributed domains operating attention and memory. (4) The intensity of the information presentation at virtual displays influenced young children's performances, but not adults'. The results may explain why some children cannot perform well / benefit from teaching/learning activities via 2/3-dimensional settings: the ability to utilize the amount of spatial-temporal information varies widely across development, in particular when children cannot manipulate the intensity of the information they are exposed to. Missing the third dimension (e.g. depth) in virtual tasks is challenging for both young and older children in which the majority of them seem to fail to compensate. Evolutionarily our coping systems seem to be more advanced for extracting spatial-temporal information from real environments as opposed to virtual. This may challenge in particular the research measuring young children's performances from computerized displays.

KEYWORDS

Space, Time, Spatial and Temporal Reasoning, Representation, Virtual, Development

1. INTRODUCTION

The terms *space* and *time* are quite ambiguous, as their qualities are susceptible to various interpretations. Neither time nor space has appearances. A mathematical space, for instance, qualifies us to represent a set of observations and quantitative measures (Gray, 1989); a topological space axiomatizes the shape of sets of points in terms of neighborhoods, enabling concepts such as wires, holes, convergence and continuity (Bourbaki, 1940). In Euclidian geometry, space is axiomatised in terms of rigid lines with fixed lengths, enabling concepts such as fixed trajectories in spacetime and geometric shapes like triangles and squares (see Euclid's elements). A virtual space is generated by machines, where spatial-temporal qualities are presented with the aid of a set of quantized cubic grid points to simulate a virtual form of reality (e.g. Hammoud, et al., 2011). A mental space corresponds to imagery (Kosslyn, 1980, 1995), operating with the aid of working memory, a crucial property of communication and mental representations (Faunconnier, 1994).

Any kind of experience, in real or virtual space, is constituted through cognitive operations in which observable properties are registered by senses. It is our exquisite visual sensitivity for instance that enables us to distinguish an apple from a pear in various environments. Besides, looking at a static picture of an apple requires different cognitive resources than watching an apple rolling/falling dynamically, or imagining it in a different context. The pictorial forms adopt spatial properties, which are also perceptual, but in a piecemeal and discrete protocol, namely e.g. the visual system is being kept by the stimuli of an apple as spatially constant. The dynamic form instead involves temporal dimension, providing feedback for the past, current, future situations, by enabling spatial-temporal representations to be encoded in an online fashion. In both cases (pictorial or online) what *makes up* an entity/event perceptual is that its (i) qualitative (e.g. color, texture, smell, topological shape), (ii) quantitative (e.g. length, width, depth, geometrical shape), and (iii) temporal properties (e.g. speed, succession, directionality), all are embedded in three/four dimensional spacetime. I call these three components *perceptual primitives*.

In the example of apple rolling/falling, in which the temporal onsets and offsets are observable, while motionless, the qualitative and quantitative features of the apple can be afforded. Once it starts rolling/falling, various features move together, requiring its perceptual *primitives* to be bound across space and time, enabling online registrations (see e.g. Robertson, 2003). Although how binding occurs at neural level is a mystery, its role for spatial-temporal qualities in structuring the external world is fundamental (see e.g. Trehub, 2007), as our sense of physical reality is largely dependent on internal resources, rather than being developed only from sensory information. At perceptual level, for instance, identification and updating time related changes of rapid successions in the visual system stands as the main activity (see also Raymond et al., 1992). Perception, however, is not informationally encapsulated from cognition as Fodor (1983) argued. There are no known barriers preventing us to move from perception to inference, or vice versa. Instead, perception is often described as having different stages, hierarchically organized (e.g. bottom-up processing requiring the capacity of top-down processing, such as attention) (Marr, 1982). At the analytical/cognitive level, *the primitives* are representational; these are mentally abstracted, integrated or interpreted by higher level intellectual faculties, such as conceptual or schematic reasoning, imagination, or planning
(see Fugelsang and Mareschal, 2013; Tolmie and Dündar-Coecke, in press, for the distinction between early perceptual and inferential processes). Evidently, spatial-temporal analysis has multiple forms, and employs various distinct cognitive resources utilized uniquely in perceptual and analytic processes (Dündar-Coecke et al., 2019b). This is probably why deep thinking is easier when we stop watching.

Apparently, required abilities for, in particular, perceptual processes emerge very early on. Based on infants' looking time at contiguous and noncontiguous events, Leslie and Keeble (1987) found that even six months old infants are susceptible to spatial-temporal characteristics of events and object interactions (se also Oakes & Cohen, 1990). These abilities become more recognizable during toddlerhood in the sense that preschoolers take into account spatial-temporal contiguity in their inference (see e.g. Schlottmann, 1999). Moreover, children and adults seem to use the same principles (e.g. priority, contiguity, succession) to infer cause-effect relations (see Bullock et al., 1982 for children, and Michotte, 1946/1963 for adults). Thus, we need to bear in mind that the majority of research investigating spatial-temporal analysis has been conducted in real world environments and employed actual materials (e.g. machines, toys, pictures, real objects). We know very little about whether perception of spatial-temporal qualities relies on the same principles in virtual and physical environments, or more specifically what happens when perceptual primitives are presented on a computer screen. Knowing how perceptual experiences are organized in the real world may not be sufficient to understand virtual reality and effects on perceptual/inferential experiences. If we could identify how perceptual primitives in these processes work and what the boundaries are, we could use this knowledge for teaching and learning practices, and we would even design a language that allows communicating with virtual perceptual experiences (see Carr & England's 1995 proposal of 'perceptual language').

According to Carr and England (1995) virtual space is the first level of virtualization, followed by the virtual image, and virtual environments. Regarding the first, the user perceives a three-dimensional, but flat layout of objects in space, which is akin to picture viewing. Virtual environment is the most inclusive and provides the largest variety of information sources to the senses. However, even in this inclusive setting, the sense of reality is constructed from the symbolic, geometric, and dynamic information presentations indirectly. In this environment, although many aspects of the actual forms can be imitated identically, a user actually interacts with the objects via an interface (Saha et al., 1994).

A few studies have attempted to compare human perception in the real versus virtual environments. Lampton et al. (1995), for instance, found that humans are less accurate in estimating distance in virtual environments than in the real world. Witmer and Kline (1998) investigated the factors influencing perceived distance estimates. They conducted two experiments to assess the contribution of various distance cues, including visual, cognitive, and proprioceptive cues. In the first experiment, participants were static and they needed to estimate the distance to a cylinder placed at various points. The effects of floor texture/patterns, and object size were also considered. In the second experiment, participants were asked to move and they needed to estimate the route segmented and total route distances. The effect of movement was considered. The authors found that traversing a distance improved distance estimate, and the errors were smaller in the physical world. In the virtual environment when the participants moved faster, their estimates were less accurate. Another study compared the fidelity of virtual versus real environment. Adult participants explored a virtual room by using a head mounted display. They were asked to estimate the dimensions of the room in meters, and afterwards they answered a questionnaire aiming to explore their perception of the physical properties of the room. The authors found that people perceived the virtual properties quite accurately compared to its actual size, except for the height dimension. However, in this study, participants' movement was restricted, as previously it was found to affect perception (e.g. walking speed, size of the environment). Cheng et al. (2014) also concluded that human performance in a virtual environment was less accurate with a greater error rate. Saleeb (2015) found that virtual dimensions are perceived as smaller than their physical counterparts, indicating discrepancies in human appreciation of metrics regarding the virtual and physical dimensions.

Virtual space obviously scales metrics differently, in which a user needs to integrate in perceptually different widths, depths, heights, and speeds. There is some evidence that extraction of spatial-temporal dimensions continuously is difficult even in actual environments. Testing 107 5-to-11-year-olds individually, the previous study showed that children did well when the tasks segmented object motion in the real environment. In this segmented version, changes in spatial-temporal information were presented proportionally following a logical consecutive order (e.g. liquid flowed from an upper flask to a lower flask in five consecutive stages, and the liquid level changed in both flasks as a function of liquid flow by time). In another task, spatial-temporal information was presented on a computer screen (children were asked to compare the speed of the three bunnies and judge the duration with the distance taken). The majority of children, in particular the young ones, failed to extrapolate spatial-temporal qualities from this computerized displays. Response profiles for each age group, and one-way ANOVAs showed age-related increases, but growth occurred later, with no difference between Year 1 and Year 3 children, though significantly differed from Year 5. Accurate responses in this task depended on processing the successive spatial states for each object, with perceptual resources needed to be attained for visually enriched loadings over time (Dündar-Coecke et al., 2019a). However, this study did not say anything about the environmental effect (virtual vs. actual) on spatial-temporal analysis.

It is common for even toddlers to start watching cartoons on televisions/tablets, dealing with the intense information presented. Furthermore, recent trend is for psychologists/educationalists to use computerized tasks to measure children's competences. Nevertheless, decades-old research has ignored the impact of virtual versus physical space on the ability to extract spatial-temporal information; in particular we know almost nothing about its development. The present study compared young children's response profiles with adults'. The aim was to understand whether children's failure was related to (a) differences in processing spatial-temporal characteristics in virtual and actual space, or (b) whether it is more to do with the fact that the intensity of the information load differed in virtual and actual spaces, or (c) whether extrapolating future states was simply difficult for children. If option 'a' is more likely, this will highlight the importance of the *primitives* and the characteristics of virtual and physical spaces in inducing perceptual processes. If 'b' and 'c' are more likely, this will call for a cognitive approach, suggesting that age related changes in spatial-temporal cognition are highly linked to changes in e.g. attentional processes, and therefore performance in the tasks are the consequences of individual's cognitive competences. If option 'c' is more likely, regarding the temporal horizon, children must have found it difficult to locate future relations, as assembled in memories. The past may be chronologically easier to comprehend -even in deterministic systems- because the future is less supported by past experience (see e.g. McCormack, 2015 for a review). The present study therefore aimed to provide further evidence on these by employing younger children's performance on the three tasks to obtain comparable results against previously investigated primary age trends. The sample also includes adults for the sake of extending the comparability and elaborating whether immature and mature forms of spatial-temporal analysis exist.

2. METHOD AND RESULTS

2.1 Method

The study utilized an experimental design employing three age groups, two spanning the English nursery and reception class age range (4 and 5-year-olds), and the third involving adults. Three tasks were given to all participants in random order within a single one-to-one session, followed by a short conversation aiming to obtain their further thoughts on the tasks.

2.1.1 Participants

Children were recruited from two schools, a nursery, and a primary, located in Oxford, UK. Adult participants who volunteered to take part were also recruited from the same city. Covering a range of socioeconomic background, the sample included 17 nursery children (N), mean age = 46.4; sd=3.04 months; 19 reception age children (R), mean age = 64.74, sd = 3.9 months; and 16 adults (A), mean age = 36.6, sd = 11.3 years. The sample consisted of typically developing children and adults with no known cognitive disability.

2.1.2 Materials and Procedure

Test sessions took place in a working room, or with some children out of class in a quiet area within their schools. Each participant took an average of approximately 8 minutes to test (min = 5, max = 13). All responses were recorded manually on score sheets at the time, and participants' explanations noted for later checking. For the experiments, the extraneous variables were kept constant so as not to influence participants' responses, such as the laptop, procedure, the researcher conducting the experiments, explanations of the tasks, materials, brightness of the screen, participants' distance from the computer etc. The clockwork toys generated a reasonable amount of mechanical noise, but participants were requested to ignore that detail and focus on their movement.

2.1.3 Measures

Virtual speed task 1 (VS1). The initial version of this task was developed and used in Dündar-Coecke, et al. (2019b) with 17 trials. On a Macintosh laptop (resolution 1440 x 900 pixels) participants saw computer animations of three bunnies (red, yellow, black) racing towards a carrot from different start positions at different speeds (Figure 1a), with the animation stopping before they reached it. Children judged which bunny would arrive at the carrot first. The task began with two practice items, followed by 13 trials gradually increasing in difficulty: the stop time reduced, from 4 to 2 seconds, as did the difference between the three bunnies in start point and relative speed, making differences in arrival time harder to distinguish, and the period available within which to track the differences shorter. Each time children were asked "Which bunny would be the winner?" The number of correct responses was recorded (0-13). At the end, participants were asked to judge the difficulty level of the task, and make comments if they had any.

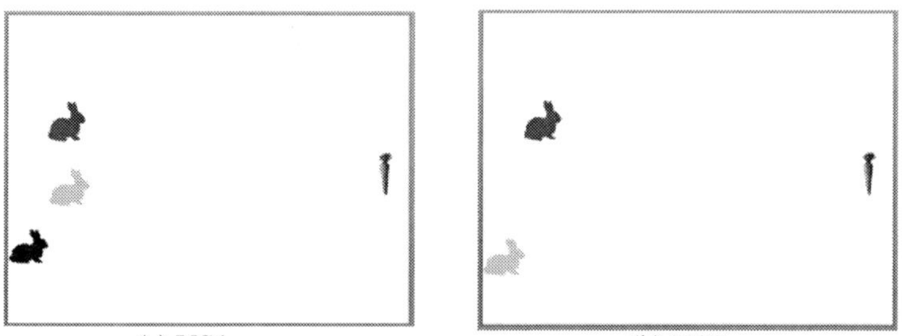

(a) VS1 (b) VS2

Figure 1. Example configurations of bunnies at the start of (a) VS1, (b) VS2 tasks

Virtual speed task 2 (VS2). This task was exactly the same as the previous speed task but with one difference: rather than three bunnies, participants saw computer animations of two bunnies (red and yellow to ensure the visual discernibility) racing toward the target item from different start positions at different speeds (Figure 1b). The original speed task used in Dündar-Coecke et al.'s (2019a) study ranged in difficulty, positively skewed with a long tail in young children's responses, indicating that for the majority of primary school children (5-to-11-year-olds) in particular for younger age groups, the task was difficult. Further analyses showed that the majority of children struggled with 8 trials consistently. These 8 trials were chosen to elaborate whether the intensity of the information load played role in this. These 8 trials were demonstrated with less intensity by cancelling one bunny located in the middle in all the trials to keep the distance as constant. Therefore the distance between the two bunnies widened. The number of correct responses was ranged between 0 and 8. Similarly, participants were asked to judge the difficulty level of the task, and make comments if they had any.

Actual speed task (AS). This task was adopted from Piaget (1969/2006) who demonstrated that primitive/early understanding of space and time was highly dependent on duration-distance judgments. Participants compared three clockwork toys in each trial (e.g. a snail, a ladybird, and a doggy, Figure 1c), differing on speed, duration and distance towards a tunnel. The participants were shown half of the run, and the other half was hidden under a cardboard tunnel so that participants did not see the entire run, nor the winner. Durations of travels varied between either 6 or 8 seconds, but the visible parts were ranged from 3 to 4 seconds with varying distances. The experimenter used a plastic ruler to make sure that participants observed a maximum of the first four seconds of the race. In total nine clockwork toys were used; two of them were replaced in each trial to avoid a conditioning effect. The task began with one practice item, in which a clockwork toy was introduced and an explanation was given as to how it moves toward the tunnel. The practice trial was followed by 5 trials gradually increasing in difficulty (e.g. the speed of the ladybird, crocodile, and the monkey were slightly different; the crocodile was the fastest, the ladybird in the middle, and the monkey slightly slower). These three toys were shown in single trials separately. The last two trials included two of them at the same time to increase the difficulty (e.g. ladybird, monkey, doggy). Once the winding keys were set up, the three objects were put behind the cardboard wall with varying distances/angles from the tunnel therefore the race was started for each object at the same time. Each time only one item travelled the longer distance with highest speed. This task aimed to replicate the results of the first virtual task. Participants needed to guess the winner from the distance to the end point and velocity of the object. The three objects traveled either (a) a different distance with the same time, or (c) the same distance with a different time. The number of correct responses was ranged between 0 and 5 over five trials.

2.2 Results

Analyses utilized data from all 52 participants who completed testing appropriately. The observed power for ANOVA was 0.90, for regression analyses it was 0.98.

The means for each age group (Table 1) illustrated that young children did not perform well (proportionate to the maximum) on VS1, but instead they relatively performed well on VS2, and well on AS tasks. A one-way ANOVA showed significant age-related progression on VS1 and VS2 performance, however, for the VS1 differences between the groups was highly significant $F(2,51)=35.525$, $p<.001$, partial eta squared=.418, Welch and Brown-Forsythe robust tests were also highly significant ($p<.001$), indicating later growth for responses in this task.

Table 1. Mean score (standard deviation) by age group on VS1 (max=13), VS2 (max=8), and AS (max=5)

Tasks	Nursery	Reception	Adults
VS1	5.3 (3.2)	8.7 (2.8)	12.9 (0.4)
VS2	6.3 (1.8)	7.4 (0.9)	8.0 (0.0)
AS	4.2 (1.4)	4.8 (0.9)	5.0 (0.0)

Zero-order correlations showed that there were no significant associations between the tasks and either gender or their socioeconomic status (SES). Only age highly correlated with VS1 (=r.767, $p<.001$) and VS2 ($r=.516$, $p<.001$) respectively, confirming the ANOVA results; VS1 highly correlated with VS2 ($r=.733$, $p<.001$) and moderately with AS (.364, $p<.05$). However, VS2 did not associate with AS ($r=.102$. $p>.05$).

When controlling for age, the patterns remained similar with a slight reduction in correlations r(partial)=.613, p<.001; and .214, p<.01, suggesting that age was not the only factor, but the characteristics of the tasks did also matter. Participants' feedback on this matter elicited the potential implications as discussed below.

Table 2. Zero-order and partial correlations

	VS1	VS2	AS
Age	.767***	.516***	.305***
VS1	1	.733***	.364**
VS2	.613***	1	.102
AS	.214	-.068	1

Zero-order correlations above diagonal, N=52; partial correlations below diagonal; *p<.05, **p<.01, ***p<.001

Further regression analyses showed that age explained the majority of variance (58.8%) in VS1 performance (β=.767, p<.001); 26.6% variance in VS2 (β=.516, p<.001), and nearly 9% in AS performance (β=.305, p<.05), neither SES or gender was significant, confirming the high correlations of age effect for VS1 and slightly less for VS2, but non significant for AS, suggesting that age effect disappeared in the actual speed task.

3. CONCLUSION

A series of spatial-temporal tasks were employed with virtual versus actual materials, with one computerized task that involved relatively intensive loading, another that involved less, to elaborate whether children's and adults' ability to extract spatial-temporal information differed in real versus virtual space. Both virtual tasks missed the third dimension (depth); other spatial-temporal qualities were manipulated in each trial to see whether depth was compensated with distance and duration. The results highlighted two factors playing a role in processing perceptual properties in virtual and physical space: (1) age effect, and (2) task characteristics.

Participants from all age groups did well (the youngest group relatively well) with the physical presentations, but responses on the virtual tasks did highly vary across development. In particular young children found comparing the speed of the three objects on a computerized display most difficult. Thirteen out of seventeen nursery children declared that when the objects were fast, the three-bunny version was harder to follow. Four reception children expressed similar feelings, and some of them talked about an interaction factor between distance and speed, making some trials in the second version of the virtual task harder to judge: perceived duration was distorted when the distance between the two fast objects widened then.

The actual space task results indicated that some reception children were capable of distinguishing between distance and duration. This finding contradicts with Piaget's (1969/2006; see also Piaget & Inhelder, 1971) view who found that young children judged the duration with the distance taken, and argued that this was the result of their confusion between spatial and temporal dimensions, as they assumed longer distance would be equal to longer duration. His view was that young children do not reliably distinguish between more complex spatial-temporal characteristics such as velocity until about age nine. Contrary, other studies found that young children demonstrate early implicit knowledge of time, speed, and duration when the tasks involved more practical elements with which children have direct contact in their life (see e.g. Bullock et al., 1982; Dündar-Coecke et al., 2019; Wilkening, 1981). According to Siegler and Richards (1979), distance-travelled cue in young children's judgment is affected by spatial characteristics, what develops by age is that once children get older they rely less on spatial elements in their temporal judgments. Later Arlin (1989) isolated the spatial cue by lifting objects of different weights for fixed durations. He found that spatial cues did not affect duration judgments alone, unlike older ones young children's judgments were affected by other types of manipulations.

In particular, the virtual speed tasks required the ability to deal with the type of spatial-temporal manipulations, indeed highly relying on cognitive resources such as attention, memory consistent with Arlin's finding. This also resonates with the cognitive account, namely age related changes in spatial-temporal cognition linked to changes in memory and attentional processes (see also Driot-Volet, 2011), supporting the argument that children's perceptions were not rigidly encapsulated from higher-level inference. This was the case in particular for the virtual tasks.

Comparing children's and adults' response profiles of the actual versus computerized speed, young children did not seem capable of dealing with asymmetrical manipulations of virtual space, and they seem to be weak in their approximations. Probably for that reason, most young children requested to repeat some of the trials. Note that the trials were not repeated. This finding can justify the option 'a' highlighting the importance of the characteristics of virtual and physical space affecting perceptual processes.

Children's struggle with the virtual tasks may be relevant to their inability to predict future positions of the objects (cf. Burns et al., 2018; Friedman, 2003; McCormack & Hanley, 2011). Though, children did not find it difficult to predict future relations with the actual materials. One can ask whether sequencing the past is inherently easier than predicting the future in virtual space. The present study cannot provide an answer for this question, but children's performances on the virtual tasks can be analyzed as follows: virtual tasks required children to calibrate the horizontal distance and speed. In these tasks the perceptual cues were limited; in particular, the third dimension (depth) was not available. It is unknown whether the third dimension would support children's estimations of the future positions, but given that the missing dimension is one of the quantitative aspects of the perceptual primitives, this highlights the importance of completeness of spatial-temporal information in fostering distinct cognitive capacities.

Evidently, the characteristics of the spaces did matter in predicting future outcomes, and extracting spatial-temporal information from virtual setting seems to be much harder for children. It is probable that various reasons play a role in this: (1) processing virtual spatial-temporal qualities may computationally be intensive, (2) perceptual primitives seem to be considered as immaterial, fast, and hypothetical, (3) calibrating these seem to be more effortful than their real-world counterparts. The results resonate with Reiner's (2018) findings underlying the involvement of other higher mental domains to support performance in virtual environments. Now we have a slight idea about why this occurs: in line with the literature showing differences in perception of virtual versus actual properties, and the results here showing that young children are more likely to struggle with extracting spatial-temporal information from virtual space, I argue that *evolutionary our ability to extract spatial-temporal information from real environment may be more advanced.* This has clear implications for educational implementations for the reason that children's problem solving abilities can vary due to individual differences. This variance may increase in an unfavorable way when the role of the intensity of information presentation in virtual versus actual environments is ignored.

ACKNOWLEDGEMENT

This research was funded by an award from UK Economic and Social Research Council.

REFERENCES

Arlin, M., 1989. The effects of physical work, mental work, and quantity on children's time perception. *Perception & Psychophysics*, 45, 209–214.

Bourbaki, N., 1940. Topologie générale (general topology). Paris, Hermann.

Buchsbaum, D. et al., 2015. Inferring action structure and causal relationships in continuous sequences of human action. *Cognitive Psychology*, 76, 30-77.

Bullock, M. et al., 1982. The development of causal reasoning. In W.J. Friedman (Ed.), *The developmental psychology of time*. Academic Press, New York. pp. 209-254.

Burns, P. et al., 2018. The development of asymmetries in past and future thinking. *Journal of Experimental Psychology: General*, 148(2), 272-288.

Carr, K.T., & England, R. 1995. *Simulated and virtual realities: elements of perception.* UK: Taylor and Francis.

Cheng, K.B. et al., 2014. Manually locating physical and virtual reality objects. *Human Factors: The Journal of the Human Factors and Ergonomics Society*, DOI:0018720814523067.

Droit-Volet, S. 2011. Child and time. In A. Vatakis, A. Esposito, M. Giagkou, & F. Cummins (Eds.), *Multidisciplinary aspects of time and time perception*. Springer-Verlag, Germany. pp. 151–173.

Dündar-Coecke, S., et al. 2019. Children's reasoning about causal processes: the role of verbal and nonverbal ability. British Journal of Educational Psychology. DOI: 10.1111/bjep.12287

Dündar-Coecke, S., et al. 2019. The role of spatial and spatial temporal analysis in children's causal cognition of continuous processes. Manuscript to appear.

Faunconnier, G. 1994. *Mental spaces: aspects of meaning construction in natural language*. Cambridge University Press, New York.

Friedman, W. J. 2003. The development of a differentiated sense of the past and future. In: R. V. Kail (Ed.), *Advances in child development and behaviour, Volume 31*. Academic Press, San Diego. pp. 232-272.

Fodor, J. A., 1983. *The Modularity of Mind*. Cambridge, MA: MIT Press.

Fugelsang, J., & Mareschal, D., 2013. The development and application of scientific reasoning. In D. Mareschal, B. Butterworth, & A. Tolmie (Eds.), Educational neuroscience. Wiley-Blackwell. pp. 237-267.

Gray, J. 1989. *Ideas of space - Euclidean, non-Euclidean, and relativistic.* (2nd edition). Clarendon Press, Oxford.

Hammoud, R. et al. 2011. *Machine vision beyond visible spectrum*. Springer-Verlag, New York.

Kosslyn, S.M. 1980. *Image and mind*. Harvard University Press, Cambridge MA.

Kosslyn, S.M. 1995. Mental imagery. In S.M. Kosslyn & D. Osherson (Eds.), *Visual cognition*. MIT Press, Cambridge MA. pp. 267-296.

Lampton, D.R., et al., 1995. Distance estimation in virtual environments. Proceeding of the Human Factors and Ergonomics Society 39th Annual Meeting, 39, 1268-1272.

Leslie, A., & Keeble, S. 1987. Do six-month-old infants perceive causality? *Cognition*, 25, 265–288.

Marr, D., 1982, *Vision*. San Francisco: W.H. Freeman.

McCormack, T. 2015. The development of temporal cognition. In R. M. Lerner, L. S. Liben, & U. Mueller (Eds.), *Handbook of Child Psychology and Developmental Science, Volume 2: Cognitive Processes* (7th ed., Vol. 2). Wiley-Blackwell. UK. pp. 624-670.

McCormack, T., & Hanley, M. 2011. Children's Reasoning About the Temporal Order of Past and Future Events. *Cognitive Development*, 26(4), 299-314.

Michotte, A.E. 1946/1963. *The perception of causality*. New York: Basic Books.

Piaget, J. 1969/2006. *The child's conception of time*. Routledge, UK.

Piaget, J., & Inhelder, B. 1971. *The child's conception of space*. Routledge & Kegan Paul, London.

Raymond, J. E., Shapiro, K. L., & Arnell, K. M. (1992). Temporary suppression of visual processing in an RSVP task: an attentional blink? *Journal of Experimental Psychology: Human Perception and Performance*, 18, 849-860.

Reiner, M. 2018. Is virtual/augmented reality beneficial for learning? EEG mental load indices associated with learning in 2D compared to 3D displays. European Association for Research in Learning and Instruction SIG 22: Neuroscience & Education, London, UK.

Robertson, L. C. 2003. Binding, spatial attention and perceptual awareness. *Nature Reviews Neuroscience*, 4, 93-102.

Saha, P.K. et al. 1994. Topology preservation in 3D digital space. *Pattern Recognition*, 27(2), 295–300.

Saleeb, N. 2015. Effects of the differences between virtual and physical perception of space on building information modelling. In WIT Transactions on The Built Environment, Vol. 149. UK: WIT Press.

Schlottmann, A. 1999. Seeing it happen and knowing how it works: how children understand the relation between perceptual causality and underlying mechanism. *Developmental Psychology*, 35, 303–317.

Siegler, R. S., & Richards, D. D. 1979. Development of time, speed, and distance concepts. *Developmental Psychology*, 15, 288–298.

Tolmie, A., & Dündar-Coecke, S., in press. Conceptual development in science. In: Thomas M, Mareschal D, Dumontheil I, editors. *Educational neuroscience: A lifespan approach*. Oxford: Wiley.

Trehub, A. 2007. Space, self and the theater of consciousness. *Consciousness and Cognition*. 16, 310–330.

Wilkening, F. 1981. Integrating velocity, time and distance information: A developmental study. *Cognitive Psychology*, 13, 231-247.

Witmer, B., & Kline, P. 1998. Judging perceived and traversed distance in virtual environments. Presence, 7(2), pp. 144-167.

A UNIPOLAR CONCENTRATION OF ENGLISH AND THE MULTILINGUAL-SEMILINGUAL PARADOX

Fusa Katada
Waseda University, Faculty of Science and Engineering
3-4-1 Okubo, Shinjuku-ku, Tokyo 169-8555 Japan

ABSTRACT

'We have the right to talk and think in our own language.' This self-evident slogan is ever challenged in the digital age of the 21st century. 'Talking and thinking' is most effectively trained and achieved by formal education carried out in one's own language. However, multilingual children growing up in multilingual societies would have to adjust their own language to a language of education in schooling. This paper clarifies scientific grounds that in such situations the main root of learning and thinking through language is discontinuous. It is claimed that the students may face semilingualism, defined as 'linguistic competence insufficiently developed for complex conceptual thinking'. Multilingualism and semilingualism are two sides of one coin, and semilingualism is affecting many parts of the world. This is due to the established eminence of English as a global lingua franca (ELF), which serves as their language of education. This paper is qualitative in nature, pointing out discrepancies between the politically empowered unipolar concentration of English and cognitively suited languages for sustainable development of conceptual thinking. It is intended to serve as a reference point for educators and professionals who are responsible for raising human resources in the digitalized global age.

KEYWORDS

Multilingualism, Semilingualism, Language for Conceptual Thinking, Mother-tongue-based Education

1. INTRODUCTION

Believing in the importance of cultural and linguistic diversity for sustainable societies, the General Conference of UNESCO approved February 21 as International Mother Language Day, a day to celebrate all mother languages spoken in the world (UNESCO Paris, 1999). The idea is to promote linguistic and cultural diversity and multilingualism in all aspects of public life, and particularly in education (UNESCO Bangkok, 2005). This conforms to the growing awareness of the importance of promoting primary education in children's mother language (UNESCO, 2010). However, there are nearly 7,000 languages currently spoken in the world (Gordon, Jr., 2005), so it is unrealistic to expect that every child can be educated in his/her mother language. Given the established eminence of English as a global lingua franca (ELF), it seems inevitable that multilingual communities choose English as their language of education. What problems then do children encounter when the school language is not the same as their mother language?

This paper clarifies scientific grounds for why mother-tongue-based education is important for sustainable development of conceptually complex thinking and that when children face schooling in a language other than their own, the main root of learning and thinking is discontinuous. It is claimed that the students may face the semilingual state of mind, defined as 'linguistic competence insufficiently developed for conceptual thinking'. *Multilingualism* and *semilingualism* are two sides of one coin. Due to the politically empowered unipolar concentration of English, English has come to be the world second language that serves as the language of education in many multilingual communities. Semilingualism is thus a global issue now.

This paper is qualitative in nature. It is expected to serve as a conceptual reference point for educators and professionals who are responsible for raising human resources in the digitalized global age. It also intends to raise the term 'semilingualism' to the level of academic terminology, so that research on this serious state of mind may advance further.

2. THE MULTILINGUAL-SEMILINGUAL PARADOX

2.1 IMLD (UNESCO 1999) and the Gravity of Mother-tongue-based Education

Shaheed Minar is a martyr monument at the University of Dhaka, which commemorates people who demonstrated for the recognition of Bengali as one of the two national languages of East Pakistan (the other was Urdu) and were shot dead by police in the capital of present-day Bangladesh. This disaster happened on 21 February, 1952. Nearly a half century after this incident, on 17 November, 1999, the General Conference of UNESCO proclaimed 21 February as International Mother Language Day (IMLD), a symbolic day to celebrate language diversity, to promote the preservation and protection of all languages used by people of the world.

The UNESCO office in Bangkok (2005) uttered a message that stresses the role of language in education for sustainable development of societies; there is a growing awareness that languages play a vital role in process of integration into all aspects of public life but particularly in education; the awareness strengthens co-operation and contributes to attaining quality education for all, building inclusive knowledge of societies and preserving cultural heritage, and mobilizing political will to apply the benefits of science and technology to sustainable development; supporting language diversity is also about supporting inclusion and acknowledging that language diversity helps to enrich us all, that this diversity of language is a treasure, not a barrier.

Language in 'language diversity' virtually means 'mother-tongue' (that is, the child's first language, L1) spoken in the world. Below are teachers' voices for mother-tongue based education that have been publicized by the UNESCO office.

> "Mother tongue education is not translation-teaching. It is a teaching method that uses children's mother tongue language for the medium of education to stimulate their cognitive skills, creative skills, and confidence." (Suraida A-wae, a Patani-Malay speaker in Thailand)

> "Mother tongue education is like the lower rungs of the ladder. Without it, children are trying to jump up onto the higher rungs and often fall in the attempt." (Gohar Rahman, a Gawri speaker in Pakistan)

The UNESCO office continued that in the context of education it is impossible to teach the majority of people to read and write in a language they don't understand, and that it is easier for you to learn *a second language* if you have learnt your first language well.

This message recognizes the difficulty of promoting education in all mother languages spoken in the world. Multilingual communities would have to go through contraction of the multiple local languages (mother-tongues) to just a few languages to carry out education, and these languages are learnt as their *second language* (L2).

2.2 A Unipolar Concentration of English as a Second Language of the World

Given the established eminence of English as a global lingua franca (EFL) especially in academic discourse in the 21st century, it seems inevitable that English is chosen as their language of instruction, which is equivalent to a *second language* in the above UNESCO's suggestion. Evidently this appears in another teacher's voice:

> "Learning English is important to be globally competitive, but we have to consider that the main root of learning is through our first language." (Rasmila M. Cosain, a Maranao speaker in the Philippines)

In these UNESCO's messages and teachers' voices, it is given as self-evident that mother-tongue based education (MTBE) is important and with no specific evidence. To see related issues and problems, the importance of MTBE should be grounded scientifically. The next section clarifies why MTBE is so important when everyone seems to agree that English is important as a global language of the world.

2.3 Scientific Bases for Mother-tongue-based Formal Education

2.3.1 Verbal Thought: L.S. Vygotsky Revisited

In his most influential theory of child development, Vygotsky (1934) claims that *thought* and *speech* have different genetic roots. At around 2 years from the child's birth, *thought* and *speech* begin to join to initiate a new form that is distinct from either *thought* or *speech*. According to him, a prelinguistic phase in the development of *thought* and a preintellectual phase in the development of *speech* are externally observable. This is because younger children are only really able to "think out loud." At around 3 to 4 years of age, *ego-centric speech* appears, which is an observable sign for *thought* and *speech* coming together to join. It lasts for a few years and then disappears at around 6 to 7 years of age. The disappearance of ego-centric speech is a sign that the merger of the linguistic phase and the intellectual phase is completed. When the two phases are merged, *thought* becomes *verbal* in a form known as *thought in language*, and *speech* is *rational*. Afterwards, due to its ability to bear *concepts*, *language* organizes *thinking*.

Note that, in most of the world school systems, 6 to 7 years old accords with the age when primary schooling begins. It is inevitable that a sprouting *oral ability* for thought in language is a presupposition to formal education.

2.3.2 Written Language in School for Cognitive Development: J.S. Bruner Revisited

Based on the study on schooled vs. unschooled children among the Wolof in Senegal, Bruner (1966; 1971) stresses the importance of *written language* in school. He claims that schooling and exposure have a significant effect on the development of the ability to perform more sophisticated cognitive operations: categorization and preservation problems. The hypothesis here is that school is operating on grouping operations through the training embodied in *written language*. This hypothesis has a theoretical base; that is, the *written language* provides an occasion in which one must deploy language out of the immediate context of reference. Writing virtually forces a remoteness of reference on the language user. In other words, *writing* is training in the use of linguistic contexts that are independent of immediate context, and moreover, understanding and expressing in *written language* is training for the development of *thought*. Note that *literacy*, as opposed to *orality*, is a key to formal education.

2.3.3 The Rationale for Mother-Tongue-Based Formal Education

The fusion of a prelinguistic phase and a preintellectual phase is an age appropriate cognitive developmental phenomenon that takes place at around 2 to 3 years old; the fusion comes to its completion at around 6 to 7 years old; and primary schooling begins. For sustainable development of the child's learning, it would be ideal if the language acquired early enough be used continuously in school as a medium of instruction. This is because such a language has most likely been gone through the ego-centric speech; it can be assumed to be tightly fused with thought; and thus it functions best as a tool for thinking. As Figure 1 illustrates, such a language is the child's mother-tongue (i.e. his/her L1) acquired and used before 6-7 years old.

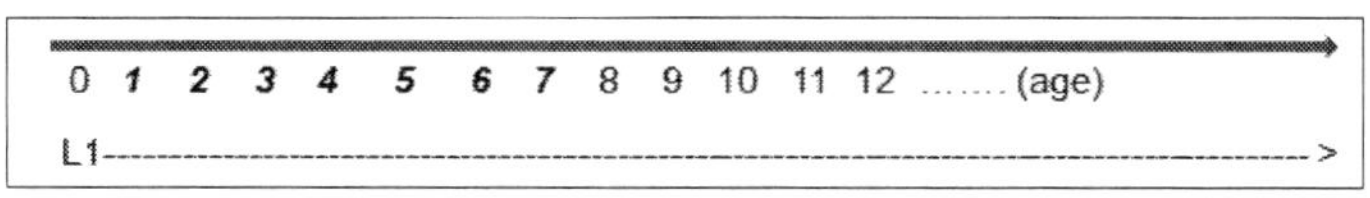

Figure 1. Age line and L1 as a language of education

For the child to be trained in written language in school, his/her L1 must be a written language having its own script. It is thus apparent that an ideal situation is created when two conditions (1) and (2) are met:

(1) the mother-tongue (L1) serves as a language of education, and

(2) the mother-tongue (L1) is a written language, having its own script.

By (1) *verbal though* in the mother-tongue is ensured. By (2) textbooks can be developed in the mother-tongue, and training for the development of thought in written language is ensured. We may then expect that the main root of learning, shaped up by literacy-based formal education, grow continuously throughout life.

Simplest cases that meet the two conditions may be found in monolingual communities with literacy traditions. For example, the Japanese culture has been considered near monolingual and meets the two conditions: (1) the child's mother-tongue, which is Japanese, is continuously used as a language of education in all levels of education, from elementary to higher education, and (2) Japanese is a written language, having its own scripts (Kanji and Kana) used for centuries. It is anticipated that on the basis of Japanese as the language of education, the main root of learning in Japanese, shaped up by literacy based formal education, can continuously grow. However note that due to the globalized movements of people, it is no longer true that Japan is a monolingual society. The country embodies multilingual populations and it is subjected to all issues raised in this paper.

2.3.4 Confirmation from School Sites

In her summary of mother-tongue based bilingual/multilingual education, Ball (2010) refers to the studies by Thomas & Collier (2002), which show that six to eight years of education in a language are necessary to develop the level of literacy and verbal proficiency required for academic achievement in secondary school. Research shows that children's ability to learn a second or additional languages (e.g., a lingua franca and an international language) does not suffer when their mother tongue is the primary language of instruction throughout primary school. Fluency and literacy in the mother tongue lay a cognitive and linguistic foundation for learning additional languages. When children receive formal instruction in their first language throughout primary school and then gradually transit to academic learning in the second language, they learn the second language quickly. If they continue to have opportunities to develop their first language skills in secondary school, they emerge as fully bilingual (or multilingual) learners.

Key to the successful bilingualism (or multilingualism) in learning seems to be the mother-tongue based (MTB) instruction throughout primary schooling. Reality, however, is that many parts of the world are not ensured the MTB instruction, especially due to the linguistic complexity.

2.4 Multilingualism and Semilingualism as Two Sides of One Coin

2.4.1 Extraordinary Multilingual Communities: One Representative Case from the Philippines

The Philippines is an archipelago nation consisting of over 7,000 islands, positioned off the southeastern coast of Asia, directly east of Vietnam and northeast of Malaysia. The nation covers 298,170 km^2 and has a population counting nearly 105 million. 182 living languages are identified, 175 among which are indigenous languages, abbreviated here as IP-language. Official languages are Filipino (the standardized version of Tagalog) and English. About 19 IP-languages are designated as auxiliary official languages and used as a language of education for the first 3 years of primary education before English comes into play. For the majority of children in the nation, IP-languages (their mother-tongues) are not used in school.

The area on which this study reports is Davao del Sur in Mindanao, the southern island of the Philippines. The area has a population of 633,000 and at least 40 indigenous languages are spoken. The language environment surrounding children in the school district is summarized in Table 1.

Table 1. Language environment surrounding children in Davao del Sur

	Language used	*Nature of language*
L1	IP-language	Mother-tongue spoken at home
L2	Bisaya	Neighborhood language
L3	Cebuano	Language of education from Grade 1 to 3
L4	Filipino	National language, taught from Grade 1
L5	English	Language of education from Grade 4, onward

First, children are born and raised in diverse mother-tongue (L1) environments. They are then exposed to Bisaya (L2), a neighborhood language, when they are grown big enough to be around outside, at about 2 years old. Elementary school education is carried out in Cebuano from Grade 1 to Grade 3. Thus, children, unless their mother-tongue is Cebuano, must switch from their mother-tongue (L1) to Cebuano (L3) for the first three years of elementary schooling. The teachers are not always the speakers of the children's mother tongues; thus, the teacher-student communication is usually difficult. In addition, Filipino (the standardized version of Tagalog) is designated as the national language; it is one of the subjects taught to children from Grade 1 and onward; Filipino is their fourth language (L4). Finally, in Grade 4, the language of education is switched from Cebuano to English; English is their fifth language (L5). For the rest of the education system throughout the nation, English serves as a ‘medium of instruction’.

2.4.2 Problems Anticipated in Multilingual Communities

Linguistic complexities in the area described in the previous section is schematically shown in Figure 2.

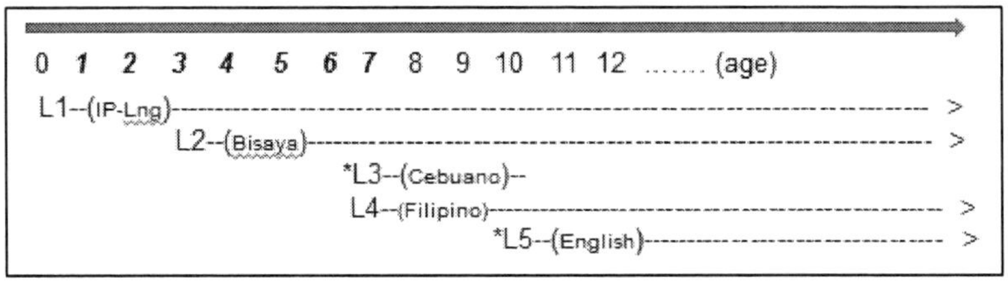

Figure 2. Linguistic complexities: an example from Davao del Sur

What would happen then to the main root of learning in children living with such complexities?

The apparent anticipation is the following. First, the fusion of a prelinguistic phase and preintellectual phase proceeds through the children’s IP-language spoken at home (that is their L1) or Bisaya (their L2) to which children are exposed early enough in the neighborhood. In other words, a language that is ready to organize thinking in them would be their IP-language or Bisaya. Either of them, however, is used as a language of education; the first three years of primary schooling (Grade 1 – 3) is carried out in Cebuano, which is switched to English in the fourth year (Grade 4). It can be anticipated that the main root of learning, to be shaped up by formal education, is discontinuous twice in the early schoolhood: once, upon the entrance to of the elementary school when children encounter Cebuano, and twice, in the beginning of the 4th year when Cebuano is taken over by English for the rest of their schooling. It is obvious that English is not an ideal, most natural language for the children to develop verbal thought (or conceptual thinking) in. Although language is not the only factor affecting learning abilities, a linguistic factor remains most influential in the children’s sustainable cognitive development.

2.4.3 Defining *Semilingualism*

Children living in multilingual communities may be multilingual performers but only at the conversational level. Their verbal thought is not necessarily ensured to fully develop in all languages they have learnt to speak. Here, two levels of language faculty are proposed: the language of thought and the language of communication. The term *semilingualism* is suggested here to refer to the cognitive linguistic state of the child’s learning foundation. *Semilingual* is defined as ‘*linguistic competence insufficiently developed for complex conceptual thinking*’. In short, people may be multilingual at the level of conversation but semilingual at the level of verbal thought. In other words, semilingualism may be hidden in multilingualism; they are two sides of one coin.

In educational settings, language diversity (i.e. mother-tongue diversity) must be reduced to just a few languages of instruction, which may be referred to as *language contraction*. The children whose mother-tongue is not the same as the language of education may fall in the above defined semilingualism. This pitfall is a challenge to the principle of International Mother Language Day, which stresses the importance of language in education. Given English as the virtual second language of the world which plays a role of language of education, *semilingualism* must be a universal concern in the digitalized age.

3. MATHEMATICAL REPRESENTATIONS

An apparent shortcoming of the study presented so far is that there is no scientific evidence we may provide for the *semilingual* state of mind. Children’s achievement in school in comparison among relevant groups of children such as in Bruner (1971) may constitute for one type of evidence. However, possible factors affecting the ability to learn is not only language. Strictly speaking then, it is difficult to narrow down possible parameters to just language and standardize levels of *semilingualness*. The purpose of this chapter is then to express the linguistic state of the child's mind in a mathematical format, taking up English representing a second language (L2) of the world, which functions as the language of education, as well as a global lingua franca (ELF) for communication purpose.

3.1 Direct Communication in L1 vs. Indirect Communication in L2 (ELF)

It is self-evident that it is the native speakers of a given language (L1) who enjoy their extraordinary linguistic competence in their language and all the benefits in social competition. In this sense, L1 belongs to the native speakers of this L1. English as a global lingua franca (ELF), on the other hand, is a product of the globalized discourse that can be characterized as a disembedded 'neutral' language of a communication means with no identification potential. There are no native speakers of ELF itself. In this sense ELF does not belong to anyone. This is another way of saying that ELF belongs to anyone who uses it. Languages other than the speakers' L1 and the speakers (or language users) can be expressed in functional forms. (The earliest formulation is presented in Katada (2019).)

In Figure 3, ELF is expressed as a function of L1, as in (a). A user of ELF (a non-native speaker of English) is in turn expressed as a function of ELF, as in (b), which is a function of L1. A native speaker of L1 is a function of this L1, as in (c).

(a) $ELF(L1_i)$
(b) $Speaker\{ELF(L1_i)\}$
(c) $Speaker(L1_i)$

where *i* ranges over diverse natural languages (mother-tongues)

Figure 3. Speaker as a Function of Language

Representation (a) yields varieties of ELF according to diverse natural languages spoken in the world ($L1_i$). In a conventional term this is what we call 'world Englishes'. In (b) a native language $L1_i$ is embedded in ELF, which shows remoteness of $L1_i$ to the speaker of $L1_i$-based ELF. This is in contrast with directness of $L1_i$ to its native speaker represented in (c). A source of frustration when the nonnative English speaker had to speak English can be read off in terms of this remoteness in (b).

Communication between two speakers of different native languages is illustrated in Figure 4. They communicate using ELF, which is a common linguistic means but with different L1-based. After all, ELF is a means to allow only indirect communication among people.

$$Speaker1\{ELF(L1_i)\} — Speaker2\{ELF(L1_j)\}$$

where i and j range over diverse natural languages, and $i \neq j$

Figure 4. Indirect Communication via ELF (English as a Lingua Franca)

Indirect communication is in contrast with direct communication illustrated in Figure 5. Strictly speaking, direct communication is possible only between the speakers of the same native language (L1).

$$Speaker1(L1_i) — Speaker2(L1_j)$$

where i and j range over diverse natural languages, and $i = j$

Figure 5. Direct Communication via the Same L1 (Mother-tongue)

3.2 Direct vs. Indirect Access to Verbal Thought (Conceptual Thinking)

Likewise for the educational settings, the child can be represented as a function of the language he/she uses. In Figure 6, (a) represents children who have direct access to the verbal thought in their L1 (mother-tongue), and (b) represents children who had to use a second language (L2), which is a function of their L1.

(a) Child(L1): direct (strong) access to verbal thought via L1.
(b) Child{L2(L1)}: indirect (weak) access to verbal thought via L2

Figure 6. Access to Verbal Thought (Conceptual Thinking)

In other words, the access to verbal thought (conceptual thinking) through L2 (English) is indirect and thus weaker than it is through L1.

4. CONCLUSION

The current linguistic situation of the world may be expressed in terms of *three Ds of a linguistic chain*—linguistic diversity, linguistic disparity, and linguistic divide, which is developed from the earliest thought presented in Katada (2002). *Linguistic diversity* refers to the fact that nearly 7,000 languages are spoken on the globe (Gordon, Jr., 2005). Among them, only a few languages are chosen to function as languages of formal education. Due to its established eminence, English is a typical medium of instruction in the globalized age. English is not only a global lingua franca in higher academic discourse but also a language of education chosen for primary education in many multilingual communities. This triggers *linguistic disparity* against the nonnative English world where English is not an ideal language to develop verbal thought (conceptual thinking); the problem of *semilingualism* may arise, which is defined as 'linguistic competence insufficiently developed for complex conceptual thinking'. This is compared to the native English world where English is the mother-tongue (L1) that is naturally tied to verbal thought. In general, it is not easy to expect that the nonnative English world achieves the same level of English used for complex thinking. Education delivered in the form of English thus institutionalizes the disparity in thought development. The result is *linguistic divide*, a social outlook, which would affect people throughout life, from their student's life to their long coming professional life.

This paper is qualitative in nature. Scientific evidence for the *semilingual state of mind* is not easy to come by, and thus mathematical representations are provided. Research on the topic should advance further seeking relevant evidence. The students' performance records before and after the time when the mother-tongue-based education policy was adopted and its practice had begun in 2008 in the aforementioned area might constitute for one type of evidence. The language awareness questionnaire survey followed by Focus Group Discussion might contribute to constituting for another type of evidence for the linguistic state of mind. All possible research methodologies on semilingualism are completely open. The present paper is intended to serve as a conceptual reference point for concerned people including educators who are responsible for sustainable development of their students, professionals who face global competitions in the 21st century, and language researchers and computer specialists who would try to elucidate the semilingual state of mind and seek for possible solutions with not excluding the possible use of advanced information technologies (cf. Katada, 2019).

ACKNOWLEDGEMENT

This study is supported by Japan Society for Promotion of Science (JSPS), Grant-in-Aid for Challenging Research (Exploratory) No. 19K21790 (Principal Investigator: Fusa Katada). My appreciation goes to Siverlyn Camposano at SPAMAST in Davao del Sur for her interest and collaboration for the planned advancement of research on the multilingual issues addressed in this paper. I would also like to thank two anonymous CELDA reviewers who furnished helpful referential comments. All shortcomings are mine.

REFERENCES

Ball, J., 2010. Educational equity for children from diverse language backgrounds: mother tongue-based bilingual or multilingual education in the early years: summary. Presentation to UNESCO International Symposium: Translation and Cultural Mediation, Paris: UNESCO, 22/23 February 2010, on the occasion of the 11th International Mother Language Day in collaboration with the International Association for Translation and Intercultural Studies, 2010 International Year for the Rapprochement of Cultures. Retrieved 25 April 2019 from: http://dspace.library.uvic.ca/handle/1828/2457.

Bruner, J.S., 1966. *Toward a Theory of Instruction*. Harvard University Press, Cambridge, Massachusetts, USA.

Bruner, J.S., 1971. *The Relevance of Education.* W.W. Norton and Company Inc., New York, USA.

Gordon, R.G., Jr., 2005. *Ethnologue: Languages of the World, 15th Edition*. SIL International, Dallas, Texas, USA.

Katada, F., 2002. The linguistic divide, autolinguals, and the notion of education-for-all. *Proceedings of the International Conference on Computers in Education*. DOI: 10.1109/CIE.2002.1186327.

Katada, F., 2019. Autolingualism in the digital age: the emergence of cyber lingua franca and its impact on language education. *Society for Information Technology & Teacher Education International Conference 2019*. 1520-1528.

Thomas, W.P. and Collier, V.P., 2002. A national study of school effectiveness for language minority students' long-term academic achievement. Goerge Masan University, Center for Research on Education, Diversity & Excellence. Retrieved 18 November 2009 from: http://www/crede.ucsc.edu/research/llaa/1.1_final.html.

Vygotsky, L.S., 1934. *Мышление и речь*. (*Thought and Language*, edited and translated by Hanfmann, E. and Vakar, G., 1962. MIT Press, Cambridge, Massachusetts and Wiley, New York, USA.

UNESCO, 1999. *Draft Report of Commission*, p.38. UNESCO, Paris, France.

UNESCO, 2005. *Advocacy Belief on Mother Tongue-based Teaching and Education for Girls.*UNESCO, Bangkok, Thailand.

UNESCO, 2010. *Why and How Africa Should Invest in African Languages and Multilingual Education: An Evidence- and Practice-based Policy Advocacy Brief.* UNESCO Institute for Lifelong learning, Hamburg, Germany.

CHESS TRAINING EFFECT ON META-COGNITIVE PROCESSES AND ACADEMIC PERFORMANCE

Carla Meloni and Rachele Fanari
Department of Education, Psychology, Philosophy
University of Cagliari, Italy

ABSTRACT

The aim of this study is to examine, in an educational context, the influence of chess training on academic performance (written text comprehension and recall and mathematical problem-solving ability) and on meta-cognitive skills (approach to studying and study strategies availability). A sample of 85 children attending primary school participated in the study: 48 children in the experimental group and 37 in the control group. The experimental group took part to a chess training (a 30-hour chess program) during school hours; the control group carried out a sport program. The results show that after the chess training, the two groups did not differ in their approach to studying, in their use of more or less functional study strategies, and in their written text recall and comprehension ability; instead, a significant difference emerged between the two groups in mathematical problem solving: The experimental group children showed a greater ability to represent a math problem and to categorize it than the control children. The results will be discussed in light of the debate about the transfer of specific domain skills to general domain skills.

KEYWORDS

Chess Training, Math Problem, Reading Comprehension, Meta-Cognitive Ability

1. INTRODUCTION

In several European countries, projects involving the introduction of chess instruction in primary school are promoted. Many schools offer chess as an optional subject, while for some schools chess teaching is a part of the standard school program; this also happens following the favorable opinion of the European Parliament itself that promotes the chess game as an important educational tool (Binev, Attard-Montalto, Deva, Mauro, & Takkula, 2011).

The hypothesis behind these choices is that the skills acquired in this specific field can improve academic performance, both in mathematics and reading, and may lead to an improvement even in general domain of cognitive skills. The idea is, therefore, that the specific skills acquired in the chess practice can be transferred to other domains (see Sala & Gobbet, 2016 for a discussion).

Transfer is a process that occurs when skills acquired in a given domain are transferred to another specific or general domain, but the exact nature of the transfer process is not yet entirely clear.

In 1901, Thorndike and Woodworth formulated the hypothesis that transfer depends on the number of features shared between two domains. More recently, Anderson (1990) stated that transfer is a function of the degree of overlap of the cognitive elements present in two tasks, an idea suggesting that the transfer from one specific task to another is often limited. Sternberg (2000) suggested a different approach to the transfer issue: transferable abilities are those constituting the basis of intelligence (general abilities as the verbal or visuo-spatial abilities) that can be applied in different domains but that, being innate, cannot be increased through practice.

Some experimental evidence (for example, Ericsson & Charness, 1994) has shown that the higher the level of expertise in a given specific domain, the more the transfer is limited. Generic learning skills (learning strategies, problem-solving methods, and reasoning techniques), on the other hand, are useful for more domains, but their teaching seems to have immediate, but not long-term benefits (Grotzer & Perkins, 2000).

Regarding the potential of transferring of skills acquired in chess playing to other domains, Gobet and Campitelli (2005), in a critical review, emphasized that the results of the works done on the topic, even if they seem to support a possible transfer of abilities, are often weak and contradictory due to methodological problems. Based on their review, the empirical evidence suggests that chess players tend to be smarter than non-chess players, and that, at least with children, there is a correlation between chess skills and general intelligence even if, quite surprisingly, a direct link between chess and visuospatial skills has not been identified. However, these results could be explained mainly by sample selection processes: more intelligent people are more likely to choose, and to excel, in intellectual activities such as chess.

In a recent meta-analysis, Sala, Foley, and Gobbet (2016) investigated the effects of chess programs both on cognitive abilities and school performances in primary school children. The authors concluded that the effects of chess training are more evident, even if moderate, on math performance and general cognitive skills than reading skills. At least 25–30 hours of chess training seem to be required to have positive effects. In the literature, it is often stated that chess playing improves math skills because chess practice has some elements in common with the domain of mathematics and promotes skills independent from the chess-specific context, such as the ability to understand the existence of a problem and reasoning skills.

Only a few studies have investigated the relationship between chess practice and both general meta-cognitive abilities and specific academic school skills (e.g., reading and math abilities) in the same experimental design, but one problem with these studies making it difficult to compare results and to draw clear conclusions is the significant variability of the variable considered (arithmetic vs. problem solving; reading and text comprehension; attention vs spatial abilities or meta-cognitive abilities). To our knowledge, there are only one study that have investigated the effects of chess training on meta-cognitive abilities, focused on metacognitive skills specifically related to math performance. The study, published in 2012 by Kazemi, Yektayar, and Abad found a positive effect of the use of chess programs on math meta-cognitive abilities. The authors concluded that chess instruction is a way to develop higher-order thinking skills useful for math problem solving.

Most research on meta-cognitive abilities and chess training in primary schools concentrates on the transfer of specific chess skills to specific meta-cognitive abilities used in the math domain. Less is known on chess training's influence on general meta-cognitive skills, skills that children can use in other domains, such motivation to study, organization of personal work, strategic elaboration of the learning material, flexibility of the modality of studying, ability to concentrate, anxiety and attitude toward school, and the knowledge and use of more or less functional study strategies.

The aim of our work is to fill this gap and to explore the link between chess training and both general meta-cognitive study abilities and verbal and math academic skills in primary school children.

We compared two groups of children—one group participating in a chess training and a control group—in their ability to solve math problems, to comprehend and recall a written text, and in their approach to studying and using study strategies.

Following the literature on the relationship between chess playing and academic skills, we expect chess training to influence mathematical problem-solving abilities, but not verbal skills. There is no literature on the effect of chess training on general meta-cognitive abilities of the approach to studying and on the knowledge and use of more or less functional strategies of studying. Therefore, the study of these aspects represents a particularly innovative component of our work and can cast light on the debated issue of the potential to improve general meta-cognitive abilities, useful in various domains, through the training of a specific skill.

2. METHOD

2.1 Participants

Eighty-five typically developing children were recruited from a public primary school in Cagliari, Italy. Both the school and the children's parents agreed to let the children take part in the research study and signed informed consent forms.

Forty-eight children were randomly assigned to a chess training group (mean age = 9.27 years and SD = 0.84; 24 males and 24 females), and 37 were randomly assigned to a control group (mean age = 9.25 years and SD = 0.76; 17 males and 20 females). At the start of the study, all the children were chess novices. The participants came from different classes in which the same teachers evenly rotated; thus, any teacher effects were controlled and the teaching provided to the children was the same even if the children came from different classes. After conducting the random assignment to the experimental and control groups, the teachers were asked if they believed, based on their daily experience with the children, that there were differences between the two groups related to academic performance or differences in attitudes toward school/learning. The teachers noted that the two randomly selected groups were comparable with respect to these variables.

2.2 Procedure

The children in the experimental group participated in a chess program during the school year. Chess lessons were held by a chess master once per week from November to May during school hours. Following Sala et al.'s (2016) meta-analysis results, a 30-hour program was chosen. The control group followed a sport training: specifically, an introduction to basketball.

At the end of the training, the children were presented with a test battery aimed to assess their meta-cognitive skills (approach to studying, knowledge and actual use of functional and dysfunctional strategies) and were tested on their ability to solve mathematical problems and on their level of text comprehension and text recall.

2.3 Assessment Tools

The tools used to assess children's meta-cognitive abilities were taken from the AMOS 8-15 Skills and Motivation Study Battery (De Beni, Moè & Cornoldi, 2003). The battery is composed of seven questionnaires indicating different aspects of meta-cognitive abilities involved in academic performance. The three questionnaires we used in this work were: the QAS questionnaire measuring the approach to studying, the QS1 questionnaire measuring the effectiveness of the study strategies know by the children, and the QS2 questionnaire evaluating the children's actual use of the study strategies.

The QAS questionnaire on the approach to studying investigates seven different dimensions (part A: study motivation; part B: personal work organization; part D: strategic information processing; part E: study flexibility; part N: concentration; part U: anxiety; part V: attitude toward school), for each dimension, seven different statements are presented to the child and he/she must indicate with a cross how true each written statement is to him/her (1 = not true, 2 = enough true, and 3 = very true). The QAS allows for a total score for the approach to studying ability as well as a single score for each dimension.

The second questionnaire used, QS1, identifies the children's beliefs on the effectiveness of functional and dysfunctional strategies that can be used while studying. In particular, the QS1 measures 32 studying strategies (example item: "Thinking about what you already known about the topic you are studying"), and the child is asked to read them carefully and evaluate how much these strategies, according to him/her, are useful for studying, giving each strategy a rating from 1 to 4 (1 = not useful, 2 = not very useful, 3 = useful, and 4 = very useful). The third questionnaire, QS2, detects the child's actual use of the same strategies proposed by the QS1 questionnaire. In the QS2, therefore, 32 studying strategies are proposed (example item: "If you do not understand a part of the text, read it again") and the child is asked to think about their approach to studying and to indicate how often he/she uses the activity with a rating from 1 to 4 (1 = I never use it, 2 = I use it sometimes, 3 = I use it often, and 4 = I always use it). These two last questionnaires (QS1 and QS2) allow a summary index of strategic coherence to be calculated that reflects the correspondence between utility judgments and the estimation of the use of the same strategies by children.

The tools used to assess children's school performance were the "Mathematical Problem Solving" (SPM) test (Lucangeli, Tressoldi & Cedron, 2003) used to test mathematical problem solving and a test taken from the AMOS 8-15 Battery (De Beni, Moè ,& Cornoldi, 2003) called the "Studying Test."

In the SPM, the child is presented with some mathematical problems with different difficulty levels depending on the level of schooling. The SPM evaluates the following skills: problem understanding (understanding the information present in the problem and their relationships), problem representation (the representation of information through a scheme able to integrate problem information), problem categorization (ability to identify among a series of alternatives the problem that has the same deep structure), problem-solving planning, problem-solving procedure, and self-assessment of the correctness of the used procedure.

Moreover, to evaluate the ability to understand, store, and recall information, the Studying Test was used. The test asks the children to study a written text for 30 minutes. After 30 minutes, they are involved in other activities for 10 minutes and then questions about the text are presented to evaluate three indexes: the ability to select the main aspects of the text (asking the child to choose a suitable title), the ability to identify specific information (open questions), and the ability to recognize true/false information with respect to the studied text (multiple-choice test).

2.4 Results

For the data analysis, the scores obtained in each test were calculated following the indications provided. Since the participants in the study were of different ages and school classes, the raw scores were transformed into Z points to compare children's scores, following the test norms.

We conducted six multivariate analyses of variance (MANOVAs). All the MANOVAs had the factor "training" as the independent variable with two levels: chess training and control.

The first MANOVA was carried out to analyze the effects of training on the dimensions of the approach to studying investigated by the QAS; the second, third, and fourth MANOVA were carried out to analyze, respectively: the effects of training on children's beliefs on the effectiveness of functional and dysfunctional study strategies (QS1 questionnaire), the effects of training on the actual use of functional and dysfunctional study strategies (QS2 questionnaire), and the index of strategic coherence in the usage of study strategies; the fifth MANOVA was carried out to analyze the effects of training on children's ability to understand and memorize a text, evaluated in the Studying Test. Finally, with the sixth MANOVA, we aimed to analyze the effects of training on children's ability to solve mathematical problems, evaluated through the SPM. Univariate tests were performed where necessary.

The first MANOVA did not show a significant effect of the chess training on the approach to studying dimensions investigated by the QAS: Wilks/' Lambda = 0.928, $F (7, 77) = 0.86$, $p = 0.54$, $\eta^2 = 0.072$. The children who participated in the chess training seem to approach the study in the same way as the control group.

The MANOVAs for the QS1 and QS2 questionnaires and for the index of strategic coherence were separately calculated: Wilks' Lambda (QS1) = 0.951, $F (2, 82) = 2.09$, $p = 0.13$, $\eta^2 = 0.049$; Wilks' Lambda (QS2) = 0.994, $F (2, 82) = 0.23$, $p = 0.79$, $\eta^2 = 0.006$; Wilks' Lambda (strategic coherence) = 0.979, $F (2, 82) = 0.89$, $p = 0.42$, $\eta^2 = 0.021$. The results show no significant difference between the experimental and control groups relative to the children's beliefs about the effectiveness of study strategies on the degree of their actual usage and on the degree of coherence with which they actually use study strategies they consider most effective.

From the fifth MANOVA, no effects of chess training on children's ability to understand and memorize a text (evaluated by the Studying Test) emerged: Wilks' Lambda = 0.954, $F (3, 81) = 1.31$, $p = 0.28$, $\eta^2 = 0.046$.

The sixth MANOVA, which compared the two groups of children on their ability to solve mathematical problems (SPM test), instead highlighted a difference between the experimental and control groups: Wilks' Lambda = 0.801, $F (6, 78) = 3.23$, $p = 0.01$, $\eta^2 = 0.199$. This last result has been examined in detail through a series of individual ANOVAs, one for each of the single dimensions investigated by the SPM battery.

The ANOVA findings indicate that chess training seems to primarily influence the ability to create a mental representation. This ability is measured by the SPM battery with a test in which the child must choose between a series of more or less abstract graphic representations (vignettes or diagrams) of the problem to be solved.

Another dimension in which the children in the experimental group exhibited significantly better performance than those in the control group is that of categorization, which investigates children's ability to extend their knowledge on the solution to a given problem to other similar problems. Finally, the children in the chess group achieved better results in the self-assessment dimension, showing a greater ability to objectively assess their problem-solving performance.

Table 1. Analysis of Variance for the Control and Chess Training Groups' scores in SPM Battery Sub-tests (n = 85)

	Control Group Mean	Control Group sd	Chess Training Group Mean	Chess Training Group sd	F	p-value
Problem comprehension	-0.09	1.66	0.01	1.83	0.07	0.79
Problem representation	-0.11	1.34	0.41	1.06	3.91	0.05*
Problem categorization	-0.30	0.95	0.37	0.83	11.91	0.001*
Problem-solving planning	0.25	1.05	0.26	0.83	0,00	0.98
Problem-solving execution	-0.59	0.98	-0.60	1.28	0.00	0.99
Self-evaluation	-0.41	0.65	-0.15	0.55	4.05	0.05*

Mean score, sd, F, and p-value (***p<.001, **p<.01, *p<.05)

3. DISCUSSION AND CONCLUSION

The aim of this work was to observe the effects of chess training on general meta-cognitive abilities and on skills closely related to school performance. Two groups of children were compared: an experimental group that participated in a chess training and a control group that participated in a sports program.

As for the general meta-cognitive abilities involved in learning, no significant differences emerged between the two groups in the different dimensions related to the QAS test assessing the general way in which they approach studying and some related sub-dimensions (e.g., motivation, strategic elaboration of the study material, ability to concentrate, and attitude toward schooling). No differences emerged between the two groups regarding children's beliefs about the effectiveness and the actual usage of study strategies. The studies that have explored the benefits of chess training on cognitive skills and school performance are scarce in the literature, and only one, to our knowledge, has specifically considered meta-cognitive abilities (Kazemi et al., 2012). In their study, the authors found that the effects of chess training were closely related to meta-cognitive abilities linked to math problem solving. The results of our study, in which we did not find an improvement in meta-cognitive ability after chess training, are not consistent with those of Kazemi et al. (2012). However, the skills considered in our study are quite different from the ones explored by Kazemi and colleagues: They tested meta-cognitive skills specifically involved in math problem solving, while we tested general meta-cognitive abilities applicable to any kind of subject of study. One potential explanation for our findings is that the dimensions tested in our study (e.g., motivation, attitude toward schooling, knowledge and usage of study strategies) are quite different from the skills acquired through chess practice, such as elaborating game plans. They require more than merely a simple transfer, but what Mestre (2005) defined as a far transfer, that is, a transfer between areas that are far from each other, and much more difficult to gain.

Although we have investigated only meta-cognitive abilities, our data seem to go in the direction of the studies that have investigated more general cognitive abilities, e.g., Scholz et al. (2008), who did not find an effect of training with chess on focused attention. A meta-analysis by Burgoyne et al. (2016) considered 19 studies that related cognitive abilities to chess skills and found a positive correlation between general cognitive abilities and chess practice that seemed, however, to be mediated by age and chess skill level. In particular, the younger and more inexperienced participants were, the greater the correlation with cognitive abilities. But it must to be noted that in the meta-analysis, the percentage of explained variance of cognitive abilities on chess performance is on average 6%, a fairly low value. In the already cited meta-analysis done by Sala and Gobbet (2016), the authors underlined how in the works considered, the effect size is not large enough to strongly support the hypothesis that the improvement in cognitive abilities is due to the chess itself. Moreover, the authors highlighted that most studies considered did not consider the placebo effect: very often the control groups were not involved in other activities that could enhance their cognitive abilities. Therefore, it is difficult to determine whether the (already small) effect found was due strictly to playing chess or merely to being involved in a stimulating activity. The results of Sala and Gobbet's (2016) meta-analysis regarding cognitive abilities therefore seem to support the difficulty in the transfer of chess-related abilities to general cognition.

For the study trial in which participants were asked to understand and remember written text informational content, no significant difference was found between the chess and control groups. This is an expected result: The researchers who have investigated the relationship between chess and verbal skills have not found relationships between these two abilities, the authors; explanation lies in the fact that these two types of skills do not share common elements (see Sala & Gobbet, 2016 for further discussion). However, it must be emphasized that in our work, we have considered the abilities of understanding and retaining information that have more in common with chess from the point of view of the underlying cognitive abilities than the simple reading skills investigated in other studies; despite this, however, we did not find significant effects.

Significant differences between the two groups of children have emerged, instead, in the SPM test score assessing the ability to solve mathematical problems, particularly in the dimensions of problem representation, problem categorization, and self-evaluation. Chess-training children are more capable of organizing information by creating a coherent representation of a problem and more able to categorize problems; they even demonstrate a greater capacity to extend their knowledge of a problem's structure to other similar problems to be able to solve them faster. The meta-analyses previously considered show that the domain of mathematics is the one that benefits most from chess training, leading most authors to think that these two areas involve common cognitive abilities. The literature results suggest that playing chess allows children to develop skills that can be de-contextualized, such as problem-solving skills and the ability of identifying quantitative relationships—abilities that can be transferred to the domain of mathematics. Our findings, demonstrating a difference between the experimental and control groups only in the math problem-solving domain, confirm this hypothesis.

Furthermore, our results showed that the chess players have a better capacity than the children in the control group to self-evaluate their school performance. This is in line with Aciego and Betancort's (2012) findings that chess practice improved not only cognitive skills but also the socio-emotional sphere, especially the ability to self-evaluate.

In sum, our findings confirm that chess practice can be useful for primary school children to enhance their mathematical problem-solving abilities and learning-related self-evaluation abilities even if chess practice could be of scarce use for improving meta-cognitive abilities applied to general school activity and for text comprehension, confirming literature data.

Our work has the merit of having used a sample taken from a primary school where the children were randomly assigned to an experimental group that played chess and to a control group. Often the works in this area use samples drawn from populations already selected a priori, such as children who are part of real chess clubs. In line with literature recommendations, the time extent of the training was 30 hours, and the control group was engaged in an alternative activity.

However, there are several limitations to note. The main limitation is that the participants did not undergo a pre-test to assess whether differences existed before the treatment, given that we had to limit the number of testing sessions to meet a school demand. To overcome this limitation, we used a large sample, randomly drawn from a school population and not pre-selected in a chess club. We selected classes in which the same teachers were regularly involved and asked the teachers, in advance, to evaluate whether the cognitive and academic levels of the children randomly assigned to the two groups were comparable. Nonetheless, we cannot exclude the possibility that one of the groups would start higher than the other in some of the dimensions considered. This is a serious limitation, even if the lack of a rigorous test-retest methodology is often observed in this type of work (see Sala & Gobbet, 2016 for further discussion).

Our findings suggest that the topic of the transfer of skills gained through chess practice to the academic domain is worth further investigation. Future research should be undertaken using a pre-posttest experimental design and a longitudinal approach to investigate the effects of chess practice over time.

ACKNOWLEDGEMENT

The authors would like to thank the principal of the school where the data collection took place. Special thanks go to the children, families, and teachers who participated in the study.

REFERENCES

Aciego, R., García, L., & Betancort, M. (2012). The benefits of chess for the intellectual and social-emotional enrichment in schoolchildren. *The Spanish journal of psychology*, 15(2), 551-559.

Anderson, J. R. (1990). *Cognitive psychology and its implication* (3rd ed.). New York: Freeman.

Binev, S., Attard-Montalto, J., Deva, N., Mauro, M., & Takkula, H. (2011). Declaration of the European Parliament, 0050/2011.

Burgoyne, A. P., Sala, G., Gobet, F., Macnamara, B. N., Campitelli, G., & Hambrick, D. Z. (2016). The relationship between cognitive ability and chess skill: A comprehensive meta-analysis. *Intelligence*, 59, 72-83.

De Beni, R., Moè, A., & Cornoldi, C. (2003). *AMOS 8-15. Abilità e motivazione allo studio: Prove di valutazione e orientamento* (Vol. 30). Edizioni Erickson.

Ericsson, K. A., & Charness, N. (1994). Expert performance: Its structure and acquisition. *American psychologist*, 49(8), 725.

Gobet, F., & Campitelli, G. (2006). Educational benefits of chess instruction: A critical review. In *Chess and education: Selected essays from the Koltanowski conference* (pp. 124-143). Chess Program at the University of Texas at Dallas Dallas, TX.

Kazemi, F., Yektayar, M., & Abad, A. M. B. (2012). Investigation the impact of chess play on developing meta-cognitive ability and math problem-solving power of students at different levels of education. *Procedia-Social and Behavioral Sciences*, 32, 372-379.

Lucangeli, D., Tressoldi, P. E., & Cendron, M. (1998). *SPM-Test delle abilità di soluzione dei problemi matematici*. Edizioni Erickson.

Mestre, J. P. (2005). *Transfer of learning from a modern multidisciplinary perspective*. Greenwich, CT: Information Age.

Perkins, D. N., & Grotzer, T. A. (1997). Teaching intelligence. *American psychologist*, 52(10), 1125.

Sala, G., & Gobet, F. (2016). Do the benefits of chess instruction transfer to academic and cognitive skills? A meta-analysis. *Educational Research Review*, 18, 46-57.

Sala, G., & Gobet, F. (2017). Does chess instruction improve mathematical problem-solving ability? Two experimental studies with an active control group. *Learning & behavior*, 45(4), 414-421.

Sala, G., Foley, J. P., & Gobet, F. (2017). The effects of chess instruction on pupils' cognitive and academic skills: state of the art and theoretical challenges. Frontiers in psychology, 8, 238.

Scholz, M., Niesch, H., Steffen, O., Ernst, B., Loeffler, M., Witruk, E., et al. (2008). Impact of chess training on mathematics performance and concentration ability of children with learning disabilities. *International Journal of Special Education*, 23, 138e148.

Sternberg, R. J. (Ed.). (2000). *Handbook of Intelligence*. Cambridge: Cambridge, University Press.

Thorndike, E. L, & Woodworth, R. S. (1901). The influence of improvement in one mental function upon the efficiency of other functions. *Psychological Review*, 9, 374-382.

SHORT PAPERS

DESIGN OF WEB BASED DYNAMIC ASSESSMENT SYSTEM FOR SOLVING TWO SIGMA PROBLEM

Arif Tuluk[1], Muhittin Şahin[2] and Halil Yurdugül[1]
[1]*Hacettepe University, Turkey*
[2]*Ege University, Turkey*

ABSTRACT

In 1984 Benjamin Bloom stated that one-to-one tutorial support increased students' achievement by two standard deviations (two sigma problem). In the literature for solving two sigma problem (in order to increase student achievement), many systems were developed as intelligent tutoring systems, adaptive hypermedia systems, recommender systems and etc. In addition to this, it can be said that dynamic assessment increases the students' achievement. Because one of the main objectives of the dynamic assessment is to improve the performance of learners by providing instructional aids with assessment tasks. Within the scope of this research, a web-based dynamic assessment system was designed and developed. Then, the effectiveness of the system tested with actual users. One group pretest-posttest design was used. A total of 322 secondary school 5th-grade students participated in this study. The findings were discussed in the context of two sigma problems. According to the findings, it can be said that the web-based dynamic assessment system increases student achievement approximately two standard deviations.

KEYWORDS

Two Sigma Problem, Dynamic Assessment, Web-Based Dynamic Assessment System

1. INTRODUCTION

Bloom (1984) stated that one-to-one tutorial support increased students' achievement by two standard deviations. In this context from past to present, many environments were designed and developed in order to support the students. At the same time, this perspective is closely related to "*The Zone of Proximal Development-ZPD*" in Vygotsky's theory of social constructivism. ZPD is expressed as the gap between what the student can do without help and what he can do with help (Bodrova & Leong, 1996; Vygotsky, 1978). It can be said that one of the alternatives for filling this gap is dynamic assessment. Because one of the main objectives of the dynamic assessment is to improve the performance of learners by providing instructional aids with assessment tasks. In this context, the feature that separates dynamic assessment from the static assessment can be explained by the concept of feedback. In the dynamic assessment, feedback is based on the performance of an assessment task; rather than cognitive, affective and motivational information about the performance of the students. In recent years, web-based assessment environments have also increased. Within the scope of this research, a web-based dynamic assessment system was designed and students were provided with a learning experience. As a result of this experience, the development of learning was discussed within the framework of two sigma problems. In this context this study includes, firstly, web-based dynamic assessment, the web-based dynamic assessment system presented to the students and finally the findings of the experimental research.

1.1 Dynamic Web Based Assessment

The development of dynamic assessment was greatly influenced by L.S. Vygotsky (Haywood, et al., 1990; Allal & Ducrey, 2000). Vygotsky (1978) emphasized that social context plays a role in children's learning and development. Vygotsky proposed the theory of "*Zone of Proximal Development (ZPD)*" to describe the difference between children's performance without the help of adults and their more competent peers (Vygotsky, 1978). The ZPD represents the learning potential of children. By interacting with adults or more competent peers, children's learning potentials can be revealed and learning activities can be improved. Dynamic assessment is an interactive assessment commonly given as "test-teach-retest" (Haywood & Lidz, 2007). In the dynamic assessment, individuals are given the opportunity to learn (Bransford, et al., 1987) and are included in the teaching and feedback testing process (Elliott, 2003). In educational psychology, the traditional use of dynamic assessment is to help classify examiners, select specific forms of mediation or training, and predict their true abilities (Elliott, 2003). However, Elliott (2003), Haywood and Lidz (2007) and Poehner (2008) stated that dynamic assessment can be integrated into school curriculum and education to assist educators and support learners' learning. This study attempts to combine two main educational features of dynamic assessment and, as a result, to suggest "*assessment as a learning and teaching strategy*". In other words, this idea means that learning and teaching strategies are structured around a web-based dynamic assessment and seamlessly combined with learning and teaching activities in the web-based dynamic assessment. In the process of web-based dynamic assessment, learning takes place through guidance and instruction provided by the assessment. In this research, a web-based dynamic assessment system has been developed based on the idea of "assessment as a learning and teaching strategy". Trainers are expected to create e-learning environments based on assessment, which will provide students with a more effective learning experience by taking advantage of this system. Trainers can also use this system to integrate the scaffolding assessment process simultaneously.

Sternberg and Grigorenko (2001) stated that there are two types of dynamic assessment as sandwich and cake form. Both formats are implemented as "test-teach-retest". The sandwich format dynamic assessment means that the instruction is held between the pre-test and the post-test, thus forming a sandwich-like process. In the dynamic assessment of cakes, teaching is a response to the answers given to each question by the researchers. In this research, since the assessment is considered as a learning and teaching strategy, cake-like dynamic assessment principles are adopted in designing the web-based dynamic assessment system. The main feature of the dynamic assessment of cakes is the design of successive cues with a progressive set of clues. This design is similar to the "graduated prompt approach" recommended by Campione and Brown (1985, 1987). According to Campione and Brown, the clues in the "graduated prompt approach" are presented in a predetermined order, arranged according to their disclosure levels (Bransford, et al., 1987). They start with "general hints" and gradually become "specific hints". General hints provide relatively little specific information about the solution, while a specific hint provides a detailed instruction that students can produce the right answer (Campione & Brown, 1985, 1987). In this study, the "graduated prompt approach" and the clues provided by the dynamic assessment elements were used to develop the web-based dynamic assessment system. These clues are called instructional guidance (IG) because they are used to guide and teach students. When students answer an item incorrectly, the IGs are progressively learned and learn to find the right answer step by step.

2. METHOD

2.1 Research Design

Within the scope of the research, pretest–posttest design was employed in quasi-experimental research and used without control group. This design includes a single group and the effectiveness of the application/intervention is determined by the development of pre-test and post-test.

2.2 Participants

A total of 322 secondary school 5th-grade students participated in the study. These students are located in three different provinces in Turkey to continue their education and training in secondary schools.

2.3 Web Based Dynamic Assessment System

Within the scope of this research, an online environment with the idea of dynamic assessment of the cake format proposed by Sternberg and Grigorenko (2001) was developed to design the scaffolding strategies in the web-based dynamic assessment system. If students answer the question correctly, they get an encouraging statement and a score (Figure 1a), if the wrong answers are scaffolding (Figure 1b).

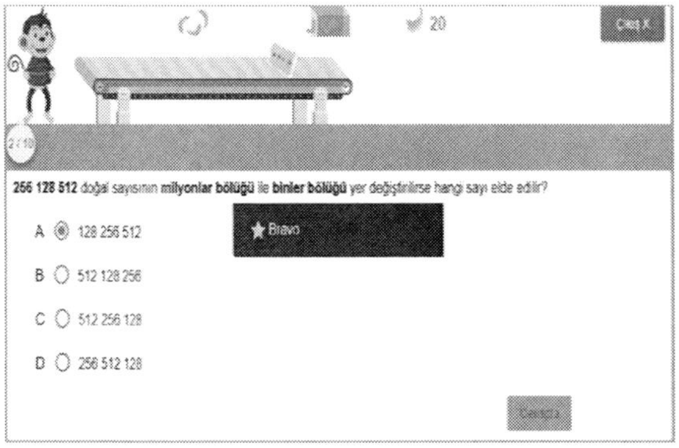

Figure 1a. Screen-shot for correct response

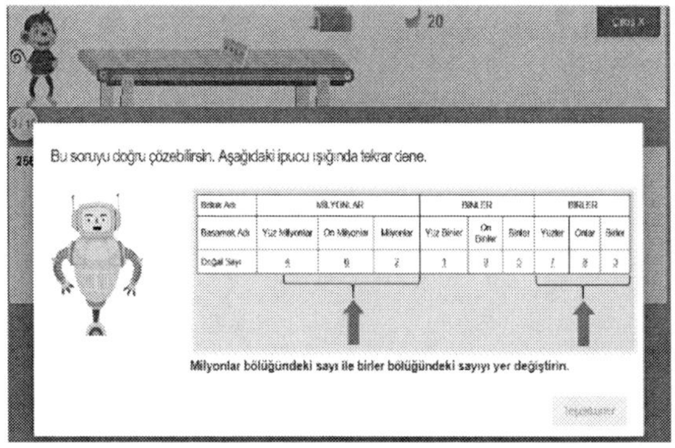

Figure 1b. Screen-shot for the wrong response

As shown in Figure 1b, when students respond incorrectly for the first time to an assessment item, a general scaffolding is offered to the students by the assessment system. Students are asked to answer the same assessment item again after the first IG. When the same assessment item responds incorrectly by the students for the second time, more specific instructional guidance is given by the system. Students who receive the second IG are required to respond to the same assessment item for the third time. If the third time is answered incorrectly, the system is presented by an even more specific IG. As the only item left in the assessment item after the third IG is left, the next assessment item is displayed after showing that the remaining item of the assessment item is correct. Students are expected to use the gains they gained here (IGs) in their next assessment tasks.

2.4 Data Collection Tools

In order to observe the development of the students, success tests developed by the researchers were applied for two different gains. Both pre-test and post-test were applied for each gain.

2.5 Data Analysis

In order to determine the development of the students, Paired Sample T-Test was employed. Additional calculations were utilized for solving two sigma problem.

3. FINDINGS

Within the scope of this research, paired sample t-test was used for each gain in order to determine the web-based dynamic assessment system achievement. The results of the analysis for the first gain are presented in Table 1.

Table 1. Results of Paired Sample T-Test for Gain 1

	n	X_{ave}	df	t	p
Pretest	322	5,88	321	-56,05	0,00
Posttest	322	7,63			

$p<0{,}01$

As can be seen in Table 1, it can be said that the achievement of students has increased statistically significantly. The results of the analysis for the first gain are presented in Table 2.

Table 2. Results of Paired Sample T-Test for Gain 2

	n	X_{ave}	df	t	p
Pretest	322	4,36	321	-54,06	0,00
Posttest	322	5,84			

$p<0,01$

As shown in Table 2, it can be said that the achievement of students has increased statistically. According to the findings, it can be said that the developed system increases the students' achievements by approximately two standard deviations.

4. CONCLUSION

One-to-one tutorial support enhances two standard deviations of student achievement (Bloom, 1984). This situation is also closely related to the ZPD established by Vygotsky (Vygotsky, 1978). Because ZPD is the difference between what an individual can do with help and without help. Within the scope of this research, a web-based dynamic assessment system has been designed and developed in order to solve two sigma problem. Within the scope of this research, an online environment with the idea of dynamic assessment of the cake format proposed by Sternberg and Grigorenko (2001) was developed to design the scaffolding strategies in the web-based dynamic assessment system. In order to test the success of the developed system, students have experienced two different gains in the system. Then, paired sample t-test was performed. According to the findings, it was found that the system was increased students' achievement approximately two standard deviations. Based on these results, it is thought that the web-based dynamic assessment system may offer a solution for two sigma problem.

REFERENCES

Allal, L., Ducrey, G.P. (2000). Assessment of-or in-the zone of proximal development. *Learning and Instruction,* 10(2), 137-152. https://doi.org/10.1016/S0959-4752(99)00025-0.

Bloom, B.S. (1984). The 2 sigma problem: The search for methods of group instruction as effective as one-to-one tutoring. *Educational Researcher,* 13(6), 4-16.

Bodrova, E., & Leong, D. J. (1996). Tools of the mind: The Vygotskian approach to early childhood education. Englewood Cliffs, NJ: Merrill/Prentice Hall.

Bransford, J. D., Delclos, V., Vye, N., Bums, S., & Hasselbring, T. (1987). Approaches to dynamic assessment: Issues, data and future directions. In C. Lidz (Ed.), Dynamic assessment: An interactional approach to evaluating learning potentials. New York: Guilford Press, 479-495.

Bransford, J. D., Brown, A. L., & Cocking, R. R. (2000). How people learn: Brain, mind, experience and school. *Expanded Edition,* Washington, DC: National Academy Press. http://nap.edu/9853.

Campione, J. C., & Brown, A. L. (1985). Dynamic assessment: One approach and some initial data. (Technical report No. 361). Bethesda, MD: National Institute of Child Health and Human Development; National Institute of Education.

Campione, J. C., & Brown, A. L. (1987). Linking dynamic assessment with school achievement. In C. S. Lidz (Ed.), Dynamic assessment: An international approach to evaluating learning potential. *The Guilford Press,* New York, 82–115.

Elliott, J. G. (2003). Dynamic assessment in educational settings: Realizing potential. *Educational Review,* 55, 15–32.

Haywood, H. C., Brown, A. L., & Wingenfeld, S. (1990). Dynamic approaches to psycho-educational assessment. *School Psychology Review,* 19, 411–422.

Haywood, H. C., Lidz, C. S. (2007). Dynamic assessment in practice. Clinical and educational applications. *Cambridge University Press,* New York.

Poehner, M. E. (2008). Dynamic assessment: A Vygotskian approach to understanding and promoting L2 development. *Springer,* New York.

Sternberg, R. J., & Grigorenko, E. L. (2001). All testing is dynamic testing. *Issues in Education,* 7, 137–170.

Vygotsky, L. S. (1978). Mind and society: The development of higher mental processes. Cambridge, MA: Harvard University Press. (Original work published in 1930, 1933, 1935).

AN EXPLORATORY STUDY OF TRIAL AND ERROR IN THE DESIGN AND PRACTICE OF UNDERGRADUATE SEMINARS IN JAPAN

Wakako Fushikida
University Education Center, Tokyo Metropolitan University, Japan

ABSTRACT

The purpose of this study is to investigate the solutions that faculty members resort to by trial and error in certain challenges presented to them in undergraduate seminars for second, third, and fourth year students. The research questions used were as follows: (1) What kind of problems do faculty members face, and (2) How faculty members try to improve their undergraduate seminars in order to provide an effective learning environment for students. Using a questionnaire, we conducted a survey on 157 faculty members and constructed the variables by factor analysis. The results indicated that faculty members usually try to set goals and activities with respect to the students' current situation or interests because they believe that the students do not have the basic knowledge and skills needed in specialized fields.

KEYWORDS

Higher Learning, Learning Community, Educational Psychology

1. INTRODUCTION

As we transition to a knowledge-based society, there is a great demand for individuals to have the abilities to survive in an unexpected future (Barnett 2012). For instance, much attention has been drawn to generic skills as the key to face and solve uncertainty problems. Though the name and usage of the skills is not uniform across countries and time periods, there is a common view that the concept of "generic skills" shows a potential for generalizability and possibility of diversion to other contexts (Australian National Training Authority 2003). Specifically, generic skills include not only basic skills such as reading, writing, thinking critically, information literacy, problem-solving skills, and human relation skills, represented by communication or teamwork, but also a sense of responsibility or flexibility. Those abilities and attitudes areexpected to be developed through interactive learning that promotes discussion and sharing of ideas among students (Ogata 2008).

In Japan, many faculty members and researchers consider an undergraduate seminar affectionately called "Zemi" as effective learning environment. It was in the nineteenth century when undergraduate seminars were born in Germany under the idea of "education through research" (Ushiogi 1986). A popular format of which is one where a faculty member and about 5 to 20 students participate in a regular meeting intended to help the students to gain a further understanding of their respective disciplines (e.g. Figure 1).

There are various activities in undergraduate seminars such as reading books and articles, conducting fieldwork, planning events or workshops, making presentations, asking questions, and writing graduation theses. Students are urged to collaboratively engage in solving practical problems and demonstrate knowledge and skills for two or three years in the same seminar (Yoshihara 2010). In other words, because of its importance as a teaching method, along with a lecture in university education, an undergraduate seminar also represents a research-oriented and a dialogue-based community of the faculty member and students, and offers students the opportunity for close interaction with faculty members. Therefore, through the seminars, the students may absorb ideas and tacit knowledge related to specialized fields through the use of daily communication.

Figure 1. Example of learning activities in a seminar
(The woman leftmost in the photo is a faculty member watching her students discuss each other.)

Recently, some researchers have reported that undergraduate seminars are also effective for students in generating motivation and satisfaction, and in fostering generic skills. However, there are only a few empirical studies on undergraduate seminars from faculty members on perspectives about design, management, and assessment. Additionally, most faculty members do not have the chance to participate in and observe other seminar classes, so they need to explore other appropriate ways for establishing their original seminar styles.

This study investigate the solutions that faculty members resort to by trial and error in certain challenges presented to them in undergraduate seminars for second, third, and fourth year students. There two research questions used were as follows: (1) What kind of problems do faculty members face while designing and managing their original seminars, and (2) How faculty members try to solve the problems and improve their seminars' styles in order to provide an effective learning environment for students.

2. METHODS

A questionnaire survey using postal mail was conducted for various faculty membersto explore their perceptions about undergraduate seminars at the end of the 2015. The seminars targeted by this study had to meet the following three prerequisites: (a) a formal name of the course is documented in the syllabus, (b) students can acquire units, (c) they are held periodically. The subjects of the study were full-time faculty members who belonged to humanities, social sciences, and integrated sciences, from universities with their headquarters located in Tokyo. The survey population had representation from 81 universities, where 525 of 14,355 faculty members were selected through a systematic random sampling.

The questionnaire items included age, gender, specialized field, age at which first seminar was started, the formal name of the seminar, scales of course design such as those of setting goals, activities, and instructions, and lastly, faculty members' practical experiences. The scales used in the questionnaires were created based on the results of previous studies and our preliminary surveys.

The purpose of this study was to clarify the common problems that faculty members encounter in undergraduate seminars, and find approaches that may be used for their improvement. First, after confirming the status of related items with extreme bias from the frequency distribution table, a correlation analysis was conducted. Second, the variables were constructed by factor analysis using the principal factor method with a promax-rotation. If an item with a communality ≤ 0.1 was seen, that item was eliminated from the list and the factor analysis was re-performed. The number of factors was decided based on the criterion of eigenvalue ≥ 1.

3. RESULTS AND DISCUSSION

Responses were received from 157 faculty members. However, cases with defects such as duplicate responses or no response to some questionnaire items were excluded. Eventually, data from the 130 viable responses were the subject of the analysis. Of the 130 faculty members, 92 were male (70.8%) and 37 were female (28.5%), with a mean age of 51.1 years (*S.D.* = 10.4). It was found that there were 30 (23.1%) faculty members from humanities, 73 (56.2%) from social sciences, and 22 (16.9%) from integrated sciences.

To the question "what kind of difficulties did you have in practicing your undergraduate seminar?", the faculty members were required to answer 10 items on a 5-point scale. Table 1 showed that most faculty members answered that the following questionnaire items were particularly difficult problems: "There is variation in students' ability and motivation (average =3.77, *S.D.* =1.00)", "Students do not read enough books" (average =3.65, *S.D.* =1.09), "Students' basic academic ability and knowledge are short" (average=3.62, *S.D.* =1.02), "Activating discussion among members" (average=3.54, *S.D.* =1.19), and "Providing instruction according to the students' current situation" (average=3.44, *S.D.* =1.06).

After conducting a factor analysis, as shown in Table 1, the first factor (Factor 1: F1) was named "Placing emphasis on learner centered activities and instructions" because a factor loads for items such as "provide instruction according to the students' current situation" and "Retaining balance between faculty members' expertise and students' interests." The second factor (Factor 2: F2) was named "shortage of basic academic literacy and motivation differences between individuals" because a factor loads for items such as "Students' are short of basic academic ability and knowledge" and "There is variation in students' ability and motivation". There is a middle level of correlation between F1 and F2 (r =.47).

Finally, F1 and F2 scores were calculated by adding together each factor questionnaire items and analyzed using a one-way inter-subject analysis of variance to reveal the effects of *years of experiences* on difficult problems in faculty members' practical experiences. The average F1 score (average=19.86, *S.E.*=.53) was significantly higher than F2 score (average=17.77, *S.E.*=.40) based on the result of a Student t-test (t (113) = 4.02, p = .00, d = .410, 95%CI = .15 – .67) . The results in Figure 1 show that there were significant differences between F2 scores (F (3, 118) = 3.072, p = .03, η^2 = .072, 95%CI = 00 –.16).

According to the Holm's sequentially rejective Bonferroni test, in the F2 scores, the score of *less than a decade* was significantly higher than the score of *more than a decade, but less than 20 years* (d = .53, 95%CI = .11 –.96) and the score of *more than 30 years* was significantly higher than the score of *more than a decade, but less than 20 years* (d = .72, 95%CI = .29 – 1.15). These findings indicate that the *less than a decade* and *more than 30 years* faculty members tended to recognize the difficulty in the design and practice of their undergraduate seminars.

Table 1. Results of factor analysis about difficult problems through faculty members' practical experience

	Questionnaire items	Average	*S.D.*	F1	F2	Communality
(k)	Providing instruction according to the students' current situation.	3.44	1.06	**.85**	-.07	.67
(i)	Allocating time required for activities properly.	3.34	1.03	**.80**	-.16	.54
(l)	Establishing the design and management of the seminar.	3.01	1.04	**.70**	.03	.50
(h)	Retaining balance between faculty members' expertise and students' interests.	3.17	1.15	**.67**	.11	.53
(j)	Activating discussion among members.	3.54	1.19	**.66**	.07	.49
(g)	Reflecting students' various interests in learning topics and activities.	3.15	1.14	**.65**	.08	.48
(a)	Students' are short of basic academic ability and knowledge.	3.62	1.02	.01	**.77**	.60
(d)	Students do not read enough books.	3.65	1.09	-.03	**.74**	.53
(c)	There is variation in students' ability and motivation.	3.77	1.00	-.06	**.75**	.53
(b)	Students' overall motivation for learning is low.	2.84	1.10	.13	**.69**	.58
(f)	Job-hunting causes negative participation and delays in the seminar activities.	3.39	1.22	-.07	**.40**	.14
		Factor contribution		3.75	3.18	
		Factor correlation			.47	
		α coefficient		.87	.75	

Figure 2. Results of the one-way analysis of variance (Error bars indicate the standard error)

4. CONCLUSION

These results indicated that faculty members try exceptionally hard to set goals and activities that cater to the students' current situations or interests, because they believe that students do not have the basic knowledge and skills needed in specialized fields. Furthermore, many faculty members seem to consider students' independent-minded stance for learning to be the most important thing, even if seminars have been thought to be professional education, based on faculty members' academic specialties in their previous studies. These findings are applicable in other educational methods, including the following elements: discussion among a faculty member and students, exploration of an academic discipline, and the sense of community.

Furthermore, beginning and expert faculty members find it extremely difficult to design and practice seminars such that students who lack some of the basic academic literacy skills and to students whose motivation levels are different between individuals. However, this research has not been able to explain the reason for the problem, so I would like to conduct additional analyses with free descriptions about faculty members' educational ideals for their seminars. It is also important to investigate the concrete process related to the above findings through periodic observation surveys of specific seminars and to offer supportive feedback to faculty members who are experiencing problems and difficulties.

ACKNOWLEDGEMENT

This work was supported by *JSPS KAKENHI Grant Numbers 26885022* and *17K1799000.*

REFERENCES

Australian national training authority (2003) Defining generic skills: At a glance, 1–12. http://www.ncver.edu.au/publications/136.html (accessed 2013.07.07)

Barnett, R. (2012) Learning for an unknown future. *Higher Education Research & Development*, 31(1):65-77.

Ogata, N. (2008) Student engagement and university education outcome. *Japanese Association of Higher Education Research* 11:45–64.

Ushiogi, M. (1997) *Kyoto teikoku daigaku no chousen.* Tokyo: Kodanshya.

Yoshihara, M. (2010) Evaluation and outcome of growth in generic skills. 2007 Basic Research (B) Evaluation of the outcome of Bachelor's Education and report of an international comparative study on fostering generic skills, 53–59.

EVALUATION OF A MOBILE PEER-EVALUATION SYSTEM FOR IN-CLASS PRESENTATIONS

Peter Gobel and Makimi Kano
Kyoto Sangyo University, Japan

ABSTRACT

Simultaneous in-class presentations are well suited to the use of peer evaluation, which also promotes greater involvement of the student audience. The problem for the teacher is how to manage peer evaluation and make it a useful part of the curriculum. PeerEval is a mobile application that allows students to anonymously evaluate presentations in real time using a Likert scale rubric and individual peer comments. The results of each evaluation are compiled in a database which is available to the teacher and the students. This short paper focuses on implementing and evaluating this app in Japanese university classrooms. The researchers sought to evaluate both the technical aspects of the software and nature of student feedback using the software. Student attitudes towards the PeerEval system were measured using a twelve-item questionnaire concerning usability of the software, their attitudes towards the system both as a presenter and as an audience member. Results are discussed regarding student perceptions of the evaluation system, overall feedback quality, and the perceived effect of feedback speed and peer comments. Further uses for a mobile peer-evaluation system are also discussed.

KEYWORDS

Peer Evaluation, Active Learning, Higher Education, Mobile Assisted Language Learning

1. INTRODUCTION

PeerEval (https://peereval.mobi/) is a peer evaluation application developed to be used with simultaneous in-class presentations. These kinds of presentations have a number of positive benefits, such as reducing speaking anxiety and promoting greater involvement of the students in the presentations (Cote, 2013). PeerEval seeks to deal with a number of drawbacks to current forms of peer evaluation such as, considerable paperwork, a reluctance to fairly evaluate peers or comment critically, and asynchronous rating.

This short paper gives an explanation of the development of the PeerEval system, a description of the use of the app, and a user evaluation of the software. Student attitudes towards PeerEval were measured using a twelve-item questionnaire concerning usability of the software and their attitudes towards the system as a presenter and as an audience member.

2. PEER EVALUATION OF PRESENTATIONS

Modern teaching practices such as poster presentations have allowed for more active learning by giving students more performance time in language classrooms. One of the drawbacks with such activities is that the teacher must, by the very nature of the activity, play a smaller role. It is almost impossible for the teacher to evaluate all students in such an activity. This situation leads to the implementation of some sort of peer evaluation. With proper planning and careful execution, peer evaluation can have a positive effect on both performance and L2 acquisition (Hansen & Liu, 2005; Gobel & Kano, 2017).

Peer assessment has been used as an alternative evaluation method for a variety of oral presentation activities (Boud, Cohen & Sampson, 1999; Patri, 2002; Shimura, 2006). It can encourage active involvement of the students, foster collaborative learning, and contribute to learner autonomy (Donato, 1994; Kessler & Bikowski, 2010; Rust, Price, & O'Donovan, 2003; Tseng & Tsai, 2010).

With the above benefits in mind, many teachers and textbooks have created paper-based rubrics for peer evaluation. While these paper-based assessment forms are useful, they pose a number of problems. One problem is the issue of anonymity. Without some privacy and anonymity, the effect of social influence may increase (Panadero, Romero, & Strijbos, 2013; Tseng, et al., 2010). In addition to this, collating paper evaluations is a time-consuming task.

Some of these problems can be alleviated by using LMS such as Moodle or Blackboard, which make it easy for students to input scores online and for the teacher to manage these scores. Such systems have been used to great effect in the peer assessment of writing (see Davies, 2000, for an overview). But it is still difficult to ensure total anonymity of feedback and comments on a forum. Some research has been done with classroom response technologies (CRT) and anonymity (Bojinova and Oigara, 2011, 2013; Raes, Vanderhoven., & Schellens, 2013), but these dealt with simple assessment scores, as opposed to written feedback. Also, CRT assessment is usually done asynchronously.

To solve these problems, PeerEval was created with a simple interface that is both flexible and anonymous in nature. The application sought to create evaluation rubrics that could be used quickly and anonymously to give quick and accurate impressions to their peers, as well as giving users immediate access to their scores and feedback. The following section describes the PeerEval system and how it has been used for in-class presentations and peer assessment.

2.1 Description of the System

There are two components: a browser-based system for the instructor to create the evaluation criteria, to upload the student name list, and to download the results; and the iOS app that the students use for their assessments. In addition, from 2018 students can access the PeerEval student system (the same as the app) on any web browser.

Teachers need to go to http://peereval.mobi, where there are two choices. Teachers may use the system without registration, but they must configure their session, conduct their class and download their results within a set time period. Teachers with login-access can create multiple rubrics, sessions and classes that remain in the system until the teacher elects to delete them.

Teachers create a session by naming the session, inputting student information and choosing or creating a rubric. Student information can be input on the webpage itself or by uploading a .csv file with all the relevant information.

Within PeerEval, teachers can choose one of the default rubrics or create their own. A set of up to six rubrics can be set up for one session, with a choice of four-point or five-point Likert scales. Each rubric consists of a title for the item, a description of the item, and a 4-5 point Likert scale (see Figure 1).

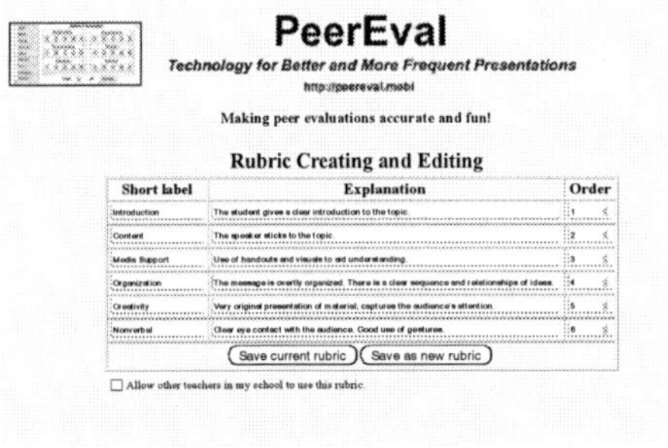

Figure 1. Rubric set up

Once a session has been fully set up, an access code is created which will be used by the students, along with their handle to access the session via the app.

Once a session has been completed, the teacher can view or download the results. The teacher can show the results instantly on the class screen if s/he is not concerned about student privacy, or print them out and supply the students with their own scores, which also show the class averages (Figure 2).

Student Scores

Name	Ending?	English only?	Good job?	Interesting?	Well-Prepared?	Average
[redacted]	3.8	3.9	3.3	3.5	3.4	3.6
Average	3.9	3.9	3.5	3.8	3.2	3.7
	interesting Very clear speech. I like love romance too!! love is interesting I like love story. love story is good I want to read this book I want to try to read.					

Figure 2. Individual score report

2.1.1 Student Attitudes towards the PeerEval App

To informally measure student attitudes towards PeerEval, a twelve-item questionnaire was created addressing affective, practical, and technical issues (Chen, 2014), and administered to students who had experience with both paper-based and PeerEval peer evaluation procedures. The rubrics for both procedures were similar. The questionnaire was divided into five questions about the PeerEval app itself, three questions comparing paper-based and app-based evaluation from the presenter's point of view, and four questions comparing paper and app-based evaluation from the point of view of the audience. The questionnaire was administered to a total of 39 students, enrolled in four separate classes. In all four classes, the students first gave short presentations and were graded using a paper-based rubric. In the following month, they gave a separate presentation and were evaluated on a similar rubric via PeerEval. Cronbach's alpha for the results was .73, indicating acceptable but weak internal consistency.

Table 1 shows the result of the questionnaire. As for Items 1-5, a 4-point Likert scale was used, 1 being "Agree," and 5 being "Don't agree." As for Items 6-12, a 4-point Likert scale was used, 1 being the strong preference to paper-based evaluation, and 4 being strong preference to the app-based evaluation. In general, students felt that the app was easy to install and use (Items 1-5). They felt that the evaluation system was clear and that the comments and feedback would help them prepare more for subsequent presentations. From the presenters' standpoint, the feedback speed was a major plus, and the ability to quickly read peer comments was viewed as helpful (Items 6-7). From the point of view of the audience, everyone preferred the privacy and feedback speed of the app and felt that the app gave them the feeling that the presentations were more interactive (Item 12). The students also felt that the app allowed them to evaluate more accurately than using paper-based methods (Items 9-11).

Table 1. Questionnaire Results

	Q1	Q2	Q3	Q4	Q5	Q6	Q7	Q8	Q9	Q10	Q11	Q12
Mean	1.76	1.72	1.92	2.00	1.75	3.6	2.96	2.48	3.64	3.48	3.12	2.96
Mode	1	1	1	1	1	4	4	1	4	4	4	3

The preliminary results of comparing PeerEval with paper-based forms of peer evaluation allowed us to consider student preferences. Students generally had a favorable impression of the system, but presenters felt audience members were paying less attention to presentations and more attention to their phones. This preliminary result suggests that rules and/or procedures should be put into place regarding when students are allowed to input their evaluations.

3. CONCLUSION

This paper briefly described a peer assessment mobile app, how it is used in context, and student attitudes towards the use of the app in reference to a paper-based rubric. The results of this preliminary study suggest that PeerEval-generated interaction quality and quantity may be different from asynchronous peer feedback.

Although PeerEval was designed to overcome rating problems with paper and LMS-based forms of peer evaluation, the present study only compared students' perceptions of paper-based and PeerEval peer evaluation procedures, without collecting data about LMS-based peer evaluation. In addition, previous studies have shown a positive effect of training in technology-based peer evaluation (Ho & Savignon, 2007) suggesting that more detailed feedback training will produce more useful, helpful, and relevant comments.

ACKNOWLEDGEMENT

The authors would like to thank the developers of the app.

REFERENCES

Bojinova, E., & Oigara, J., 2011. Teaching and learning with clickers: Are clickers good for students? *Interdisciplinary Journal of E-Learning and Learning Objects, 7,* 169-184. Retrieved from http://www.ijello.org/Volume7/IJELLOv7p169-184Bojinova772.pdf

Bojinova, E., & Oigara, J., 2013. Teaching and learning with clickers in higher education. *International Journal of Teaching and Learning in Higher Education, 25*(2), 154-165. Retrieved from https://files.eric.ed.gov/fulltext/EJ1016407.pdf

Boud, D., Cohen, R., & Sampson, J., 1999. Peer learning and assessment. *Assessment and Evaluation in Higher Education, 24*(4), 413-26. doi:10.1080/0260293990240405

Chen, T., 2014. Technology-supported peer feedback in ESL/ EFL writing classes: a research synthesis, *Computer Assisted Language Learning*, DOI: 10.1080/09588221.2014.960942

Cote, R., 2013. The role of student attitude towards peer review in anonymous electronic peer review in an EFL writing classroom. Unpublished Ph.D. Dissertation Retrieved from http://arizona.openrepository.com/arizona/bitstream/10150/307005/3/azu_etd_13017_sip1_m.pdf

Davies, P., 2000. Computerized peer assessment. *Innovations in Education and Training International, 37*(4), 346-355, doi:10.1080/135580000750052955

Donato, R., 1994. Collective scaffolding in second language learning. In J.P. Lantolf, & G. appel (Eds.), *Vygotskian approaches to second language research* (pp. 3356). Norwood, NJ: Ablex.

Gobel, P. & Kano, M., 2017. The complexities of digital storytelling: Factors affecting performance, production, and project completion. In Issa, T., Issa, T., Kommers, P., Isaias, P., & Issa, T. (Eds.), *Smart technology applications in business environments* (pp. 343-360). Hershey, PA: IGI Global. doi:10.4018/978-1-5225-2492-2

Hansen, J.G., & Liu, J., 2005. Guiding principles for effective peer response. *ELT Journal, 59*(1), 31-39, doi:10.1093/elt/cci004

Ho, M., & Savignon, S.J., 2007. Face-to-face and computer-mediated peer review in EFL writing. *CALICO Journal, 24*(2), 269290.

Kessler, G., & Bikowski, D., 2010. Developing collaborative autonomous learning abilities in computer mediated language learning: Attention to meaning among students in wiki space. *Computer Assisted Language Learning, 23*(1), 4158.

Panadero, E., Romero, M., & Strijbos, J. W., 2013. The impact of a rubric and friendship on peer assessment: Effects on construct validity, performance, and perceptions of fairness and comfort. *Studies in Educational Evaluation, 39*(4), 195-203. doi:10.1016/j.stueduc.2013.10.005

Patri, M., 2002. The influence of peer feedback on self and peer-assessment of oral skills. *Language Testing, 19,* 109-131. doi: 10.1191/0265532202lt224oa

Raes, A., Vanderhoven, E., & Schellens, T., 2015. Increasing anonymity in peer assessment by using classroom response technology within face-to-face higher education. *Studies in Higher Education, 40*(1), 178-193. doi:10.1080/03075079.2013.823930.

Rust, C., Price, M., & O'Donovan, B., 2003. Improving students' learning by developing their understanding of assessment criteria and processes. *Assessment and Evaluation in Higher Education, 28*(2), 147-164. doi:10.1080/02602930301671

Shimura, M., 2006. Peer-and instructor assessment of oral presentations in Japanese university EFL classrooms: A pilot study. *Waseda Global Forum, 3*, 99-107.

Tseng, S. C., & Tsai, C. C., 2010. Taiwan college students' self-efficacy and motivation of learning in online peer assessment environments. *The Internet and Higher Education, 13*(3), 164-169. Retrieved from https://www.learntechlib.org/p/108386/.

COMPLEX GAMIFICATION PLATFORM BASED ON MOODLE SYSTEM

Balázs Barna and Szabina Fodor[1]
[1]Dr., PhD
Corvinus University of Budapest, Hungary

ABSTRACT

Using an e-learning system as an educational tool has become a common practice among university courses. A well-structured e-learning system can not only support the course as a storage place of materials but can help the students to learn the given subjects. The Moodle (Modular Object-Oriented Dynamic Learning Environment) e-learning environment provides a wide scale of possibilities to create a student-centered, highly manageable course interface. The tool is given; however, the motivation of students is rarely satisfying. Tough the success of a course mostly depends on the teaching materials, using gamification principles can enhance the motivation level of students. The aim of this paper is to propose a structure built up from the core elements of Moodle, existing plugins and suggested developments, which could provide a properly gamified Moodle course that fosters the students to gain motivation for learning better.

KEYWORDS

Gamification, Education, e-Learning Platform

1. GAMIFICATION: MOTIVATIONAL TECHNOLOGY

For people, learning is a vital ability. Pastor-Pina et al (Pastor-Pina et al, 2015) point out that teachers can create an environment that supports learning, but the learner needs an active role to succeed. Student motivation and commitment are key factors in the learning process.

The gamification (which is the use of game design elements in non-game context (Deterding et al, 2011) combines a certain progress (e.g. work, study) with reward-based design aspects of games to create a product that is enjoyable and motivating as well as productive and efficient (O'Donovan, 2012).

Nacke and Deterding wrote (Nacke and Deterding, 2017) that several companies and design agencies offer gamification design or software-as-a-service (SaaS) packages, and organizations across the globe began exploring gamification to motivate people and improve the user experience. These applications vary between education, training, health, innovation, employee engagement, marketing etc. (Seaborn and Fels, 2015)

Most gamified systems can be built using the following components (Werbach and Hunter, 2012), (Hunicke et al, 2004):

- **Game elements**: these are the specific elements that the user is already facing when using the game for the first time: collect points, work in team, do some personalization, or perform missions;
- **Game mechanisms**: they describe how each game element interacts with each other and how the individual steps and states of the user are determined. It also includes guidelines to determine the progress of the game, as well as the expected reactions to an event;
- **Game dynamics**: these are the behavior of players and their interrelationship triggered by game elements and mechanisms. Dynamics are influenced by the nature and experience of the user. A risk-averse, inward-looking player has a different behavioral pattern than a user who is looking for particularly risky situations;
- **Fun**: adds the more or less entertaining factor to the application.

In order to create an effective game or game-like application, it must be motivating and addictive as well as providing encouragement to reach short-term goals, meanwhile it maintains the option for making a mistake or fail, along with retrying as long as the user finally succeeds (O'Donovan et al, 2013).

Considering the source of motivation, there can be intrinsic and extrinsic types from it. Intrinsic motivated users choose and do activities just by curiosity or by their own will. This kind of users are ready to make a significant mental effort during a task, and to use deeper and more effective learning strategies. On the other hand, extrinsic motivated users are only committed to activities when they are externally rewarded (such as getting good marks or avoiding failure). Generally, extrinsic motivation is easier to be created and be managed than intrinsic motivation. (Pastor-Pina et al, 2015) Idealistically, the main goal of using extrinsic motivation solutions is to turn them into intrinsic motivation within the users.

2. RELATED WORK

Several researches deal with the issue of enhancing and examining a course built up with e-learning system.

Researchers from Kaunas University of Technology (Jurgelaitis et al, 2018) created a course of 'gamified UML and system design' in Moodle environment using the core elements and a few plugins. As a result, they could report that the students are satisfied with the course, find it useful and they enjoyed the course itself.

Members of University of Alicante made a research (Pastor-Pina et al, 2015) which aim was to analyze the suitability of Moodle to implement structurally gamified teaching proposals in it. The authors stated the environment is 'not quite friendly' to help teachers to use game-elements in their courses. Tough the visual appearance of gamification can be considered as poor, a strong logical system (mainly based on conditions of accessibility of contents) can be used to create different learning paths for students.

In 2015 at Corvinus University of Budapest, an IT course has been rebased into a blended form using the Moodle supporting with gamification components, like points, badges and levels as a reward system, alternative learning paths for different style of learning methods, feedbacks and social interactions. As a result, higher participation rate could be achieved during the semester, and the students valued the gained knowledge more than those who learnt the course in a non-gamified environment. Besides the positive results, the research points out to some restrictions and lack of student-level personalization in Moodle. (Barna and Fodor, 2018).

3. MOODLE: THE GAMIFICATION PLATFORM

Common strategy for gamifying an educational course is to migrate to an e-learning environment as a first step and introduce gamification elements as a second step (Jurgelaitis et al, 2018).

Moodle is one of the most used open source learning management systems nowadays, and it is quite popular among teachers because it is free and, they can create their own online courses very easily (Pastor-Pina et al, 2015). The platform provides comprehensive logs about activities done by users on sites, tasks or the course itself (Moodle, 2016), however the satisfaction and motivation cannot be found out from these data.

3.1 Existing Elements

In the examined e-learning system several elements and plugins can be. Some of the Moodle's core elements can be useful from the aspect of gamification, such as setting restrictions for accessing documents, parts of a page or tasks. With tracking the completion and restricting the accessibility of activities, different levels can be defined, maps can be set up to explore the content of the course, or even Easter eggs can be hidden. For completing special achievements, badges and titles can be given to the users. With using grade book, the users of Moodle can check their grades and points, which can be handled as a feedback of their progress. Online social interactions can be fostered with forums and chats, and the teachers can measure the knowledge level of students with quizzes, assignments, lessons, workshops or surveys.

The list of gamification related plugins include a module that facilitates progress with a visualized levelling-up, asks back a question bank in the form of a miniature game, makes video materials interactive, implements inventory for students, and has a module that introduces a virtual currency into the course. (Moodle, 2019)

These plugins contain mostly gamification elements, thus – as mentioned in Chapter 1.1 – an effective gamified application should consist not only gamification elements, but mechanics and game-dynamics as well.

3.2 Proposed Solution

Moodle is capable of implementing various gamification elements and partial solutions to a course maker, but it does not help to follow the principles of gamification for the whole course at system level.

By combining the current plugins, the personalized auditing and motivation cannot be realized. Due to the various kinds of users, different motivation ways are needed for them. Motivation may include smaller challenges (e.g. "Practice with tests 5 days in a row for +3 points!"), displaying the progress of student, customizing the graphical interface to allow the user (with limited freedom) to change the appearance of the system (theme of design, theme of levels, etc.).

In this paper, the examined features and functions are separated by their purposes into four categories:

1) serving the main goal (learn and develop)
2) fostering the use of service (exploring)
3) providing social connections and interactions
4) enhancing the feel of personalization

The following list shows the **Core elements**, the ***Existing plugins***, and the suggested ***Additional plugins*** and improvements **(+)**.

Motivated learning by developing and recognition:

- The main function of an e-learning system is to provide **Knowledge materials** of a specific topic in a more or less structured way. Using a **Content Map** helps the students to overlook the amount and connections of the required materials. Even with an existing plugin, these materials can be enhanced into ***Interactive materials*** (e.g. attached multimedia, checking quiz whether the student understands the given knowledge or not).
- The Moodle system provides several kinds of **Tasks** which can measure the knowledge level of a student. Using ***Mini Games(+)*** as a way of practicing can make the course more interesting, but they can make the course light-minded if they are overused or they do not fit into the topic.
- With completing the tasks, the students can earn **Points**; with their accumulating points, they can achieve higher ***Levels(+)*** and better final **Grades**.
- Beside finishing a task or fill out a test, additional ***Rewards(+)*** can be set which can be used to foster proper preparation of a student, or recognize the student's learning progress (e.g. giving new color-schema). The final ***Goal*** of a course is achieving a high grade, but ***Minor goals*** should be set as well. If the course is separated into several parts, the sub-goals can be the completion of them. In order to inform the student, ***Progress Bar*** can be used to show the current completion state of the selected (minor) goal.

Motivated learning by engaging and exploring:

- Moodle allows to create **Knowledge materials** as lessons, sub-pages, contents by default. With the help of **Access management**, parts of the material-collections can be restricted to certain conditions (which depend on the actions of a student), such as completing a **Task**, or collecting a preset amount of **Points**.
- In order to motivate students to do (or at least check) several not mandatory tasks, assignments or tests, ***Challenges*** can be set up or **Badges**(+) can be given (e.g. for visiting all tasks).
- For those who are keen on exploring as much details of the site as possible, collectable **Easter Eggs(+)** can be hidden, therefore they have the urge to visit every part of the course.

Motivated learning by social connections and interactions:

- Social interactions take an important role in gamification. The Moodle provides possibilities to use **Forum** and **Chat** for sharing information between users.
- Assignments that requires **Teamwork** can also be attached to a course by default.
- Two-way communication between students and teachers is not well-supported by the core functions, but with the possibility to give ***Feedback to teachers***, the students could ***Rate*** the tasks and materials.

Motivated learning by personalization:

- The Moodle cannot give opportunity for user-level ***Personalization*** within a course, the established environment is valid for every student. With giving the opportunity for changing the appearance of the interface (e.g. color-schema, ***Theme*** of levels) to users, it can give them the feel of personalization.

- Based on the activated materials and completed tasks, ***Personalized test*** can be created automatically for the students that helps to maintain and improve their knowledge.

There are some highly gamified components that can be hardly applied in Moodle due to the visual structure of interface or due to the nature of teaching, such as storytelling, using different emotions, or forcing a leaderboard on students.

4. CONCLUSIONS AND FURTHER WORK

The use of e-learning systems takes significant role in university education. Besides providing technical environment, the urge to use them by students must be fostered as well. For this purpose, the authors suggest applying gamification principals, therefore the motivation for learning can be enhanced.

In this paper the Moodle e-learning environment has been examined in order to find out how well it is appropriate for gamifying a course with it. After examining the existing parts of Moodle, a proposed solution has been described which combinates the core elements of Moodle, the already created plugins for it and some suggested developments. The proposed concepts are aligned by how they can foster the motivated learning: by developing and recognition, by exploring, by social interactions and by personalization. The course creators can decide which of the mentioned flows and concepts they can apply for their course, and which part of the concepts should be developed.

As for further work, the authors plan to develop some of the not yet existing plugins (Sub-goals and Progress Bar), apply them in a course, and examine their effect.

ACKNOWLEDGEMENT

This article has been supported by the ÚNKP-18-3 New National Excellence Program of the Hungarian Ministry of Human Capacities.

REFERENCES

Barna, B. and Fodor, Sz., 2018. An Empirical Study on the Use of Gamification on IT Courses at Higher Education. In: *Teaching and Learning in a Digital World. ICL 2017. Advances in Intelligent Systems and Computing*. Vol 715. Springer, Cham

Deterding, S. et al, 2011. From Game Design Elements to Gamefulness: Defining "Gamification", *MindTrek '11 Procee-dings of the 15th International Academic MindTrek Conference: Envisioning Future Media Environments*, pp. 9-15.

Hunicke, R. et al, 2004. MDA: A Formal Approach to Game Design and Game Research. *Nineteenth National Conference on Artificial Intelligence*, http://www.cs.northwestern.edu/~hunicke/MDA.pdf

Jurgelaitis, M. et al, 2018. Gamified Moodle Course for Teaching UML. *Baltic J. Modern Computing*, Vol. 6(2), pp. 119-127, at: https://doi.org/10.22364/bjmc.2018.6.2.03

Moodle, 2016. Logs, at: https://docs.moodle.org/37/en/Logs, accessed: 2019. 06. 20.

Moodle, 2019. Gamification – A list of plugins that brings some aspects of gamification to Moodle courses., at: https://moodle.org/plugins/browse.php?list=set&id=88, accessed: 2019. 05. 30.

Nacke, L. E. and Deterding, S., 2017. The maturing of gamification research. *Computers in Human Behavior*, White Rose University Consortium, at: http://dx.doi.org/10.1016/j.chb.2016.11.062

O'Donovan, S., 2012. Gamification of the Games Course, at: http://pubs.cs.uct.ac.za/archive/00000771/01/ Gamification_of_the_Games_Course, accessed: 2019.01.11.

O'Donovan, S., Gain, J., Marais, P., 2013. A case study in the gamification of a university-level games development course, pp. 242, at: http://dl.acm.org/citation.cfm?id=2513456.2513469

Pastor-Pina, H. et al, 2015. Can Moodle be used for structural gamification? *INTED2015 Proceedings*, pp. 1014-1021, at: https://www.sun.ac.za/english/learning-teaching/ctl/Documents/Can moodle be used for structural gamification.pdf

Seaborn, K., and Fels, D. I., 2015. Gamification in theory and action: A survey. *International Journal of Human-Computer Studies*, Vol. 74(2), pp 14–31. at: http://doi.org/10.1016/j.ijhcs.2014.09.006

Werbach, K. and Hunter, D., 2012. *For The Win. How Game Thinking Can Revolutionize Your Business*. Wharton Digital

GOAL TREES AS STRUCTURING ELEMENT IN A DIGITAL DATA-DRIVEN STUDY ASSISTANT

Felix Weber
Osnabrück University, Germany

ABSTRACT

The Future Skills Report about the future of learning and higher Education (Ehlers & Kellermann, 2019) defines a variety of skills in which the active learner plays a central role. Starting from this perspective, our idea is to promote future skills with a digital data-driven study assistant for. As a theoretical foundation research about constructivism, self-regulation and goal-setting is reviewed and the concept of Goal Trees as structuring element of a software is derived. On a psychological level we show how Goal Trees may increase motivation and simplify study planning. On the level of user interface design, we show how Goal Trees may be used as structuring element of a digital data-driven study assistant. Consequently we outline how functionalities derived from research about goal-setting and self-regulation can be implemented in a study assistant. Finally advantages and challenges of implementing such a system are discussed.

KEYWORDS

Goal Trees, Goal Setting, E-Learning, Digital Assistant, Self-Regulation, Higher Education

1. THEORETICAL BACKGROUND

Ehlers and Kellermann (Ehlers & Kellermann, 2019) define "future skills" as the "ability to act successful on a complex problem in a future unknown context of action". As future skills related to the learners themselves and their individual development the authors identify autonomy, self-initiative, self-management, need or motivation for achievement, personal agility, autonomous learning competence and self-efficacy. The authors predict a change in higher education towards "active learning and autonomy" and a trend towards personalized curricula. Such learning conditions challenge the learner to set individual learning goals, maintain and pursue them and self-regulate their behavior based on success or failure in goal achievement.

In face of such a definition of crucial skills for the future, constructivism, a view which is around since decades, seems to be highly relevant again. Loyens and Gijbels (Loyens & Gijbels, 2008) state the core assumption of constructivism: Knowledge is constructed by an active learner. They further characterize the process of knowledge generation as "active sense-making and knowledge construction" (Gijbels & Loyens, 2009). We assume that personal interest and commitment to an education goal form a more solid foundation for active sense-making and knowledge construction than commitment by curricular obligations. Personal interest and commitment cannot be prescribed but instead must originate in the learner. Therefore, individually meaningful learning goals should be the roots of education.

Others have found that today, students entering the higher education system may often even not be able to name their personal education goals (Olos, Hoff, & Härtwig, 2014). This may originate from the fact that throughout elementary, middle, and high school students still often do not have many choices concerning learning content. Ex-cathedra teaching and other formats limiting exploratory learning are still very common. Thus, there is still a huge gap between ideal and reality of the educational system. The question arises how university students can be supported, such that autonomy, self-management and self-efficacy are increased. We propose a digital study-assistant as a tool to accompany university students in developing these skills.

The concept of self-regulated learning is explainable from different theoretical perspectives and has a self-oriented feedback loop as central feature (Zimmerman, 1989). In this loop, the learner actively develops and applies learning methods and strategies and monitors this process, the application of those and the effectiveness in terms of goal-achievement. The question arises, how the self-regulatory feedback loop can be realized in a learning software. We assume, that actively formulating learning methods, strategies and specific actions and the corresponding specific learning goal are the first half of the loop. The second half, namely a reflective process arises when goal and strategies are evaluated. We propose Goal Trees as a structuring element for the self-regulation feedback loop in our study assistant.

Goal Setting Theory by Locke and Latham has been developed since 1975. It led to knowledge about the relationship between goal setting and performance. (Locke & Latham, 1990, 1991) The underlying mechanisms of successful goal-setting according to Locke and Latham (Locke & Latham, 2002) are:

1. the direction of attention and effort towards goal-relevant actions
2. the mobilization of resources and effort for goal-relevant actions
3. the maintenance of goals over time support enduring goal striving
4. goal-directed actions as a consequence of task-relevant knowledge and strategies

Morisano and her co-workers have established a goal setting program for the context of academic learning which was evaluated with "struggling" students at McGill University in Montreal, Canada. The software-based goal setting program led to a significant increase in General Point Average (GPA) reduced negative affect, increase in self-efficacy (Morisano, Hirsh, Peterson, Pihl, & Shore, 2010). This research show that a software built on the foundation of goal-setting research has the potential to increase not only study success measured in grades, but also lead to beneficial effects on affect and self-efficacy.

The literature on goal setting makes a distinction between proximal and distal goals (Latham & Brown, 2006) which differ in their effects on performance, motivation, activity and self-efficacy. Latham and Brown (Latham & Brown, 2006) have shown that challenging distal outcome goals may be discouraging and decrease perceived self-efficacy if they are not combined with proximal learning goals. They also showed that distal outcome goals in combination with proximal goals lead to a higher GPA than distal goals alone (Latham & Brown, 2006). Using abstract distal goals, Storch and Krause (Storch & Krause, 2007) have developed a goal setting program called the "Züricher Ressourcen Modell" (Zurich Ressource Model, ZRM) in which they use abstract distal goals they call "Motto-Goals". This kind of goals has been shown to increase motivation and activity (Storch & Krause, 2007). Using proximal goals, Doran (Doran, 1981) suggests that goals which are specific, measurable, achievable, realistic and time-related are more realizable than abstract goals. According to these attributes he calls such goals "S.M.A.R.T.". It will be shown how the advantages of distal and proximal may be combined by Goal Trees.

2. THE CONCEPT OF GOAL TREES

The main research question or our research is: How can findings from former research on constructivism, goal-setting, self-regulation and self-monitoring be applied in a digital data-driven study assistance software?

Our central idea is to represent goal systems as "Goal Trees" in a software to assist University Students in the acquisition of future skills. We define Goal Trees as tree-shaped directed graphs originating in one root goal, splitting up into branch-like sub-goals until the branches terminate in leaf-like goals. The leaves are in the best case proximal goals which are specific, measurable, achievable, realistic and time-related. So the resulting network of goals has a tree-shaped structure with one goal as its root, several layers of intermediate sub-goals as branches and finally actions or S.M.A.R.T. goals as its leaves.

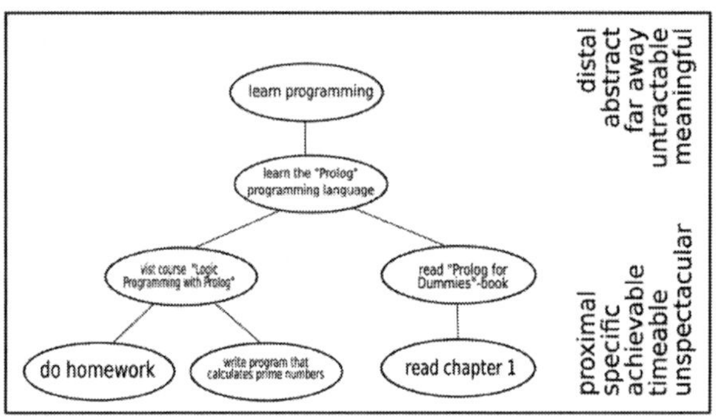

Figure 1. A practical example

A practical example (figure 1): Imagine, a student has the goal to learn the programming, which is an abstract distal goal. A sub-goal may be to master the programming language Prolog. The student may formulate the further sub-sub-goal to take the university class "Introduction to Logic Programming in Prolog", the sub-sub-goal to work through the book "Prolog for Dummies". These sub-sub-goals may be further split until actions, such as "do the homework" or "read chapter 3" result. The border between goals and actions is fluent and a question of granularity.

2.1 Advantages on the Conceptual Level

From a conceptual perspective the benefits of such Goal Trees are numerous:

- On the root level they contain distal goals of personal relevance which may lead to an increase in motivation and activity.
- The possibility to define inspiring root goals, with high personal relevance without yet knowing how to specify them, may empower students to select meaningful education goals.
- The tractability of distal goals is increased by splitting up into intermediate goals and concrete actions.
- Proximal goals may gain personal relevance because of their connection to inspiring distal goals.
- In case of conflicting actions under constraints a prioritizing according to the importance of the underlying distal goals is straight-forward.
- Action sequences can be derived by browsing the leaf level of goal trees.
- Revision of goal trees allow self-regulation by reflecting which actions/strategies led to goal achievement and which did not.
- Mechanisms from Goal Setting Theory are supported as goal maintenance is given and generation of new sub-goals and actions implement the direction of attention and strategies.

2.2 From Theory to Practical Implications for the Graphical User Interface

On the user interface level, Goal Trees (with zoom functions to increase focus) may be used as central structuring element. Consistently with constructivist learning theories, the students actively construct their individual Goal Trees, each originating in a meaningful individual root goal, such as "learn programming". The metaphor of a tree is fruitful because it reflects the growing, ongoing process of goal generation. During the ongoing iterative construction process, the study assistant may assist with hints, questions and dialogues. The following interactions are based on Locke's & Latham's goal mechanisms (Locke & Latham, 2002):

- When the student creates new goals, a dialog will ask him or her to generate concrete actions. This is a direct implementation of the goal mechanism of directing attention and effort to goal-relevant activities.
- When the student creates an action, the study assistant will ask him or her to mobilize times for the action which is a direct implementation of the goal mechanism of mobilizing time and resources for goal-relevant activities.
- The study assistant will store Goal Trees persistently and regularly remind the student to review and extend them. This is a direct implementation of the goal mechanism of goal persistence.

The following interactions are based on the goal setting program by (Morisano, 2008):

- The study assistant may ask students to define inspiring individual study goals for the distant future.
- If students have difficulties to define individual study goals, the assistant may ask them to elaborate on their ideal future, qualities admired in others, things to do better, career in the future, things to learn about and habits to be improved.
- To increase goal commitment and motivation for specific goals, the study assistant may ask the users to elaborate on impacts of the goal if achieved.
- If students have difficulties to generate sub-goals and actions, the assistant may ask them to elaborate on goal attainment, sub-goals, strategies and concrete plans and actions.
- To support goal achievement, the study assistant may ask students for potential obstacles and possible ways to overcome them for specific goals.
- To support students in self-regulation, the study assistant may ask students to define benchmarks of success for specific study goals. If due dates are mentioned in the definition, the study assistant may send reminders.
- The study assistant may ask students to rank the root goals of their Goal Trees in an order. This allows for prioritization of possibly conflicting actions.

To assist in self-regulation, the study assistant may regularly remind the student to review the Goal Trees. This is a technical implementation on self-monitoring. During review of Goal Trees, students may actively

- evaluate success or failure of applied actions / strategies
- monitor themselves whether they invested time and resources according to the Goal Tree or not
- derive new sub-goals and actions (methods, strategies and behaviors in terms of self-regulated learning)

  An important aspect for self-monitoring is critical review of strategies that failed. For this purpose it will not be possible to simply delete goals in the review process. Rather the software will encourage students to reflect why a goal could not be reached or why it does not make sense anymore. This persistence of goals may lead to meta-cognitive learning processes.

3. CONCLUSION

Goal Trees are a contribution which may serve as foundation for a graphical user interface for a study assistant that has the potential to empower students to realize, maintain and pursue meaningful education goals. At the same time, such a study assistant may convey important meta-cognitive skills.

One crucial limitation is the usage of the study assistant. A software can only be as effective as its users are motivated and consequently invest time and effort. As there is a broad variety of software available to university students, it will be a major challenge to convince students to regularly use another software. Goal attainment itself may be perceived as rewarding and our study assistant can even increase this effect by gamification and (self-set) rewards.

The potential of a goal setting tool for higher education is to empower students to think about individual inspiring education goals, to develop self-regulation abilities and increase self-efficacy. In a constructivist sense such a study assistant may help to implement a shift from curricular-driven learning for exams to interest-driven learning for life.

REFERENCES

Doran, G. T. (1981). There's a S.M.A.R.T way to write management's goals and objectives. *Management Review*, *70*(11), 35–36.

Ehlers, U.-D., & Kellermann, S. A. (2019). *Future Skills - The future of learning and higher education*. Karlsruhe.

Gijbels, D., & Loyens, S. M. M. (2009). Constructivist learning (environments) and how to avoid another tower of Babel: Reply to Renkl. *Instructional Science*, *37*(5), 499–502. https://doi.org/10.1007/s11251-009-9100-2

Latham, G. P., & Brown, T. C. (2006). The Effect of Learning vs. Outcome Goals on Self-Efficacy, Satisfaction and Performance in an MBA Program. *Applied Psychology*, *55*(4), 606–623. https://doi.org/10.1111/j.1464-0597.2006.00246.x

Latham, G. P., & Locke, E. A. (1991). Self-regulation through goal setting. *Organizational Behavior and Human Decision Processes*, *50*(2), 212–247. https://doi.org/10.1016/0749-5978(91)90021-K

Locke, E. A., & Latham, G. P. (1990). *A theory of goal setting and task performance*. Englewood Cliffs, NJ, USA: Prentice Hall.

Locke, E. A., & Latham, G. P. (2002). Building a practically useful theory of goal setting and task motivation: A 35-year odyssey. *American Psychologist*, *57*(9), 705–717. https://doi.org/10.1037/0003-066X.57.9.705

Loyens, S. M. M., & Gijbels, D. (2008). Understanding the effects of constructivist learning environments: Introducing a multi-directional approach. *Instructional Science*, *36*, 351–357. https://doi.org/10.1007/s11251-008-9059-4

Morisano, D. (2008). *Personal Goal Setting in University Students: Effects on Academic Achievement, Executive Functioning, Personality, and Mood*. McGill University, Montreal.

Morisano, D., Hirsh, J. B., Peterson, J. B., Pihl, R. O., & Shore, B. M. (2010). Setting, elaborating, and reflecting on personal goals improves academic performance. *Journal of Applied Psychology*, *95*(2), 255–264. https://doi.org/10.1037/a0018478

Olos, L., Hoff, E.-H., & Härtwig, C. (2014). *Berufliche Zielklärung und Selbststeuerung*. (L. Olos, E.-H. Hoff, & C. Härtwig, Eds.). Wiesbaden: Springer Fachmedien Wiesbaden. https://doi.org/10.1007/978-3-658-03650-8

Storch, M., & Krause, F. (2007). *Selbstmanagement - ressourcenorientiert. Grundlagen und Trainingsmanual für die Arbeit mit dem Zürcher Ressourcen Modell (ZRM). Zürcher Ressourcenmodell ZRM.*

Zimmerman, B. J. (1989). Models of Self-Regulated Learning and Academic Achievement (pp. 1–25). https://doi.org/10.1007/978-1-4612-3618-4_1

CASE STUDY OF TEACHER'S ON GOING COGNITION USING VR

Takashi Ikuta[1], Yasushi Gotoh[2] and Wataru Uchiyama[3]
[1]*Gifu Women's University*
80, Taromaru, Gifu City, Gifu, Japan
[2]*Niigata University*
8050, Ikarashi 2no-cho, Nishi ward, Niigata City, Niigata, Japan
[3]*Niigata Sogo gakuen*
494-3, Higashibori-dori, Chuo ward, Niigata City, Niigata, Japan

ABSTRACT

Teacher cognition in classroom lessons is identified by an ongoing method using virtual reality (VR) videos. There are place and time constraints in real time implementation of the ongoing method in synchronous situations. To avoid these, recorded virtual reality videos were used. As a result, the existence of non-corresponding cognition was recognized: teacher educators focused on teaching strategy, while teachers focused on children's individual reactions.

KEYWORDS

360° Camera, Teaching Skill, Lesson Cognition, Lesson Research, Ongoing Method

1. PURPOSE OF RESEARCH

Dewey (1933) discusses reflection, in a pedagogical context, as the essence of teachers' thinking. Schöne (1983) and Schavelson (1973) also argue from the teacher's classroom teaching context. There are two methods for grasping teachers' reflections :"reflection on action" which considers teachers' reflections after the class and "reflection in action" which considers their reflections in real time during classroom teaching. Since the former does not enable reflection to be grasped during the actual class, real time reflection is especially important and for this the latter i.e. "reflection in action" must be studied.

In specialist field techniques, there are those which can be transmitted using explicit knowledge and those where latent knowledge is involved. In teacher development, reflection in action including latent knowledge is important and an issue in teacher education. In teacher education although there is research (Walshe and Driver, 2019) into using video recordings for teacher training, there are few practical studies focusing on this issue as it concerns teachers' cognition. In this study the authors propose the ongoing method (OGM) with VR recorded video as a tool for understanding teachers' "reflection in action."

2. METHOD

2.1 OGM

OGM is a method that enables us to understand lesson cognition in the classroom in real time (Ikuta, 1999). In this study the authors define lesson cognition as the cognition of the decision-making process. Teachers regard a teaching event as consisting of cognition, judgment and action. The OGM method involves a process in which

1. Observers express vocally and record their cognition of the classroom lesson process in real time.

2. After the lesson, the utterances of the observers are recorded synchronously with the classroom events and their personal interpretation is described.
3. The cognition of the observers is compared and analyzed and the teachers's cognition and reflection are described.

OGM makes it possible to compare and discuss for the same lesson the real time lesson cognitions of multiple observers.

In OGM, teaching events in which multiple observers participate are divided into "cognition of different teaching events' and cognition of same teaching event." Since observers' cognitions may differ even if they are watching the same event, the features of the cognition can be clarified by dividing cognition of the same teaching event into corresponding cognition where the object and contents of the cognition are the same, and non-corresponding cognition where the contents are different. In cognition of different teaching events, the object of the observers' cognition is itself different.

OGM using video recordings means that observers can freely select place and time, but their main advantage lies in the selectivity of the field of view. In this case, a VR video was watched and utterances made according to an ongoing protocol with the objective of synchronous understanding and comparing of VR screens. This is a new method of classroom observation in which multiple observers freely record, analyze and compare their own cognition with that of other people under asynchronous conditions,

On the other hand, although courses from scenarios do exist for teacher training using VR, virtually no research uses the present approach.

2.2 Classroom Lesson VR and Participating Observers

The VR lesson scenario used was arithmetic (round numbers) 54 minute lesson at J elementary school Year 4. Two persons, a teacher educator and a teacher were present. The observer put on a VR head set, observed the lesson and recorded utterances by ongoing process (OGP). The date was November 2017. The field of view in the VR and the OGP were synchronously recorded and played back and the lesson protocol and utterances synthesized into a new scenario to be used as basic data.

3. RESULTS

3.1 Corresponding Cognition and Non-Corresponding Cognitions (OGP in Classroom Process)

The teacher educator made 51 utterances and the teacher 135. The classroom lesson was divided into introduction, main content and summary. Teaching-learning events were classed from A to M. Viewers cognitions in relation to each event were sorted into corresponding cognition and non-corresponding cognition (Table 1).

As shown in Table 1, introduction events A and B were non-corresponding cognition, and while non-corresponding cognition was intermingled in the main content stage, mid-level main content events G, H and I were continuously non-corresponding cognition. Hence there were differences in observers' cognition in relation to the main content which is the intermediate heart of the lesson.

Table 1. Viewers cognitions in relation to each event

Lesson Process	Teaching-learning event	Cognition of same teaching event	
		Corresponding cognition	Non-corresponding cognition
Introduction	A		○
	B		○
Main content	C	○	
	D		○
	E		○
	F	○	
	G		○
	H		○
	I		○
	J	○	
	K	○	
	L		○
Summary	M	○	

3.2 Changes in Number of Utterances Depending on Teaching-Learning Event

The number of utterances per teaching-learning event is shown in figure 1. There were no radical differences in overall trend between the observers. As shown in the ratio for each teaching-event in relation to total number of individual utterances, the difference in frequency ratio between the two observers is large in introduction event A, main content events F, G and J and summary event M. There was non-corresponding cognition for G and J in events where the difference was large.

Looking at non-corresponding cognition in event G, the teacher educator predicted from an early stage that since the first step of dealing with round numbers was insufficiently understood, this lack of understanding would affect the second step of estimation and pointed this out as a structural guidance issue. The teacher educator consistently saw the basic guidance framework as a problem.

Teacher educator's OGPs are as follows.

- "It looks as though the children add up the whole 3000 yen to see whether they have enough money or not. This means that the first step, which should be to understand round numbers, can't be used to learn about approximate estimations."
- "The fact that for the first step we have not consolidated former learning task has an impact."
- "Here we see that most children add up all the numbers. Clearly, they are not making an estimation."

On the other hand, the teacher was interested in what the children were thinking at various times, pointing out the link between ambiguity in the intention of the teacher's questions and children's understanding. The teacher focused on each child's individual understanding.

Teacher's OGPs are as follows.

- "In the question, "Will it all be enough?" what are the children thinking?"
- "Are children able to understand words and formulae?"
- "The child ends up not knowing what to do."

In the summary stage, although the number of statements of both participants varied greatly, both pointed out the fact that the notion of approximate estimation was not well understood by the children (corresponding cognition).

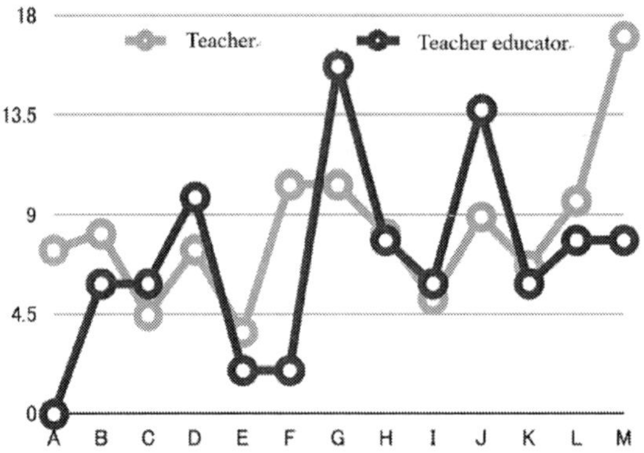

Figure 1. The number of utterances per teaching-learning event

4. DISCUSSION AND SUGGESTIONS

In these above case studies,

1) OGM with VR recorded video enables us to grasp observers' reflections in action and show that real time cognition and reflection are different.

2) These findings can provide clues about future teacher training methods because in classroom study, what participants see, their judgments and reflections, are important elements.

Looking at students and novice teachers, it becomes possible to create a method which studies classroom lesson techniques with VR images where young people compare their cognition with the cognition of experienced teachers and use differences as a clue.

3) Asynchronous teacher training with VR recorded video can be carried out in a form that is very close to real time classroom participation (Ikuta, et al., 2018) so that the immersion experience can be re-experienced thanks to VR and contribute to teacher development by its intermediary function in relation to the classroom.

ACKNOWLEDGEMENT

This work was supported by JSPS KAKENHI Grant Number 18H01061 and 19H01712.

REFERENCES

Dewy, J. 1933. *How we think: A restatement of the relation of reflective thinking to the educative process.* Heath and Company, New York, USA.

Ikuta, T. 1999. "*Jugyo wo Tennkaisuru Chikara*", in Asada. et (ed.) *Seicho suru Kyoshi,* Kaneko Shobou, Tokyo, Japan, pp. 42-54. (In Japanese)

Ikuta, T. & Uchiyama, Y. 2018. 360° camera niyoru Jugyokiroku no katuyou to igi. *Technical report of Gifi women's University Digital archive institute*. Vol. 3, No. 2, pp. 29-34. (In Japanese)

Shavelson, R.J. 1973. *The basic teaching skill: Decision making Research and Memorandum.*104. Stanford Center for Research and Development in teaching.

Schöne, D. 1983. *The Reflective Practitioner: How Professionals Think in Action.* Basic Books, New York, USA.

Theelen, H., Beemt, A. & Brok, P. 2019. Using 360-degree videos in teacher education to improve preservice teacher's professional interpersonal vision. *Journal of Computer Assisted Learning.* 2019, pp. 1-9.

Reyna J. 2018. The Potential of 360-Degree Videos for Teaching, Learning and Research, *Proceedings of INTED2018 Conference 5th-7th March 2018.* Valencia, Spain, pp. 1448-1454.

Walshe, N. & Driver, P. 2019. Developing reflective trainee teacher practice with 360-degree video. *Teaching and Teacher Education: An International Journal of Research and Studies,* Vol. 78, No. 1, pp 97-105.

EXAMINING THE IMPACT OF ONLINE CASE-BASED DISCUSSIONS ON STUDENTS' PERCEIVED COGNITIVE PRESENCE, LEARNING AND SATISFACTION

Ayesha Sadaf and Stella Kim
University of North Carolina Charlotte,
9201 University City Blvd, Charlotte, NC 28223, USA

ABSTRACT

This study examined the impact of case-based discussions on students perceived cognitive presence, learning and satisfaction in online courses. Forty-four online graduate students enrolled in an instructional design course completed an online survey. The quantitative data were analyzed using descriptive statistics and a paired-samples t-test. Qualitative data obtained from the open-ended survey responses were analyzed using constant comparative approach. The findings revealed that case-based discussions lead to high levels of cognitive presence–Triggering, integration, and resolution–than non-case-based discussion. In addition, students have a higher level of perceived satisfaction in case-based discussion than non-case-based discussions.

KEYWORDS

Cognitive Presence, Case-Based Discussions, Online Courses, Online Learning

1. INTRODUCTION

The importance of cognitive presence to generate higher-level learning in online environments has been widely reported in literature (Garrison, Anderson, & Archer 2001; Rourke & Kanuka 2009; Sadaf & Olesova, 2017). Garrison, Anderson, and Archer (2001) defined cognitive presence as "the extent to which learners are able to construct and confirm meaning through sustained reflection and discourse in a critical community of inquiry" (11). The concept of cognitive presence emerged from the Community of Inquiry (CoI) framework to guide the use of online learning environments in support of social constructivist approach to learning. Case studies hold great potential for facilitate constructivist learning through social interactions in online courses. However, little is known about online case-based discussions and their impact on cognitive presence and student learning in online courses. Therefore, the purpose of this study is to implement case-based discussions and evaluate its impact on students' cognitive presence, perceived learning and satisfaction in online courses. A quantitative research method was used for the evaluation and qualitative data were used to further explain the findings obtained from the quantitative data. The results of this study will enhance the quality of teaching and learning strategies used in online courses and provide guidelines for instructors looking to enhance cognitive presence in their online courses using online case-based discussions.

2. LITERATURE REVIEW

Given the recent rapid growth of online education, identifying "best practices" for facilitating student learning in online environments has gained considerable interest (Nistor & Neubauer, 2010). Studies have reported the effectiveness of online discussions, specifically, case-based discussions to improve student learning (Ertmer & Koehler, 2014; Sadaf & Olesova, 2017). Case-based discussions are the type of discussion that can introduce students to real-world scenarios where they can exchange opinions and interact with each other to find solutions to the problem in the case. On the other hand, non-case-based or conventional discussion are defined as posting of a question about a particular topic of discussion and asking student to respond in the context of the course (Darabi, Liang, Suryavanshi, & Yureki, 2013).

Case-based discussions introduce students to diverse perspectives and enrich the learning experience by promoting understanding, reflection, elaboration, and clarification (Ertmer & Stepich, 2002; Yew & Schmidt, 2012). During case-based instruction, students collaborate and discuss case elements with other students (Ertmer & Koehler, 2014). In a meta-analysis on effectiveness of online discussion strategies, Darabi and colleagues (2013) stated that students usually respond better when they are engaged in a purposefully structured and strategic online discussion, especially when discussion tasks involved an application scenario such as a case. Online case-based discussions have the potential to enhance cognitive presence in online courses through application of real-world scenarios across different disciplines. Although case-based discussions can help facilitate high-level learning (Darabi et al., 2013; Ertmer & Koehler, 2014; Richardson, Sadaf, & Ertmer, 2012) research related to their impact on student cognitive presence is limited.

2.1 Purpose of the Study

The purpose of this study was to examine the impact of case-based discussions on students' cognitive presence in online courses. The overall question that guided our study was this: To what extent do case-based discussions compare with non-case-based discussions impact students' levels of cognitive presence in online discussions? Specifically, our research questions included the following:

1. Is there a difference in the overall cognitive presence in online case-based and non-case-based discussions?
2. Are there differences between case-based and non-case-based discussions in terms of the impact of cognitive presence, satisfaction and perceived learning?

3. METHODS

3.1 Participants

A purposeful sample of forty-four graduate students (11 males and 32 females) enrolled in an Instructional Design course were selected to participate in this study. The sample was majority female (75%, n = 32; male: 25%, n = 11) and half (50%, n = 22) of them were more than 40 years old. The majority (59%, n=26) of the participants have taken more than 3 online courses. All of the participants rated themselves as being very comfortable with participating in online discussions.

3.2 Context of the Study

The online course was offered over a 15-week semester and delivered via a learning management system, Canvas. Students were required to engage in week-long online discussions per week. During the semester, there were thirteen online discussions on various topics–three case-based discussions and ten non-case-based discussions. The case-based discussions consisted of decision-making problems referred by Jonassen (2010) as a rational choice model, in which a group of students must compare the advantages and disadvantages of alternative solutions of the problems. Each case described a scenario in which a specific instructional design principle was applied to solve the issue. Students were required to analyze the problem situations, reflect on the concepts learned in the course and propose solutions to the issues presented in the case study.

3.3 Data Collection and Analysis

Data were collected from an online survey administered at the end of Fall 2018, Spring 2019, and Fall 2019 semesters. Students responded to two sets of CoI survey questions: one with a reflection on their case-based discussions experience and the other on the non-case-based discussions. Students' perceived learning and satisfaction were measured by adding two survey items at the end. The CoI survey was developed to measure students' perception of cognitive presence, teaching presence, and social presence (Arbaugh et al., 2008). Since the focus of this study is cognitive presence, only 12 items form the CoI survey that measure cognitive presence were used. The items employed a 5-point Likert-type scale, with 1 = strongly disagree and 5 = strongly agree. Simple demographic information was also collected such as gender, age, and prior experience with online courses. In addition, qualitative data were sought using open-ended questions in order to further explain the quantitative findings.

The quantitative data were analyzed descriptive analysis using means and standard deviations. To examine the difference between case-based and non-case-based discussions, a paired t-test was be performed for each variable separately. Qualitative data from the open-ended survey responses were analyzed using constant comparative approach (Miles & Huberman, 1994).

4. RESULTS

Results showed, in general, students' cognitive presence was higher for the case-based discussions than the non-case-based discussions for all four levels of cognitive presence–Triggering, exploration, integration, and resolution. Students' perceptions of their cognitive presence in online case-based discussions showed that students had high perceptions of their cognitive presence related to both integration (M = 4.11, SD = 0.83) and resolution (M = 4.21, SD = 0.76) compared with the non-case-based discussions. Additionally, students were more satisfied (M = 4.09, SD =.77) and learned more (M = 4.00, SD = 0.84) as compared to non-case-based discussions (see Table 1).

Table 1. Students' level of cognitive presence in case-based and non-case-based discussions (n=43)

Levels of Cognitive Presence	**Case-based discussions**		**Non-case-based discussions**	
	Mean	*SD*	Mean	*SD*
Triggering Event	4.07	0.66	3.84	0.78
Exploration	4.00	0.71	3.95	0.73
Integration	4.11	0.72	3.97	0.76
Resolution	4.20	0.70	4.02	0.79
I was satisfied with the discussions	4.09	0.77	3.80	0.82
I learned much in the discussions	4.00	0.84	3.91	1.01

The paired-samples t-test was conducted to explore the difference in the cognitive presence between case-based and non-case-based discussions. Among four levels of the cognitive presence, there were statistically significant differences in triggering events, integration, and resolution. More specifically, a higher rating was found on triggering events for case-based discussion (M = 4.0758, SD = .6623) than non-case-based discussion (M = 3.8409, SD = .7858), $t(43)$ = 2.907, $p < .01$. Also, students' responses to integration showed statistically significant higher scores on case-based discussion (M = 4.1061, SD = .7288) than non-case-based discussion (M = 3.9697, SD = .7602), $t(43)$ = 2.148, $p < .05$. Students' responses to resolution revealed significantly higher scores on case-based discussion (M = 4.2045, SD = .7052) than non-case-based discussion (M = 4.0227, SD = .7921), $t(43)$ = 2.253, $p < .05$. The second cognitive level, exploration, only exhibited a statistically non-significant difference between case-based discussion (M = 4.0076, SD = .7170) and non-case-based discussion (M = 3.9545, SD = .7352), $t(43)$ = .880, p = .384. In general, case-based discussions led to a higher level of cognitive presence than non-case-based discussion, except for exploration.

A paired-samples t-test was performed to compare perceived learning and satisfaction between case-based and non-case-based discussions. In terms of perceived learning outcomes, no significant difference was found between case-based discussion (M = 4.00, SD = .84) and non-case-based discussion (M = 3.84, SD = .96), $t(43)$ = 1.636, $p > .05$. However, students reported higher level of satisfaction on case-based discussion (M = 4.0909, SD = .7721) than on non-case-based discussion (M = 3.7955, SD = .8235), $t(43)$ = 3.301, $p < .05$. In general, these results suggest that students tend to have a higher level of satisfaction when they participate in the case-based discussion than non-case-based discussions.

In addition, comments in the open-ended survey questions revealed that students valued case discussions as meaningful and engaging. Qualitative results revealed that students enjoyed participating in case-based discussions and said that using the concepts that we learned from our readings and applying them to real life problems helped them get a better understanding of the concepts and how to use them. Students commented that, "case-based discussions helped construct explanations, solutions, and reflections on course content to understand fundamental concepts in this class." These results show that it is important to give students an authentic task such as a case or a problem to solve followed by PIM prompts can make discussions relevant to their learning. Sadaf and Olesova (2017) concluded that moving discussions through the stages of cognitive presence may lead to high levels of learning as each stage offers a process that encourages knowledge construction through deep levels of discourse among students.

5. CONCLUSION

Achieving high levels of cognitive presence is often the goal of online discussions. This study contributes to the limited body of knowledge on the notion that discussions can reach high levels of cognitive presence, progressing from *triggering* to *integration* and *resolution* phases, when instructors require students to provide a solution to cases or lead a discussion to a meaningful resolution of ideas. Looking at the results, one may conclude that students are more satisfied and perceive to achieve high levels of cognitive presence using case-based discussions. In this regard, online instructors can use case-based discussions that ask students to explore the problems, find and justify their solutions to facilitate high-levels of cognitive presence that may lead to deeper constructivist learning among students. Overall, the findings in this study are valuable because they contribute to further effective design of online asynchronous discussions through the use of case-based real-world scenarios for learning a specific discipline.

This study has some limitations that may lead to future research efforts. First, this study is limited in generalizability of findings due to small sample size and participants representing only one program and university. Follow-up studies could utilize large sample size with data collected across programs or institutions to further refine the results and implications of this study. In addition, research investigating the relationship between the levels of question prompts and the levels of cognitive presence in students' postings and the discourse facilitated in follow-up responses would be a promising direction for future studies.

REFERENCES

Darabi, A., Liang, X., Suryavanshi, R., & Yurekli, H. (2013). Effectiveness of online discussion strategies: A meta-analysis. *American journal of distance education, 27*(4), 228-241.

Ertmer, P.A., & Koehler, A.A. (2014). Online case-based discussions: Examining coverage of the afforded problem space. *Educational Technology Research and Development, 62*(5), 617-636.

Ertmer, P. A., & Stepich, D. A. (2002). Initiating and maintaining meaningful case discussions: Maximizing the potential of case-based instruction. *Journal on Excellence in College Teaching, 13*(2/3), 5-18.

Garrison, D.R., Anderson, T., & Archer, W. (2001). Critical thinking, cognitive presence, and computer conferencing in distance education. *The American Journal of Distance Education, 15*(1), 7–23.

Jonassen D.H. (2010). *Learning to Solve Problems: A Handbook.* Routledge, NewYork.

Miles, M. B., & Huberman, A. (1994). *Qualitative data analysis: An expanded sourcebook.*

Nistor, N., & Neubauer, K. (2010). From participation to dropout: Quantitative participation patterns in online university courses. *Computers & Education, 55*(2), 663-672.

Richardson, J. C., Sadaf, A., & Ertmer, P. A. (2013). Relationship between types of question prompts and critical thinking in online discussions. In *Educational communities of inquiry: Theoretical framework, research and practice* (pp. 197-222). IGI Global.

Rourke, L., & Kanuka, H. (2009). Learning in communities of inquiry: A review of the literature. *Journal of Distance Education, 23*(1), 19-48.

Sadaf, A., & Olesova, L. (2017). Enhancing cognitive presence in online case discussions with questions based on the practical inquiry model. American Journal of Distance Education, 31(1), 56-69.

Yew, E. H., & Schmidt, H. G. (2012). What students learn in problem-based learning: A process analysis. *Instructional Science, 40*(2), 371-395.

NUMERACY SKILLS EMPOWERMENT FROM PRESCHOOL

Maria Lidia Mascia, Maria Chiara Fastame, Mirian Agus and Maria Pietronilla Penna
Department of Pedagogy, Psychology, Philosophy, University of Cagliari, Italy

ABSTRACT

The development of numerical abilities was examined in 59 children aged 5 years divided into three groups: one control group ($n = 15$) and two experimental groups (pencil-and-paper mathematical training: $n = 29$: computerized mathematical training: $n = 15$). The participants were assessed both before and after a battery of validated tests assessing numerical abilities (BIN test) and fluid intelligence (CPM test). The three groups showed similar values in the pre-test assessment regarding these two dimensions. A gain between post-test and pre-test scores was calculated; this result underlines significant differences between experimental groups and the control group in the four areas evaluated by the BIN test. This study shows the efficacy of both computer-assisted and pencil-and-paper training in enriching numerical intelligence; pencil-and-paper mathematical training seems to be more effective in some areas. This aspect leads us to reflect about this result and to deepen the research with subsequent experiments.

KEYWORDS

Early Numeracy Learning, Psychoeducational Training, Preschool, Cognitive Empowerment, Educational Technology

1. INTRODUCTION

A wide literature has documented that the effect of developmental factors on numeracy competence (i.e. the ability to use numerical information to perform different daily life activities, such as counting, seriation and number comparison tasks) begins in early infancy and continues along the whole life span, predicting not only academic achievements (e.g. Watt et al., 2014) but also some aspects of later life quality, such as mental health (e.g. Fastame et al., 2019).

With the early life span, there is evidence that low kindergartner numeracy performance predicts later mathematics achievement in primary school (e.g. Geary et al., 1999). Therefore, if it is crucial to identify the contribution of the concurrent psychological processes underpinning number processing, such as visuospatial working memory, processing speed and non-verbal reasoning (Jenks et al., 2012), in order to detect early possible atypical developmental trajectories of these cognitive functions, then the development of specific psychoeducational interventions enhancing numeracy skills in early childhood may favour later mathematics achievement during formal schooling (Melhuish et al., 2008). Relative to the psychological interventions designed to enrich cognitive processes in childhood, Holmes and Gathercole (2013) emphasize the contribution of so-called brain training as an educational aid to enhance the cognitive processes underpinning different academic achievements. Moreover, a further trend of research (e.g. Prins et al., 2011; Chen et al., 2013) highlighted that using cognitive interventions based on the use of new technologies is more effective than the traditional pencil-and-paper method for cognitive empowerment because videogame-like activities enhanced both cognitive function efficiency and pupil motivation.

Relative to the Italian context, there is evidence for the effectiveness of combined pencil-and-paper and computer-assisted interventions, including both visuospatial and numeracy tasks, for the empowerment of mathematics skills in kindergartners (Agus et al., 2015). Moreover, Mascia et al. (2015) trained one group of 5-year-old children with a computer-assisted mathematical programme and a further group with the same computerized intervention combined with a pencil-and-paper numeracy programme; a third group did not receive any specific training (i.e. control group). After the end of training, compared with the control participants both trained groups benefitted from the psychoeducational interventions; however, no significant differences in terms of numeracy efficiency were found between the two trained groups. This suggests that the combination of computer-assisted and pencil-and-paper mathematical training was not more effective.

However, to our knowledge, no studies have been conducted to test the separate impacts of similar pencil-and-paper and computerized interventions aimed at enriching mathematics skills in kindergartners.

This study was mainly aimed at examining the effect of the presentation modality (i.e. computer-assisted versus pencil-and-paper) on the enhancement of numeracy skills in 5-year-old children. Therefore, one group of kindergartners was presented with the computerized version of 'Intelligenza numerica I' training whereas another group was trained using the pencil-and-paper version. A further group of 5-year-old children was used as the control group.

It was hypothesized that pupils in the experimental groups might obtain higher scores in the assessment of numerical abilities than pupils in the control group.

2. METHOD

2.1 Participants, Materials and Procedure

Fifty-nine pupils (29 males, 49.2%; mean age 65.8 ± 4.03 months) attending the last year of kindergarten in Italian schools (Sardinian area) were divided into three groups: the control group (n = 15) and two experimental groups (pencil-and-paper mathematical training: n = 29; computerized mathematical training: n = 15). The activities aiming to enrich numerical knowledge were developed collectively during 10 weekly meetings that each lasted approximately 1 hour. The psychoeducational training consisted of activities developed by Lucangeli and colleagues (Lucangeli, Poli & Molin 2003, 2010) in 'Sviluppare l'intelligenza numerica I' and 'L'intelligenza numerica I'. In the control group, pupils followed the classical activities proposed by their teachers. Assessment was carried out by the presentation (at pre-test and post-test sessions) of Raven's Colored Progressive Matrices (CPM: Raven, 1958) and the BIN numerical intelligence scale (Molin, Poli & Lucangeli, 2007) to achieve a measure of the pupils' fluid intelligence and numerical knowledge. The BIN test is used to investigate four principal areas: lexical, semantic, pre-syntactic and counting. Each area is evaluated with specific activities, such as reading and writing.

2.2 Findings

These three groups showed similar values in the pre-test assessment regarding fluid intelligence and numerical knowledge (lexical area: K-W χ^2 = 2.396, df = 2, p = .302; semantic area: K-W χ^2 = 1.971, df = 2 p = .373; counting area: K-W χ^2 = .381, df = 2, p = .827; pre-syntactic area: K-W χ^2 = 1.252, df = 2, p = 5.35; CPM: K-W χ^2 = 3.589, df = 2, p = .166). In order to assess the effect of training in numerical abilities, the gain was computed by applying the *[(Post-test score – Pre-test score) / Pre-test score]* ratio. Kruskal-Wallis (K-W) non-parametric statistical analyses were applied, using the training group as independent variable and the gains computed for each scale of the BIN test as dependent variables. The outcomes are shown in Table 1.

Results for the lexical area (i.e. assessing the ability to read and write Arabic numbers and the skill to join the number-word to the exact digit) and the pre-syntactic area (i.e, appraising the capability to link numbers to their number representation and to order several quantities) show an effective empowerment in both experimental groups. Pupils engaged in the pencil-and-paper activities show higher scores in the semantic area (i.e. evaluating the ability to associate numerical sizes, dots and Arabic digits) and the counting area (i.e. assessing the ability to recite the number-word sequence forward and backward, as well as knowledge of the order of Arabic digits from 1 to 5). This study shows the efficacy of both computer-assisted and pencil-and-paper training for enriching numerical intelligence, highlighting some differences between the experimental groups that use different training formats.

Table 1

Variable	K-W χ^2	df	*p*	Pairwise comparison	W	*p*	Mean (SD) Control	Mean (SD) Pencil-and-paper	Mean (SD) Computerized
gain_BIN Lexical area	6.02	2	.049	Control / Pencil-and-paper	3.089	.029	.060	.514	.591
				Control / Computerized	3.073	.030	(.303)	(.717)	(.750)
				Pencil-and-paper / Computerized	.441	.755			
gain_BIN Semantic area	9.21	2	.010	Control / Pencil-and-paper	4.03	.004	.238	.887	.387
				Control / Computerized	2.29	.105	(.961)	(1.470)	(.911)
				Pencil-and-paper / Computerized	-2.19	.121			
gain_ BIN Counting area	6.57	2	.037	Control / Pencil-and-paper	3.63	.010	.079	1.110	.238
				Control / Computerized	2.21	.119	(.627)	(1.870)	(.464)
				Pencil-and-paper / Computerized	-1.07	.451			
gain_ BIN Pre-syntactic area	21.12	2	<.001	Control / Pencil-and-paper	6.153	< .001	-.175	1.620	1.460
				Control / Computerized	5.214	< .001	(.433)	(2.460)	(2.340)
				Pencil-and-paper / Computerized	.386	.785			

3. CONCLUSION

Literacy reflects the efficacy of our psychoeducational intervention in empowering the knowledge in numeracy learning starting from preschool. Psychoeducational intervention can be carried out both by pencil-and-paper and computerized formats (Agus, Mascia, Fastame e Penna, 2016; Mascia, Agus, Fastame e Addis, 2016). The latter training format underlines the importance that educational technology has in society today. Technology includes a set of electronic tools and applications that provide teaching materials and support cognitive processes in order to improve learning goals (Geiger, Goos & Dole, 2015). It should be emphasized that the choice of format must always be accompanied by a study of learning based on an integrated design and usability that is functional and accessible (Penna & Stara, 2010). We can therefore conclude that digital technology, as an indispensable presence in our society and in the life of all active users of schools, is a reality that cannot be overlooked or underestimated. It is necessary to know its potential and its criticality, and introduce it into everyday teaching in a conscious and responsible way (Sung, Chang & Liu, 2016). However, in our study, it is necessary to underline how Italian schools are not yet prepared for the use of educational technology; in particular, this is evident in the lack of adequate and recent digital tools. Nowadays children use increasingly updated multimedia tools (Silverman, Kim, Hartranft, Nunn & McNeish, 2017); in future studies it would be interesting to let the child use not only the computer but also videogames in order to enhance numeracy with greater interactivity. In this way we can also improve learning motivation and performance, for example, by using the touch-screen tablet application (Kamaruzaman, Nor & Azahari, 2016).

ACKNOWLEDGEMENT

The authors would like to thank the schools and the children who participated in the study.

REFERENCES

Agus, M., Mascia, M. L., Fastame, M. C., & Penna, M. P. (2016). Difficoltà matematiche: percorsi di potenziamento delle abilità numeriche e visuo-spaziali. *Psicologia dell'educazione*, 2, 29-37.

Agus, M., Mascia, M. L., Fastame, M. C., Melis, V., Pilloni, M. C., & Penna, M. P. (2015). The measurement of enhancement in mathematical abilities as a result of joint cognitive trainings in numerical and visual-spatial skills: A preliminary study. In *Journal of Physics: Conference Series* (Vol. 588, No. 1, p. 012041). IOP Publishing.

Chen, Y., Lin, C., Wei, T., Liu, C., & Wuang, Y. (2013). The effectiveness of multimedia visual perceptual training groups for the preschool children with developmental delay. *Research in Developmental Disabilities*, 34, 4447-4454.

Fastame, M. C., Manca, C., Penna, M.P., Lucangeli, D., & Hitchcott, P.K. (2019). Numeracy Skills and Self-Reported Mental Health in People Aging Well. *Psychiatric Quarterly*. doi: 10.1007/s11126-019-09655-y

Geary, D. C., Hoard, M. K., & Hamson, C. O. (1999). Numerical and arithmetical cognition: Patterns of functions and deficits in children at risk for a mathematical disability. *Journal of Experimental Child Psychology*, 74, 213–239. doi:10.1006/jecp.1999.2515

Geiger, V., Goos, M., & Dole, S. (2015). The role of digital technologies in numeracy teaching and learning. *International Journal of Science and Mathematics Education*, 13(5), 1115-1137.

Holmes, J., & Gatherchole, S. E. (2013). Taking working memory training from the laboratory into school. *Educational Psychology: An International Journal of Experimental Educational Psychology.* doi: 10.1080/01443410.2013.797338

Jenks, K. M., Van Lieshout, E. C. D. M., & De Moor, J. M. (2012). Cognitive correlates of mathematical achievement in children with cerebral palsy and typically developing children. *British Journal of Educational Psychology*, 82, 120–135. doi:10.1111/j.2044-8279.2011.02034.x

Kamaruzaman, M. F., Nor, H. M., & Azahari, M. H. H. (2016). Using touchscreen technology to support basic numeracy learning process for high functioning children with autism. *The Turkish Online Journal of Educational Technology*, 632-639.

Lucangeli, D., Poli, S. & Molin, A. (2003). L'intelligenza numerica, Edizioni Erickson. Lucangeli, D., Poli, S. & Molin, A., 2010. Sviluppare l'intelligenza numerica I, Edizioni Erickson.

Mascia, M. L., Agus, M., Fastame, M. C., & Addis, A. (2016). Enhancement in Mathematical Abilities: A System Approach. Towards a Post-Bertalanffy Systemics. SE-25 Contemporary Systems Thinking ed G Minati, MR Abram and E Pessa.

Melhuish, E. C., Phan, M. B., Sylva, K., Sammons, P., Siraj-Blatchford, I., & Taggart, B. (2008). Effects of the home learning environment and preschool center experience upon literacy and numeracy development in early primary school. *Journal of Social Issues, 64*(1), 95-114.

Molin, A., Poli, S. & Lucangeli, D. (2007). Batteria Intelligenza Numerica 4-6 [Battery for Numerical Intelligence], Edizioni Erickson.

Penna, M. P., & Stara, V. (2010). Opinions on computers, and efficacy of a computer-based learning: A pilot study. *Education and Information Technologies*, 15(3), 181-204

Prins, P. J., Dovis, S., Ponsioen, A., Ten Brink, E., & Van Der Oord, S. (2011). Does computerized working memory training with game elements enhance motivation and training efficacy in children with ADHD?. *Cyberpsychology, behavior, and social networking*, 14, 115-122.

Raven, J.C. (1958). Guide to using the Coloured Progressive Matrices, Oxford, England: H. K. Lewis & Co

Silverman, R., Kim, Y. S., Hartranft, A., Nunn, S., & McNeish, D. (2017). Effects of a multimedia enhanced reading buddies program on kindergarten and Grade 4 vocabulary and comprehension. *The Journal of Educational Research*, 110(4), 391-404.

Sung, Y. T., Chang, K. E., & Liu, T. C. (2016). The effects of integrating mobile devices with teaching and learning on students' learning performance: A meta-analysis and research synthesis. *Computers & Education*, 94, 252-275.

Watts, T. W., Duncan, G. J., Siegler, R. S., & Davis-Kean, P. E. (2014). What's past is prologue: Relations between early mathematics knowledge and high school achievement. *Educational Researcher*, 43(7), 352-360.

MENTORING: A FOCUS ON ETHNIC IDENTITY DEVELOPMENT AMONG AFRICAN AMERICAN MALE COLLEGE FRESHMEN IN THE DIGITAL AGE

John W. Hatcher III
Southeastern Louisiana University
SLU 10549, Hammond, LA. 70402, USA

ABSTRACT

This study explored a process of mentoring African American males transitioning from high school to college. The researcher used Phinney and Ong's (2007) conceptualization and measurement of ethnic identity development employing the Multi-Group Ethnic Identity Measure-Revised survey. This research is intended to provide insight into the potential impact of mentoring on a group of African American male students who are navigating their first year of college, while discovering who they are. The use of digital sources assisted in the communication and relationship building processes that helped to support the mentorship effort. This is the initial phase of an ongoing study.

KEYWORDS

Mentoring, African American Males, Digital Age

1. INTRODUCTION

This study is significant as it will provide stakeholder groups with practical ways in which to engage African American male students in positive and supportive relationships, while guiding them towards graduation, as well as, their development of ethnic identity in the digital age. Identity development has been a challenge for African American males in the United States of America. Hatcher (2015) stated, "...these young males currently lead the nation [U.S.A.] in some of the most alarming statistics." These categories include, but are not limited to lower academic achievement rates, lower graduation rates, and higher dropout rates than their Caucasian and Asian counterparts (Brown, 2005 & Fox & Swatt, 2008). African American males are experiencing higher rates of homicides (Fox & Swatt, 2008), while their life expectancy is declining (Anderson, 2006). These quality-of-life indicators highlight the ethnic identity development crisis among the African American male population.

Ethnic identity is a foundational aspect of one's identity, which is the critical crisis of Erik Erikson's (1968) fifth stage of human development (Identity versus Role Confusion). The underlying structures of Erikson's theory is that in each of the eight stages of development there are specific relationships that should develop, as well as, specific crises that needs to be resolved. The effective response to the identity question "who am I?" is predicated on the appropriate development of critical relationships and the resolution of the corresponding crises in each developmental stage. One of these critical relationships is that of the father's role in the child's development of their identity. However, Freek (2017) cited the absence of fathers as a major crisis and contributes to lower rates of academic achievement, increased behavioral problems, less motivation, and role confusion. The U.S. Census Bureau (2017) reported that almost two thirds of African American children under the age of 18 live in a households without a father figure. It is for this reason that the researcher focused on the role of the mentor in the process of ethnic identity development among African American male students using available technology to build and support respectful and trusting relationships. The origin of the term mentor has roots in the classical literature of Homer's Odyssey, in which, Mentor was left in Odysseus' stead to develop his son Telemachus, in Odysseus' absence. Mentoring is a fundamental form of human development where one person invests time and resources in support of the development of their mentee. Mentors today provide expertise to less experienced persons in order to enhance their education, advance their careers, and build supportive networks. "Mentoring can be defined as a significant, long-term, beneficial effect on a person's life or style, generally as a result of personal, one-on-one contact (www.aleanjourney.com)." The focus of mentoring in this study is to develop ethnic identity through the use of modern technology.

2. BODY OF PAPER

The researcher was assigned as the instructor and advisor to a college orientation course that every freshmen entering the host university must take. The purpose of the course is to support students while they are in the process of transitioning from high school into college and to advise them with regard to their scheduling, academic status, organizational interest, and overall navigation of their first year in college. The goal of the course is to increase the student's connection to the university through their advisor, in order to increase the retention rates and ultimately the graduation rates of all students. The purpose of this research was to report the initial findings of an ongoing process of mentoring. The instructor became the mentor and was responsible for building a positive and professional relationship with each student in order to support their successful transition. The class was made up of n= (15) African American male students who were recruited as a convenient sample by the mentor during the summer prior to the start of their first semester of college. It is important to note that the instructor is an African American male educator with more than 25 years of experience in PreK-24 education. The class was scheduled to meet once a week for 16 weeks and for one hour and fifteen minutes each session. Given the amount of content for the course and the amount of time needed to build strong, positive, and appropriate working relationship with each student, the mentor initiated a mentorship effort to increase the amount of contact time with students. Mentoring can be a support for African American male student's success in college. Mentoring can have a tiered approach which includes adult-to-adult, mentor-to-student, and student-to-student, "mentoring approaches will create a supportive environment and community for the African American male that provides them with guidance and advice (Gardenhire, Cerna, & Ivery, 2016)." The Sons of Promise Mentoring initiative employed each of the three types of mentoring relationships in order to create a viable support system for these college freshmen. Mentoring discussions can aid faculty members with the identification of at-risk students early in the semester (Pawley, 2018). Identification of student needs enables faculty to engage students with relevant advice, review of difficult concepts, and augment the course with the critical knowledge regarding their ethnic identity development.

2.1 Ethnic Identity Development

The underpinnings of this study are based in Erik Erikson's (1968) theory of psych-social development and Phinney's research on ethnic identity development. Erikson theorized that the primary journey in life is the development of individual identity and posits that identity development is the critical task of the adolescent stage of development. Erikson (1968) stated that identity development took place, "in the core of the individual and yet also in the core of his communal culture." It is essential to understand that ethnic identity is a type of individual or personal identity that influences all other aspects of identity. In the context of responding to the "Who am I?" question, the adolescent person must experience a sense of wholeness and congruence between that which he perceives about himself and what he believes others perceive about him (Erikson, 1968). Marcia's (1993) research bridges Erikson's eight stages of psycho-social developmental theory with Phinney's (1992) ethnic identity theory. Marcia extended Erikson's model of development by focusing on the adolescent stage of development and introduced four identity status groups.

Phinney (1992) developed the Multi-group Ethic Identity Measure survey instrument to measure ethnic identity status based on Marcia's (1966) study of identity in adolescence, wherein Marcia proposed the four stages of a linear process of identity development. Marcia (1993) would later modify his findings to reflect four status groups citing various pathways to connect to Erikson's fifth stage of psycho-social development, which is "Identity versus Role Confusion." The identity achieved status group has both committed to an identity and explored that same identity. This is the desired status group for resolving the crisis of identity. The moratorium status group has explored the meaning of a particular identity; however, they have not yet committed to that identity. The foreclosure status group, on the contrary, has committed to an identity without having explored that identity. This happens when an individual settles on an identity that has been projected upon them, yet they have not explored the whole of what is the meaning of that identity. The identity diffusion status group has neither committed to nor explored the proposed identity. The identity diffusion status group is considered to be in the state of an identity crisis or role confusion as Erikson put it.

Figure 1 is an illustration of how Phinney's theory assigned ethnic identity status groups. Phinney measured ethnic identity development status from the constructs of commitment and exploration. Phinney and Ong (2007) used a developmental approach to the study of identity development. Phinney and Ong stated: "We propose that a developmental approach, which focuses on the process of ethnic identity formation, can provide a theoretically and psychometrically sound basis for measuring the core aspects of ethnic identity" (p. 13). These two constructs are the basis for Phinney's study of ethnic identity development. The Multi-group Ethnic Identity Measure-Revised (MEIM-R) survey was administered to the class during the first month of class to measure each student's ethnic identity development status.

		COMMITMENT	
		High	**Low**
EXPLORATION			
	High	ID Achievement	Moratorium
	Low	Foreclosure	ID Diffusion

Figure 1. The Four Ethnic Identity Statuses

The MEIM-R is made up of six items created to assess individual's commitment to and exploration of their ethnic identity. Three items assess the commitment construct and three items assess the exploration construct. Each item is rated on a five point Likert scale, one (1) was Strongly Disagree and five (5) was Strongly Agree. The mean score from each construct is calculated in order to determine a high or low rating and ethnic identity status.

2.2 Mentoring in the 21st Century

Researchers have reported that technology has changed the way people conduct their personal and professional relationships in very fundamental ways (Guy, 2002). There are still questions about whether technology has made measureable improvement to the quality of our relationships. Most people will agree that technology does have the potential to affect the quality of life for many people. Guy (2002) stated the following about mentoring in the 21st Century, "I explore the relationship of technology to mentoring through what is called tele-mentoring, the electronic version of mentoring (p. 27). He went on to further state that, "A key assumption that guides this exploration is that technology is altering the nature of human relationships, particularly mentoring relationships..." The researcher used a variety of technology applications to support and sustain his mentoring relationship with the student participants. Table 1. illustrates the variety of technology applications used, the percentage of student participants who used that technology applications, and a brief description of the technology application.

Researchers say that educational aspects of mentoring include intervention, advising, and individualized development plans. Palmer, Davis, and Thompson (2010) observed intersectionality between building a community and mentoring where underrepresented students can become involved in the university. The various applications of technology were used in three main communication formats with and among the mentorship group. The formats used for whole group communication included Email and GroupMe. They were used to send notices, updates, and reminders to the entire group. The small group communication took place via Email, text message, Messenger, & FaceBook and they were used for the same reason as whole group, yet with specific members of the group, such as, the leadership team. Phone calls, text message, FaceTime, Messenger, Messenger Games (Chess), and LinkedIn were all used in one-on-one communication between the mentor and an individual students.

Table 1. Digital Resources Used for Communication

Digital Application	Percentage of Students Using Tech. App. to Communicate (#)		Description
Email	100	(15)	Electronic mail application
Phone Call	100	(15)	A telephone communication via telephone network
GroupMe	73.33	(11)	Group text messaging to a set of telephones
Text Msg.	60	(9)	Text messaging, or texting, composing and sending electronic messages
FaceTime	26.67	(4)	a proprietary Video- telephony product developed by Apple Inc.
Messenger	26.67	(4)	is a messaging app
Games (Chess)	26.67	(4)	Videogames played by and between users
Facebook	20	(3)	an online social media network
LinkedIn	.67	(1)	a business service that operates via websites and mobile apps

3. DISCUSSION

In this study there were six (6) students who were rated in the Identity Achievement status group, five (5) who were rated in the Foreclosure status groups, and four (4) who were rated in the Identity Diffusion status group. In addition to the mentor who oversaw the group, the students rated in the Identity Achievement status group were mentored by upperclassmen. Student participants who were rated in the Foreclosure and Identity Diffusion status groups were guided toward adult mentors and mentors with greater experience. The additional mentors provided another layer of support for these African American male students who were in their first year of transition from high school into college. The additional volunteer mentors were all African American males. The mentoring initiative supported student's efforts to become involved in area of interest on campus as the lead mentor advised students to explore the university. The students' exploration allowed them to access the support systems that were available outside of their classroom. Examples were the Sons of Promise Mentorship Organization, which included adult mentors, such as, the Vice President of Student Affairs, the Dean of Students, and upperclassmen who became mentors. Exposure to activities on campus aided students with developing a relationship and commitment to the university. Braxton, Doyle, Hartley, Hirschy, Jones, & McLendon (2014) stated that involvement while at the university leads to a subsequent commitment to completion of the student's degree. When seeking a model to describe human development through social interaction such as mentoring and especially social interaction in digital communication environments the notion of identity will often emerge. The researcher acknowledges that identity focuses on the individual's perceptions of self and ethnicity describes an individual's inclusion within a cultural group. The various digital applications enabled the lead mentor to nurture and maintain positive and supportive relationships with his students based on the technology available to each student, as well as, their individual preference to communicate.

4. CONCLUSION

In the digital age much of one's identity has been reduced to creating profiles that include ethnicity, age, gender, interest groups, and sexual orientation, while ethnic identity development is explored through Google searches and documentaries found on Netflix. Online learning is taking place in both formal and informal settings. The use of technology in the classroom is used to assess student learning and has become commonplace, while Youtube has become the digital tutor and mentor for students in the digital age. This study explored the role of a mentor with regards to the development of ethnic identity through the use of various technology applications. Those who endeavor to become a mentor in the digital age must continue to engage face-to-face interactions; however, they must also be savvy in the use of technology applications that will support the types of communication that work for both the mentor and the mentee. The researcher in this study had to employ a variety of technology applications in order to build and maintain positive and supportive relationships with the student participants over the course of one year. Providing opportunities for students to explore their self-identifying ethnic identity has guided student participants toward answering the "who am I" question. The researcher will continue to investigate the ethnic identity of the participants in this study as they matriculate through their college experience. The MEIM-R survey will be administered each year students are in school in order to monitor participant's ethnic identity development status. Finally, follow-up interviews will be conducted to give voice to the African American male students participating in this ongoing study.

ACKNOWLEDGEMENT

I would like to acknowledge the Sons of Promise Mentorship Organization and every student participant who participated in this study. Your time, efforts, and continuous support aids the development of ethnic identity and improvement of academic achievement for those you serve. Thank you!

REFERENCES

Anderson J. L., 2006. An evaluation of African-American health status with gender comparison. *California Journal Health Promotion,* Vol. 4, No. 2, pp 168-174.

Braxton, J. M. et al, 2014. *Rethinking College Student Retention*. Jossey-Bass, San Francisco, CA

Brown, D.F. 2005. The significance of congruent communication in effective classroom management. *The Clearing House,* Vol.79, No.1, pp 12-15.

Cobb-Payton F., 2003.Rethinking the Digital Divide. *Communications of the ACM*, Vol. 46, No.6, pp 89-91.

Erikson E., 1968. *Identity: Youth and crisis*. Norton, New York, NY.

Fox J. et al, 2008. *The recent surge in homicides involving young Black males and guns*. Northeastern University, Boston, MA.

Freek F., 2017. Responding to the challenge of father absence and fatherlessness in the South Africa context: A case study involving concerned fathers from the North West Province. *Stellenbosch Theological Journal*. Vol. 3, No. 1, pp 89-113.

Gardenhire A. et al, 2016. Boosting college success among men of color: Promising approaches and next steps. *Manpower Demonstration Research Corporation.* Retrieved October 12, 2019 from https://www.mdrc.org/sites/default/files/MenofColor_b.pdf

Guy, T., (2002). Tele-mentoring: Shaping Mentoring Relationships for the 21st Century. Retrieved October 12, 2019 from http://www.calpro-online.org/eric/docs/mott/mentoring5.pdf

Hatcher J. et al, 2015. The African-American adolescent male identity development crisis: A mixed-methods design exploring the relationship between ethnic identity development status and student achievement. *Journal of African American Males in Education*, Vol. 1, No. 6.

Marcia J., et al, 1993. *Ego identity: A handbook for psychosocial research.* Springer, New York, NY.

McMahon T., 2016. Mentoring is Vital to Developing Lean Thinking. *A Lean Journey*. Retrieved October 12, 2019 from aleanjourney.com/2016/03/mentoring-is-vital-to-developing-lean.html

Palmer R. T., et al 2010. Theory meets practice: HBCU initiatives that promote academic success among African Americans in STEM. *Journal of College Student Development, Vol.51*, pp 440-443.

Pawley A. L., 2018. Learning from small numbers: Studying ruling relations that gender and race the structure of U.S. engineering education. *Journal of Engineering Education,* Vol.108, pp 13-31.

Phinney J., 1992. The multigroup ethnic identity measure: A new scale for use with adolescents and young adults from diverse groups. *Journal of Adolescent Research,* Vol. 7, No. 2, 156–176.

Phinney J., et al, 2007. Conceptualization and measurement of ethnic identity: Current status and future directions. *Journal of Counseling Psychology,* Vol. *54,* No. (3), pp 271–281.

Prince Z., 2016. Census Bureau: Higher Percentage of Black Children Live with Single Mothers. *U.S. Census Bureau.* Retrieved October 12, 2019 from afro.com/census-bureau-higher-percentage-black-children-live-single-mothers/

DIGITAL ETHNICITY – EMERGING PROFILES

Nan B. Adams and Thomas A. DeVaney
Southeastern Louisiana University, USA

ABSTRACT

Digital Ethnicity is a model developed to provide an organized method to define human interaction with digital communication technologies and the result of these interactions on cultural development. The ultimate goal for the development of Digital Ethnicity as a concept is to describe those aspects of digital ethnicity that influence society. These digital ethnic aspects are intended to guide thinking and provide insight into the social and educational needs of rapidly changing societal groupings by providing guidance for leaders and educators to address the biological, social and cognitive changes brought about by pervasive use of digital communication technologies. Digital Profiles have emerged by certain demographic characteristics – most notably, age and gender. This paper discusses these emerging profiles.

KEYWORDS

Social Aspects of Technological Change, Digital Communication, Learning Theory, Ethnicity

1. INTRODUCTION

Much of current literature focuses on various effects the rapid and pervasive emergence of social media has on our everyday lives. Ethnographies, how to interact with the Internet of Things (IoT) and casting the future as no longer human seem to dominate the discussion. This de facto conversation is interesting, but often misses cohesion and reflects an observation or response to some undefined phenomenon rather than an attempt to organize these effects to guide action. The reality is that the influence of these digital communication technologies referred to as social media is changing human actions and beliefs. The construction of our social reality is in flux. For over a decade, the majority of the world's population 'text' rather than 'talk'; couples fall in love online and meet after the fact; gender identity is becoming a choice made not by biology but by a screen name or the physical appearance of an avatar. Pew Research Center (2017) reported 2/3rds of Americans get at least some of their news from social media – and for the first time, 55% of these Americans are ages 50 or older. For the under 50 demographic, 74% of Americans of all races get news on social media sites. Facebook is the most commonly cited social media site, but Twitter, YouTube and Snapchat are sites on the rise. As a result of this phenomenal use of social media, social groups are formed in these virtual spaces that provide new kinds of common identity to previously disparate individuals. The Digital Ethnicity Model has yielded Digital Profiles based on certain demographic characteristics. These emerging Digital Profiles may provide insight into understanding into how society is changing under the influence of digital tools.

2. BODY OF PAPER

Akin (2016) wrote about the 'cyber effect' and discussed 'when humans and technology collide'. She discussed that "some changes have occurred so quickly that it has become difficult to tell the difference between passing trends, still evolving behavior, and somethings that's already become an acceptable social norm (p.4)." She observed the significant need to study the cyber effect along with the challenges this poses for systematic academic study of this phenomenon and terms this an accelerated form of socialization. As the concept of Digital Ethnicity is explored, differences in gender use of computers and social media are of interest to development of Digital Ethnicity Profiles.

In a meta-analysis of 71 studies utilizing 644 different measures, Kay concluded that "actual computer behaviour has been studied far less than frequency of computer use, yet it is specific behaviour that can help uncover clues and nuances with respect to gender differences" (2008, p.19). In 2015, different computer activities were found to be used by different genders, with males performing more gaming and surfing the net, and females more email and communication-type activities (Fairlie, 2015).

The rapid increase in use of social media over the past 15 years reveals similar complexities. The difference between genders consistently reveals that females are more engaged with social media than males. According to Pew Research (2019), in 2010, 39% of males were engaged with at least one social media site, whereas 46% of females were engaged. This trend has held. The same longitudinal study by Pew indicates that in 2019, 65% of males are engaged regularly on at least one social media site, compared to 78% of females.

Differences of computer and social media use by Age have also been documented. According to the Pew Research Center surveys of social media use, there are substantial differences in social media use by age. Some 88% of 18- to 29-year-olds indicate that they use any form of social media. That share falls to 78% among those ages 30 to 49, to 64% among those ages 50 to 64 and to 37% among Americans 65 and older. Statista (2019) publishes similar statistics, listing 100% of 18-19 year olds having internet access. That number falls to 97% of 30-49 year-olds, then 88% of 50-64 year-olds, and reveals that 73% of those over the age of 65 have internet access.

The question arises – how does increased use of computers and social media that has developed a level of seamless interconnectedness influence the development of our society – more specifically, how does it impact how people belong to that society? Restated - How does interaction with computers and other digital communication technologies, commonly called social media, influence ethnicity? What ethnic profiles may be developed using the Digital Ethnicity Model?

2.1 Aspects of Ethnicity – The Underlying Theory and Working Model

Longstreet (1978) developed a functional model for the 5 aspects that may be used to describe her concept of ethnicity. These aspects are (a) verbal communication, (b) nonverbal communication, (c) orientation mode, (d) social value patterns, and (e) intellectual mode. A brief description of each follows:

1. **Verbal communication** may be described as the structure a person uses when communicating orally. The rules or patterns for this oral communication are learned by children prior to the development of their abstract intellectual abilities. The ability to learn language seems to be a universal capacity of humankind [8, p. 42].
2. **Nonverbal Communication** may be described as a system of facial expression, body movements and spatial arrangements that communicate meaning to others [8, p. 59].
3. **Orientation Mode** refers to patterns of behavior used, regardless of the presence of others, as ways of orienting oneself to the differing contexts of one's usual environment. It may be described as the way one communicates with themselves [8, p. 74]. The orientation mode may be the most complex of the described modes. This mode is influenced by the social environment but ultimately becomes the ways one becomes comfortable in their own environment when no communication takes place.
4. **Social Value Patterns** are based on the sets of persistent behaviors that a group expects from its members and upon which it places certain values and upholds with certain beliefs [8, p. 89].
5. **Intellectual Modes** are described by Longstreet as the most emotionally charged aspect of ethnicity. This mode is not intended to deal with human innate intelligence, but rather reflect the way we externalize our thoughts, how we approach a problem, what gets our full attention, what details we are most likely to recall. Intellectual modes link intellectual performance to past experiences [8, pp. 106-107].

When seeking a model to describe human development through social interaction, and especially social interaction in digital communication environments, the notion of identity often emerges. The authors wish to acknowledge that identity focuses on the individual's definition of self [3], whereas ethnicity describes an individual's place or believed inclusion within a cultural group. This inquiry focuses on the individuals as they relate to a group.

When constructing a scale to describe those aspects of ethnicity that may be influenced by early and pervasive interaction with digital communication technologies, consideration of which aspects to investigate was a challenging task. Longstreet (1978) predicted a variety of contextual ethnicities that may be distinct ethnicities. These distinct and specialized ethnicities were described as being grounded in one or more of the identified 5 Aspects of Ethnicity.

2.2 Digital Ethnic Profiles

To explore the data for possible profiles related to age and gender, a series of two-way analyses of variance was conducted. Each analysis identified statistically significance differences based on age (IM: $p = .009$; SVP: $p < .001$; IM: $p < .001$). The results further indicated that agreement increased as the age category increased which suggests different perceptions within each domain based on age. Concerning gender, the analysis of variance results indicated statistically significance differences between male and female respondents for SVP and OM and no statistically significant differences with respect to IM. However, unlike consistency identified in the results for age, the results indicated higher SVP values among females while females had lower values concerning OM. Finally, the results indicated there was not a statistically significant interaction between age and gender for any of the domains (IM: $p = 783$; SVP: $p = .380$; OM: $p = .923$). These results are illustrated in the figures below.

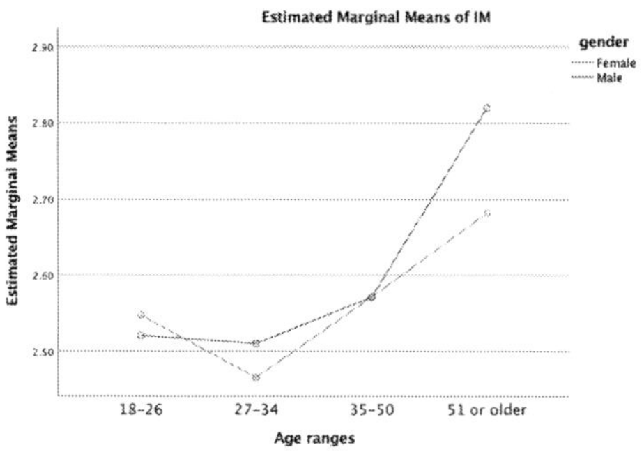

Figure 1

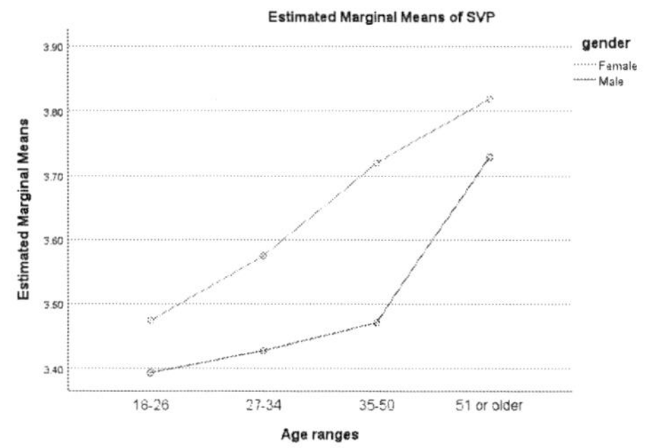

Figure 2

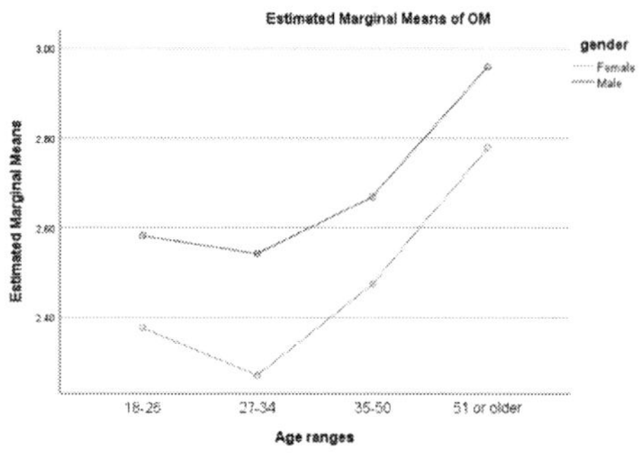

Figure 3

2.3 Discussion of Results

The aspects of ethnicity identified by this investigation of the specialized ethnicity termed Digital Ethnicity include (a) Orientation Mode, (b) Intellectual Mode, and (c) Social Value Patterns. As with other specialized ethnicities described by the Longstreet (1978) model, Digital Ethnicity is rooted in the combined aspects of Verbal Communication and Non-Verbal Communication that have been termed Communication Mode for the concept of Digital Ethnicity. The Digital Ethnicity Scale was constructed to validate the model of Digital Ethnicity (2009).

Analysis of survey data reveals significant differences by gender exist with regard to Orientation Mode and Social Value Patterns. There is little variation within Intellectual Mode with regard to gender, which may be interpreted as an indication that we are all part of the same society or national ethnic group and therefore our intellectual mode has been shaped by our surroundings – schools that share standardized planned development programs, television and other media sources with synchronized information presented in somewhat standard formats. The differences by Orientation Mode and Social Value Patterns may reflect the individual in relationship to the group and reveal relationships to 1) personal preferences and how we comfort ourselves (orientation mode) and 2) those values held as a result of our relationship to our surroundings (social value patterns).

Females returned higher means for Social Value Patterns, which indicates they have stronger agreement with the statements, which reflect stronger ties to the societal norms reflected by the survey. For example, posting private information is not acceptable, downloading music without paying for it is not acceptable, etc. Males have stronger agreement with orientation mode items, which indicates more set patterns of behavior and less flexibility for changes in preferred orientations. Because there are apparent differences and they swap for SVP and OM, it gives evidence that there are different profiles based on the three areas for male and female.

With regard to differences by age – the patterns are consistent with each age group returning similar results across the 3 identified aspects of Intellectual Mode, Orientation Mode and Social Value Patterns. This bodes well for development of Digital Ethnic Profiles. The largest difference by age occurs with those less than 50 years old and those older than 50 years, with the 3 age ranges of 18-26, 27-34 and 35-50 somewhat combined with less variability to each other and more variability with those over 50 years of age. This tracks previous research (Adams, 2004) that suggested a difference in ways of knowing may exist between those born before or after 1970.

3. CONCLUSION

The pervasive use of Social Media coupled with the current lack of guidelines or policy to ensure the ethical and truthful dissemination of information through these digital Social Media communication platforms underpin the central need for utilizing the identified aspects of Digital Ethnicity model as a tool describe phenomena to guide our futures. The development of Digital Ethnic Profiles provide guidance for understanding different mindsets held by different individuals as participation in the emerging global society increases.

REFERENCES

Adams, N., DeVaney, T., & Longstreet, W., Investigating aspects of an emerging digital ethnicity: Development of the Digital Ethnicity Scale (DES). *Computers in Human Behavior*, 26 (2010) 1822-1830.

Adams, N., Digital Intelligence Fostered by Technology. Journal of Technology Studies, (Spring 2004) 93-98.

Aiken, M., (2017). The Cyber Effect. New York: Spiegel & Grau

Erikson, E. (1968). *Identity: Youth and crisis*. New York, NY: W. W. Norton.

Fairlie, R.W. Do Boys and Girls Use Computers Differently, and Does It Contribute to Why Boys Do Worse in School than Girls? Discussion Paper No. 9302 August 2015 IZA DP No. 9302

Kay,R.H. (2008). Exploring Gender Differences in Computer-Related Behaviour: Past, Present, and Future. 10.4018/978-1-59904-774-4.ch002.

Longstreet, W. S. (1978). *Aspects of ethnicity*. New York, NY: Teachers College Press.

Pew Research (2019)(https://www.pewinternet.org/chart/social-media-use-by-gender/).

Shearer, E., & Gottfried, J. (2017). News Use Across Social Media Platforms 2017. Pew Research Center. Retrieved from http://www.journalism.org/2017/09/07/news-use-across-social-media-platforms-2017/

Statista (https://www.statista.com/statistics/266587/percentage-of-internet-users-by-age-groups-in-the-us/)

MIRELE: A MIXED-REALITY SYSTEM FOR LEARNING A TASK DOMAIN

Zardosht Hodaie, Sajjad Taheri and Bernd Brügge
Technical University of Munich. Faculty of Informatics. Chair for applied Software Engineering
Boltzmannstr. 3, 85748 Garching b. München, Germany

ABSTRACT

MIRELE is an interactive tabletop for situated domain learning that helps students learn names of the physical objects and their relationships by projecting the names, relationships, and additional information onto the real objects. It is build based on camera-projector system and offers a domain-independent fast authoring system. Using the authoring system, the teachers can create the learning materials themselves without any programming. MIRELE is designed for domain-independence, unobtrusiveness and usability for manual activities, and offers a simple low-cost solution that can be utilized very fast in the classroom.

KEYWORDS

Interactive Tabletops, Situated Vocabulary Learning, AR Authoring

1. INTRODUCTION

An essential part of learning any domain is learning its vocabulary, concepts, and the relationships between them. In this paper we focus on the domain of manual-procedural activities (MPAs) (Hodaie, Haladjian & Bruegge 2018). Manual-procedural activities involve manipulating real physical objects by following a given procedure. Examples of MPAs are numerous, such as repairing a motor, assembling a part, and different crafts. In all these activities we a) manipulate physical objects and materials either directly by hands, or indirectly using tools; and b) follow steps of a given procedure, either by looking it up in the instruction manual, or knowing it by heart, or imitating an instructor. As part of learning a manual-procedural activity, a student must learn the names of the objects, materials, and tools, and how they relate to each other. Acquisition of this domain knowledge is part of every Vocational Education and Training program (Rauner et al. 2012).

A motivation behind our work is the current refugee crisis facing the European countries. Many of the refugees are skilled professionals that could be integrated into the local economies. However, a challenge towards incorporating them quickly into the job market is the language barrier. These professionals already know their corresponding domain of work, but they don't know the vocabulary in the language of the host country. So our system aims to aid them in faster learning of their technical vocabulary.

In this paper we propose a mixed-reality system based on a camera-projector setup to assist vocabulary and concept learning. Our assumption is that a mixed-reality system that involves the real objects and provides a situated (Lave & Wenger 1991) and embodied (Abrahamson & Lindgren 2014) learning experience will be more effective in learning and retention of the vocabulary and concepts of a domain.

The system consists of three main components: an interactive tabletop that recognizes and tracks real objects and projects names and different additional information onto them; A domain-independent authoring system that allows teachers to create learning content without any programming; A simple GUI for creating object recognition components.

2. RELATED WORK

The Bloom's Taxonomy of learning objectives considers acquiring knowledge as the basis of all other cognitive processes of learning (Krathwohl 2002). The knowledge itself is further categorized into factual knowledge (e.g. terminology), conceptual knowledge (e.g. categories and interrelations between concepts), and procedural knowledge (e.g. methods and procedures for doing something).

There is evidence in the literature that affordances such as embodiment and interactivity provided by Augmented Reality (AR) and tangible user interfaces improve learning and knowledge acquisition (Schneider et al. 2010, Diegmann et al. 2015). Manches et al. (2009) discuss the perceptual and manipulative properties of physical objects and how these properties can support learning for children. Working with physical objects and hands-on learning is also an integrated part of engineering disciplines (Carlson & Sullivan 1999). Accordingly, we argue that when the domain of learning is the physical world, such as tools and objects required for accomplishing a physical task, interacting with the real objects will benefit the learning performance.

Another related area of research for our work is the situated vocabulary learning. Several systems have utilized the pedagogical theories of hands-on, authentic, and situated learning (Ozverir & Herrington 2011) in the field of vocabulary learning. Ogata et al. (2004) use RFID tags on objects and environment attached sensors in order to track user's environment and present the relevant vocabulary and phrases. Santos et al. (2016) created a marker-based mobile vocabulary learning app and showed a slight improvement in learning gain as well as a significant positive attitude of the users toward learning. Vazquez et al. (2017) created a mixed-reality app using Microsoft Hololens that uses cloud-based object recognition to enable a serendipitous language learning experience with dynamic content.

Our approach is distinguished from related work in two aspects. We offer a fast and domain-independent authoring system that allows flexible definition of learning content directly by teachers. Additionally, we offer a simple GUI for fast creation of object recognition components that can be used in the system. As a result, our system is not limited to hard-coded pre-defined content, and can be used directly by teachers of different domains.

3. MIRELE

Figure 1 (left) shows use cases of MIRELE. The system has two actors: the teacher and the student. Teachers can define learning content in the Authoring mode. This learning content is presented in Training mode to the student. The teacher can also define exercises that are presented to the student in Exercise mode.

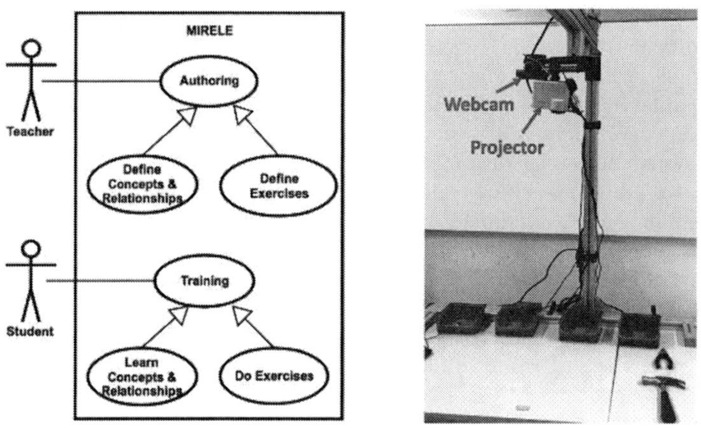

Figure 1. Use case of MIRELE and the camera-projector setup

We considered the following design goals in creating MIRELE: Low-cost, easy to setup, and easy-to-use system; and fast and domain-independent authoring. Accordingly, we chose a camera-projector setup, because the required equipment can easily be acquired with comparatively low price in the consumer market. Furthermore, this setup allows for easy hands-free interaction without the need for bulky and tethered head-mounted displays. The same setup is used by the teachers to create the learning content quickly using a graphical user interface. Figure 1 (right) shows our camera- projector setup.

MIRELE has two modes: Authoring and Training. In Authoring mode, the teacher interacts with the camera-projector setup and authoring GUI on a PC to create learning contents. This step includes defining objects and their annotations and defining exercises. The annotations can be different multi-media content like text, arrows, video, and audio. In Training mode, the student interacts with the tabletop by putting and manipulating objects on the table, or selecting the objects and annotations using a tracked selection stick. In Training mode, the content defined by the teacher is projected on the tabletop.

Learning content are presented as AR annotations projected onto the objects on the tabletop. This include textual annotations, arrows, circles, checkboxes, images, audio, and video snippets. Each annotation can be either attached to an object or placed on a fixed position on the tabletop. Furthermore, the teacher can define named relationships between objects. In Training mode, the relationships are shown as straight labeled lines between objects. For example, different kinds of pliers can be grouped together using relationship lines.

The system does not consider the semantics of the content. The teacher defines what are the learning content and their semantics. This can be names of the materials, objects, and tools, names of the parts of an object, and different relationships between objects and which objects are required for a task. Similarly, exercises are defined as membership questions. For example, "Which objects are needed to accomplish task X?". The system considers the content merely as different kinds of AR annotations.

In order to dynamically project annotations onto the physical objects, the table needs to know which objects are on the table, where are their positions, and what are their orientations. This is achieved using object recognition components. For each set of objects in a domain, that are involved in a learning session, the teacher needs first to create and include the required object detectors. An object detector is either based on a machine learning model (marker-less object detection) or based on markers. In the case of marker less object detection, we offer a simple UI in which the teacher selects objects that need to be detected. The program then creates an object detection package that include a trained ML model. Depending on the hardware used, this process may take a long time, up to several hours. For marker-based object detection, the teacher associates physical objects with the markers, by selecting them in the UI and assigning a marker ID to them. In addition to object detection, the system also offers detection of a selection stick, using which the student can interact with objects and annotation. For example, selecting an object can trigger an audio annotation that names the object. Or selecting a video annotation will start playing it.

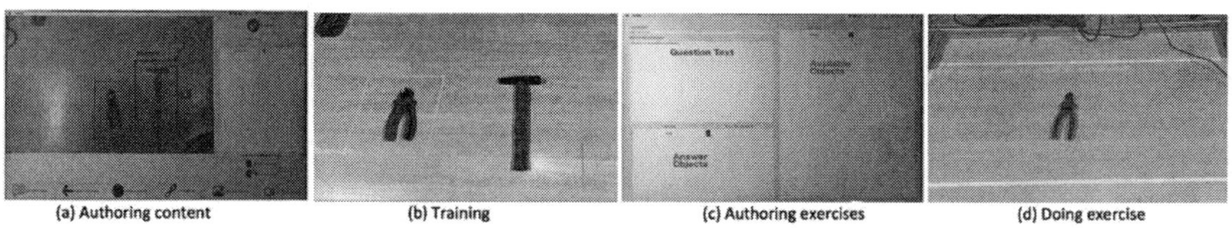

Figure 2. The system screenshots (see text for descriptions)

Figure 2 shows the screenshots of the systems in different modes. In Authoring mode (Figure 2a), the teacher sees a top-view of the table provided by the camera and graphically interacts with it to define the content. The teacher puts the objects on the table and selects them to be tracked by the systems. He then adds different kinds of annotations like textual descriptions, arrows, or video snippets attached to the objects or at fixed positions on the scene. In the Training mode (Figure 2b), the student puts the objects on the table, the system detects the objects and projects the annotations provide by the teacher onto them. The student can select objects and annotation, for example selecting a video annotation that demonstrates how to use a tool. The system also projects the relationships between objects as labeled straight lines. The teacher defines exercises as questions that have objects as answer (Figure 2c). The exercise consists of a question text and a set of objects as the correct answer. For example, "Which tool do you use to pull out a nail?" and for the correct answer the student should put the "pincer" on the table. It is also possible to define an exercise as a multiple-choice question using checkboxes, or as a selection task, in which the student should select the right object. In exercise mode (Figure 2d), the system projects the question on the table. The student answers the question by putting objects on the table. The system detects the objects put on the table and gives feedback on correctness of the answer.

4. CONCLUSION AND FUTURE WORK

In this paper we introduced our ongoing work on MIRELE, an interactive tabletop intended to support learning of a task domain in manual-procedural activities. MIRELE offers a simple authoring tool for the interactive tabletop, using which the teachers themselves can create learning content, without depending on programmers. We believe this low-cost and simple system will lower the entrance barrier for teachers to experiment with new possibilities of augmented reality and tangible interaction in the classroom. Furthermore, the authoring system together with the domain-independence focus of MIRELE allows rapid creation of learning materials for different domains. We believe this opens new opportunities for research on the use of augmented reality in the classroom, that is conducted directly by pedagogical experts themselves and in which the cost and effort of content creation is significantly reduced.

We are currently conducting a pilot between-subject user study to evaluate the effectiveness of MIRELE for learning the vocabulary of simple task domain consisting of 10 tools from a typical house-hold toolbox in German language. Our assumption is that the participant who learn with physical objects will perform better in terms of retention of the object names compared to those who use a paper-based learning material. In the next step, we plan to conduct usability studies with teachers of a vocational school, in order to evaluate how they use MIRELE and get feedback for improving its feature set.

REFERENCES

Abrahamson, D. and Lindgren, R., 2014. *Embodiment and embodied design.* The Cambridge handbook of the learning sciences, 2, pp.358-376.

Carlson, L.E. and Sullivan, J.F., 1999. Hands-on engineering: learning by doing in the integrated teaching and learning program. *International Journal of Engineering Education*, 15(1), pp. 20-31.

Diegmann P., Schmidt-Kraepelin M., van den Eynden S., Basten D., 2015. Benefits of augmented reality in educational environments—A systematic literature review, In *Proc. 12th Int. Conf. Wirtschaftsinformatik*, pp. 1542-1556.

Hodaie, Z., Haladjian, J. and Bruegge, B., 2018, June. TUMA: Towards an Intelligent Tutoring System for Manual Procedural Activities. In *International Conference on Intelligent Tutoring Systems* (pp. 326-331). Springer.

Krathwohl, D.R., 2002. A revision of Bloom's taxonomy: An overview. Revising Bloom's Taxonomy. Theory into practice, 41(4), pp. 212-218. The H.W. Wilson Company.

Lave, J. and Wenger, E., 1991. Situated learning: Legitimate peripheral participation. Cambridge university press.

Manches A., O'Malley C., Benford S. 2009. Physical manipulation: evaluating the potential for tangible designs. In Proceedings of the 3rd International Conference on Tangible and Embedded Interaction. ACM, 77–84.

Ogata, H., Akamatsu, R. and Yano, Y., 2004. Computer supported ubiquitous learning environment for vocabulary learning using RFID tags. In *IFIP World Computer Congress*, TC 3 (pp. 121-130). Springer, Boston, MA.

Ozverir, I. and Herrington, J., 2011, June. Authentic activities in language learning: Bringing real world relevance to classroom activities. In *EdMedia+ Innovate Learning* (pp. 1423-1428). Association for the Advancement of Computing in Education (AACE).

Rauner, F., Heinemann, L., Maurer, A. Haasler, B., 2012. *Competence Development and Assessment in TVET (COMET): Theoretical framework and empirical results* (Vol. 16). Springer Science & Business Media.

Santos, M.E.C., Taketomi, T., Yamamoto, G., Rodrigo M., and Kato, H., 2016. Augmented reality as multimedia: the case for situated vocabulary learning. *Research and Practice in Technology Enhanced Learning*, 11(1), p.4.

Schneider, B., Jermann, P., Zufferey, G. and Dillenbourg, P., 2010. Benefits of a tangible interface for collaborative learning and interaction. *IEEE Transactions on Learning Technologies*, 4(3), pp. 222-232.

Vazquez, C.D., Nyati, A.A., Luh, A., Fu, M., Aikawa, T. and Maes, P., 2017, May. Serendipitous language learning in mixed reality. In *Proceedings of the 2017 CHI Conference Extended Abstracts on Human Factors in Computing Systems* (pp. 2172-2179). ACM.

LIFELONG SELF-DIRECTED LEARNING IN THE DIGITAL AGE: AN ORIENTATION OF CURRENT SOFTWARE TOOLS SUPPORTING EXPERTS IN MAINTAINING AND UPDATING THEIR KNOWLEDGE

Jodie Freeman[1], Andreas Raabe[1], Felix Schmitz[2] and Sissel Guttormsen[2]
[1]*University Clinic for Neurosurgery, Neuro Centre, University hospital of Bern, Switzerland*
[2]*Institute of Medical Education, Medical Faculty, University of Bern, Switzerland*

ABSTRACT

To guarantee high-quality services, health professionals are required to successfully maintain their extensive knowledge base. M, health professionals are forced to consistently stay up-to-date in their field in which new knowledge is evolving continuously. Hence, there is a strong need for effective support during their lifelong, self-directed learning processes as a means of maintaining and updating medical-related expert knowledge. From the literature, self-organisation, -management, -assessment, and collaboration activities have been defined to be of high relevance for these learning processes.

The increasing speed of technological development has led to the development of a plethora of digital tools with varying features aimed at supporting professionals in their self-directed learning. In light of the increased number of tools available, we aim to give orientation on some of the most popular tools available to support health and other professionals in their self-directed learning. Results show that three main categories of digital tools related to self-directed learning can be identified: reference-management systems, learn-and-test tools, and collaborating tools. Our results further show that within the current landscape, there is no one tool that covers all tasks related to self-directed learning. We conclude that one single digital tool, combining all the features supporting self-directed learning in one simple easy to use manner may better support health and other professionals in maintaining and updating their expert knowledge. Future development should focus in particular on suitable combinations of features supporting self-directed learning, as implemented within one tool.

KEYWORDS

Self-Directed Learning, Health Professionals, Software Tools

1. INTRODUCTION

Health professionals are required to stay up to date in their field in which new knowledge is evolving continuously (Kompen, 2019). In addition to updating new areas of expertise, health professionals also have to maintain their existing knowledge base enabling them to be lifelong learners (Teunissen and Dornan, 2008). A systematic review (Murad et al., 2010) identified self-directed learning (SDL) as the most appropriate methodology for maintaining and updating levels of expertise and promote lifelong learning; hence SDL has been advocated as an effective and efficient activity for health professionals (Kompen, 2019). Aspects of SDL include self-analysis, self-assessment, self-evaluation and collaboration (Costa and Kallick, 2004). Learners who self-assess themselves enhance continuous lifelong SDL in which technology is reducing the effort needed to find, organise, manage and interact with information (Costa and Kallick, 2004). The emerging problems and challenges for experts practicing SDL are manifold. For example, learners must quickly identify relevant digital information from insurmountable range of sources coupled with the need to store, manage and retrieve these documents quickly and efficiently, in which the traditional means of managing information (e.g. individually storing data in electronic filing systems) are ill-suited to the realities of the digital age (Bryan, 2015). Current restrictions in working hours and changes in the organisation of health care make it ever more necessary for health professionals to utilise their time productively and learn more efficiently (Teunissen and Dornan, 2008).

The digital age is profoundly changing the ways in which we learn with the use of technologies (Kompen, 2019), in particular how we search, select, use and interact with information for our professional development. Printed textbooks and journals are increasingly being replaced by PDF versions and additional digital sources, such as videos, web pages, blogs, etc. Developments in digital technology, and the speed at which they emerge, drive innovation and new applications that touch our lives in different and often profound ways (Khosrow-Pour, 2018). Given the increased use of fast changing digital technologies in the workplace, new skills needs have emerged (Khosrow-Pour, 2018). The use of these technologies has contributed to transforming learning and skills development into a lifelong process. From this perspective, learners have to continually improve and evolve with technology to benefit from the support in their learning. Manganello et al., (2013) found that many software tools require training to fully exploit the learning power of these technologies, highlighting that it may be more beneficial to develop a single, easy to use interface, which provides the SDL functionalities needed to support learning without having to master complex technological skills.

The increasing speed of technological development has led to the development and advancement of a plethora of digital tools that claim to support learning and combat the challenges the increasing rate of information has brought about. There is a lot more recognition in SDL for learners to utilize technology and the current research shows a growth in digital software aimed at the various learning needs of professionals (Kompen et al., 2019). Research highlights that digital tools can support SDL in many ways, helping learners skillfully "*access the expanding house of knowledge in the Web 2.0 and beyond environment*" (Bryan, 2015. Pg. 44). Hence, digital tools can also increase the speed of accessing information, increase confidence in the learner and responsibility for what they learn. In addition, with digital tools learners have the potential to collaborate, share content and establish new online communities, which support SDL both, in formal and informal settings (Bryan, 2015). However at present, there is no one tool that assists learners in reordering, classifying, interacting with proper knowledge resources and sharing them with learners with similar needs thus more than one digital tool is needed to support their SDL needs (Manganello et al, 2013). Therefore, the aim of this paper is to give orientation on some of the most popular current digital tools used by professionals to support their SDL. We also seek to show which precise features of those tools actually correspond with SDL-related principles. Hence, these research questions (RQ) are formulated:

RQ1: *Which digital tools are used most frequently by health professionals in order to support their SDL?*

RQ2: *Which of those tools are made up of features linked with SDL-related principles as mentioned in the existing literature?*

2. METHODS

To give an overview of current digital tools' SDL-related features, it firstly had to be defined, which tools should be analysed according to our questions. Based on existing opinions of researchers (n= 5 experts at our university clinic) a selection of tools used by professionals were identified. We identified 9 Tools that could be clustered as management systems, learn-and-test tools, and collaborating tools (e.g. for writing a paper together). To further validate our first selection of tools, a comparison was made with the learning tools available amongst students and post-doctorates as identified by the Head of Library and research services at the University of Bern. The selection of tools as set out in this paper were confirmed as current tools that support learning within research institutions. The most frequently named tools were:

- *Endnote* (https://endnote.com/) as representative for reference-management systems
- *Authorea* (https://www.authorea.com) as representative for collaboration tools
- *Brainscape* (https://brainscape.com) as representative for learn-and-test tools

In a second step, we used the data bank *AlternateTo* (https://alternativeto.net/); with this data bank one can query software tools that have comparable features to a respective competitor. Importantly, the query results are ranked based on an online-community, which means that the higher a tool is listed the more favourable it is rated by the community. Accordingly, we searched for alternatives for the three mentioned tools – and chose the two first, and thus most popular, digital tools per category in the list of the query results.

In a third step, the features offered by the resulting nine digital tools (see Table 1) were independently analysed by two experts along the following SDL-related tasks: (i) finding, storing, retrieving information,

(ii) self-organisation, (iii) self-management, (iv) self-assessment, and (v) sharing/collaborating. According to Costa and Kallick (2004), these tasks refer to as the most central components of SDL.

In the fourth step, directly after the ratings were completed, the two raters were tasked with reaching a consensus in the case of differences in their ratings. They discussed the few cases in which features were similar to reformulate them into one single feature and excluded features when agreed that they are irrelevant to the domains of SDL. Based on consensus between the raters, final univocal allocations were determined.

In the fifth and final step, we compared the digital tools by opposing their SDL-based features in a matrix.

3. RESULTS

The findings highlight that there is no single tool that offers all SDL-related features linked with supporting self-directed, lifelong learning. Instead the tools offer a set of features that support one or two certain component(s) of the learning process. For details, see Table 1.

Table 1. Prominent software tools and their SDL-related features

		Digital tool								
SDL-related aspect	Feature	Brainscape	Cram	Studyblue	Citavi	Endnote	Mendeley	Authorea	Evernote	Scrivemers
Finding, storing, retrieving information	add files	no	no	no	yes	yes	yes	yes	yes	yes
	(advanced) search	no	no	no	yes	yes	yes	no	yes	yes
	cloud access	no	no	no	yes	yes	yes	yes	yes	yes
Self-organising	creating chaper tree	no	no	no	yes	no	yes	no	yes	yes
	add chapter /sub-chapter	no	no	no	yes	no	yes	no	yes	yes
	Searching for stored files	no	no	no	yes	yes	yes	yes	yes	yes
	sort, filter	no	no	no	yes	yes	yes	yes	yes	yes
	tagging	no	no	no	yes	yes	yes	yes	yes	no
Self-managing	task list	no	no	no	yes	no	yes	yes	yes	yes
	annotations	no	no	no	yes	yes	yes	no	yes	yes
Self-assessing	creating flashcards	yes	yes	yes	no	no	no	no	no	no
	flashcards shared by professionals	yes	yes	yes	no	no	no	no	no	no
	create own lessons	yes	no	yes	no	no	no	no	no	no
	scoring	yes	yes	yes	no	no	no	no	no	no
sharing / collaborating	share contents	yes	yes	yes	yes	yes	yes	yes	yes	yes
	link sharing via email/text message	no	no	no	yes	yes	yes	yes	yes	yes
	ask online community questions	no	no	yes	no	no	no	no	no	yes
	connect with users through their profile	yes	no	yes	no	no	yes	yes	yes	no
	online/realtime collaboration (e.g. writing a paper together)	no	no	yes	no	no	no	yes	yes	yes
	templates	yes	yes	yes	no	no	no	yes	yes	yes

Note: Brainscape, Cram and Studyblue are associated with 'learn-and-test' tools; Citavi, Endnote and Mendely are reference management systems; Authorea, Evernote and Scriveners are mainly associated with tools for online collaboration.

4. DISCUSSION

Within this study, we provided an overview of the most popular digital tools for health professionals, which are used for SDL-related purposes. Our two research questions are clarified: Firstly, the questioned health professionals most frequently use reference-management systems for their daily work. Nonetheless, they also use collaboration and 'learn-and-test' tools. Secondly, the tools that we evaluated only offer a set of features that support one or two component(s) of the SDL process. These components specifically include knowledge management, self-assessment and collaboration, which seem to address major needs of health professionals.

Our findings show that there are a range of digital tools available to support professionals in their learning, with different tools offering a variety of features. However, based on our main finding, the tools we analysed do not offer a combination of features covering all the aspects of SDL at once. The need to support various functions within one tool is supported by previous literature denoting the importance of combining a range of varying features to create a successfully functional personal learning environment (Attwell, 2007) that supports SDL in a holistic sound manner (Kompen, 2019). Each digital tool analysed in this study supports one or two component(s) of SDL and therefore a varying choice of tools and their features (which in turn support different components of SDL) would need to be combined in response to individual learning needs, aims and goals (Attwell, 2007). We assume that health professionals are not supported optimally, when they have to use a set of various tools in order to be fully supported in their SDL, further research should explore this assumption.

Further, it should be investigated, which functions of the SDL activities ideally can be implemented in one single tool, without resulting in an overload of functions and low usability. Previous findings show that when technology aimed at supporting the user get too complex, the acceptance of the learner suffers (Khosrow-Pour, 2018), suggesting that a tool, which combines the various features for how we store, manage, assess knowledge, and collaborate with others may be too complex to handle resulting in reduced efficiency. In addition, if digital tools are over complicated with too many features, research shows that learners become frustrated and spend more time learning to use the tools than actually learning from relevant materials (Khosrow-Pour, 2018).

Taken together, it might be worthwhile to design a digital tool that, on the one hand, offers a combination of all features of SDL (cf. Costa and Kallick, 2004). On the other hand, the concept of such a tool must also focus on the tool's usability in order to reduce the time spent learning the software as well as to make it easy and satisfactory to use (Teunissen and Dornan, 2008). Consequently, future research should focus on how to design digital tools that include all central components of SDL by also providing a strong alignment with the actual needs and ICT competencies of health professionals (Teunissen and Dornan, 2008).

4.1 Limitations

This study has some limitations. Foremost, we were not able to systematically identify all digital tools that, at present, address SDL-related features. Findings are based on a selection of corresponding tools. Still, the selection made in this study is likely to be representative, as it is based on the typical target population and their habits, as well as on a much broader online-community. We conclude that our results are generalisable.

Another potential limitation is that the scope of the selected tools also represents an inherent selection of features. For instance, a reference-management system is normally not built for self-assessment reasons. Nonetheless, this issue does not derogate our main finding that there is no one prominent tool available at present that covers all central components of SDL; users only use digital tools available on the current market.

5. CONCLUSION

This study offers an orientation of prominent digital tools used by health professionals for SDL-related reasons. Most importantly, we could not identify a single digital tool that covers all components of SDL as discussed in the literature. Hence, future research should focus on how to design a tool that offers more features linked with SDL-related components in one solution – by bridging the gap between usability, knowledge management and human learning principles, also addressing the domain-specific needs of health professionals.

REFERENCES

Attwell G., 2007. Personal learning environments: the future of eLearning? *Elearning Papers*, Vol. *2*, No. 1, pp 1-8.

Bryan V.C. 2015. Self-directed learning and technology. *The Education Digest*, Vol. 80, No. 6, pp 42-44.

Costa, A. L. and Kallick, B., 2004. *Assessment Strategies for Self-Directed Learning.* Sage Publications, California.

Khosrow-Pour M., 2018. *Handbook of Research on Challenges and Opportunities in Launching a Technology-Driven International University. Advances in Higher Education and Professional Development.* IGI Global, USA.

Kompen T. et al, 2019. Personal learning Environments based on Web 2.0 services in higher education. *Telematics and Informatics*, Vol. 38, pp 194-206.

Manganello, F et al, 2013. PKS: An ontology-based learning construct for lifelong learners. *Journal of Educational Technology & Society*, Vol 16, pp 104-117

Murad, M.H et al, 2010. The effectiveness of self-directed learning in health professions education: a systematic review. *Medical Education*, Vol 44, No 11, pp1057-1068

Teunissen, P. W. and Dornan, T., 2008. Lifelong learning at work. *British Med. Journal*, Vol. 336, No. 7645, pp 667-669.

EDUCATION SYSTEM FOR ELECTRONIC CIRCUIT CONSTRUCTION INVOLVING SOLDERING ON A CIRCUIT BOARD

Atsushi Takemura
Tokyo University of Agriculture and Technology
2-24-16 Naka-cho, Koganei-shi, Tokyo 184-8588, Japan

ABSTRACT

This paper proposes a novel education system for learning electronic circuit construction involving soldering on a universal circuit-board. This system enables a student to efficiently design the layout of circuit components on a circuit board and helps the student securely construct the circuit by soldering the circuit components in accordance with the designed layout. Web-based instructions are utilized for wiring and soldering the circuit components on the lower surface of the circuit-board based on automated recognition of circuit images during the circuit construction. The effectiveness of the proposed system was verified by 40 undergraduate students at Tokyo University of Agriculture and Technology. The comparison tests between two groups that comprised students that used or did not use the proposed system demonstrated the effectiveness of the system.

KEYWORDS

Web-Based Education, Circuit Construction, Soldering

1. INTRODUCTION

Knowledge of electronic circuit construction and practical applications, such as signal processing, machine control, and robotics, are of critical importance for a modern technology education. Recently, several educational support systems have been developed to improve students' understanding of electronic circuits and their ability for circuit construction (Reisslein, 2013; Rodriguez-Sanchez, 2016; Garcia-Zubia, 2017). However, these education tools are limited in scope and are only suitable for specific circuits within a subject area. To improve applicability to a broader array of circuit types, an educational system for supporting virtual and physical circuit-construction was developed (Takemura, 2018). These conventional systems allow a student to construct a circuit using a breadboard (Figure 1(a)). Here, soldering of the circuit components (e.g., devices and cables) is not performed and the components' terminals are only plugged into the holes on the upper surface of the breadboard. This breadboard-based construction is suitable for beginners' education because of the safety and reusability. However, the solder-less circuit on a breadboard is inferior in the stability and practical use and therefore, is applicable only to trial construction or construction of small-scale circuits for elementary education. To overcome the shortcoming of the conventional systems, a novel education system for learning electronic circuit construction involving soldering on a universal circuit-board (Figure 1(b)) is proposed. In addition, a web-based instruction set for wiring and soldering on the lower surface of the circuit-board based on a circuit image-processing technique is included.

The rest of this paper is organized in the following manner. Section 2 describes the technical features of the proposed system for instruction of circuit construction with soldering on a universal circuit-board. Section 3 describes the experimental methodology to evaluate the proposed system. Section 4 summarizes the results of the experiments at actual university laboratories. This section also describes the quantitative evaluation of the proposed system. Finally, Section 5 provides the conclusions.

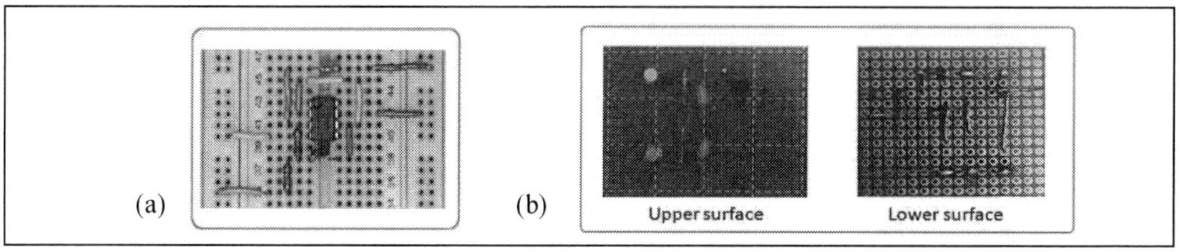

Figure 1. Examples of constructed circuits on the two types of circuit boards: (a) constructed circuit on a solder-less breadboard, and (b) constructed circuit soldered on a universal circuit-board

2. TECHNICAL FEATURES OF THE SYSTEM

Figure 2 illustrates the technical features of the proposed system for learning circuit construction involving soldering on a universal circuit-board. This system consists of the individual students' mobile PC and the remote analysis system. A student uses his mobile PC to construct a virtual circuit by handwriting using a graphic editor (Takemura, 2018). Based on the layout of the circuit components on the virtual circuit, the student can efficiently construct a physical circuit by placing circuit devices on the upper surface of the circuit-board and wiring and soldering on the lower surface. The remote analysis system can automatically recognize the structures of the virtual and physical circuits by image processing (e.g., segmentation and pattern recognition) of the constructed circuit images (Figure 2B(3)). In this study, based on the circuit structures obtained from the image processing, an image analysis-based process was developed for automating instructions on demand for wiring and soldering on the lower surface of the circuit-board (Figure 2B(4)). In addition, the developed system enables individual students to simulate their constructed circuits' behaviors (Figure 2B(6) and B(7)). This circuit simulation is obtained from the translation of the recognized circuit structure into a general circuit description language (simulation program with integrated circuit emphasis (SPICE)) (Rabaey, 2012). Moreover, differences of the SPICE information between the correct circuit and the constructed circuit can identify errors in the student's circuit.

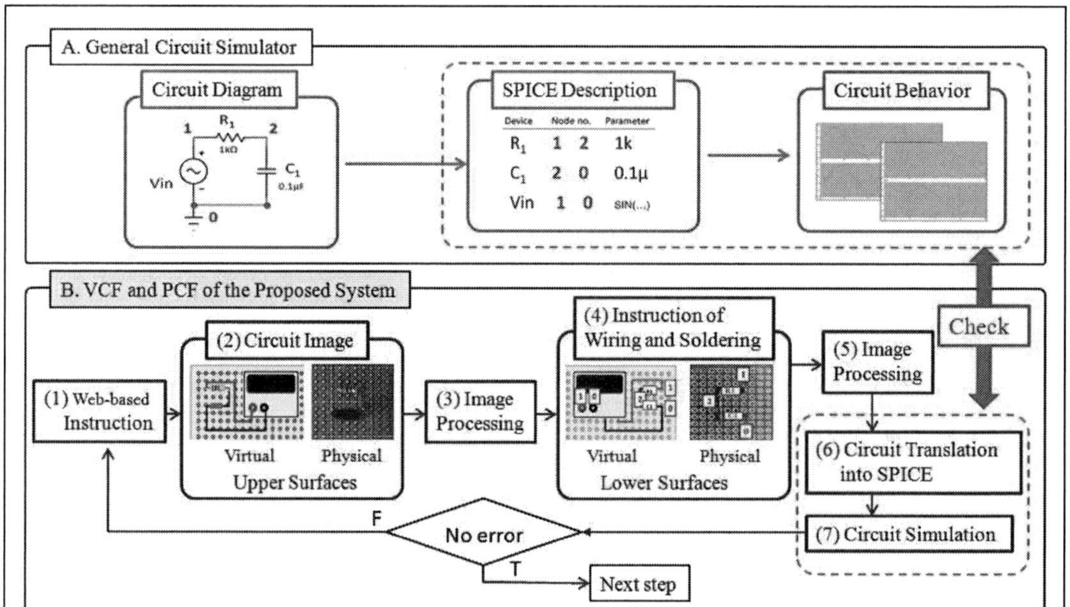

Figure 2. Schematic of the proposed workflow for circuit construction

2.1 Web-based Instructions for Circuit Construction

The proposed education system provides individual students with circuit diagrams and specifications of the circuit to be constructed available through common web-based databases. Based on the information obtained from the circuit translation, the proposed system sends messages to individual students during circuit construction and instructs them to inspect and correct their results in the following manner:

1) When incorrect components or faulty wiring and soldering are detected from a circuit image, the analysis system indicates the errors and instructs the student to check and correct them.

2) When the analysis system detects a serious error (e.g., short circuit), the system sends the student a critical warning to correct the incorrect section.

3) The analysis system requests the student to check whether the simulated behavior of the constructed circuit corresponds to the circuit's specification.

2.2 Virtual Circuit Construction Function

Figure 2B also shows the virtual circuit construction function (VCF) of the proposed system. The VCF aids in designing the layout of circuit devices on the upper surface of the universal circuit-board and provides instructions on wiring the circuit devices and the soldering positions. Using a graphic editor, a student can design the layout of the circuit components as an image of the upper surface of a circuit-board by placing virtual circuit components downloaded from a database. As shown in Figure 2B(2), the student draws colored lines to indicate the wiring of each device. Based on the recognition of the virtually constructed circuit, the proposed system can automatically provide instructions for wiring and soldering on the lower surface of the circuit-board (Figure 2B(3) and (4)). This function also simulates the circuit operation and individual students can observe the circuit behavior on their tablet-type PCs. The presence and location of incorrect components in the virtual circuit are determined by analyzing the difference of the SPICE information between the correct circuit and the virtual circuit. When faulty parts or incorrect behavior of the virtual circuit is indicated, the system provides the student with instructions or warnings as described in Section 2.1. Conversely, when correct circuit behavior and components are indicated, the system instructs the student to construct a physical circuit using the function described below.

2.3 Physical Circuit Construction Function

Figure 2B also illustrates the physical circuit construction function (PCF) of the proposed system. In accordance with the layout of the virtual circuit preliminary constructed using VCF, a student constructs the physical circuit and transmit an image to the remote analysis system (Figure 2B(2)). This function automatically performs image processing to recognize the circuit's structure and translates the structure into SPICE. Based on the recognized circuit information, the PCF can instruct the wiring and soldering on the image of the lower surface of the circuit-board (Figure 2B(3) and 2B(4)). This function also enables the simulation of the circuit operation, and individual students can observe the circuit behavior on their tablet-type PCs. To detect faulty parts in the physical circuit and simulate the circuit behavior, the PCF performs the same processes as the VCF. The presence and location of incorrect components in the circuit are determined by analyzing the difference of the SPICE information between the correct circuit and the physically constructed circuit. When the system indicates faulty parts or incorrect behavior of the physical circuit, the system provides the student the web-based instruction for correcting them. If no faults are identified, the system indicates that the student can proceed with further experiments using the physical circuit.

3. METHODOLOGY FOR EVALUATING THE PROPOSED SYSTEM

The effectiveness of the proposed combination of virtual and physical systems was evaluated by the comparison of two groups of students aged 19–21 at Tokyo University of Agriculture and Technology.

Group-1 was comprised of 20 students instructed to construct an audio amplifier circuit, as shown in Figure 3(a), by conventional methods. Group-2 consisted of 20 students who performed the same circuit construction using the new system. Groups-1 and -2 were evaluated in 2018 and 2019, respectively. The system for the circuit construction used by the students in Group-2 is shown in Figure 3(b). Prior to the experiments, questionnaires were provided to ascertain the degrees of individual students' experience in circuit construction with soldering. Based on this, each student was subdivided into three experience categories as listed below:

A: Experienced in circuit construction with soldering in addition to practice exercises at school
B: No experience except for practice exercises at school
C: No experience

The number of students belonging to each experience category is shown in Figure 3(c) and indicates that the majority of students belonged to category B. All students had learned construction of elementary circuits with soldering as part of compulsory education in junior high schools in Japan and therefore there were no students belonging to category C.

The students in Group-1 were tasked to construct circuits based on the conventional method listed below within a time limit of 3.5 h:

(G1-1) Lecture on circuit construction and soldering by an instructor (0.5 h)
(G1-2) Physical circuit construction using the necessary circuit components provided by the instructor
(G1-3) The instructor inspects the constructed circuit. If an incorrect part is discovered, this student corrects it under the instructor's guidance (2 h for (G1-2) and (G1-3))
(G1-4) Measurement of the characteristics of the constructed circuit using experimental equipment (1 h)

The individual students in Group-2 were tasked to construct circuits using the proposed new system within 3.5 h according to the following processes:

(G2-1) Lecture on circuit construction and soldering by an instructor (0.5 h)
(G2-2) Construction of the circuit using VCF and PCF
(G2-3) The instructor inspects the physical circuit. If an incorrect part is discovered, this student corrects it under the instructor's guidance (2 h for (G2-2) and (G2-3))
(G2-4) Measurement of the characteristics of the constructed circuit using experimental equipments (1 h)

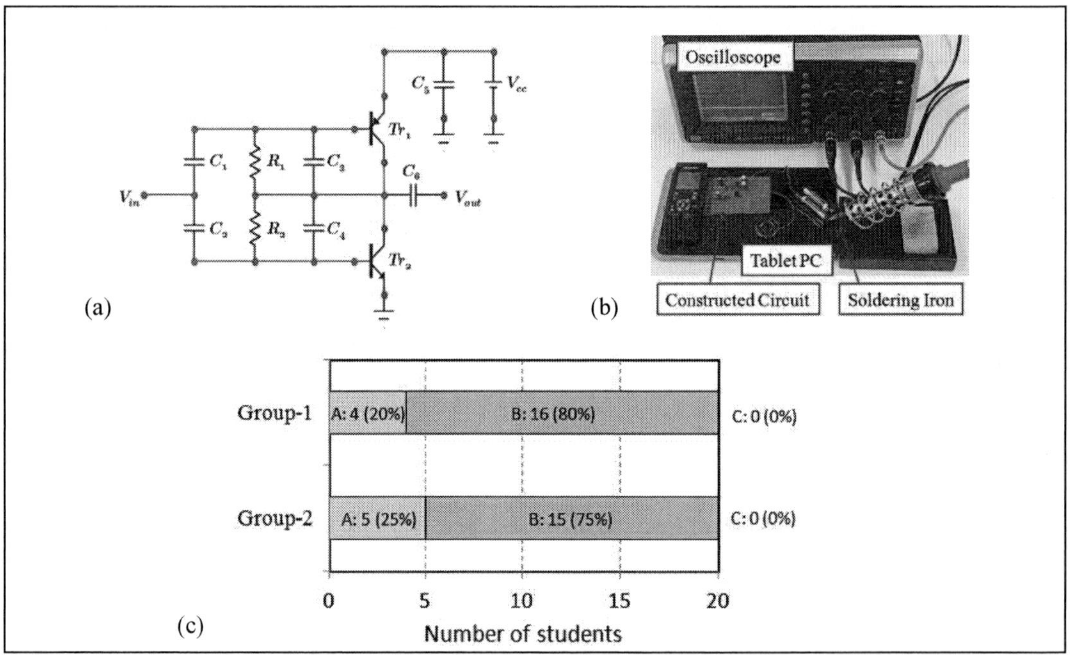

Figure 3. Method for evaluation of the proposed system; (a) circuit diagram of an audio amplifier to be constructed in this experiment, (b) system used for circuit construction with Group-2, and (c) distribution of experience categories in circuit construction with soldering for each group

4. RESULTS AND DISCUSSION

Comparison of testing results between Group-1 and Group-2 were evaluated to show the impact of the proposed system on the experiment described in Section 3. Figure 4 shows examples of the constructed circuits and simulation results obtained from a student in Group-2. Figure 4(a) shows the images of the constructed circuit corresponding to the diagram shown in Figure 3(a). Based on the layout of the virtually constructed circuit using VCF (Figure 4(v1)), the physical circuit (Figure 4(p1)) was constructed using PCF. Figure 4(b) shows the results of automated circuit recognition of the circuit images and the web-based instruction for wiring and soldering on the lower surface of the circuit-board. Figure 4(c) shows the results of the virtual measurement; the circuit translation into SPICE was obtained from the circuit recognition, and the translated SPICE enables the student to simulate the circuit's behavior.

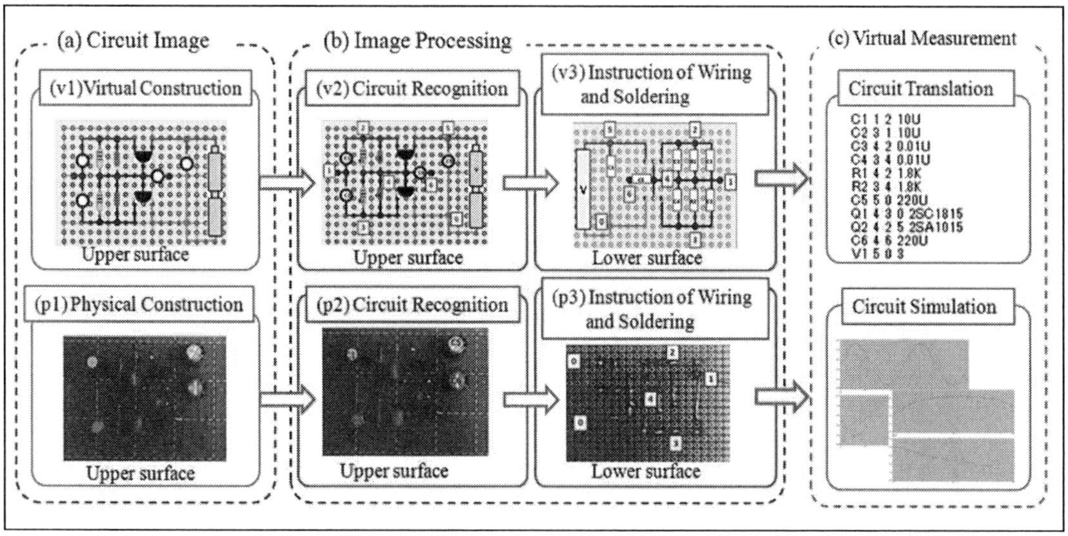

Figure 4. Results of the construction and simulation of the virtual and physical circuits constructed by a student in Group-2 using VCF and PCF of the proposed system

Figure 5(a) shows that the averages and ranges of the required time for the circuit construction of each experience category in Group-2 were shorter than that of Group-1. The average required time of the students in category B in Group-2 was close to that of category A in Group-1. These results indicate that the use of the proposed system decreased the time for circuit construction with soldering regardless of the students' experience. Figure 5(b) indicates the occurrence of errors in the constructed circuits that were discovered by the instructors during the process. As shown in this figure, ten (50%) students in Group-1 had errors in circuit construction that were observed by the instructor. Conversely, no errors in the circuits constructed by the students in Group-2 were noted. These results indicate the effectiveness of the proposed system for circuit construction with soldering on a universal circuit-board.

Through the evaluation process, positive responses were obtained from the instructors, which provide further validation of the effectiveness of the proposed system. These comments show that:

- The proposed system can improve the accuracy and efficiency of circuit construction with soldering.
- Combination of VCF and PCF is effective for avoiding serious errors that could cause accidents (e.g., a short circuit or inappropriate power supply) when operating the physical circuits.
- The web-based instructions given during VCF and PCF decrease an instructor's load and also increase safety of experiments involving circuit construction with soldering.

From the students in Group-2, the positive responses indicating the usefulness of the proposed system were obtained and include:

- VCF was a useful tool as the image of the virtual circuit layout helped to efficiently construct the physical circuit.

- The automated instructions based on the circuit image-processing increased the efficiency for wiring and soldering on the lower surface of the circuit-board.

To improve the applicability and usefulness of the system, the following studies should be implemented:

- evaluation test by beginners with no experience in soldering
- application to larger scale circuits

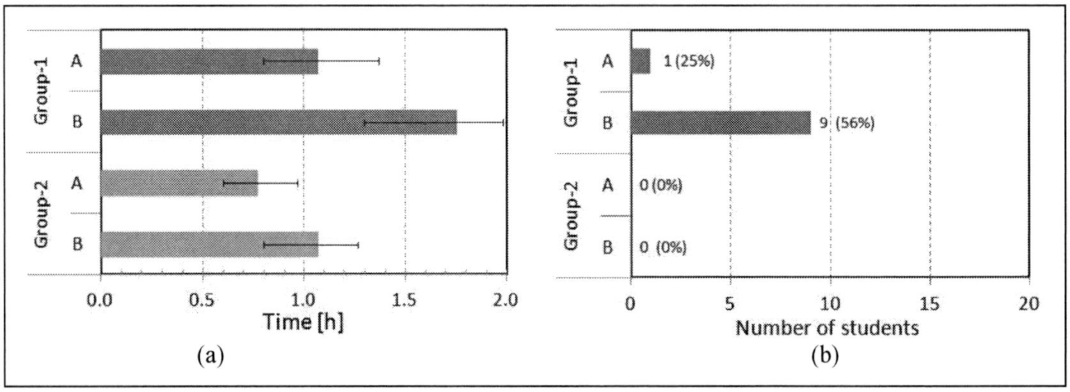

Figure 5. Results of the comparison test between Group-1 and Group-2; (a) average and range of the required time for the circuit construction of each group and experience degree, (b) the number of students whose circuits included errors

5. CONCLUSION

A novel web-based education system for circuit construction involving soldering on a universal circuit-board is demonstrated. The proposed system automatically recognizes the image of constructed circuits and can instruct the student in wiring and soldering on the lower surface of the circuit-board. A comparison study between two groups of university students demonstrated the effectiveness of the proposed system for accurate circuit construction with soldering on a circuit-board. Improvement of the web-based construction and image processing techniques are necessary for the applicability to more complex and larger scale circuits.

ACKNOWLEDGMENT

This study was partly supported by a Grant-in-Aid for Scientific Research (KAKENHI) 19K03079 from the Japan Society for the Promotion of Science.

REFERENCES

Garcia-Zubia, J., et al., 2017, Empirical analysis of the use of the VISIR remote lab in teaching analog electronics, *In IEEE Trans. Education*, Vol. 60, No. 2, pp. 149–156.

Rabaey, J. M., The Spice Page, <URL: http://bwrc.eecs.berkeley.edu/Classes/IcBook/SPICE/> (accessed July 18, 2019).

Reisslein, J., et al., 2013, Circuits kit K–12 outreach: impact of circuit element representation and student gender, *In IEEE Trans. Education*, Vol. 56, No. 3, pp. 316–321.

Rodriguez-Sanchez, M. C., et al., 2016, An embedded systems course for engineering students using open-source platforms in wireless scenarios, *In IEEE Trans. Education*, Vol. 59, No. 4, pp. 248–254.

Takemura, A., 2018, e-Learning system for electronic circuit construction using handwriting recognition and mixed reality technique, *Proc. IADIS Conference e-Learning 2018*, pp. 161–166, Madrid, Spain.

BENEFITS AND RISKS OF ICTS AND THEIR APPLICATIONS: AN ATTEMPT TO ANALYZE FREE DESCRIPTIVE ANSWERS

Yukiko Maruyama
Tokai University
Hiratsuka Kanagawa, Japan

ABSTRACT

This paper presents the results of an attempt to analyze the benefits and risks of information and communication technologies (ICTs) and their applications, as perceived by university students. A survey was conducted using questionnaire with a free descriptive answering format. Responses were analyzed via text mining and correspondence analysis; in this manner, explanations of students' perceptions could be deduced. As the survey conducted here was preliminary, the sample size was small; further analysis with a larger number of participants is necessary.

KEYWORDS

ICT, Risk, Benefit, Text Mining, Correspondence Analysis

1. INTRODUCTION

Over the past several decades, various ICTs and their applications have been developed. As Brey (2018) states, "Technology has become integral to the fabric of society, and helps to shape its quality" (p.39), technology has huge impact on our society. In particular, ICTs and their applications rapidly infiltrate our society and influence our lives in various situations. It can be seen that the diffusion of ICTs simultaneously provides both advantages and disadvantages to different groups of people, possibly creating division and conflict. For this reason, we should accept ICTs carefully. While creating rules and regulations comprise one method of mediating such conflicts, legislations tend to be delayed. As such, individuals need to acquire the appropriate skills to make decisions on such issues by themselves and to participate in legislation in an informed manner. These decisions should be made not only for individual benefit but also for the benefit of society as a whole. Hence, a fundamental approach to handling this situation is to evaluate the value of every type of ICT and its applications.

Benefit and/or risk perceptions are regarded as factors that influence the acceptance of emerging technologies, even those unrelated to ICT. There have been many studies examining this (Bearth and Siegrist 2016, Liu et al. 2019, Wilson et al. 2017). While the ability to accurately perceive the benefit and risk factors of technologies is essential to evaluate their value, it is difficult to sufficiently analyze these factors. It is supposed that perceptions depend on subjective experiences and attitudes toward technologies. Sato and Tabata (2018) investigated risk perceptions to Internet use for older adults and university students; the results of their semi-structured interviews revealed notable differences in risk and benefit perceptions between the two groups. The results showed that perceived benefits and risks differed based on respondents' personal Internet usage patterns. Moreover, it is probable that the characteristics of the technologies themselves influence users' perceptions. It is possible that some users could accurately perceive the risks of certain technologies but not others.

To support people's acquisition of such situation-specific skills, education is expected to play a significant role. It is desirable to establish appropriate curriculum and lesson plans to foster students' abilities. As the first step to achieving this, it is important to understand students' current perceptions of the benefits and risks of various ICTs. To compare the students' perceived benefits and risks of multiple ICTs will show that what kind of characteristics are hardly noticed by students. As mentioned above, some research has investigated users' perceived benefits and risks for specific ICTs; however, there are few studies that have simultaneously investigated them for multiple ICTs. Moreover, it is difficult to gain a clear understanding of students' perceptions of benefit and risk factors for multiple ICTs. This study aims to gain a general overview of the benefits and risks of multiple ICTs and their applications as perceived by university students. Text mining for free descriptive answer text by university students and the correspondence analysis were attempted. This paper present results from the preliminary survey analysis attempt.

2. SURVEY

The survey used in this study was administered via a questionnaire to thirteen university students in April 2019. The participants were from an expanded minor ICT-related educational program, indicating that they had greater interest in ICT than average university students. The questionnaire included 19 questions related to the usage, risks, and benefits of ICTs (robots, self-driving cars, drones, AI, big data, and AI speakers) and 3 questions related to their consent to participating in the survey. In this paper, 12 questions related to benefit and risk of ICTs are focused on. The questions were in the following format: "What factors concerning the usage of robot (self-driving car, drone, AI, big data or AI speaker) do you think are beneficial/risky?" Participants were asked to answer by freely describing all the ideas they could think of.

Responses were input as electronic data for analysis. At the input stage, obvious typological errors were corrected. For response data related to both benefits and risks, word extraction and correspondence analysis were performed using KH Coder (Higuchi 2016, Higuchi 2017).

3. RESULTS AND DISCUSSION

Figure 1 shows correspondence analysis results for perceived benefits. It can be seen that "drone" and "robot" are located close to one another; and words such as "danger," "job," "work," and "use" were located close to these two items. This suggests that participants consider the availability of drones and robots for use in dangerous situations to be beneficial. In addition, "reduce," "labor cost," "people," and so on are located near "robot," and "easy," "sky," "place," "congestion," and so on are located near "drone." This allows us to conclude that participants seemed to think that these two items, especially robots, can serve as an alternative to people.

"AI" was located close to "drone" and "robot" on the Dimension 1–2 plane, but it was relatively far from these two items on the Dimension 1–3 plane. However, "big data" was located relatively close to "AI," as compared to other ICTs. "Accurate" was located close to these two items, implying that participants saw accuracy as a common benefit of AI and big data.

"AI speaker" and "self-driving car" are located far from every other item. "AI speaker" was characterized by "communication," "voice," "search," and "ask." Although an AI speaker is application of AI, participants seemed to perceive more practical benefits in it. "Self-driving car" was characterized by "reduce," "decrease," "accident," "risk," "load," "drive," "old," and "human error." Participants seemed to consider load reduction to be a benefit of self-driving cars. Unlike robots and drones, self-driving cars seem to be considered as assistants, rather than alternatives, to people.

Figure 2 shows correspondence analysis results for perceived risks. "Robot" and "self-driving car" are located closely; words such as "bug," "malfunction," "dementia," and "prevent" were located near these two items, implying that participants were concerned about technical imperfection. Moreover, they seemed to consider cognitive decline to be a risk of using robots or self-driving cars as alternatives or assistants to people.

"Drone" and "AI speaker" are located relatively close to one another. "Mischief" and "wiretap" were relatively close to these two items, implying that participants were concerned about malicious acts by users. Unlike for robots and self-driving cars, participants were more conscious of intentional threats by users.

"Big data" was characterized by "data," "personal information," and "management." Participants were more concerned with managing data than how big data is used. "AI" was located relatively far from any other words.

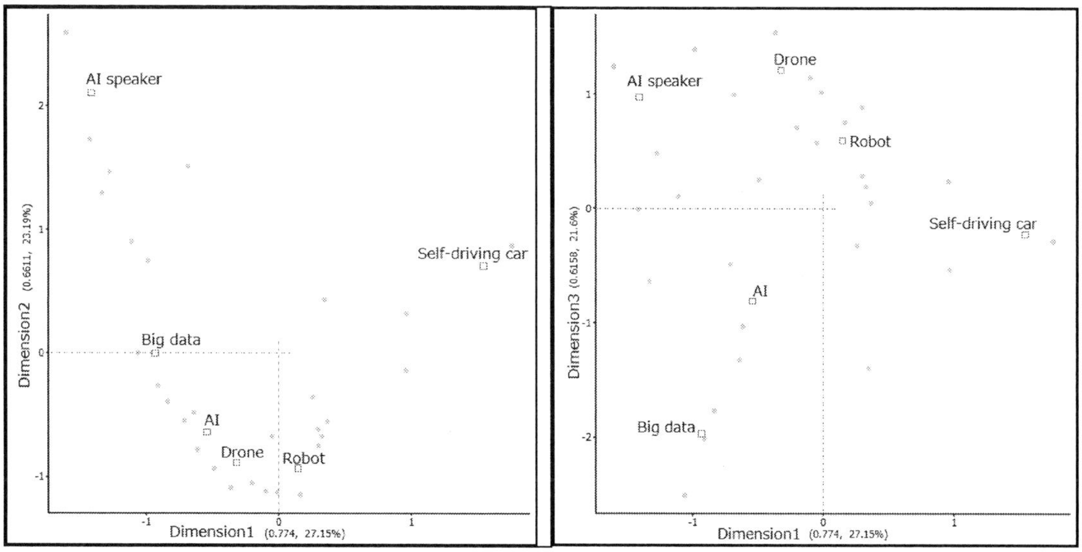

Figure 1. Results of correspondence analysis of perceived benefits for ICTs

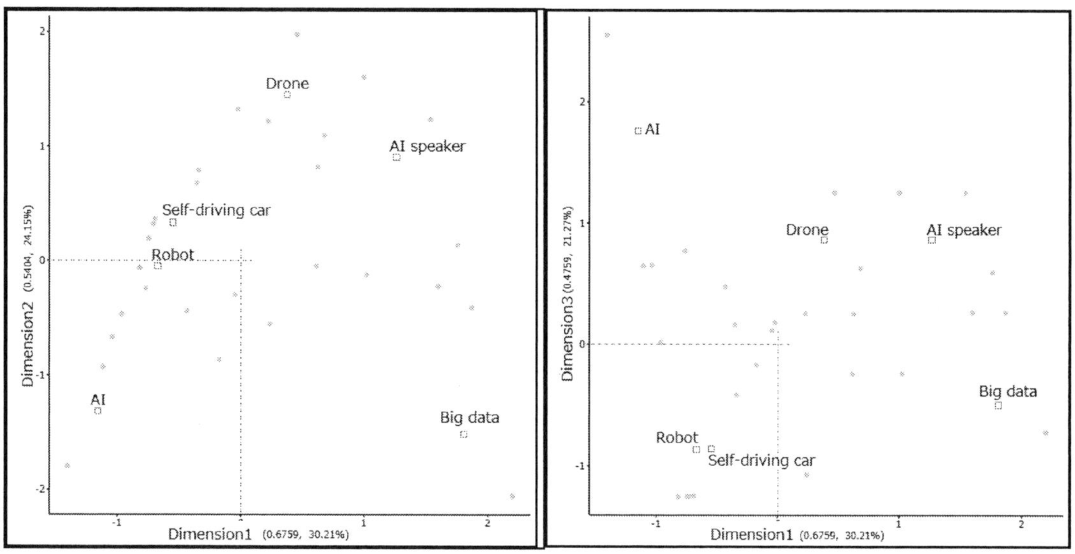

Figure 2. Results of correspondence analysis of perceived risks for ICTs

4. CONCLUSION

This study aims to gain a general overview of the benefits and risks perceived by university students' for multiple ICTs and their applications. Analysis of survey results was attempted using text mining and correspondence analysis. The following conclusions could be deduced from the results of our analysis.

1) Participants considered the availability for use in dangerous situations to be a benefit of drones and robots.

2) Participants saw accuracy as a common benefit of both AI and big data.

3) Participants seemed to perceive more practical benefits.

4) Participants seemed to consider the reduction of load on people to be a benefit of self-driving cars.

5) Participants were concerned about technical imperfections.

6) Participants were more conscious of intentional threats by users in drones and AI speakers.

6) Participants were more concerned with managing data themselves than how big data is used.

The sample size in this study was small because the survey presented here was preliminary. Further analysis with a larger number of participants is necessary.

REFERENCES

Bearth, A., and Siegrist, M., 2016. A risk or benefit perceptions more important for public acceptance of innovative food technologies: A meta-analysis. *Trends in Food Science & Technology*, Vol. 49, 14-23.

Brey, P., 2018. The strategic role of technology in a good society. *Technology in Society*, Vol. 52, pp 39-45.

Higuchi, K., 2016. A Two-Step Approach to Quantitative Content Analysis: KH Coder Tutorial Using Anne of Green Gables (Part I). *Ritsumeikan Social Science Review*, Vol. 52, No. 3, pp. 77-91.

Higuchi, K., 2017. A Two-Step Approach to Quantitative Content Analysis: KH Coder Tutorial Using Anne of Green Gables (Part II). *Ritsumeikan Social Science Review*, Vol. 53, No. 1, pp. 137-147.

Liu, P., Ma, Y. and Zuo, Y., 2019. Self-driving vehicles: Are people willing to trade risks for environmental benefits? *Transportation Research Part A*, Vol. 125, pp. 139-149.

Sato, H., and Tabata, N., 2018. Characteristics of risk perception to Internet use for older adults. *Shinshu studies in humanities*, Vol. 5m pp. 29-39. (In Japanese)

Wilson, C., Hargreaves, T., and Hauxwell-Baldwin, R., 2017. Benefits and risks of smart home technologies. *Energy Policy*, Vol. 103, pp. 72-83.

A DISTRIBUTED CONTENT ADDRESSABLE NETWORK FOR OPEN EDUCATIONAL RESOURCES

Stephen Downes
National Research Council Canada,
Ottawa, Ontario, Canada

ABSTRACT

We introduce Content Addressable Resources for Education (CARE) as a method for addressing issues of scale, access, management and distribution that currently exist for open educational resources (OER) as they are currently developed in higher education. CARE is based on the concept of the distributed web (dweb) and, using (for example) the Interplanetary File System (IPFS) provides a means to distributed OER in such a way that they cannot be blocked or paywalled, can be associated with each other (for example, as links in a single site, or as newer versions of existing resources) creating what is essentially an open resource graph (ORG), and when accessed through applications such as Beaker Browser, can be cloned and edited by any user to create and share new resources.

KEYWORDS

Open Educational Resources, Distributed Web, Dat, Interplanetary File System, Open Resource Graph, Content-based Addressing

1. INTRODUCTION

The distributed web potentially solves issues proponents of decentralization have long sought to address. One challenge is traffic, which overloads a single server. A second issue is latency, or the lag created by accessing resources half a world away. Additionally, some resources may be subject to national policies creating the need to differentiate access. And finally, if the centralized source is unavailable for some reason, then access for the entire world is disrupted.

For the World Wide Web, many of these challenges are addressed with Content Distribution Networks (CDN). (Benghozi & Simon, 2016) In essence, a CDN creates a local version of a website in different geographical regions. When a person in that region requests a resource, they are served a copy of the resource from the local server, rather than the original from a server much further away. This reduces traffic on the home server and makes access faster for the end user. Companies such as Cloudflare and Akamai now serve as much as half the content traffic on the internet (yet they are almost invisible to end-users).

The solution proposed by advocates of the distributed web is in many respects very similar. Content is stored on multiple servers. And when a web user requests that content, it is served from the nearest server. In the distributed web, however, rather than belonging to a company such as Akamai, these servers are individual users' computers. This model, called the peer-to-peer web, has a history of continuous development including services such as Napster, Gnutella, Tor and BitTorrent. (Troncoso, Isaakidis, Danezis & Halpin, Harry, 2017) These are called 'peers' and the system as a whole is called a 'peer-to-peer' (P2P) network.

More recently, a set of proposals called "Web3" (corresponding to a JavaScript library called Web3.js) (Stark, 2018) applies methods of chaining encrypted data structures to create what may be characterized as a "stateful" distributed web. "The ability to easily and efficiently transfer value P2P is at the heart of finance and efficient markets. If you can't hold state in the Internet, you can't transfer value without centralized institutions acting as clearing entities." (Voshmgir, 2018). Beyond obvious applications such as distributed token networks such as Bitcoin or Ethereum, Web3 may offer a response to the issues of centralization and commercialization afflicting OER.

2. CONTENT ADDRESSABLE RESOURCES FOR EDUCATION

2.1 Open Web and Open Educational Resources

The open internet began as email lists and Usenet groups. It grew through blogs and personal websites, from humble personal pages to sprawling websites such as Wikipedia. The open internet thrived in the age of social networks, online classrooms, and massive open online courses. When we think of the internet, we usually think of the internet as 'open', and this openness is most often found in the form of open resources.

The philosophy of 'open' that characterized the early internet was also reflected in the concept of open education. "Open education is a philosophy about the way people should produce, share, and build on knowledge. Proponents of open education believe everyone in the world should have access to high-quality educational experiences and resources, and they work to eliminate barriers to this goal." (opensource.com; Colpaert, 2018) This access is often supported by means of Open Educational Resources.

Open Educational Resources (OER) are teaching, learning and research materials that reside in the public domain or have been released under an open license that permits no-cost access, use, adaptation and redistribution by others with no or limited restrictions. (UNESCO, 2002) There is a large base of literature and practice associated with OER. (Weller, 2016) Numerous repositories containing OER have been developed. (Atenas & Havemann, 2013).

2.2 Challenges to Open Educational Resources

In today's internet, however, we see companies and institutions pushing back against openness. Proprietors of copyright content such as music, videos, articles and research publications have demanded that internet services block access to free copies of this content, and that they require payment for access to these resources. (Aversa, Hervas-Drane & Evenou, 2019) In addition, content owners and vendors began making money through advertisements. Both subscription-based and advertising-based models encouraged the growth of technology that herded users into content silos and that tracked and analyzed their behaviour. (Papadopoulos, Snyder & Livshits, 2019).

The challenges faced by the open web are reflected in the challenges faced by OER. For example, providers of massive open online courses (MOOCs) have begun to create barriers, charging first for certification and then for access to content itself. (Shah, 2017) In the world of OER the same thing happened with open textbook publisher Flat World Knowledge started charging for access. (Lederman, 2012) The temptation to monetize OER is always present for centralized services like Open Stax, Alison, Top Hat and Lumen Learning. (Aspesi, et.al., 2019)

By dint of subscription fees, value-added services, or advertising and surveillance, these services must contemplate one business model after another based on enclosing open content and requiring some form of authentication to access. And as David Bollier says, the enclosure of open content is one of the greatest threats to the internet. "Enclosure is about dispossession. It privatizes and commodifies resources that belong to a community or to everyone, and dismantles a commons-based culture." (Bollier, 2011).

The practical application of OER in education today faces numerous challenges, a number of which were described by Sukaina Walji and Cheryl Hodgkinson-Williams (Walju & Hodgkinson-Williams, 2018).

- While OER are being created, we are seeing limited re-use, and almost no adaptation to create new or localized resources
- Licensing remains a mystery to many people, and there isn't clarity about what license to use, how to license, or even whether certain licenses are actually OER
- It is not easy to create and upload OER to repositories, nor is it easy to use OER in the context of a course or the creation of course materials.
- Models for support and sustainability of OER remain elusive, and projects continue to depend on uncertain sources such as institutional funding, foundations and national or international bodies.

Additional problems exist, for example:

- OER remain hard to discover; there isn't a good way to search for OER, and learning object metadata (LOM) is difficult to use, and didn't actually facilitate discovery
- Individual OER often lacked educational support materials such as quizzes, assignment banks, or other materials

- There is no mechanism for ensuring the quality of OER or the appropriateness of OER in a given educational context.

As Tim Berners-Lee wrote recently, “for all the good we’ve achieved, the web has evolved into an engine of inequity and division; swayed by powerful forces who use it for their own agendas.” (Berners-Lee, 2018) His own project, Solid, is a tentative first step toward re-decentralizing that new web.

2.3 Content Addressing

One major difference between the traditional World Wide Web and Web3 lies in how these resources are addressed. On the traditional web and in CDNs, we use the location of a resource. The URL corresponds to an IP address (for example, http://www.downes.ca corresponds to 167.99.39.236) and to retrieve a resource, the browser sends a request to that address. However, in the distributed web we use content-based addressing. In essence, we search for resources based on what it is rather than where it is.

The content of a resource (whether it’s text, a web page, an image, whatever) is used as input to a hash algorithm that produces a scrambled string of characters - the hash - of the resource. Depending on the algorithm and the length of the hash produced, each hash is an essentially unique identifier for that resource. So instead of using a URL to request a resource, we use this unique identifier. (Sicilia, Sánchez-Alonso & Barriocanal, 2016). A peer sends a request to the closest peer, which either sends us the resource, or passes the request along to more peers. A content receiver can verify fidelity by using the hash algorithm to ensure the hash of the content received is the same as the hash of the content that was requested.

One significant current project implementing such a protocol is called Dweb (for ‘distributed web’ or ‘decentralized web’). (Ayala, 2018) It’s being called the next big step for the World Wide Web. The Dweb is based on the dat protocol, (https://www.datprotocol.com/) which is essentially a mechanism for finding and distributing content-addressable resources by their hash. We may see more and more resources with addresses like this in the future:

dat://502bdf152d00a35f9785f78d107b9037b5eca9354bcf593e7b4995f9be97a614/

This address is in fact the dat:// address for the first Content Addressable Resource for Education (CARE). If you access this resource using a peer-to-peer Dweb application you will find a set of pages containing the National Research Council’s Vision and Principles statement (in both official languages, set to photos I took myself). CARE, along with the associated concepts of CARE Packages and CARENet, is a new type of Open Educational Resource.

2.4 Peer Applications

In order to participate in the distributed web, it is necessary to have a peer application. This is an application that runs on your computer and communicates with other nodes in a P2P network to share resources. One such application is the Beaker Browser. The browser allows users to explore Dweb resources, ‘clone’ those resources locally, and create or edit new resources. Beaker manages Dweb functionality like creating hashes and chaining resources together. (Robinson, Hand, Madsen, Buus & McKelvey, 2018).

Beaker also helps users with a dat name service. Hash addresses (like the one above) are long and difficult to remember. A name service allows us to associate a simple string with a hash address (in exactly the same way the Domain Name Service (DNS) associates URLs with IP addresses). So an address in Beaker might look like this: dat://enoki.site/ For more Dweb resources open a Beaker browser to this website: dat://taravancil.com/explore-the-p2p-web.md

The dat:// protocol is only one of a number of current projects based on creating a content-addressable distributed web. One of the other major initiatives is called the blockchain. In the case of the blockchain, the resources in question are entries in financial ledgers. Another initiative, Git (with services based on the protocol like GitHub and GitLab), chains resources in different versions or branches of a software development project. An ambitious project to bring all these under a single umbrella is called the Interplanetary File System (IPFS) along with the associated project, Inter Planetary Linked Data (IPLD).

2.5 Content Addressable Resources for Education

Content Addressable Resources for Education (CARE) is proposed as a new medium for free and open learning resources, essentially replacing OER as it exists today. The differences will be as follows:

- Because CARE are content-addressable, they are stored and access in the web as a whole, rather than in a specific location, and hence cannot be blocked or paywalled
- As part of the distributed web, CARE are also associated with each other (for example, as links in a single site, or as newer versions of existing resources) creating what is essentially an Open Resource Graph (ORG).
- Accessed through applications such as Beaker Browser, CARE can be cloned and edited by any user to create and share new resources.

While we have seen more traditional contents, such as books, media and music, being distributed through IPFS and Dweb, it is important to underline that CARE consist not only of educational content, but interactive applications and service interfaces as well.

As demonstrated in Figure 1, a high-level overview of CARE, resources are uploaded into IPFS, where they receive a content-based address. This address is stored on an Ethereum blockchain. In order to upload, retrieve, view and edit OER, an application similar to Beaker is employed, using IPFS and Web3 Javascript libraries (this application will be demonstrated at the conference).

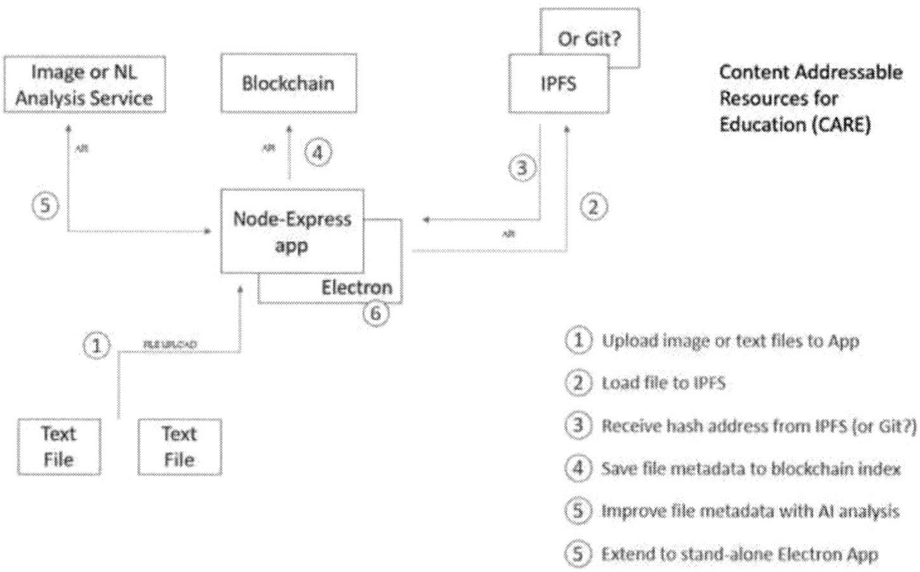

Figure 1. Content Addressable Resources for Education network diagram

3. CONCLUSION

In our work thus far, we have found the distributed web is very much in flux and that practical applications will depend on the resolution of some significant issues. Among them are:

- Speed - though the distributed web can be very fast, in practice, it often isn't, partially because of the time it takes to locate individual content-addressed content, and partially because upload speeds can be very slow for average users. In response, many people look to the cloud to host Dweb or IPFS nodes.
- Ease of Use - while it may seem that creating and sharing a web resource using Beaker or IPFS should be easy, in practice (as E-Learning 3.0 participants experienced first-hand) it can be daunting, especially since applications don't always work and guides are minimal.

- Finding resources - there isn't yet a good Dweb search engine. Additionally, resources can disappear when a host goes offline. This has led to the development of semi-centralized intermediaries such as Hashbase (https://hashbase.io/) (which make money by offering always-open nodes).
- Acceptance - many institutions officially disapprove of peer-to-peer services and block .torrent and other P2P traffic; additionally, many P2P sites are associated with blockchain and may therefore also be blocked by institutional internet services
- Appropriation for questionable and possible illegal content and services. With no central point of origin, there is no means to control these types of content, which raises questions about both their legality and their vulnerability.

Future work will be focused on addressing speed issues with a set of known CARE repositories functioning as IPFS nodes (known as CARE Net) and the development of multi-part CARE resources (known as CARE Packages). The emphasis will be to facilitate not only discovery but to also develop mechanisms for content creation through remixing and reusing existing resources.

REFERENCES

Aspesi, C., et al, 2019. SPARC*Landscape Analysis: The Changing Academic Publishing Industry – Implications for Academic Institutions. In *Copyright, FairUse, Scholarly Communication, etc*., 99.

Atenas, J. and Havemann, L., 2013. Quality assurance in the open: an evaluation of OER repositories. *INNOQUAL: The International Journal for Innovation and Quality in Learning*, 1(2) pp. 22–34

Aversa, P., Hervas-Drane, A. and Evenou, M., 2019. Business model responses to digital piracy. *California Management Review*, 61(2), pp. 30-58.

Ayala, D., (2018. Introducing the Dweb. *Mozilla Hacks* (weblog), July 31, 2018.

Benghozi, P. and Simon, J., 2016. Out of the Blue: The Rise of CDN Networks. *Communications & Strategies*, 1, issue 101, p. 107-128.

Berners-Lee, T., 2019. One Small Step for the Web… *Inrupt* (web site). October 23, 2018.

Bollier, D., 2011. The Commons, Short and Sweet. Weblog post, July 15, 2011.

Colpaert, J., 2018. Exploration of affordances of Open Data for Language Learning and Teaching. *Journal of Technology and Chinese Language Teaching*, 9(1), 1–14.

Lederman, D., 2012 Fleeing from 'Free'. *Inside Higher Ed*, November 5, 2012.

Papadopoulos, P; Snyder, P. and Livshits; B., 2019. Another Brick in the Paywall: The Popularity and Privacy Implications of Paywalls. *arXiv*:1903.01406

Robinson, D. C., et al, 2018. The Dat Project, an open and decentralized research data tool. *Scientific Data* volume 5, Article number: 180221 (2018).

Shah, D., 2017. Coursera Experiments with A Single Subscription Price for the Entire Catalog. *Class Central*, November 8th, 2017.

Sicilia, M. Á., Sánchez-Alonso, S. and Barriocanal, E., 2016. Sharing Linked Open Data over Peer-to-Peer Distributed File Systems: The Case of IPFS. In *Metadata and Semantics Research: 10th International Conference*, MTSR 2016, Göttingen, Germany, November 22-25, 2016, Proceedings, pp.3-14.

Stark, J., 2018. Making Sense of Web 3. L4 Blog, *Medium*. June 6, 2018.

Troncoso, C., et al, 2017. Systematizing Decentralization and Privacy: Lessons from 15 Years of Research and Deployments. *Proceedings on Privacy Enhancing Technologies* 2017 (4):404–426. De Gruyter.

UNESCO, 2002. UNESCO Promotes New Initiative for Free Educational Resources on the Internet. Web site.

Voshmgir, S., 2018. Token Economy: How Blockchains and Smart Contracts Revolutionize the Economy. *BlockchainHub Berlin Edition* 27 Jun 2019.

Walju, S. and Hodgkinson-Williams, C., 2018. Conversation with Sukaina Walji and Cheryl Hodgkinson-Williams. Video. Week 5 of *E-Learning 3.0*, November 21, 2018.

Weller, M., 2016. Different Aspects of the Emerging OER Discipline. *Revista Educacao e Cultura Contemporanea*, 13(31), 404-418.

REFLECTION PAPER

EMBEDDING VIRTUAL REALITY INTO COMPETENCE RECOGNITION

Merja Drake
Haaga-Helia University of Applied Sciences
Ratapihantie 13, FIN 00520 Helsinki, Finland

ABSTRACT

Nearly every third present occupation will disappear by the year 2030. While today's workplaces play a significant role in competence recognition, a degree is only one part of developing skills and competences (Ministry of Education and Culture 2019). Therefore, we need to shape the politics of lifelong learning's core, which is expertise instead of degrees.
Virtual reality (VR) can offer both educators and businesses an exciting possibility for optimising competences and learning processes (Melo, Bentley, McAllister & Cortez 2019). The use of VR has been studied to some extent, but mainly in school and university contexts. Its use has been limited in terms of employment training and competence recognition (Huang, Rauch & Liaw 2010); therefore, this area requires further study.
The aim of this research is to develop and test the use of VR in identifying needed competences in working life and in supporting employment training so that language skills are a minimum constraint. The main target group is immigrants in Finland. This ongoing research will be conducted in a Living Lab.

KEYWORDS

Virtual Reality, Competence Recognition, Life Long Learning

1. INTRODUCTION

Futurist speaker Thomas Frey (2019) claims that 'Businesses today care far less about someone's degree or underlying coursework and far more about whether they've been able to pass the necessary certification tests'. He also thinks that we will soon have micro colleges to meet this need. Our working, teaching and living environments are indeed changing at an accelerated pace. Nearly every third present occupation will disappear by the year 2030. While today's workplaces play a significant role in competence recognition, a degree is only one part of developing skills and competences (Ministry of Culture and Education 2019). Therefore, we need to shape the politics of lifelong learning's core, which is expertise instead of degrees.

Immigrants are predicted to play a key role in maintaining an adequate level of Finland's working-age population. Four of five foreigners who are living in Finland are of working age; however, the employment rate of working-age immigrants is considerably lower than that of the general population (Eronen et al. 2014). One of the biggest obstacles to employing immigrants is a lack of language skills. The bigger an economic advantage that is provided, the faster more immigrants will be employed. If young people stay outside education and outside working life, it has the negative effects, which will last for ~5–7 years. (Åslund & Rooth 2007).

Per the Organisation for Economic Co-operation and Development's (OECD) 2018 report, earlier attempts to employ immigrants have not been successful, and new bold initiatives to solve the problem need to be developed. The objective of the current project is to develop and test the use of virtual reality (VR) in identifying needed competences in working life and in supporting employment training, especially for immigrants, so that language skills are a minimum constraint. The goal is also to increase the awareness of companies, including recruitment agencies, in using VR for recruiting, work training and task orientation.

2. LITERATURE REVIEW

Per the VR Society (2019), 'Virtual reality is the term used to describe a three-dimensional, computer-generated environment, which can be explored and interacted with by a person. That person either becomes part of this virtual world or is immersed within this environment and, whilst there, is able to manipulate objects or perform a series of actions'. VR is an immersive experience meaning human is deeply concentrated on his tasks and not realising being in a virtual world. Immersion can help learning by reducing external disturbing factors. (Witmer, Jerome & Singer 2005.) VR is said to elaborate problem-solving capability and improve learning engagement (Zhen, Xie & Liu 2018)

Kulik, Kunert, Beck and Frölich (2017) suggest that virtual learning should be highly interactive because people learn by doing. VR learning can include collaborative interaction with others if it can focus on the environment, but learning also necessitates individual autonomy. Huang et al. (2013) claim that VR learning enhances interpersonal communication as well as a service mindset.

VR could be particularly useful for training immigrants because instructions need not necessarily be linguistic. Instead, training modules can be produced so that the correct modes of action are firstly demonstrated before being practiced. In addition, exercises can be repeated safely, and knowledge can also be verified on a virtual world screen. The biggest obstacles to using VR are the cost and human resources (Kavanagh et al. 2017). However, decreasing software and equipment costs are making more experiments possible.

3. RESEARCH QUESTIONS AND METHOD

The objective here is to develop a VR-based fast-track model for competence recognition together with immigrant organisations and entrepreneurs to open new employment avenues. The research method is based on the Living Lab approach, which is a user-centred ecosystem that aims to produce innovations, new products and new services in collaboration with users, citizens, companies and researchers (Chesbrough 2003). The idea of the Living Lab is to solve everyday problems and boost the economy by practice-based innovation, rapid development and testing of users (Pallot et al. 2011). We will build the ecosystem with companies, immigrant organisations, local employment authorities and educational institutions, while we alone will develop the VR recognition system, test it and use it. Once it provides competence recognition, companies will be able to employ the most suitable candidates. We will conduct three different employment experiments, with each lasting six months. In total, over 100 immigrants aged 24 to 64 and 50 companies will participate in the ecosystem.

Our research questions will include the following: 1) What is the best way to develop a competence recognition model using VR to employ immigrants in a particular field or position? 2) What kind of competence recognition model best serves participating companies in finding the proper expertise? 3) How satisfied are the immigrants and the company representatives with the competence recognition model?

The research data will be drawn from brainstorming, co-creation workshops and developing and testing workshops of the competence recognition system. We will collect additional data both during and after the employment experiment by interviewing both immigrants and the representatives of the companies. The data will be analysed by content analysis. The project is financed by the European Social Fund.

REFERENCES

Åslund, O. & Rooth, D-O. 2007. *Do When and Where Matter? Initial Labour Market Conditions and Immigrant Earnings* (0000). The Economic Journal, vol. 117, no. 518, pp. 422–448, March. <https://ssrn.com/abstract=978574 or http://dx.doi.org/10.1111/j.1468-0297.2007.02024.x>.

Chesbrough, H. W. 2003. *Open innovation: The new imperative for creating and profiting from technology*. Boston: Harvard Business School Press.

Eronen, A., Härmälä, V., Jauhiainen, S., Karikallio, H., Karhinen, R., Kosunen, A., Laamanen, J-P. & Lahtinen, M. 2014. *Maahanmuuttajien työllistyminen. Taustatekijät, työnhaku ja työvoimapalvelut.* (*Labour Market of Immigrants in Finland)* Työ- ja elinkeinoministeriön julkaisuja. Työ ja yrittäjyys 6/2014.

Frey, T. 2019. *Are certifications more valuable than college degrees?* <https://futuristspeaker.com/future-of-education/are-certifications-more-valuable-than-college-degrees/>.

Huang, H-M., Rauch, U. & Liaw, S-S. 2010. *Investigating Learners' Attitudes toward Virtual Reality Learning Environments: Based on a Constructivist Approach.* Computers & Education, vol. 55, no. 3, pp. 1171–1182, Nov.

Kavanagh, S., Luxton-Reilly, A., Wunche, B. & Plimmer, B. 2017. *A systematic review of Virtual Reality in education.* Themes in Science & Technology Education, vol. 10, no. 2, pp. 85–119.

Kulik, A., Kunert, A., Beck, S. & Frölich, B. 2017. Collaborative virtual reality for joint learning experiences. Proceedings CSCL, pp. 721–722.

Melo, M., Bentley, E., McAllister, K. & Cortez, J. 2019. *Pedagogy of Productive Failure: Navigating the Challenges of Integrating VR into the Classroom.* Journal of Virtual Worlds Research. vol. 12, no. 1, pp. 1–21.

Ministry of Education and Culture 2019. *Jatkuvan oppimisen kehittäminen (Developing lifelong learning).* http://urn.fi/URN:ISBN:978-952-263-641-6.

OECD 2018. *Working Together: Skills and Labour Market Integration of Immigrants and their Children in Finland.,* Paris: OECD Publishing. <https://doi.org/10.1787/9789264305250-en>.

Pallot, M., Trousse, B., Senach, B. & Scapin, D. 2011. *Living Lab Research Landscape: From User-Centered Design and User Experience towards User Cocreation.* First European Summer School 'Living Labs', Inria (ICT Usage Lab), Userlab, EsoceNet, Universcience, Aug 2010, Paris, France. <https://hal.inria.fr/inria-00612632>.

Virtual Reality Society 2019. *What is virtual reality*?. https://www.vrs.org.uk/virtual-reality/what-is-virtual-reality.html retrieved 10.10.2019.

Witmer, B., Jerome, C. & Singer, M. 2005. *The Factor Structure of the Presence Questionnaire*. Presence: Volume 14. Number 3, pp. 298-312.

Zheng, L., Xie, T. & Liu, G. 2018 *Affordance of Virtual Reality for Collaborative Learning.* 2018 International Joint Conference on Information, Media Na Engineering (ICIME).